Of the People

Of the People

A HISTORY of the
UNITED STATES
with Sources

VOLUME 1 • TO 1877

Third Edition

James Oakes
City University of New York Graduate Center

Michael McGerr
Indiana University–Bloomington

Jan Ellen Lewis
Rutgers University, Newark

Nick Cullather
Indiana University–Bloomington

Jeanne Boydston
University of Wisconsin–Madison

Mark Summers
University of Kentucky–Lexington

Camilla Townsend
Rutgers University–New Brunswick

Karen M. Dunak
Muskingum University

New York   Oxford
Oxford University Press

Oxford University Press is a department of the University of Oxford.
It furthers the University's objective of excellence in research,
scholarship, and education by publishing worldwide.

Oxford   New York
Auckland   Cape Town   Dar es Salaam   Hong Kong   Karachi
Kuala Lumpur   Madrid   Melbourne   Mexico City   Nairobi
New Delhi   Shanghai   Taipei   Toronto

With offices in
Argentina   Austria   Brazil   Chile   Czech Republic   France   Greece
Guatemala   Hungary   Italy   Japan   Poland   Portugal   Singapore
South Korea   Switzerland   Thailand   Turkey   Ukraine   Vietnam

Copyright © 2017, 2013, and 2011 by Oxford University Press

Published by Oxford University Press
198 Madison Avenue, New York, New York 10016
http://www.oup.com

Oxford is a registered trademark of Oxford University Press.

ISBN: 978-0-19-025488-9

Printing number: 9 8 7 6 5

Printed in the United States of America
on acid-free paper

Jeanne Boydston
1944–2008
Historian, Teacher, Friend

Brief Contents

Contents

CHAPTER 1   Worlds in Motion, 1450–1550   2

CHAPTER 3 The English Come to Stay, 1600–1660   **58**

Chapter 4 Primary Sources

CHAPTER **5** The Eighteenth-Century World, 1700–1775   **120**

CHAPTER **6**   Conflict in the Empire, 1713–1774   **152**

CHAPTER 7 Creating a New Nation, 1775–1788   182

CHAPTER 9   A Republic in Transition, 1800–1819   250

CHAPTER 11   Reform and Conflict, 1820–1848   324

CHAPTER 13   The Politics of Slavery, 1848–1860   **382**

AMERICAN PORTRAIT: **Frederick Douglass   384**

The Political Economy of Freedom and Slavery   385

A Changing Economy in the North   385

AMERICAN LANDSCAPE: **City of Broad Shoulders and Broader Implications:**
Chicago   387

The Slave Economy   389
The Importance of the West   390

Slavery Becomes a Political Issue   391

Wilmot Introduces His Proviso   391
A Compromise Without Compromises   392
The Fugitive Slave Act Provokes a Crisis   393
The Election of 1852 and the Decline of the Whig Party   394

Nativism and the Origins of the Republican Party   394

The Nativist Attack on Immigration   394
The Kansas-Nebraska Act Revives the Slavery Issue   396
The Labor Problem and the Politics of Slavery   397
"Bleeding Kansas"   399

AMERICA AND THE WORLD: **Slavery as a Foreign Policy   400**

STRUGGLES FOR DEMOCRACY: **The Settling and Unsettling of Kansas   401**

A New Political Party Takes Shape   402

The First Sectional Election   402
The Dred Scott Decision   403
The Lecompton Constitution Splits the Democratic Party   404
The "Irrepressible" Conflict   404

The Retreat from Union   406

John Brown's War Against Slavery   406
Northerners Elect a President   407

Conclusion   410

Chapter 13 Primary Sources

CHAPTER **14** A War for Union and Emancipation, 1861–1865 **412**

Appendices

Features

AMERICAN PORTRAIT

AMERICAN LANDSCAPE

AMERICA AND THE WORLD

STRUGGLES FOR DEMOCRACY

Preface

We are grateful that the first and second editions of *Of the People* have been welcomed by instructors and students as a useful instructional aid. Enhanced with even greater emphasis on American democracy and diversity, the third edition includes a new democracy feature and a version of the text is available with end-of-chapter primary source documents, both textual and visual, which help students draw connections among topics and think critically. In preparing the third edition, our primary goal has been to maintain the text's overarching focus on the evolution of American democracy, people, and power; its strong portrayal of political and social history; and its clear, compelling narrative voice. To that end, the broad representation of Native Americans, African Americans, and other minority groups in this text shows the full diversity of the American people. One of the text's strengths is its critical-thinking pedagogy because the study of history entails careful analysis, not mere memorization of names and dates.

History continues, and the writing of history is never finished. For the third edition, we have updated the following elements based on the most recent scholarship:

- **Chapters 10 and 11** integrate content on slavery and national development, as well as the politics of slavery and the abolition movement.
- **Chapters 13 through 15** were restructured and now include increased coverage of westward expansion, the growth of railroads and what this meant in terms of economic growth for the North and South (as well as the political economy of the Civil War), the emergence of the Republican Party, and a revised explanation for Reconstruction's demise.
- **Chapter 30** now covers the span of years between 1989 and 2001 and includes increased coverage of domestic terrorism, an expanded discussion of African Americans in the post–civil rights era, as well as gay and lesbian rights.
- The **Epilogue** covers the onset of the war on terror, from September 11, 2001, to the present and provides an account of the Obama administration through 2014, the nation's continuing response to challenging economic circumstances, including income inequality, and national security issues such as the controversy surrounding government surveillance and the emergence of ISIS.

At Gettysburg, Pennsylvania, on November 19, 1863, President Abraham Lincoln dedicated a memorial to the more than 3,000 Union soldiers who had died turning back a Confederate invasion in the first days of July. There were at least a few ways that the president could have justified the sad loss of life in the third year of a brutal war dividing North and South. He could have said it was necessary to destroy the Confederacy's cherished institution of slavery, to punish Southerners for seceding from the United States, or to preserve the nation intact. Instead, at this crucial moment in American history, Lincoln gave a short, stunning speech about democracy. The president did not use the word, but he offered its essence. To honor the dead of Gettysburg, he called on Northerners to ensure "that government of the people, by the people, for the people, shall not perish from the earth."

With these words, Lincoln put democracy at the center of the Civil War and at the center of American history. The authors of this book share his belief in the centrality of democracy; his words, "of the people," give our book its title and its main theme. We see American history as a story "of the people," of their struggles to shape their lives and their land.

Our choice of theme does not mean we believe that America has always been a democracy. Clearly, it has not. As Lincoln gave the Gettysburg Address, most African Americans still lived in slavery. American women, North and South, lacked rights that many men enjoyed; for all their disagreements, white southerners and northerners viewed Native Americans as enemies. Neither do we believe that there is only a single definition of democracy, either in the narrow sense of a particular form of government or in the larger one of a society whose members participate equally in its creation. Although Lincoln defined the Northern cause as a struggle for democracy, Southerners believed it was anything but democratic to force them to remain in the Union at gunpoint. As bloody draft riots in New York City in July 1863 made clear, many Northern men thought it was anything but democratic to force them to fight in Lincoln's armies. Such disagreements have been typical of American history. For more than 500 years, people have struggled over whose vision of life in the New World would prevail.

It is precisely such struggles that offer the best angle of vision for seeing and understanding the most important developments in the nation's history. In particular, the democratic theme concentrates attention on the most fundamental concerns of history: people and power.

Lincoln's words serve as a reminder of the basic truth that history is about people. Across the 30 chapters of this book, we write extensively about complex events. But we also write in the awareness that these developments are only abstractions unless they are grounded in the lives of people. The test of a historical narrative, we believe, is whether its characters are fully rounded, believable human beings.

The choice of Lincoln's words also reflects our belief that history is about power. To ask whether America was democratic at some point in the past is to ask how much power various groups of people had to make their lives and their nation. Such questions of power necessarily take us to political processes, to the ways in which people work separately and collectively to enforce their will. We define politics quite broadly in this book. With the feminists of the 1960s, we believe that "the personal is the political," that power relations shape people's lives in private as well as in public. *Of the People* looks for democracy in the living room as well as the legislature, and in the bedroom as well as the business office.

Focusing on democracy, on people and power, we have necessarily written as wide-ranging a history as possible. In the features and in the main text, *Of the People* conveys both the unity and the great diversity of the American people across time and place. We chronicle the racial and ethnic groups who have shaped America, differences of religious and regional identity, the changing nature of social classes, and the different ways that gender identities have been constructed over the centuries.

While treating different groups in their distinctiveness, we have integrated them into the broader narrative as much as possible. A true history "of the people" means not only acknowledging their individuality and diversity but also showing their interrelationships and their roles in the larger narrative. More integrated coverage of Native

Americans, African Americans, Latinos, and other minority groups appears throughout the third edition.

Of the People also offers comprehensive coverage of the different spheres of human life—cultural as well as governmental, social as well as economic, environmental as well as military. This commitment to comprehensiveness is a reflection of our belief that all aspects of human existence are the stuff of history. It is also an expression of the fundamental theme of the book: the focus on democracy leads naturally to the study of people's struggles for power in every dimension of their lives. Moreover, the democratic approach emphasizes the interconnections between the different aspects of Americans' lives; we cannot understand politics and government without tracing their connection to economics, religion, culture, art, sexuality, and so on.

The economic connection is especially important. *Of the People* devotes much attention to economic life, to the ways in which Americans have worked and saved and spent. Economic power, the authors believe, is basic to democracy. Americans' power to shape their lives and their country has been greatly affected by whether they were farmers or hunters, plantation owners or slaves, wage workers or capitalists, domestic servants or bureaucrats. The authors do not see economics as an impersonal, all-conquering force; instead, we try to show how the values and actions of ordinary people, as well as the laws and regulations of government, have made economic life.

We have also tried especially to place America in a global context. The history of America, or any nation, cannot be adequately explained without understanding its relationship to transnational events and global developments. That is true for the first chapter of the book, which shows how America began to emerge from the collision of Native Americans, West Africans, and Europeans in the fifteenth and sixteenth centuries. It is just as true for the last chapter of the book, which demonstrates how globalization and the war on terror transformed the United States at the turn of the twenty-first century. In the chapters in between these two, we detail how the world has changed America and how America has changed the world. Reflecting the concerns of the rest of the book, we focus particularly on the movement of people, the evolution of power, and the attempt to spread democracy abroad.

Abraham Lincoln wanted to sell a war, of course. But he also truly believed that his audience would see democracy as quintessentially American. Whether he was right is the burden of this book.

New to the Third Edition

"Struggles for Democracy" Feature

This feature focuses on moments of debate and public conversation surrounding events that have contributed to the changing ideas of democracy, as well as the sometimes constricting but overall gradually widening opportunities that evolved for the American people as a result. It appears in each chapter.

Number of Chapters

The book has been condensed from 31 to 30 chapters: content from former Chapter 12, Slavery and the Nation, 1790–1860, has been distributed throughout Chapters 10 and 11 in order to improve the chronological sequence of Volume I. Chapter 30, The Globalized Nation, has been revised to cover the span of years from 1989 to 2000.

Epilogue

We have made the addition of an Epilogue, "A Nation Transformed," which covers the span of years from 2001 to 2014 and includes a limited number of features.

New Additions to "American Portrait," "American Landscape," and "America and the World" Features

These popular boxed features from the second edition have been updated with five new "American Portraits" and six new "American Landscapes." "America and the World" remains as a feature in select chapters.

Photos

Approximately 10 percent of the photos have been revised throughout the chapters.

Primary Sources

A version of the text is available with end-of-chapter primary source documents, both textual and visual, designed to reinforce students' understanding of the material.

Hallmark Features

- Each chapter opens with an **"American Portrait"** feature, a story of someone whose life in one way or another embodies the basic theme of the pages to follow.
- Select chapters include an **"American Landscape"** feature, a particular place in time where issues of power appeared in especially sharp relief.
- To underscore the fundamental importance of global relationships, select chapters include a feature on **"America and the World."**
- Focus questions at chapter openings
- Time Lines in every chapter
- "Who, What": This list of chapter-ending key terms helps students recall the important people and events of that chapter.
- Critical-thinking pedagogy: All chapters end with both Review Questions, which test students' memory and understanding of chapter content, and Critical-Thinking Questions, which ask students to analyze and interpret chapter content.

Supplements

For Students

Oxford University Press offers a complete and authoritative package of supplementary material for students, including print and new media resources designed for chapter review, primary source reading, essay writing, test preparation, and further research.

Student Companion Website at www.oup.com/us/oakes
The open-access Online Study Center designed for *Of the People: A History of the United States*, Third Edition helps students to review what they have learned from the textbook as well as explore other resources online. Note-taking guides help students focus their

attention in class, whereas interactive practice quizzes allow them to assess their knowledge of a topic before a test.

- **Online Study Guide,** including
  - Note-taking outlines
  - Multiple-choice and identification quizzes (two quizzes per chapter, 30-question quizzes—*different* from those found in the Instructor's Manual/Test Bank)
- **Primary Source Companion and Research Guide,** a brief online Research Primer, with a library of annotated links to primary and secondary sources in US history.
- **Interactive Flashcards,** using key terms and people listed at the end of each chapter; these multimedia cards help students remember who's who and what's what.

Oxford First Source

Oxford First Source is an online database—with custom print capability—of primary source documents for the US History Survey Course.

These documents cover a broad variety of political, economic, social, and cultural topics and represent a broad cross section of American voices. Special effort was made to include as many previously disenfranchised voices as possible. The documents in this collection are indexed by date, author, title, and subject, allowing instructors to identify and select documents best suited for their courses. Short documents (one or two pages) are presented in their entirety while longer documents have been carefully edited to highlight significant content.

Each document is introduced with a short explanatory paragraph and accompanied with study questions. The collection includes an *Introduction to Reading and Interpreting Primary Documents*, which introduces students to the concept of primary documents and explains several methods for reading, interpreting, and understanding them. It also explains how to set documents into their historical context and how to incorporate primary documents into papers, exams, and other assignments.

For Instructors

For decades American history professors have turned to Oxford University Press as the leading source for high-quality readings and reference materials. Now, when you adopt Oakes's *Of the People: A History of the United States*, Third Edition, the Press will partner with you and make available its best supplemental materials and resources for your classroom. Listed here are several resources of high interest, but you will want to talk with your sales representative to learn more about what can be made available and about what would suit your course best.

Ancillary Resource Center (ARC) at www.oup-arc.com

This convenient, instructor-focused website provides access to all of the up-to-date teaching resources for this text—at any time—while guaranteeing the security of grade-significant resources. In addition, it allows Oxford University Press to keep instructors informed when new content becomes available. The following items are available on the ARC:

- Digital copy of **Instructor's Manual**

- Computerized **Test Bank** including:
    - **Quizzes** (two per chapter, one per half of the chapter, content divided somewhat evenly down the middle of the chapter: 30 multiple-choice questions each)
    - **Tests** (two per chapter, each covering the entire chapter contents, offering 10 identification/matching; 10 multiple choice; five short answer; two essay)
- Chapter-by-chapter **PowerPoint Presentations** with images and videos to illustrate important points
- **Sample Syllabi**
- **Chapter Outlines**
- **In-Class Discussion Questions**
- **Lecture Ideas**
- **Oxford's Further Reading List**

Dashboard

Online homework made easy! Tired of learning management systems that promise the world but are too difficult to use? Oxford offers you Dashboard, a simple, nationally hosted, online learning course—including study, review, interactive, and assessment materials—in an easy-to-use system that requires less than 15 minutes to master. Assignment and assessment results flow into a straightforward, color-coded grade book, allowing you a clear view into your students' progress. The system works on every major platform and device, including mobile devices.

Available for sale on its own or as a package. Contact your local Oxford University Press representative to order *Of the People*, Third Edition + the Access Code Card for Dashboard. Please use the following package ISBNs to order.

Of the People, Third Edition, Volume 1 without sources: 978-0-19-049833-7
Of the People, Third Edition, Volume 2 without sources: 978-0-19-049834-4
Of the People, Third Edition, Volume 1 with sources: 978-0-19-049824-5
Of the People, Third Edition, Volume 2 with sources: 978-0-19-049825-2

A complete **Course Management cartridge** is also available to qualified adopters. Instructor's resources are also available for download directly to your computer through a secure connection via the instructor's side of the companion website. Contact your Oxford University Press sales representative for more information.

Other Oxford Titles of Interest for the US History Classroom

Oxford University Press publishes a vast array of titles in American history. The following list is just a small selection of books that pair particularly well with Oakes's *Of the People: A History of the United States*, Third Edition. Any of these books can be packaged with *Of the People* at a significant discount to students. Please contact your Oxford University Press sales representative for specific pricing information or for additional packaging suggestions. Please visit www.oup.com/us for a full listing of Oxford titles.

WRITING HISTORY: A GUIDE FOR STUDENTS, FOURTH EDITION, BY WILLIAM KELLEHER STOREY, PROFESSOR OF HISTORY AT MILLSAPS COLLEGE

Bringing together practical methods from both history and composition, *Writing History* provides a wealth of tips and advice to help students research and write essays for history classes. The book covers all aspects of writing about history, including **finding topics and researching** them, **interpreting source materials, drawing inferences from sources, and constructing arguments.** It concludes with three chapters that discuss writing effective sentences, using precise wording, and revising. Using numerous examples from the works of cultural, political, and social historians, *Writing History* serves as an ideal supplement to history courses that require students to conduct research. The third edition includes expanded sections on peer editing and topic selection, as well as new sections on searching and using the Internet. *Writing History* can be packaged with Oakes's *Of the People: A History of the United States*, Third Edition. Contact your Oxford University Press sales representative for more information.

THE INFORMATION-LITERATE HISTORIAN: A GUIDE TO RESEARCH FOR HISTORY STUDENTS, SECOND EDITION, BY JENNY PRESNELL, INFORMATION SERVICES LIBRARY AND HISTORY, AMERICAN STUDIES, AND WOMEN'S STUDIES BIBLIOGRAPHER, MIAMI UNIVERSITY OF OHIO
This is the only book specifically designed to teach today's history student how to most successfully select and use sources—primary, secondary, and electronic—to carry out and present their research. Written by a college librarian, *The Information-Literate Historian* is an indispensable reference for historians, students, and other readers doing history research. *The Information-Literate Historian* can be packaged with Oakes's *Of the People: A History of the United States*, Third Edition. Contact your Oxford University Press sales representative for more information.

Acknowledgments

We are grateful to our families, friends, and colleagues who encouraged us during the planning and writing of this book. We would like once again to thank Bruce Nichols for helping launch this book years ago. We are grateful to the editors and staff at Oxford University Press, especially our acquisitions editor, Brian Wheel, and our development editor, Maegan Sherlock. Brian's commitment made this text possible and Maegan deftly guided the development of the third edition. Thanks also to our talented production team, Barbara Mathieu, senior production editor, and Michele Laseau, art director, who helped to fulfill the book's vision. And special thanks go to Linda Sykes and Danniel Schoonebeek, who managed the photo research; to Leslie Anglin, our copyeditor; to Gina Bocchetta, Brian Wheel's editorial assistant; and to the many other people behind the scenes at Oxford for helping this complex project happen.

The authors and editors would also like to thank the following people, whose time and insights have contributed to the first, second, and third editions.

Supplement Authors

Diane Boucher
Fitchburg State University
Dashboard

Daniel Covino
Graduate Student, Harvard Graduate
School of Education
Dashboard

Laura Graves
South Plains College
Instructor's Manual

Volker Janssen
Fullerton University
PowerPoint Slides and Test Bank

Andre McMichael
Western Kentucky University
Student Companion Website

Expert Reviewers of the Third Edition

Greg Hall
Western Illinois University

Ross A. Kennedy
Illinois State University

Randall M. Miller
Saint Joseph's University

David W. Morris
Santa Barbara City College

Adam Pratt
University of Scranton

Judith Ridner
Mississippi State University

Robert A. Smith
Pittsburg State University

Timothy B. Smith
University of Tennessee at Martin

Linda D. Tomlinson
Fayetteville State University

Gerald Wilson
Eastern Washington University

Expert Reviewers of the Second Edition

Marjorie Berman
Red Rocks Community College–Lakewood

Will Carter
South Texas Community College

Jonathan Chu
University of Massachusetts, Boston

Sara Combs
Virginia Highlands Community College

Mark Elliott
University of North Carolina–Greensboro

David Hamilton
University of Kentucky

James Harvey
Houston Community College

Courtney Joiner
East Georgia College

Timothy Mahoney
University of Nebraska–Lincoln

Abigail Markwyn
Carroll University

Brian Maxson
Eastern Tennessee State University

Matthew Oyos
Radford University

John Pinheiro
Aquinas College

James Pula
Purdue University–North Central

John Rosinbum
Arizona State University

Christopher Thrasher
Texas Tech University

Jeffrey Trask
University of Massachusetts–Amherst

Michael Ward
California State University–Northridge

Bridgette Williams-Searle
The College of Saint Rose

Expert Reviewers of the First Edition

Thomas L. Altherr
Metropolitan State College of Denver

Luis Alvarez
University of California–San Diego

Adam Arenson
University of Texas–El Paso

Melissa Estes Blair
University of Georgia

Lawrence Bowdish
Ohio State University

Susan Roth Breitzer
Fayetteville State University

Margaret Lynn Brown
Brevard College

W. Fitzhugh Brundage
University of North Carolina–Chapel Hill

Gregory Bush
University of Miami

Brian Casserly
University of Washington

Ann Chirhart
Indiana State University

Bradley R. Clampitt
East Central University

William W. Cobb Jr.
Utah Valley University

Cheryll Ann Cody
Houston Community College

Sondra Cosgrove
College of Southern Nevada

Thomas H. Cox
Sam Houston State University

Carl Creasman
Valencia Community College

Christine Daniels
Michigan State University

Brian J. Daugherity
Virginia Commonwealth University

Mark Elliott
University of North Carolina–Greensboro

Katherine Carté Enge
Texas A&M University

Michael Faubion
University of Texas–Pan American

John Fea
Messiah College

Anne L. Foster
Indiana State University

Matthew Garrett
Arizona State University

Tim Garvin
California State University–Long Beach

Suzanne Cooper Guasco
Queens University of Charlotte

Lloyd Ray Gunn
University of Utah

Richard Hall
Columbus State University

Marsha Hamilton
University of South Alabama

Mark Hanna
University of California–San Diego

Joseph M. Hawes
University of Memphis

Melissa Hovsepian
University of Houston–Downtown

Jorge Iber
Texas Tech University

David K. Johnson
University of South Florida

Lloyd Johnson
Campbell University

Catherine O'Donnell Kaplan
Arizona State University

Rebecca M. Kluchin
California State University–Sacramento

Michael Kramer
Northwestern University

Louis M. Kyriakoudes
University of Southern Mississippi

Jason S. Lantzer
Butler University

Shelly Lemons
St. Louis Community College

Charlie Levine
Mesa Community College

Denise Lynn
University of Southern Indiana

Lillian Marrujo-Duck
City College of San Francisco

Michael McCoy
Orange County Community College

Noeleen McIlvenna
Wright State University

Elizabeth Brand Monroe
*Indiana University–Purdue
University Indianapolis*

Kevin C. Motl
Ouachita Baptist University

Todd Moye
University of North Texas

Charlotte Negrete
Mt. San Antonio College

Julie Nicoletta
University of Washington–Tacoma

David M. Parker
California State University–Northridge

Jason Parker
Texas A&M University

Burton W. Peretti
Western Connecticut State University

Jim Piecuch
Kennesaw State University

John Putman
San Diego State University

R. J. Rockefeller
Loyola College of Maryland

Herbert Sloan
Barnard College, Columbia University

Vincent L. Toscano
Nova Southeastern University

William E. Weeks
San Diego State University

Timothy L. Wood
Southwest Baptist University

Jason Young
SUNY–Buffalo

Expert Reviewers of the Concise Second Edition

Hedrick Alixopulos
Santa Rosa Junior College

Guy Alain Aronoff
Humboldt State University

Melissa Estes Blair
Warren Wilson College

Amanda Bruce
Nassau Community College

Jonathan Chu
University of Massachusetts–Boston

Paul G. E. Clemens
Rutgers University

Martha Anne Fielder
Cedar Valley College

Tim Hacsi
University of Massachusetts–Boston

Matthew Isham
Pennsylvania State University

Ross A. Kennedy
Illinois State University

Eve Kornfeld
San Diego State University

Peggy Lambert
Lone Star College-Kingwood

Shelly L. Lemons
St. Louis Community College

Carolyn Herbst Lewis
Louisiana State University

Catherine M. Lewis
Kennesaw State University

Daniel K. Lewis
California State Polytechnic University

Scott P. Marler
University of Memphis

Laura McCall
Metropolitan State College of Denver

Stephen P. McGrath
Central Connecticut State University

Vincent P. Mikkelsen
Florida State University

Julie Nicoletta
University of Washington Tacoma

Caitlin Stewart
Eastern Connecticut State University

Thomas Summerhill
Michigan State University

David Tegeder
Santa Fe College

Eric H. Walther
University of Houston

William E. Weeks
University of San Diego

Kenneth B. White
Modesto Junior College

Julie Winch
University of Massachusetts–Boston

Mary Montgomery Wolf
University of Georgia

Kyle F. Zelner
University of Southern Mississippi

Expert Reviewers of the Concise First Edition

Hedrick Alixopulos
Santa Rosa Junior College

Guy Alain Aronoff
Humboldt State University

Melissa Estes Blair
Warren Wilson College

Amanda Bruce
Nassau Community College

Jonathan Chu
University of Massachusetts–Boston

Paul G. E. Clemens
Rutgers University

Martha Anne Fielder
Cedar Valley College

Tim Hacsi
University of Massachusetts–Boston

Matthew Isham
Pennsylvania State University

Ross A. Kennedy
Illinois State University

Eve Kornfeld
San Diego State University

Peggy Lambert
Lone Star College–Kingwood

Shelly L. Lemons
St. Louis Community College

Carolyn Herbst Lewis
Louisiana State University

Catherine M. Lewis
Kennesaw State University

Daniel K. Lewis
California State Polytechnic University

Scott P. Marler
University of Memphis

Laura McCall
Metropolitan State College of Denver

Stephen P. McGrath
Central Connecticut State University

Vincent P. Mikkelsen
Florida State University

Julie Nicoletta
University of Washington Tacoma

Caitlin Stewart
Eastern Connecticut State University

Thomas Summerhill
Michigan State University

David Tegeder
Santa Fe College

Eric H. Walther
University of Houston

William E. Weeks
University of San Diego

Kenneth B. White
Modesto Junior College

Julie Winch
University of Massachusetts–Boston

Mary Montgomery Wolf
University of Georgia

Kyle F. Zelner
University of Southern Mississippi

James Oakes has published several books and numerous articles on slavery and antislavery in the nineteenth century, including *The Radical and the Republican: Frederick Douglass, Abraham Lincoln, and the Triumph of Antislavery Politics* (2007), winner of the Lincoln Prize in 2008. Professor Oakes is Distinguished Professor of History and Graduate School Humanities Professor at the City University of New York Graduate Center. In 2008 he was a fellow at the Cullman Center at the New York Public Library. His new book is *Freedom National: The Destruction of Slavery in the United States* (February 2013).

Michael McGerr is the Paul V. McNutt Professor of History at Indiana University–Bloomington. He is the author of *The Decline of Popular Politics: The American North, 1865–1928* (1986) and *A Fierce Discontent: The Rise and Fall of the Progressive Movement, 1870–1920* (2003), both from Oxford University Press. He is writing *"The Public Be Damned": The Kingdom and the Dream of the Vanderbilts.* The recipient of a fellowship from the National Endowment for the Humanities, Professor McGerr has won numerous teaching awards at Indiana, where his courses include the US Survey; War in Modern American History; Rock, Hip Hop, and Revolution; Big Business; The Sixties; and American Pleasure. He has previously taught at Yale University and the Massachusetts Institute of Technology. He received his BA, MA, and PhD from Yale.

Jan Ellen Lewis is Professor of History and Dean of the Faculty of Arts and Sciences, Rutgers University, Newark. She also teaches in the history PhD program at Rutgers, New Brunswick, and was a visiting professor of history at Princeton. A specialist in colonial and early national history, she is the author of *The Pursuit of Happiness: Family and Values in Jefferson's Virginia* (1983) as well as numerous articles and reviews. She has coedited *An Emotional History of the United States* (1998), *Sally Hemings and Thomas Jefferson: History, Memory, and Civic Culture* (1999), and *The Revolution of 1800: Democracy, Race, and the New Republic* (2002). She has served on the editorial board of the *American Historical Review* and as chair of the New Jersey Historical Commission. She is an elected member of the Society of American Historians and the American Antiquarian Society. She received her AB from Bryn Mawr College and MAs and PhD from the University of Michigan.

Nick Cullather is a historian of US foreign relations at Indiana University–Bloomington. He is author of three books on nation building: *The Hungry World* (2010), a story of foreign aid, development, and science; *Illusions of Influence* (1994), on US–Philippines relations; and *Secret History* (1999 and 2006), a history of the CIA's overthrow of the Guatemalan government in 1954. He received his PhD from the University of Virginia.

Jeanne Boydston was Robinson-Edwards Professor of American History at the University of Wisconsin–Madison. A specialist in the histories of gender and labor, she was the author of *Home and Work: Housework, Wages, and the Ideology of Labor in the Early*

American Republic (1990); coauthor of *The Limits of Sisterhood: The Beecher Sisters on Women's Rights and Woman's Sphere* (1988), and coeditor of *Root of Bitterness: Documents in the Social History of American Women*, second edition (1996). Her most recent article is "Gender as a Category of Historical Analysis," *Gender History* (2008). She taught courses in women's and gender history, the histories of the early republic and the antebellum United States, and global and comparative history, and she was the recipient of numerous awards for teaching and mentoring. Her BA and MA were from the University of Tennessee, and her PhD was from Yale University.

Mark Summers is the Thomas D. Clark Professor of History at the University of Kentucky–Lexington. In addition to various articles, he has written *Railroads, Reconstruction, and the Gospel of Prosperity* (1984), *The Plundering Generation* (1988), *The Era of Good Stealings* (1993), *The Press Gang* (1994), *The Gilded Age; or, The Hazard of New Functions* (1997), *Rum, Romanism and Rebellion* (2000), *Party Games* (2004), and *A Dangerous Stir* (2009). At present, he has just completed a book about a Tammany politician, *Big Tim and the Tiger.* He is now writing a survey of Reconstruction and a book about 1868. He teaches the American history survey (both halves), the Gilded Age, the Progressive Era, the Age of Jackson, Civil War and Reconstruction, the British Empire (both halves), the Old West (both halves), a history of political cartooning, and various graduate courses. He earned his BA from Yale and his PhD from the University of California–Berkeley.

Camilla Townsend is Professor of History at Rutgers University–New Brunswick. She is the author of four books, among them *Malintzin's Choices: An Indian Woman in the Conquest of Mexico* (2006) and *Pocahontas and the Powhatan Dilemma* (2004), and is the editor of *American Indian History: A Documentary Reader* (2010). The recipient of fellowships from the National Endowment for the Humanities and the John Simon Guggenheim Memorial Foundation, she has also won awards at Rutgers and at Colgate, where she used to teach. Her courses cover the colonial history of the Americas, as well as Native American history, early and modern. She received her BA from Bryn Mawr and her PhD from Rutgers.

Karen M. Dunak is Assistant Professor of History at Muskingum University in New Concord, Ohio. She is the author of *As Long as We Both Shall Love: The White Wedding in Postwar America* (2013), published by New York University Press. She currently is working on a project that investigates the process by which the ideals of Second Wave feminism became mainstream. Her courses include the US Survey, Gender and Sexuality in US History, 1950s America, and various other topics related to modern US history. She earned her BA from American University and her PhD from Indiana University.

Of the People

Malinche, Cultural Translator

When the Native American woman who would later be known as La Malinche was a little girl, she listened to the poems and histories of her people on starlit evenings. Her father was a nobleman from Coatzacoalcos, on the Gulf of Mexico; his people had lived there for generations in adobe houses built around communal court-yards. Her mother, though, was lowborn, maybe even a captive con-cubine, and this made the child vulnerable. Trouble came when she was still young. The powerful Aztecs from the Central Valley of Mexico were expanding their dominion, and she was either taken in battle or, more likely, given away as a preemptive peace offering to the invaders. Then the Aztecs sold her to the Mayas, and she lived with them for years as a slave.

When strangers from across the sea came on huge canoes with cloth sails, the Mayas attacked them—and lost the battle. Once again the girl was given away as a peace offering. This time, she found herself among the newly arrived Spaniards, who baptized her "Marina." The Indians heard the name as "Malina" (as they had no "r") and called her "Malintzin" to convey respect. The Spaniards heard "Malinchi" or "Malinche" (as they had no "tz" sound), and so we still call her today. We will never know what her mother had once named her. She had become someone different, and she soon dis-covered her potential importance to her new captors. Her native language was Nahuatl, the same tongue spoken by the Aztecs, and by now she also spoke the coastal Mayan dia-lect. The Spaniards had with them one Jerónimo de Aguilar, who had lived for years among the Mayas as a shipwreck victim and also spoke their language. In a perfect translation chain, Hernando Cortés spoke to Aguilar, who spoke to Malinche, who in turn spoke to the Aztecs. She was a gifted young woman and learned Spanish quickly, soon becoming the only translator needed.

Malinche told the Spaniards about the Aztec capital where Moctezuma ruled, and she helped to guide them there. She had no reason to protect the Aztec people; after all, they had threatened her own family and caused her enslavement. And she had every reason to work cooperatively with the newcomers. If she did, they would treat her well. If not, they would use her as a sexual slave. She also soon saw that the Spanish were brutal on the battlefield and learned that there were many thousands more of them ready to come. Often she advised indigenous villages that they passed to make peace with the strangers rather than fight them. She said, quite rightly, that they could be useful friends but would make dangerous enemies. When they reached the Aztec capital, she translated adroitly between Cortés and Moctezuma, refusing to be intimidated, and helped Cortés determine what to do at each stage.

Hernando Cortés probably would not have been able to bring down the Aztecs with-out the help of Malinche. And yet if he had failed, some other Spaniard almost certainly would eventually have found some other captive woman to act as translator and mediator, for the domineering Aztecs had many enemies.

Like many people who have been forced to become cultural mediators, Malinche survived as best she could. She bore a son by Cortés, and when, after the conquest, she demanded a Spanish husband for her own protection, he saw her married to one of his lieutenants. She later bore her husband a daughter. Malinche died when she was about 30 of one of the diseases brought by the Europeans, but not before she had helped her children enter the Spanish world on a firm footing, with wealth and position. She knew by then that the New World she had helped to create was proving dangerous to indigenous people, even those who befriended the Spaniards. She may have had fears for the future, but she could not have had any real regrets about the past, for at the time, she had had very few options. She had done the best she could in an extraordinarily difficult situation.

The Worlds of Indian Peoples

For most of human history, there were no people in the Americas. Archaeologists have found that modern humankind (*Homo sapiens*) originated in Africa about 400,000 years ago. In a sense, all people alive today are ultimately African, as we are all descended from those early humans. Some of them migrated northward and eventually populated Europe and Asia. Mutations occurred along the way, yielding populations who looked different but still had almost all of their genetic material—and their natures and abilities—in common.

Great Migrations

In the last Ice Age, arctic glaciers expanded so extensively that the world's sea level dropped, perhaps by as much as 350 feet. This phenomenon created a land bridge (called "Beringia") between Siberia in Asia and Alaska in America. Humans hunting mammoths and other big game traveled along the new corridor into America. Linguistic evidence indicates that there were three great waves of migration. Archaeologists argue fiercely about when the first one occurred. Most agree it was about 12,000 BCE, but there are a few sites that may suggest otherwise. The Monte Verde site in Chile—where a child's footprint next to a hearth has been forever preserved—seems to have been inhabited a thousand years earlier, for example. Eventually, about 9000 BCE, the ice melted, the sea level rose, and the land bridge disappeared, closing off the Old World from what would later be called the New. The people living in the Americas, known now as Paleo-Indians, at first remained what they had been—hunter-gatherers who moved in small groups of no more than about 25, generally choosing their spouses from other bands whom they met in passing.

Because of the end of the Ice Age, the climate began to shift, yielding distinct changes in lifestyle. At the start of the Archaic period (approximately 8000 BCE), most of the large mammals that were hunted for food went extinct. Overhunting may have contributed to their disappearance, but climactic shifts probably explain the demise of species like the woolly mammoth. The men learned to hunt and trap smaller species, and the women foraged more determinedly for edible and useful plants. They moved through their environment in seasonal cycles, making satisfying and productive lives for themselves for many generations. By the time of Columbus's voyage, there were hundreds of indigenous groups in the Americas.

The Emergence of Farming

As temperatures rose and more species of plants appeared, people around the world began to experiment with planting the seeds of their favorite types. They continued to follow the game as they always had, but then returned to the same place months later to harvest what they had planted. In some places, the available plants proved so rich in protein—containing the amino acids necessary to support life—that human populations gradually ceased to be nomadic hunter-gatherers and became full-time farmers instead. In other places, the available plants were not nutritious enough to enable a major change in lifestyle. In Southwest Asia, for example, in the area traditionally known as "the Fertile Crescent," located between the Tigris and the Euphrates Rivers, wheat, barley, and peas were all native to the region, and all were protein-rich. Not surprisingly, humans' early efforts to domesticate plants in this part of the world led relatively rapidly to the adoption of farming as a full-time occupation by about 8000 BCE. In New Guinea, to take a contrary example, the native plants included bananas and sugarcane, both delicious but not rich in protein. People planted them occasionally, but they continued their hunting-and-gathering lifestyle.

In the Americas, there were also very few plant species rich in the amino acids needed to synthesize protein. The ancestor of today's corn, which first appeared in what is today Mexico, was an exception to some extent, but the kernels at that time were extremely tiny, and they were missing some key amino acids. During the Archaic period (8000 BCE–2000 BCE), a number of groups did experiment with growing it (as well as squash and other plants). However, it took many generations of selective planting to create the ears of corn we know today. It took people even longer to discover that if they ate corn together with beans, they were left as well-nourished as if they had eaten meat. (The beans provided the amino acids missing from corn: together, they form a complete protein.) Once these breakthroughs had occurred, more societies adopted full-time agriculture.

The Cradle of the Americas

Mesoamerica, the area stretching from the Rio Grande to today's Panama, has been called "the Cradle of the Americas" because it was here that the hemisphere's first technologically advanced civilizations emerged. They appeared wherever corn became the centerpiece of a farming culture, beginning in about 2000 BCE. In every part of the ancient world, numerous technological innovations followed the advent of full-time farming. A sedentary lifestyle in which only a portion of the population was engaged in full-time food production enabled the emergence of such things as complex architecture, large ceramics, forges, irrigation techniques, and detailed recordkeeping. Mesoamerica was no exception.

By about 200 CE, two distinct zones of Mesoamerican culture had emerged. In the Yucatan Peninsula, the Classic Mayan civilizations flourished. The central basin of Mexico saw a succession of prominent states, beginning with the city of Teotihuacan—the breathtaking ruins of which still stand—and ending with the Aztec Empire,

AMERICAN LANDSCAPE

Tenochtitlan

When the Spanish reached Tenochtitlan, they found a city so beautiful that it "seemed like an enchanted vision." Built on an island in a lake, and linked to the shore by extraordinary causeways, it was nevertheless larger than any city in Europe at that time. In the center were Moctezuma's palaces (including a zoo and a library), the public buildings, and huge pyramid temples sitting atop high platforms. All of these buildings were painted glistening white, then decorated in bright colors and surrounded by magnificent gardens, and all were kept immaculately clean.

The society was arranged hierarchically, and the higher the status of the family, the better the housing. Nobles and the families of especially successful warriors lived in well-decorated two-story stucco homes, whereas ordinary people inhabited more modest dwellings, with those of the poorest built of wood and straw. Such houses were without any furnishings beyond reed mats for sleeping, straw baskets and chests, a few cooking pots, and the stones on which the women in the family ground maize. Each home had several rooms opening onto a courtyard, where family activities took place. Most people lived in extended family groupings—one or two nuclear families together—of 10 to 15 people. Married children, for example, often lived with the parents of either the bride or groom, or a wealthy man might have several wives, each with her own room in the complex.

Work was assigned by gender. Every woman, whatever her age or class, spent much of the day weaving. Girls were taught by their mothers how to spin and weave and how to grind corn and prepare meals. Fathers taught their sons an artisanal craft, but all young men also stood ready to go to war when needed. The heart of Tenochtitlan's economic life was the market at Tlatelolco, on the north side of town. It served 25,000 people daily, selling not only food, clothing, and household goods but also luxuries such as craftwork made of feathers, gold, and precious stones. People sold their services, too, as barbers, fortune-tellers, scribes, and even prostitutes. Each kind of good and service was assigned its own section of the market, making it easier for customers to compare quality and price. The state regulated the market, setting an upper limit on prices and taxing each transaction. Stretching away from the market, the people of well-organized neighborhoods pursued their daily pastimes, and across the lake in the surrounding countryside, farmers tilled the soil and grew the life-sustaining corn and beans. Along the roads winding toward the city came the people of conquered city-states, either to pay their tribute or buy goods in the thriving marketplace.

dominant when the Europeans arrived. We know a great deal about the Mayas and Aztecs because they had their own pictoglyphic writing traditions, and they wrote down more about their culture when they learned the Roman alphabet from Spanish priests in the sixteenth century. In reading these individuals' writings, sometimes we stumble eerily into a moment from the past. One day in about the year 800, for example, a skilled Mayan artisan crafted a cup for drinking hot chocolate as a gift for a young prince. In the midst of the complicated paintings on the cup, which had religious and astronomical significance, he composed a poem in glyphic writing. He ended it by connecting the earthly world to the divine world, honoring both a powerful prince and a creator god: "He who gave the open space its place/who gave Jaguar Night his place/was the Black-Faced Lord, the Star-Faced Lord."

Scholars studying the writings and other remains of ancient Mesoamerican peoples have helped dispel some of the myths about them. Like people everywhere, they could be gentle and had senses of humor, but they were also competitive and often fought for dominance. They sometimes sacrificed prisoners of war to the gods, but they were not inherently more violent than other humans; they did *not* routinely sacrifice thousands of people at a time, as was once believed. In general, victors in political power struggles preferred that outsiders choose to ally with them rather than be destroyed. The more scholars learn about individual ethnic groups in the pre-Columbian period, the clearer it becomes that they were nearly all based on alliances formed between disparate groups in a more remote past. As bands grew to become chiefdoms—and in some cases, actual states—they governed themselves successfully by allowing the different subunits to have a voice in the increasingly complex polity. Constituent groups negotiated with each other and rotated between them the duties of going to war, for example, or working on a temple. In some regards Mesoamerican native cultures thus constituted the hemisphere's first democracies although they were ruled by chiefs.

The Northern World Takes Shape

In the pre-Columbian period, North America was peripheral to Mesoamerica. Due to the centrality of farming in Mesoamerica, the population there was many millions strong (scholars debate the exact number), while the population of all of North America was about 1 million. Because a desert covered northern Mexico, the culture centered on corn did not travel northward as easily as comparable crops had once traveled from the Fertile Crescent throughout Europe and Asia. But ancient Mesoamerican migrants and traders did eventually spread their valuable commodities, largely through canoe travel along the coasts and eventually even across the Gulf of Mexico.

Beginning as early as 100 CE, small villages began to be established in what we call the American Southwest following the Mexican model. The Anasazi, the Mogollon, and the Hohokam cultures all experimented with agriculture and built houses around court-yards. Later, the climate and their nomadic enemies caused most of them to return to hunting and gathering for a time. The Anasazi, however, persistently circled back to planting corn and eventually built their remarkable cliff dwellings and the towns of Chaco Canyon, among them the 800-room complex at Pueblo Bonito. This extraordinary architectural wonder seems to have been built largely for ceremonial purposes; thousands of people working over generations were dedicated to its construction.

Meanwhile, the Mississippi River had long functioned as a great highway for the exchange of goods and ideas. Once corn reached the mouth of the river, it was not long before it spread northward. We call the style of culture that traveled up the artery of the river "Mississippian." Mississippian sites, ranging from about 800 CE to 1500 CE, included the region's more ancient funerary mounds, as well as Mexican-style ball courts

Image of Community of Cahokia The community at Cahokia, at eye level, as envisioned by a modern-day graphic artist. The town was surrounded by a stockade, which enclosed the mounds, plazas, temples, and homes.

next to grand pyramids, central courtyards, and, of course, corn farming. Cahokia, a city-state located near the point where the Missouri River runs into the Mississippi, rose to become the greatest power in the region for a time, exacting tribute from surrounding villages. In the eleventh century, the town boasted about 10,000 people. After that, its power declined and its people abandoned the site; perhaps the powerful lords had made too many enemies, or perhaps a terrible drought struck, or both.

Even as Cahokia saw its demise, however, Mississippian culture spread into the American Southeast, and corn also traveled up the Ohio River to the Great Lakes, to the ancestors of the Iroquoian peoples. By the time the Europeans met the cultures of the Eastern Woodlands, many of them had been part-time farmers for a few hundred years, although they also continued to rely on hunting deer and gathering wild plants. Those groups who farmed most successfully saw their populations rise relative to their neighbors. The Iroquoian peoples in particular translated this into political power by resolving their internal differences through democratic discussion and presenting a united face to the world. It seems that at least a century before the Europeans arrived, the leader Deganawidah helped them found the entity later known as the League of Five Nations. Women, whose work in agriculture was deemed highly important, had a voice in the selection of chiefs.

Some parts of North America were not subject to the influence of Mexican culture and corn. The peoples of the far north, relatively few in number, survived through expert hunting. The Great Plains were largely uninhabited, for in a world without horses, their vastness and aridity seemed impenetrable, except for a few people who piled their goods onto a chamois pulled by dogs. A few corn farmers nestled around the edges of the prairies, and sometimes enterprising men drove roaming herds of buffalo over cliffs to harvest the meat. Many of these people lived in villages of earthen lodges. Farther west, along the coast of California and in the Pacific Northwest, large numbers of people lived by fishing and processing acorns. They built lodges and totem poles out of wood and painted them with bright colors. On the Columbia Plateau, a great annual trade fair centered on the buying and selling of dried salmon. Even here, although the people had not become farmers, some Mexican influence was felt. Travelers brought luxury goods to trade, like turquoise jewelry, which had come from the lands to the south.

These northwestern fisher peoples would be among the last to come face-to-face with Europeans. The newcomers were approaching from the south and east.

The Worlds of Christopher Columbus

In the world into which Christopher Columbus was born, Europe was peripheral. Great overland trade caravans and the sea routes of the Indian Ocean connected the known world. The Middle Eastern merchants at the center formed the hub (see Map 1–1). The goods of China were in greatest demand. Europeans constituted the least powerful element of the world's trade system. Princes and merchants there longed to be able to compete with other players on the world stage, and some desperately sought ways of doing so.

The *Reconquista*

Middle Eastern economic power had spurred the spread of the Islamic faith after its inception in the seventh century. By the year 711, most of the Iberian Peninsula (today's Spain and Portugal) had fallen to Muslim conquerors of Arab and Berber descent (called "Moors" by Christians). The new authorities were generally tolerant of those they had vanquished and allowed Christian and Jewish subjects to coexist peacefully alongside Muslims. Toward the end of the eleventh century, however, dissatisfied descendants of the ousted ruling families began a concerted effort toward reconquest, or *reconquista*. In 1085, Alfonso VI of Castile retook Toledo. "Inspired by God's grace," he wrote triumphantly, "I moved an army against this city, where my ancestors once reigned in power

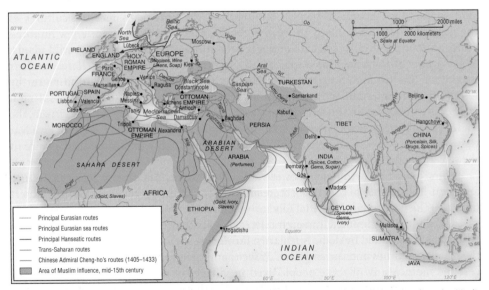

Map 1–1   World Trade on the Eve of Discovery For a thousand years, world trade centered on the Mediterranean. European, Arab, and Asian traders crisscrossed much of the Eastern Hemisphere, carrying spices, silks, and cottons from Asia; linens, woolens, and wine from Europe; and gold and slaves from Africa.

and wealth, deeming it acceptable in the sight of the Lord." Over the course of the next four centuries, other Christian princes followed Alfonso's lead. In these years, warfare shaped all aspects of Iberian society. The priests who proclaimed the *reconquista* a holy struggle against the Moorish infidel and the soldiers who waged such wars were elevated to positions of prestige. The surest path to wealth and honor lay in plunder and conquest.

By the time the Italian-born Christopher Columbus arrived in Spain in 1485, the Muslim rulers had been ejected from the entire peninsula, except Granada. The 1469 marriage of Isabel, princess of Castile, and her cousin Ferdinand, prince of Aragon, had unified the heart of what would soon be the nation of Spain. Although Isabel was only 18 when she married (and her husband a year younger), she had already shown herself to be a woman of boldness and determination, and because Castile was more powerful than Aragon, she was able to dictate the terms of the marriage contract. Together, she and Ferdinand launched a final campaign against the Moors. In 1492, Isabel and Ferdinand defeated the Muslim ruler at Granada. Muslims who chose to remain in Spain had to convert to Christianity. The noblemen surrounding Ferdinand and Isabel then insisted that the monarchs banish the roughly 150,000 Jews living in Spain. Jews could depart, convert, or face public execution.

The Age of Exploration

The same energy that fueled the *reconquista* animated many Europeans in this era to attempt to expand their power. Some organized the Crusades; some expanded militarily into Ireland and others into the region around the Baltic Sea. Merchants and ambitious princes dreamed of finding a way to circumvent the Muslim traders who were the middlemen in a thriving trade with the Far East. Europe's nobility and prosperous urban peoples desired the East's sugar, spices, fabrics, jewels, and precious metals. They were dazzled by the Italian Marco Polo's accounts of his journeys between 1275 and 1292 to the cities of China. So it was that European explorers set off in search of new routes to Asia.

In the fifteenth century, for the first time, Europeans had the necessary technology to be able to travel far from home in numbers. While Norsemen had briefly established a settlement in Newfoundland in about the year 1000, it had remained an isolated event. Now times had changed. The printing press, invented by Johannes Gutenberg in the middle of the century, allowed the rapid spread of information—like Marco Polo's text, as well as valuable maps. Through the traditional international trade routes, Europeans had gleaned gunpowder (originally from China) and navigational tools such as the compass (from the Arabs). They took the cannons they had originally learned of in the East and mounted them on ships so that they might make demands of people they encountered. The seafaring Portuguese absorbed all they had seen of other people's boats and designed the caravel, a ship that could sail faster than any previous vessel, making it possible to go farther with limited food and water.

Indeed, throughout the fifteenth century, having expelled the Muslims from their territory more rapidly than the Spaniards, the Portuguese had been gradually exploring the hitherto unknown coast of Africa. Prince Henry the Navigator encouraged many of these expeditions. By the 1470s, the Portuguese had discovered the kingdom of Benin (where Nigeria now is), and by the 1480s, they had rounded the southern tip of Africa at a point they named the Cape of Good Hope. This left them prepared to sail on to Asia and establish trading posts.

New Ideas Take Root

Because of the existence of the Sahara Desert, Europeans had previously known very little about Africa. Myths and stories had abounded, coming to Europe through the trade networks. Muslim merchants had established caravan routes across the desert and influenced the establishment of such states as the Mali and then the Songhay Empires (home of the fabled Timbuktu). But educated Europeans had learned from the works of the ancient Greeks that people could not live below the "burnt" zone and thus imagined that cities like Timbuktu were literally at the edge of the habitable world. It was therefore quite surprising to them to learn of such places as the densely populated, agricultural Benin as the Portuguese traveled farther down the African coast. And they were impressed to find that craftsmen in the neighboring Yoruba city-states produced stunningly beautiful items of bronze and ivory, including weapons (see Map 1–2).

However, even these kingdoms were no match, technologically speaking, for the Europeans. It would not have been possible, for example, for them to have come to explore Portugal. Because of a lack of protein-rich plants and domesticable animals, sub-Saharan Africans had turned to full-time farming significantly later than Eurasians and North Africans. When the Europeans found them in the fifteenth century, their technological power was roughly on a par with that of the ancient Sumerians of the Fertile Crescent, when they, too, had been relatively new to farming. The Portuguese thus found that the Africans were eager to trade desirable natural resources like gold, ivory, and also human slaves in exchange for textiles, metal goods like guns, and other items from the workshops of the North.

In these early years, the Portuguese sailors brought back only a few hundred Africans annually from their exploratory voyages and sold them in Mediterranean markets as household servants. They did not immediately imagine that the trade would grow, not associating slavery with Africans in particular. (The Latin root of the word "slave" referred to Slavic peoples taken in war.) In Africa, as almost everywhere on earth, there existed an ancient practice of selling prisoners of war into slavery. These slaves were mostly women and children who worked as domestics in other people's households. Theirs was not an enviable fate, but they generally were not treated cruelly, and their children were not usually considered slaves.

However, after Portugal gained control of the island of Madeira, off the coast of Africa, in the 1420s, and Spain seized the Canary Islands at the end of the century, businessmen conceived the idea of large-scale sugar cultivation based on slave labor. Enslaved Africans on the islands did not live in their captors' households or become enmeshed in ties of affection; and if they had any children, they became slaves, too. The new concept of chattel slavery was emerging. In the coming centuries, plantation slavery would strip the African continent of much of its population and bring new suffering to the Americas.

In the late fifteenth century, the findings of the Portuguese explorers led Christopher Columbus to think that if the experts had been wrong in their assumption that no people lived south of the Sahara, they might have been wrong about other things. Perhaps the globe was much smaller than they believed. It might be possible for a ship to travel west and arrive in the East before its food and water supplies ran out. And if the continent to the south of Europe was full of seemingly conquerable peoples, perhaps there was similar territory to the south of Asia. Such lands could be taken and used as a foothold in seeking the riches of the East. Columbus set about attempting to convince others of his theories.

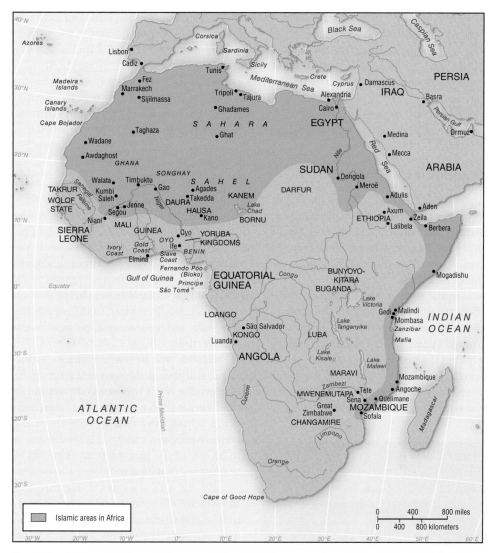

Map 1–2 Africa in the Age of Discovery Before 1450, Europeans knew little of Africa. Until that time, trade between Africa and Europe was controlled by Islamic traders whose empire extended across North Africa. In the middle of the fifteenth century, the Portuguese reached the western coast of Africa and began importing both trade goods and a small number of slaves. *Source:* Mark Kishlansky et al., *Societies and Culture in World History* (New York: Harper Collins, 1995), p. 414.

Collision in the Caribbean

Exactly which part of the Old World would encounter the New, and when, was largely a matter of chance. In the early fifteenth century, the Chinese emperor had sent ships to explore beyond their usual routes in the Indian Ocean, but he had eventually concluded it was not worth the cost of investing in expensive fleets, as the world's merchants seemed so bent on coming to his country in any case. In the late fifteenth century, Europeans were experiencing heady successes in their efforts to navigate the globe and compete with the once-dominant Muslim states. Still, there remained many obstacles to their reaching the unknown New World. We have often been taught that Columbus was one of the few who understood that the world was not flat. That is myth, however. All educated Europeans in his era knew the world was round. They also knew it was too big for their small ships to circumnavigate. Columbus was simply wrong in his hopeful calculations, which were based on ignorance. So it was that the monarchs of Spain and Portugal, and then of France and England, all initially turned Columbus down when he asked that they back his proposed venture.

Columbus's First Voyage

Then suddenly in 1492, after the fall of Granada, Queen Isabel summoned Columbus. With the wars over, she had money available and had decided to take a chance. The Portuguese had just rounded the southern tip of Africa, and Italian merchants had far more positive relations with Muslim merchants than Spanish ones did at present. She was desperate to prevent her newly unified country from falling into economic dependence on others.

In the accord that both sides signed, it is evident that Columbus was being sent on more than a trade mission. The monarchs were also clearly interested in the possibility that he might conquer a foothold in the East. He was to sail not due west, but southwest, toward Asian lands they hoped would be weaker than China. Columbus was also granted the position of governor-general of all the lands that he might conquer. Needless to say, he was also to conduct trade with China, and after deducting for expenses, he could keep one-tenth of the income from the enterprise, with the monarchy retaining the rest. The amount spent on the voyages, though larger than any individual merchant could afford, was relatively small in the context of Spain's budget; it would prove to be one of the shrewdest investments in the history of nations.

By his calculations, Columbus was sure his tiny fleet would be at sea no more than a few weeks. After nearly six weeks, with supplies dwindling, the men grew dangerously restless. They occasionally saw seagulls and tufts of grass in the water, but no land. Then, at two hours after midnight on October 12, 1492, a lookout spotted land. It was an island, and they named it San Salvador, after Jesus Christ the savior.

Christopher Columbus There are no surviving images of Christopher Columbus taken from life, but this painting was completed while people who remembered him well still lived.

Columbus believed they were off the coast of China, Japan, or India. Not understanding that he had found an unknown continent, he called the people they met "Indians." He conducted a ceremony to take possession of the island in the name of Ferdinand and Isabel. When the Indians came to see the newly arrived strangers, he presented gifts to initiate trade. The people responded with alacrity, bringing cotton and parrots to exchange for what the Spaniards offered. Columbus wrote in his journal, "They should be good and intelligent servants, for I see that they say very quickly everything that is said to them; and I believe that they would become Christians very easily, for it seemed to me that they had no religion. Our Lord pleasing, at the time of my departure, I will take six of them from here to Your Highnesses in order that they may learn to speak." Modern readers often stop at this point, chagrined but not surprised by Columbus's evident condescension and the Native Americans' apparent innocence. Reading further in the journal, however, the picture becomes more complicated. The Indians did, of course, have a religion, a language, and a set of diplomatic understandings of their own, and they did not respond positively to everything the newcomers did. In frustration, Columbus seized a number of them with brutal violence.

Columbus and his men visited the islands in the area over the next three months. The Arawak (or Taino) people who lived there had been farmers for a few hundred years. They grew corn and beans, lived in settled villages, and had begun to weave cotton into cloth. They had no metal weapons of any kind, and their towns could not withstand concerted attacks by the Spaniards. Other Indians, relative newcomers coming up from today's Venezuela, were in the process of conquering some of the smaller islands for themselves. These were the Caribs who later gave the Caribbean its name. They were much vilified by the Spaniards due to the effectiveness of their guerilla warfare tactics. After a futile search for China, hampered not only by geographic realities but also by an absolute inability to communicate, Columbus decided to return to Spain. He traded for as much gold jewelry and wild cotton, and as many exotic birds as he could. Then he set sail for home, bearing the cargo, the kidnapped Indians, and his exciting news to an eager Spanish court.

The Origins of a New World Political and Economic Order

Columbus was treated like a hero upon his return. Large investments were readily forthcoming, and within a year he embarked again. (He would sail two more times before he died.) Over a thousand people accompanied him this time. They were to settle the islands and from there continue to seek the fabulous wealth of China and Japan. This time, they would even be able to gather information from the indigenous people, as some of those they had brought back to Europe had learned to speak Spanish.

It soon became clear that the vast treasures Columbus had anticipated were not actually at hand. The people who had accompanied him, however, expected to be rewarded, and the queen and king who had financed his expedition awaited profits. Therefore, Columbus packed off more than 500 Indians to be sold as slaves in Europe and distributed another 600 or so among the Spanish settlers of Hispaniola for them to use to establish plantations and gold mines. The level of violence increased considerably. One man wrote home with relish about a young Indian woman whom he had brought on board a ship and brutally raped.

Yet as the monarch who had driven the Muslims and then the Jews out of Spain, Isabel took seriously her responsibilities to evangelize and care for her Indian subjects.

Isabel and her successors also had political and economic goals, all of which they attempted to reconcile by insisting that the Indians who inhabited the islands seized by the Spanish were her vassals, subjects of the Spanish crown. Like other vassals in Spain and its growing empire, the Indians were to be technically free, although they could be required to both work and pay tribute to the crown. Isabel instructed the governor to impose European-style civilization and Christianity on them. They were to be "made to serve us through work, and be paid a just salary," and in order to assure their salvation, "they must live in villages, each in a house with a wife, family and possessions, as do the people of our kingdoms, and dress and behave like reasonable beings." Humane treatment and freedom from slavery would thus depend on the Indians' willingness to abandon their religion and customs and adopt those of the Spanish.

With the Spanish monarchy refusing to sanction the enslavement of friendly Indians, settlers had to devise an alternate means of getting labor from them. Out of this struggle a New World political economy emerged. For the first several years, the Spanish simply demanded a certain amount of tribute from the Tainos as a whole. Individual Spaniards found this arrangement insufficiently lucrative, and across the island of Hispaniola, they began subduing individual *caciques* (chiefs) and demanding that they compel their people to work for whomever the governor named. The settlers received neither land—which had to be obtained from Spanish royal officials through grant or purchase—nor actual ownership of the Indians. They possessed only the right to compel the Indians they held in *encomienda* (as the system was called) to work for them. In exchange, each *encomendero*, or holder of an *encomienda*, was to ensure that the Indians received Christian instruction and lived in godly villages. Theoretically, the colonists thus complied with Isabel's insistence that friendly Indians be made vassals of the crown rather than slaves. But although the system appeared to give due regard to the rights and spiritual requirements of the native people, they were in fact subjected to overwork and abuse even if they could not legally be bought and sold as slaves. This form of exploitation, though akin to European serfdom, was unique to the New World.

The Division of the World

Meanwhile, in Europe, the report of Christopher Columbus had touched off a veritable frenzy of international competition. In 1493, at the request of the Spanish monarchs, Pope Alexander VI confirmed Spanish dominion over all the lands that Columbus had explored and commanded the Spanish "to lead the peoples dwelling in those islands and countries to embrace the Christian religion." The Portuguese feared that they might lose control of Madeira and the nearby Azores and other current or future settlements on islands off the coast of Africa, so they complained to the pope. In 1494, the office of the pope arranged for both parties to sign the Treaty of Tordesillas, giving Spain all lands to be discovered to the west of an imaginary line 270 leagues west of the Azores, and Portugal all lands east of it. The treaty later formed the basis for Portugal's claim to Brazil, which her explorers accidentally reached in 1500. In the same period, in 1497, Henry VII of England, who deeply regretted having rejected Columbus's overture, sent off John Cabot to sail past Greenland and seek a "Northwest Passage" to the East. Cabot came to Newfoundland, concluded it must be part of Asia, and claimed it for England.

An Italian merchant named Amerigo Vespucci joined some of the expeditions sailing off to explore these new lands. In 1499, he saw the northeast coast of what we now know is South America. He still believed he was seeing some part of the Asian world, but he and his companions were increasingly convinced that these were significant southern territories—either an extensive peninsula or even a severed southern landmass—not previously heard of, as Columbus had predicted. A few years later, an embellished version of his letters was published. At the time, many intellectuals questioned whether the newly discovered lands actually fell within the Asian world or constituted an entire, previously unknown continent separating the great ocean into two. In 1507, a German cartographer concluded that the latter must be true. He published a map that circulated widely because it was the first to assert the geographic truth so unmistakably. He named the new landmass after Amerigo Vespucci, whom he wrongly believed to have been the first European to see it, and the unlikely label stuck.

Onto the Mainland

Even after the Europeans had become convinced that they were nowhere near the mainland of Asia, they continued their exploratory missions with zeal. In a little more than a quarter of a century, the population of the Caribbean islands had collapsed. The Spaniards who had arrived first divided its arable lands among themselves. Therefore, newly arriving European settlers, seeking both land and slaves, continued to sail beyond charted territories. In 1513, the crown issued the *Requerimiento*, or "Requirement," a document drafted by legal scholars and theologians. It promised all Indians that if they accepted Christianity, including the authority of the pope and the Spanish monarch, the conquerors would leave them in peace; but if they resisted, the conquerors would have the right to make war on them and capture and enslave prisoners. Some evidence suggests that explorers read the document in Latin to uncomprehending Indians, then proceeded to wage what could now be defined as a "just war" against them. The Indians learned to tantalize the Spaniards with accounts of glittering empires a little farther west, just far enough away to get the dangerous strangers out of their territory. It was not long before the Spaniards were convinced that there was a large continent to be found. Eventually, they discovered the Aztec Empire in Mexico and the Inca Empire in Peru, each of which rivaled the most fantastic images from literature and legend.

The First Florida Ventures

Ambitious Spaniards set off on their exploratory missions in all directions (see Map 1–3). They crossed Central America at one point and saw the Pacific, and they touched on the northern coasts of South America. Juan Ponce de León was the first European explorer to reach the mainland that would later be called the United States. In March 1513 he reached the Atlantic shore of the land he named Florida, which he mistakenly thought was another island. He and his men sailed around Florida to the Gulf Coast, encountering hostile Indians who probably had already heard about the Spanish slave traders. On the west coast of Florida, he met the Calusas, the most powerful ethnic group in the region. When Ponce de León returned with another expedition in 1521, they were ready for him. The Calusas attacked. Ponce de León was wounded by an arrow and returned to Cuba to die.

In Florida, the diseases the Spaniards brought with them struck the densely settled agricultural population particularly hard, and explorers routinely pillaged local villages and enslaved those whom they captured. Of the hundreds of small tribes, each with its own history, politics, economy, and culture, all that remains today are the names that the Spaniards recorded.

The Conquest of Mexico

For almost 30 years, the fabled cities of gold sought by the Spaniards proved elusive. However, the capital of a great empire really was nearby, and its ruler, through his network of spies, soon learned of the coming of the strangers. His name was Moctezuma II (later renamed "Montezuma" by the English), and he was the sixth in a line of powerful Aztec kings. The Mayan states in the Yucatan had long ago declined from their former glory and now existed as relatively small, separate chiefdoms. But the star of the central basin of Mexico had risen. Waves of nomadic invaders from the north (that is, the southwestern part of the future United States) had regularly brought new blood and new ideas to the famed farming regions of central Mexico, and there they had been incorporated (as Europe sometimes incorporated the Vikings, or China the Mongolian hordes). Moctezuma's people, the Mexica (pronounced Me-SHEE-ka), arriving 200 years previously, had constituted the last wave of invaders. After several generations of jockeying for power with other local chiefs, through strategic alliances and extraordinary military bravado, they had launched the most powerful state yet known in the Americas.

Moctezuma's power was still growing. At the start of his reign, he had led the invasion of areas including the Coatzacoalcos region, the home of Malinche. Other ethnic groups were always offered the prospect of joining the empire voluntarily at first by paying an annual tribute. They were then left alone as largely self-governing entities. Only if they resisted did the Aztec lord bring his military might and that of his subject states and allies to bear. Great resistance was punished harshly: prisoners were taken as sacrifices for the gods, who in exchange for all they did for humankind demanded the greatest gift of all, that of human life.

In 1517 and 1518, two different Spanish expeditions rounded the Yucatan Peninsula and touched on the coast of central Mexico in Mayan territory. Aztec merchants lived in the area, and through them, Moctezuma would have heard of the events. In 1519, Hernando Cortés followed the paths they had charted. He was both luckier and bolder than his predecessors. After a skirmish with the Mayas, he was given 20 women as a peace offering, and among them was the young woman, Malinche. With her at his side translating, explaining, and bargaining for food, Cortés was able to learn the whereabouts of the Aztec capital and begin to make his way upward into the mountains along the paths that led to the city. Messengers from the outskirts of his territories brought Moctezuma the news.

As Cortés and his entourage of about 500 made their way toward the city of Tenochtitlan (on the site of present-day Mexico City), they worked to form alliances with Moctezuma's avowed enemies, or with people recently conquered by him and still smarting from their defeat. When the Spaniards were occasionally attacked, they attacked back, sending mounted and armored men galloping through villages with long spears and torches, wreaking destruction, until the people sued for peace and declared themselves willing to join the Spanish.

Moctezuma himself probably ordered some of the attacks as he tested the strangers' military capabilities. He then sent messengers offering to pay the Spaniards an annual

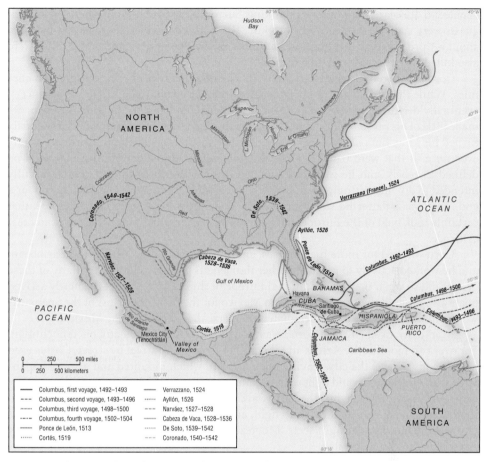

Map 1–3　The Spanish Exploration In the 50 years after Columbus's first voyage, Spanish explorers traveled across most of the southern half of the United States.

tribute if they would stay away (essentially what those whom he could defeat offered him). This, however, was not what the Spaniards wanted. They pressed forward, and Moctezuma decided to let them and their new indigenous allies enter the city. Politically, he could not afford a battle with major casualties close to home, and if he let them enter, he might be able to work out an arrangement satisfactory to both parties. In November 1519, Hernando Cortés and Moctezuma II met formally and exchanged ostentatious greetings on a grand causeway leading over the lake that surrounded the beautiful island city of Tenochtitlan.

For the next few months, the Spaniards were the unwelcome yet honored guests of Moctezuma. They visited all parts of the city and asked for and were given large quantities of gold. Both sides schemed to learn more of each other and gain control of the situation. Eventually, Cortés had his men seize Moctezuma and hold him prisoner. He then proceeded to issue orders to the populace through his new hostage. Not long after, some jumpy Spaniards panicked at the sight of a religious dance put on by warriors in full regalia and slaughtered all the performers. This was enough for the Mexica people. They decided to disregard the words of their king. Surrounding the building where their hated guests were staying, they moved in to kill. The terrified Spaniards broke out, but only about a third escaped. An unknown number of the Spaniards' indigenous allies were also killed, as well as Moctezuma himself.

Cortés gathered his shattered forces in Tlaxcala, home of the Aztecs' greatest enemies. While the Tlaxcalans publicly debated whether or not to continue the alliance—eventually deciding that they should—Cortés penned a letter to the king of Spain. He made little of his present plight and also made the claim that Moctezuma had voluntarily turned his kingdom over to him on the day they met and had been in Cortés's custody ever since. If that were true, then the warriors who had just driven him out could be defined as rebels, and he would be justified in bringing them to heel, which he fully intended to do. Interestingly, he made no claim at all that the Aztecs had taken him for a god. That was a flattering story invented by Spaniards many years later, a fiction that certainly took hold of the European imagination, but for which there was never any real evidence.

Cortés waited for more men, horses, and supplies from Europe and the Caribbean, and he worked actively to persuade other indigenous groups to join him. Many of these groups did so when they saw additional European ships arrive. One of the newly arrived boats also brought the smallpox virus to Mexico for the first time. Most of the Spaniards were immune, but the disease decimated the Tlaxcalans as well as the Mexica.

Eventually, in April 1521, Cortés was ready to launch a great assault on Tenochtitlan. For over two months, the Aztecs and their allies fought him street by street. Cortés used his cannons to level the city, leaving open areas in which mounted and armored Spaniards with long lances could fight with impunity against their adversaries. "Bit by bit they came pressing us back against the [city] wall," an Aztec warrior later remembered. When there were almost no warriors left to fight, and the starving women and children in the city were reduced to eating insects, Moctezuma's successor sought peace. The mighty Aztec state had been defeated.

The Establishment of a Spanish Empire

In many ways, the Aztecs' experiences were similar to those of most Native Americans in their early dealings with Europeans. An early period of tentative, even fumbling European exploration was followed by a formal, ceremonial exchange. Then came a brief time of mutual curiosity and trade, before European intentions became fully clear to the indigenous and a crisis erupted in which they violently rejected the outsiders. After a setback of greater or lesser extent, however, the Europeans always collected themselves and ultimately asserted their authority. The Indians strategized creatively and fought bravely, but they could not compete with European technology. The problem was that people who had only recently become farmers (or in some cases were still hunter-gatherers) were pitted against people who were the cultural heirs of 10,000 years of sedentary living. One side had such things as horses, protective metal armor, far-shooting crossbows, and ships constantly bringing new men and supplies, while the other side did not. The people of the central basin of Mexico had been farming longer than anyone else in the Americas, and not surprisingly, they were able to put up the most dramatic fight against the Europeans. However, even they could win only a battle, not a long, drawn-out war.

STRUGGLES FOR DEMOCRACY

Native Americans Debate the Question of the Europeans

Before a great pyramid temple, surrounded by sunbaked adobe buildings, the nobles of Tlaxcala (Tlash-KA-la) met to discuss the fate of the Spaniards. It was July 1520 (in the European calendar), and the invading Spaniards under Hernando Cortés had just been driven from the Aztec capital of Tenochtitlan; about two thirds of them had been killed. Dying at their sides had been hundreds of Tlaxcalans who chose to ally with the Europeans. Now the Tlaxcalan council had to decide if they should protect the Spaniards who had fled back to them or turn on their former allies.

When the newcomers first appeared from the east more than a year before, the Tlaxcalans met them in battle, but they soon learned that they could not defeat the metal-clad warriors mounted on large beasts, wielding long spears and shooting fire arrows from a distance. The Indians' stone arrows shattered when they hit their enemies' armor, and the Spaniards could storm into their villages on horseback, skewer people, set fire to buildings, then escape unhurt themselves. Within days the Tlaxcalans had made peace, offering to help the Spaniards move against the Aztecs, who were the Tlaxcalans' longtime enemies. They sent hundreds, perhaps thousands of warriors to Tenochtitlan. The Spaniards, however, were ejected from the powerful Aztec capital a few months later, and many of the Tlaxcalan allies died.

The exhausted and impatient Spanish survivors waited for two weeks while the Tlaxcalans' democratic process unfolded. Many people were allowed to have a say in the public forum in order for consensus to emerge. Tlaxcala consisted of four sub-kingdoms, each ruled by its own chief, or *tlatoani*, meaning "he who speaks on behalf of others." Sometimes the four units worked together on internal, domestic tasks, such as the building of roads; they always operated in tandem in their diplomatic dealings with outsiders and the making of war. Regarding the present occasion, it was not merely a question of allowing each of the four chiefs to speak. Each chief was supported by the heads of the noble lineages within his domain; to retain power, the chief needed to be sure that each man felt he was heard and respected. The four subunits took turns allowing men to step forward and voice their thoughts. Sometimes the highest nobles interjected a summary or underscored a central point to keep the group moving gradually toward a resolution.

Some of the nobles believed they had learned enough about Spanish capability to be sure they would win in the end; they noted that they had it on good authority from Indians who were learning Spanish that more Europeans, horses, and weapons were on their way. Others believed the power of the Spanish was exaggerated, that the Aztecs' recent victory demonstrated that the Europeans could be defeated, and that their present weakness provided the Tlaxcalans a perfect opportunity to destroy them. One young prince named Xicotencatl (SHEE-ko-ten-kat), the son of the chief of the second most *continued* powerful quadrant, had engaged in negotiations with the Aztecs: the Aztecs promised, he said, that if they turned on the Spanish now, the Aztecs would make the Tlaxcalans their closest allies. Having resisted Aztec authority themselves for so long, it was tempting to the Tlaxcalans to become the Aztecs' partners in ruling the land. Others, however, cautioned that the Aztecs could not be trusted.

The debate went back and forth until the vast majority had decided it was safer to hold fast to the Spaniards and help them survive until more Europeans arrived. Xicotencatl did not agree, but his father did, and he expressed willingness to abide by the community's decision. His people had taught him that governance was more effective when power was shared.

After defeating the Aztecs, the Spaniards continued to wage war against other ethnic groups, but it did not take many years to subdue most of Mexico, leaving only the most remote areas still independent and unconquered. Meanwhile, the Europeans built ships on the Pacific coast and began to make their way down the side of the continent. In the 1530s, they discovered and conquered the astounding Inca Empire (centered in today's Peru), another farming kingdom, whose network of roads had covered much of the Andes. Now the Spaniards had at least nominal control of the lands stretching from the tip of South America to halfway up what is now the United States, excepting only the Portuguese colony of Brazil.

Both Mexico and Peru were found to contain vast deposits of silver, and Colombia contained a significant amount of gold. This yielded extraordinary profits for both Spanish investors and the crown (as collector of the tax called the King's fifth). The Indians everywhere were given out in *encomienda* to work on the plantations of the Spaniards.

The plantations produced widely varying crops, but the most profitable one was sugar. As its cultivation spread, so did the demand for labor, as producing sugar was extremely labor intensive at certain seasons. The *encomienda* system could not meet the demand. By the second half of the sixteenth century, Indian laborers in sugar had been replaced by enslaved Africans. Brazil and some of the Caribbean colonies were largely dedicated to its cultivation. For the first time, Africans became yet another commodity to be transported across the seas, robbing Africa of its population and adding to the wealth of the Old World.

The Return to North America

After the conquest of Mexico, the Spaniards resumed their exploration of Florida with heightened expectations. There were several ventures, the most significant ones led by Lucas Vázquez de Ayllón, Pánfilo de Narváez, and Hernando de Soto. In 1526, Ayllón explored the South Carolina coast and established a short-lived town on the coast of Georgia. Two years later, Narváez landed near modern-day Tampa with 400 men. Battles and shipwrecks, however, destroyed the expedition. Ultimately, only four men survived: three Spaniards and an enslaved North African. They washed up on the shores of Texas.

By good luck, they came to be accepted as healers and, eight years later, walked down into Spanish Mexico from the north.

The Spaniard who left the greatest mark on the southeastern part of the future United States was Hernando de Soto. He had participated in the assault on the Inca Empire in Peru, which provided him with a small fortune and the belief that more wealth could be found in exploring unknown territories. He and his forces landed near Tampa in 1539. His party of about 600 soldiers spent the next four years exploring the area, which was densely populated by Mississippian tribes, and eventually reached the Mississippi River.

De Soto took whatever food, treasure, and people he wanted in his journey. Some communities fought back fiercely, whereas others attempted to placate the invaders. The region never really recovered from the expedition's depredations: deaths from disease, the destruction of many chieftains, and losses incurred in battles made it impossible for ruling families to continue to command tribal members to produce food surpluses and build great towns. On the other hand, the resistance on the part of the Indians took its toll on the Spaniards as well. Only about 300 of them made it back to Mexico, and de Soto himself died en route in 1542.

In the Southeast, the Spanish never found the great sought-after cities of gold resembling the Aztec and Inca capitals. And because much of the land did not seem suitable for large-scale agriculture, and most of the peoples were still nomadic hunter-gatherers for part of each year—who therefore could not be given out in *encomienda*—Spain never colonized most of the territory de Soto saw. Instead, military outposts, such as St. Augustine, were established to protect the more valuable lands to the south. To prevent rival nations from claiming the northern reaches of its empire, Spain did not disclose the geographic information it had secured from expeditions like de Soto's. This secrecy ultimately weakened Spain's claim to the region, however, because such claims traditionally depended on the right of prior exploration.

In the meantime, another group of Spaniards was setting out northward from Mexico City, toward the southwestern part of the future United States. They had heard tales of the Seven Cities of Cíbola, supposedly filled with gold and gems. In May 1539, a party guided by Esteban the Moor—one of the four survivors of the Narváez expedition, who had survived because they had attained the status of healers—reached the Zuni Pueblo in today's New Mexico. The inhabitants of the town no longer interpreted Esteban to be a healer; they killed him when he approached. A year later, another aspiring conquistador, Francisco Vásquez de Coronado, arrived at Zuni with about 300 Spaniards, 1,000 Indian allies, and 1,500 horses and pack animals. They took the pueblo and several others by force and later traveled west to the Grand Canyon and east as far as Wichita, Kansas, coming within 300 miles of de Soto's expedition.

Timucua Indians, 1591 Here they celebrate the defeat of the enemy.

Unprepared for the cold winter of 1540–1541, Coronado's party depleted the food and supplies of the Indians near their camp at Bernalillo. When a Spaniard raped an Indian woman, the Pueblos rebelled. By the time they were put down, at least 100 Indians had been burned at the stake and about 13 villages destroyed. To the relief of the local people, silver was shortly thereafter discovered in Mexico and became the focus of the settlers' attention for many years. The Southwest had proved disappointing to them; they left and did not return in numbers until the 1590s. A warning of the struggles to come, however, had been given to both sides.

The Consequences of Conquest

Some of the most important changes produced by contact between Europeans and Native Americans were wholly unintentional. Most indigenous communities needed the effort of all members to provide a food supply. Even those who demanded tribute from others were well aware of this. European demands often tipped a delicate social balance, though the newcomers did not realize it. The Europeans also unintentionally introduced new diseases that spread rapidly. If the biological effects of human contact were felt immediately, however, the consequences of plant and animal exchange took much longer. New breeds of animals were introduced into the Americas, and plants were exchanged between the Americas and Europe. The American landscape was forever changed, as domestic animals trampled grasslands and increasing acreage was turned over to the cultivation of Old World crops.

Demographic Disaster

The violent warfare that made conquest possible turned out to be only a small part of the problem faced by indigenous peoples. Although the *encomienda* system at first satisfied the Spanish settlers, it proved disastrous for the Indians. They could not produce the surplus necessary to support the Europeans in addition to feeding their own families. Besides facing the direct effects of malnutrition, the dislocation of their normal way of life was deeply disturbing, and the birthrate began to fall.

Within a few years after the appearance of Europeans, the Native American population began to decline, and the introduction of the smallpox virus to Hispaniola in 1518 hastened the process. Soon, no more than a thousand of the island's original half million inhabitants survived. Disease worked the same terrible destruction on the nearby islands of Cuba, Puerto Rico, and Jamaica. Sickness followed the Spanish and other Europeans wherever they went in the Americas, making conquest that much easier for them. Epidemics also spread to and decimated native populations that had not yet encountered Europeans.

Europeans did not set out to kill off the Native Americans, but the diseases they brought with them did just that. Isolation had protected the native peoples from the diseases of the Old World, whereas centuries of trade had caused Europeans, Africans, and Asians to become exposed to the microbes present in one another's environments and thus acquire some biological defenses. Without such immunities, Indians were overcome by wave after wave of European diseases, including smallpox, typhus, and influenza. Scholars debate the exact number of deaths, but it is clear that over the course of the first century, the indigenous population dropped by about 90 percent—in some places more, in some less. The psychological trauma inflicted by such events is almost impossible for those who have not experienced them to imagine. A Cakchiquel Indian remembered the spread of an epidemic in his native Guatemala in 1521 that killed a substantial proportion of his community. "After our fathers and grandfathers succumbed, half of the people fled to the fields. The dogs and the vultures devoured the bodies. . . . Your grandfathers died, and with them died the son of the king and his brothers and kinsmen. So it was that we became orphans, oh my sons! . . . We were born to die."

The Columbian Exchange

In what historians have called the Columbian Exchange, plants and animals, as well as human beings and their diseases, were shared between the two worlds connected in 1492, eventually transforming them both. Along with the 1,500 Spaniards who joined him on his second voyage, Columbus brought horses, pigs, cattle, sheep, and goats, as well as wheat, sugarcane, and seeds for fruits and vegetables (see Map 1–4). And he returned to Europe with a variety of plants hitherto unknown there.

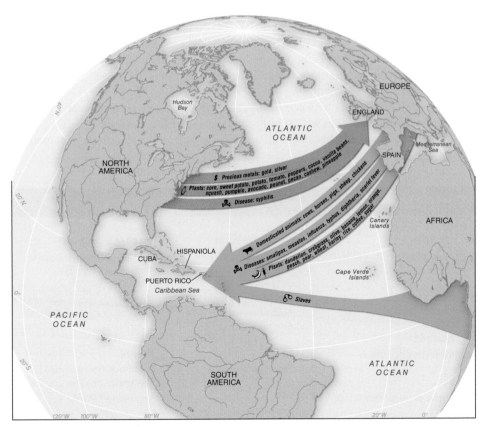

Map 1–4 The Columbian Exchange The exchanges of plants, animals, and diseases dramatically altered both the Old World and the New.

The introduction of the new plants and animals had the negative effect of sometimes overrunning native farm fields and other ecosystems, but the new species also had some positive effects. Indians often adopted Old World life forms to their own purposes. American Southwestern and Plains Indians took to the horse, for example, which changed their way of life, making them more productive hunters and more dangerous enemies. Mounted Indians could easily kill more buffalo than they needed for their own subsistence, creating a surplus they could trade for European goods.

The Old World was also profoundly transformed by plants introduced from the Americas. Some plants that we associate with Europe came from the Americas. We might identify potatoes with Ireland, tomatoes with Italy, and fine chocolate with France, but none of these foods was produced in Europe before the sixteenth century. Moreover, the cultivation of American foods (particularly potatoes and corn) in the Old World, as well as of Old World foods (such as wheat) in the New, is often thought to have made possible the dramatic growth in world population that occurred in the ensuing centuries (see Figure 1–1).

Men's and Women's Lives

Every society has its own notion of the proper relationship between the sexes; this is one of the ways it establishes order. When one society conquers another, not only do different notions of gender come into conflict, but gender itself becomes one of the instruments of conquest. Conquerors often demonstrate dominance through rape, and the conquistadors wrote without self-consciousness of the ways in which they used native women whom they seized as commodities.

Yet not all encounters between European men and native women were violent. In many indigenous societies as well as in Europe, people were accustomed to using sexual relationships and marriage to cement alliances between prominent families—sometimes

Time Line

▼C.12,000 BCE
Indian peoples arrive in North America

▼711 CE
Moors invade Iberian Peninsula

▼1275–1292
Marco Polo travels in Asia

▼1434
Portuguese arrive at West Coast of Africa

▼1492
Spanish complete the *reconquista*, evicting Moors from Spain

Jews expelled from Spain

Columbus's first voyage to America

▼1493
Columbus's second voyage

▼1494
Treaty of Tordesillas divides New World between Spain and Portugal

▼1496
Spanish complete conquest of Canary Islands

▼1497
John Cabot arrives in North America

▼1498
Columbus's third voyage to America, reaches South American coast

▼1500
Portuguese arrive in Brazil

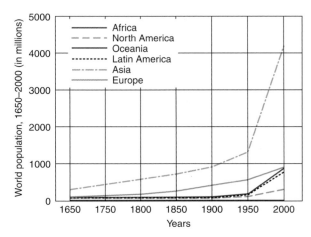

Figure 1–1 World Population, 1650–2000 These rough estimates of world population suggest the way that the colonization of the New World affected world population. The introduction of Old World disease led to population decline in the Americas, while the enslavement of millions of Africans led to population decline in Africa. At the same time, foods from the New World made possible the population increase of Europe and Asia.

Source: Based on Alfred W. Crosby Jr., *The Columbian Exchange: Biological and Cultural Consequences of 1492* (Westport, CT: Greenwood Pub. Co., 1972), p. 166.

at great personal cost to the young women involved. Thus, for example, after Cortés defeated the Tlaxcalans, whose kingdom stood on the path to the Aztec capital, the Tlaxcalans presented a number of young women as part of the peace agreement. A page from a Tlaxcalan codex (a pictorial account painted on bark or paper) illustrates the ceremony. In the picture, Cortés sits on a chair, his officers behind him. In front of him is the Tlaxcalan leader, also backed up by his nobles. Malintzin stands addressing the Tlaxcalan women, who include elegantly dressed nobles, intended to be accepted as wives for Spanish leaders. The group also includes the daughters of lesser nobles, as well as some commoners intended as slaves.

Several decades later, the names and fates of some of the elite women were still remembered by both sides. Tlecuiluatzin, a daughter of Xicotencatl, an important Tlaxcalan chief, was renamed doña Luisa and became the mistress of Pedro de

▼**1504**
Columbus's fourth voyage to America ends

▼**1508**
Spanish conquer Puerto Rico

▼**1513**
Spanish *Requerimiento* promises freedom to all Indians who accept Spanish authority
Spanish conquer Cuba
Ponce de León reaches Florida
The Laws of Burgos attempt to regulate working conditions of Indians

▼**1518**
Spanish introduce smallpox to New World

▼**1519**
Cortés lands on Yucatan coast

▼**1519–1522**
Ferdinand Magellan's crew sails around the world

▼**1521**
Tenochtitlan falls to the Spanish
Ponce de León returns to Florida

▼**1526**
Ayllón explores South Carolina coast and establishes fort in Georgia

▼**1528**
Narváez explores Florida

▼**1539–1543**
De Soto and his party explore Southeast, arriving at Mississippi, devastating the Indians and their land

▼**1540–1542**
Coronado explores Southwest

Defeat of the Tlaxcalans Here, Malinche stands next to Cortés, receiving the Tlaxcalan women who have been presented to them as gifts from a defeated people.

Alvarado, second in command after Cortés. She accompanied him to Guatemala, and although they were not married, their children entered the higher ranks of Spanish society in the New World. Many of the first generation of elite *mestizo* (or mixed) sons, including Malinche's son by Cortés, were brought up in their fathers' households and even sent to Spain for their education, while the daughters generally found prominent husbands.

This state of affairs did not last, however. Indigenous women continued to bear children by European men, but once there were more Spanish women in the colonies, fewer such women ended up married, and fewer of the children received places of honor when they reached adulthood. Nevertheless, many of the relationships between the Spaniards and Native American women were consensual. The women had few options, given the devastation in their communities, and their cultures had instilled the idea that true strength lay in survival, rather than choosing death over compromise. The mestizo population grew larger every year.

Conclusion

Within a half century after Columbus's arrival in the New World, both the world he had come from and the one he had reached had been transformed into a new, global political economy (see Map 1–5). Thanks to the decision made by Queen Isabel, Spain dominated exploration, colonization, and exploitation of the New World. The wealth that Spain extracted from her colonies encouraged rival nations to enter into overseas ventures. Eventually France, England, the Netherlands, Sweden, and Russia all established New World colonies. Because Spain (along with Portugal, which claimed Brazil) had such a head start, rival nations would have to settle for the lands Spain left unclaimed.

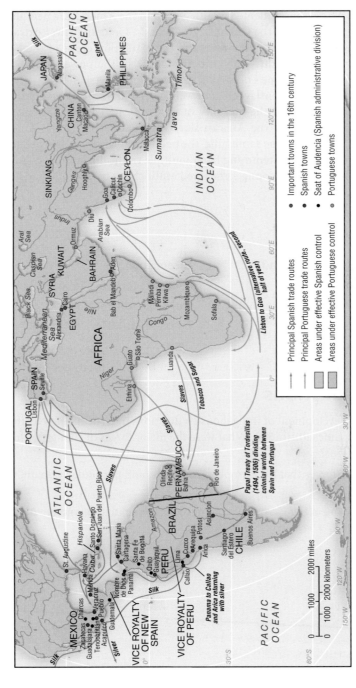

Map 1–5 A New Global Economy By 1600, both Spain and Portugal had established empires that reached from one end of the globe to the other.

In the wake of the unprecedented wealth gained in the Americas, a new global economy was established, linking the Old and New Worlds. Gold and silver extracted from its empire sustained Spain's rise to power, and the plantation crops of the New World made many Europeans wealthy. Thus, the divergence in the power of the two hemispheres grew wider, and Europe's power also grew relative to Asia's.

Native Americans faced enslavement or were given out in *encomienda*. As the native population was depleted and the morality of enslaving native populations was questioned, Europeans turned to the African slave trade. Suffering in the Americas was therefore intense, and yet at the same time, the people who survived learned to carry on with their lives. Ways of life stemming from multiple traditions unfolded, and cultures evolved in creative ways. The young girl named Malinche, it turned out, had been pointing the way.

Who, What

Francisco Vásquez de Coronado 23

Hernando Cortés 4

Malinche (Malintzin, doña Marina) 4

Juan Ponce de León 17

Hernando de Soto 22

Encomienda 16

Political economy 16

The *Requerimiento* 17

Tenochtitlan 18

Review Questions

1. Describe the development of indigenous civilizations in Central and North America from Archaic times until 1500. What were the major forces of change within these early populations?

2. What were the forces that led European countries, and particularly Spain, to explore the New World?

3. What was the impact of European conquest on the population and environment of the New World?

Critical-Thinking Questions

1. Compare older ways of explaining the conquest (such as Moctezuma's supposed belief that Hernando Cortés was a god) with scholars' more recent explanations. What beliefs about Native Americans does each set of explanations reflect?

2. How would Native American men and women have experienced conquest differently?

3. Compare Spain's treatment of Muslims and Jews in Spain following the *reconquista* with the country's later treatment of conquered Native Americans in the New World. Do you think these groups received similar or different treatment? Why?

For further review materials and resource information, please visit www.oup.com/us/oakes

CHAPTER 1: WORLDS IN MOTION, 1450–1550

Primary Sources

1.1 AZTEC PRAYER TO TLALOC (PRE-CONQUEST)

The Nahuas began to arrive in central Mexico in the 900s. They migrated from what is today Arizona and New Mexico and settled among people who had been farmers for at least two millennia. One of the last groups to arrive, the Mexica (Me-SHEE-ka), had risen to great power by the time the Spanish came, ruling over hundreds of other city-states. We know them now as the Aztecs. They had a remarkable literary culture, including poetry, songs, histories, and prayers. However, it was an oral culture and would probably be lost to us today were it not for the efforts of Christian missionaries. In the 1560s, forty years after the Spanish conquest, a Franciscan named Bernardino de Sahagún orchestrated a project in which Nahuatl-speaking assistants interviewed Indian elders about their former lives. The work was eventually taken to Florence, Italy, and thus became known as the Florentine Codex.

Uncan mitoa in tlatolli: in uel iniollocopa quitoaia in iquac quitlatlauhtiaia in tlaloc ...
Auh iz nelle axcan ca ie tlaihiiouitoc in tonacaiutl, ca ie ma uilantoc in teteu inueltiuh: in
tonacaiutl ca ie teuhpachiuhtoc, ca ie tocatzaoalquimiliuhtoc ca ie tlaihiiouia, ca ie
tlaciaui ...

Here are told the words which they uttered from their hearts when they prayed to Tlaloc [the rain god]:

Behold now, earthly life lies suffering, the elder sister of the gods lies outstretched. Earthly life lies covered with dust, wrapped in cobwebs. There is fatigue, exhaustion.

Behold the common folk, who are the tail and the wings.[1] They are disappearing. Their eyelids are swelling, their mouths drying out. They become bony, twisted, stretched. Thin are the commoners' lips and blanched are their throats. With pallid eyes live the babies, the children, those who totter, those who crawl, those who spend their time turning dirt and potshards in their hands, those who live with their eyes bent to the ground, those who lie on the boards, who fill the cradles. All the people face torment, affliction. They witness that which makes humans suffer.

Already there are none who are passed over; all the little creatures are suffering. The troupial bird, the roseate spoonbill drag their wings. They are upended, tumbled headfirst. They open and close their beaks [from thirst]. And the animals, the four-footed ones of the lord of the near, of the nigh, just wander here and there. They can scarcely rise; to no purpose is the ground licked. They are crazed for water. Already there is death, all are perishing. The common folk and the animals are dying.

Uncan mitoa: in quenin ticitl quitlatlauhtiaia, in piltzintli in ooallacat ...
Auh in otlalticpac quiz piltzintli: niman tzatzi in ticitl, tlacaoatza, quitoznequi: ca ouel
iaot in cioatzintli, ca onoquichtic, ca otlama, ca ocacic in piltzintli ...

---

[1] This metaphor was used to express the crucial importance of the commoners to all of society.

Here is told how the midwife exhorted the baby who had been born:

When the baby had arrived on earth, then the midwife shouted; she gave war cries, which meant that the woman had fought a good battle, had become a brave warrior, had taken a captive, had captured a baby.

Then the midwife spoke to it. . . . You have suffered exhaustion, you have suffered fatigue, my youngest one, my precious noble child, precious necklace, precious feather, precious one. You have arrived. Rest, find repose. Here are gathered your beloved grandfathers, your beloved grandmothers, who await you. Here into their hands you have arrived. Do not sigh! Do not be sad! Why have you come, why have you been brought here? Truly you will endure the sufferings of torment and fatigue, for our lord has ordered, has disposed that there will be pain, affliction, misery [in our lives on earth]. There will be work, labor for morning and evening sustenance. [But] there is sweat, weariness and labor so that there will be eating, drinking, and the wearing of raiment. Truly you will endure . . .

Source: Charles Dibble and Arthur J. O. Anderson, eds., *General History of the Things of New Spain*, Book 6: *Rhetoric and Moral Philosophy* (Salt Lake City: University of Utah Press, 1969), pp. 35–36, 167–168. (We have amended their translations.)

1.2 VISUAL DOCUMENT: CHACO CULTURE NATIONAL HISTORICAL PARK, PUEBLO BONITO

The corn that sustained Mesoamerican civilization eventually spread outward through long-distance trade. For example, in the San Juan River basin and especially in Chaco Canyon in the northwestern corner of today's New Mexico, people experimented with agriculture from the ninth to the eleventh century, adopting it for a few generations and then, when times were tougher, breaking into small nomadic groups. They built impressive stone-and-wood villages organized around *kivas*, large communal ceremonial chambers. The largest of these sites is now called Pueblo Bonito. Archaeologists have

confirmed that the people who lived there were well aware of their history. A small original construction became the ceremonial heart of the large village, which was built around it several generations later. There the people concentrated their burials, reliquaries, and precious goods, which included products brought from as far away as Mexico. At the town's height, as many as a thousand people lived there.

Source: Getty Images/DEA/SIOEN/Contributor and Getty Images/Education Images/Contributor

1.3 KING FERNANDO AND QUEEN ISABELLA OF SPAIN, "GRANADA CAPITULATIONS" (1492)

In 1492, King Fernando and Queen Isabella of Spain defeated the last Muslim kingdom on the Iberian Peninsula, freeing them to turn their attention to international trade. They signed a business contract with a Genoese explorer named Christopher Columbus, who believed he could reach Asia by sailing west. They promised him a percentage of all the profits, and later, at his request, they also agreed that he could govern any territories he might conquer. They were all imagining he might conquer territories on the outskirts of Asia. This document, called the "Granada Capitulations," was signed April 30, 1492.

Sir Fernando and Lady Isabel, by the grace of God king and queen of Castile, Leon, Aragon, Sicily, Granada, Toledo, Valencia, Galicia, the Balearics, Seville, Sardinia, Cordoba, Corsica, Murcia, Jaen, the Algarve, Algeziras, Gibraltar and the Canary Islands, count and countess of

Barcelona, lords of Vizcaya and Molina, dukes of Athens and Neopatria, counts of Roussillon and Cerdagne, marquises of Oristano and Goceano.

Because you, Christopher Columbus, are going at our command with some of our ships and personnel to discover and acquire certain islands and mainland in the Ocean Sea, and it is hoped that, with the help of God, some of the islands and mainland in the Ocean Sea will be discovered and acquired by your command and expertise, it is just and reasonable that you should be remunerated for placing yourself in danger for our service.

Wanting to honor and bestow favor for these reasons, it is our grace and wish that you, Christopher Columbus, after having discovered and acquired these islands and mainland in the Ocean Sea, will be our admiral of the islands and mainland that you discover and acquire and will be our admiral, viceroy and governor of them. You will be empowered from that time forward to call yourself Sir Christopher Columbus, and thus your sons and successors in this office and post may entitle themselves sir, admiral, viceroy and governor of them.

You and your proxies will have the authority to exercise the office of admiral together with the offices of viceroy and governor of the islands and mainland that you discover and acquire. You will have the power to hear and dispose of all the lawsuits and case, civil and criminal, related to the offices of admiral, viceroy, and governor, as you determine according to the law, and as the admirals of our kingdoms are accustomed to administer it. You and your proxies will have the power to punish and penalize delinquents as well as exercising the offices of admiral, viceroy, and governor in all matters pertaining to these offices. You will enjoy and benefit from the fees and salaries attached, belonging and corresponding to these offices, just as your high admiral enjoys and is accustomed to them in the admiralty of our kingdoms. . . .

Source: Granada Capitulations, Granada, April 30, 1492, as translated in Geoffrey Symcox and Blair Sullivan, eds., *Christopher Columbus and the Enterprise of the Indies* (Boston: Bedford, 2005), pp. 60–61.

1.4 AZTEC PRIESTS, STATEMENT TO THE FRANCISCAN FRIARS (1520s)

In 1524, three years after the conquest of Tenochtitlan, a group of twelve Franciscan friars representing the twelve apostles arrived in Mexico. They orchestrated a series of official meetings with high-ranking Aztec political leaders and priests. On several of these occasions, the Europeans took notes. Years later, in the 1560s, another Franciscan rewrote these notes as though the exchange he was recording had occurred on a single occasion, though he was really creating a composite picture. Here is a direct translation from the Nahuatl of what he claimed the Aztec priests said after having listened for several hours to the messages of the Christians. Notice that what has truly angered them is not so much the idea of a new god as the demand that they abandon the old.

You say that we do not recognize the being who is everywhere, lord of heaven and earth. You say our gods are not true gods. The new words that you utter are what confuse us; due to them we feel foreboding. Our makers [our ancestors] who came to live on earth never uttered such words. They gave us *their* laws, their ways of doing things. They believed in the gods, served them and honored them. They are the ones who taught us everything, the gods' being served and respected. Before them we eat earth [kiss the ground]; we bleed; we pay our debts to the gods, offer incense, make sacrifice. . . . indeed, we live by the grace of those gods. They rightly made us out of the time, the place where it was still dark. . . . They give us what we go to sleep with, what we get up with [our daily sustenance], all that is drunk, all that is eaten, the produce, corn, beans, green maize, chia. We beg from them the water, the rain, so that things grow upon the earth.

The gods are happy in their prosperity, in what they have, always and forever. Everything sprouts and turns green in their home. What kind of place is the land of Tlaloc [the rain god]? Never is there any famine there, nor any illness, nor suffering. And they [the gods] give people virility, bravery, success in the hunt, [bejeweled] lip rings, blankets, breeches, cloaks, flowers, tobacco, jade, feathers and gold.

Since time immemorial they have been addressed, prayed to, taken as gods. It has been a very long time that they have been revered, since once upon a time in Tula, in Huapalcalco, Xochitlapan, Tlamohuanchan, in Teotihuacan, the home of the night. These gods are the ones who established the mats and thrones [that is, inherited chieftainships], who gave people nobility, and kingship, renown and respect.

Will we be the ones to destroy the ancient traditions of the Chichimeca, the Tolteca, the Colhuaca, the Tepaneca? [No!][2] It is our opinion that there is life, that people are born, people are nurtured, people grow up, [only] by the gods' being called upon, prayed to. Alas, o our lords, beware lest you make the common people do something bad. How will the poor old men, the poor old women, forget or erase their upbringing, their education? May the gods not be angry with us. Let us not move towards their anger. And let us not agitate the commoners, raise a riot, lest they rebel for this reason, because of our saying to them: address the gods no longer, pray to them no longer. Look quietly, calmly, o our lords, at what is needed. Our hearts cannot be at ease as long as we cannot understand each other. We do not admit as true [what you say]. We will cause you pain. Here are the towns, the rulers and kings who carry the world. It is enough that we have lost political power, that it was taken from us, that we were made to abandon the mats and thrones. We will not budge; we will just end [this conversation]. Do to us whatever you want. This is all with which we return, we answer, your breath, your words, o our lords.

Source: Miguel León Portilla, ed., *Coloquios y doctrina cristiana* (Mexico City: UNAM, 1986). This edition provides a facsimile of the original document; we have translated from the original Nahuatl into English.

1.5 ALVAR NÚÑEZ CABEZA DE VACA, DESCRIBING NORTH AMERICA (1535)

In 1528, a Spanish exploratory expedition wrecked off the coast of Florida. The survivors met with a hostile Indian population and eventually fled from them in rafts that they built. Ultimately, only four men survived—three Spaniards and one North African, who had been a slave. They lived for years along the coast of what is today Texas, where they gained a reputation as healers among the local people. In 1535, they wandered into Spanish settlements in northern Mexico and re-entered European society. One of them, Alvar Núñez Cabeza de Vaca, wrote a long narrative about his experiences among people who had never seen a white man—or a black man—before.

The Indians from the Island of Malhado . . . are warlike people, and they have as much cunning to protect themselves from their enemies as they would have if they had been raised in Italy and in continuous war. When they are in a place where their enemies can attack them, they set up their houses at the edge of the most rugged woods and of the greatest density they find there. And next to it they make a trench and sleep in it. All the warriors are covered with light brush, and they make their arrows. And they are so well covered and hidden that even if their heads are uncovered, they are not seen. And they make a very narrow path and enter into the

---

[2]Nahuatl texts are full of rhetorical questions, the answer to which is always meant to be a resounding "No!"

middle of the woods. And there they make a place for their women and children to sleep. And when night comes, they light fires in their houses, so that if there should be spies, they would believe that they are in them. And before dawn, they again light the same fires, and if by chance their enemies come to attack the houses themselves, those who are in the trench surprise them and from the trenches do them much harm without those outside seeing them or being able to find them. . . . While I was with the ones of Aguenes, they not being warned, their enemies came at midnight and attacked them and killed three of them and wounded many others, with the result that they fled from their houses forward through the woods. And as soon as they perceived that the others had gone, they returned to them. And they gathered up all the arrows that the others had shot at them, and as secretly as they could, they followed them and were near their houses that night without being perceived. And in the early morning they attacked them and they killed five of them and injured many others, and made them flee and leave their houses and their bows with all their possessions . . .

The manner in which they fight is low to the ground. And while they are shooting their arrows, they go stalking and leaping about from place to place, avoiding the arrows of their enemies, so much so that in such places they manage to suffer very little harm. The Indians are more likely to make fun of crossbows and harquebuses [than to fear them] because these weapons are ineffective against them in the flat, open areas where they roam free. They are good for enclosed areas and wetlands, but in all other areas, horses are what must be used to defeat them, and are what the Indians universally fear. Whoever might have to fight against them should be advised to prevent them from perceiving weakness or greed for what the [Indians] have. And as long as war lasts, they must treat them very badly, because if they know that their enemy has fear or some sort of greed [that may affect their decisions] they are people who know how to recognize the times in which to . . . take advantage of the fear [or greed] of their enemies.

Source: Rolena Adorno and Patrick Charles Pautz, eds., *The Narrative of Cabeza de Vaca* (Lincoln: University of Nebraska Press, 2003), pp. 127–129.

Colonial Outposts

1550–1650

COMMON THREADS

Why did each colonizing European nation have a somewhat different relationship with Native Americans? How did this phenomenon cause the empires of Spain, France, Holland, and England to develop in different ways?

What did it mean for the English in North America that they came late to the business of establishing an overseas empire?

How might you chart the paths that each nation took toward offering greater self-determination for some groups and less for others?

Paquiquineo Finds His Way Home

The son of a chieftain, Paquiquineo was a young man, perhaps still a teenager, when the Spanish picked him up in 1561 on one of their exploratory expeditions. The Europeans often abducted young Indians and took them back to their own nations so that they could serve as translators and guides. Sometimes the process worked the other way around, and Europeans who were members of expeditions were accidentally left behind. To survive, they learned the Native Americans' language and customs. If and when they were ever reunited with their countrymen, they were valuable as interpreters. In the early years of colonization, those who had learned the ways of another culture gained influence far out of proportion to their numbers.

Don Luis did not see his own people again for 10 years. First the Spanish took him to Spain, where King Philip II asked him to convert to Christianity. He refused and asked only that he be taken home. The king, recognizing him as a fellow prince, agreed and sent him off in the next convoy to Mexico with orders that he be returned to his homeland on the expedition's return to Spain, following the winds. In Mexico, while he was staying with the Dominican Order, Paquiquineo became dangerously ill and decided to accept baptism. He was renamed don Luis de Velasco after the viceroy, who became his godfather. Unfortunately for him, the head of the order decided that such an astute young man would be invaluable as an intermediary in conversion efforts in North America, and would not let him leave. Years later, don Luis managed to travel to Havana, from there back to Spain, and then back to Havana, where he persuaded some Jesuits that he would help them establish a Christian mission among his own people on the North American mainland.

In 1570, less than a week after the Jesuits and their Indian convert had settled in Virginia, don Luis returned to his own people and customs. He scandalized the Jesuits by taking several wives, a privilege of Indian men of high rank. The Jesuits had expected don Luis to act as an intermediary with his people, securing them supplies and favorable treatment, so they threatened to bring the wrath of Spain down upon him. Paquiquineo had learned too much about Europeans during his time among them to doubt their ability to do this. He knew that his people had to act quickly if they were to act at all.

The Powhatans killed eight of the nine people at the mission. According to Indian custom, a young boy named Alonso was spared, although don Luis apparently argued for his death also. Knowing that the Spanish would someday return, he wanted no witnesses. As don Luis predicted, the Spanish did come back. They retrieved Alonso, through him ordered don Luis to appear for an inquest, and began executing other Indians when he failed to appear. Don Luis never returned to the Spanish, and in frustration, they sailed home.

In 1607 the English planted their first permanent colony on the mainland at Jamestown among people who were kin to don Luis's people. Throughout the seventeenth century, the English heard rumors about a Powhatan Indian who had spent time in the Spanish colonies.

During this period of American history, no sharp geographic or cultural line separated the Indians and Europeans. Indians such as don Luis lived among the Europeans, and Europeans such as Alonso spent time with the Indians. Even before permanent colonies were established, each group thus knew the other moderately well. Although the customs and practices of the other group often seemed odd and even ungodly, they were never completely alien. By the time actual settlements were established, there were usually already people who could act as go-betweens.

Pursuing Wealth and Glory Along the North American Shore

The search for wealth and prestige soon propelled other European nations to cross the Atlantic. In the minds of European leaders, riches, glory, and power were almost inseparable. As the English explorer Sir Walter Raleigh explained, "Whosoever commands the sea commands the trade; whosoever commands the trade of the world commands the riches of the world, and consequently the world itself." Most of the North American colonies established by European nations in the first half of the seventeenth century were outposts in the global economy. Despite significant differences, these colonies all shared certain elements: First, they were intended to bring in the greatest amount of revenue to the mother country at the lowest cost. Second, success depended on harmonious relations with—or elimination of—local Indians. Third, colonial societies slowly developed their own distinctive patterns, depending on which route they followed to prosperity.

European Objectives

At first, Europeans believed that Columbus had reached Asia. By the time they understood that he had discovered a new land, the Spanish were well on their way to conquering native peoples and stripping them of their wealth. Their success inspired other European nations to search for new sources of gold and silver in the regions Spain had not yet claimed. They also continued to seek a path through the Americas to Asia. For northern Europeans, colonization was not a goal for almost a century, and even then their colonies were designed primarily to provide a quick return on investment, not to transplant Europeans onto foreign soil.

The nations of northern Europe were unwilling to invest in permanent settlements for good reason. A foreign colony was costly. It involved procuring and provisioning a ship, providing a settlement with food and equipment, and resupplying it until it could turn a profit. Spain had been lucky: Isabel and Ferdinand's risk paid off relatively quickly because they found a hospitable climate, deposits of precious metals, and, most important, sedentary farming peoples who were already accustomed to a political hierarchy and to paying tribute to others. The northern European nations could not afford expeditions comparable to that of Columbus when it became clear that the North American world was very different from New Spain in these key regards.

Northern European nations learned what they knew of the North American world by sponsoring small, economical expeditions designed to establish trade and seek a sea route to Asia. Would-be explorers sold their services to the highest bidder. John Cabot, who sailed for England, was, like Columbus, born in Genoa, Italy. (His real name was Giovanni Caboto.) Before coming to England, he had spent time in Muslim Arabia, Spain, and Portugal, apparently looking for sponsors for a voyage to Asia. He found them in the English port city of Bristol, from whence he sailed in 1497. He landed in Newfoundland and claimed the territory for England.

Soon both England and France sent fishing expeditions to the waters off Newfoundland (see Map 2–1). The population of northwestern Europe exploded in the sixteenth and seventeenth centuries, creating an increased demand for fish, and fishing expeditions to Newfoundland were relatively inexpensive to sustain.

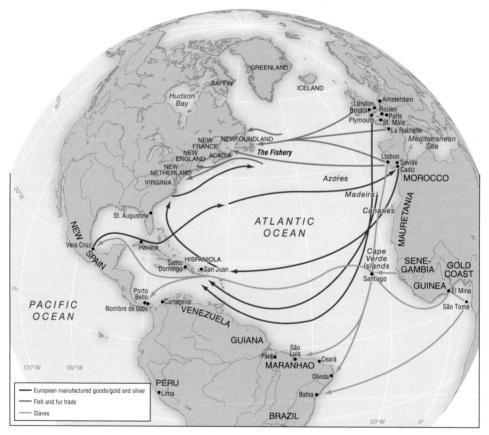

Map 2–1   North Atlantic Trade Routes at the End of the Sixteenth Century Hundreds of entrepreneurs from England, France, and Portugal sent ships to fish off the coast of Newfoundland to feed the growing population of Europe. The fur trade grew out of the Newfoundland fishing enterprise when fishermen who built winter shelters on the shore began trading with local Algonquian Indians (green lines). At the same time, European cities sent food, cloth, and manufactured goods to New Spain, in return for gold and silver (red lines). After 1580, the Portuguese began transporting slaves from Africa to sell in Brazil and New Spain (yellow lines). *Source:* D. W. Meinig, *The Shaping of America* (New Haven, CT: Yale University Press, 1986), vol. 1, p. 56.

The French colony of New France, planted in the St. Lawrence River region of Canada, grew out of the French fishing ventures off Newfoundland. Although early French explorers discovered neither gold nor a Northwest Passage to Asia, French fishermen found that the Indians were willing to trade beaver pelts at prices so low that a man could make a fortune in a few months' time.

The Huge Geographical Barrier

At first, North America seemed little more than an obstacle on the way to Asia. In 1522 Ferdinand Magellan's expedition had completed the first round-the-world voyage for Spain, proving finally that one could get to the East by heading west. Other nations then became interested in finding a way through, rather than around, North America. Two years after Magellan's voyage, the Italian Giovanni da Verrazano sailed on behalf of France. He explored the coast from South Carolina to Maine and was the first European to see New York Harbor. To Europeans, however, all that Verrazano had discovered was a huge barrier between Europe and Asia.

On that "huge barrier" of North America lived Indians, some wary and some friendly. Unfamiliar with Indian customs, Europeans often could not distinguish hospitality from malice. When Algonquian Indians attempted to dry out one of Verrazano's sailors, who had almost drowned, by setting him near a campfire, Verrazano feared that they "wanted to roast him for food." In the early years of exploration, survival often depended on local Indians, yet because the Europeans were looking either for treasure or for a Northwest Passage and were not necessarily thoughtful students of human nature, they tended to see cultural differences rather than similarities.

Between 1534 and 1542, King François I of France financed Jacques Cartier to make three expeditions to seek a route through North America and to look out for any riches along the way. All three came to naught. On their second trip, the French sailed up the St. Lawrence River as far as the town of Hochelaga (near present-day Montréal). The Iroquoian speakers there told of a wealthy land to the west. Although the Indians may have been trying to deceive the French, it is possible that the shiny metal they spoke of was the copper that the Hurons to the west mined and traded. The winter was brutal. Even with food and care from the Indians, at the end of the winter almost a quarter of the party was dead. The French found that their survival depended on the native peoples.

Later expeditions fared as badly. The region was cold and remote. The French quarreled with their Indian hosts and fought among themselves. Because their early attempts at finding easy riches failed, the French were in effect demonstrating that European profits in North America would have to rest on exploration, conquest of the natives, and colonization. Needless to say, this principle of European colonialism was gradually established without the consent of the Indians who inhabited the land.

Spanish Outposts

Throughout the sixteenth century, European nations jockeyed for power on their own continent. Because most of these nations were at war with each other, North America was often a low priority. But when the fighting in Europe abated, the Europeans looked across the Atlantic in hopes of gaining an advantage over a rival nation or finding a new source of wealth.

Soon the French and English, who found no gold or jewels along the coast, discovered an easier source of wealth—stealing from the Spanish. Every season, Spanish ships laden with treasure from Mexico and South America moved out of the Caribbean into the Atlantic and north along the coast until they caught the trade winds home. By the middle of the sixteenth century, French ships were lying in wait off Florida or the Carolinas. Because it was cheaper than exploration, preying on Spanish ships became a national policy.

To prevent these costly acts of piracy, King Philip II established a series of forts along both coasts of Florida. At the same time, a group of Huguenots (French Protestants) established a colony, Fort Caroline, near present-day Georgia. For the new commander of the Spanish forts, Pedro Menéndez de Avilés, the task was to destroy the French settlement. On a September morning in 1565, 500 Spanish soldiers surprised the French at Fort Caroline. Although the French surrendered and begged for mercy, they were slaughtered. The religious and nationalist conflicts of Europe had been transplanted to North America (see Map 2–2).

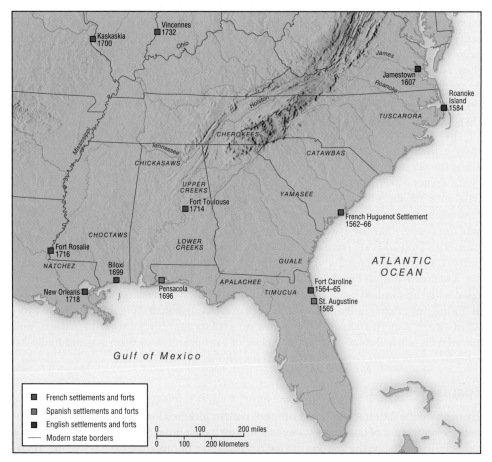

Map 2–2 European Colonization of the Southeast Beginning in the second half of the sixteenth century, the French, Spanish, and English established settlements in the Southeast. *Source:* Charles Hudson, *The Southeastern Indians* (Knoxville: University of Tennessee Press, 1976), pp. 430–431.

One of the forts established by the Spaniards, St. Augustine, settled in 1565, is the oldest continuously inhabited city of European origin in the United States. Most of Menéndez's ambitious plans for Spanish settlements, however, were undermined by local Indians whom the Spanish alienated. After attacks by the Orista Indians in 1576 and by England's Francis Drake a decade later, the Spanish abandoned all of their Florida forts except St. Augustine. They faced the reality that this was not a territory either of silver mines or of sedentary Indians who could easily be given out in *encomienda*. Spanish dreams of an empire in this part of North America had been reduced to a small coastal garrison designed to protect the far richer territories to the south. Although the Spanish would later establish other missions in Florida, their presence was peripheral to Spain's American empire.

New France: An Outpost in Global Politics and Economics

The Spanish had given up hopes of an empire along the southeast coast of North America, but they had at least succeeded in scaring off the French from there. After the massacre at Fort Caroline, the French once again turned their focus to the St. Lawrence River. By the beginning of the seventeenth century, the French had discovered the beaver trade. The pelts found a ready market in Europe, where they were turned into felt hats. A trade that began almost as an accident on fishing expeditions soon became the basis for the French empire in modern Canada. The French were drawing the Indians into a global economy, a process that dramatically changed not only the world of the North Americans but that of the Europeans as well.

The Five Nations of Iroquois and the Political Landscape

The French intruded on a region where warfare among Indian tribes had recently been widespread. At least a century previously, five Iroquoian-speaking tribes living in today's New York State (see Map 2–3) had ended a period of feuding among themselves by establishing a league called the Five Nations. The members of this alliance were bound to keep peace among themselves and to coordinate a common defense against outsiders. Their new policy, combined with a relatively dense population due to their practicing agriculture for part of the year, easily rendered them the dominant political entity in the region. They made war against the Algonquian-speaking tribes living primarily to the north of the St. Lawrence, but they also attacked other Iroquoian-speaking groups and may even have annihilated some, such as the Hochelegans. The Hurons, for example, although speakers of an Iroquoian language, were the avowed enemies of the Five Nations when the French arrived. Such schisms would have serious consequences indeed when the Europeans became a factor in the political landscape.

However, despite the endemic warfare, we must not imagine a world of unending violence. Casualties tended to be light, which was not the case in European wars. Most often, the goal was not to kill as many of the enemy as possible, but to take young women and children captive so that they might be adopted to replace deceased clan members. Furthermore, these wars focused violence outward. The cruelty that Indians practiced on their enemies shocked Europeans, but unlike in European society, violence or even crime within a clan or extended family was virtually unknown.

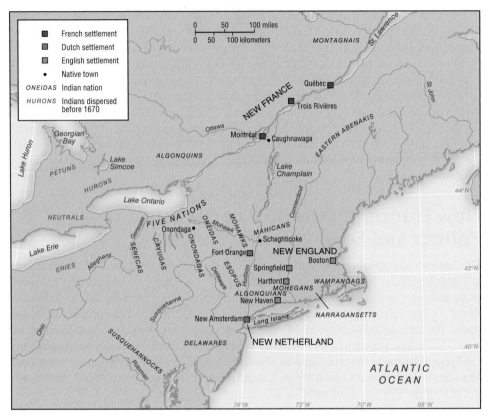

Map 2–3   The Iroquois Region in the Middle of the Seventeenth Century By the middle of the seventeenth century, the French, Dutch, and English had all established trading posts on the fringe of the Iroquois homeland. In the Beaver Wars (ca. 1648–1660), discussed later in the chapter, the Iroquois lashed out at their neighbors, dispersing several Huron tribes. *Source:* Matthew Dennis, *Cultivating a Landscape of Peace* (Ithaca, NY: Cornell University Press, 1993), p. 16.

Champlain Encounters the Hurons

After Cartier's last voyage in 1541, the French waited more than half a century before again attempting to plant a settlement in Canada. They were preoccupied with a brutal civil war. In 1594, Henry of Navarre, a Huguenot, emerged the victor, converted to Catholicism, and in 1598 issued the Edict of Nantes, which granted limited religious toleration to the Huguenots. The French could once again look to North America.

The French had continued to fish off Newfoundland, sending ships to the mainland to trade for beaver pelts. The French crown now realized that extending commerce with the Indians could increase its power and wealth. Several early efforts to establish a permanent trading settlement failed, but in 1608, Samuel de Champlain and a small band retraced Cartier's route up the St. Lawrence River and established a post at Québec (see Map 2–4). Champlain, after several attempts, finally established the first French foothold in Canada, created a trading network along the St. Lawrence River, and learned how to live among people with a culture different from his own.

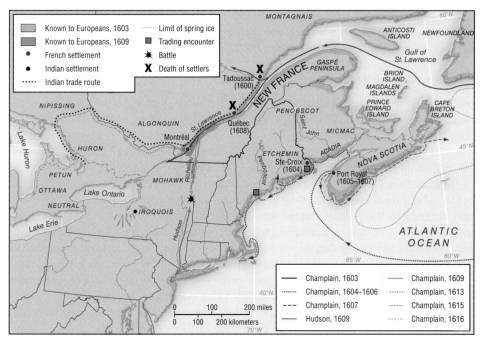

Map 2–4 French Exploration and Settlement, 1603–1616 Between 1603 and 1616, Samuel de Champlain and other French explorers made numerous trips up the St. Lawrence River and along the New England coast as far south as Cape Cod. They established several settlements, and they traded with local Indians and fought with them as well.

As the French government provided them with little support, Champlain's party depended on the aid of their Montagnais Indian hosts (an Algonquian-speaking tribe). To survive in New France, they had to adapt to Indian customs and assist their Indian benefactors in wars against their enemy. Killing the enemy in warfare was relatively easy for an experienced soldier such as Champlain. Indian forms of torture, however, seemed barbaric, not because Europeans did not engage in torture—it was even a part of court-room protocol to accept evidence elicited under torture—but because Europeans usually did not practice it against other soldiers.

Over the next several years, Champlain established a widespread fur trade in the region, linking the French and the Indians in a transformed transatlantic economy. Peasants were brought to New France in 1614 to raise food for the traders; Jesuits were sent to convert the Native Americans. The missionaries were more successful than the peasants. The persistence and adaptability of the missionaries and their ability to make Catholicism meaningful to Native Americans, as well as their encouragement of trading relationships, eventually gained them many converts.

After Champlain's original trade monopoly expired, his group competed with other Frenchmen in the fur trade. The French government was too busy with conflicts at home and abroad to support any of these outposts. To maintain a competitive edge, each summer Champlain pushed farther up the St. Lawrence River from his base at Québec to intercept the Indian tribes who were bringing pelts to the east. Each winter he also sent some of his men to live among the western Hurons and Algonquians to learn their languages and customs. These Indians already traded widely in corn, fish, nets, wampum, and other items. As French traders and Huron and Algonquian hunters created a trade network, each group became dependent on the others.

Creating a Middle Ground in New France

Indians and French traders accommodated each other's cultural practices. Together they created a middle ground neither fully European nor fully Indian, but rather a new world built from two different traditions. A middle ground came into being in other places in America as well, whenever Europeans and Indians needed each other and, at least for the present, could not achieve what they wanted through the use of force.

As the French drew the Native Americans into a global trade network, the Indians began to hunt more beaver than they needed for themselves, depleting the beaver population. Some historians believe that the introduction of European goods and commerce destroyed Native American cultures from within by making them dependent on those goods and inducing them to abandon their own crafts. Others have pointed out that the trade had different meanings for the French and for the Indians. For the French, trade was important for its cash value; for the Indians, trade goods were important both for the practical uses to which they could be put and for their symbolic value in religious ceremonies.

A métis (or mixed) culture soon emerged. Traders and priests learned to sleep on the cold ground without complaint and to eat Indian foods such as sagamité, a sort of corn-meal mush in which a small animal had been boiled. Many French traders found Indian wives. Most Native Americans accepted the taking of more than one wife, so they were not troubled if the French also had wives at home. Moreover, the Hurons were accustomed to adopting members of different ethnic groups, and the French were not averse to racial mixing. Both the Indians and the French believed mixed marriages strengthened trading and military alliances.

The French were drawn into their Huron and Algonquian allies' political world as well. To keep the furs flowing east, they had to join war parties (usually against the Iroquois), finance their allies' battles, and purchase their loyalty with annual payments the Indians considered "presents" and the French thought of as the price of diplomacy. The French and their Indian allies manipulated each other for their own benefit, and there were costs and benefits on both sides.

The arrival of the French stimulated competition among regional tribes for the positions of brokers between the French and the other Indians with furs to trade. The pace and nature of Indian warfare changed dramatically, for a new motive: control of the lucrative fur trade. Through diplomacy and the liberal dispensing of presents, French officials were usually able to quell the infighting among their allies, but not between their allies and the Five Nations. After the Dutch and English established colonies to the south and made alliances with the Iroquois, maintaining the loyalty of Huron and Algonquian allies became the major French objective in North America in the seventeenth and eighteenth centuries. Because they were receptive to Indian customs, the French were the best diplomats in North America, and their Indian allies the most loyal, but the latter paid dearly in lives lost to warfare and disease.

An Outpost in a Global Political Economy

New France began as a tiny outpost. By the end of the seventeenth century, it had increased in both size and importance. Its French population reached 2,000 in 1650 and

STRUGGLES FOR DEMOCRACY

The French and the Indians Learn to Compromise

Should we speak of democracy when people are forced to negotiate because no individual or group has enough power to force all others to acquiesce to their will? That is far from our usual understanding of *democracy*, in which formalized institutions guarantee that different voices will be heard. Nevertheless, the lack of extreme power on the part of any one group in early America may have helped engender our modern democracy. Europeans maintained outposts of empire; they were far, both literally and figuratively, from being at the center of empire, and as a result they learned to compromise. In the fur-trading regions of Canada, for example, negotiated settlement was the norm for many decades.

Never was this clearer than in the case of murder. Among the Native Americans, if someone was murdered by a fellow tribal member or ally, the killer and his people could atone for the death by offering gifts to the bereaved family or by presenting them with a captive to be adopted. (If someone was killed by an enemy tribe, it was tantamount to a declaration of war.) Among the French, a murder was not resolved by the killer and the kinfolk, but by the state. And the state demanded as punishment the death of the killer.

In the hunting season of 1682–1683, tensions percolated in the Keewenaw Peninsula of today's Lake Superior. The local Algonkian-speaking Sault Chippewas were embittered because disease had been running rampant, recent Iroquois attacks had gone unavenged by their French allies, and the French were beginning to trade directly with the Siouan peoples to the west, eliminating the need for the Sault Chippewas to act as middlemen. During this time, the sons of a local chief and a Menominee friend came across two French fur traders whom they robbed and killed. Daniel Dulhut, an officer at the nearest French fort, heard of the event and sent out a party of soldiers to capture the chief, Achiganaga, and all of his sons. Achiganaga's people immediately offered to pay a heavy gift price, including two captive slaves to be adopted by the French.

Dulhut rejected the offer. He wanted the men to stand trial in a French court, but taking the captives through their own people's country to Montreal would be an impossible task; even if his soldiers managed it, they would then have to live with immense Chippewa hostility. Dulhut demanded that the local indigenous groups meet, and once they were assembled, he forced them to serve as a sort of jury at a trial. Achiganaga's son and his friends freely acknowledged what they had done, confident that their proffered gift would be accepted. But the French demanded that the other Indians present execute them. The Indians knew that if they did so, they would in effect be declaring war on the Sault Chippewas and the Menominee, and thus refused. Dulhut offered a compromise: he would not ask that they kill the whole group who had conspired in the murders, but just two of them. If they had been from an enemy group, this would have been an acceptable punishment—a life for a life.

continued

STRUGGLES FOR DEMOCRACY *continued*

When it became clear that Dulhut himself was prepared to carry out the executions, the chief of a different Chippewa group tried to avert war by praising him for his mercy in deciding to demand the deaths of only two of the men. He tried to convey to the others that they should accept this plan, lest their relations with the French deteriorate further. Dulhut went ahead and killed Achiganaga's son and his Menominee friend. Because this occurred in Ottawa territory, the Ottawa were deemed responsible by their Indian peers. Their chiefs scrambled to present expensive wampum belts as gifts to Achiganaga and the Menominee chief in an effort to avert war. In a set of remarkable gestures, Dulhut himself gave a great feast for the Ottawa, "to take away the pain I have caused them by pronouncing the death sentence" on their lands, and then presented Achiganaga himself with many gifts. The French traders who lived in the region had persuaded him that it was imperative that he live according to Indian custom as well as French law. Otherwise, the reprisals would be terrible. This was not the lesson the French officer had expected to learn when he came to America, but living with a new reality taught him to let go of some of his expectations. Later, when Europeans once again attempted to assert more control, the settlers would find that they themselves had come to value more open, democratic negotiations.

19,000 in 1714. In the same years, the Huron population decreased dramatically, cut in half by epidemics and warfare. The death of many of Huronia's leaders resulted in internal conflict and political instability that left the Hurons vulnerable to their Indian enemies and increasingly dependent on their French allies. At the same time, the French depended on the Hurons and Algonquians to keep bringing them furs. The Hurons operated solely as middlemen, acquiring beaver pelts from other tribes rather than hunting for them.

By the middle of the seventeenth century, the local beaver supply began to diminish. Before the arrival of the French, the Indians had trapped only enough for their own use. The huge European demand, however, led Indians to kill more beaver than could be replaced by natural reproduction. As a result, Europeans (or their Indian middlemen) extended trade routes north and west, drawing larger numbers of Indians into the emerging global economy.

The European demand for beaver coats and hats was insatiable. To increase trade, the French expanded domestic manufacturing of cloth, metal implements, guns, and other goods attractive to the Indians. This pattern, in which the mother country produced goods to be sold or traded in foreign colonies for raw materials, was replicated by England and Holland. None of these nations found either the treasures or the settled Indian populations that Spain did in Mexico and Peru. Instead, they found new products, such as beaver pelts, for which there was a growing demand in Europe.

A new economic theory called mercantilism guided the growth of European nation-states and their colonies: its objective was to strengthen the nation-state by making the economy serve its interests. According to the theory, the world's wealth, measured in gold and silver, could never be increased. As a result, each nation's economic objective must be to secure as much of the world's wealth as possible. One nation's gain was necessarily another's loss. Colonies were to provide raw materials and markets for manufactured goods for the mother country. National competition for colonies and markets was not only about economics but also about politics and diplomacy. The nation's strength would depend on its ability to dominate international trade.

New Netherland: The Empire of a Trading Nation

In many ways, the Dutch venture into North America resembled that of France. It began with an intrepid explorer in quest of a Northwest Passage and a government unwilling to invest heavily in a North American colony. Unlike the French, however, the Dutch government assigned the task of establishing a trading settlement almost entirely to a private company. And because Holland was a Protestant nation, there were no activist Catholic missionaries to spread their religion and oppose the excesses of a commercial economy. Even more than the French and Spanish colonies, New Netherland was shaped by the forces of commerce.

Colonization by a Private Company

The Netherlands had an unusual history in the context of Europe. The seven provinces hugged the coast, and the economy was dominated by merchants whose sailing ventures made them quite cosmopolitan. It had neither a powerful landed aristocracy nor an oppressed peasantry. It was thus no accident that it was home to such Renaissance thinkers as Erasmus and later Descartes. Jews expelled from Spain found a home there, as did zealous Protestants fleeing England. However, being a small, coastal territory also had its disadvantages: the Netherlands was subject to frequent invasion. Most recently, the powerful Spanish had annexed the country, and in the early 1600s the Dutch were in the midst of fighting for their political independence (which they would win in 1648). If anything, their political struggles made them even more ambitious to participate actively in international trade.

It was by chance that the Dutch and not the British claimed the Hudson River valley. Henry Hudson, an English explorer, sailed several times for the English, attempting to find the Northwest Passage by sailing over the North Pole. In 1609 Hudson persuaded a group of Dutch merchants who traded in Asia, the Dutch East India Company, to finance a venture. Sailing on the *Halve Maen* (Half Moon, in English), Hudson headed toward the Chesapeake Bay, which he believed offered a passage to the Pacific. He sailed along the coast, anchoring in New York Harbor and trading with local Algonquian Indians. He pushed up the river as far as Albany, where he discovered that the river narrowed, apparently disproving his theory about a water passage through North America.

The opportunity to profit from the fur trade soon drew investors and traders to New Netherland. Within two years of Hudson's "discovery" of the river that bears his name, Dutch merchants returned to the region, and in 1614 a group called the New Netherland Company secured from their government a temporary monopoly of trade between the Delaware and Connecticut Rivers. The profits drew other Dutch merchants. In 1621 the Dutch West India Company obtained a permit and soon established settlements at Fort Orange (present-day Albany) and New Amsterdam (present-day New York City), purchasing Manhattan from local Algonquian Indians for 60 florins' worth of merchandise. Thirty families arrived in

1624 to serve the fur trade, either by trading with Indians or by providing support for the traders. All profits went to the Company, with the settlers given small salaries.

Until the Company was willing to offer better terms to settlers, the colony grew very slowly. There were 270 inhabitants in 1628 and 500 in 1640. In 1629, the Company began to offer huge plots of land (18 miles along the Hudson River) and extensive governing powers to *patroons*, men who would bring 50 settlers to the new colony. It also offered smaller grants of land to individuals who would farm the land and return to the Company one-tenth of what they produced. Both approaches placed restrictions on land ownership and self-government, and neither was successful. So in 1640, the Company offered greater rights of self-government and 200 acres to anyone who brought over five adult immigrants. This policy worked better. With its tolerant social attitudes, New Netherland soon became a magnet for peoples from many cultures and nations. As the colony grew, it expanded up the Hudson from the island of Manhattan into New Jersey and Long Island and south to the Delaware River.

The ethnic diversity of the colony increased even further when in 1655 it absorbed the small colony of New Sweden, a privately financed trading outpost on the Delaware that failed when it could not return a quick profit. The varied population of New Netherland was united by no single religion or culture that could have established social order. In most European nations at the time, social order was maintained by a combination of state authority and cohesive religious structures and values. In New Netherland, however, both of these were relatively weak. The governors were caught between the Company, which expected to earn a profit, and the settlers, who wanted to prosper themselves. Peter Stuyvesant, governor from 1647 until the English took over in 1664, was the most successful of the governors, but even he could not fully control New Netherland's people.

In one year alone, when the population numbered less than 1,000, there were 50 civil suits and almost as many criminal prosecutions. The rate of alcohol consumption seems to have been the highest of any North American colony. In 1645, there were only between 150 and 200 houses in New Amsterdam—but 35 taverns! Stuyvesant was unsuccessful in regulating either social life or the economy. He attempted to set prices on such commodities as beer and bread, but he was overruled by the Company, which feared that

Peter Stuyvesant A man of strong character, Peter Stuyvesant did his best to govern the Dutch colony of New Amsterdam effectively.

economic controls would thwart further immigration. In a pattern that would prevail in all of the Dutch and English North American colonies, commerce triumphed.

Slavery and Freedom in New Netherland

The settlers, the Company, and the government of the Netherlands all wanted to make themselves wealthy through commerce. This desire led to the introduction of African slavery into New Netherland. The fur trade did not prove as lucrative as investors had hoped, and the Company found that colonists tended to abandon agriculture for trade. The Company decided that the primary function of New Netherland should be to provide food for its more lucrative plantation colonies in Brazil and the Caribbean. Earlier in the century, the Dutch had seized a portion of northern Brazil from Portugal and developed a sugar-plantation slave economy, which it transplanted to islands in the Caribbean. By that time they had also entered the transatlantic slave trade. In fact, a Dutch warship dropped off the first 20 Africans at the English colony of Jamestown in 1619 in return for food. With its own plantation colonies needing slave labor, the Netherlands became a major player in the slave trade, transporting Africans to the colonies of other nations as well.

In the context of the lucrative Dutch trade in sugar and slaves, New Netherland was only a sideshow. Hoping to make the colony profitable, the Company turned to enslaved Africans. By 1664, there were perhaps 700 slaves in the colony, a considerable portion (about 8 percent) of New Netherland's population.

The Netherlands was perhaps the most tolerant nation of its day, and the Dutch Reformed Church accepted Africans, as well as Indians, as converts, provided they could demonstrate their knowledge of the Dutch religion. The Church did not oppose the institution of slavery, however. Moreover, the strict nature of Dutch Calvinism placed limits on the Church's tolerance. It insisted that its followers be able to read and understand the Bible and the doctrines of the Church.

The primary force for religious tolerance in New Netherland was, in fact, the Dutch West India Company, which saw it as necessary to commercial prosperity. When the head of the Dutch Reformed Church in New Netherland and Governor Stuyvesant attempted to prevent the entry of 23 Dutch Jews expelled from Portuguese Brazil, they were reversed by the Company.

After some early mistakes, the Company also came to advocate a policy of fairness to the local Indian tribes, with the ultimate goal of maintaining peace. They insisted that land must be purchased from its original owners before Europeans could settle on it. Because some settlers were coercing Indians to sell their land cheaply, in 1652 Stuyvesant forbade purchases of land without government approval.

It might appear puzzling that the Dutch, who encouraged toleration of religious minorities and justice toward Native Americans, would also introduce and encourage slavery in North America. The Dutch were not motivated, however, by abstract ideals. Their primary goal was profit through trade: religious and cultural toleration, amicable relations with local Indians, and African slavery all served that end.

The Dutch-Indian Trading Partnership

In the 40 years of New Netherland's existence, its most profitable activity was the fur trade. As the French had done, the Dutch disrupted the balance among regional Indian tribes. The arrival of the Europeans heightened long-standing local animosities. Tribes came to rely on their European allies not only for goods but also for weapons and even soldiers to fight their enemies.

The Dutch began trading near Albany around 1614 and built Fort Orange there a decade later. This small outpost was in a region inhabited by the Mahican tribe, an Algonquian-speaking people who gave the Dutch access to the furs trapped by other Algonquian tribes to the north. The Dutch were assisting the Mahicans in their trade rivalry with the Mohawks (one of the Five Nations of Iroquois) when they were attacked—and defeated—by the Mohawks. The Mohawks, however, asked for peace: their objective was not to eliminate the Dutch but to secure them as trade partners.

By 1628 the Mohawks had defeated the Mahicans and forced them to move into Connecticut, establishing the Mohawks as the most powerful force in the region. The Dutch and the Mohawks abandoned their former hostility for a generally peaceful trading partnership.

By the 1660s, however, New Netherland was in serious economic trouble. The underlying problem was an oversupply of wampum, beads made from the shells of clams. Indians had placed a high value on wampum well before the arrival of Europeans, and the Dutch provided the tools to mass-produce it. They also helped the Indians establish a trade in wampum itself, in which wampum was traded to the Dutch for European goods. The Dutch then exchanged the wampum for furs from the Mohawks and other Indians, shipping the furs to the Netherlands for more European goods. By the middle of the seventeenth century, perhaps as many as 3 million pieces of wampum were in circulation in the area.

By the 1640s English traders in New England had cornered the market in wampum, just when New Englanders were ceasing to use the beads as money. The traders then dumped them into the Dutch market by buying up huge quantities of European goods with them. Almost immediately, the price of manufactured trade goods skyrocketed (due to their relative scarcity) and the value of wampum fell (due to its plentiful supply), leaving the Dutch with too few of the former and too much of the latter. Competition among Dutch traders increased, pressure on Iroquois trade partners mounted, and profits fell. The economic crisis tipped the delicate balance of violence on the frontier and precipitated a major war.

The Beaver Wars

As the Dutch economic position faltered, the balance of power among many northeastern tribes collapsed. The Iroquois, dependent on the failing Dutch merchants for guns, were now vulnerable. Western Iroquois tribes came under assault from the Susquehannocks, a tribe to the south, while the Mohawks in the east faced renewed pressure from the Mahicans. Simultaneously, the Hurons had cut the Iroquois off from trade with the French to the north. Pressured, the Iroquois lashed out in desperate hostilities, known as the Beaver Wars, which raged between 1648 and the 1660s. They attacked almost all of their Indian neighbors and pushed the last French-allied Hurons to the west.

This warfare was horrendous for all sides. As Indian fought Indian, Europeans ultimately gained the upper hand. The Five Nations won the Beaver Wars, but their victory was hollow. Although the Hurons had been dispersed west, the Iroquois could not secure the French as trade partners. Once the Hurons were gone, the French began trading with other Algonquian tribes to the east. Although the Iroquois remained a powerful force until almost the end of the eighteenth century, the Beaver Wars marked an important turning point. The Indians were never able to replace population lost to warfare, even by raiding other tribes. By the middle of the seventeenth century, the pace of European colonization was increasing, filling the land once hunted by Indians.

Even before the English conquered New Netherland in 1664, the Iroquois were looking for new trade partners. They found them in the English. The transition in New Netherland from Dutch to English rule was relatively quiet. The Dutch had established the colony hoping to make money through trade. Having failed, they had little incentive to fight for its control.

England Attempts an Empire

England came late to empire building. The English did not achieve the necessary political unity until the second half of the sixteenth century. Between 1455 and 1485, England was torn by a dynastic struggle, the Wars of the Roses. King Henry VII and his son, Henry VIII, consolidated the power of the state by crushing resistant nobles. When the pope refused to let Henry VIII terminate his sonless marriage to Catherine of Aragon (a daughter of Ferdinand and Isabel), the king made Protestantism the official religion of the nation, banned Catholicism, and confiscated the land and wealth of the Catholic Church. Henry's daughter Mary, who reigned from 1553 through 1558, reinstated Catholicism, burning Protestants at the stake and throwing the nation into turmoil. Order was finally established under the rule of Henry's other daughter, Elizabeth I (reigning from 1558 to 1603), who reestablished Protestantism and strengthened the state. She, too, did not hesitate to use violence to subdue internal dissent, but in her case, she had the majority of the people behind her rather than against her. She succeeded in stabilizing a political entity worthy of being called a nation, but because the English came late to colonization, they found that the most profitable territories in the Americas were already claimed by others.

Competition with Spain

Queen Elizabeth, although an ardent nationalist, was unwilling to risk her treasury on North American adventures. Others, however, were convinced that a New World empire, even in the inhospitable north, could bring England wealth and glory. By the end of the sixteenth century, nationalists, such as two cousins both named Richard Hakluyt, were making the case for an overseas empire. The Hakluyts united nationalism, mercantilism, and militant Protestantism. They argued that if England had colonies for raw materials and as markets for manufactured goods, it could free itself from economic dependency on Spain and other nations. Moreover, colonies could drain off the growing numbers of the unemployed. The Hakluyts also believed that North American Indians could be relatively easily converted to English trade and religion, assuming they would prefer these to Spanish "pride and tyranie." The English could simultaneously strike a blow against Catholic Spain and advance "the glory of God." Although the Hakluyts' dream was never realized, their plans for an English mercantile empire became a blueprint for colonization.

England's first move was not to establish colonies but to try stealing from the Spanish. The English Crown did not have the money to found a colonial empire that would not immediately deliver profits, and Elizabeth I was unconvinced by colonial propagandists. Most concerned about international power politics in Europe, she was willing to let individual Englishmen try to poach on the Spanish. Her goal was to weaken Spain more than to establish a North American empire.

As early as the 1560s, John Hawkins tried to break into the slave trade, but the Spanish forced him out. The English moved on to privateering, that is, state-sanctioned piracy. In 1570 Sir Francis Drake set off for the Isthmus of Panama on a raiding expedition. Drake was motivated by dreams of glory and a conviction that his Protestant religion was superior to all others. Working in one of Hawkins's slaving expeditions, he had learned to hate the Spanish.

In years to come, Drake led the second expedition to sail around the world, crossed the Atlantic many times, helped defeat the huge Spanish naval fleet, the Armada, and became an architect of England's colonial strategies. He was the English version of the conquistador. His venture into Panama failed to produce any treasure, but it inspired a group of professional seamen, aggressive Protestants, and members of Elizabeth's court to plan for an English colonial empire. This group won the cautious queen's support. The success of Drake's round-the-world expedition (1577–1580) spurred further privateering ventures. He brought back to England enough treasure to pay for the voyage and proof that the Spanish empire was vulnerable. From 1585 to 1604, the English government issued licenses to privateers, sometimes as many as 100 per year. Each venture was financed by a joint-stock company, a relatively new form of business organization that was the forerunner to the modern corporation. These companies brought together merchants who saw privateering as a way to broaden their trade and gentlemen who saw it as a way to increase their incomes.

Rehearsal in Ireland

At the end of the sixteenth century, England embarked on a campaign to bring Ireland, which its people had first invaded in the twelfth century, under its full control. The conquest of Ireland between 1565 and 1576 became the model for England's colonial ventures. Ireland presented the monarchy with the same political problem that all early-modern rulers faced, that is, a set of powerful nobles who put their own interests ahead of those of the nation. Building the nation meant bringing the nobles into line.

England not only subdued the Irish leaders and their people but also forcibly removed some of them to make way for loyal Englishmen, who were given land as a reward for their service to the queen. By paying her followers with someone else's land and financing military expeditions from joint-stock companies, England made the conquest of Ireland relatively cheap. It showed a skeptical queen that establishing colonies was in England's interest, provided that the venture was paid for privately—by privateering, by charters to individuals, or by joint-stock companies.

The English conquest of Ireland provided not only practical experience in how to organize and finance a colonial venture but also a view of cultural difference that was later applied to the Indians. Although the Irish were Catholics and hence fellow Christians, the English thought that people who behaved as the Irish did must be barbarians. According to the English, the Irish "blaspheme, they murder, commit whoredome, hold no wedlocke, ravish, steal, and commit all abomination without scruple of conscience." These attitudes were used to justify an official policy of terrorism. In two grisly massacres, one in the middle of a Christmas feast, hundreds of men, women, and children were slaughtered. The English governor, Sir Humphrey Gilbert, ordered that the heads of all those killed resisting the conquest be chopped off and placed along the path leading to his tent so that anyone coming to see him "must pass through a lane of heads." The English justified such acts by referring to the supposed barbarism of the Irish people. These ideas, similar to early Spanish depictions of the Indians of the Americas, were carried to the New World, England's next stop in its expanding empire.

Indians on the Thames

When we think about the cultural encounter between the Old World and the New, we tend to imagine European men coming ashore in a wilderness and meeting Native American people. Often, however, the encounter consisted of Indians docking at European cities for the first time. Over the course of the first century after contact, the colonizers brought hundreds of Native Americans back to Europe with them. Some of these Native Americans went on to take leading roles in the unfolding dramas.

The phenomenon began with Columbus and the Spaniards, but English colonizers also regularly kidnapped Indians. In 1530, an English captain explored the coast of Brazil (not yet firmly under Portuguese control) and reported that "one of the savage kings of the country was contented to take ship with him and to be transported into England." The indigenous man was brought to the court of Henry VIII. "The King and all the Nobilitie did not a little marvaile." The English spent a year teaching him their language, but when they tried to take him home, so that he might aid them in their efforts to profit in Brazil, "the said Savage king died at sea."

Other English explorers followed suit. Sir Walter Raleigh, for example, in the course of the explorations leading to the founding of Roanoke, ordered that two indigenous boys be taken from the Carolina coast. They were known as Manteo and Wanchese. Now we know that the latter was hiding his true name from those who had kidnapped him: the word he gave them simply meant "boy" in his own language. The two lived in Raleigh's home for two years until the expedition sailed.

Sometimes indigenous people coming to London from the Spanish world did not disclose their Indian origins. Martín Cortés, Malinche's son by the conqueror, was given to Philip II as a page when he was a young man, and in 1554, he accompanied Philip to London for his marriage to Queen Mary. He lived at court, where no one would have guessed that his mother had grown up in an indigenous chieftainship on the coast of Mexico.

At the start of the seventeenth century, when the English became more active in colonization, interest in Native Americans spiked. In 1603 Bartholomew Gosnold seized some Indians from the Rappahannock River and had them perform daring feats on canoes on the Thames for riveted audiences. (They died of the plague shortly after, and their people were still asking angrily about them when John Smith arrived in their country.) In *The Tempest*, Shakespeare has one character complain of others' selfishness: "When they will not give a doit [a coin] to a lame beggar, they will lay out ten to see a dead Indian." And in *Henry VIII* (1613), a man responds to the sight of a gathering mob by saying, "Have we some Indian with the great tool come to court, the women so besiege us?" When Pocahontas came to London in 1616, she was the talk of the town, and the Virginia Company used her presence to secure investments.

In 1614, an English explorer of the Massachusetts coast seized about 14 Indians to sell in Spain. One of them was later taken to London, working for a shipbuilder. He traveled to Newfoundland with some

continued

fishermen, back to London, and then in 1619 sailed with a captain planning to go farther south, to New England. This was Tisquantum, known as "Squanto." No wonder the Pilgrims were greeted by an Indian saying very distinctly, in English, "Welcome."

It is easy to imagine the agonizing loneliness of these Indians and to be angry at the ways in which they were being used. (If only they had left us diaries and letters!) But we must remember that they also took action and made choices that sometimes had significant consequences. Some of the indigenous in Spain came to know religious men who later advocated for them, and the behavior of don Luis helped convince Spanish authorities that it was worthless to attempt to colonize North America. Wanchese harbored rage against the English

and, once home, was instrumental in leading his people away from an alliance, thereby contributing to the destruction of the colony at Roanoke. Pocahontas died in England, but one of her father's advisers accompanied her on the trip. He returned home to warn his countrymen of the danger they faced and to encourage a great rebellion against Jamestown that later followed. Squanto offered his services to the Pilgrims in order to benefit his own clan, but in doing so, he also ensured the colony's survival.

These people were undoubtedly impressed by what they saw in Europe, but they were far from overwhelmed by it. Instead, they used their knowledge to strategize about how best to react to the Europeans.

The Roanoke Venture

Roanoke, England's first colony in what became the United States, was a military venture, intended as a resupply base for privateers raiding in the Caribbean. In 1584 Walter Raleigh received a charter to establish a colony in North America. Only 30 years old at the time, Raleigh was the half-brother of the late Sir Humphrey Gilbert. Elizabeth agreed to let Raleigh establish a combination colony and privateering base north of Spain's settlement at St. Augustine. Raleigh's scouts had found a potential site at Roanoke Island on the Outer Banks of today's North Carolina and had brought back to England two Indians, Manteo and Wanchese. Elizabeth gave the enterprise some support. She knighted Raleigh but refused to let the hotheaded young soldier lead the expedition himself.

The Roanoke expedition left Plymouth in April 1585 under the command of Sir Richard Grenville, an aristocrat who had fought in Ireland. Half of the crew of 600 were probably recruited or impressed (i.e., forcibly seized) from the unemployed poor of Britain. Little value was attached to their lives. When one of the ships separated from the fleet and found its supplies running low, 20 men were dropped off at Jamaica—only 2 of whom were ever heard from again—and another 32 were later left on an island in the Outer Banks.

Roanoke was a poor port, dangerous for small ships and inadequate for larger ones. When the primary ship was almost wrecked and a major portion of the food supply lost, Grenville's fleet departed for England. Colonel Ralph Lane, another veteran of war in Ireland, was left in charge as governor. He was supposed to look for a better port, build a fort, and find food for the 100 men left under his command.

The Arrival of the English at Roanoke This image derives from a 1585 sketch by the artist John White.

Roanoke was established to gain an advantage over the treasure-filled Spanish ships traveling back to Spain. The men left on the island prepared for an attack by Spain and pointed the fort's guns out to sea. Raleigh intended to send another supply ship that summer, but the queen insisted he sail instead to Newfoundland to warn the English there about a probable sea war with Spain. The first settlers of Roanoke were ill equipped to build a self-sustaining colony. Half soldiers and gentlemen and half undisciplined and impoverished young men, no one knew how to build or support a town. Unable to find gold or provide for themselves, the colonists turned to the local Roanoke Indians (an Algonquian-speaking tribe), whom they soon alienated.

The Roanokes were familiar with Europeans through their contacts with the Spanish and through the stories of Wanchese, who had run away from the English and returned home. They were ready to trade with them. However, the English need for more food than the natives could easily supply led to tensions. Thinking that an Indian had stolen a silver cup, the English retaliated by burning an empty village and the surrounding cornfields, which fed both Indians and English. The Indians had to balance the benefits of trade against the costs of English aggression. After a failed ambush attempt, the Roanokes decided to withdraw from Roanoke Island, leaving the English to starve. When Lane learned of this plan, he attacked the Indians, beheading their chieftain Wingina. Indian-English relations deteriorated further, and Wanchese became an avowed enemy.

Not all the colonists, however, treated the Roanokes as an enemy to be conquered. Much of what we know about the Roanoke Colony and its Indian neighbors is due to the work of two sympathetic colonists. John White, a painter, and Thomas Hariot, who later became a great mathematician, were sent to survey the region and describe its inhabitants and natural features. Their illustrations, maps, and descriptions provide the most

John White's Watercolor of an Algonquian Village Much of what we know about Algonquian life at the time of the Roanoke expedition comes from the paintings of John White, who was a member of the expedition. Here we see a small village, surrounded by a tall stockade.

accurate information that we have about the people of this region before the arrival of large numbers of Europeans.

By June 1585, it was clear that Roanoke had failed in its mission. When Drake and his fleet appeared on their way back from a looting expedition in the Caribbean, the colonists decided to return to England, leaving behind only 15 men.

Yet the English advocates of colonization were not ready to give up. The original plan for a military-style base had failed, but a new vision of colonization would now be tried. Raleigh's commitment was lukewarm, for Roanoke had already cost £30,000 without returning a cent. John White, the painter, remained enthusiastic and assembled a group of settlers. It included 110 people—men, women, and children—who were prepared to raise their own crops, and also one loyal Roanoke Indian, Manteo. In exchange for their investment, Raleigh granted each man 500 acres of land. The new expedition arrived in July 1587. The second attempt to establish a colony at Roanoke was probably doomed by the poisoned relations with the Indians. White

Time Line

▼1400–1600

Five Iroquois nations create the Great League of Peace

▼1561

Spanish abduct don Luis de Velasco

▼1562

John Hawkins tries to break into the slave trade

▼1565

Spanish establish settlement at St. Augustine
Spanish destroy French settlement at Fort Caroline

▼1565–1576

The English conquer Ireland

▼1570

Paquiquineo returns home to Virginia

▼1577–1580

Francis Drake sails around the world for England

▼1584

Walter Raleigh receives charter to establish colony at Roanoke

▼1585

First settlement at Roanoke established

soon found that the 15 men who had remained had been attacked by Roanokes. As the survival of the colony now depended on support from England, the colonists, who included White's daughter and granddaughter, sent White back to act as their agent in England. No European ever saw any of the colonists again.

The Abandoned Colony

No one had planned to abandon the little colony. Raleigh assembled a supply fleet the next spring, but a sea war looming with the Spanish Armada prevented it from leaving. Finally, in August 1590, after the Armada had been defeated, White arrived in Roanoke only to find everyone gone. There were signs of an orderly departure, and the word CROATOAN, Manteo's home island, was carved in a post. White assumed that was where the group had gone. Short of water and with a storm brewing, the fleet decided to put out to sea and return the next year. They never got there.

The colony of Roanoke was not "lost," as legend usually puts it; it was abandoned. Serving no useful economic or military purpose, the people of Roanoke were entirely expendable. John White could not obtain the help of backers and seems to have died shortly thereafter. Raleigh and Queen Elizabeth soon after had a falling out, and he was placed under arrest. After he was released, he did send at least one search party, but no one was ever found. In 1603, Queen Elizabeth died, and her successor, James I, had Raleigh arrested as a traitor in his efforts to make peace with Spain.

What happened to the abandoned colonists? In 1607, the English returned to the region, establishing a permanent colony at Jamestown, on the Chesapeake. In 1608, Englishmen heard that many Roanoke colonists had made their way up to Virginia and settled among the friendly Chesapeake Indians before being attacked by the Powhatans. In fact, over the next two generations, there were numerous reports of sightings of people with "perfect yellow hair" or "white skin" at various places. One scholar has mapped these purported appearances and finds that a good number fall along a well-known trading path. This makes perfect sense. The seminomadic Algonquian-speaking people who either attacked the colonists or absorbed them peacefully would never have been able to keep such a large group together. The vulnerable newcomers would have been immediately dispersed, just like any other large group of prisoners or starving

▼**1587**
Second attempt to found colony at Roanoke

▼**1590**
English settlers at Roanoke have disappeared

▼**1607**
English establish permanent colony at Jamestown

▼**1608**
Samuel de Champlain establishes a fort at Quebec

▼**1609**
Henry Hudson arrives at New York, sailing for the Netherlands

▼**1614**
Dutch begin trading in Albany region
French settlers arrive in New France

▼**1621**
Dutch West India Company established

▼**1624**
First Dutch families arrive at Manhattan

▼**1648–1660s**
Beaver Wars fought

▼**1664**
English take over New Amsterdam

A cheife Heroroans wyfe of Pomeoc.
and her daughter of the age of. 8. er.
10. yeares.

Portrait of an Algonquian Mother and Child by John White This beautiful picture illustrates the indulgence of Algonquian mothers and the sensitivity of the English artist who painted this one.

migrants, and traded along well-worn routes. Theories abound about the fate of the colonists, but this is the only one that has common sense and the realities of Native American life on its side.

The English were beginning to learn that they could not rely on the Indians for food. Unlike the Spanish, they had not found densely settled farming communities who were accustomed to paying tribute. As a result, the English colonies would have to grow their own food. Consequently, the history of the English in North America would by and large be that of the growth of the English population (augmented by Africans and other European immigrants) and the steady decline of the original inhabitants.

Conclusion

European nations established colonies to achieve a political or economic advantage over their rivals. Most of these nations had only recently been unified by force, an experience that gave them the energy to establish colonies and a military model they could use for colonization. The distinctive domestic history of each nation, however, shaped its relations with the Indians it encountered, just as the distinctive societies of the Indian nations shaped their interactions with Europeans. The Spanish came prepared for a new *reconquista*, and the crown helped sponsor well-armed forces in the New World. There they found large, highly organized groups of native peoples, who had amassed treasure and were accustomed to working for others. The French found no such peoples, but they learned that the Indians there were expert providers of beaver pelts. Rather than uselessly attempting to conquer the nomadic and seminomadic hunters, they worked on establishing alliances to guarantee the trade and became entangled in the Indians' own conflicts. The Dutch, experienced as merchants, also recognized that the goodwill of the Indians was vital for a flourishing trade, and their businessmen worked to make New Amsterdam a crossroads in the international beaver economy. The English, like the Dutch, arrived on the scene late, but rather than joining the northern beaver economy as merchant traders, they still dreamed of competing with Spain in the warmer climes. They did so largely by preying on Spanish ships. The English thought it would be relatively easy to convince the Indians to grow food for them, as the Spanish had done, but they had misunderstood the nature of the societies they were dealing with.

Out of these different interactions between natives and newcomers, a North Atlantic political economy began to emerge, shaped by the forces of trade and the quest for power. Europeans, Indians, and eventually Africans were drawn into a global economy in which the nations of the world competed for advantage. The early years of American colonial history were shaped by impersonal forces that built empires and subjugated peoples. But they were also shaped by individuals. Some set out to find new worlds, whereas others were forced into them. Captives such as Paquiquineo, Wanchese, and Manteo; explorers such as Jacques Cartier and Henry Hudson; soldiers such as Sir Francis Drake and Samuel de Champlain; the poor dragooned into sailing for Roanoke and left there to die; and Huron women who married French traders: all of them left their mark on the New World, even before the English planted their first permanent colonies in North America.

Who, What

Jacques Cartier 37

Samuel de Champlain 40

Sir Francis Drake 50

Five Nations of Iroquois 39

Walter Raleigh 35

Peter Stuyvesant 46

Joint-stock company 50

Mercantilism 44

Privateering 50

Wampum 42

Review Questions

1. What were the key European objectives in exploring North America in this period? To what extent did England, France, and the Netherlands achieve their objectives?

2. What do we know about the precontact history of the Five Nations of Iroquois? How did this history affect the world of colonial America? How did the European colonial ventures affect the Iroquois?

3. What was the "middle ground," and how was it created?

Critical-Thinking Questions

1. What were the ramifications of the northern Europeans failing to find cities equivalent to Tenochtitlan anywhere in North America?

2. Did the English, French, and Dutch have profoundly different attitudes toward the Indians at the outset? If the English had been the ones to spearhead the beaver trade, do you think that English traders and trappers might have married Huron women?

3. Early on, the Dutch faced the need to democratize their colony to some extent. Did other colonies of the era face a similar need? Why or why not?

For further review materials and resource information, please visit www.oup.com/us/oakes

CHAPTER 2: COLONIAL OUTPOSTS, 1550–1650
Primary Sources

2.1 LETTER FROM FRAY PEDRO DE FERIA TO PHILLIP II, KING OF SPAIN, ABOUT PAQUIQUINEO (1563)

Paquiquineo, a Native American boy, was kidnapped from the Chesapeake by Spanish explorers in 1561. He and a companion were taken to Spain, where they met the king. Paquiquineo refused to convert to Christianity and begged the monarch to send him home. His wish was granted, but he was sent first to Mexico; from there he was to be taken to the northern territories. While in Mexico, he became a Christian and was baptized "don Luis de Velasco," in honor of the viceroy. The following letter offers insight into his frustrating experiences among his captors. It was written by the head of the Dominican order in Mexico City soon after Paquiquineo had been left to his keeping. The friar was alight with zeal: he had in his hands a young man whom he believed would be a perfect intermediary in a major effort to proselytize in the northern territories.

Your Holy Royal Majesty:

In the last fleet there came to New Spain two Indians whom Captain Antonio Velázquez brought before Your Majesty, and whom Your Majesty ordered Captain Pedro Menéndez to return to their homeland as they were not baptized at the time they left the kingdom [of Spain]. As soon as they arrived in this city they got so sick and arrived at such a point that it was not thought they would escape death. For that reason, having learned of their desire to be baptized, as they had asked for it more than once, they were given the sacrament of baptism. Our lord was moved to give them back their health. The religious [brothers] of this your Convent of Santo Domingo begged your Viceroy to keep them here among us so we might instruct them in the things of our holy Catholic Faith and also so that they would become tied by affection to the friars. It was done, and thus they have been and still are among us, and have been treated like sons and taught the things of our faith. Seeing that they are now Christians and members of the church, and that if they were returned to their land alone without ministers who could keep them from straying from the faith and from Christian law, and if they were to return to their rites and idolatries and thus lose their souls, then their baptism would have caused them to be damned. Permitting all of that to happen would seem to be a great inhumanity, even a grave offense against our Lord, and a disservice to Your Majesty. It is believed that your desire to return them to their land depended on their being pagans, as they were when they left you. Considering as well the fine presence and capacity of this Indian, and what he tells us of his land, that it is well populated with peaceful people, and believing as we do that Our Lord has arranged all of this business and sent this Indian so that he may be the means of saving all of that land, your viceroy, with the zeal of a true Christian and a Catholic and a vassal of Your Majesty . . . communicated with the Provincial and other leading men of our Dominican Order what we might do assuming we received the permission of Your majesty so that the excellent opportunity we had been offered by means of the conversion of this Indian would not be lost. Thus the Order offered to send religious brothers on this project. . . . And to be more effective your Viceroy, desirous of being of service to Our Lord and to Your Majesty, offered to pay expenses himself . . . There then arrived the moment to deal with the captain [of the royal convoy] Pedro Menéndez about the necessary measures for the execution of this business . . . Because he did not have the necessary orders, or because Our Lord ordered it otherwise, wanting the expedition to be better guided by Your Majesty's hands, he denied the departure of the religious . . .

The Archbishop[1] then ordered Pedro Menéndez not to return the Indians to their homelands since no ministers would go with them. If he wanted to bring them back to Spain to go before Your Majesty, of course he could do that. The Indians were at full liberty to go to Spain and even encouraged to do so, but they said that if they were not going to return to their land, they preferred to stay here than to go all the way to Spain. Thus they remained here and are still among us, who take care to teach them the doctrine and all that is appropriate. Your Viceroy takes a special interest in them and oversees their good treatment. . .

Understanding the desire that exists on the part of the Order to serve Our Lord and Your Majesty and the opportunity that exists just now to save those people [of the northern territory] and the misfortune it would be if this opportunity were lost, it seems Your Majesty was well served. Those people are peaceful, and it is believed that they would be even more so if this Indian were to go there and give an account of what he has seen and the benefits he has received. No more than forty or fifty men would have to go with the religious, in one ship, which would be able to pacify the people there. . . . May Our Lord keep the holy person of Your Majesty and augment your territories for his service . . . Mexico City, February 13, 1563.

Fray Pedro de Feria

Source: Archivo General de Indios, Seville, Spain. Record Group Mexico, vol. 280, February 1563. Our own translation.

2.2 RICHARD HAKLUYT, EXCERPT FROM *THE PRINCIPAL NAVIGATIONS, VOYAGES, TRAFFIQUES, AND DISCOVERIES OF THE ENGLISH NATION* (1589–1600)

Towards the end of Queen Elizabeth I's reign, two cousins, both named Richard Hakluyt, became involved in the project of advancing English explorations and conquests overseas. The elder Hakluyt became known to merchants and geographers for his immense collection of letters and documents related to English interactions abroad, and the younger eventually published the collection in three volumes in 1598, 1599, and 1600. The latter Hakluyt conceived of his project as showing the way to young Englishmen who also wished to pursue exploration and conquest. The original spelling has been retained in the case of this document in order to show how differently the English language of earlier centuries reads.

---

[1]The Archbishop at the time was a Dominican. He was a friend of the Provincial of the Order and strongly in favor of any plan that would help the Dominicans gain influence in the New World.

"A brief relation of two sundry voyages made by the worshipful M. William Haukins [Hawkins] of Plimmouth, father to Sir John Haukins knight, late treasurer to her Majesties Navie, in the yeere 1530 and 1532"

Olde M. William Haukins of Plimmouth, a man for his wisedome, valure, experience, and skill in sea causes much esteemed, and beloved of K. Henry the 8, and being one of the principall Sea captaines in the West partes of England in his time, not contented with the short voyages commonly then made onely to the knowne coasts of Europe, armed out a tall and goodly shippe of his owne of the burthen of 250 tunnes, called the Paule of Plimmouth, wherewith he made three long and famous voyages unto the coast of Brasil, a thing in those dayes very rare, especially to our Nation. In the course of which voyages he touched at the river of Sestos upon the coast of Guinea, where hee trafficqued with the Negros, and tooke of them Elephants teeth, and other commodities which that place yeeldeth: and so arriving on the coast of Brasil, he used there such discretion, and behaved himself so widely with those savage people, that he grew into great familiarity and friendship with them. Insomuch that in his second voyage, one of the savage kinds of the countery of Brasil, was contented to take ship with him, and to be transported hither into England: whereunto M. Haukins agreed, leaving behind in the Countery as a pledge of his safetie and returne again, one Martin Cockeram of Plimmouth. This Brasilian king being arrived, was brought up to London and presented to K. Henry the 8, lying as then at White-hall: at the sight of whom the King and all the Nobilitie did not a little marvaile, and not without cause: for in his cheeks were holes made according to their savage maner, and therein small bones were planted, standing an inch out from the said holes, which in his owne Countery was reputed for a great braverie. He had also another hole in his nether lip, wherein was set a precious stone about the bignes of a pease: All his apparel, behavior, and gesture, were very strange to the beholders.

Having remained here the space almost of a whole yeere, and the king with his sight fully satisfied, M. Hawkins [sic] according to his promise and appointment, purposed to convey him againe into his courntrey: but it fell out in the say, that by the change of aire and alteration of diet, the said Savage king died at sea, which was feared would turn to the losse of the life of Martin Cockeram his pledge. Neverthelesse, the Savages being fully persuaded of the honest dealing of our men with their prince, restored againe the said pledge, without any harme to him, or any man of the company: which pledge of theirs they brought home againe into England, with their ship freighted, and furnished with the commodities of the countery. Which Martin Cockeram, by the witnesse of Sir John Hawkins, being an officer in the towne of Plimmouth, was living within these fewe yeeres.

Source: Richard Hakluyt, *The Principal Navigations, Voyages, Traffiques, and Discoveries of the English Nation*, edited by Irwin R. Blacker (New York: Viking, 1965), pp. 39–40.

2.3 VINCENT BIGOT, ACCOUNT OF GANDEAKTENA BECOMING A CHRISTIAN (1679)

Many Native American people resisted the pressure brought to bear by Christian missionaries to accept Christianity; others chose to convert. In French Canada, the most famous convert was Catherine Tegahkouita, or Kateri as she is usually called today. It has traditionally been assumed that she was simply susceptible to influence by the missionaries, for better or for worse, depending on one's perspective. The story, however, is more complicated: her mother was an Algonkian captive taken by the Iroquois. When her father and his family died of smallpox, she was left without immediate kin and thus was interested in joining a new community that would be more supportive of her. Kateri was not alone. In 1679, a Jesuit recounted the story of Gandeaktena; she is much less famous to us today, but the account of her life is worth reading nonetheless, as several elements of her story are comparable to Kateri's.

The Queen of virtues has been wonderfully displayed in the person of a poor slave, taken prisoner by the Iroquois from the Chat nation. We shall undoubtedly be touched by the graces that god was pleased to confer upon this Captive, and by the singular virtues—and, above all, the Charity toward God and her neighbor—that she displayed before the eyes of the savages and the French at la prairie de la Magdelaine. Here is the narrative:

God having permitted that Gentaienton, a village of the Chat nation, should be taken and sacked by the Iroquois, Gandeaktena, which is the name of the one of whom we are speaking, was taken into slavery together with her mother and brought to Onniout. There the misfortune of her country proved the blessing of our Captive; and her slavery was the Cause of her preparing herself to receive through baptism the liberty of the children of God. The innocence in which she had lived, even before intending to become a Christian, seemed to have prepared her to receive this grace; and it is an astonishing fact that, in the midst of the extreme Corruption of the Iroquois, she was able, before being illumined by the light of the gospel, to keep herself from participating in their debaucheries, although she was their slave.

Some years after her coming to Onneiout, father Bruyas also came thither to preach the gospel. On the day after his arrival, he made known in public the reason of his coming. Our slave was at once Inwardly influenced by God, and so keenly affected with the desire of paradise and the fear of hell, that she Immediately resolved to spare no pains in acquiring the one and avoiding the other. She showed no less Constancy in the prosecution of her purpose than promptitude in forming it; and although she encountered great obstacles, there was none that she did not succeed in overcoming. Her extreme modesty, which would not permit her to visit the father all alone; the refusal of all whom she asked to bear her company; the determination, sudden and unexpected, of her husband[2] to take her with him to the war; the work assigned to her by the woman whose slave she was, —that of going to the fishery, after her husband had sent her back from the expedition,—served only to bring to view the power of the spirit by which she was urged forward. This spirit, rendering her

---

[2]Captured girls and young women usually had the option of marrying into the tribe.

careful to Seek the favorable opportunity of corresponding to the divine inspiration, prevailed upon her to embrace at last what the providence of God rather than chance placed in her way. For, on her return from the fishery, she met one of her Companions who was on her way to the prayers. She went with her; and on arriving at the Cabin of the father, she repeated the prayers. The father noticed her, and judged from her modest countenance that there was something about this Young woman that was quite out of the common; this determined him to address to her some words of encouragement in private. From that time she never failed to come to pray to God in the Chapel. She learned in a very short time the prayers, and the mysteries of our faith; but, reflecting on the Corrupt morals and licentiousness of the Iroquois, and wisely Concluding that she would experience much difficulty in securing her salvation if she lived among them, she resolved to leave them and come to live with the French. She commended the matter to God, and spoke of her plan to her mother, to her father-in-law, and to her husband, after his return from the war. She won them all over, as well as certain others of her neighbors, and came with them to Monseigneur Bishop of Canada, who, after they had been instructed, baptized them all. These blessed successes with which God had accompanied the Conversion of our Catherine—for that is the name she received at baptism—and that little band of persons whom she had attracted to the faith, and the train of events, made it apparent that he had from that time appointed her, and was Directing her, to become Instrumental in the salvation of many Iroquois; for he gave her the thought of going to dwell at la prairie de la Magdelaine, where, two months ago, a settlement had been Started. She went there, in fact, together with those with whom she had been baptized—12 in number,—and gave the first Impulse to the mission which is now so flourishing.

No advance was made in these small beginnings for 2 or 3 years; but, at length they attained much renown, especially among the Iroquois nations, so that more than 200 Iroquois have come since that time to establish themselves at la prairie de la Magdelaine, in order to live there as good Christians. And it is a surprising Thing that God should have willed that they [the Iroquois] should Spare the life of Catherine in order that, afterward, she might obtain for them eternal salvation, and that thus their slave might become their instructress in the faith. She was that indeed, not only at the outset of her Conversion, but all the remainder of her life, through the rare examples of virtue which she furnished them.

Source: Vincent Bigot, revised by Claude Dablon, "Relation of What Occurred Most Remarkable in the Mission of the Fathers of the Society of Jesus in New France, in the year 1679," in Reuben Gold Thwaites, ed., *The Jesuit Relations and Allied Documents*, vol. LXI (Cleveland, Ohio: Burrows Brothers, 1896), pp. 195–199.

2.4 JOHN HECKEWELDER, ACCOUNT OF THE ARRIVAL OF THE DUTCH AT MANHATTAN

The Delawares and Mahicans lived on the coast of today's New Jersey and in the Hudson River Valley region when the Dutch first arrived at Manhattan in 1609. Gradually, as more Europeans arrived, they were pushed westward, taking their memories and stories with them. By the middle of the eighteenth century, they were living in the Ohio Valley. There, a Moravian missionary named John Heckewelder came to live among them and learn their language. Accounts of his indicate that the Indians told him of the arrival of the Dutch at Manhattan as a humorous tall tale.

A great many years ago, when men with a white skin had never yet been seen in the land, some Indians who were out a fishing, at a place where the sea widens, espied at a great distance something remarkably large floating on the water, and such as they had never seen before. These Indians immediately returning to the shore, apprised their countryman of what they had observed, and pressed them to go out with them and discover what it might be. They hurried out together, and saw with astonishment the phenomenon which now appeared to their sight, but could not agree upon what it was; some believed it to be an uncommonly large fish or animal, while others were of opinion it must be a very big house floating on the sea. At length the spectators concluded that this wonderful object was moving towards the land, and that it must be an animal or something else that had life in it; it would therefore be proper to inform all the Indians on the inhabited island of what they had seen, and put them on their guard. Accordingly they sent off a number of runners and watermen to carry the news to their scattered chiefs, that they might send off in every direction for the warriors, with a message that they should come on immediately. These arriving in numbers, and having themselves viewed the strange appearance, and observing that it was actually moving towards the entrance of the river or bay; concluded it to be a remarkably large house in which the Mannitto (the Great or Supreme Being) himself was present, and that he probably was coming to visit them. By this time the chiefs were assembled at York island, and deliberating in what manner they should receive their Mannitto on his arrival. Every measure was taken to be well provided with plenty of meat for a sacrifice. The women were desired to prepare the best victuals. All the idols or images were examined and put in order, and a grand dance was supposed not only to be an agreeable entertainment for the Great Being, but it was believed that it might, with the addition of a sacrifice, contribute to appease him if he was angry with them. The conjurers were also set to work, to determine what this phenomenon portended, and what the possible result of it might be. To these and to the chiefs and wise men of the nations, men, women and children were looking up for advice and protection. Distracted between hope and fear, they were at a loss what to do; a dance, however, commenced in great confusion. While in this situation, fresh runners arrived declaring it to be a large house of various colors, and crowded with living creatures. It appears now to be certain, that it is the great Mannitto, bringing them some kind of game, such as he had not given them before, but other runners soon after arriving declare that it is positively full of human beings, of quite a different color from that of the Indians, and dressed differently from them; that in particular one of them was dressed entirely in red who must be the Mannitto himself. They are hailed from the vessel in a language they do not understand yet they shout or yell in return by way of answer, according to the custom of their country; many are for running off to the woods, but are pressed by others to stay, in order not to give offence to their visitor, who might find them out and destroy them. The house, some say large canoe, at last stops, and a canoe of a smaller size comes on shore with the red man, and some others in it; some stay with his canoe to guard it. The chiefs and wise men, assembled in council, form themselves into a large circle, towards which the man in red clothes approaches with two others. He salutes after their manner. They are lost in admiration [stunned surprise]; the dress, the manners, the whole appearance of the unknown strangers is to them a subject of wonder; but they are particularly struck with him who wore the red coat all glittering with gold lace,[3] which they could in no manner account for. He, surely, must be the great Mannitto, but why should he have a white skin? Meanwhile, a large *Hackhack* [gourd] is brought by one of his servants, from which an unknown substance is poured out into a small cup or glass, and handed to the supposed Mannitto. He drinks—has the glass filled again, and hands it to the chief standing next to him. The chief receives it, but only smells the contents and passes it on to the next chief, who does the same. The glass or cup thus passes through the circle, without the liquor being tasted by any one, and is upon the point of being returned to the red clothed Mannitto, when one of the Indians, a brave man and a great warrior, suddenly jumps up and harangues the assembly on the impropriety of returning the cup with its contents. It was handed to them, says he, by the Mannitto, that they should drink out of it, as he himself had done. To follow his example would be pleasing to him; but to return what he had given them might provoke his wrath, and bring destruction on them. And since the orator believed it for the good of that nation that the contents offered them should be drunk, an as no one else would do it, he would drink it himself, let the consequence be what it might; it was better for one man to die, than that a whole nation should be destroyed. He then took the glass, and bidding the assembly a solemn farewell, at once drank up its whole contents. Every eye was fixed on the resolute chief, to see what the effect the unknown liquor would produce. He soon began to stagger, and at last fell prostrate on the ground. His companions now bemoan his fate, he falls into a sound sleep, and they think he has expired. He wakes again, jumps up and declares, that he has enjoyed the most delicious sensations, and that he never before felt himself so happy as after he had drunk the cup. He asks for more, his wish is granted; the whole assembly then imitate him, and all become intoxicated.

After this general intoxication had ceased, for they say that while it lasted the whites had confined themselves to their vessel, the man with the red clothes returned again, and distributed presents among them, consisting of beads, axes, hoes, and stockings such as the white people wear. They soon became familiar with each other, and began to converse by signs. The Dutch made them understand that they would not stay here, that they would return home again, but would pay them another visit the next year, when they would bring them more presents and stay with them awhile; but as they could not live without eating, they should want a little land of them to sow seeds, in order to raise herbs and vegetables to put into their broth. They went away as they had said, and returned in the following season, when both parties were much rejoiced to see each other; but the whites laughed at the Indians, seeing that they knew not the use of the axes and hoes they had given them the year before; for they had these hanging to their waists as ornaments, and the stockings were made use of as tobacco pouches. The whites now put the handles to the former for them, and cut trees down before their eyes, hoed up the ground, and put the stockings on their legs.

---

[3]Note that this is not really how the Dutch officers dressed in 1609. It is, however, how British officers dressed in the eighteenth century, when the story was recorded.

Here, they say, a general laughterr ensued among the Indians, that they had remained ignorant of the use of such valuable implement, and had born the weight of such heavy metal hanging to their necks, for such a length of time. They took every white man they saw for an inferior mannitto attendant upon the Supreme Deity who shone superior in the red and laced clothes. As the whites became daily more familiar with the Indians, they at last proposed to stay with them, and asked only for so much ground for a garden lot, as, they said the hide of a bullock would cover or encompass, which hide was spread before them. The Indians readily granted this apparently reasonable request; but the whites then took a knife, and beginning at one end of the hide, cut it up to a long rope, not thicker than a child's finger, so that by the time the whole was cut up, it made an great heap; they then took the rope at one end, and drew it gently along, carefully avoiding its breaking. It was drawn out into a circular form, and being closed at its ends encompassed a large piece of ground. The Indians were surprised at the superior wit of the whites, but did not wish to contend with them about a little land, as they had still enough themselves. The white and red men lived contentedly together for a long time, though the former from time to time asked for more land, which was readily obtained, and thus they gradually proceeded higher up the mahicannittuck [Hudson River], until the Indians began to believe that they would soon want all their country, which in the end proved true.

Source: John Heckewelder, *An Account of the history, manners, and customs of the Indian nations, who once inhabited Pennsylvania and neighboring states* (Philadelphia: Historical Society of Pennsylvania, 1876 [1819]), pp. 71–75 and 321–322.

COMMON THREADS

After the failure at Roanoke, how were the English finally able to plant successful colonies?

Why did the Jamestown Colony almost fail, and why did the New England ones succeed almost immediately? Can the Chesapeake or the New England experience be considered more "typical" of what would become the United States?

What were the similarities and differences in each region's relations with Native Americans?

How and why did slavery become more prominent in the Chesapeake?

What role did religion play in shaping the Puritan colonies?

What elements of democracy existed in the New England and Chesapeake colonies?

The Adventures of John Smith

John Smith has attained almost mythical stature, but he was once a real person. In the 1590s, he was a rebellious adolescent in the English countryside. His yeoman father apprenticed him to a merchant in the nearby seaport town of King's Lynn. Then his father died, and young John seized the opportunity to leave his master. He made his way to the Netherlands and joined the rebel army there engaged in fighting for independence from Spain. Later, he hired himself out to Archduke Ferdinand of Austria to fight Ottoman Turks in Hungary. He was taken prisoner on the battlefield, sold as a slave, and sent to work on a farm in Tartary. He escaped on a stolen horse and got to Christian Russia, and from there he was able to return home.

Back in London by 1606, John Smith found everyone talking about plans for a colony in "Virginia." He wanted to go. His experiences in faraway countries apparently convinced officers of the Virginia Company to name him as one of the council members who were to direct the colony at Jamestown. Later, he would even briefly become president of the council.

The expedition touched land in April 1607. Because the colony starved and struggled, the daring Smith decided to make his way up the Chickahominy River in the dead of winter to try to persuade the Indians to give the settlers corn. He was captured by a party of Powhatans and taken to Werowocomoco, the seat of the paramount chief, named "Powhatan" for his people. Through signs and pantomime, he and the high chief tried to glean information about each other's purposes. Over the course of several weeks, Smith was encouraged to spend time with one of Powhatan's less important daughters, born to him by an ordinary woman, not a noblewoman. This was Pocahontas, then aged 10 or so. She quickly picked up the English phrases he taught her. In early January 1608, the Indians returned their prisoner to the fort at Jamestown, satisfied to have made inroads in forging an alliance with the newcomers.

Smith wrote a report almost immediately and sent it back to London. He said nothing about the purported events that have since become so famous—that Powhatan intended to bash his brains out, but his lovely daughter threw herself over him to save him. In fact, Smith said nothing about this in any of the several works he published in the ensuing decade. He told the illogical story 17 years later, when Pocahontas and everyone else involved were dead. He made the claim in the wake of an Indian rebellion, when Powhatan's kindred were viewed as the devil incarnate, and Pocahontas, who by then had been to London and was a celebrity, was seen as exceptional among all her people.

Furthermore, it is notable that in Smith's accounts of his exploits around the world, he never failed to mention that at each critical juncture, a beautiful young woman had fallen in love with him and interceded on his behalf. He claimed it happened in Turkey, in Russia, and in France. He always said that these beautiful girls had been willing to die for him—a sign of a woman's love in old medieval tales.

What Smith *did* talk about earlier on—and which was probably true—was that Powhatan had involved him in a special ceremony, which scholars now interpret as a ceremony of political adoption. Powhatan, in short, was willing to draw the English into his world and use them in any way he saw fit. The 10-year-old Pocahontas may even have been present as the only possible partial translator.

Smith was injured in a gunpowder accident not long after, and he seized the moment to leave the floundering colony and return to England. He became involved in the burgeoning efforts to colonize New England, but he did not settle there. He ended up making his living by writing about his travels and about the Americas, dying in 1631.

Smith was a man of his age. He was no friend to the Indians and often advocated violence. In fact, when Pocahontas saw him years later while she was visiting London, she accused him of having lied about his own and other Englishmen's intentions. On the other hand, he was unusual in that he did know the Indians as real people and respected them as adversaries. Smith never made the mistake of believing that the Indians of Virginia would be happy to do whatever the English wanted or of seeing them as subhuman. His detailed 1608 report, written before he allowed his fantasies to run away with him and before he was trying to sell books, remains one of the best sources of information we have about the important cultural encounter at Jamestown.

The First Chesapeake Colonies

When Queen Elizabeth died in 1603, she was succeeded by her Scottish cousin, King James I, who immediately signed a treaty with Spain ending decades of warfare. With peace established, all those who had lived off privateering and warfare had to look for another source of income. They joined with old advocates of colonization to establish new colonies in North America. In 1606, James granted charters to two groups of English merchants and military men, one in London and the other in Plymouth. The Plymouth group would colonize the northern coast, and the Londoners the Chesapeake region. Each operation was chartered as a private company, which would raise money from shareholders and finance, populate, and regulate its colonies.

Founding Virginia

In 1606, the Plymouth-based company deposited some settlers at the mouth of the Kennebec River in today's Maine, but the climate defeated them within a season. The Virginia Company (named in honor of the recently deceased, never-married queen) had wealthy London backers and met with greater success. Just before Christmas in 1606, it sent out three ships under Captain Christopher Newport, a one-legged veteran Atlantic explorer. When the ships arrived at Virginia on April 26, 1607, the colonists learned that they were to be governed by a council of seven men. Unfortunately, two of them, Edward Maria Wingfield, an arrogant gentleman and investor in the company, and Captain John Smith, the equally arrogant but considerably more capable soldier of fortune, despised each other. By the end of the summer, another council member had been executed because he was supposedly a double agent for the Spanish. The early history of Jamestown was marked by internal wrangling. External conflict soon developed as well, as the colonists antagonized their Indian hosts. Almost everything that could go wrong did.

The experience of Roanoke notwithstanding, the English still hoped to find a land like Mexico, filled with gold and other less glamorous raw materials. Whatever limited manufacturing was needed could be performed either by English criminals, sent over to work as their punishment, or by indentured servants, English men and women from the lowest ranks of society who agreed to work for a set period to pay their transportation expenses. The colonists expected to trade with the local Indians, who would be the primary suppliers of food.

The Virginia Company planned to get the colony up and running within seven years. During that period, all colonists would work for the Company, which would give them food and shelter. At the end of that time, they would receive grants of land. The Company evidently thought the colony would need a great deal of direction, for about one-third of the original settlers were gentlemen, that is, members of the elite, a proportion of the colony's population that was six times higher than it was in England.

The Company also sent skilled laborers, many with skills of little use in the colony, such as tailors, goldsmiths, and a perfumer. Some were thought necessary to support the gentlemen. Others were to work the gold and precious gems colonists hoped to find. Farmers and ordinary laborers, on the other hand, were in short supply, for it was assumed that the Indians would fill these roles.

Starving Times

Poor planning and bad luck placed the colonists on swampy ground with bad water. The salty water of the James River could be poisonous, and in summer it became a breeding ground for typhoid and dysentery. Some historians have argued that these diseases left the survivors too weak to plant food, whereas others note that many of the healthy seemed to prefer prospecting for gold. The colonists depended on the resentful Powhatan Indians for food, and the resulting malnutrition made the effects of disease worse. These factors, along with skirmishes with the Powhatans, led to appallingly high mortality rates. By September 1607, half of the more than 100 original colonists were dead, and by the following spring only 38 were still alive. Although the Company sent over more colonists, they continued to die off at extraordinary rates. As late as 1616, the English population was only 350, although more than five times that number had emigrated from England (see Table 3–1).

The Fort at Jamestown This nineteenth-century engraving of Jamestown in 1607 shows the difficulties of unloading goods from a ship in the earliest days of settlement.

Table 3-1 English Population of Virginia, 1607–1640

Population in Virginia Colony	Immigration to Virginia Colony
104 (April 1607)	104 (April 1607)
38 (Jan. 1608)	
	120 (Jan. 1608, 1st supply)
130 (Sept. 1608)	
	70 (Sept. 1608, 2nd supply)
200 (late Sept. 1608)	
100 (spring 1609)	
	300 (Fall 1609, 3rd supply)
	540 (1610)
450 (April 1611)	
	660 (1611)
682 (Jan. 1612)	
350 (Jan. 1613)	
	45 (1613–1616)
351 (1616)	
600 (Dec. 1618)	
	900 (1618–1620)
887 (Mar. 1620)	
	1,051 (1620–1621)
943 (Mar. 1621)	
	1,580 (1621–1622)
1,240 (Mar. 1622)	
	1,935 (1622–1623)
1,241 (April 1623)	
	1,646 (1623–1624)
1,275 (Feb. 1624)	
1,210 (1625)	
	9,000 (1625–1634)
4,914 (1634)	
	6,000 (1635–1640)
8,100 (1640)	total: 23,951

Source: Data from Carville Earle, *Geographical Inquiry and American Historical Problems* (Stanford, CA: Stanford University Press, 1992), and Virginia Bernhard, "Men, Women, and Children at Jamestown: Population and Gender in Early Virginia, 1607–1610," *Journal of Southern History,* 58 (1992).

Note: Although about 24,000 men and women immigrated to Virginia between 1607 and 1640, in 1640 the population stood at only 8,100. Most of the inhabitants fell victim to disease, although the Indian uprising of 1622 took 347 lives.

Troubled Relations with the Powhatans

In Virginia, the English encountered the powerful paramount chieftaincy of the Powhatan Indians. Originally a small tribe of Algonquian-speaking Indians like many others in the region, the Powhatans had attained great power when, through a series of politically motivated marriages, a young chief of theirs had inherited the rulerships of several other tribes, some through his mother and some through his father. This man, called Powhatan in honor of his people, took his larger-than-usual force of warriors and made a series of strategic attacks, then followed up by taking a wife from each of numerous chiefly families in the area. At the time of the arrival of the English, Powhatan's chieftaincy included about 20,000 Indians, divided into about three dozen tribes.

Powhatan hoped to use the English to buttress his power by trading for metal goods and textiles, but he recognized that the strangers might constitute a threat. In his negotiations first with Smith and then with others, he attempted to tie the English into his world as his vassals. But, of course, the English hoped for the inverse. At one point, the English put a fake crown on the kneeling Powhatan's head, imitating the ceremonies in which feudal princes pledged allegiance to a king. The Indians, however, remained unmoved by the ceremony.

With his large force, Lord De La Warr immediately set out to subjugate the Indians. He ordered Powhatan to return all English captives taken in prior skirmishes. When Powhatan refused, De La Warr ordered an attack on an Indian village. The English killed about 75 inhabitants, burned the town and its cornfields, and captured the wife of a chieftain and her children. As the English sailed back to Jamestown, they threw the children overboard and shot them as they swam in the water. So opened the First Anglo-Powhatan War, the first of three conflicts between 1610 and 1646.

During this war, an English captain kidnapped the daughter of Powhatan named Pocahontas and brought her back to Jamestown. The English knew her because she and Smith had taught each other some of their languages when he was briefly held captive during the colony's first year, and she later had visited the fort. She had been a child then and now was a young woman. The English placed her in the care of a minister, hoping to convert her and render her "a perfect Interpreter." However, she remained unconverted. In the summer of 1614, the English took their hostage upriver to Powhatan's town and threatened to harm her if he did not do as they asked and agree to pay tribute in corn. The two sides were at an impasse. Suddenly John Rolfe, a young widower who had apparently tutored Pocahontas in English, asked for her hand in marriage. Messengers were sent to Powhatan, and he agreed. In permitting his daughter to marry an Englishman, Powhatan was adopting a means he had used to establish his powerful chieftaincy. Young Algonquian women frequently married with the enemy for their people's sake. Pocahontas agreed, and three days later announced she had converted to Christianity. The marriage of John Rolfe and Pocahontas ushered in a brief period of peace, but it could not last.

Toward a New Economic Order and the Rise of Democracy

The tide finally turned against the Powhatans, not because of a failure in diplomacy or the politics of marriage, but because the English finally found a way to make money in Virginia. Pocahontas's husband, John Rolfe, developed a strain of tobacco that found a ready market in England. It transformed the colony almost overnight. Within three years, Virginia was shipping 50,000 pounds of tobacco to England per year. Suddenly Virginia

Powhatan and English Dwellings These are reconstructions of typical Powhatan Indian and English homes, ca. 1607. Both are dark and small.

experienced an economic boom. By 1619, a man working by himself was making £200 in one crop, and a man with six indentured servants could make £1,000, money only the nobility was accustomed to. Once fortunes this large could be made, the race to Virginia was on.

All that was needed to make money in Virginia was land and people to work it. In 1616 the Virginia Company, which had land but no money, offered land as dividends to its stockholders. Those already living in Virginia were given land, and anyone who came over (or brought another person over) was to be granted 50 acres a head (called a headright). The Company was moving toward private enterprise, away from the corporate, company-directed economy of the early years. The leadership of the colony also gave itself grants, laying the basis for its own wealth and power. It was far easier to obtain land in Virginia than in England.

To attract settlers, the Company replaced martial law with common law, guaranteeing colonists all the rights of the English people. The colonists were also granted greater rights to self-government than were enjoyed by those who lived in England. The first elected representative government in the New World, the Virginia House of Burgesses (renamed the General Assembly after the American Revolution), met in Jamestown on July 30, 1619.

These inducements attracted 3,500 settlers to Virginia in three years, three times as many as had come in the preceding ten years. By accident more than planning, Virginia had found the formula for a successful English colony. It was one that all other colonies generally followed: offering colonists greater opportunities to make money and greater rights of self-government than they had at home. These changes came too late, however, to rescue the Virginia Company, which went bankrupt in 1624. King James I dissolved the Company and turned Virginia into a royal colony under his control.

Toward the Destruction of the Powhatans

As the new colonists spread out, establishing private plantations, English settlers claimed all the Indians' prime farmland on both sides of the James River and began to move up its tributaries (see Map 3–1). At the same time, the Powhatans became increasingly

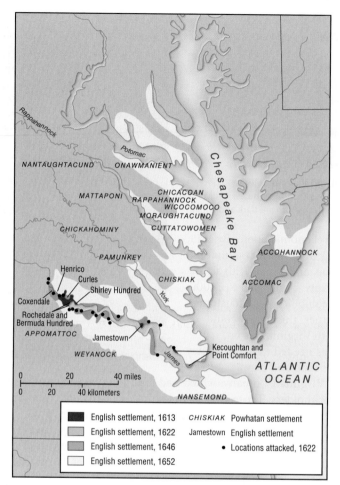

Map 3–1   English Encroachments on Indian Land, 1613–1652 After John Rolfe's development of a marketable strain of tobacco, the English spread out through the Chesapeake region, encroaching steadily on Indian land. Tobacco planters preferred land along the rivers, for casks filled with tobacco bound for England were more easily transported by ship. *Source:* Frederic Gleach, *Powhatan's World and Colonial Virginia* (Lincoln: University of Nebraska Press, 1997), and James Horn, *Adapting to a New World: English Society in the Seventeenth-Century Chesapeake* (Chapel Hill: University of North Carolina Press, 1994).

dependent on English goods such as metal tools. Moreover, as the English population began to grow its own food, it had less need of Indian food, the only significant commodity the Indians had to trade. The Indians slowly accumulated a debt to the English and lost their economic independence.

After Powhatan died, his more militant brother, Opechancanough, decided to get rid of the English. He wanted to convince them to go home or at least to limit their spreading. On the morning of March 22, 1622, in an extraordinarily well-planned attack, the Indians struck at most of the plantations along the James River, killing about one-quarter of the colonists. The Second Anglo-Powhatan War, which continued for another 10 years, had begun. This war marked a turning point in English policy. Although some of the English recognized that the Indian attack had been caused by their "own perfid-iouse dealing," most decided that the Indians were untrustworthy and incapable of being converted to the English way of life. Therefore, a policy of extermination was justified. Some were almost happy that the Indians had attacked; John Smith concluded that the massacre "will be good for the Plantation, because now we have just cause to destroy them by all meanes possible." Until this point, the English had claimed only land that the Indians were not currently farming. Now they seized territory the Indians had just cleared and planted. In only 15 years' time, the English and Indians in Virginia had become implacable enemies.

Indian resistance only made the English more determined to stay, and with the tobacco economy booming, settlers poured into Virginia. They spread across the Chesapeake to the Eastern Shore and north to the Potomac River. The aged Opechanca-nough, determined to make one final push, struck again on April 18, 1644, killing about 400 and taking many prisoners.

The Third Anglo-Powhatan War ended, however, in the Indians' total defeat two years later. Opechancanough was killed. The English took complete possession of the land between the James and York Rivers. Henceforth, no Indian was allowed to enter this territory unless he was bringing a message from a chief. Any English person who shel-tered an Indian without permission was to be put to death. The land north of the York River was set aside for the Indians, making it the first American Indian reservation. Soon, English settlers moved into that region, too. It was not the last time that the English settlers would break a treaty with the Indians.

A New Colony in Maryland

Virginia's original plan to make money from trading with the local Indians was not en-tirely forgotten. When tobacco prices dipped in the 1620s, trade became attractive once again. By the late 1620s, an outpost had been established at the northern end of the Chesapeake Bay to obtain beaver furs from the Susquehannocks. Sir George Calvert, the first Lord Baltimore and a Catholic, saw the commercial potential of this region and in 1632 persuaded King Charles I, a Catholic sympathizer, to grant him the land north of the Potomac and south of the Delaware that was "not yet cultivated and planted." This territory became Maryland, the first proprietary colony, that is, a colony owned literally by an individual and his heirs. (Virginia was originally a charter colony, held by a group of private shareholders. Unlike royal colonies, in charter and proprietary colonies the English Crown turned over both financing and management to the shareholders or pro-prietors.) Maryland, named after the Catholic queen of England, remained the heredi-tary possession of the Calvert family until the American Revolution, although the majority of the settlers were not Catholics.

As the first proprietary colony, Maryland established a pattern for subsequent proprietorships. The proprietor had extensive powers to grant land and make laws by himself, but perhaps because Calvert knew he would have to compete for settlers with Virginia, which had a representative government, he agreed to a representative assembly. In 1649 that assembly passed the Act of Toleration, which said that no one would be "compelled to the beliefe or exercise of any other Religion against his or her consent." Even though religious toleration was extended only to Christians, Maryland was among the most tolerant places in the world. Moreover, this right was extended to women as well as men. (This experiment in religious toleration faced a crisis, however, in 1689, when Coode's Rebellion overthrew the proprietor, making Maryland temporarily a royal colony and, in 1702, establishing the Anglican Church. In 1715 the Calvert family was restored to power. See Chapter 4 for more on the effects of England's "Glorious Revolution" in America.)

Although Maryland's population increased slowly, the familiar political economy emerged quickly. As in Virginia, attracting colonists required greater opportunities and freedoms—of self-government and of religion—than they enjoyed in England. Even during the conflict with the Powhatan Confederacy, the booming tobacco economy drew settlers to Virginia and, after about 1650, to Maryland as well. Although they had separate governments, Virginia and Maryland had similar political economies, based on tobacco. The defeat of the Indians made more land available for cultivation; the colonies needed only people to work it.

The Political Economy of Slavery Emerges

Chesapeake society in the first half of the seventeenth century was shaped by four forces: weak government, the market for tobacco, the availability of land, and the need for labor. Because government was weak, the forces of plantation agriculture were unchecked, and the profit motive operated without restraint. Those who could take advantage of these opportunities—male and female both—profited wildly, whereas the poor, both white and African, were without defense. In this environment the political economy of slavery took root.

The Problem of a Labor Supply

Once the crises of the early years had passed, the Chesapeake's greatest problem was securing laborers to produce tobacco. As soon as John Rolfe brought in his first successful crop, the Virginia governor began pressing England to send him its poor. The Virginia Company also encouraged the emigration of women, for the young colony was primarily male. No matter how many colonists came, however, the demand for labor always outstripped the supply. By 1660, 50,000 Britons, mostly single men in their 20s, had migrated to the Chesapeake, but the population was still only a little over 35,000. Because of disease and malnutrition, the death rate remained extraordinarily high. It did not help that most of the colonists came from impoverished backgrounds and arrived alone and friendless to face a harsh new situation.

The profits from tobacco were so great and the risk of death so high that landowners squeezed out every penny of profit as quickly as they could. Those with land and servants to work it could become rich overnight. Colonial officials, including members of the legislature, discovered a variety of ways to make themselves wealthy. Great wealth, however, could be achieved only by the labor of others, and the demand for labor was almost insatiable. Perhaps 90 percent of those who migrated to the Chesapeake in the seventeenth century came as servants, and half died before completing their term of service. In England, servants had some basic protections, but in Virginia, working conditions were deadly brutal. In 1623, Richard Frethorne, a young Virginia servant "with weeping tears" wrote to his parents in England, "We must work early and late for a mess of water gruel and a mouthful of bread and beef."

AMERICA AND THE WORLD

The English Enter the Slave Trade

By the sixteenth century, slavery did not exist in England, and its people prided themselves on their "free air." History books in the Anglo-American world have tended to blame the Portuguese and the Spanish for initiating the African slave trade and the Dutch merchants for developing it. Yet by the eighteenth century, British shipping dominated the trade, and English merchants made immense profits from it. Slavery eventually took root everywhere in the Americas, including the English colonies. English traders entered the business as soon as it was feasible to do so, and their actions sped the rise of slavery in the Americas, which in turn encouraged the trade.

In 1562, John Hawkins, from a wealthy seafaring family in Plymouth, decided to break into the Portuguese slave trade. He seized hundreds of Africans, as well as valuable trade goods, from Portuguese ships along the Guinea coast of West Africa and took them to Santo Domingo on Hispaniola to sell. Even after paying the necessary bribes to Spanish officials—as trade with England was illegal—the profits were enormous. Queen Elizabeth I, who had been against the slave trade, began to pay attention, and she later invested Crown resources. On his second voyage, Hawkins experimented with attacking African villages himself, but he found the costs to be high: in one incident, he seized 10 Africans but lost 7 crew members. Hawkins eventually learned that Africans could be his allies in the trade. An emissary from an African king approached him with a proposition: help the king defeat his enemies and share in the slaves taken as booty. Hawkins

agreed and ended up with hundreds of captives. It was the beginning of a hideous guns-for-slaves cycle that would eventually cripple Africa. For Hawkins, ironically, the voyage ended badly. The Spaniards in the Caribbean, having been punished for their prior illegal dealings with him, refused his merchandise. Then they attacked his fleet off the coast of Veracruz, Mexico, and killed and imprisoned nearly all his men. Hawkins himself barely made it home to England.

It was the lack of a ready legal market in the New World that made the business impossible for the time being. In the first half of the seventeenth century, however, that situation changed as the English established colonies on the mainland of North America and on certain Caribbean islands. In 1630, wealthy Puritans established the colony they hoped would make England rich on Providence Island, off the coast of Nicaragua. The investors had in mind the widespread production of cash crops that grew readily in tropical climates. After only four years, the investors abandoned the importation of indentured English servants and filled the land with Africans—whom enthusiastic captains found they could buy along the Central American coast. After the Pequots lost a war with the New Englanders, Pequot prisoners were also sold on Providence Island. One man wrote with abhorrence of the turn of events; his Puritan brethren were unmoved. Only the constant rebellions frightened them, so they took steps to curb the total number relative to the number of English. Yet by the time the Spanish navy destroyed the colony *continued* in 1641, there were more than 380 African slaves and fewer than 350 English settlers.

From 1640 on, the numbers of African slaves grew in Barbados and other English island colonies, and after the 1660s in the Chesapeake as well. As soon as they were available cheaply enough, slaves became widespread wherever cash crops could grow—even in a Puritan colony. The English slave trade had blossomed.

Servants might be beaten so severely that they died, or they might find their indentures (the contract that bound them to service for a period of usually seven years) sold from one master to another. They found little protection from the courts. They were not, in fact, slaves. They would become free if they outlived their period of indenture; they retained all of the rights of English people, and their servitude was not hereditary. But they were far worse off than servants in England.

Some colonists tried to resolve the problem of the labor shortage by purchasing Indian slaves who had been captured by other Indians in wars farther west, but there were not nearly enough of these to meet the demand (see Chapter 4).

The Origins of African Slavery in the Chesapeake

Other New World plantation societies in which labor was in short supply had already turned to African slavery, so it was probably only a matter of time until the Chesapeake did as well. Historians do not know precisely when slavery was first practiced on a widespread basis in the Chesapeake, but Africans first arrived in Virginia in 1619, when a Dutch ship sailing off course sold its cargo of "twenty Negars" to the Virginians. As long as life expectancy was low, it was generally more profitable for a planter to purchase an indentured servant for a period of seven years than a slave for life. Not until life expectancy improved toward the end of the seventeenth century were significant numbers of African slaves imported into the Chesapeake.

All the English plantation colonies followed the same pattern in making the transition from white servitude to African slavery. The transition was quick in some places and slow in others; in Virginia, it took about three-quarters of a century. The primary factors dictating how readily English colonists adopted African slavery were the need for plantation laborers and the availability of African slaves at a good price. If there was any discussion about the justice of slavery, the English claimed that slavery was an appropriate punishment for certain crimes and for prisoners taken in just wars. No white people were ever enslaved in the English colonies, however. It was a practice reserved for "strangers," primarily foreigners of a non-Christian religion. At first, some of the Africans who ended up in the colonies were those who came as the domestic servants of well-to-do colonists, not as chattel slaves. In addition, some buyers in the early years allowed Africans to earn their freedom as did English indentured servants. Still, all the British colonies eventually practiced permanent chattel slavery, and it became critical to plantation economies. African slaves were even brought back to the British Islands, and by the middle of the eighteenth century, 2 percent of London's population was African.

Even before they had substantial contact with African people, the English and other northern Europeans probably harbored prejudice against dark-skinned people. By the second half of the sixteenth century, the English were depicting Africans in derogatory terms, saying that Africans were unattractive, with "dispositions most savage and brutish," a "people of beastly living" who "contract no matrimonie, neither have respect to chastity." Northern Europeans considered African women particularly monstrous, sexually promiscuous, and neglectful of their children. Although these views were not explicitly used to justify slavery, they formed the basis for the racism that would develop along with the slave system.

During the first half of the seventeenth century, African slavery and white and African servitude existed side by side. The Chesapeake was a society with slaves, but it was still not a slave society. The first clear evidence of permanent and generalized enslavement of Africans in the Chesapeake dates to 1639, when the Maryland Assembly passed a law guaranteeing "all the Inhabitants of this Province being Christians (Slaves excepted)" all the rights and liberties of "any natural born subject of England." The first Virginia law recognizing slavery, passed in 1661, said that any English servant who ran away with an African would have to serve additional time not only for himself but for the African as well. Such Africans were clearly already understood to be slaves for life and hence were incapable of serving any additional time.

Such laws reveal the great familiarity that existed between white and black servants. Slaves and white servants worked together, enjoyed leisure together, had sexual relations with each other, and ran away together. As late as 1680, most of the plantation laborers were still white indentured servants. There is no evidence that they were kept separate from Africans by law or inclination.

As long as the black population remained small, the color line was blurry. Not until late in the seventeenth century were laws passed that restricted free African Americans. In fact, in 1660, Anthony Johnson, an African who had arrived in Virginia as a servant in 1621, owned both land and African slaves. In the 40 years that he had been in Virginia, slavery had become institutionalized and recognized by the law, but laws separating the races had yet to be enacted.

Gender and the Social Order in the Chesapeake

The founders of England's colonies hoped to replicate the social order they had known at home. As early as 1619, the Virginia Company began to bring single women to the colony to become brides of the unmarried planters. As in England, it was expected that men would perform all the "outside" labor, including planting, farming, and tending large farm animals. Women would do all the "inside" work, including preserving and preparing food, spinning and weaving, making and repairing clothing, and gardening. In English society, a farmer's wife was not simply a man's sexual partner and companion; she was also the mistress of a successful household economy. Both men and women were vital to the society the English wanted to create in the Chesapeake.

However, the powerful tobacco economy transformed both the economy and society of the New World. With profits from tobacco so high, women went directly into the tobacco fields instead of the kitchen. Children were in the fields as soon as they could work. Only when a man became wealthy did he hire a servant—often a woman—to replace his wife in the fields. As a result, for many years, Virginia society lacked the

The First African Arrivals Exercise Some Rights

One day in 1654, an African American family living on Virginia's Eastern Shore met on their plantation for a family conference. They were all free; in fact, they themselves owned a few slaves. One of these slaves, a man named John Casor, had recently complained that he was really an indentured servant and should have been given his liberty by now. A court investigator reported that "Anthony Johnson's son-in-law, his wife and his own two sons persuaded the old Negro Anthony Johnson to set the said John Casor free."

To modern readers, the Johnson family saga seems a remarkable one. Anthony Johnson arrived as a slave in Virginia in 1621, aboard one of the first ships to bring Africans to the new colony. The following year, the plantation where he worked was attacked by the Powhatan Indians in the uprising of 1622, but Johnson managed to escape death. That same year, he married another newly arrived African named Mary. They went on to spend forty years together and had at least four surviving children. Within a few years, they found a way to gain their freedom—probably by being allowed to raise their own cattle on the side and keep the proceeds. After he was free, Johnson put the money he made into buying slaves and indentured servants, and eventually was able to claim 250 acres of land under the headright system (through which colonists were given 50 acres for each person they brought into the colony). Then in 1653, the Johnson family experienced catastrophe: a

fire on their plantation left them nearly destitute. Fortunately, however, they had gained their community's respect and liking over the years, and the court allowed them tax relief for a significant period so they might put themselves back on their feet. And they did indeed collect themselves.

Anthony Johnson found a way to empower himself. Within a few decades, however, it became impossible for any black man in Virginia, no matter how enterprising, to achieve what he achieved. An extraordinary legal constriction of the rights of Africans occurred. From the time of their first arrival, Africans had generally been viewed as slaves for life, unlike indentured servants; nevertheless, the lines of demarcation were at first somewhat fuzzy. Many Africans were freed by their masters after years of service or were encouraged to buy themselves, and once they were free, no laws forbade them from participating in community activities like anyone else. In the 1660s, as the colony became more dependent on plantation agriculture and slave labor, this began to change. The Virginia Assembly gradually passed laws disenfranchising the region's black population on multiple levels. Most of the laws applied to enslaved people only and came to be called "the slave code." But free blacks were not immune. By the 1690s, any slave who became a freedman was required to leave Virginia within six months. And in 1705, people of African descent living in the colony were specifically prohibited from holding office or giving grand jury testimony. For people of African descent, the Virginia Assembly, rather than being an entity that enabled them to voice their concerns, was the instrument that destroyed their hard-won freedoms. By then, the Johnson family had moved away.

"comforts of home" that women produced, such as prepared food, homemade clothing, and even soap. Tobacco was everything.

Colonial society also weakened patriarchal controls. Chesapeake governments tried—but failed—to control immigrant women, insisting, for example, that a woman receive government permission before marrying and prosecuting for slander women who spoke out against the government or their neighbors. But colonial government was relatively weak, and women, far from their own fathers, found themselves unexpectedly free from traditional restrictions.

Although women without the protection of fathers were vulnerable in seventeenth-century plantation societies, in a world where men outnumbered women three or four to one, women were often in a position of relative power. Local governments struggled to impose order by prosecuting women for adultery, fornication, and giving birth to illegitimate children. The public, however, was more tolerant of sexual misconduct than government officials were. The first generation of women to immigrate to the Chesapeake region married relatively late—in their mid-20s or later. As a result, they had relatively few children, and it was many decades before Chesapeake society reproduced itself naturally. Perhaps half of all children born in the colony died in infancy, and one marriage partner was also likely to die within seven years of marriage. At least until 1680 or so, to be a widow, widower, or orphan was the normal state of affairs. Widows who inherited their husband's possessions were powerful and in demand on the marriage market. Children, however, often lost their inheritances to a stepparent.

A Bible Commonwealth in the New England Wilderness

In 1620, 13 years after the founding of the Virginia Colony, England planted another permanent colony at Plymouth; 9 years after that, it planted one at Massachusetts Bay. In many ways the Virginia and Massachusetts colonies could not have been more different. The primary impetus behind the Massachusetts settlement was religious. Both the Pilgrims at Plymouth and the much more numerous Puritans at Massachusetts Bay sought to escape persecution and to establish new communities based on God's law as they understood it. The Puritans and Pilgrims were middle class, and their ventures were well financed and capably planned for the benefit of the settlers. The environment was much more healthful than that of the Chesapeake, and the population reproduced itself rapidly. Relations with the Indians were better than in the Chesapeake. Nonetheless, despite the colonies' differences, the Puritan movement was in fact originally a product of the same growth of national states in Europe and the expansion of commerce that led to the European exploration of the New World and the foundation of Jamestown. Furthermore, the Puritans themselves often demonstrated the same tendencies as other Englishmen.

The English Origins of the Puritan Movement

In Europe during the sixteenth century, ordinary people and powerful monarchs had vastly different reasons for abandoning the Roman Catholic Church in favor of one of the new Protestant churches. In England, these differing motives led to 130 years of conflict, including a revolution and massive religious persecution. In the 1530s, Henry VIII established his own state religion, the Church of England, for political rather than for pious reasons. After many years of marriage to Catherine of Aragon, Henry still did not have a male heir. With one of Catherine's ladies-in-waiting, Anne Boleyn, already pregnant, Henry pressed the pope for an annulment of his marriage. In 1533, the pope refused the annulment, and Henry removed the Catholic Church as the established religion of England, replacing it with his own Church of England. He confiscated Catholic Church lands, which he redistributed to members of the English nobility in return for their loyalty. In one move, Henry eliminated a powerful political rival, the Roman Catholic Church, and consolidated his rule over his nobility.

Replacing the Catholic Church did not bring stability, however. Henry's successors alternated between Protestantism and Catholicism. Under the reign of Catherine's daughter Mary, hundreds of Protestants left the country to avoid persecution. When Mary's Protestant sister, Elizabeth, ascended the throne, these exiles returned, having picked up the Calvinist doctrine of predestination on the Continent. John Calvin, the Swiss Protestant reformer, insisted that even before people were born, God foreordained "to some eternal life and to some eternal damnation." Although the Church of England adopted Calvin's doctrine of predestination, it never held to it thoroughly enough or followed through on other reforms well enough to please those who called themselves Puritans. And because the monarch viewed challenges to the state religion as challenges to the state itself, religious dissenters were frequently persecuted.

What Did the Puritans Believe?

Like all Christians, Puritans believed that humanity was guilty of the original sin committed by Adam and Eve when they disobeyed God in the Garden of Eden. They believed that God's son, Jesus Christ, had given his life to pay (or atone) for the original sin and that as a consequence, all truly faithful Christians would be forgiven their sins and admitted to heaven after they died. Unlike other Christians, Calvinists insisted there was nothing that people could do to guarantee that God, by an act of "grace," would grant them the faith that would save them from hell.

Protestants rejected the hierarchy of the Catholic Church, maintaining that the relationship between God and humanity should be direct and unmediated. Because every person had direct access to the word of God through the Bible, Protestants promoted literacy and translated the Bible into modern languages.

As Calvinists, Puritans wanted to "purify" the Church of England of all remnants of Catholicism, including rituals and priestly hierarchy. Furthermore, Anglicans (members of the established Church of England) had come to think that Catholics were partly right—that believing Christians *could* earn their way to heaven by good works, a doctrine the Puritans labeled Arminianism. Puritans, in contrast, continued to insist that salvation was the free gift of God and that human beings could not force God's hand. Individuals could only prepare for grace by reading and studying the Bible, so that they understood God's plan, and by attempting to live the best lives they could. Because they could never be certain of salvation, Puritans always lived with anxiety.

Puritanism contained a powerful tension between intellect and emotion. On the one hand, Puritanism was a highly rational religion, requiring all of its followers to study the Bible and listen to long sermons on fine points of theology. As a result, Puritans, male and female, were highly literate. On the other hand, Puritans believed that no amount of book learning could get a person into heaven, and that grace was as much a matter of the heart as of the mind. The Puritan movement always struggled to contain this tension, as some of its believers embraced a more fully rational religion and others abandoned book learning for emotion.

Puritans believed that church membership was only for those who could demonstrate that they were saved. As they were persecuted for their faith, they came to believe that, like the Israelites of old, they were God's chosen people—that they had a covenant or agreement with God, and that if they did his will, he would make them prosper.

The Puritans first attempted to reform the Church of England. Once they saw that the Church would resist more reformation and was moving further from the Calvinist principle of predestination, some Puritans began to make other plans.

The Pilgrim Colony at Plymouth

The first Puritan colony in North America was established in 1620 at Plymouth, by a group of Puritans known as the Pilgrims, "Separatists" who had given up hope of reforming the Church of England. The Pilgrims had already moved to Holland, thinking its Calvinism would offer a better home. It was hard for the Pilgrims to fit themselves into Holland's economy, however, and they found their children seduced by "the manifold temptations of the place."

By 1620 the Pilgrims were ready to accept the Virginia Company of London's offer of land in America for any English people who would pay their own way. With the colony at Jamestown foundering and the Company looking for other opportunities, it filled two ships, the *Mayflower* and the *Speedwell*, with the Pilgrims from Holland, other interested Puritans, and a large number of non-Puritans also willing to pay their own way.

The leaking *Speedwell* had to turn back, but the *Mayflower* arrived at Plymouth, Massachusetts, in November 1620, far north of its destination and outside the jurisdiction of the Virginia Company. Because the Pilgrims had landed in territory that had no legal claim and no lawful government, 41 of the adult men on board signed a document known as the Mayflower Compact. The men bound themselves into a "Civil Body Politic" to make laws and govern the colony and also to recognize the authority of the governor. Although the Compact provided a legal basis for joint government and to a large extent allowed for self-determination on the part of the people, it was by no means a wholly democratic document. By design, it excluded those who were not "Saints," or Puritans, from the body politic. Some of the non-Puritans (called "Strangers") had been talking about mutiny, so the Pilgrims wanted to make their power secure.

Only one of the 102 passengers had died en route, but only half of the party survived the harsh first winter. Years later the second governor, William Bradford, remembered the Pilgrims' ordeals. The Indians, he complained, were "savage barbarians . . . readier to fill their sides full of arrows than otherwise." And their new home was "a hideous and desolate wilderness, full of wild beasts and wild men."

In fact, the Plymouth Colony would never have survived had it not been for the assistance of friendly Indians. Like the French in New France and unlike the English at Jamestown, the Pilgrims established diplomatic relations both because they were good diplomats and because the local Indians desperately needed foreign allies. Before the Pilgrims' arrival, Plymouth Bay had been inhabited by as many as 2,000 people. Then European fishermen and traders introduced some fatal disease—possibly viral hepatitis—which was carried along the trading network and killed 90 percent of the local population. Indians "died in heapes as they lay in their houses," their villages filled with the bones of the unburied dead. So recently had Patuxet and Pokanoket Indians inhabited the region that the Pilgrims were able to supplement their meager supplies by rummaging Indian graves, homes, and stores of grain.

The world was vastly changed for Native Americans who survived. Tisquantum, or "Squanto," a Patuxet, had spent the plague years in Europe, having been kidnapped by an exploring Englishman (see Chapter 2). He had only recently made his way back and found that his tribe had almost entirely disappeared. The once-powerful Pokanokets, led by Massasoit, were now paying tribute to the Narragansetts, who had escaped the deadly disease. Squanto persuaded Massasoit that the English might be allies against the Narragansetts. Thus, in the spring of 1621, Squanto offered his assistance to the Pilgrims and showed them how to grow corn.

From the Indian perspective, this assistance was a diplomatic initiative, enabling a treaty between the Pokanokets and the Pilgrims. It worked for the English, too, however. By the time Squanto died in 1622, he had helped secure the future of the Pilgrims' Plymouth Colony. Plymouth remained a separate colony until 1691, when it was absorbed into the larger, more influential Massachusetts Bay Colony. Plymouth demonstrated that New England could be inhabited by Europeans and that effective diplomatic relations with local Indians were critical for a colony's survival.

The Puritan Colony at Massachusetts Bay

In England, increasing numbers of people considered themselves Puritans and yet were not Separatists, like the Pilgrims. Many dreamed of founding colonies, but they wanted to serve as models to other Englishmen, not sever themselves from them. In February 1630, an English Puritan noted in his diary that the faithful had recently sent off ships to New England as well as to a place near Mexico. He was referring to Providence Island, off the coast of Nicaragua. Many Puritans were wealthy landowners and merchants who could not endure to think that the great wealth of the Americas should go mostly to Spain. They wanted an English colony in the tropics and so found an uninhabited island upon which to establish a plantation economy. They first envisioned a labor force of indentured servants, as in the Chesapeake, but rapidly moved to African slavery, with only one Puritan voicing serious opposition. In 1641, the Spanish navy destroyed the fledgling colony.

In the meantime, friends and relatives of the Providence Island Puritans had remained focused on New England and the transport of Puritan settler families. In 1629, the Massachusetts Bay Company, a group of London merchants, had received a charter from King Charles I to establish a colony. The investors in the joint-stock company would have full rights to a swath of land reaching from Massachusetts Bay west across the entire continent. Along with Puritans looking for a new home where they could govern themselves, the company included some who hoped to turn a profit from trade. By the end of the year 1630, Boston and 10 other towns had been founded. By the early 1640s, between 20,000 and 25,000 Britons (not all of them Puritans) had migrated to the Puritan colonies of Plymouth, Massachusetts Bay, Connecticut, Rhode Island, and New Hampshire. Although fewer than half as many migrated to New England as to the Chesapeake region, by 1660 both had populations of a similar size—around 35,000.

New England was able to catch up and keep pace with the Chesapeake for three reasons. First, New England was a much more healthful region. Long, cold winters killed the mosquitoes that carried fatal diseases, and the water supply was good. Second, Puritans migrated as families. Ninety percent came as part of a family group, a pattern almost exactly the reverse of that in the Chesapeake. In such circumstances, the population soon reproduced itself. Third, most of the settlers were not desperate; they had resources to help them make the transition. Most were prosperous members of the middle range of society. Many of the men were professionals—craftsmen, doctors, lawyers, and ministers—people who profited from the changing English economy of the late sixteenth and early seventeenth centuries. Again, the contrast with the Chesapeake was dramatic. There, the vast majority of migrants were people with few skills and dim prospects.

The New England Way

The Puritans of Massachusetts Bay Colony were men and women with a mission. Their first governor, John Winthrop, set out the vision of a Bible commonwealth in a sermon he preached aboard the *Arbella* in the spring of 1630, even before the ship docked at Boston. God, Winthrop said, had entered into a covenant with the Puritans, just as they had entered into a covenant with one another. Together they had taken enormous risks and begun an extraordinary experiment to see whether they could establish a society based on the word of God: "We shall be as a city upon a hill, the eyes of all people are upon us. So that if we shall deal falsely with our God in this work we have undertaken, and so cause Him to withdraw his present help from us, we shall be made a story and a by-word through the world." This broad vision shaped the development of New England's society.

Elizabeth Paddy Wensley Far from the grim Massachusetts settler we imagine, Elizabeth Paddy Wensley dressed stylishly by the standards of the 1670s. A mother of five, she was married to the wealthy Boston merchant John Wensley.

This communal vision made early New Englanders relatively cohesive. Each town was created by a grant of land by the Massachusetts General Court (the name given to the legislature) to a group of citizens. The settlers in turn entered into a covenant with one another to establish a government and distribute the land they held collectively. This was not a modern democracy, for Puritans believed in hierarchy, and their vision was more communal than individualist. Nonetheless, there was considerably more economic equality and cohesion than in most parts of the world.

At first, the new towns divided up only a portion of the land that they held, reserving the rest for newcomers and the children of the original founders. The land was distributed unequally, according to social status and family size (see Table 3-2). Although New England society was relatively egalitarian, with only a small gap between the richest and poorest, the Puritans set out to create a social hierarchy. The rich and powerful were supposed to take care of the poor, and Puritan towns did assist all those who could not care for themselves. Each town administered itself through a town meeting, a periodic gathering of the adult male property owners to attend to the town's business. In the past, historians pointed to the democratic elements in the town meeting as the source of American democracy. More recently, historians have emphasized undemocratic elements. Participation was restricted to adult male property holders, who were only 35 percent of the adult residents, once women are considered. In addition, the habit of deference to the powerful, prosperous, and educated was so strong that a small group of influential men tended to govern each town. Moreover, Puritans abhorred conflict, so great social pressure was used to ensure harmony and limit dissent. If democracy means the right to disagree and majority rule in open elections, then the New England town meeting was not fully democratic. However, even with all these restrictions, the New England town meeting was far more democratic than any form of government in England at the time, where the vast majority of men, not to mention women, were excluded from political participation.

Table 3-2 Distribution of Land in Rowley, Massachusetts, 1639–ca. 1642

Acres	No. of Grants
over 250	0
201–250	1
151–200	1
101–150	0
51–100	7
21–50	22
20 or less	63
No record	1
Total	95

Source: David Grayson Allen, In *English Ways: The Movement of Societies and the Transferal of English Local Law and Custom to Massachusetts Bay in the Seventeenth Century* (Chapel Hill: University of North Carolina Press, 1981), p. 32.

Note: Between 1639 and 1642, the town of Rowley, Massachusetts, distributed a little over 2,000 acres to 95 families—an average of just 23 acres per family—even though the grant to the town was for many thousand acres. Although most grants were for fewer than 20 acres, some families received considerably more. The founders of Rowley wanted to re-create the hierarchical social order they had known in England.

Changing the Landscape to Fit the Political Economy

The Puritans' corporate social vision was generally compatible with a capitalist political economy. Although land was distributed to towns, once those towns transferred parcels of the land to individual farmers, the farmers were free to leave it to their heirs, to sell it to whomever they pleased, and to buy more land from others. Any improvements on the land (from clearing away trees to building homes, fences, dams, or mills) remained the property of the owners. These practices followed English law.

The contrast with Indian patterns of land use was dramatic. Indians held their land communally, not individually. The entire group had to consent to its sale. At first, when Indians "sold" land to the Puritans, they thought that they were giving them the right to use the land only and to share the land with them. They might allow the Puritans to build a village, plant, and hunt, while they retained similar rights over the same parcel of land, including the right to allow it to be used by several groups of Europeans at once.

The Puritans' notion of exclusive land rights was a cornerstone of their political economy. Because a man could profit from the improvements made on his land and pass those improvements on to his heirs, he had incentives to make them. Moreover, not only the land but its products became commodities to be sold. Thus, like other European colonists, the Puritans turned their Indian neighbors into commercial hunters. For centuries, the Indians had taken only as many beaver as they needed, but now that they found themselves fenced out of their former lands, they could no longer live part of the year by farming and became more committed to hunting. Overhunting led to the disappearance of beaver in the region.

The Puritans themselves cleared the forests of trees. They found a ready market for timber in England, as New England's trees were much taller and straighter than any known in Europe. The English navy came to depend on New England for its masts. Although the bounty of the land had seemed limitless, by 1800 much of southern New England had been stripped of its forests and native wildlife.

Prosperity did not come to Massachusetts immediately. For the first decade, the colony maintained a favorable balance of trade with England only by sending back the money that new immigrants brought with them in return for goods from the mother country. New England's cold climate made it impossible to develop a cash crop such as tobacco. In the 1640s and 1650s, the government encouraged local manufacturing (to cut down on imports) and export of raw materials. Through government policy and individual initiative, New Englanders eventually made great profits from selling timber, wood products, and fish and by acting as merchants. In the meantime, successful family farms were the mainstay of the local economy.

The Puritan Family

Like most early-modern western Europeans, Puritans thought of the family as the society in microcosm, or "a little Church, and a little commonwealth." There was no sharp distinction between home and the wider world. Although Harvard College was founded in 1636 (to train ministers) and the Massachusetts General Court established a system of public education in 1647, most early instruction and virtually all vocational teaching took place at home. Parents were required to teach their children to read the Bible.

The family was also the center of the Puritans' economy. Farmers, of course, worked at home, as did almost all craftsmen. Women also performed tasks critical to the survival of the family. Although tasks were assigned by gender, in the absence of her husband a woman could assume his responsibilities, selling the products he had made or even fighting off Indians. The family, like society, was a hierarchy, with the husband at the top and his wife as his "deputy."

Puritans lived in fear of lawlessness, and they used the family as an instrument of order. Puritans considered excessive affection and particularly excessive maternal love a danger. Children were subjected to strict discipline not out of cruelty but from deep religious convictions. Considering that Puritan women bore on average eight or nine children and that families were confined in small houses over long New England winters, this harmony was probably necessary for survival.

Despite the importance of control, Puritan households were hardly prisons. If Puritans believed that men were the natural heads of the household and that women bore particular responsibility for Eve's original sin, they also believed that both were equally capable of God's grace. Puritans distrusted the passion of love, which could lead to impulsiveness and disorder. They had great respect, however, for the natural affection that grew over the course of marriage and encouraged playfulness when it helped rather than impeded social harmony.

So successful were the early Puritans in establishing tight-knit communities that only two years after their great migration to America had begun, Reverend Thomas Welde could write proudly back to England, "[H]ere I find three great blessings, peace, plenty, and health. . . . I profess if I might have my wish in what part of the world to dwell I know no other place on the whole globe of the earth where I would be rather than here."

Dissension in the Puritan Ranks

Yet not everyone lived in such bliss. The Puritan movement embodied tensions that created individual and social turmoil. Puritans had difficulty balancing emotion and intellect, the individual and the community, spiritual equality and social hierarchy, and anxiety over salvation and the satisfaction of thinking oneself a member of a chosen people. The Puritans also had no mechanisms for handling dissent, which they interpreted as a replay of original sin. The migration to a strange land, populated by people they thought of as savages, as well as the pressure of thinking that the whole world was watching them, only increased the Puritans' desire to maintain a strict order.

Roger Williams and Toleration

The Massachusetts Bay Colony was only a year old when trouble appeared in the person of Roger Williams, a brilliant and obstinate young minister. No sooner had he landed than he announced that he was really a Separatist and would not accept appointment at a church unless it repudiated its ties to the Church of England. Massachusetts Bay was already walking a fine line between outward obedience to the laws of England and inner rejection of the English way of life, and an explicit repudiation of the established church was thought to be an act of political suicide.

Without a church of his own, Williams began preaching to those who would listen. Saying that the king had no right to grant land owned by the Indians, he questioned the validity of the Massachusetts charter and argued for strict separation of church and state, as well as strict separation of the converted and the unconverted. Williams went so far as to advocate religious toleration, with each congregation or sect governing itself completely free from state interference.

These doctrines were heresy to both Puritan church and state. In 1635, when Williams violated an order to stop preaching his unorthodox views, the magistrates decided to ship him immediately to England, where he might be imprisoned or even executed. John Winthrop warned Williams of his fate, giving him time to sneak away to Narragansett Bay, outside the jurisdiction of Massachusetts Bay. Williams and some followers established the new colony of Rhode Island, which was chartered in 1644. The colony, which became a refuge for dissenters of all sorts, was referred to by Massachusetts Puritans as "the sewer of New England."

Anne Hutchinson and the Equality of Believers

One of Puritanism's many tensions concerned the position of women. By insisting on the equality of all true believers before God and the importance of marriage, Protestantism and especially its Puritan branch undermined the starkly negative image of women that prevailed in sixteenth-century Europe. When Puritan ministers preached that women and men were both "joynt Heirs of salvation" and that women, rather than being a "necessary evil," were in fact "a necessary good," they were directly criticizing both the Catholic legacy and common folk belief.

Puritanism extended women respect, but it also insisted they be subordinate to men. In their hierarchical society, woman's position was clearly beneath that of man. Puritanism struggled to find the balance between women's spiritual equality and their earthly subordination: although most Puritan women deferred to male authority, others seized the opportunity that Puritanism seemed to offer. Without exception, the Puritan authorities put them back in their place.

Anne Hutchinson was just over 40 when she, her husband, and their 12 children followed the Reverend John Cotton to Massachusetts Bay. Cotton was a popular preacher who placed particular emphasis on the doctrine of predestination. Hutchinson pushed that doctrine to its logical, if unsettling, conclusion. She claimed that she had experienced several direct revelations, one telling her to follow Cotton to Boston. At informal Bible discussion meetings at her Boston home, which even the new governor attended, Hutchinson challenged the Puritan doctrine of "preparation": if God had truly chosen those whom he would save, it was unnecessary for Puritans to prepare themselves for saving grace by leading sin-free lives. Nor was good behavior a reliable sign of salvation. Hutchinson did not favor sin; she simply believed her neighbors were wrong in thinking that good works would save them. She accused them of the heresy of Arminianism. By claiming that the Holy Spirit spoke directly to her, Hutchinson opened herself to charges of another heresy, antinomianism.

Hutchinson's views were so popular that many residents—possibly a majority—became her followers. Once she accused certain ministers of being unconverted, the colony leaders mounted a campaign against her and her allies. In 1637 they moved the site of the election for governor outside Boston, where her strength was greatest, so that John Winthrop could win. Then, after her most prominent ally among the ministers had been banished, Hutchinson was put on trial for slandering the ministry, convicted, and ordered to leave the colony. Followed by 80 other families, she and her family found temporary refuge in Roger Williams's Rhode Island. (She later moved to New Netherland, where she was killed in an Indian war.) The fact that Hutchinson's ideas came from a woman made them even more dangerous to the Massachusetts leadership. John Winthrop suggested that she might be a witch. Without any evidence at all of sexual misconduct, ministers asserted that Hutchinson and her female followers were driven by lust and that unless they were punished, it would lead to communal living, open sex, and the repudiation of marriage.

It is sometimes asserted that Puritans came to New England in search of religious freedom, but they never would have made that claim. They wanted the liberty to follow their own religion but actively denied that opportunity to others. Puritans insisted on their right to keep out nonbelievers. "No man hath right to come into us," John Winthrop wrote, "without our consent."

Puritan Indian Policy and the Pequot War

The Puritan dissidents were all critical of the Puritans' Indian policy. Roger Williams insisted on purchasing land from the Indians instead of simply seizing it, and the men in the Hutchinson family refused to fight in the Pequot War of 1637. The Puritans had been fortunate in settling in a region in which the Indian population had recently been decimated and in having the English-speaking Squanto's diplomatic services. The Puritan communities expanded so rapidly, however, that they soon intruded on land populated by Indians who had no intention of giving them exclusive rights to it.

Within a few years of the founding of the Massachusetts Bay Colony, small groups of Puritans were spreading out in all directions (see Map 3–2). The Reverend John Wheelwright, Anne Hutchinson's brother-in-law and most ardent supporter, took a party into what is now New Hampshire. Others settled in Maine. In 1638, New Haven, Connecticut, was founded by the Reverend John Davenport and a London merchant, Theophilus Eaton, who purchased land from local Indians. Four years earlier, the first Puritan settlers had reached the Connecticut River in western Massachusetts. In 1636 the Reverend Thomas Hooker led his followers to the site of Hartford, Connecticut.

The Pequot War grew out of conflicts among Europeans about who would govern the fertile Connecticut River valley and among Native Americans about who would trade with the Europeans. Until the arrival of the English, the Dutch had controlled trade along the Connecticut River. They had granted trading privileges to the Pequots, which frustrated other tribes, who could trade only through these middlemen. When the English arrived, the Pequots' enemies attempted to attract them to the valley as trading rivals to the Dutch. The Pequots, afraid of losing their monopoly, made the mistake of inviting Massachusetts Bay to establish a trading post in the region. They were counting on their ability to control not only their Indian enemies but also the Dutch and English. As hundreds of settlers poured in, the Pequots became alarmed. They appealed to their one-time enemies, the Narragansetts, to join with them to get rid of the English. The Narragansetts, however, had already been approached by the Puritans to join them in fighting the Pequots. That is where the Narragansetts calculated that their long-term advantage lay. They themselves were in desperate need of land, having been squeezed beyond endurance by the English settlements. Their leaders recognized the greater power of the English as allies than the Pequots.

Time Line

▼**1533**
Henry VIII breaks with Roman Catholic Church, establishes Church of England

▼**1603**
Queen Elizabeth I dies, succeeded by King James I

▼**1606**
James I grants two charters for North American settlement to Virginia Company

▼**1607**
English found Jamestown

▼**1608**
John Smith named president of Virginia's council

▼**1609**
John Smith returns to England

▼**1610–1614**
First Anglo-Powhatan War

▼**1612–1617**
John Rolfe develops a marketable strain of tobacco

▼**1614**
John Rolfe and Pocahontas marry

▼**1616**
Virginia Company offers a 50-acre headright to each immigrant

Map 3–2 New England in the 1640s This map shows the land settled by each of the New England colonies, the regions inhabited by Indian tribes, and the region of Dutch settlement. *Source:* John Murrin et al., *Liberty, Equality, Power* (Orlando, FL: Harcourt College Publishers, 1995), p. 73.

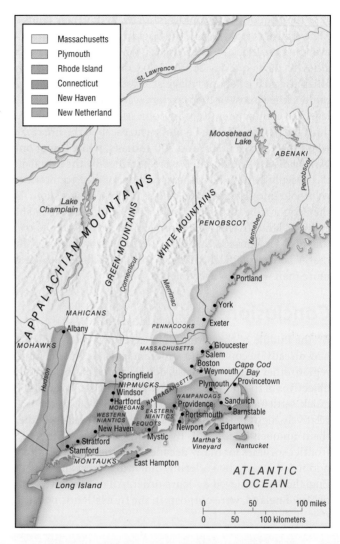

▼**1619**
First meeting of Virginia General Assembly
First Africans arrive in Virginia
Virginia Company pays for transportation of women to Virginia

▼**1620**
Pilgrims found colony at Plymouth; Mayflower Compact signed

▼**1622–1632**
Second Anglo-Powhatan War

▼**1624**
Virginia Company dissolved; Virginia becomes a royal colony

▼**1625**
James I dies, succeeded by King Charles I

▼**1629**
Massachusetts Bay Company receives charter to establish colony in North America

▼**1630**
Massachusetts Bay Colony founded

▼**1632**
George Calvert receives charter for Maryland

continued

The Pequots were caught in a rivalry for their lands between the parent colony in Massachusetts and the new offshoot in Connecticut. The Connecticut group struck first, avenging an attack by the Pequots, which in itself was in revenge for an attack on their allies. At dawn on May 26, 1637, 90 Connecticut men accompanied by 500 Narragansett allies attacked a Pequot village at Mystic filled with women, children, and old men. The raiders knew most of the warriors were away from home. As his men encircled the village, the commander, Captain John Mason, set a torch to the wigwams, shouting, "We must burn them." Those Pequots who escaped the fire ran into the ring of Mason's party, who killed between 300 and 700 Indians, while losing only two of their own men. The Narragansetts' Indian allies were horrified by the brutal attack.

Deeply demoralized, the remainder of the Pequot tribe was easily defeated. Prisoners were sold into slavery in the colony of Providence Island. By 1638, the Puritans declared the Pequot tribe dissolved, and in 1639 Connecticut established its dominance over the Pequots' land. In that year Connecticut established its own government, modeled after that of Massachusetts. In 1662 it became a royal colony. The Puritans had demonstrated that where ecological changes were insufficient to destroy the Indians, they were more than willing to use violence.

Conclusion

By the middle of the seventeenth century, the New England and Chesapeake colonies had already become quite different. Although the forces of capitalism shaped each region, other factors—disease, demographic patterns, relations with the Indians, and the objectives of the founders—left their distinctive imprints. The early history and relatively quick settlement of New England was shaped by the extraordinary cohesiveness and relatively high social standing and degree of wealth of the Puritan settlers, which made them uniquely successful. By contrast, New France and New Netherland were rough frontier societies for many decades, and the Chesapeake colonies were still raw outposts, populated largely by suffering indentured servants and African slaves long after New England had achieved a secure order. All of the North American colonies, except those of New England, were outposts in the transatlantic political and economic order, created

Time Line *continued*

▼**1636**
Harvard College founded
Roger Williams exiled from
    Massachusetts

▼**1637**
Anne Hutchinson and her
    followers exiled
Pequot War

▼**1638**
New Haven founded

▼**1639**
First law mentioning slavery,
    in Maryland
Connecticut establishes
    its government

▼**1644**
Rhode Island receives charter

▼**1644–1646**
Third Anglo-Powhatan War

▼**1647**
Massachusetts establishes
    system of public education

▼**1649**
Act of Toleration passed
    in Maryland

▼**1661**
First Virginia law mentioning
    slavery

▼**1691**
Plymouth Colony absorbed
    into Massachusetts

to enrich their mother countries and enhance those countries' power. New England was the exception, but so successful was New England in achieving a stable society that we sometimes forget that it was the exception and not the rule.

Who, What

Anne Hutchinson 81

Pocahontas 60

Powhatan 60

Captain John Smith 60

Squanto 76

Roger Williams 80

John Winthrop 77

Anglo-Powhatan Wars 64

Antinomianism 81

Arminianism 75

Calvinism 75

Charter colony 67

Headright 65

Indentured servants 62

Pequot War 82

Proprietary colony 67

Royal colony 65

Review Questions

1. What were the objectives of the founders of Virginia? Why did the colony survive, in spite of poor planning?

2. What were the objectives of the founders of the Puritan colonies at Plymouth and Massachusetts Bay? Compare the early years of these colonies to those of the Virginia Colony.

3. What role did gender play in the social order of the Chesapeake and New England colonies?

Critical-Thinking Questions

1. Were the more amicable native-white relations in early New England, as compared to those in Virginia, the result of greater tolerance on the part of the New Englanders or greater willingness to compromise on the part of the Indians?

2. What factors other than religious commitment help explain the success of the Puritan colonies in Massachusetts?

3. Which society was more democratic in its original formulation, the New England colony or the Chesapeake colony? Explain your answer.

4. Are you more impressed by the ease or the slowness that the Chesapeake demonstrated in adopting African slavery? Explain your answer.

For further review materials and resource information, please visit www.oup.com/us/oakes

CHAPTER 3: THE ENGLISH COME TO STAY, 1600–1660
Primary Sources

3.1 JOHN SMITH, "A TRUE RELATION OF SUCH OCCURRENCES AND ACCIDENTS OF NOTE, AS HATH HAPNED IN VIRGINIA" (1608) AND "THE GENERAL HISTORIE OF VIRGINIA" (1624)

In late 1607, John Smith left the Jamestown settlement and traveled up the Chickahominy River to trade for corn. He was captured by a kinsman of Powhatan, the paramount chief of the local tribes, and was taken to Werowocomoco, the "village of the king." A few weeks later the Indians returned Smith to Jamestown with messages for his leaders stating that they wanted to open up trade. In early 1608, a few weeks after his captivity ended, Smith sent a report to the colony's backers in London describing what had happened to him. In 1624, he wrote about the events again, this time in the third person, and embellished them extensively. In the intervening years, Powhatan's daughter, Pocahontas, had been to London and become something of a celebrity, so Smith included her in the drama, though she was only about nine years old in 1608. In 1622, the Virginia Indians launched an offensive against the white colonists, which changed their reputation with the colonists and those in London, thus requiring some rewriting on Smith's part. In 1624, Smith was free to write what he wanted because Powhatan, Pocahontas, and all the principals of the story had since died. The old English spelling has been retained in this selection to situate readers in that century.

1608

Arriving at Werawocomoco, their Emperour proudly lying upon a Bedstead a foote high upon tenne or twelve Mattes, richly hung with many Chaynes of great Pearles about his necke, and covered with a great Covering of rahaughcums [that is, raccoon pelts]: At his head sat a woman, at his feete another, on each side sitting upon a Matte upon the ground were raunged his chiefe men on each side the fire, tenne in a ranke, and behinde them as many young women, each a great Chaine of white Beades over their shoulders, their heades painted in redde, and [he] with such a grave and Majesticall countenance, as drove me into admiration to see such state in a naked Salvage, . . . hee kindly welcomed me with good wordes, and great Platters of sundrie Victuals, assuring mee his friendship, and my libertie within foure dayes; hee much delighted in [his kinsman] Opechancanoughs relation of what I had described to him, and oft examined me upon the same [subjects]. Hee asked me the cause of our coming; I tolde him, being in fight with the Spaniards our enemie, being over powred, near put to retreat, and by extreame weather put to his shore . . .

1624

At last they brought him to Meronocomoco [sic], where was Powhatan their Emperor. Here more then two hundred of those grim Courtiers stood wondering at him, as [if] he had been a monster; till Powhatan and his trayne had put themselves in their greatest braveries [ie finest attire]. Before a fire upon a seat like a bedsted, he sat covered with a great robe, made of Rarowcun skinnes, and all the tayles hanging by. On either hand did sit a young wench of 16 or 18 yeares, and along on each side the house, two rowes of men, and behind them as many women, with all their heads and shoulders painted red; many of their heads bedecked with the white downe of Birds, but every one with something; and a great chayne of white beads about their necks. At his entrance before the King, all the people gave a great shout. The Queene of Appamatuck was appointed to bring him water to wash his hands, and another brought him a bunch of feathers, in stead of a Towell to dry them; having feasted him after their best barbarous manner they could, a long consultation was held, but the conclusion was, two great stones were brought before Powhatan; then as many as could layd hands on him, dragged him to them, and thereon laid his head, and being ready with their clubs, to beate out his braines, Pocahontas the Kings dearest daughter, when no intreaty could prevaile, got his head in her armes, and laide her owne upon his to save him from death; whereat the Emperour was contented he should live to make him hatchets, and her bells, beads, and copper . . .

Source: Philip Barbour, ed., *The Complete Works of John Smith* (Williamsburg, VA: Institute of Early American History and Culture, 1986), I: 53 and II: 150–151.

3.2 LETTER FROM RICHARD FRETHORNE TO HIS PARENTS ABOUT LIFE IN VIRGINIA (1623)

Almost nothing is known about Richard Frethorne, other than what a letter he sent home to his parents tells us. Frethorne was a young indentured servant who arrived in Jamestown in December of 1622, a few months after a major uprising by the indigenous population which left about a quarter of the colonists dead. Life in Virginia was not what he had expected, and he wrote to beg his parents to try to buy him out of his indenture. Someone apparently turned the missive over to the Company, as it was found in their records. The spelling here has been modernized, as the original is too idiosyncratic to read with ease.

Loving and kind father and mother,

My most humble duty remembered to you, hoping in God of your good health, as I myself am at the making hereof. This is to let you understand that I your child am in a most heavy case by reason of the nature of the country is such that it causeth much sickness, as the scurvy and the bloody flux and divers other diseases, which maketh the body very poor and weak. And when we are sick, there is nothing to comfort us, for since I came out of the ship, I never ate anything but peas and loblolly (that is, water gruel). As for deer or venison, I never saw any since I came into this land. There is indeed some fowl, but we are not allowed to go and get it, but must work hard both early and late for a mess of water gruel and a mouthful of bread and beef. . . . People cry out day and night—Oh that they were in England without their limbs— and would not care to lose any limb to be in England again, yea, though they beg from door to door. For we live in fear of the enemy every hour, yet we have had a combat with them on the Sunday before Shrovetide, and we took two alive and make slaves of them. But it was by policy, for we are in great danger, for our plantation is very weak by reason of the dearth and sickness of our company. . . . we are but 32 to fight against 3000 if they should come. And the nighest help that we have is ten miles of us, and when the rogues overcame this place last they slew 80 persons. How then shall we do, for we live even in their teeth [that is, close by]? They may easily take us, but that God is merciful and can save with few as well as with many . . .

And I have nothing to comfort me, nor there is nothing to be gotten here but sickness and death, except that one had money to lay out in some things for profit. But I have nothing at all—no, not a shirt to my back but two rags, nor no clothes but one poor suit, nor but one pair of shoes, but one pair of stockings, but one cap, but two bands. My cloak is stolen by one of my own fellows. . . . I have not a penny, nor a penny worth, to help me to either spice or sugar or strong waters, without which one cannot live here. For as strong beer in England doth fatten and strengthen them, so water here doth wash and weaken these here, only keeps life and soul together. But I am not half a quarter so strong as I was in England, and all is for want of victuals: for I do protest unto you that I have eaten more in a day at home than I have allowed me here for a week. You have given more than my day's allowance to a beggar at the door . . .

If you love me, you will redeem me suddenly, for which I do entreat and beg. And if you cannot get the merchants to redeem me for some little money, then for God's sake get a gathering [that is, take up a collection] or entreat some good folks to lay out some little sum of money in meat and cheese and butter and beef. . . .

Good father, do not forget me, but have mercy and pity my miserable case. I know, if you did but see me, you would weep to see me. . . . Wherefore, for God's sake, pity me. I pray you to remember my love to all my friends and kindred. I hope all my brothers and sisters are in good health, and as for my part I have set down my resolution that certainly will be; that is, that the answer of this letter will be life or death to me. Therefore, good father, send as soon as you can . . . I thought no head had been able to hold so much water as hath and doth daily flow from mine eyes. But this is certain: I never felt the want of father and mother till now; but now, dear friends, full well I know and rue it, although it were too late before I knew it. Your loving son, Richard Frethorne
Virginia, 3rd April, 1623.

Source: Susan Kingsbury, ed., *The Records of the Virginia Company*, vol. 4 (Washington, D.C.: U.S. Government Printing Office, 1935), pp. 58–62.

3.3 EXCERPTS FROM ANNE HUTCHINSON'S TRIAL TRANSCRIPT (1637)

When the Massachusetts Bay Colony was still very young, Anne Hutchinson, a merchant's wife, held meetings in her house for those who wished to discuss religion. She was accused of promoting a schism, or division within the spiritual community, and on November 7, 1637, was brought to trial in Boston. She stonewalled the prosecution by avoiding their questions, arguing that she had not actually been accused of any specific wrongdoing. Nevertheless, she was found guilty and banished from the colony.

Gov. John Winthrop:
Mrs. Hutchinson, you are called here as one of those that have troubled the peace of the commonwealth and the churches here: you are known to be a woman that hath had a great share in the promoting . . . those opinions that are the cause of this trouble, and to be nearly joined not only in affinity and affection with some of those the court had taken notice of and passed censure upon, but you have spoken divers thing . . . very prejudicial to the honour of the churches and ministers thereof, and you have maintained a meeting and an assembly in your house that hath been condemned by the general assembly as a thing not tolerable nor comely in the sight of God nor fitting for your sex, and notwithstanding that was cried down you have continued the same. Therefore we have thought good to send for you to understand how things are, that if you be in an erroneous way we may reduce you that so you may become a profitable member here among us. Otherwise if you be obstinate in your course that then the court may take such

course that you may trouble us no further. Therefore I would entreat you to express whether you do assent and hold in practice to those opinions and factions that have been handled in court already, that is to say, whether you do not justify Mr. Wheelwright's sermon and the petition.

Mrs. Anne Hutchinson:

I am called here to answer before you but I hear no things laid to my charge.

Source: David Hall, ed., *The Antinomian Controversy, 1636–1638: A Documentary History* (Durham, NC: Duke University Press, 1990).

3.4 LETTER FROM ANNE BRADSTREET TO HER CHILDREN (UNDATED)

Anne Dudley Bradstreet, born to a prosperous London family, came to the Massachusetts Bay Colony in 1630 where first her father and then her husband later served as governor. She was well educated and, in 1650, a volume of her poems was published in London under the title *The Tenth Muse Lately Sprung Up in America*. It was met with a positive reception. This letter to her children is undated but was probably written later in her life.

To My Dear Children

This book by any yet unread,
I leave for you when I am dead,
That being gone, here you may find
What was your living mother's mind.
Make use of what I leave in love
And God shall bless you from above.

A.B.

My dear children,—

I, knowing by experience that the exhortations of parents take most effect when the speakers leave to speak, and being ignorant whether on my death bed I shall have opportunity to speak to any of you much less to all, thought it the best whilst I was able to compose some short matters (for what else to call them I know not) and bequeath to you, that when I am no more with you, yet I may be daily in your remembrance (although that is the least in my aim in what I now do) but that you may gain some spiritual advantage by my experience. I have not studied [that is, aimed] in this you read to show my skill, but to declare the Truth, not to set forth myself, but the Glory of God. If I had minded the former it had been perhaps better pleasing to you, but seeing the last is the best, let I be best pleasing to you.

The method I will observe shall be this—I will begin with God's dealing with me from my childhood to this day.

In my young years, about 6 or 7 as I take it, I began to make conscience of my way, and what I knew was sinful as lying, disobedience to parents, etcetera, I avoided it. If at any time I was overtaken with the like evils, it was a great trouble. I could not be at rest 'till by prayer I had confessed it unto God. I was also troubled at the neglect of private duties, though too often tardy that way. I also found much comfort in reading the Scriptures, especially those places I thought most concerned my condition, and as I grew to have more understanding, so the more solace I took in them.

In a long fit of sickness which I had on my bed, I often communed with my heart, and made my supplication to the most high who set me free from that affliction.

But as I grew up to be about 14 or 15, I found my heart more carnal, and sitting loose from God, vanity and the follies of youth took hold of me.

About 16, the Lord laid his hand sore upon me and smote me with the small pox. When I was in my affliction, I besought the Lord, and confessed my pride and vanity and he was entreated of me, and again restored me. But I rendered not to him according to the benefit received.

After a short time I changed my condition and was married and came into this country, where I found a new world and new manners, at which my heart rose. But after I was convinced it was the way of God, I admitted to it and joined to the church at Boston.

After some time I fell into a lingering sickness like a consumption, together with a lameness, which correction I saw the Lord sent to humble and try me and to do me good: and it was not altogether ineffectual.

It pleased God to keep me a long time without a child which was a great grief to me, and cost me many prayers and tears before I obtained one, and after him gave me many more, of whom I now take the care, that as I have brought you into the world, and with great pains, weakness, cares and fears brought you to this, I now travail in birth again of you till Christ be formed in you.

Among all my experiences of God's gracious dealings with me I have constantly observed this, that he hath never suffered me long to sit loose from him, but by one affliction or another hath made me look home, and search what was amiss—so usually thus it hath been with me that I have no sooner felt my heart out of order, but I have expected correction for it, which most commonly hath been upon my own person, in sickness, weakness, pains, sometimes on my soul, in doubts and fears of God's displeasure, and my sincerity towards him. Sometimes he hath smote a child with sickness, sometimes chastened by losses in estate, and these times (through his great mercy) have been the times of my greatest getting and advantage, yet I have found them the times when the Lord hath manifested the most love to me. Then have I gone to searching, and have said with David, Lord search me and try me, see what ways of wickedness are in me, and lead me in the way everlasting: and seldom or never but I have found either some sin I lay under which God would have reformed, or some duty neglected which he would have performed. And by his help I have laid vows and bonds upon my soul to perform his righteous commands.

If at any time you are chastened of God, take it as thankfully and joyfully as in greatest mercies. For if ye be his, ye shall reap the greatest benefit by it. It has been no small support to me in times of darkness, which the Almighty hath hid his face from me, that yet I have had abundance of sweetness and refreshment after affliction and more circumspection in my wailing after I have been afflicted. I have been with God like an untoward child, that no longer than the rod has been on my back (or at least in sight) but have been apt to forget him and myself too. Before I was afflicted I went astray, but now I keep thy statutes.

I have had great experience of God's hearing my prayers, and returning comfortable answers to me, either in granting the thing I prayed for, or else in satisfying my mind without it; and I have ben confident it hath bene from him, because I have found my heart through his goodness enlarged in thankfulness to him.

I have often been perplexed that I have not found that constant joy in my pilgrimage and refreshing which I supposed the most of the servants of God have, although he hath not left me altogether without the witness of his Holy Spirit, who hath oft given me his word and set to his seal that it shall be well with me. I have sometimes tasted of that hidden manna that the world knows not, and have set up my Ebenezer, and have resolved with myself that against such a promise, such tastes of sweetness, the fates of Hell shall never prevail. Yet have I many sinkings and droopings, and not enjoyed that felicity that sometimes I have done. But when I have been in darkness and seen no light, yet have I desired to stay myself upon the Lord. And, when I have been in sickness and pain, I have thought if the Lord would but lift up the light of his countenance upon me, although he ground me to powder, it would be but light to me. Yea, often have I thought were it Hell itself and could there find the love of God toward me, it would be a Heaven. And, could I have been in Heaven without the love of God, it would have been a Hell to me. For, in Truth, it is the absence of presence of God that makes Heaven or Hell.

Many times hath Satan troubled me concerning the verity of the Scriptures, many times by atheism. How could I know whether there was a God if I never saw any miracles to confirm me, and those which I read of, how did I know, but they were feigned. That there is a God my reason would soon tell me by the wondrous works that I see, the vast frame of the Heaven and the earth, the order of all things, night and day, summer and winter, spring and autumn, the daily providing for this great household upon the earth, the preserving and directing of all to its proper end. The consideration of these things would with amazement certainly resolve me that there is an Eternal Being.

But how should I know he is such a God as I worship in Trinity, and such a Saviour as I rely upon? Though this hath thousands of times been suggested to me, yet God hath helped me over. I have argued thus with myself. That there is a God I see. If ever this God hath revealed himself, it must be in his word, and this must be it or none. Have I not found that operation by it that no humane invention can work upon the soul? Hath not judgments befallen diverse who have scorned and contend it? Hath it not been preserved through all ages maugre [that is, despite] all the heathen tyrants and all of the enemies who have opposed it? Is there any story but that which shows the beginning of times, and how the world came to be as we see? Do we not know the prophecies in it fulfilled which could not have been so long foretold by any but God himself?

When I have got over this block, then have I another put in my way. That admit this be the true God whom we worship, and that be his word, yet why may not the popish religion be the right? They have the same God, the same Christ, the same word. They only interpret it one way, we another.

This hath sometimes stuck with me, and more it would, but the vain fooleries that are in their religion, together with their lying miracles, and cruel persecutions of the saints, which admit were they as they term them, yet not so to be dealt withal.

The consideration of these things and many the like would soon turn me to my own religion again.

But some new troubles I have had since the world has been filled with blasphemy, and sectaries, and some who have been accounted sincere Christians have been carried away with them, that sometimes I have said, "Is there faith upon the earth?" And I have not known what to think; but then I have remembered the words of Christ that so it must be, and that, if it were possible, the very elect should be deceived. "Behold," saith our Saviour, "I have told you before," that hath stayed my heart, and I can now say, "Return, o my soul, to thy rest, upon this rock Christ Jesus will I build my faith, and if I perish, I perish." But I Know all the powers of Hell shall never prevail against it. I know whom I have trusted, and whom I have believed, and that he is able to keep that I have committed to his charge.

Now to the King, immortal, eternal, and invisible, the only wise God, be honor and glory for ever and ever. Amen.

This was written in much sickness and weakness, and is very weakly and imperfectly done; but if you can pick any benefit out of it, it is the mark which I aimed at.

Source: Adelaide Amore, ed., *A Woman's Inner World: Selected Poetry and Pose of Anne Bradstreet* (Lanham, MD: University Press of America, 1982).

De Yndio y Mestiza

Continental Empires

1660–1720

COMMON THREADS

What forces—political, economic, military, social, and cultural—gave shape to the English empire in the New World? Which of these forces figured in the conscious plan of empire, and which shaped the empire nonetheless?

How did imperial politics—in particular the contest between England and France, and England's larger geopolitical objectives—affect the lives of ordinary men and women in the colonies?

What is a slave society, and how did Virginia become one?

Which European institutions transplanted easily to North America, and which did not?

OUTLINE

AMERICAN PORTRAIT

Tituba Shapes Her World and Saves Herself

Her name was Tituba. Some say she was a Yoruba from Africa, but contemporary evidence indicates that she was an Indian, either an Arawak from Guyana or some other ethnicity from the Spanish Caribbean. Had she not been accused of practicing witchcraft in Salem, Massachusetts, in 1692, she surely would have been forgotten by history. Whether she came from South America or Africa, she was torn away from her home and sent to work on a sugar plantation on the Caribbean island of Barbados, which the English had colonized almost 50 years before. Whatever her birthplace, Tituba lived for years in an African-majority society and absorbed African customs.

Tituba was probably a teenager when she was taken by her owners to Massachusetts in 1680. She had been purchased by a young, Harvard-educated Barbadian, Samuel Parris. Parris's father had failed as a planter, and now he himself had failed as a merchant. In 1689 Parris moved his wife, their three children, Tituba, and her enslaved husband, John Indian, to Salem Village, where he had taken up a new profession, the ministry.

Three years later, all of their lives changed forever when one of Parris's daughters, Betty, and her cousin Abigail, "fell afflicted" and began to behave strangely. Betty began to experience strange and seemingly inexplicable pains, which spread to other young women. When neither doctors nor ministers could cure them, a neighbor asked Tituba to bake a "witchcake" out of rye flour and the girls' urine. This was "white magic," intended to uncover the identity of the witch who was thought to be bewitching Betty and the others. Their suffering, however, only got worse. Parris now questioned the girls: Who was bewitching them? This time the girls had an answer: two older, rather marginal white women—and Tituba.

The three women were charged with the capital offense of witchcraft. Under duress, the first woman, Sarah Good, implicated the second, Sarah Osborne. Osborne steadfastly denied her guilt and was returned to jail. Finally, Tituba was summoned. As a slave, she was particularly vulnerable. Perhaps calculating the odds carefully, Tituba slowly began to embroider a story. She named only two names—Sarah Good and Sarah Osborne. She talked about a tall, white-haired man in Boston who made her sign a mysterious book and about conspiring with other, unnamed witches.

Responding to the hints of her Puritan interrogators, Tituba confirmed that she had made a covenant with the devil, the tall man in Boston. But she also added elements that came from African and Indian cultures, such as a "thing all over hairy, all the face harye & a long nose. . . ." Tituba's tales of witches' meetings, flying to Boston on a broomstick, and wolves and birds and hairy imps persuaded her interrogators that their colony was beset by witches. A children's game spiraled into panic, but Tituba escaped with her life. Having spent her life as a prisoner in other people's lands, she had combined their cultures with her own, crafting them into a strategy for survival.

Colonial America in the second half of the seventeenth century was remarkably unstable. Without secure colonial governments, colonial societies were torn by conflicting cultural and economic forces. In some ways, Tituba was a victim of these crosscurrents. She was in Salem because Samuel Parris failed as a merchant, unable to succeed in the world's economy. Tituba's freedom was sacrificed so that other, more powerful people could become prosperous. Instability, however, creates opportunity as it creates danger. By melding her own culture and that of her captors, Tituba became a cultural shape-shifter, and she was able to save herself when she faced accusations of witchcraft. Though more dramatic, Tituba's story is like that of many Americans of the late seventeenth century. Caught in the crosscurrents of cultural and economic transformation, they adapted their cultural inheritances to new circumstances.

The Plan of Empire

Trying to make sense of the haphazard development of Britain's American colonies, the English political theorist Edmund Burke explained in 1757, "The settlement of our colonies was never pursued upon any regular plan; but they were formed, grew, and flourished, as accidents, the nature of the climate, or the dispositions of private men happened to operate." In comparison, the Spanish and French governments more actively directed their colonies, though the portions of their empires that would one day become the United States were so marginal that they, too, received relatively little attention. The British colonies were all private ventures, chartered by the government but little supervised or supported. So long as mainland colonies contributed little to the national wealth and cost the government less, they received the loosest of controls and were permitted to develop each in its own way.

The result was a period of significant instability at the end of the seventeenth century, as local colonial governments struggled to control their inhabitants, police their borders, and establish successful economies. In many of the colonies, elites vied for control, whereas in others poor people rose up against insecure leadership. As expanding populations and aggressive traders pushed against native populations, violence exploded. At the edges of empire, the British, French, and Dutch—and their Indian allies—collided. In the midst of these struggles, colonists such as Tituba found themselves caught in—and taking advantage of—the crosscurrents.

Turmoil in England

In the middle of the seventeenth century, the British government was thrown into turmoil as Parliament and the king struggled over the future direction of the nation. Two issues were at stake: religion and royal power. The uneasy balance that Elizabeth I had established between Puritans and the Church of England collapsed under her successors James I (1603–1625) and Charles I (1625–1649). Archbishop of Canterbury William Laud moved the Church of England away from the Calvinist belief in predestination, brought back worship that smacked of Catholicism, and persecuted Puritans, prompting Presbyterian Scotland to revolt.

Parliament refused to appropriate the funds that King Charles requested to quash the revolt. Instead, in 1628, Parliament passed the Petition of Right, which reasserted such basic freedoms as no taxation except by act of Parliament, no arbitrary arrest or imprisonment, and no quartering of soldiers in private homes. After years of stalemate, in 1642 Charles raised an army and moved against the Parliament, beginning the English Civil War. It concluded in 1647 with Parliament's victory. Two years later, Charles was beheaded. Oliver Cromwell, a Puritan, ruled as Lord Protector until his death in 1658. When Cromwell's son and successor proved an inept leader, Charles II was invited to reclaim the crown in 1660.

Although the monarchy had been restored, its authority had been diminished. Britain had been transformed into a constitutional monarchy in which the power of the Crown was balanced by that of Parliament. Britain also found a middle way between Calvinist Protestantism and Catholicism. When the Catholic King James II (1685–1688) tried to fill the government with Catholics and to rule without the consent of Parliament, he was removed in a bloodless revolution, known as the Glorious Revolution (1688). It brought Mary, James's Protestant daughter, and her Protestant husband, William of Orange (Holland), to the throne.

The Political Economy of Mercantilism

After the reassertion of Parliament's authority in 1688, the British state became increasingly strong and centralized. Britain then embarked on a course that would make it the world's most powerful nation by the early nineteenth century.

Throughout the political turmoil of the seventeenth century, Britain's economic policies were guided by a theory called mercantilism, which held that the chief object of a nation's economic policies was to serve the state. Mercantilism was developed to facilitate the consolidation of the new European nation-states, which required vast amounts of money to support their growing military and bureaucracies. Mercantilists considered the economy and politics as zero-sum games; one side's gain was another's loss. Wealth was defined exclusively as hard money, that is, gold and silver. With only a finite amount of gold and silver in the world, a nation could best improve its position by capturing a share of other nations' money. Mercantilism thus led to rivalry between nations. Between 1651 and 1696, the mercantilist British government passed a series of trade regulations, the Navigation Acts, requiring that all goods shipped to England and its colonies be carried in ships owned and manned by the English (including colonists). All foreign goods going to the colonies had to be shipped via Britain, where they could be taxed, and some colonial products (tobacco, sugar, indigo, and cotton, to start) had to be sent first to England before being shipped elsewhere. In mercantilist doctrine, the mother country was to produce finished products, and the colonies, raw materials. Hence, when the colonies began to manufacture items such as woolen cloth and hats, Parliament restricted those industries.

New Colonies, New Patterns

Lacking tight English control, each colony developed differently. In the second half of the seventeenth century, two important new English colonies, Pennsylvania and South Carolina, were established, and New Netherland was seized from the Dutch. As a rule, the most successful colonies offered the most opportunity to free white people and the greatest amount of religious toleration.

New Netherland Becomes New York

By the middle of the seventeenth century, the British were ready to challenge their chief trade rival, the Dutch, whom they defeated in three wars between 1652 and 1674. The Navigation Acts cut the Dutch out of international trade, and Britain began to challenge Dutch dominance of the slave trade. In 1663 King Charles II chartered the Royal Africa Company to carry slaves out of Africa to the British West Indies. Britain also made a move for New Netherland.

James, the Duke of York and King Charles II's younger brother, persuaded Charles to grant him the territory between the Connecticut and Delaware Rivers (present-day Pennsylvania, New Jersey, New York, and part of Connecticut), which was occupied by the Netherlands. In 1664 James sent a governor, 400 troops, and several warships that easily conquered the small colony of New Amsterdam. In 1665 James gave away what is now New Jersey to two of his royal cronies, Lords John Berkeley and George Carteret, and in 1667 New York's governor gave the territory on the western side of the Connecticut River to Connecticut. New Netherland had become New York.

The new colony was part Dutch (in New York City and along the Hudson) and part English (on Long Island, where New England Puritans had migrated). The first governors attempted to satisfy both groups. The governors confirmed Dutch landholdings, including huge estates along the Hudson, and guaranteed the Dutch religious freedom. The governors also distributed 2 million more acres of land, most of it in enormous chunks called manors. The owners of these manors, like feudal lords, rented land to tenants and set up courts on their estates.

If religious toleration attracted diverse peoples to the region, feudal land policies and England's failure to restore self-government kept others away. Without an elective legislature to raise taxes, the governors, following English mercantilist policy, used customs duties to raise the revenue necessary to run the colony and send a profit to James. These attempts to regulate trade and direct the economy angered local merchants and harmed the economy. Eventually, James gave in to popular discontent and, in 1683, allowed New York to have an elective assembly.

At its first meeting, this group of English and Dutch men passed a "Charter of Libertyes and Priviledges," which, had the king approved it, would have guaranteed New Yorkers a number of civil liberties and the continuing right to self-government by their elected assembly. The charter expressed the principles of liberalism starting to spread through both Britain and the Netherlands. Liberalism places an emphasis on individual liberty and holds that all human beings are equally entitled to enjoy the freedom and fulfillment to be found in their social lives—their work, families, and churches. The charter would have guaranteed all free men the right to vote and to be taxed only by their elective representatives. It also provided for trial by jury, due process, freedom of conscience for Christians, and certain property rights for women, the latter two items reflecting Dutch practices. However, the king refused to approve the charter on two grounds: it would give New Yorkers more rights than any other colonists, and the New York Assembly might undermine the power of Parliament. Without secure self-government, New Yorkers fell to fighting among themselves, and political instability in combination with feudal land holdings slowed New York's population growth.

New Amsterdam/New York

Today it is called Wall Street, and it represents the center of world finance, but in 1660, it was literally a wall that marked the northernmost edge of settlement on the island of Manhattan. Although some of the street grid remains—and today's Broad Street was once a huge canal—most of the other traces of the Dutch settlement of New Amsterdam have disappeared.

Lower Manhattan did not become a business and commercial center until the nineteenth century, however. Until then, it was a little urban village, first Dutch and then English. Even after the English takeover in 1664, the town retained its Dutch character and distinctive Dutch architectural styles. The original New Amsterdam was home to a variety of crafts- and tradespeople: not only the merchants, brokers, lawyers, and shipmasters one would expect in a commercial port but also druggists, painters, printers, tailors, and boardinghouse keepers. The homes and workshops were built in the Dutch style, out of red and yellow brick, with leaded-glass casement windows and terracotta tiles on the roofs. The comfortable feel of such homes was not unlike a middle-class home in Amsterdam.

Because buildings often functioned as both homes and workshops, they might contain not only the nuclear family but also the employees of the family business and slaves, both Indian and African. (In 1703, 40 percent of New York's households contained African slaves.) If New Amsterdam and its successor, New York, looked and felt like a European town, the presence of large numbers of Africans and Indians gave the little settlement a distinctive New World character.

From its earliest years, New Amsterdam was an urban village in a global economy, home to immigrants and natives, all buying and selling in a global market. The Kierstede family built its house at the corner of what today are Pearl and Whitehall Streets, looking out on the East River. Hans Kierstede, a German religious refugee, came to New Amsterdam and served as its first surgeon. His wife, Sara Roelofs, had been born in Amsterdam and lived as a child near present-day Albany, where she played with the local Indians and learned their languages. In New Amsterdam, she built a backyard shed where Indian women crafted goods to sell in the market across the street from the Kierstedes' home. In 1664, Sara Roelofs Kierstede served as a translator when Peter Stuyvesant negotiated a treaty with the local Indians. The Lenape Indian Sachem Oratam was so pleased with her translating abilities that he gave her some 2,000 acres of land on the Hackensack River, in present-day Bergen County, New Jersey.

When archeologists excavated the family home late in the twentieth century, they found bits and pieces of the cultures that mixed on the island of Manhattan: pipes made in Holland and imported even after the English takeover; a German wineglass; a piece of a sword; hair curlers for curling wigs; whistles carved from clay pipes and traded to the Indians for furs; and ceramic gambling tokens, similar to ones found at plantations in the South and the West Indies.

New Amsterdam was a crossroads of empire. There people—and goods—from both sides of the Atlantic, Europeans, Indians, and Africans, met and traded with each other, creating a new world made out of bits and pieces from each of their cultures.

Diversity and Prosperity in Pennsylvania

Pennsylvania demonstrated the potential of a colony that offered both religious toleration and economic opportunity. Its founder, William Penn, was a Quaker and the son of one of King Charles II's leading supporters. After his restoration to the throne, Charles had a number of political debts to repay, and giving away vast chunks of North America was a cheap way of doing it. As a Quaker, Penn was eager to get out of England. In 1661 alone, 4,000 English Quakers were jailed, and Penn was imprisoned four times. The Quakers were a radical sect of Protestants who believed that God offered salvation to all and placed an "inner light" inside everyone. Hardworking, serious, and moral, Quakers rejected violence and refused to serve in the military or pay taxes for its support.

Penn received his charter in 1681. To raise money, he sold land to a group of wealthy Quaker merchants, who received government positions and economic concessions in return. To attract ordinary settlers, Penn promised self-government (although stacked in favor of the merchant elite), freedom of religion, and reasonably priced land.

In 1682, when Penn arrived at Philadelphia (Greek for "city of brotherly love"), the colony already had 4,000 inhabitants. Penn had clear ideas about how he wanted his colony to develop. He expected the orderly growth of farming villages, neatly laid out along rivers and creeks, and mapped the settlement of the city along a grid, with each house set far enough from its neighbors to prevent the spread of fires. He wanted harmonious relations with local Indians.

Penn's policies attracted a wide variety of Europeans. Soon Pennsylvania was populated by self-contained communities, each speaking a different language or practicing a different religion. Pennsylvania's early history was characterized by rapid growth and prosperity. However, this progress undermined Penn's plans for a cohesive, hierarchical society. People lived where and how they wanted, pursuing the economic activities they found most profitable.

While moving away from the inequalities of the Old World, Pennsylvania replicated those of the New World. Many of its European immigrants were indentured servants or redemptioners, people who worked for a brief period to pay back the ship's captain for the cost of transportation to the colony. And by 1700, the Pennsylvania Assembly had passed laws recognizing slavery, although not unanimously. That slavery could take root in a colony where some questioned its morality suggests both the force of its power in shaping early America and the weakness of the opposition.

Indians and Africans in the Political Economy of Carolina

Like Pennsylvania and Maryland, South Carolina was a proprietary colony. One of the proprietors, Anthony Ashley Cooper, the Earl of Shaftesbury, and his secretary, John Locke, drafted the Fundamental Constitutions for the new colony. Locke later became a leading political philosopher, and the Constitutions reflect the liberal, rights-guaranteeing principles that he later developed more fully.

The Constitutions provided for a representative government and widespread religious toleration. At the same time, they embodied the traditional assumption that liberty could be guaranteed only in a hierarchical society. Shaftesbury and Locke tried to set up a complex hierarchy of nobles at the top and hereditary serfs at the bottom. The Constitutions also recognized African slavery, and Carolina was the first colony that introduced slavery at the outset. The Constitutions never went into full effect, for the first Carolina representative assembly rejected many of its provisions. Predictably, the attempt to transplant a British-style nobility failed. The only aristocracy that the Carolinas developed was one of wealth, supported by the labor of slaves.

The first settlers arrived at Charles Town (later moved and renamed Charleston) in 1670. The area had a semitropical climate, wonderfully fertile soil, and a growing season of up to 295 days a year. The region had once been explored by the Spanish, who still claimed it. It was inhabited by mission Indians, that is, Indians who had converted to Catholicism.

As happened so often when Europeans arrived, Indian tribes competed to trade with them, and rival groups of Europeans struggled to dominate the trade. In the colonial period, Indian wars usually pitted one group of Europeans and their Indian allies against another group of Europeans and their native allies, with the Indians doing most of the fighting. Such wars were an extension of Europe's market economy: Indians fought for European goods, and Europeans fought for a monopoly over Indian products. The

Chickasaw Map This eighteenth-century French copy of a Chickasaw map represents an indigenous conception of the local political landscape.

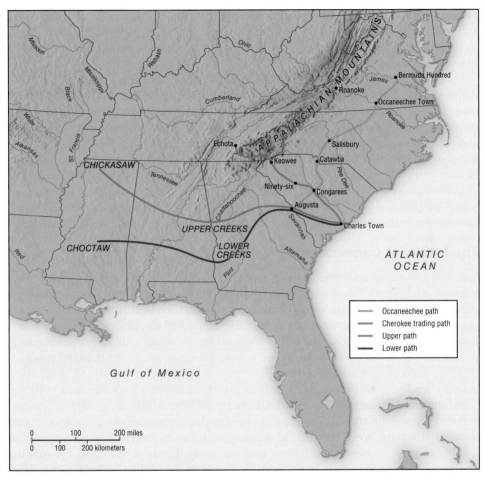

Map 4–1 **Trade Routes in the Southeast** Beginning in the seventeenth century, English traders from Virginia and later Carolina followed several paths to trade with Southeastern Indians as far west as the Mississippi.
Source: Adapted from W. Stitt Robinson, *The Southern Colonial Frontier* (Albuquerque: University of New Mexico Press, 1979), p. 103.

English were particularly successful in achieving dominance because of their sophisticated market economy. London's banks had perfected the mechanisms of credit, which financed a fur trade in the forests half a world away.

The Westos elbowed their way ahead of other tribes by offering the Carolina traders a commodity more valuable even than deerskins: Indian slaves. In fact, until about 1690, slaves were the most valuable commodity sold by the Carolina colony.

Carolina merchants quickly established control over the entire Southeast (see Map 4–1), pushing out the Spanish, the French, and even the Virginians. At the same time, Indian tribes fought to become the chief slave supplier. In 1680, in the Westo War, the Carolina traders sent their allies, the Savannah Indians, out to destroy the Westos, who were the Virginians' link to the Native American trade of the Southeast. The Carolinians vanquished the Spanish by sending in other Indian allies to destroy the mission towns. In this way, the Carolina traders eliminated their European rivals. At the same time, the Chickasaws emerged to replace the Westos and, like them, obliterated less powerful tribes in order to obtain a steady supply of slaves. All together, between 1670 and 1715, somewhere between 25,000 and 50,000 Indians were enslaved, with many more killed in the slaving raids. The slave trade increased dramatically the level of violence among Native Americans.

This violence was turned against the Carolinians in the Yamasee War (1715–1716). Although the Yamasees had been reliable trading partners for 40 years and had fought with the British in Queen Anne's War (see later in the chapter), South Carolina traders cheated them out of their land and enslaved their women and children. In retaliation, the Yamasees and their allies attacked, pushing the settlers almost back to Charleston before they were stopped. The war killed 400 white South Carolinians (7 percent of the population, more than in King Philip's War in New England), crippled the Indian slave trade, forced the colony to abandon frontier settlements, and revealed the fragility of the entire South Carolina venture. When international war began again in 1739, the frontier regions were, as they had been a quarter of a century earlier, dangerous and unstable for settlers, traders, and Indians alike.

The Barbados Connection

Carolina was part of a far-flung Atlantic political economy based on trade, plantation agriculture, and slavery. Many of the early Carolina settlers had substantial experience with African slavery in Barbados, a small Caribbean island settled in 1627 that within a decade became a major source of the world's sugar. By then, it had an African majority and was Britain's first slave society. By the end of the seventeenth century, Barbados was the most productive of all Britain's colonies, its per-person income much higher than in England.

This income was not shared equally, however. Owners of the largest plantations became fabulously wealthy, and even lesser planters enjoyed a high standard of living. Conditions for African slaves, however, were brutal. The British magnified differences between Europeans and Africans to enhance the distinction between landowners and slaves. Barbadians were the first to portray Africans as beasts, and the racism of Caribbean planters was intense. Slave codes were the harshest of any in the Atlantic world, prescribing that male slaves convicted of crimes could be burned at the stake, beheaded, starved, or castrated. When Caribbean slavery was imported into Carolina, these attitudes came with it. The Carolina slave code was the harshest in North America. Laws and attitudes separated whites from blacks, but differences among Europeans were minimized, as some restrictions against Irish Catholics and Jews were lifted after Barbados became a slave society. In 1650, Barbados allowed the immigration of Jews and other religious minorities six years before England did. As in the Chesapeake, increasing freedom for Europeans developed alongside the enslavement of Africans.

The sugar plantations of Barbados and Britain's other Caribbean islands made their extraordinary profits from the labor of African slaves. British planters worked Africans harder than European indentured servants. Profits came from keeping labor costs down, as well as from the growing demand for sugar. It is important to remember that the New World slave system would not have grown as it did without European demand for plantation crops. African slaves were imported into Carolina from the outset, but only after 1690 did the colony develop a staple crop—rice—that increased the demand for slave labor. After rice became the region's major cash crop, African slaves became more valuable. By 1720, Africans composed more than 70 percent of Carolina's population. With a black majority, a lethal environment, and wealth concentrated in an elite, Carolina resembled the Caribbean islands more than it did the other English colonies on the mainland. In only a few decades, Carolina had become a slave society, not simply a society with slaves: slavery stood at the center of everything.

The Transformation of Virginia

At the same time that a newly vigorous England was planting new colonies, those established earlier were reshaped. In the final quarter of the seventeenth century, the older colonies experienced political and sometimes social instability, followed by the establishment of a lasting order. In Virginia, the transition was marked by a violent insurrection known as Bacon's Rebellion. Significantly, the rebels sought not to overthrow the social and political order but to secure a legitimate government that could protect economic opportunity. In its aftermath, Virginia became a slave society.

Social Change in Virginia

As Virginia entered its second half-century, the health of its population finally began to improve. Apple orchards had matured, so Virginians could drink cider instead of impure water. Ships bringing new servants arrived in the fall, a healthy time of year. Increasingly, they lived to serve out their periods of indenture and set out on their own to plant tobacco. However, most of the best land in eastern Virginia had already been claimed, and the land to the west was occupied by Indian tribes with peace treaties with the English. In addition, the government was controlled by a small clique of men using it as a means of getting rich. Taxes, assessed in tobacco, were extraordinarily high, and as taxes rose, the price of tobacco began to fall. Caught in a squeeze, many ordinary planters went to work for others as tenants or overseers.

Still, servants kept coming to the colony, most from the lower ranks of society. Restless and unhappy, they joined in a series of disturbances beginning in the middle of the century. The elite responded by lengthening the time of service and stiffening the penalties for running away.

Bacon's Rebellion and the Abandonment of the Middle Ground

When the revolt came, it was led not by one of the poor or landless but by a member of the elite. Nathaniel Bacon was young, well educated, wealthy, and a member of a prominent family. Bacon made an immediate impression on Virginia's ruling clique, and Governor Berkeley invited him to join the colony's Council of State. For unknown reasons, Bacon cast his lot with Berkeley's enemies among the elite. The instability of elites created political factions in a number of colonies. When ruling elites, such as Berkeley's in Virginia, levied exorbitant taxes and ignored their constituents, they left themselves open to challenge.

The contest between Bacon and Berkeley might have remained minor had not Bacon capitalized on the discontent of the colony's freedmen (men who had served out their indentures). In 1676, Bacon's Rebellion was triggered by a routine episode of violence on the middle ground inhabited by Indians and Europeans. Seeking payment for goods they had delivered to a planter, a band of Doeg Indians killed the planter's overseer and tried to steal his hogs. Over the years, Europeans and Indians who shared the middle ground had adapted the Indian custom of providing restitution for crimes committed by one side or the other. Although this practice resulted in sporadic violence, it also helped maintain order. But this time, the conflict escalated, as Virginians sought revenge, prompting further Indian retaliation.

Soon an isolated incident escalated into a militia expedition of 1,000 men, an extraordinarily large force at the time. For six weeks the war party laid siege to the reservation of the Susquehannocks, a tribe drawn unwillingly into the conflict, who in turn avenged themselves on settlers on the frontier.

When Berkeley refused to fight the Susquehannocks, the frontier planters were infuriated. They complained that their taxes went to Berkeley's clique instead of being used to police the frontier. Planter women used their gossip networks to spread the idea that Berkeley was "a greater friend to the Indians than to the English."

With his wife's encouragement, Nathaniel Bacon agreed to lead a wholesale war on "all Indians whatsoever." After his rebels massacred some formerly friendly Occoneechees, Bacon marched on the government at Jamestown with 400 armed men, demanding to fight "all Indians in general, for that they were all Enemies." Berkeley agreed, and then changed his mind, but it was too late. By then Bacon was in control, and Berkeley fled to the eastern shore.

By the time a royal commission and 1,000 soldiers arrived in January 1677 to put down the disorder, Bacon had died, and Berkeley had regained control. Twenty-three rebel leaders were executed, then the king removed Berkeley from office. After Bacon's death, support for the rebellion quickly dissipated.

After Bacon's Rebellion, the government remained in the hands of the planter elite, but the rebels had achieved their primary objective. The frontier Indians had been dispersed, and their land was now free for settlement. Those in power became more responsive to white freedmen. Other factors also improved economic conditions: tobacco prices began to climb, and planters replaced servants with slaves.

Virginia Becomes a Slave Society

With new colonies such as New York and Pennsylvania offering greater opportunity to poor whites, the supply of European indentured servants to the Chesapeake dried up just when more Africans were becoming available. Britain entered the slave trade on a large scale at the end of the seventeenth century, authorizing private merchants to carry slaves from Africa to North America in 1698. It seemed planters could not get enough slaves to meet their needs. In 1680, only 7 percent of Virginia's population was African in origin, but by 1700 the proportion had increased to 28 percent, and half the labor force was enslaved (see Table 4–1). Within two decades, Virginia had become a society in which slavery was central to the political economy and the social structure. With the bottom tier of the social order enslaved and hence unable to compete for land or wealth, opportunity for all whites necessarily improved.

As the composition of Virginia's labor force changed, so did the laws to control it. Although all slave societies had certain features in common, each colony enacted its own slave code to maintain and define the institution. By 1705, Virginia had a thorough slave code in place.

All forms of slavery have certain elements in common: perpetuity, kinlessness, violence, and the master's access to the slave's sexuality. First, slavery is a lifelong condition. Second, a slave has no legally recognized family relationships. Third, slavery rests on violence or its threat, including the master's sexual access to the slave.

American slavery added other elements. First, slavery in all the Americas was hereditary, passed on from a mother to her children and to their children, for all time. Second, compared with other slave systems, including that of Latin America,

Table 4-1 Population of British Colonies in America, 1660 and 1710

	1660			1710		
Colony	White	Black	Total	White	Black	Total
Virginia	26,070	950	27,020	55,163	23,118	78,281
Maryland	7,668	758	8,426	34,796	7,945	42,741
Chesapeake	33,738	1,708	35,446	89,959	31,063	121,022
Massachusetts	22,062	422	22,484	61,080	1,310	62,390
Connecticut	7,955	25	7,980	38,700	750	39,450
Rhode Island	1,474	65	1,539	7,198	375	7,573
New Hampshire	1,515	50	1,565	5,531	150	5,681
New England	33,006	562	33,568	112,509	2,585	115,094
Bermuda	3,500	200	3,700	4,268	2,845	7,113
Barbados	26,200	27,100	53,300	13,000	52,300	65,300
Antigua	1,539	1,448	2,987	2,892	12,960	15,852
Montserrat	1,788	661	2,449	1,545	3,570	5,115
Nevis	2,347	2,566	4,913	1,104	3,676	4,780
St. Kitts	1,265	957	2,222	1,670	3,294	4,964
Jamaica				7,250	58,000	65,250
Caribbean	36,639	32,932	69,571	31,729	136,645	168,374
New York	4,336	600	4,936	18,814	2,811	21,625
New Jersey				18,540	1,332	19,872
Pennsylvania				22,875	1,575	24,450
Delaware	510	30	540	3,145	500	3,645
Middle Colonies	4,846	630	5,476	63,374	6,218	69,592
North Carolina	980	20	1,000	14,220	900	15,120
South Carolina				6,783	4,100	10,883
Lower South	980	20	1,000	21,003	5,000	26,003
Totals	109,209	35,852	145,061	318,574	181,511	500,085

Source: Jack P. Greene, *Pursuits of Happiness* (Chapel Hill: University of North Carolina, 1988), pp. 178–179.

manumissions—the freeing of slaves—in the American South were quite rare. Finally, slavery in the South was racial. Slavery was reserved for Africans and some Indians. The line between slavery and freedom was defined as one of color.

Slave codes also defined gender roles. Two early pieces of legislation denied African women the privileges of European women. A 1643 statute made all adult men and African women taxable, assuming that they (and not white women) were performing productive labor in the fields. In 1662, another law said that children were to inherit the status of their mother, not their father.

The same laws that created and sustained racial slavery also increased the freedom of whites. New World plantation slavery was developed in a world in which the freedom of most Europeans also was limited in various ways. In fact, two-thirds of the Europeans who migrated to British America before the American Revolution were unfree—servants or redemptioners. (When Africans are added, virtually all of whom were enslaved, the

Table 4-2 Codifying Race and Slavery

1640—Masters are required to arm everyone in their households except Africans (Virginia)

1643—All adult men and African women are taxable, on the assumption that they were working in the fields (Virginia)

1662—Children follow the condition of their mother (Virginia)

1662—Double fine charged for any Christian who commits fornication with an African (Virginia)

1664—All slaves serve for life; that is, slavery is defined as a lifelong condition (Maryland)

1664—Interracial marriage banned; any free woman who marries a slave will serve that slave's master until her husband dies, and their children will be enslaved (Maryland)

1667—Baptism as a Christian does not make a slave free (Virginia)

1669—No punishment is given if punished slave dies (Virginia)

1670—Free blacks and Indians are not allowed to purchase Christian indentured servants (Virginia)

1670—Indians captured elsewhere and sold as slaves to Virginia are to serve for life; those captured in Virginia, until the age of 30, if children, or for 12 years, if grown (Virginia)

1680—In order to prevent "Negroes Insurrections": no slave may carry arms or weapons; no slave may leave his or her master without written permission; any slave who "lifts up his hand" against a Christian will receive 30 lashes; any slave who runs away and resists arrest may be killed lawfully (Virginia)

1682—Slaves may not gather for more than four hours at other than owner's plantation (Virginia)

1682—All servants who were "Negroes, Moors, Mollattoes or Indians" were to be considered slaves at the time of their purchase if neither their parents nor country were Christian (Virginia)

1691—Owners are to be compensated if "negroes, mulattoes or other slaves" are killed while resisting arrest (Virginia)

1691—Forbidden is all miscegenation as "that abominable mixture"; any English or "other white man or woman" who marries a "negroe, mulatto, or Indian" is to be banished; any free English woman who bears a "bastard child by any negro or mulatto" will be fined, and if she can't pay the fine, she will be indentured for five years and the child will be indentured until the age of 30 (Virginia)

1691—All slaves who are freed by their masters must be transported out of the state (Virginia)

1692—Special courts of "over and terminer" are established for trying slaves accused of crimes, creating a separate system of justice (Virginia)

1705—Mulatto is defined as "the child of an Indian, the child, grandchild, or great grandchild of a negro" (Virginia)

1705—Africans, mulattoes, and Indians are prohibited from holding office or giving grand jury testimony (Virginia)

1705—Slaves are forbidden to own livestock (Virginia)

1705—"Christian white" servants cannot be whipped naked (Virginia)

1723—Free blacks explicitly excluded from militia (Virginia)

1723—Free blacks explicitly denied the right to vote (Virginia)

Note: Slavery is a creation of law, which defines what it means to be a slave and protects the master's rights in his slave property. Slave codes developed piecemeal in the Chesapeake, over the course of the seventeenth century. Legislators in the Chesapeake colonies defined slavery as a racial institution, appropriate only for Africans, and protected it with a series of laws, which, in the process, also created a privileged position for whites.

total increases to 90 percent.) The increase in freedom for whites was the product of several sorts of policies. First, it depended on the widespread availability of cheap land, which whites could obtain only by dispossessing the Indians who inhabited it. Second, it depended on British government policies, such as permitting self-government in the colonies, which were designed to attract immigrants. Third, it depended on specific laws that improved the conditions of whites, often at the same time limiting the freedom of blacks. For example, in 1705 Virginia made it illegal for white servants to be whipped without an order from a justice of the peace (see Table 4–2).

New England Under Assault

New England's prosperity led to problems, both internal and external. How would a religion born in adversity cope with good fortune? A combination of internal colonial conflicts and a growing population encroaching on Indian lands led to the region's deadliest Indian war in 1675.

Social Prosperity and the Fear of Religious Decline

In many ways, the Puritan founders of the New England colonies saw their dreams come true. Although immigration virtually halted as the English Revolution broke out, natural increase kept the population growing, from about 23,000 in 1650 to more than 93,000 in 1700. Life expectancy was higher than in England, and families were larger.

Most New Englanders enjoyed a comfortable, if modest, standard of living. By the end of the century, the simple shacks of the first settlers had been replaced by two-story frame homes. By our standards, these homes would still have been almost unbearably cold in the winter, when indoor temperatures routinely dropped into the 40s. Still, New Englanders were beginning to enjoy the prosperous village life their ancestors had once known in England.

For Puritans, such good fortune presented a problem. Prosperity became a cause for worry, as people turned their minds away from God to more worldly things. In the 1660s and 1670s, New England's ministers preached a series of jeremiads, lamentations about spiritual decline. They criticized problems ranging from public drunkenness and sexual license to land speculation and excessively high prices and wages. If New Englanders did not change their ways, the ministers predicted, "Ruine upon Ruine, Destruction upon Destruction would come, until one stone were not left upon another."

Most of the churches were embroiled in controversy in the 1660s concerning who could be members. The founders had assumed that most people, sooner or later, would have the conversion experience that entitled them to full church membership. By the third generation, however, many children and grandchildren of full members had not had the experience of spiritual rebirth. In 1662 a group of ministers adopted the Half-Way Covenant, which set out terms for church membership and participation. Full church membership was reserved for those who could demonstrate a conversion experience. Their offspring could still be "half-way" members of the church, receiving its discipline and having their children baptized. Those who wished to maintain the purity and exclusivity of the church resisted. Rather than settle this question, the Half-Way Covenant aggravated tensions always present in the Puritan religion.

Turmoil broke out as well in the persecution of Quakers, despite Charles II's having issued a protection order. In 1660, Massachusetts had executed the Quaker Mary Dyer, who had returned to Boston after her banishment. The Quakers had been brazen in their defiance of authority, not only returning to the colony when they knew it meant certain death but also even running naked through the streets or in church.

King Philip's War

Although New England's colonies developed along a common path, conflicts among them were intense and led to the region's deadliest Indian war. As in Bacon's Rebellion, the underlying cause of the war was the steady encroachment of English settlers on Native American lands. In the 1660s, Rhode Island, Massachusetts, and Plymouth all

King Philip's (Metacom)'s Map, 1668 A map of the lands that Metacom (known by New Englanders as King Philip) sold in 1668. Note that Metacom's understanding of what it meant to "sell" land differed from English conceptions of property ownership. He insisted that the Indians who were living on the land could continue to do so.

claimed the land occupied by the Wampanoags, Massasoit's tribe, now ruled by his son Metacom, known by the colonists as King Philip. By 1671, the colonies had resolved their dispute and ordered King Philip and his people to submit to the rule of Plymouth. No longer able to play one colony against another, King Philip prepared for war, as did the colonists of all the colonies except Rhode Island, which attempted to mediate. In June 1675 King Philip's men attacked the Plymouth village of Swansea.

During the next year, New Englanders attacked entire villages of noncombatants, and the Indians retaliated in kind. At the beginning of the war, New Englanders looked down on the Indians' traditional methods as evidence of depravity, saying they fought "more like wolves than men." By the end of the war, however, both sides committed brutalities, including scalping and putting their victims' heads on stakes. That was the fate of King Philip. His wife and nine-year-old son were sold into slavery, along with hundreds of captives.

The New Englanders won King Philip's War, but the cost was enormous. The casualty rate was one of the highest for any American war ever. About 4,000 Indians died, many of starvation after the New Englanders destroyed their cornfields. The war eliminated any significant Native American presence in southeastern New England and killed 2,000 English settlers (1 out of every 25). The Indians pushed to within 20 miles of Boston, attacked more than half of New England's towns, and burned 1,200 homes. It took the region decades to rebuild.

Indians and the Empire

New England's relations with Indian tribes were not simply a local concern. They were of deep interest to the British Empire, as Andros's participation demonstrated. The British government had to balance the desires of its colonists against the empire's larger objectives. As the French expanded their presence in North America, using friendly Indians to check their advance became one of those objectives. In 1673 the French explorers Jacques Marquette and Louis Joliet had traveled down the Mississippi River as far south as the Arkansas River, and nine years later René-Robert Cavelier, Sieur de La Salle, reached the mouth of the river and named the surrounding territory Louisiana, in honor of King Louis XIV. Biloxi was founded in 1699, New Orleans in 1718, and the forts at Cahokia and Kaskaskia several years later. The French and their Indian allies controlled the Great Lakes region and the eastern shore of the Mississippi all the way to its mouth, while the British were confined to the East Coast.

This geopolitical reality dictated Britain's Indian policy. Andros saw a role for Native Americans as trade partners and allies in Britain's conflict with the French. He welcomed the Indian survivors of King Philip's War into New York and refused to send them back to New England for execution and enslavement, thus becoming the "father" who offered protection to his Indian "children." The British and the Iroquois, who dominated all the other tribes in the region, joined in a strong alliance known as the Covenant Chain, which enhanced the positions of both New York and the Iroquois. The Iroquois became the middlemen between other tribes and the merchants at Albany and were allowed to push as far north and west against French-allied tribes as they could.

With New York dominating the British-Indian alliance, the New England colonies were effectively hemmed in. New York used the Mohawks to make a claim to Maine and blocked New England's movement to the west. Albany became the undisputed center of the Indian trade. In every way, King Philip's War proved exceedingly costly for the New England colonies.

The Empire Strikes

As Britain regained political stability at the end of the seventeenth century, it tried to bring more order to its "accidental empire" by making the colonies play a larger role in its governance. As the Glorious Revolution that removed King James II from the British throne secured constitutional government for Britain's subjects on both sides of the Atlantic, it also made Britain strong and stable enough to challenge France for world supremacy. Between 1689 and 1763, the Anglo-French rivalry drew the colonies into four international wars that shaped them in important ways.

The Dominion of New England

When James II ascended the throne, he decided to punish New England for its disloyalty to the Crown during the Puritan Revolution. There were also reports that New Englanders were defying the Navigation Acts by smuggling. In France, Louis XIV had centralized his administration and brought both his nation and his empire under firm control, and James decided to try similar tactics. In North America, he began unilaterally to revoke the charters of the colonies. By 1688, Massachusetts, Plymouth, Connecticut, New York, New Jersey, New Hampshire, and Rhode Island had been joined together into the Dominion of New England, and Edmund Andros was named its governor.

Before James II and Andros were deposed by the Glorious Revolution of 1688, they wreaked considerable havoc in New England. Massachusetts, New York, and Maryland all suffered revolts. James's attempt to strengthen rule over the colonies failed, but it marked a turning point: the colonies' last period of significant political instability before the eve of the American Revolution.

James's attempt to tighten control affected Massachusetts most seriously. He ordered it to tolerate religious dissenters; some feared he would impose Catholicism on the colony. He took away liberties that residents had enjoyed for over half a century: juries were now to be appointed by sheriffs, town meetings were limited to once a year, and town selectmen could serve no more than two two-year terms. All titles to land had to be reconfirmed, with the holder paying Andros a small fee. Andros claimed the right to levy taxes on his own and began seizing all common lands. Some Boston merchants allied themselves with Andros, hoping to win his favor. This alliance revealed a growing rift in the region between those who welcomed commerce and a more secular way of life and those who wished to preserve the old ways. Most people in Massachusetts, however, despised Andros and feared the road he was leading them down.

The Glorious Revolution in Britain and America

The Glorious Revolution made it clear that Parliament, not an autocratic monarch, would henceforth play the leading role in government. It also determined, after almost a century and a half of conflict, that the Anglican religion would prevail. The Glorious Revolution ushered in a period of remarkable political stability that enabled Britain to become the world's most powerful nation.

In the next century Britain's North American colonies looked to this moment in British history as a model of constitutional government. Their understanding of events in Britain was shaped by political philosopher John Locke's *Two Treatises of Government* (1690). Since the time that he and Shaftesbury had written Carolina's Fundamental Constitutions more than 20 years earlier, Locke had become increasingly radical. The *Treatises* boldly asserted fundamental human equality and universal rights and provided the political theories that would justify a revolution.

The *Treatises* have become the founding documents of political liberalism and its theory of human rights. Locke argued that governments were created by people, not by God. Man was born "with a Title to perfect Freedom," or "natural rights." When people created governments, they gave up some of that freedom in exchange for the rights that they enjoyed in society. The purpose of government was to protect the "Lives, Liberties," and "Fortunes" of the people who created it, not to achieve glory or power for the nation or to serve God. Moreover, should a government take away the civil rights of its citizens, they had a "right to resume their original Liberty." This right of revolution was Locke's boldest and most radical assertion. Once news of the Glorious Revolution reached Massachusetts, its inhabitants poured into the streets, seized the government, and threw the despised Andros in jail. They proclaimed loyalty to the new king and lobbied for the return of their charter. Rhode Island and Connecticut soon got their charters back, but Massachusetts, which was perceived as too independent, was made a royal colony in 1691, with a royal governor. Although Massachusetts lost some of its autonomy and was forced to tolerate dissenters, the town meeting was restored. At the same time, New Hampshire became a royal colony.

The citizens of Maryland and New York also took the opportunity presented by the Glorious Revolution to evict their royal governors. In Maryland, tensions between the tobacco planters and the increasingly dictatorial proprietor, Charles Calvert, Lord Baltimore, had been building for several decades. Four-fifths of the population was Protestant, but the colony's government was dominated by Catholics, who allocated to themselves the best land. When Protestant planters protested, Baltimore imposed a

Maryland's Colonists Demand a New Government

In 1688, King James II of Britain fell in what came to be known as the Glorious Revolution. As a result, in 1689, rebellions against the authorities occurred in three British colonies—New York, Massachusetts, and Maryland. Though the rebellions collapsed in Boston and New York, in Maryland, the rebels set up their own governing assembly and were eventually recognized as the legitimate colonial government. This was a significant marker in early American history, though whether it signaled a step forward in the forging of democracy is still debated.

In England, the Glorious Revolution occurred when the king's second wife bore a son, which caused the largely Protestant population to fear that their Catholic king would establish a Catholic dynasty. Rebel leaders invited his Protestant daughter, Mary (from his first marriage), and her Dutch husband, William of Orange, to invade their island nation, and they did so successfully, with little bloodshed. In Maryland, some comparable issues were at stake. Maryland had been established as a proprietary colony in the hands of the Catholic Calvert family; for decades it had served as a haven not only for Catholics but other relatively disempowered sects as well. Key governing positions remained in the hands of Calvert family or their close connections, and this led to periodic outbursts of resentment and even rebellion among the largely Protestant settlers.

After James II was overthrown, the Catholic colonial government of Maryland did not immediately recognize the Protestant William and Mary as their sovereigns. Crises at the apex of a powerful state often make room for rebellion among the populace, which happened in the colonies. The fact that the reigning authorities of Maryland were also Catholic strengthened the rebellion. Rumors spread that the colonial government had not only failed to move quickly to support William and Mary but also had in fact entered into negotiations with the Catholic French king and had requested that they send Indians from their inland territories to massacre the discontented Protestant settlers of Maryland. Of course, there was not a shred of truth to these rumors, but many people believed them. Fear of Indian attack was a central part of colonial life.

In July of 1689, within two months of receiving the news from London, a man named John Coode stepped forward to lead the people in marching on the state house in St. Mary's City. Coode was born in Cornwall in 1648 and came to Maryland as a young Anglican minister but found himself unfit for such a profession. He married a wealthy widow and set himself up as a planter. He had protested the Calvert family government before, and now he found a far larger and more enthusiastic audience for his complaints. Surrounded by hundreds of armed men, the proprietary government stepped down without firing a shot. In August, Coode took the remarkable and politically dangerous step of calling for the election of a new assembly. The people were not only protesting; they *continued* were choosing to constitute their own governing body, without waiting for word from the king.

Fortunately for Coode and his cohort, in February of 1690 they received official word from William and Mary that the new assembly could continue to govern. They had been doing an excellent job of maintaining the peace, and the new Protestant monarchs had little desire to side publicly with the Calvert family. Results were different in New York and Massachusetts, where the rebel governments were dissolved. In Maryland, the people had demonstrated that in certain circumstances, they had the power to reject an imposed government and replace it with one of their own choosing. Despite this, the change did not open up new economic opportunities for the common man or woman, and already successful Protestant settlers gained more political power than they had had before. Catholics and Quakers suddenly found themselves legally excluded from holding office. Increasing the power of the majority to govern the country ended up putting certain minorities more at risk, since they no longer had a royal power supporting them. Was this democracy or the tyranny of the majority?

property qualification for voting and appointed increasingly dictatorial governors. When news of the Glorious Revolution reached Maryland in 1689, a group led by John Coode, a militia officer, took over the government in a bloodless coup (known as Coode's Rebellion), proclaimed loyalty to William and Mary, and got the new government in Britain to take away Baltimore's proprietorship. In 1691, Maryland became a royal colony, and in 1702, the Anglican Church was made the state church, ending Maryland's experiment with religious toleration.

New York's rebels were less successful. A group of prosperous Dutch traders led by Jacob Leisler took over the government. Unlike Coode in Maryland, Leisler was not willing to cede power to the new king's appointees. As a result, the new governor put the rebel leaders on trial, and Leisler and his son-in-law were executed, their bodies decapitated and quartered.

The Rights of Englishmen

Although the Glorious Revolution restored self-government to the North American colonies, the colonists and their British governors interpreted that event somewhat differently. Colonists felt it gave them all the rights of Englishmen. These rights were of two sorts: civil rights, from trial by jury to freedom from unreasonable searches, and the rights of self-government, including taxation only by their own elected representatives, self-rule, and civilian, not military, rule. The colonists believed that their legislatures were the local equivalent of Parliament and that, just as the citizens of Britain were governed by Parliament, so they should be governed by their own elective legislatures.

The British government held differently. First, it believed that the colonies were dependents of the mother country that needed a parent's protection and that owed that parent obedience. Second, the good of the empire as a whole was more important than that of any one of its parts. A colony was valued, as one British official put it, by what it contributed to "the gain or loss of *this* Kingdom." Third, colonial governments were subordinate to the British government. Finally, the British government had complete jurisdiction over every aspect of colonial life. The views of Britain and its colonists of how the empire should function radically diverged.

Conflict in the Empire

Between 1689 and 1713, Britain fought two wars against France and her allies, King William's War (1689–1697) and Queen Anne's War (1702–1713). Competition for the Indian alliances and the colonies' struggle over trade and territory made the European-Indian borderline uncertain and dangerous.

King William's War and Queen Anne's War followed a similar pattern. Each was produced by a struggle for power between France and England, and each resulted in a stalemate. The North American phase of each war began with a Canadian-Indian assault on isolated British settlements on the northern frontier (see Map 4–2). King William's War started with the capture of the British fort at Pemaquid, Maine, and the burning of Schenectady, New York, and Falmouth, Maine. Queen Anne's War began in 1704 with a horrific raid on Deerfield, Massachusetts, in which half the town was torched and half the population was killed or captured.

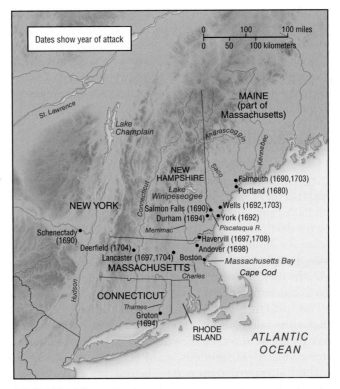

Map 4–2   Frontier Warfare During King William's and Queen Anne's Wars During these international conflicts, the New England frontier was exposed to attack by French Canadians and their Indian allies.
Source: Adapted from Alan Gallay, ed., *Colonial Wars of North America, 1512–1763* (New York: Garland, 1996), p. 247.

In the first war, the British colonies responded with massive retaliation, sending raiding parties into ambitious but ultimately unsuccessful attacks on Québec. In 1690 Massachusetts governor Sir William Phips set out to seize Québec in an attack by land and sea. The failed expedition cost 1,000 lives and £40,000 and drove American colonists away from the northern frontier.

Queen Anne's War followed much the same course. Canadian-Indian attacks on frontier villages were met with raids on Indian villages. Again, New England attempted a two-pronged attack on Québec. When 900 troops (and 35 female camp followers) were killed as their ships sank in the St. Lawrence River, the commander canceled the expedition. Like King William's War, Queen Anne's War ended badly for New Englanders who had been eager to remove the twin threats of Catholicism and French-backed Indians to the north.

The imperial wars merged with and were survived by long-standing conflicts with Indian tribes. In North America, European rivals almost never confronted each other directly but instead mobilized their Indian allies and made war on those of their adversaries. These tactics, in addition to an expanding colonial population and the Native American attempt to monopolize trade, made conflict on the frontiers endemic.

Massachusetts in Crisis

If the imperial wars provide a window into international tensions, the Salem witchcraft trials reveal a society in crisis internally, one coping with economic development, the conflict between old and new ways of understanding the world, and the threats presented by political instability, imperial war, and conflict with the Indians. In 1692 Massachusetts executed 20 people who had been convicted of witchcraft in Salem. Even in a society that believed in witchcraft, the execution of so many people at once was an aberration that revealed deep tensions.

The Social and Cultural Contexts of Witchcraft

Although the majority of New England's colonists were Puritan, many seem to have believed in magic. They subscribed to such tenets of Puritanism as predestination, but they also believed that they could use supernatural powers to predict the future, protect themselves from harm, and hurt their enemies. Although the ministry identified the use of magic with the devil, Tituba's folk religion and that of New Englanders were not incompatible. Before the development of scientific modes of explanation for such catastrophes as epidemics, droughts, and sudden death, people looked for supernatural causes.

In 1692, the inhabitants of Massachusetts were unusually anxious. They were without an effective government because they had not yet received their new charter. King William's War had just begun, with the French Catholics of Canada and their Algonquian Indian allies raiding the northern and eastern frontiers. Slaves reported that the French were planning to recruit New England's Africans as soldiers. These sources of stress increased underlying tensions, many of which concerned gender. Although men and women both attempted to use magic, the vast majority of those accused of witchcraft were women. Almost 80 percent of the 355 persons officially accused of practicing witchcraft were women, as were an even higher proportion of the 103 persons actually put on trial. Because most of these women had neither sons nor other male heirs, they could control property, which made them an anomaly in Puritan society. By the end of the seventeenth century, local land was an increasingly scarce commodity, and any woman who controlled it could be seen as threatening to the men who wanted it.

In addition, declining opportunity also disrupted the tight Puritan social order. Because land was scarce, it became difficult for young couples to start out. Consequently, the age of marriage increased, and the number of women who were pregnant on their wedding days began to climb, as did the number of women who gave birth without marrying at all. Courts increasingly shifted the burden of child support from fathers to mothers. By the end of the seventeenth century, New Englanders were more inclined than ever to hold women responsible for sin.

Witchcraft at Salem

In this context of strain and anxiety, on February 29, 1692, magistrates John Hathorne and Jonathan Corwin went to Salem to investigate recent accusations of witchcraft. By the time the investigation and trials ended, 156 people had been jailed and 20 executed. As in previous more minor witchcraft scares, most of the accused were women past the age of 40, and most of the accusers were women in their late teens and 20s.

Most of the accused fell into categories that revealed the stresses in Puritan society. Many, like Sarah Good, were the sort of disagreeable women who had always attracted accusations of witchcraft. Others had ties to Quakers or Baptists. Several were suspiciously friendly with the Indians. As a dark-skinned woman from an alien culture, Tituba was also vulnerable. Notably, some of the accusers had been orphaned or displaced by the recent Indian wars, and they described the devil they feared as "a Tawney, or an Indian color." In addition, most of the accusers lived in Salem Village, an economic backwater, whereas most of the accused lived in or had ties to the more prosperous merchant community of Salem Town. The pattern of accusations suggested resentment on a variety of levels.

By late September, accusations were falling on wealthy and well-connected men and women, such as the wife of the governor. Accusers were paraded from town to town to root out local witchcraft, and other people were drawn to Salem like medieval pilgrims. Finally, the leading ministers of Boston, most of whom believed in witchcraft but had been skeptical of the trials, stepped in, and the governor adjourned the court. No one was ever convicted of witchcraft in New England again.

The End of Witchcraft

The epidemic of panic and resentment was eventually brought under control. Although many colonists continued to believe in witchcraft, magic, and the occult, by the end of the seventeenth century they more often believed that the universe was orderly and that events were caused by natural, and knowable, forces. By the eighteenth century, educated people took pride in their rational understanding of nature and disdained a belief in the occult as mere superstition. This change in thinking reflected a new faith not only in human reason but also in the capacity of ordinary people to shape their lives. Increasing numbers of people, especially those who were well educated, prosperous, and lived in cities, believed that they could control their destinies and were not at the mercy of invisible evil forces. The seed of individualism had been planted in New England's rocky soil.

The witchcraft trials ended New England's belief in itself as a covenanted society with a collective future. Because Puritans had believed that God had chosen them for a mission, they read special meaning into every event, from a sudden snowstorm to an Indian attack. By the eighteenth century, however, they began to evaluate events separately, rather than always as part of God's master plan.

Empires in Collision

As late as the middle of the eighteenth century, Native Americans still outnumbered Europeans on the North American continent. At the end of the seventeenth century in the territory that became the United States, Britain was the only European power with a substantial presence (see Map 4–3). The French and Spanish both had mainland outposts north of the Rio Grande, but these nations concentrated their resources on more valuable colonies: for the Spanish, Mexico and Latin America, and for the French, the West

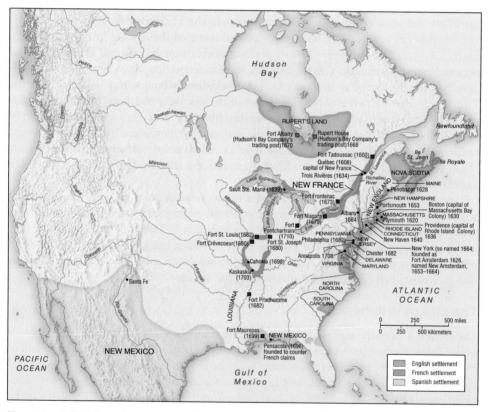

Map 4–3   Colonial North America, East of the Mississippi, 1720 This map shows the expansion of European settlement. English settlement was concentrated in a strip down the East Coast from Maine to North Carolina, with pockets of settlement in Canada and Carolina. French settlements formed a ring along the St. Lawrence River, from the Great Lakes south along the Mississippi, and along the Gulf Coast. The Spanish had outposts along the Gulf and in Florida. *Source:* Adapted from Geoffrey Barraclough, ed., *The Times Concise Atlas of World History* (Maplewood, NJ: Hammond, 1994), p. 67.

Indies. Nonetheless, imperial ambitions brought European powers into conflict in North America, where they jostled against each other and the Native Americans.

France Attempts an Empire

After its civil wars of religion ended early in the seventeenth century, France was free to establish foreign colonies. After 1664, France's minister Jean-Baptiste Colbert tried to formulate a coherent imperial policy, directed from Paris. He envisioned a series of settlements, each contributing to the wealth of the nation through the fur trade and fishing in North America and plantation agriculture in the West Indies. France tried to direct the development of its New World empire, but it could not control small settlements so far away.

Colbert attempted to control every aspect of life in Québec. He subsidized emigration and had female migrants investigated to make sure that they were healthy and morally sound. To encourage reproduction, dowries were offered to all men who married by the age of 20. Agriculture developed and the population grew, more from natural increase than immigration. Colbert's attempt to make Québec a hierarchical society on the Old World model failed, however. First, very few French men and women were willing to settle in Canada. Between 1670 and 1730, perhaps fewer than 3,000 moved to mainland North America (and only a few thousand more to the West Indies). Second, those who did move resisted being controlled from Paris.

Eventually, Native Americans were more successful than Colbert in shaping the fur trade, the mainstay of the Québec economy. The French depended on their Indian trading partners to supply them with furs and serve as military allies. When Indians tried to trade their furs to the British, the French built forts—at considerable cost—to intercept them. French traders smuggled furs to the British in return for British fabrics that the Indians preferred. Moreover, to maintain the allegiance of their Algonquian allies, the French gave them gifts of ammunition, knives, cloth, tobacco, and brandy. When the declining revenues from the fur trade are balanced against all these costs, it is questionable whether Canada was of any economic benefit to France, which maintained the fur trade more for political than for economic reasons.

It was for political reasons that France established outposts in present-day Louisiana and Mississippi, including Fort Biloxi (1699), Fort Toulouse (1717), and New Orleans (1718), all in the territory named Louisiana. (At the same time France built a number of forts in the north—such as Fort Niagara [1720] and Fort St. Frédéric [1731]—to guard against English encroachments.) When the French explorer La Salle reached the mouth of the Mississippi River in 1682 and claimed it for France, the Spanish mainland empire was cut in two, and the British faced a western rival. British traders had pushed into the lower Mississippi region looking for deerskins and Indian slaves. When the French arrived, tribes such as the Choctaws and Mobilians looked to the French for protection from the British and their allies. Within several decades, the French had established trading posts as far north as the Illinois Territory. Farther west, French settlement of the lower Mississippi Valley led to conflict with the Natchez Indians, whom they conquered and sold into slavery.

The early history of the Louisiana Colony resembled that of the British settlement at Jamestown. As in Virginia, the first settlers were ill suited to the venture, top-heavy with military personnel and pirates. Louisiana itself was so unattractive that it could not

The French Settlement at Biloxi The French outpost at Biloxi was moved to higher ground in 1720. Here we see both temporary dwellings, thrown up in haste, and a more permanent storehouse to the left, with the entire settlement a hive of activity.

attract colonists, so France began deporting criminals to the colony. Debilitated by the unhealthful environment, colonists could not even grow their own food. Caught up in wars on the continent, the French did not adequately support the colony, so its survival depended on the generosity of local Indians. After African slaves began to be smuggled into the colony from the Caribbean, in 1719 France permitted the importation of African slaves, but the colony still foundered.

Unlike the Chesapeake, colonial Louisiana never developed a significant cash crop. Because the colony was not important to French economic interests, French mercantilist policies protected Caribbean plantations at the expense of those in Louisiana. Although Louisiana had a slave majority by 1727, it was not a slave society. Louisiana's economy was one of frontier exchange among Europeans, Indians, and Africans, rather than one of commercial agriculture. Marginal to France's empire, Louisiana was largely ignored, and Europeans, Indians, and Africans depended on each other for survival. They intermarried and worked together. As late as 1730, Native Americans still made up more than 90 percent of the population, and social and economic relations remained fluid.

The situation could not have been more different in France's Caribbean empire. There, by the end of the eighteenth century, most of the native population had been killed by disease or war. It was soon replaced by African slaves. By 1670, the islands of Martinique and Guadeloupe were producing significant amounts of sugar with African slave labor. Between 1680 and 1730, 380,000 Africans were imported into those islands and the French colony of Saint-Domingue on the island of Santo Domingo, where they outnumbered Europeans by an astonishing ratio of 7.6 to 1. By the middle of the eighteenth century, Saint-Domingue was producing more sugar than any colony in America and would become the world's greatest producer of coffee. In a few decades, the French West Indies had been transformed into slave societies, in which slavery shaped every aspect of life. They were by far the most valuable part of France's New World empire.

The Spanish Outpost in Florida

Like France's colony at Louisiana, Spain's settlement at St. Augustine, Florida, was intended to be a self-supporting military outpost. Unable to attract settlers and costly to maintain, Florida grew so slowly and unsteadily that the Spanish considered abandoning it and moving the population to the West Indies.

When the British established their colony at Carolina, however, Florida again became important to Spain—and it gained a new source of settlers in runaway slaves. The British and Spanish began fighting, usually using Indian and African surrogates. Spanish raiders seized slaves from Carolina plantations, paid them wages, and introduced them to Catholicism. Soon, as Carolina's governor complained, slaves were "running dayly" to Florida. In 1693, Spain's king offered liberty to all British slaves who escaped to Florida.

The border between the two colonies was violent—and, for Africans, a place of opportunity. Africans gained valuable military experience and, in 1738, about 100 former slaves established the free black town of Gracia Real de Santa Teresa de Mose near St. Augustine. Mose's leader was the Mandinga captain of the free black militia, Francisco Menéndez. A former slave who had been reenslaved, he persisted in petitioning for his freedom. Spain freed Menéndez and other Africans like him and reiterated the policy that British slaves who escaped to Florida should be free. The persistence of Menéndez and the other escaped slaves established the first free black community on the North American continent.

Conquest, Revolt, and Reconquest in New Mexico

In the West, New Mexico developed into a colonial outpost on the far edge of a world empire, irrelevant to Spain's economy or political power. Early in the seventeenth century, the Spanish considered abandoning the settlement, but Franciscan missionaries persuaded Spain to stay so the priests could minister to the Native Americans. In the eastern half of the continent, Indians could play the European powers against each other, but in the West, only Spain was a presence, reducing the Pueblo Indians' leverage. When the Pueblo Indians rose up against the Spanish at the end of the seventeenth century, the survival of New Mexico was in doubt.

Spain had established its colony in New Mexico by conquest. Although Coronado's party had explored the region from Arizona to Kansas (1541–1542), it had not planted a permanent settlement. In 1598, Juan de Oñate was appointed governor and authorized to establish a colony. Like his great-grandfather Cortés, Oñate persuaded some local Pueblos to accept him as their ruler, and others he overcame by force. His harsh means proved effective, and the Spanish soon dominated the entire Southwest. In 1610 they established their capital at Santa Fe, and the colony, called New Mexico, began to grow slowly. The New Mexico Colony was to serve as an outpost against the French, just as St. Augustine was to defend against the English. The most important "business" in the colony was to convert the Pueblo Indians to Catholicism.

Franciscan priests established a series of missions in New Mexico. Although there were never more than 50 or so Franciscans at any time, they claimed to have converted about 80,000 Indians in less than a century. Most of these conversions, however, were in name only. The Indians deeply resented the priests' attempts to change their customs and beliefs. By forcing the Indians to adopt European sex roles and sexual mores, the Franciscans undermined not only Pueblo religion but also their society.

Spanish rule fell harshly on the Pueblos. Although Spanish law forbade enslavement of conquered Indians, some Spanish settlers openly defied it. More common was the *encomienda* system. Oñate rewarded his lieutenants by naming them *encomenderos*, which entitled them to tribute from the Indians living on the land they had been awarded. Some *encomenderos* also demanded labor or personal service. Women working in Spanish households were vulnerable to sexual abuse by their masters. Facing such burdens, the Indian population declined from about 40,000 in 1638 to only 17,000 in 1670.

A combination of Spanish demands for labor and tribute and a long period of drought left the Pueblos without the food surpluses that they had been selling to the nomadic Apaches and Navajos. Those tribes began to raid the Pueblos, taking by force what they could no longer get by trade. Under siege, Pueblos turned once again to their tribal gods and religious leaders.

When the Spanish punished the Indians who returned to their traditional religion, they pushed the Pueblos into revolt. A medicine man named Popé united the leaders of most of the Pueblos, promising that if the Indians threw out the Spanish and prayed again to their ancient gods, food would be plentiful. Indians would never have to work for the Spanish again, he said, and Indian customs would be restored.

The Pueblo at Acoma The Acoma Pueblo sits atop a mesa that rises 400 feet aboveground. In January 1699, Spanish soldiers destroyed the pueblo and killed 800 of its inhabitants, in retaliation for the killing of a dozen soldiers. All the male survivors over the age of 12 and all female survivors were sentenced to 20 years of servitude to the Spanish, and the men over the age of 25 each had a foot cut off as well. The pueblo was rebuilt after its destruction.

Pope's revolt began on August 10, 1680, when the Spanish were low on supplies. First, the Indians seized all horses and mules, immobilizing the Spanish. Next, they blocked the roads to Santa Fe. Then they destroyed all the Spanish settlements, one at a time. At day's end, more than 400 Spanish had been killed. The Pueblos laid siege to Santa Fe, forcing Spanish survivors to retreat to El Paso. In the most successful Indian revolt ever in North America, the Spanish had been driven from New Mexico.

The Pueblos held off the Spanish for 13 years, until the mid-1690s, but the struggles took a heavy toll. Contrary to Pope's promise, the drought continued. Warfare took more lives, and the population continued to drop.

The revolt taught the Spanish lessons. The new Franciscan missionaries were far less zealous than their predecessors. The *encomienda* was not reestablished, and brutal exploitation was less common. Slowly the Spanish colony began rebuilding (see Map 4–4).

The population was divided into four groupings, from a small elite at the top to enslaved Indians at the bottom. The elite, a hereditary aristocracy of 20 or so families, included government officials. They developed codes of honor to distinguish themselves from lower orders. This local nobility prided itself on its racial purity, considering white

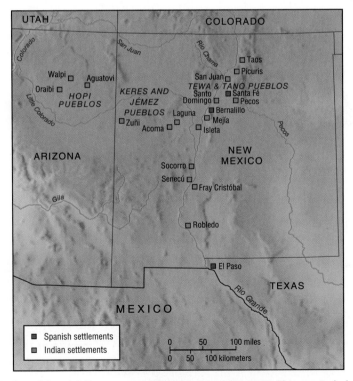

Map 4–4   Region of Spanish Reconquest of New Mexico, 1692–1696 This map includes the pueblos reconquered by the Spanish, as well as Spanish settlements. *Source:* Adapted from Oakah L. Jones Jr., *Pueblo Warriors and Spanish Conquest* (Norman: University of Oklahoma Press, 1966), p. 37.

Eighteenth-Century Spanish Illustrations of New World Racial Mixture In this case, the union of an Indian ("Yndio") and a "Mestiza" produces a "Coyote" child. The Spanish were much more attentive to color distinction than were the English, and they developed a large vocabulary so that they could make these distinctions with great precision.

skin a clear sign of superiority. It scorned those of mixed blood, many of whom, of course, were the illegitimate children of elite Spanish men and the Indian women they coerced. Aristocratic men placed a high value on the personal qualities of courage, honesty, loyalty, and sexual virility. Female honor consisted of extreme modesty and sexual purity.

The second group was landed peasants, most of them *mestizos*, half-Spanish and half-Indian. In this highly color-conscious colonial society, the *mestizos* often prized the Spanish part of their heritage and scorned the Indian. Next came the Pueblo Indians, living in their own communities. The *genízaros*, Indians who had left their own communities by choice or whose ancestors had been enslaved, lived in Spanish settlements. Sometimes these urban immigrants were outcasts, such as women who had been raped

Time Line

▼**1598**
Juan de Oñate colonizes New
   Mexico for Spain

▼**1610**
Santa Fe established

▼**1627**
Barbados settled

▼**1628**
Parliament passes Petition
   of Right

▼**1642–1647**
English Revolution

▼**1649**
King Charles I beheaded

▼**1651–1696**
Navigation Acts passed
   to regulate trade

▼**1652–1674**
Three Anglo-Dutch Wars

▼**1660**
British monarchy restored,
   Charles II crowned king

▼**1662**
Half-Way Covenant

▼**1664**
British seize New Netherland,
   renaming it New York

▼**1665**
New Jersey established

▼**1669**
Fundamental Constitutions
   written for South Carolina

▼**1670**
Carolina settled

▼**1673**
Marquette and Joliet explore
   Mississippi for France

▼**1675–1676**
King Philip's War

▼**1676–1677**
Bacon's Rebellion

▼**1680**
Pueblo Revolt in New Mexico
   reestablishes Indian rule
Westo War, Carolina defeats
   the Westos

by Spanish men. A century after their first conquest, the Pueblo Indians had in some regards begun to adopt the values of their conquerors.

Native Americans and the Country Between

Spain paid little attention to its impoverished outposts in New Mexico, leaving them vulnerable to the Indians to the east. When the French in Louisiana started arming their Comanche, Wichita, and Pawnee trading partners, New Mexicans—Spanish and Pueblos alike—were challenged.

The Indians of the Great Plains, however, profited from the conflict, obtaining guns from the French and horses from the Spanish. After the Pueblo revolt, the Spanish left behind hundreds of horses that Pueblo and Apache Indians passed on to the Plains Indians. By the middle of the eighteenth century, all the Plains Indians were on horseback, which transformed their lives dramatically. They became more effective buffalo hunters, thus making them better fed, clothed, and housed. Their new mobility gave them an increasing sense of freedom, too. But the horses—and the better living conditions they helped make possible—attracted other Indians to the Great Plains. In fact, most of the Indians we now associate with the Great Plains—Sioux, Arapaho, Cheyenne, Blackfoot, Cree—did not arrive there until the eighteenth century.

The result was increased warfare among the Plains Indians, and those with the best access to horses fared the best. For example, the Comanches came to dominate the southern plains, from western Kansas to New Mexico, where they intruded on both the Apaches and the Spanish. The Comanches raided the Apaches, taking not only their horses but also their women and children as captives, some of whom they sold as slaves— *genízaros*—to the Spanish. The Comanches cut the Apaches off from French traders to

▼**1681**
William Penn granted charter for Pennsylvania

▼**1683**
New York's assembly meets for first time

▼**1685**
King Charles II dies and James, Duke of York, becomes King James II

▼**1686**
Massachusetts, Plymouth, Connecticut, Rhode Island, and New Hampshire combined in Dominion of New England; New York and New Jersey added two years later

▼**1688**
Glorious Revolution

▼**1689**
Leisler's Rebellion in New York, Coode's Rebellion in Maryland
William and Mary become King and Queen of Britain; Dominion of New England overthrown

▼**1689–1697**
King William's War

▼**1690**
Publication of John Locke's *Two Treatises of Government*

▼**1691**
Massachusetts made a royal colony
Maryland made a royal colony
New Hampshire made a royal colony

▼**1692**
Salem witchcraft trials

▼**1696**
Reconquest of New Mexico

▼**1702–1713**
Queen Anne's War

▼**1715–1716**
Yamasee War

▼**1718**
French establish settlement at New Orleans

the east. The Apaches in turn moved west and south, bringing them into conflict with the Pueblos and the Spanish. In defense, the Spanish built a string of armed settlements in current-day Texas, but they could not withstand the Comanches, and even the New Mexican settlements were endangered.

Eventually, the new horse-centered way of life took its toll. Although some tribes grew stronger at the expense of others, all suffered from the increasing violence. European diseases proved deadly as well. Under such pressures, gender roles changed. Men sought distinction as warriors, demonstrating success by the number of scalps or captives they seized. Yet so many fell in battle that they were soon outnumbered by women, which led to an increased frequency of polygamy, as surviving warriors took multiple wives. As men's status as warriors and hunters rose, that of women—the agriculturalists—fell.

Conclusion

After a period of considerable instability, by the beginning of the eighteenth century, almost all of the British North American colonies had developed the societies that they would maintain until the American Revolution. For the most part, the colonies were prosperous, with a large white middle class. The efforts to replicate a European hierarchical order had largely failed. Each region had found a secure economic base: farming and shipping in New England, mixed farming in the middle colonies, and single-crop planting in the southern ones. The southern colonies had become slave societies, although slavery was practiced in every colony. For the most part, the colonies had figured out how to control their own populations, whether by affording them increased opportunity and political rights, in the case of Europeans, or by exercising tighter control, in the case of enslaved Africans. These strong economic foundations, when combined with political stability, were the preconditions for the rapid population growth of the eighteenth century, when the British population on the mainland would far surpass that of the French and Spanish colonies. The French and Spanish colonies on the mainland were still little more than frontier outposts, although both nations maintained imperial visions for North America. Native Americans remained a strong presence, but the competition among the European powers—and even the individual colonies—for the loyalty of the Indian tribes, their trade, and their land remained a source of conflict.

Who, What

Review Questions

1. What was Britain's plan of empire? What role were the American colonies supposed to play in it?

2. What effect did political turmoil and the change of leadership in Britain have on the American colonies in the second half of the seventeenth century?

3. Describe Indian-white relations in the American colonies in the second half of the seventeenth century. Why was competition between the colonies an important element?

Critical-Thinking Questions

1. Many of the American colonies experienced a period of political instability in the last quarter of the seventeenth century. In many cases, ranging from the Salem witch trials to Popé's Rebellion of 1680, the sources of the instability appear specific and local, yet they may also reveal a pattern. To what extent were these instances of instability local, and to what extent may they reveal larger processes at work in the colonies of European imperial powers?

2. In this period, a number of colonies became slave societies. What forces propelled these changes? Were different outcomes possible?

3. What patterns, if any, do you see in Native Americans' accommodation and resistance to European expansion in North America in this period?

**For further review materials and resource information,
please visit www.oup.com/us/oakes**

CHAPTER 4: CONTINENTAL EMPIRES, 1660–1720
Primary Sources

4.1 THE NAVIGATION ACT OF 1651

The Navigation Act of 1651 was the first in a series of acts that would number nearly 200 and end with the American revolutionary crisis. The act laid out a system later called *mercantilism,* which ensured a favorable balance of trade for Britain by forcing the colonies to ship certain raw materials to the mother country and pay for manufactured goods of greater value in exchange. This maximized the inflow of specie—gold and silver—for the mother country.

For the increase of the shipping and the encouragement of the navigation of this nation, which under the good providence and protection of God is so great a means of the welfare and safety of this Commonwealth: be it enacted by this present Parliament, and the authority thereof, that from and after the first day of December, one thousand six hundred fifty and one, and from thence forwards, no goods or commodities whatsoever of the growth, production or manufacture of Asia, Africa or America, or of any part thereof; or of any islands belonging to them, or which are described or laid down in the usual maps or cards of those places, as well of the English plantations as others, shall be imported or brought into this Commonwealth of England, or into Ireland, or any other lands, islands, plantations, or territories to this Commonwealth belonging, or in their possession, in any other ship or ships, vessel or vessels whatsoever, but only in such as do truly and without fraud belong only to the people of this Commonwealth, or the plantations thereof, as the proprietors or right owners thereof; and whereof the master and mariners are also for the most part of them of the people of this Commonwealth, under the penalty of the forfeiture and loss of all the goods that shall be imported contrary to this act; as also of the ship (with all her tackle, guns and apparel) in which the said goods or commodities shall be so brought in and imported; the one moiety to the use of the Commonwealth, and the other moiety to the use and behoof of any person or persons who shall seize the goods or commodities, and shall prosecute the same in any court of record within this Commonwealth.

And it is further enacted by the authority aforesaid, that no goods or commodities of the growth, production, or manufacture of Europe, or of any part thereof, shall after the first day of December, one thousand six hundred fifty and one, be imported or brought into this Commonwealth of England, or into Ireland, or any other lands, islands, plantations or territories to this Commonwealth belonging, or in their possession, in any ship or ships, vessel or vessels whatsoever, but in such as do truly and without fraud belong only to the people of this Commonwealth, as the true owners and proprietors thereof, and in no other, except only such foreign ships and vessels as do truly and properly belong to the people of that country or place, of which the said goods are the growth, production or manufacture; or to such ports where the said goods can only be, or most usually are first shipped for transportation; and that under the same penalty of forfeiture and loss expressed in the former branch of this Act, the said forfeitures to be recovered and employed as is therein expressed.

And it is further enacted by the authority aforesaid, that no goods or commodities that are of foreign growth, production or manufacture, and which are to be brought into this Commonwealth in shipping belonging to the people thereof, shall be by them shipped or brought from any other place or places, country or countries, but only from those of their said growth, production, or manufacture, or from those ports where the said goods and commodities can only, or are, or usually have been first shipped for transportation; and from none other places or countries, under the same penalty of forfeiture and loss expressed in the first branch of this Act, the said forfeitures to be recovered and employed as is therein expressed.

Source: "The Navigation Act, Ordinance of 1651, October 9th, 1651," in *American History Leaflets: Colonial and Constitutional. Number 19, Extracts from the Navigation Acts 1645–1696,* edited by Albert Bushnell Hart and Edward Channing (New York: A. Lovell and Company, 1895), pp. 6–7.

4.2 LETTER FROM WILLIAM PENN TO HIS BACKERS (1683)

William Penn was the son of a wealthy English admiral. As a young man, he converted to the Quaker faith and suffered imprisonments. In 1682, the King paid a debt to Penn's father by giving him lands in the New World, and the younger Penn immediately set off to govern them, founding "Pennsylvania" that same year. In 1683, after touring the lands and meeting with the Lenni Lenape, or Delaware Indians, he wrote a letter describing his experiences with them to his backers in London. That same year, a printed version was published. In 1684, Penn returned to England but went back to Pennsylvania for an extended stay from 1699 to 1701.

August 6, 1683

. . . Every King hath his Council, and that consists of all the Old and Wise men of his Nation, which perhaps is two hundred People: nothing of Moment Is undertaken, be it War, Peace, Selling of Land or Traffick, without advising with them; and which is more, with the Young Men too. 'Tis admirable to consider, how Powerful the Kings are, and yet how they move by the Breath of their People.

I have had occasion to be in Council with them upon Treaties for Land, and to adjust the terms of Trade; their Order is thus: The King sits in the middle of an half Moon, and hath his Council, the Old and Wise on each hand; behind them, or at a little distance, sit the younger Fry, in the same figure. Having consulted and resolved their business, the King ordered one of them to speak to me; he stood up, came to me, and In the Name of his King saluted me, then took me by the hand, and told me, That he was ordered by his King to speak to me, and that now it was not he, but the King that spoke, because what he should say, was the King's mind. He first pray'd me, To excuse them that they had not yet complied with me the last tie; he feared, there might be some fault in the Interpreter, being neither Indian nor English; besides, it was the Indian Custom to deliberate, and take up much time in Council, before they resolve; and that If the Young People and Owners of the Land had been ready as he, I had not met with so much delay. Having thus introduced his matter, he fell to the Bounds of the Land they had agreed to dispose of, and the Price (which now is little and dear, that which would have bought twenty Miles, not buying now two). During their time that this Person spoke, not a man of them was observed to whisper or smile; the Old, Grave, the Young, Reverend In the Deportment; they do speak little, but fervently, and with Elegancy: I have never seen more natural Sagacity, considering them without the help (I was agoing to say, the spoil) of Tradition; and he will deserve the Name of Wise, that Outwits them in any Treaty about a thing they understand.

When the Purhase was agreed, great Promises past between us of Kindness and good Neighbourhood, and that the Indians and English must live In Love, as long as the Sun gave light. Which done, another made a Speech to the Indians, in the Name of all the Sachamakers or Kings, first to tell them what was done; next, to charge and command them, To Love the Christians, and particularly live In Peace with me, and the People under my Governement:

That many Governors had been in the River, but that no Gouvernour [sic] had come himself to live and stay here before; and having now such a one that had treated them well, they should never do him or his any wrong. At every sentence of which they shouted, and said, Amen, In their way.[1]

The Justice they have Is Pecuniary: In case of any Wrong or evil Fact, be it Murther itself, they Attone by Feasts and Presents of their Wampum, which Is propositioned to the quality of the Offence or Person Injured, or of the Sex they are of: for in case they kill a Woman, they pay double, and the Reason they render is, That she breedeth Children, which men cannot do. 'Tis rare that they fall out, if Sober; and if Drunk, they forgive It, saying, It was the Drink, and not the Man, that abused them.

We have agreed, that in all Differences between us, Six of each side shall end the matter: Don't abuse them, but let them have Justice, and you win them: The worst Is, that they are the worse for the Christians, who have propagated their Vices, and yielded them Tradition for ill, and not for good things, but as low an Ebb as they're at, and as glorious as the Condition looks, the Christians have not out-liv'd their sight with all their Pretensions to an higher Manifesta-tion: What good then might not a good People graft, where there is so distinct a Knowledge left between Good and Evil? I beseech God to incline the Hearts of all that come into these parts, to out-live the Knowledge of the Natives, but a fixt Obedience to their greater Knowledge of the Will of God; for it were miserable indeed for us to fall under the just censure of the poor Indian Conscience, while we make profession of things so far transcending.

Source: Albert Book Myers, ed., *William Penn's Own Account of the Lenni Lenape or Delaware Indians* (Somerset, NJ: Middle Atlantic Press, 1970 [1683]), pp. 36–41.

4.3 MARY ROWLANDSON, EXCERPTS FROM *THE SOVEREIGNTY AND GOODNESS OF GOD* (1682)

In 1675 and 1676 a brutal war was waged between the Massachusetts colonists and the New England Indians. Initially, the Indians scored some major victories, but they did not have permanent access to food, ammunition, and new recruits as the colonists did. During the war, Mary Rowlandson, a clergyman's wife and mother of four, was kid-napped along with several of her children from Lancaster, Massachusetts, and experi-enced, together with her captors, the hunger that plagued the Indians as they retreated.

My Child being even ready to depart this sorrowful world, they bade me carry it out to another Wigwam (I suppose because they would not be troubled with such spectacles) Whither I went with a very heavy heart, and down I sat with the picture of death in my lap. About two houres in the night, my sweet Babe, like a lamb departed this life, on *Feb. 18. 1675*, it being about six years and five months old. . . . I cannot but take notice, how at another time I could not bear to be in the room where any dead person was, but now the case [was] changed; I must and could ly down by my dead Babe, side by side all the night after. I have thought since of the wonderfull goodness of God to me, in preserving me in the use of my reason and senses, in that distressed time, that I did not use wicked and violent means to end my own miserable life. In the morning . . . I went to take up my dead child in my arms to carry it with me, but they bid me let it alone: there was no resisting, but goe I must and leave it. . . . I took the first opportunity I could get, to go look after my dead child: when I came I askt them what they had done with it? Then they told me it

---

[1]This paragraph was not in the original letter. Penn did not actually stay for many years, but he hoped to.

was upon the hill: then they went and shewed me where it was, where I saw the ground was newly digged, and there they told me they had buried it. *There I left that Child in the Wilderness, and must commit it, and my self also in this Wilderness-condition, to him who is above all.* God having taken away this dear Child, I went to see my daughter *Mary*, who was [for a while] at this same *Indian Town*, at a *Wigwam* not very far off, though we had little liberty or opportunity to see one another; she was about ten years old. . . . When I came in sight, she would fall a weeping; at which they were provoked, and would not let me come near her, but bade me be gone; which was a heart-cutting word to me. I had one Child dead, another in the Wilderness, I knew not where, the third they would not let me come near to. . . .

[two weeks later]

On the Saturday, they boyled an old Horses leg which they had got, and so we drank of the broth, as soon as they thought it was ready . . . The first week of my being among them, I hardly ate anything; the second week, I found my stomach grow very faint for want of something; and yet it was very hard to get down their filthy trash: but the third week, though I could think how formerly my stomach would turn against this or that, and I could starve or die before I could eat such things, yet they were sweet and savory to my taste. . . . And here I cannot but take notice of the strange providence of God in preserving the heathen: They were many hundreds, old and young, some sick, and some lame, many had *Papooses* at their backs, the greatest number at this time with us, were *Squaws*, and they traveled with all they had, bag and baggage, and yet they got over the River; and on *Munday*, they set their *Wigwams* on fire, and away they went: On that very same day came the English Army after them to this River, and saw the smoak of their Wigwams, and yet this River put a stop to them . . .

On *Munday* (as I said), they set their *Wigwams* on fire, and went away. It was a cold morning, and before us there was a great Brook with ice on it; some waded through it, up to the knees & higher, but others went till they came to a Beaver dam, and I amongst them, where through the good providence of God, I did not wet my foot.[2] I went along that day mourning and lamenting, leaving farther my own Country, and traveling into the vast and howling Wilderness, and I understood something of Lot's Wife's[3] Temptations, when she looked back: We came that day to a great Swamp, by the side of which we took up our lodging that night. When I came to the brow of the hill, that looked toward the Swamp, I thought we had been come to a great Indian Town (though there were none but our own Company). The Indians were as thick as the trees; it seemed as if there had been a thousand Hatchets going at once: if one looked before one, there was nothing but Indians, and behind one, nothing but Indians, and so on either hand, I myself in the midst, and no Christian soul near me. . . .

On the morrow morning we must go over the River, i.e. Connecticot, to meet with King *Philip*, two *Cannoos* full, they had carried over, the next Turn I myself was to go; but as my foot was upon the *Cannoo* to stop in, there was a sudden out-cry among them, and I must step back; and instead of going over the River, I must go four or five miles up the River farther Northward. Some of the *Indians* ran one way, and some another. The cause of this rout was, as I thought, their espying some *English Scouts*, who were thereabout. In this travel up the river, about noon the Company made a stop, and sat down; some to eat, and others to rest them. As I sate amongst them, musing of things past, my son *Joseph* unexpectedly came to me: we asked of each others welfare, bemoaning our dolefull condition, and the change that had come upon us. . . . I asked him whither he would read; he told me, he earnestly desired it. I gave him my Bible,[4] and he lighted upon that comfortable scripture, Psal. 118.17, 18. *I shall not dye but live,*

---

[2]Whether or not Rowlandson got wet in making the crossings became extremely important to her as the cold was almost unendurable when she was soaked.

[3]Lot's wife was warned not to look back or she would be turned to a pillar of salt. See Genesis 19:26.

[4]Rowlandson had not been able to leave carrying anything except her child, but an Indian had later given her a Bible taken in the spoils of battle.

and declare the works of the Lord: the Lord hath chastened me sore, yet he hath not given me over to death. Look here, Mother (sayes he), did you read this? . . . We traveled on till night; and in the morning, we must go over the River to *Philip's* crew. When I was in the Cannoo, I could not but be amazed at the numerous crew of Pagans that were on the Bank on the other side. When I came ashore, they gathered all about me, I sitting alone in the midst: I observed they asked one another questions, and laughed, and rejoyced over their Gains and Victories. Then my heart began to fail: and I fell a weeping which was the first time to my remembrance that I wept before them. Although I had met with so much Affliction, and my heart was many times ready to break, yet could I not shed one tear in their sight: but rather had been all this while in a maze [that is, amazed, stunned], like one astonished: but now I may say as Psal. 137.1 *By the rivers of Babylon, there we sat down: yea, we wept when we remembered Zion.* There one of them asked me, why I wept, I could hardly tell what to say: yet I answered, they would kill me: No, said he, none will hurt you. Then came one of them and gave me two spoon-fulls of Meal to comfort me, and another gave me half a pint of Pease; which was more worth than many Bushels at another time.[5] Then I went to see King *Philip*, he bade me come in and sit down, and asked me whether I would smoke . . .

Source: Mary Rowlandson, *The Sovereignty and Goodness of God, Together with the Faithfulness of His Promises Displayed* (Cambridge, MA: Samuel Green, 1682).

4.4 DECLARATION OF A PUEBLO INDIAN CAPTURED BY THE SPANIARDS (1680)

The Spanish had been a strong presence in New Mexico since 1598. In 1680, a rebellion broke out that was so successful for the Pueblo Indians that the surviving Spanish were forced to flee and were unable to retake the territory for a full 12 years. The leaders of the rebellion were well organized, orchestrating the timing across a wide region, and the movement had broad popular support. In the midst of the uprising, the Spanish sent out military parties in a desperate attempt to gather useful information and save Spanish sites. Their agenda essentially failed, but the Spanish did manage to capture some Indians for questioning.

In the place of El Alamillo, jurisdiction of El Socorro, on the 6th day of the month of September, 1680, for the prosecution of this case, and so that an Indian who was captured on the road as the camp was marching may be examined, in order to ascertain the plans, designs, and motives of the rebellious enemy, his lordship, the señor-gobernador and captain-general, caused the said Indian to appear before him. He received the oath from him in due legal form, in the name of God, our Lord, and on a sign of the cross, under charge of which he promised to tell the truth concerning what he might know and as he might be questioned. Having been asked his name and of what place he is a native, his condition, and age, he said that his name is Don Pedro Nanboa,[6] that he is a native of the pueblo of Alameda, a widower, and somewhat more than eighty years of age. Asked for what reason the Indians of this kingdom have rebelled, forsaking their obedience to his Majesty and failing in their obligation as Christians, he said that for a long time, because the Spaniards punished sorcerers and idolaters, the nations of the Teguas, Tao, Pecuríes, Pecos and Jemez had been plotting to rebel and kill the Spaniards

---

[5] It was worth so much because the company was starving.

[6] The use of the title "don" by a native man in this period indicates that he was of high or noble status within his own community.

and the religious [Franciscans], and that they had been planning constantly to carry it out, down to the present occasion. Asked what he learned, saw and heard in the juntas and parleys that the Indians have held, what they have plotted among themselves, and why the Indians have burned the church and profaned the images of the pueblo of Sandia, he said that he has not taken part in any junta, nor has he harmed any one; that what he has heard is that the Indians do not want religious [friars] or Spaniards. Because he is so old he was in the cornfield[7] when he learned from the Indian rebels who came from the sierra that they had killed the Spaniards of the jurisdiction and robbed all their haciendas, sacking their houses. Asked whether he knows about the Spaniards and religious who were gathered in the pueblo of La Isleta, he said that it is true that some days ago there assembled in the said pueblo of La Isleta the religious of Sandia, Jemez, and Zia, and that they set out to leave the kingdom with those of the said pueblo of La Isleta and the Spaniards—not one of whom remained—taking along their property. The Indians did not fight with them because all the men had gone with the other nations to fight at the villa [in the capital] and destroy the governor and captain-general and all the people who were with him. He declared that the resentment which all the Indians have in their hearts has been so strong, from the time this kingdom was discovered, because the religious and the Spaniards took away their idols and forbade their sorceries and idolatries; that they have inherited successively from their old men the things pertaining to their ancient customs; and that he has heard this resentment spoken of since he was of an age to understand. What he has said is the truth and what he knows, under the oath taken, and he signs and ratifies it, it being read and explained to him in his language through the interpretation of Captain Sebastián Montaño, who signed it with his lordship, as the said Indian does not know how, before me, the present secretary. Antonio de Otermín, (rubric); Sebastián Montaño (rubric); Juan Lucero de Godoy (rubric); Luis de Quintana (rubric). Before me, Francisco Xavier, secretary of government and war (rubric).

Source: "Declaration of one of the rebellious Christian Indians who was captured on the road. El Alamillo, September 6, 1680." In Charles Wilson Hackett, ed., *Revolt of the Pueblo Indians of New Mexico and Otermín's Attempted Reconquest, 1680–1682* (Albuquerque: University of New Mexico Press, 1942), pp. 60–62.

4.5 ROBERT CALEF, EXCERPTS FROM *MORE WONDERS OF THE INVISIBLE WORLD* (1700)

As the witch hunts of 1692 unfolded in the colony of Massachusetts, many residents looked on in horror. Some colonists later wrote about the experience, while some collected other people's testimonies regarding the events that occurred in the ensuing months and years. Robert Calef, a Boston merchant, sent an extensive manuscript back to London in 1697. When it was published in 1700, Puritan minister Increase Mather had copies burned in Harvard Yard.

May 24, 1692. Mrs. Cary of Charlestown [Massachusetts], was examined and committed. Her husband Mr. Nathaniel Cary has given account thereof, as also of her escape, to this effect,

I having heard [for] some days, that my wife was accused of witchcraft, being much disturbed at it, by advice, we went to Salem Village, to see if the afflicted did know her; we arrived there, 24 May, it happened to be a day appointed for examination; accordingly soon after our

---

[7]Don Pedro meant that because of his advanced age, he had been left to till the fields rather than invited to join the war party.

[8]Those accused of witchcraft were jeered at, yelled at.

arrival, Mr. Hathorne and Mr. Corwin, etc., went to the meeting house, which was the place appointed for that work, the minister began with prayer, and having taken care to get a convenient place, I observed, that the afflicted were two girls of about ten years old, and about two or three others, of about eighteen. One of the girls talked most, and could discern more than the rest. The prisoners were cavalled in one by one, and as they came in were cried out of,[8] etc. The prisoner was placed about 7 or 8 foot from the justices, and the accusers between the justices and them; the prisoner was ordered to stand right before the justices, with an officer appointed to hold each hand, lest they should therewith afflict them, and the prisoner's eyes must be constantly on the justices; for if they looked on the afflicted, they would either fall into their fits, or cry out of being hurt by them; after examination of the prisoners, who it was afflicted these girls, etc., they were put upon saying the Lord's prayer, as a trial of their guilt; after the afflicted seemed to be out of their fits, they would look steadfastly on some one person, and frequently not speak; and then the justices said they were struck dumb, and after a little time would speak again; then the justices said to the accusers, "which of you will go and touch the prisoner at the bar?" then the most courageous would adventure, but before they had made three steps would ordinarily fall down as in a fit; the justices ordered that they should be taken up and carried to the prisoner, that she might touch them; and as soon as they were touched by the accused, the justices would say, they are well, before I could discern any alteration; by which I observed that the justices understood the manner of it. Thus far I was only as a spectator, my wife also was there part of the time, but no notice taken of her by the afflicted, except once or twice they came to her and asked her name.

But I having an opportunity to discourse [with] Mr. Hale (with whom I had formerly an acquaintance) I took his advice, what I had best to do, and desired of him that I might have an opportunity to speak with her that accused my wife; which he promised should be, I acquainting him that I reposed my trust In him.

Accordingly he came to me after the examination was over, and told me I had now an opportunity to speak with the said accuser, viz. Abigail Williams, a girl of 11 or 12 years old; but that we could not be in private at Mr. Parris's house, as he had promised me; we went therefore into the alehouse, where an Indian man attended us, who it seems was one of the afflicted: to him we gave some cider, he showed several scars, that seemed as if they had been long there, and showed them as done by witchcraft, and acquainted us that his wife, who also was a slave, was imprisoned for witchcraft. And now Instead of one accuser, they all came in, who began to tumble down like swine, and then three women were called in to attend them. We in the room were all at a stand, to see who they would cry out of; but in a short time they cried out, Cary; and Immediately after a warrant was sent from the justices to bring my wife before them, who were sitting in a chamber nearby, waiting for this.

Being brought before the justices, her chief accusers were two girls; my wife declared to the justices, that she never had any knowledge of them before that day; she was forced to stand with her arms stretched out. I did request that I might hold one of her hands, but it was denied me; then she desired me to wipe the tears from her eyes, and the sweat from her face, which I did; then she desired she might lean herself on me, saying, she should faint.

Justice Hathorne replied, she had strength enough to torment those persons, and she should have strength enough to stand. I speaking something against their cruel proceedings, they commanded me to be silent, or else I should be turned out of the room. The Indian before mentioned, was also brought in, to be one of her accusers; being come In, he now (when before the justices) fell down and tumbled about like a hog, but said nothing. The justices asked the girls, who afflicted the Indian? They answered she (meaning my wife) and now lay upon him; the justices ordered her to touch him, In order to his cure, but her head must be turned another way, lest instead of curing, she should make him worse, by her looking on him, her hand being guided to take hold of his; but the Indian took hold on her hand, and pulled her down on the floor, In a barbarous manner; then his hand was taken off, and her hand put on his, and the cure was quickly wrought. I being extremely troubled at their inhumane dealings, uttered a hasty speech (that God would take vengeance on them, and desired that God would deliver us out of the hands of unmerciful men). Then her Mittimus was writ. I did with difficulty and charge obtain the liberty of a room, but no beds In It; if there had [been], [she] could have taken but little rest that night. She was committed to Boston prison; but I obtained a habeas corpus to remove her to Cambridge prison, which is in our County of Middlesex. Having been there one night, next morning the jailer put Irons on her legs (having received such command) the weight of them was about eight pounds; these irons and her other afflictions, soon brought her into convulsion fits, so that I thought she would have died that night. I sent to entreat that the irons might be taken off, but all entreaties were in vain, if it would have saved her life, so that in this condition she must continue. The trials at Salem coming on, I went thither, to see how things were there managed; and finding that the spectre evidence was there received, together with Idle if not malicious stories, against people's lives, I did easily perceive which way the rest would go; for the same evidence that served for one, would serve for all the rest. I acquainted her with her danger; and that if she were carried to Salem to be tried, I feared she would never return. I did my utmost that she might have her trial in our own county, I with several others petitioning the judge for it, and were put in hopes of it; but I soon saw so much, that I understood thereby it was not intended, which put me upon consulting the means of her escape; which through the goodness of God was effected, and she got to Rhode Island, but soon found herself not safe when there, by reason of the pursuit after her; from thence she went to New York, along with some others that had escaped their cruel hands; where we found his Excellency Benjamin Fletcher, Esqu., governor, who was very courteous to us. After this some of my goods were seized In a friend's hands, with whom I had left them, and myself Imprisoned by the sheriff, and kept in custody half a day, and then dismissed; but to speak of their usage of the prisoners, and their Inhumanity shown to them, at the time of their execution, no sober Christian could bear; they had also trials of cruel mockings; which is the more, considering what a people for religion, I mean the profession of it, we have been; those that suffered being many of them church members, and most of them unspotted In their conversation, till their adversary the devil took up this method for accusing them.

Source: Robert Calef, *More Wonders of the Invisible World* (London, 1700), as found in Frances Hill, ed., *The Salem Witch Trials Reader* (New York: Da Capo Press, 2000), pp. 68–71.

1. Hon.ble Peter Manigault

2. Taylor, an Officer

Mr. Peter Manigault and his Friends,

The Eighteenth-Century World

1700–1775

‡ Isaac God
ytmore, an

AMERICAN PORTRAIT

George Whitefield:
Evangelist for a Consumer Society

In 1740 there were no more than 16,000 people living in Boston, yet on October 12, some 20,000 people filled the Common to hear an English minister preach. Everywhere he went, the crowds were unprecedented—8,000 in Philadelphia, 3,000 in the little Pennsylvania village of Neshaminy. Those who could not see the evangelist in person read about him in the newspapers. If there was one binding experience for the American people in the decades before the Revolution, it was George Whitefield's ministry.

Born in Bristol, England, in 1714, George Whitefield would become not only a leading preacher of the Great Awakening of religion in the American colonies but also one of the most influential preachers in the history of Christianity. Because of the growth of the market economy, men and women on both sides of the Atlantic could now participate in a consumer culture that offered many ways to spend money and leisure time. To those schooled in a traditional Calvinist religion, the consumer society was both attractive and frightening. Could one serve God and oneself at the same time?

At 17, when Whitefield discovered he had no aptitude for trade, the career he had chosen, the boy from a poor family faced a personal crisis. One morning, he blurted out, "God intends something for me which we know not of." Whitefield then prepared for the ministry. He enrolled at Oxford University, paying his way by working as a servant to wealthy students. He became friendly with the Methodists, a group of religious young men planning a mission to the new colony of Georgia. Under their influence, Whitefield turned his back on consumer culture. "Whatsoever I did," Whitefield explained, "I endeavoured to do all to the glory of God." Whitefield was determined to share what he had learned with all who would hear.

Whitefield helped create a mass public that broke down the boundaries of small communities in which each minister or priest had typically addressed only his own congregation. The crowds Whitefield drew were often so large that he preached outdoors, with a voice so loud that Benjamin Franklin calculated that it could be heard by 25,000 people at a time. Although Whitefield spoke directly to the heart of each individual, he also drew together entire communities in a way no one had ever done before.

Whitefield embodied the great contradictions of his age without threatening the political or economic order that sustained them. He appealed to men as well as women, to the poor as well as the rich, to slaves as well as their masters, and to those who were suffering from capitalism as well as those who were benefiting from it. Whitefield's strategy was to criticize the individual without attacking the system. In Philadelphia, he preached, "Do not say, you are miserable, and poor, and blind and naked, and therefore ashamed to come, for it is to such that this Invitation is now sent. The Polite, the Rich, the Busy, Self-Righteous Pharisees of this Generation have been bidden already, but they . . . are too deeply engaged in going one to his Country House, another to his Merchandize."

He censured the religious leadership, but not the church itself. Cruel slave masters were condemned, but not the institution of slavery. He showed people how to acquire the self-discipline that would enable them either to succeed in a competitive market or to bear failures with Christian resignation. He helped them experience religion as an intense personal feeling and find meaning in a time of rapid economic transformation.

A world traveler who called Georgia his home, Whitefield died in Newburyport, Massachusetts, in 1770, preaching to the end. Five years later, a band of Continental army officers dug up his corpse. The body had decayed, but his clothing was still intact. The soldiers snipped pieces of it to take with them as protection.

The Population Explosion of the Eighteenth Century

George Whitefield could speak to the hearts of the American colonists because he understood their world. As the colonies matured, they were tied in to the North Atlantic world and brought dramatic changes. One of the most important changes was the increase in population, from both immigration and natural increase. This population produced products for the world economy and provided a market for them as well, and its boom was both the product of American prosperity and the precondition for its further growth.

The Dimensions of Population Growth

The population in the American colonies grew at a rate unprecedented in human history, from just over 250,000 people in 1700 to more than 1 million by 1750. The rate of growth was highest in the free population in prosperous farming regions, but it was rapid everywhere, even among slaves.

Much of the colonies' population growth was caused by their unquenchable thirst for labor. They attracted an extraordinary number of immigrants, and when free labor did not meet the demand, unfree labor (slaves, indentured servants, and redemptioners) filled the gap. Increasingly, these immigrants reflected the broad reach of the North Atlantic political world. At the beginning of the eighteenth century, the population of the American colonies was primarily English in origin. By the beginning of the American Revolution, the population had changed significantly. There were small numbers of people with Finnish, Swedish, French, Swiss, and Jewish heritage, and large numbers of Welsh, Scotch-Irish, Germans, Dutch, and Africans. The foundation for American diversity had been laid.

Bound for America: European Immigrants

In the eighteenth century, about 425,000 Europeans migrated to the colonies, with large numbers from Scotland, Ireland, Wales, and Germany. The largest numbers of European immigrants were Scotch-Irish, that is, Scottish people who had moved to Northern Ireland to escape famine in their own country. As many as 250,000 came to seek a better life and to escape the religious persecution they experienced as Presbyterians in an Anglican society. At first, Massachusetts invited the Scotch-Irish to settle on its borders, as a buffer between the colony and the Indians. Once the impoverished Scotch-Irish began to arrive in large numbers, however, the English inhabitants worried that they would have to provide for them. In 1729 a Boston mob turned away a shipload of Scotch-Irish immigrants, and in 1738 the Puritans of Worcester burned down a Presbyterian church. Thereafter, the vast majority of Scotch-Irish immigrants headed for the more welcoming middle colonies and the South.

Going where land was the cheapest, the Scotch-Irish settled between the English seaboard settlements and the Indian communities to the west, from Pennsylvania to Georgia (see Map 5–1). As their numbers increased, the Scotch-Irish pressed against the Indians,

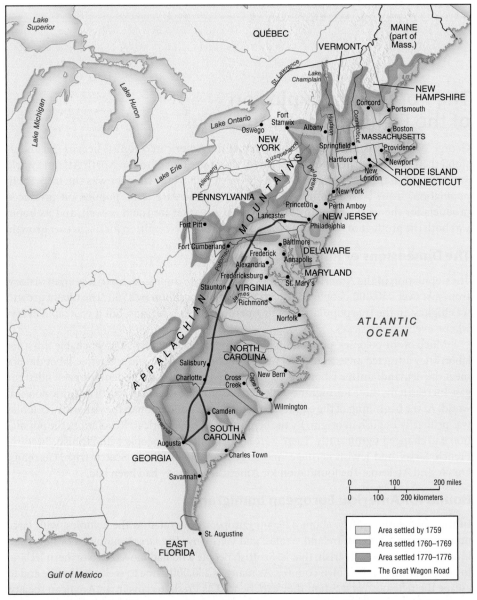

Map 5–1   Expansion of Settlement, 1720–1760 By 1760, the colonial population made up an almost continuous line of settlement from Maine to Florida and was pushing west over the Appalachian Mountains.

seizing their lands. Like the Scotch-Irish, most German migrants settled in the backcountry from Pennsylvania to the Carolinas. Between 1700 and the start of the Revolution, more than 100,000 Germans arrived, and by 1775, a third of Pennsylvania's population was German. Including not only Lutherans and Catholics but also Quakers, Amish, and Mennonites, Germans established prosperous farming communities wherever they settled. Indeed, colonies such as Pennsylvania that welcomed the widest variety of immigrants became not only the most prosperous but also the ones in which prosperity was most widely shared. Unlike most seventeenth-century migrants, a large proportion of eighteenth-century migrants were artisans drawn to America by the demand for their labor. The majority of European migrants to the colonies were unfree—not only indentured servants and redemptioners but also the 50,000 British convicts whose sentences were commuted to a term of service in the colonies. Most English and Welsh migrants were single men between the ages of 19 and 23 who came as indentured servants. The Scotch-Irish migration included a larger number of families, and three-fourths of the Germans came in family groups. For all, the passage to America, which could take three months or more, was grueling and profoundly unhealthy. Once the migrants arrived, servants and convicts were sold for terms of service at auctions (see Figure 5–1).

Bound for America: African Slaves

The increase in the African population was even more dramatic than that of Europeans. In 1660 there were only 2,920 African or African-descended inhabitants of the mainland

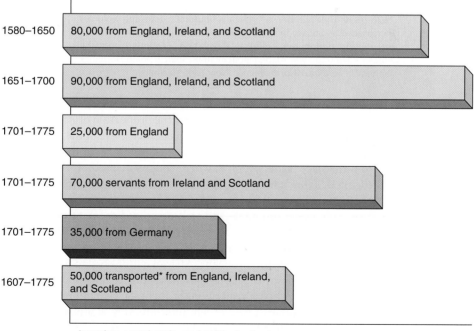

1580–1650   80,000 from England, Ireland, and Scotland

1651–1700   90,000 from England, Ireland, and Scotland

1701–1775   25,000 from England

1701–1775   70,000 servants from Ireland and Scotland

1701–1775   35,000 from Germany

1607–1775   50,000 transported* from England, Ireland, and Scotland

*convicts, vagabonds, and political prisoners

Figure 5–1   The Importation of Servants from Europe into British America, 1580–1775 By the time of the American Revolution, 350,000 servants had been imported into the colonies, most of whom came from the British Isles. *Source:* Richard S. Dunn, "Servants and Slaves," in Jack P. Greene and J. R. Pole, *Colonial British America* (Baltimore: Johns Hopkins, 1984), p. 159.

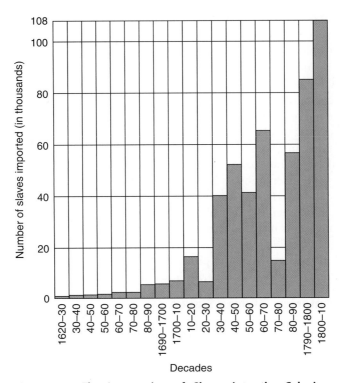

Figure 5–2 The Importation of Slaves into the Colonies, 1620–1810 The number of Africans imported into the colonies increased dramatically in the eighteenth century, and, except for an interruption during the American Revolution, continued until the African slave trade was made illegal in 1808. *Source:* Helen Hornbeck Tanner, *The Settling of North America* (New York: Macmillan, 1995), p. 51.

colonies. A century later there were more than 300,000. The proportion of Africans grew most rapidly in the southern colonies, to almost 40 percent on the eve of the Revolution. By 1720 South Carolina had an African majority. Most of the increase in the African population came from the slave trade. By 1808, when Congress closed off the importation of slaves to the United States, about 523,000 African slaves had been imported into the nation (see Figure 5–2).

The African slave trade was a profitable and well-organized segment of the world economy. Until the eighteenth century, when demand from the New World increased, the transatlantic slave trade was controlled by Africans, in the sense that slaves were brought to the coast by other Africans for sale to Europeans. African nations had to participate in this activity because it was the only way they could purchase guns, and without guns, they were vulnerable to neighbors who had already bought them. Some nations supplied a steady stream of slaves, whereas others offered them intermittently, stopping when they had enough arms to defend themselves for a while. Most slaves were captives of war, and as the demand for slaves increased, the tempo of warfare in Africa intensified in response. The New World preferred male slaves, leaving most of the female captives to the African slave market, where they became domestic slaves or plural wives to wealthier Africans.

The Slave Ship

We do not usually think of a ship as part of a landscape, but the slave ship was one of the most important places in the eighteenth century. It was at once a floating factory, prison, and fortress. It was there that Africans were transformed into slaves.

Any ship, small or large, could be made into a slave ship. Because the cost of transporting slaves across the Atlantic was so high, accounting for three-quarters of the price of a slave, slave merchants tried to crowd as many Africans as possible into each ship—300, 400, or even 600. The English were particularly efficient, carrying twice as many slaves as crew members and half again as many slaves per ship as the other nations, thereby increasing the profits.

To maximize the number of Africans on each ship, platforms were built between decks, thus doubling the surface area upon which the slaves could be placed. With perhaps only four and a half feet between the platform and the ceiling, the Africans could not stand up. They were packed so tightly that they could not move from side to side. Even the smallest spaces were filled with children.

Packing so many human beings into such tight quarters created the risk of suffocation. But if the hatches were kept open, the Africans might escape confinement and overpower the crew. Hence, grates were placed over the hatches, and small air openings were cut into the sides of the ship. Later, some ships used large funnel tubes to carry air below decks.

Men and women were kept separate, divided by partitions. Male slaves were shackled and confined below deck for most of each day. Chained together and without enough room to stand up, many were unable to reach the large buckets that served as latrines. Some captains let the slaves lie in their own filth until the voyage's end. Heat and disease compounded the misery. One ship's doctor reported that the slaves' deck "was so covered with the blood and mucus which had proceeded from them in consequence of the flux, that it resembled a slaughterhouse." The women were left unshackled but were often prey to the sailors' lust. When slaves were brought above deck, some would jump overboard. Captains stretched netting around their ships to prevent such suicides.

To protect the crew in case of insurrection, slave ships often had thick, 10-foot-high walls—barricados—to separate the crew from the human cargo. Armed sailors patrolled atop the barricado. Ship captains gathered their human cargo from different regions, each with its own language, to make sure that the captives could not communicate with each other and foment rebellion. At the same time, the captains had to be careful not to bring together groups who might fight each other. With resistance from the enslaved the norm, ship captains used terror to maintain order. Flogging—a punishment for sailors as well—was common. Some captains used instruments of torture, such as the thumbscrew, "a dreadful engine, which, if the screw be turned by an unrelenting hand, can give intolerable anguish." The object was not only to punish the disobedient but also to

continued

AMERICAN LANDSCAPE *continued*

frighten their shipmates. That was surely the result after some of the Africans aboard the *Brownlow* rebelled. The captain dismembered the rebels with an axe "till their bodies remained only like a trunk of a tree when all the branches are lopped away," and he threw the severed heads and limbs at the other slaves, chained together on the deck.

Such terror hardened captain and crew. Few sailors signed on to a slave ship if they had better options, and one captain described his crew as the "very dregs of the community." The life of a sailor was hard enough; service on a slave ship—a floating prison—was even harder. Yet even the lowest sailor was superior to the enslaved. Even though many sailors were dark-skinned men from Asia, the Caribbean, or India, at sea, they were all known as "white people." Over time, both captain and crew became practiced in the ways of cruelty. Silas Todd was apprenticed to a slave ship captain at the age of 14 and hoped to become a captain himself. Then, ashore in Boston in 1734, he was "saved" in the Great Awakening. Had he not been, he later reflected, he might have become "as eminent a savage" as the captains under whom he had served.

Enslaved Africans Bound for the New World This group is being force marched by an African slave trader from the interior of Africa to a European trading post on the coast.

Because African slaves were unwilling and sometimes rebellious passengers on the ships that transported them across the Atlantic, European slave ships needed larger crews and heavier weapons than usual. This resistance by slaves increased the cost of transporting them so much that the higher prices may have spared half a million Africans' enslavement.

As bad as the voyage to America was for indentured servants, the trip for enslaved Africans was worse. Perhaps 10 percent died before reaching the African coast. Many had never seen an ocean or a white man, and both sights terrified them. They were confined in pens or forts for as long as half a year while waiting for a ship.

The voyage, or "middle passage," proved lethal to many more. As the slave trade became more efficient in the eighteenth century, the mortality rate dropped, from perhaps 20 percent to half that amount. Those who survived were ready to begin their lives as New World slaves.

The Great Increase of Offspring

Most of the extraordinary increase in the colonies' population, European and African alike, came not from immigration or the slave trade but from natural increase.

For European Americans, population increase was mainly due to the lower age of marriage for women and the higher proportion of women who married. In England, for example, as many as 20 percent of women did not marry by age 45, compared with only 5 percent in the colonies. The age of marriage for women in the colonies was also considerably lower, with women marrying in their late teens or early 20s, compared to the late 20s in England. Because more women married, and married earlier, they bore more babies, on average seven or eight each, with six or seven surviving to adulthood. As a rule, the more economic opportunity, the earlier the age of marriage for women and men, and the more children. In the better climate, more children survived to adulthood, but child mortality rates were high. Thanks to rapid population growth, the American population was exceptionally young.

In many ways, the African American population resembled the European American population. Slaves born in the colonies married young and established families as stable as slavery permitted. By the time they were 18, most slave women had had their first child. They might not form a lasting union with the father, but within a few years many settled into long-lasting relationships with the men who would father the rest of their children. Slave women bore between six and eight children, on average. With child mortality even higher for African Americans than for European Americans, between 25 and 50 percent of slave children died before reaching adulthood. Even so, the slave population more than reproduced itself, and by the middle of the eighteenth century it was growing more from natural increase than from the importation of slaves. Only a tiny fraction of the Africans sold into slavery in the Americas ended up in mainland British colonies. Nonetheless, when slavery was abolished after the Civil War, the United States had the largest population of African descent in the New World.

The Transatlantic Economy: Producing and Consuming

In the eighteenth century, as the colonies matured, they became capitalist societies in an Atlantic trade network. More and more, people produced for the market, so that they could buy the goods the market had to offer. Throughout the Atlantic world, ordinary people reshaped their lives so they could buy more goods. Historians talk about two economic revolutions in this period: a consumer revolution—a steady increase in the demand for and purchase of consumer goods—and an industrious revolution (not *industrial* but *industrious* revolution), in which people worked harder and organized their households (their families, servants, and slaves) to produce goods for sale so that they would have money to pay for items they wanted. Income went up only slightly in the eighteenth century, yet people were buying more. In the process, they created a consumer society, in which most people eagerly purchased consumer goods.

The Nature of Colonial Economic Growth

Throughout human history, population growth has usually led to a decline in the standard of living as more people compete for a finite supply of resources. In the American colonies, however, population growth led to an expansion of the economy, as more of the continent's abundant natural resources were brought under human control. The standard of living for most free Americans probably improved, although not dramatically. As the economy matured, a small segment—urban merchants and owners of large plantations—became wealthy. At the same time, the urban poor and tenant farmers began to slip toward poverty.

All of these changes took place, however, without any significant changes in technology (such as the power looms that would be invented later in the century). Most wealth was made from shipping and agriculture. Eighty percent of the colonies' population worked on farms or plantations, areas with no major technological innovations. Virtually all gains in productivity came instead from labor: more people were working, and they were working more efficiently.

The economy of colonial America was shaped by three factors: abundance of land and shortages of labor and of capital. The plantation regions of the South and the West Indies were best situated to take advantage of these circumstances, and the small-farm areas of New England were the least suitable. Tobacco planters in the Chesapeake and rice and indigo planters in South Carolina sold their products on a huge world market. Their large profits enabled them to purchase more land and more slaves to work it.

Because northern farmers raised crops and animals that were also produced in Europe, profits from agriculture alone were too low to permit them to acquire large tracts of land or additional labor (see Table 5–1). Northerners had to look to other opportunities for wealth. They found them in trade, exchanging their raw goods for European manufactured ones and selling them to American consumers.

The Transformation of the Family Economy

In colonial America, the family was the basic economic unit, and all family members contributed to it. Work was organized by gender. On farms, women were responsible for the preparation of food and clothing, child care, and care of the home. Women grew vegetables and herbs, provided dairy products, and transformed flax and wool into clothing. Daughters worked under their mothers' supervision, perhaps spinning extra yarn to be sold for a profit.

Men worked the rest of the farm. They raised grain and maintained the pastures. They cleared the land, chopped wood for fuel, and built and maintained the house, barn, and other structures. They took crops to market. Men's and women's work were complementary and necessary for survival. For example, men planted apple trees, children picked apples, and women pressed the apples into cider. When a husband was disabled,

Table 5-1 How Wealthy Were Colonial Americans?

Property-Owning Class	New England	Mid-Atlantic Colonies	Southern Colonies	Thirteen Colonies
Men	169	194	410	260
Women	42	103	215	132
Adults 45 and older	252	274	595	361
Adults 44 and younger	129	185	399	237
Urban	191	287	641	233
Rural	151	173	392	255
Esquires, gentlemen	313	1,223	1,281	572
Merchants	563	858	314	497
Professions, sea captains	271	241	512	341
Farmers only, planters	155	180	396	263
Farmer-artisans, ship owners, fishermen	144	257	801	410
Shop and tavern keepers	219	222	195	204
Artisans, chandlers	114	144	138	122
Miners, laborers	52	67	383	62

Source: Alice Hanson Jones, *Wealth of a Nation to Be: The American Colonies on the Eve of the Revolution* (New York: Columbia University Press, 1980), p. 224.

Note: Numbers given are in pounds sterling.

ill, or away from home, his wife could perform virtually all of his tasks as a sort of "deputy husband." Men almost never performed women's work, however, and men whose wives died remarried quickly to have someone to care for the household and children.

The eighteenth century's industrious revolution transformed the family economy: when people decided to produce goods to sell, they changed their family economies. Historians believe that increased production in this period came primarily from the labor of women and children, who worked harder and longer than they had before.

Sources of Regional Prosperity

The South, the most productive region, accounted for more than 60 percent of colonial exports (see Map 5–2). Tobacco was its chief cash crop. Next came cereals such as rice, wheat, corn, and flour, and then indigo, a plant used to dye fabric.

Slave labor accounted for most of the southern agricultural output and was organized to produce for the market. When tobacco profits began to slip because of falling prices and the depletion of the soil, planters worked their slaves harder and, in the Chesapeake, began to plant corn and wheat. By diversifying their crops, planters were able to make maximum use of their slave labor force by keeping slaves busy throughout the year.

The work routine of slaves depended on the crops they tended. On tobacco plantations, where careful attention to the plants was necessary to ensure high quality, planters

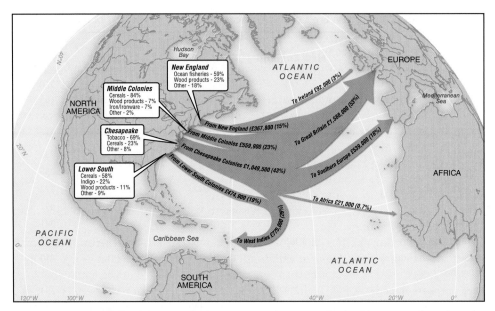

Map 5–2   Exports of the Thirteen Colonies, ca. 1770 Almost two-thirds of the exports from the colonies came from the South, and more than one-half went to Great Britain alone. Tobacco and grains were the most important exports of all. *Source:* Jacob Cooke, ed., *Encyclopedia of North American Colonies* (New York: Scribner's, 1993), pp. 1, 514.

or white overseers worked the slaves in small gangs carefully selected and arranged to maximize productivity.

In the rice-growing lower South, however, the enslaved were usually assigned specific tasks, which they would work at until the job was completed. Rice growing required far less supervision than did tobacco planting. Because many Africans had grown rice in Africa and had likely taught Europeans how to grow it in America, rice planters let the slaves set their own pace. Once finished for the day, the enslaved people could use their time as they pleased. Many planted gardens to supplement their own diets or to earn a small income. Slaves trafficked in a wide range of products, from rice, corn, chickens, hogs, and catfish to canoes, baskets, and wax.

The inhabitants of the middle colonies grew prosperous by raising and selling wheat and other grains. The ports of Baltimore, Philadelphia, Wilmington, and New York became thriving commercial centers that collected grain from regional farms, milled it into flour, and shipped it to the West Indies, southern Europe, and other American colonies. Farmers relied on indentured servants, cottagers, and slaves to supplement the labor of family members. Cottagers were families who rented out part of a farmer's land, which they worked for wages.

As long as land was cheap and accessible, the middle colonies enjoyed the most evenly shared prosperity on the continent. Most inhabitants fell into the comfortable middle class, with the gap between the richest and the poorest relatively small. Pennsylvania, which offered both religious toleration and relatively simple ways to purchase land, was particularly prosperous. The energy that elsewhere went into religious conflict here fueled work and material accumulation. Gottlieb Mittelberger, who endured a horrendous journey to Pennsylvania, described his new home as a sort of paradise: "Our Americans live more quietly and peacefully than the Europeans; and all this is the result of the liberty which they enjoy and which makes them all equal."

When land became expensive or difficult to obtain, however, conflict might ensue. In the 1740s and 1750s, both New Jersey and New York experienced land riots when conflicting claims made land titles uncertain. In the Chesapeake and southeastern Pennsylvania, increasing land prices drove the poor into tenancy or to the urban centers. Widespread prosperity led Americans to expect that everyone who wished to would be able to own a farm. When land ownership was not fully possible, tension and anger grew.

New England was also primarily a farming region. Here, however, male family members, rather than indentured servants, cottagers, or slaves, provided most farm labor. Although farms in some regions, such as the Connecticut River valley, produced surpluses for the market, most farm families had to look for other sources of income to pay for consumer goods.

Town governments in New England encouraged enterprise, sometimes providing gristmills, sawmills, and fields on which cattle could graze. The region prospered, and New Englanders came to expect their governments to enhance the economy. Agricultural exports were relatively slight, although both grain and livestock were sold to the slave plantations of the West Indies, which received more than 25 percent of the American colonies' exports (and more than 70 percent of New England's).

The other major colonial exports in the eighteenth century were fur and hides. By the eve of the Revolution, 95 percent of the furs imported into England came from North America—most of them provided by Indians, who traded them to European middlemen.

Merchants and Dependent Laborers in the Transatlantic Economy

Almost all colonies participated in a transatlantic economy. In each region, those most involved in the market were those with the most resources: large planters in the southern colonies, owners of the biggest farms in the middle colonies, and urban merchants in the northern colonies. The wealthiest never made their fortunes from farming or planting alone but always added income from activities such as speculating in land, practicing law, or lending money.

If some economic development was spurred from above, by enterprising individuals or by governments, much was also created by ambitious ordinary men and women. New England's mixed economy of grain, grazing, fishing, and lumbering required substantial capital improvements such as gristmills, sawmills, and tanneries to be profitable. By the beginning of the eighteenth century, shipbuilding was a major activity, and by 1775, one-third of the English merchant fleet had been built in the colonies.

The shipbuilding industry, in turn, spurred further economic development, such as lumbering, sail making, and rope making. Linked economic development occurs when an enterprise is tied to a variety of other local businesses. Furthermore, the profits generated by shipbuilding and trade were reinvested in sawmills to produce more lumber, in gristmills to grind grain into flour, and, of course, in more trading voyages. The growth of shipping in port cities such as Boston, Newport, New York, Philadelphia, and Charleston created an affluent merchant class, but trading was a risky business, and few who tried it rose to the top. One ship lost to a storm could ruin a merchant, as could a sudden turn in the market. Insurance companies were born as a result.

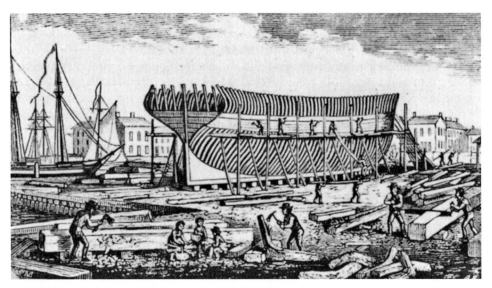

A Ship Being Built in New York Carpenters put together a ship for the growing trade out of colonial port cities.

The seafaring trades led capitalist development. A wealthy, risk-taking merchant class emerged, as well as another distinguishing mark of a capitalist economy, a wage-earning class. As long as there was a labor shortage in the colonies, workers had an advantage. By the beginning of the eighteenth century, however, rapid population increase led to a growing supply of labor. Although they were free to shop around for the best wages, workers became part of a wage-earning class, dependent on others for employment and income. Only a small portion of Americans were wage earners on the eve of the Revolution, but they were a sign of things to come.

Consumer Choices and the Creation of Gentility

Under the British mercantilist system (see Chapter 4), the colonies were supposed to export raw materials to the empire and import finished products back, sending West Indian sugar, tobacco, wheat, lumber, fish, and animal pelts to Britain in exchange for cloth and iron. Yet within this general pattern, individual men and women made choices about what to buy.

On both sides of the Atlantic, demand for plantation products and consumer goods was insatiable. At first only the wealthy could afford such luxuries as sugar and tobacco. But as more and more labor was organized to produce for the market, ordinary people had the added income needed to purchase luxury products. Tea, imported into both Britain and the colonies from Asia, became, like tobacco and sugar, a mass-consumed luxury. By the time of the Revolution, annual sugar consumption in England had skyrocketed to 23 pounds per person, and tobacco consumption was about 2 pounds per person. Demand for these plantation products led directly to the traffic in African slaves.

As plantation products flowed to England, so manufactured goods came back to the colonies. Consumer behavior on both sides of the Atlantic was similar: people smoked tobacco; sweetened their tea with sugar; and bought more clothing, household items, books, and every sort of manufactured goods.

This consumer revolution was not due to higher wages. Instead, people chose to work harder and chose work that brought in money. They decided what they would do with that money—they chose to buy particular items. Increasingly, people bought items that their friends and neighbors could see and that they could use in entertaining them. In seventeenth-century America, extra income was spent on items of lasting value, such as tablecloths and bed linens kept folded away in a chest, to pass on to one's children. In the eighteenth century, men and women bought more clothing made out of cheaper, less durable fabrics. Until this time, most people had only a few outfits. The wealthy, of course, always had large wardrobes made from fine fabrics. In the eighteenth century, however, fabric prices fell, and clothing made from cheaper fabrics satisfied growing consumer demand. Then people needed new pieces of furniture in which to store their new garments. Chests of drawers, or dressers, first available to the wealthy in the 1630s and 1640s, had, by 1760, become a standard item for the middle class.

People became increasingly interested in how they appeared to others. Ordinary people began to pay attention to the latest fashions, once a concern only of the wealthy. By 1700, two new items made it easier for those with the time and money to attend to their appearance: the dressing table and the full-length mirror. For the first time, people could see how they looked, head to toe. Washing oneself and styling one's hair or periwig became standard rituals for all who hoped to appear "genteel."

In the eighteenth century, the prosperous on both sides of the Atlantic created and tried to follow the standards of a new style of life, gentility. Gentility represented all that was polite, civilized, refined, and fashionable. It was everything that vulgarity, its opposite, was not. Gentility meant not only certain sorts of objects, such as a dressing table or a bone china teapot, but also the manners needed to use such objects properly. Standards of gentility established boundaries between the genteel and the vulgar. Those who considered themselves genteel looked down on those whose style of living seemed unrefined and became uncomfortable when required to associate with social inferiors.

Yet if the public display of gentility erected a barrier between people, it also showed the vulgar how to become genteel. All they needed to do was to acquire the right goods and learn how to use them. Throughout the colonies, ordinary people began to purchase goods that established their gentility. Even relatively poor people often owned a mirror, a few pieces of china, or a teapot. The slaves executed in New York City in 1741 (discussed subsequently) were probably conspiring not to burn the city down but to steal clothing and other fancy goods they could resell to poor people in the underground economy. This mass consumption and widespread distribution of consumer goods created and sustained the consumer revolution.

The consumer revolution had another egalitarian effect: it encouraged sociability. Throughout the Atlantic world, men and women, particularly those with a little leisure and money (perhaps half the white population), began to cultivate social life. Many believed that the purpose of life was the sort of society they created during an evening shared with friends and family in their parlors.

To put all of their guests on an equal footing, people began to purchase matching sets of dinner plates, silverware, glasses, and chairs. Until the eighteenth century, the most important people at the table—the man of the house, his wife, and high-ranking men—got the best chairs. Children, servants, and those of lower social standing sat on stools, benches, or boxes, or they stood. Dishes, utensils, and mugs rarely matched. Matched sets of tableware and chairs underscored the symbolic equality of all guests.

1. Honᵇˡᵉ Peter Manigault
2. Taylor, an Officer
3. Demare — do —
4. Captᵇ Massou

Mʳ Peter Manigault and his Friends.
Drawn by One of them (Mʳ Roupell) about the year 1754 from which this Copy is now
made in August 1854.
By his Great-Grand-Son Louis Manigault
Charleston Sᵒ Cᵃ

5. Mʳ Isaac Godin
6. Coytmore, an Officer
7. Colᵉ Probart Howarth
8. Mʳ George Roupell

The New Gentility In 1750 in Charleston, South Carolina, Mr. Peter Manigault and his friends toasted each other, demonstrating their civility and their knowledge of the rules of polite behavior, including how to drink punch from a stem glass.

The newest and most popular consumer goods made their way quickly to America—forks, drinking glasses, and teapots, each with its own etiquette. Such rules were daunting for the uneducated, but once they were mastered, a person could enter polite society anywhere in the Atlantic world and be accepted. The eighteenth-century capitalist economy created a trade not only in goods and raw materials but in styles of life as well.

Historians debate the effects of the consumer revolution, but on balance it was a democratic force. Ordinary men and women and even slaves came to think it was their right to spend their money as they pleased. As one Bostonian put it in 1754, the poor should be allowed to buy "the Conveniencies, and Comforts, as well as Necessaries of Life . . . as freely as the Rich." After all, "I am sure we Work as hard as they do . . . ; therefore, I cannot see why we have not as good a natural Right to them as they have."

The Varieties of Colonial Experience

Although the eighteenth-century industrious and consumer revolutions tied the peoples of the North Atlantic world together, climate, geography, immigration, patterns of economic development, and population density made for considerable variety. Although the vast majority of Americans lived in small communities or on farms, an increasing number lived in cities that played a critical role in shaping colonial life. At the same time, farming regions were maturing, changing the character of rural life, and the growing population continued to push at the frontiers, leading to the founding of Georgia, the last of the thirteen colonies.

Creating an Urban Public Sphere

At the end of the seventeenth century, Boston, with 7,000 people, was the only town that was much more than a rural village. By 1720, Boston's population had grown to 12,000, Philadelphia had 10,000 inhabitants, New York had 7,000, and Newport and Charleston almost 4,000 each. Forty years later, other urban centers had sprung up, each with populations around 3,000—Salem, Marblehead, and Newburyport in Massachusetts; Portsmouth, New Hampshire; Providence, Rhode Island; New Haven and Hartford, Connecticut; Albany, New York; Lancaster, Pennsylvania; Baltimore, Maryland; Norfolk, Virginia; and Savannah, Georgia. By the eve of the Revolution, Philadelphia had 30,000 residents, New York had 25,000, and Boston had 16,000 (see Map 5–3). All of these cities were either ports or centers for the fur trade. Colonial cities were centers of commerce; that was their reason for being.

Social life in colonial cities was characterized by two somewhat contradictory trends. On the one hand, nowhere in the colonies was social stratification among free people more pronounced. By the eve of the American Revolution, each city had an affluent elite, made up of merchants, professionals, and government officials, and each city also had a class of indigent poor. On the other hand, cities brought all classes of society together at theaters, in taverns, and at religious revivals such as the one led by George Whitefield. This civic life became one of the seedbeds of the Revolution because it provided a forum for the exchange of ideas.

Affluent city dwellers created a life as much like that of London as they could. They imported European finery and established English-style institutions, founding social clubs, dancing assemblies, and fishing and hunting clubs. Although many of these associations were for men only, some brought men and women together. Such organizations helped the elite function as a class.

Urban associations reflected the ideals of the Enlightenment (see "The Ideas of the Enlightenment," later in this chapter). Some, such as the Masons, a European fraternal order with branches in all the major colonial cities, espoused the ideal of universalism, that all people were by their nature fundamentally the same. Other institutions advocated self-improvement. Whereas some urban institutions separated out the elite and others challenged the ruling hierarchy, still others brought together all members of society in a "public sphere." City dwellers could see stage plays in Williamsburg by 1716, in Charleston and New York by the 1730s, and in Philadelphia and Boston by the 1740s. Taverns brought all ranks even closer. By 1737, Boston had 177 taverns, one for every 99 inhabitants. (Between 30 percent and 40 percent were owned by women, usually widows.) Taverns became true public institutions in which people could meet and discuss the issues of the day.

Newspapers also played a critical role in creating a public sphere and extending it beyond the cities. The first newspaper was the *Boston News-Letter,* which appeared in

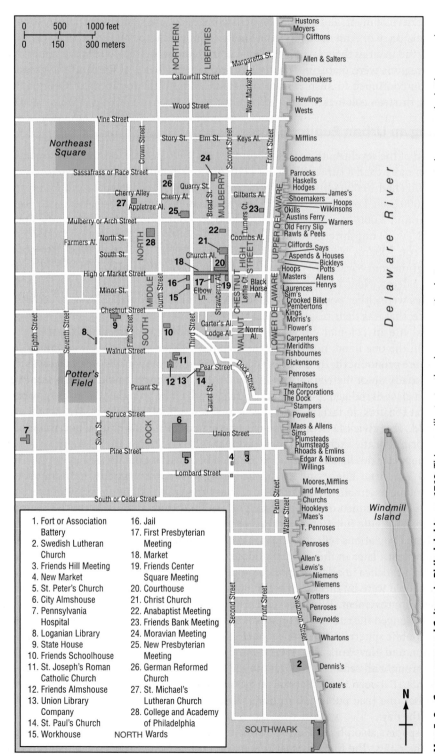

Scale bars:
0 — 500 — 1000 feet
0 — 150 — 300 meters

NORTHERN
LIBERTIES

Margaretta St.
Callowhill Street
Wood Street
Vine Street
New Market St.

Northeast Square

Story St. Elm St. Keys Al. Front Street
Sassafrass or Race Street
Cherry Alley
Cherry Al.
Appletree Al.
Mulberry or Arch Street
Crown Street
Quarry St.
Second Street
MULBERRY
Bread St.
Gilberts Al.
Turners Ct.
UPPER DELAWARE

Farmers Al.
North St.
South St.
High or Market Street
Minor St.
Chestnut Street
NORTH
MIDDLE
SOUTH
Fourth Street
Church Al.
Coombs Al.
HIGH STREET
WALNUT
CHESTNUT
Letitia Ct.
LOWER DELAWARE
Black Horse Al.
Elbow Ln.
Strawberry Al.
Third Street
Carter's Al.
Lodge Al.
Norris Al.

Eighth Street
Seventh Street
Potter's Field
Sixth St.
Fifth Street
Walnut Street
Pear Street
Pruant St.
Laurel St.
Dock Street
Spruce Street
Union Street
Pine Street
Lombard Street
South or Cedar Street
DOCK

Penn Street
Water Street
Second Street
Front Street
Swanson Street

SOUTHWARK

Delaware River

Windmill Island

Hustons
Moyers
Clifftons
Allen & Salters
Shoemakers
Hewlings
Wests
Mifflins
Goodmans
Parrocks
Haskells
Hodges
James's
Shoemakers
Hoops
Okills
Wilkinsons
Austins Ferry
Warners
Old Ferry Slip
Rawls & Peels
Cliffords
Says
Aspends & Houses
Bickleys
Hoops
Potts
Masters
Allens
Henrys
Laurences
Sim's
Crooked Billet
Pembertons
Kings
Morris's
Flower's
Carpenters
Meridiths
Fishbournes
Dickensons
Penroses
Hamiltons
The Corporations
The Dock
Stampers
Powells
Maes & Allens
Sims
Plumsteads
Plumsteads
Rhoads & Emlins
Edgar & Nixons
Willings
Moores,Mifflins and Mertons
Churchs
Hookleys
Maes's
T. Penroses
Penroses
Allen's
Lewis's
Niemens
Niemens
Trotters
Penroses
Reynolds
Whartons
Dennis's
Coate's

N ↑

1. Fort or Association Battery
2. Swedish Lutheran Church
3. Friends Hill Meeting
4. New Market
5. St. Peter's Church
6. City Almshouse
7. Pennsylvania Hospital
8. Loganian Library
9. State House
10. Friends Schoolhouse
11. St. Joseph's Roman Catholic Church
12. Friends Almshouse
13. Union Library Company
14. St. Paul's Church
15. Workhouse

16. Jail
17. First Presbyterian Meeting
18. Market
19. Friends Center Square Meeting
20. Courthouse
21. Christ Church
22. Anabaptist Meeting
23. Friends Bank Meeting
24. Moravian Meeting
25. New Presbyterian Meeting
26. German Reformed Church
27. St. Michael's Lutheran Church
28. College and Academy of Philadelphia

NORTH Wards

Map 5–3 Commerce and Culture in Philadelphia, ca. 1760 This map illustrates the close connection between commerce—note how many docks there are along the Delaware River—and culture. By 1760, Philadelphia was home to churches of many different denominations, as well as an array of enlightened institutions— a hospital, a college, and two libraries. *Source:* Lester Cappon, ed., *The Atlas of Early American History* (Princeton, NJ: Princeton University Press, 1976), p. 10.

1704. By the time of the Revolution, 39 newspapers were being published, and the chief town in each colony except Delaware had at least one newspaper.

Strict libel laws prohibited the printing of opinions critical of public officials, or even the truth if it cast them in a bad light. John Peter Zenger, editor of the *New-York Weekly Journal*, was tried in 1735 for criticizing the governor. Zenger's flamboyant attorney, Andrew Hamilton, persuaded the jury that they should rule not simply on the facts of the case (Zenger had criticized the governor) but on whether the law itself was just. When the jury ruled in Zenger's favor, cheers went up in the courtroom. Although it would be many years before freedom of the press would be guaranteed by law, the Zenger case was a milestone in the developing relationship between the public and government officials. The verdict expressed the belief that in the contest between the two, the press spoke for the people, and hence it was the people themselves, not government, that would hold the press accountable.

City dwellers came to think of themselves as a "public" that had certain rights or liberties, such as making their views known and enjoying a fair price for their goods. At times, working people, acting as a public, and sometimes with support from the elite, used mob action to assert their political views. Mobs in both New York and Boston reacted violently to press gangs that scoured the waterfront for additional hands for the Royal Navy. By the time of the Revolution, city dwellers had a long history of asserting their rights in public.

The Diversity of Urban Life

Periodic downturns in the urban economy, especially after the middle of the century, led to increased activism by workers and the urban poor. Colonial politics had been premised on the deference of the less powerful to their social and economic "betters," but by the middle of the eighteenth century, the increasing wealth of those at the top and the appearance of a small class of permanently poor at the bottom of the economic hierarchy began to undermine the assumption of a common interest and that the wealthy and well educated could be trusted to govern for the benefit of everyone.

Although by today's standards the colonial population, even in the cities, was remarkably equal economically, in the eighteenth century it became more stratified. At the beginning of the eighteenth century, none of the cities had a substantial number of poor people. In New York, in 1700, there were only 35 paupers, almost all of whom were aged or disabled. Over the course of the century, however, colonial wars sent men home disabled and left many women widowed and children orphaned. Each city responded to the growth in poverty by building almshouses for the poor who could not support themselves and workhouses for those, including women and children, who could. In Philadelphia and New York about 25 percent of the population was at or below the poverty level, and in Boston perhaps as much as 40 percent of the population was living at or near subsistence. Many colonists feared that colonial cities were coming to resemble London, with its mass of impoverished and desperate poor.

All the major cities had slaves, and in some cities the black population was considerable. By 1746, 30 percent of New York City's working class consisted of enslaved people. After a serious slave revolt in 1712 and a rumored revolt in 1741, the white population responded with harsh punishments (but without halting the slave trade). In the wake of the 1712 revolt, which had left 9 white men dead, city officials executed 18 convicted rebels, burned 3 at the stake, let 1 starve to death in chains, and broke 1 on the wheel, a medieval instrument of torture. Six more committed suicide. The response to a rumored slave insurrection in 1741 resembled Salem's witchcraft trials: 18 slaves and 4 whites were hanged, and 13 slaves were burned at the stake.

New York enacted a stringent slave code after the 1712 revolt, and Boston and Pennsylvania imposed significant import duties on slaves. Nonetheless, the importation of slaves continued into all the port cities, where they were in demand as house servants and artisans. Almost all of Boston's elite owned at least one slave, as did many members of the middle class. Wealthy white artisans often purchased slaves instead of enlisting free whites as apprentices.

In Charleston, where more than half the population was enslaved, many masters let their slaves hire themselves out in return for a portion of their earnings. Such slaves set their own hours, chose their own recreational and religious activities, and participated in the consumer economy by selling their products and making purchases with the profits. Some whites complained about the fancy dresses of the black women at biracial dances attended by "many of the first gentlemen" of Charleston. Interracial sex in Charleston seems to have been common. Although white city dwellers were troubled by what they called the "impudence" of urban slaves, urban slavery flourished.

The Maturing of Rural Society

Population increases had a different impact in rural areas than in cities. During the eighteenth century, some long-settled regions became relatively overcrowded. Land that once seemed abundant had been carelessly farmed and had lost some of its fertility. This relative overcrowding, which historians call land pressure, led to a number of changes in colonial society, felt most acutely in New England. Population density increased, and with no additional farmland available, migration from farms to newly settled areas and cities increased. Both the concentration of wealth and social differentiation intensified, dividing the farm community into rich and poor.

Such broad economic changes had a direct impact on individual men and women. Families with numerous children were hard pressed if the original plot of land could not be divided into homesteads large enough for each son. (Daughters were given movable property such as farm animals, household equipment, and slaves.) Some sons migrated to cities, looking for employment. Others worked on other men's farms for wages or, in the South in particular, became tenant farmers. Daughters became servants in other women's households. In such older regions, the average age of marriage crept upward.

As young men and women in long-settled regions had to defer marriage, increasing numbers had sexual relations before marriage. In some towns, by the middle of the eighteenth century, between 30 percent and 50 percent of brides bore their first child within eight months of their wedding day. The growing belief that marriage should be based primarily on love probably encouraged some couples to become intimate before they married, especially if poverty required them to postpone marriage. Young women who engaged in sexual relations before marriage took a huge risk, however. If their lovers declined to marry them, they would be disgraced, and their futures would be bleak.

The World That Slavery Made

The rural economy of the South depended on slave labor. Whites and their black slaves formed two distinctive cultures, one in the black-majority lower South and the other in the Chesapeake region. In both regions, the most affluent slave masters sold their crops on the international market and used the profits to buy elegant furniture and the latest London fashions.

Chesapeake planters modeled themselves after English country gentlemen, whereas low-country planters imitated the elite of London. Chesapeake planters designed their plantations to be self-sufficient villages, like English country estates. Because slaves produced most of the goods and services the plantation needed, planters such as William Byrd II imagined themselves living "in a kind of independence on everyone but Providence." But unlike English country gentlemen, southern slave owners were wholly dependent on both slave labor and the vagaries of the market for their fortunes. South Carolina planters used their wealth to build elegant homes in Charleston and other coastal cities, where they spent much time and established a flourishing urban culture. By the eve of the Revolution, the area around Charleston was the most affluent in the mainland colonies. In spite of their affluence, the southern planter elite never achieved the secure political power enjoyed by their English counterparts. In England the social elite dominated the government: not only the hereditary positions but also the appointive and elective ones. With noble rank inherited and voting rights limited to male property owners, the English government was remarkably stable. The colonial elite, however (in the North as well as the South), were cut off from the top levels of political power, which remained in England. The colonists were at the mercy of whichever officials the Crown happened to appoint.

Unable to count on support from above, the colonial elite needed to guarantee the loyalty of those below them. In Virginia, the elite acted as middlemen for lesser planters, advancing them credit and marketing their tobacco. In general, they wielded their authority with a light hand, and punishments for crimes committed by whites were light.

Although members of the Virginia gentry tried to distance themselves from their slaves, whom they considered "vulgar," some whites crossed the color line in a dramatic way, despite eighteenth-century racial views. Sexual relations between whites and blacks were common. Several prominent Virginians acknowledged and supported their mixed-race children. Some interracial relationships were affectionate; most were coerced. All the resulting offspring were in a vulnerable position; like all slaves, they were dependent on the will of whites.

In the low country, the absenteeism of the planters combined with the task system to give plantation slaves an unusual degree of autonomy. As a majority, slaves in the low country were better able to retain their own religions, languages, and customs than were those in the Chesapeake. For example, the Gullah language, still spoken today on the Sea Islands off the coast of South Carolina and Georgia, combined English, Spanish, Portuguese, and African languages.

The mainland colonies' bloodiest slave revolt, the Stono Rebellion, took place in 1739 in South Carolina. The uprising was led by about 20 slaves born in Kongo (present-day Angola). The rebels were probably Catholics, for the king of Kongo, converted by the Portuguese, made Catholicism his nation's religion. Early in the morning of September 9, the rebels broke into a store near the Stono Bridge, taking weapons and ammunition and killing the storekeepers. The rebels moved south toward St. Augustine, killing whites and gathering blacks into their fold. Although the main body of the rebels was dispersed that evening and many were executed on the spot, skirmishes took place for another week, and the last of the ringleaders was not captured for three years.

The authorities reacted with predictable severity, putting dozens of slave rebels "to the most cruel Death" and revoking many liberties the slaves had enjoyed. A prohibitive duty was placed on the importation of slaves, and the immigration of white Europeans was encouraged. Although slave imports dropped significantly in the 1740s, by 1750 they rose to pre-Stono levels.

Georgia: From Frontier Outpost to Plantation Society

Nowhere was the white determination to create and maintain a slave society stronger than in the colony of Georgia. It is sometimes said that the introduction of slavery in North America was an unthinking decision, that the colonies became slave societies slowly, as individual planters purchased Africans already enslaved, and without society as a whole ever committing itself to slavery. Although there is some truth to this analysis, it is not accurate for Georgia, where the introduction of slavery was a purposeful decision.

The establishment of the English colony at South Carolina had, of course, made the Spanish nervous because of its proximity to their settlement at St. Augustine, Florida. With the French founding of New Orleans (1718) and Fort Toulouse (1717), Carolinians felt increasingly threatened. They were therefore eager for the English to establish a colony to the south, which would both serve as a buffer between Florida and South Carolina and, if extended far enough west, cut the French colonial empire in two.

The British Crown issued a 21-year charter to a group of trustees led by James Oglethorpe, who had achieved prominence by bringing about reforms in England's debtors' prisons. The colony, Georgia, was designed as a combination philanthropic venture and military-commercial outpost. Its colonists, who were to be drawn from Britain's "deserving poor," were supposed to protect South Carolina's borders and to make the new colony a sort of Italy on the Atlantic, producing wine, olives, and silk.

Unfortunately, Oglethorpe's humanitarianism was not matched by an understanding of the world economy. Because it was well known that excessive indulgence in alcohol was undermining the cohesion of many Indian tribes, Oglethorpe had banned liquor from the colony. However, without a product to sell, the colony could not prosper. South Carolina's wharves, merchants, and willingness to sell rum enabled it to dominate the trade with local Indians. Oglethorpe had also banned slavery for humanitarian reasons (making it the only colony expressly to prohibit slavery). As a result, Georgia farmers looked enviously across the Savannah River at South Carolinians growing rich off slave labor. The settlers were also angry that, contrary to colonial practice, women were not allowed to inherit property and that Georgia's trustees had made no provision for self-government. Georgia, despite its founders' noble intentions, lacked everything that the thriving colonies enjoyed: a cash crop or product, large plots of land, slaves to work the land, and laws of its own devising.

Never able to realize their dream of a colony of small and contented farmers, the trustees surrendered Georgia back to the Crown in 1752. With Oglethorpe's laws repealed and slavery introduced, the colony soon resembled the plantation society of South Carolina. Savannah became a little Charleston, with its robust civic and cultural life and its slave markets.

The Head and the Heart in America: The Enlightenment and Religious Awakening

American life in the eighteenth century was shaped by two movements, the Enlightenment and a series of religious revivals known as the Great Awakening. In many ways, these movements were separate, even opposite, appealing to different groups of people. The Enlightenment was a transatlantic intellectual movement that held that the universe could be understood and improved by the human mind. The Great Awakening was a transatlantic religious movement that held that all people were born sinners, that all could feel their own depravity without the assistance of ministers, and that all were equal in the eyes of God. Although the movements might seem fundamentally opposite, with one emphasizing the power of the human mind and the other disparaging it, both criticized established authority and valued the experience of the individual. Both contributed to the humanitarianism that emerged at the end of the century.

The Ideas of the Enlightenment

The roots of the Enlightenment can be traced to the Renaissance and its spirit of inquiry and faith in science that led explorers like Columbus halfway around the globe. Men and women of the Enlightenment, on both sides of the Atlantic, contrasted the ignorance, oppression, and suffering of the Middle or "Dark" Ages, as they called them, and their own enlightened time. Thomas Jefferson described the earlier period as "the times of Vandalism, when ignorance put everything in the hands of power and priestcraft." Enlightened thinkers believed fervently in the power of rational thinking and scoffed at superstition.

People of the Enlightenment believed that God and his world were knowable. Rejecting revelation as a guide, the Enlightenment looked instead to reason. Jefferson's "trinity of the three greatest men the world had ever produced" included not Jesus Christ but Isaac Newton, the scientist responsible for modern mathematics and physics; Francis Bacon, the philosopher who outlined the scientific method; and John Locke, the political philosopher of democracy. The Enlightenment was interested in knowledge not for its own sake but for the improvements it could make in human happiness.

Enlightenment thinkers were more interested in what all people had in common than in what differentiated them. No passage in the Bible was more important to them than Genesis 1:27: "So God created man in his own image." It was the basis not only for overcoming Calvinism's belief in humanity's innate depravity but also for asserting the principle of human equality. The Enlightenment encouraged a broad toleration of religion. Benjamin Franklin said that "if the Mufti of Constantinople were to send a missionary to preach Mahometanism to us, he would find a pulpit at his service."

Humanity's duties were clear and simple. Chief among them, according to Benjamin Franklin, was "doing good to [God's] other children." In fact, people served God best not by praying, which, as Thomas Paine put it, "can add nothing to eternity," but "by endeavouring to make his creatures happy." Scientific inquiry and experiments such as Franklin's with electricity all had as their object the improvement of human life.

Although there had been some improvements in the quality of life, life in the eighteenth century was still violent and filled with pain. The Enlightenment responded to the pain and violence of the world in two ways. First, it attempted to alleviate and curtail them. Scientists eagerly sought cures for diseases. The Reverend Cotton Mather of Boston learned about the procedure of inoculating against smallpox (using a small amount of the deadly virus) from a scientific article and from his African slave Onesimus, who knew of its practice in Africa. An epidemic gave him an opportunity to try out the technique. The revulsion against pain and suffering also encouraged humanitarian reform, such as James Oglethorpe's reform of English debtors' prisons and, eventually, the anti-slavery movement.

Men and women of the Enlightenment also cultivated a stoic resignation to the evils they could not change and a personal ideal of moderation, so that they would neither give nor receive pain. The gentility and politeness of the urban elite were expressions of this ideal of moderation. Both gentility and the Enlightenment were espoused by the same set of people, the urban elite: professionals, merchants, and prosperous planters tied in to the global economy.

The Economic and Social Foundations of Democracy

Enlightenment thinkers began to study the connections among society, politics, and the economy. John Locke, the English philosopher, was the first to link these in a theory. He argued that there was a systematic connection between social institutions (such as the family), political institutions, and property rights. He began with the claim that each person has the right to life and the right to preserve that life. To sustain their lives, people form families, and to support themselves and their families, they labor. The basic right to life thus gives people the right to the product of their labor: property. To protect their lives and their property, people create governments. They give up some of their liberty but receive protection of their lives and property in return.

Locke also developed a new economic theory. His idea that money has no intrinsic value was a departure from mercantilism, which said that the value of money was fixed. In the second half of the eighteenth century, Scottish philosophers such as Francis Hutcheson and Adam Smith carried Locke's ideas even further, arguing that human beings should be free to value the things that made them happy.

Using happiness as their standard for human life, the Scots argued that people should be free to produce. Adam Smith's influential *The Wealth of Nations* (1776) was both a critique of mercantilism and a defense of free markets and free labor. For Smith and other Enlightenment theorists, the best incentive to hard work was the increased wealth and comforts it would bring. Human beings were happiest, they said, when they lived under free governments, which protected private property but left the market largely unregulated. These ideas became increasingly popular around the time of the Revolution.

Enlightened Institutions

The Enlightenment spurred the creation of institutions that embodied its principles. Humanitarianism led to the building of the Pennsylvania Hospital in 1751 and the Eastern State Mental Hospital at Williamsburg in 1773. In 1743 Benjamin Franklin proposed a society of learned men, modeled after the Royal Society of London, to study and share information about science and technology. He also helped establish the Library Company of Philadelphia in 1731, the first lending library in the colonies. Philadelphia acquired a second library in 1751 when the Quaker James Logan bequeathed his library,

STRUGGLES FOR DEMOCRACY

Books Become More Accessible

In the eighteenth century, very few people had ever held a book in their hands. Even fewer had had the experience of reading and recognizing a connection between themselves and someone who lived either long ago or far away, or of quickly and efficiently gaining access to desired knowledge or expertise. These forms of empowerment were reserved for the very wealthy.

In July 1731, Benjamin Franklin and some of his friends and colleagues met in Philadelphia to try to change that situation. They were members of a philosophical club called the Junto. Most were avid readers of the newspapers and leaflets that came off the ships coming in from England, and they had learned of an interesting recent development in London and other British towns. Libraries were relatively rare, even in Europe, and where they did exist in connection with certain institutions, they were not open to the public, and the books did not circulate. In the last few decades, however, that had begun to change, as collectives formed to buy books that all members of the group would then have access to. Inspired, fifty members of the Junto promised to contribute 40 shillings each to start a circulating library. In addition, each man committed himself to giving 10 more shillings per annum to buy newly printed works and to maintain the collection. Their motto was a Latin phrase meaning "To support the common good is divine."

The master tradesmen, doctors, and small merchants who belonged to the Junto were certainly not poor, but they were not wealthy enough to buy large numbers of books, which were expensive at the time. By creating this institution, these men would have access to Enlightenment thinking in regards to law, science, and other subjects to an extent that they never could have managed on their own. Their ambitions of improving "the common good," however, extended beyond their own collectivity. They were also thinking of the improvement of the people of Philadelphia in general. The library was open to everyone on Saturday evenings from four to eight o'clock. Members could borrow books freely; visitors who were not members could also borrow a book, but they had to leave some sort of collateral, something of value that could be sold if the book was never returned.

The founding of "the Library Company," as the new institution was called, inspired the establishment of more libraries, both in Philadelphia and in other colonies. Circulating libraries grew increasingly common in America, and due to their presence, Enlightenment ideas spread far more rapidly than they otherwise would have. Only about 10 percent of the Library Company's books concerned theology, whereas in traditional institutional libraries—such as Harvard's—most of the titles were religious in nature. Instead, the Library Company offered books on history, geography, and science. Furthermore, the majority of the books were in English, rather than Latin, because the purpose in this case was not for readers to display their erudition but to gain access to what they viewed as practical knowledge. Eventually, circulating libraries helped to spread the patriots' ideas during the American Revolution. The *continued*

Library Company, for example, loaned out its copy of Thomas Paine's *Common Sense*.

Of course, those who came to the library to read were generally middle-class citizens or even well-to-do. They were not the very poor, slaves, or former slaves, nor were they women. However, expanding access to knowledge from a tiny group to a substantially larger one was a necessary first step in democratizing access to education. Later, in the nineteenth century, the circulating library supported by subscription inspired the creation of the public libraries we know today.

books and building both, to the city. By the time of the Revolution, Newport, New York, Charleston, and Savannah all had libraries.

The Enlightenment had a significant effect on organized religion as well. The Anglicans, in particular, were receptive to its ideals of moderation and rationalism. In England, John Tillotson, the Archbishop of Canterbury, preached a comforting and simple Christianity: God was "good and just" and required nothing "that is either unsuitable to our reason or prejudicial to our interest . . . nothing but what is easy to be understood, and is as easy to be practiced by an honest and willing mind."

This message became popular in the colonies, even among Congregationalist ministers, who abandoned the Calvinism of their forefathers. John Wise, the minister of Ipswich, Massachusetts, insisted that "to follow God and to obey Reason is the same thing." Arminianism, the belief that salvation was partly a matter of individual effort rather than entirely God's will, enjoyed a new popularity. Harvard University became a hotbed of liberal theology, and, in response, religious conservatives founded Yale University in 1701 to guarantee ministers a proper Calvinist education.

Origins of the Great Awakening

The problem with rational religion was that it was not emotionally fulfilling. In addition, rapid population growth had left the colonies without enough churches and ministers. Popular demand for more and better religion led to a series of revivals known as the Great Awakening, which swept through the colonies between 1734 and 1745. At first, church leaders looked with pleasure on the stirrings of spiritual renewal. In the winter of 1734–1735, some of the rowdiest young people in Northampton, Massachusetts, who carried on parties for "the greater part of the night," began seeking religion at the church of a brilliant young minister, Jonathan Edwards. Everyone rejoiced at such signs of spiritual awakening.

The Grand Itinerant

When George Whitefield arrived in Philadelphia in 1739, the local ministers, including those of his own Anglican church, welcomed him. Whitefield drew audiences in the thousands everywhere he spoke. In the 15 months of his grand tour, he visited every colony from Maine to Georgia, met all the important ministers, and was heard at least

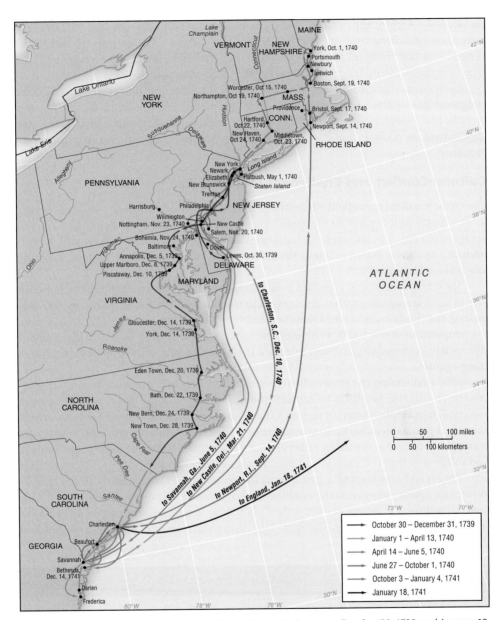

Map 5–4   George Whitefield's Itinerary   In the 15 months between October 30, 1739, and January 18, 1741, Whitefield covered thousands of miles, visiting every colony from New Hampshire to Georgia, and stopping in some states such as Pennsylvania, South Carolina, and Georgia several times.

once by most of the people of Massachusetts and Connecticut (see Map 5–4). He spoke to the entire community—rich, poor, slave, free, old, young, male, and female—acting out simple scripts based on biblical stories. The message was always the same: the sinfulness of man and the mercy of God.

In a calculated move, perhaps to increase his audiences, Whitefield began speaking out against some in the ministry, accusing them of being unconverted. He started with the deceased Archbishop of Canterbury, John Tillotson. Following his lead, Gilbert Tennent, on a preaching tour of New England, warned about "The Danger of an Unconverted Ministry." Tennent implied that some ministers were in it for the money and that true Christians should leave their churches for those of honest preachers.

Even sympathetic ministers were shocked by these accusations, which turned their congregations against them and split their churches. Some leading ministers, who already had reservations about the revivalists because of their emotional style, now condemned the revival. That only made the revivalists more popular and attracted larger crowds.

Cultural Conflict and Challenges to Authority

The Great Awakening walked a fine line between challenging authority and supporting it, which may well explain its widespread appeal. It antagonized the most powerful and arrogant but did not challenge the fundamental structures of society. By attacking ministers but not government officials, the revivalists criticized authority without suffering any real consequences.

The Great Awakening appealed to all classes of people. Its greatest impact, however, was in areas facing the greatest change—in particular, cities (especially among the lower orders), the frontier, and older towns beginning to suffer from overcrowding. Here lived the people most disrupted by economic changes. Disturbed by an increasingly competitive society, men and women were attracted to the democratic fellowship of the revivalist congregation.

While criticizing the materialism and competitiveness of eighteenth-century society, the revival told people to look inside themselves for change, not to the structures of society. For example, a woman named Sarah Osborn blamed herself for her woes, which she saw as punishment for her sinful singing and dancing. After her spiritual rebirth, she trusted in God and accepted her poverty. Spiritual rebirth provided such people the joy and fulfillment that their world had been unable to supply.

The revival also walked a fine line in its treatment of slavery. Early in his travels, Whitefield spoke out against the cruelties of slavery and harangued slaveholders. At the same time, however, he maintained a slave plantation in South Carolina and pestered the trustees to permit slavery in Georgia. Like many slave owners after him, Whitefield

Time Line

▼1701
Yale founded

▼1704
First newspaper, *Boston News-Letter*, published in colonies

▼1712
Slave revolt in New York City

▼1717
French build Fort Toulouse

▼1718
French found New Orleans

▼1731
Library Company, first lending library in colonies, erected in Philadelphia

▼1733
Georgia founded

▼1734
Great Awakening begins

▼1735
John Peter Zenger acquitted of libeling New York's governor

argued that it was immoral to enslave Africans, but not to own them, provided that one treated them well and Christianized them. By linking humanitarianism, Christianity, and slavery, the Great Awakening anchored slavery in the South, at least for the time being.

Although it is hard to say whether slaves were treated more humanely on the plantations of evangelicals, beginning in the 1740s large numbers of slaves were converted to Christianity, and by some point in the nineteenth century virtually all slaves had become Christians. Although some may have converted to please their masters and to get Sundays off, blacks were attracted to evangelical religion for the same reason that whites were. It offered them a way to order and find meaning in their lives.

To a great extent, poor whites and slaves, especially in the South, had been left out of the society that more prosperous people had created. Evangelical religion placed the individual in a community of believers. It offered slaves the opportunity for church discipline and personal responsibility on almost the same terms as whites and gave some blacks the possibility of leadership in a biracial community. Africans grafted some of their religious practices, such as shouting and ecstatic visions, onto the revival, so that worship in southern Baptist and Methodist churches became a truly African American phenomenon.

What the Awakening Wrought

The opponents of the Great Awakening feared that it would turn the world upside down, but the leaders of the revival disciplined their own wildest members, such as New London's James Davenport. Davenport had led his flock through the streets late at night, singing at the tops of their lungs. They also made a bonfire to rid themselves of heresy, by burning the books of their opponents, and idolatry, by burning the clothes they were wearing. The stripping party was stopped by evangelicals in the crowd, and Davenport was brought back to his senses by his fellow ministers. In general, the Great Awakening took colonial society in the direction in which it was already heading: toward individualism. Church after church split into evangelical and traditional factions, and new denominations appeared. Choosing a religion became a personal matter, and colonies with established churches tolerated dissenters. Religion, as a general force, was strengthened, making the colonies simultaneously the most Protestant and the most religiously diverse culture in the world.

▼**1739**
Stono Rebellion
George Whitefield begins his
    American tour

▼**1741**
Thirty-five people executed
    in New York City after slave-
    revolt scare

▼**1748**
College of New Jersey
    (Princeton) founded

▼**1751**
Pennsylvania Hospital built
    in Philadelphia

▼**1752**
Georgia becomes a Crown
    colony

▼**1754**
Columbia College founded

▼**1766**
Queens College (Rutgers)
    founded

▼**1773**
Eastern State Mental Hospital
    built in Williamsburg

The Great Awakening also spurred the establishment of educational institutions. Princeton, chartered in 1748 as the College of New Jersey, grew out of an evangelical seminary. Next came Brown in 1764, and Rutgers, chartered in 1766, to advance "true religion and useful knowledge." Dartmouth was established in 1769, building on a former school for Native Americans run by evangelicals. Columbia College, chartered in 1754, represented the Anglicans' response. The focus of higher education was slowly shifting from preparation for the ministry to the training of leaders more generally. The Great Awakening diminished the power of ministers while increasing the influence of personal religion.

At the height of the Awakening, religious enthusiasm was both attacked and defended. Yet the conflict was hardly a battle of the pious against the godless or the well-educated against the uninformed. Jonathan Edwards, one of the greatest minds of his age, drew from the Enlightenment, as well as from Calvinist ideas. For Edwards, however, reason and good habits were not enough, and reason had to be supplemented by emotion, in particular the emotion of God's grace. By insisting that religious salvation and virtue were more matters of the heart than of the head, Edwards opened the way for a popular religion that was democratic, intensely personal, and humanitarian.

Conclusion

Eighteenth-century America was part of an expanding world market and a capitalist political economy. A growing population sustained a vigorous economy, one that produced for and purchased from the world market. As participants in an "industrious revolution," white Americans worked themselves and their slaves harder to purchase consumer goods. These new goods enabled people to live more genteelly and to cultivate a social life. Especially in the cities, this new emphasis on social life spawned an array of institutions in which people could acquire and display learning and gentility. The benefits of the economy were not shared equally, however. Enslaved people produced for the market economy but were denied its rewards. The increasing stratification of urban society and land pressures in rural regions meant many were too poor to profit from the expanding economy.

The eighteenth-century world spawned two different but related intellectual responses, the Enlightenment and the Great Awakening. Both were critical in shaping the eighteenth-century colonial world, and both paved the way for the Revolution. The Enlightenment led some to believe that rational thought and the scientific method would conquer human ills. At the same time, the Great Awakening reminded men and women that life was short and ultimately beyond their control. In different ways, the Enlightenment and the Great Awakening both encouraged the individualism that would characterize American life.

Who, What

Review Questions

1. What were the primary sources of population increase in the eighteenth century? Compare the patterns of population growth of Europeans and Africans in the colonies.

2. What was the "industrious revolution"? How did it shape the development of the colonial economy? What were the other key factors shaping the development of the colonial economy? What effect did this development have on the lives of ordinary men and women?

3. What were the primary changes in urban and rural life in the eighteenth century?

Critical-Thinking Questions

1. Was the development of the eighteenth-century consumer culture a democratizing force—or the opposite?

2. Why were some eighteenth-century men and women drawn to the ideas of the Enlightenment while others were drawn to the Great Awakening?

3. Analyze the relationship between humanitarianism and slavery, which developed at the same time.

For further review materials and resource information, please visit www.oup.com/us/oakes

CHAPTER 5: THE EIGHTEENTH-CENTURY WORLD, 1700–1775

Primary Sources

5.1 BENJAMIN FRANKLIN, *THE AUTOBIOGRAPHY OF BENJAMIN FRANKLIN* (1771–1790)

Benjamin Franklin began writing his autobiography in 1771 and returned to the task periodically until he died in 1790. In this selection from the first pages, he describes how he came to read and write with the flair that made him one of the eighteenth century's leading men of letters. The excerpt provides some insight into life in the first half of the eighteenth century in Boston, Massachusetts, despite the fact that it was written at a much later date.

From a child I was fond of reading, and all the little money that came into my hands was ever laid out in books. Pleased with the *Pilgrim's Progress*, my first collection was of John Bunyan's works in separate little volumes. I afterward sold them to enable me to buy R. Burton's Historical Collections; they were small chapmen's books, and cheap, 40 or 50 in all. My father's little library consisted chiefly of books in polemic divinity, most of which I read, and have since often regretted that, at a time when I had such a thirst for knowledge, more proper books had not fallen in my way since it was now resolved I should not be a clergyman. Plutarch's *Lives* there was in which I read abundantly, and I still think that time spent to great advantage. There was also a book of De Foe's, called an *Essay on Projects,* and another of Dr. Mather's, called *Essays to do Good,* which perhaps gave me a turn of thinking that had an influence on some of the principal future events of my life.

This bookish inclination at length determined my father to make me a printer, though he had already one son (James) of that profession. In 1717 my brother James returned from England with a press and letters to set up his business in Boston. I liked it much better than that of my father, but still had a hankering for the sea. To prevent the apprehended effect of such an inclination, my father was impatient to have me bound to my brother. I stood out some time, but at last was persuaded, and signed the indentures when I was yet but twelve years old. I was to serve as an apprentice till I was twenty-one years of age, only I was to be allowed journeyman's wages during the last year. In a little time I made great proficiency in the business, and became a useful hand to my brother. I now had access to better books. An acquaintance with the apprentices of booksellers enabled me sometimes to borrow a small one, which I was careful to return soon and clean. Often I sat up in my room reading the greatest part of the night, when the book was borrowed in the evening and to be returned early in the morning, lest it should be missed or wanted. . . .

There was another bookish lad in the town, John Collins by name, with whom I was intimately acquainted. We sometimes disputed, and very fond we were of argument, and very desirous of confuting one another, which disputatious turn, by the way, is apt to become a very bad habit, making people often extremely disagreeable in company by the contradiction that is necessary to bring it into practice; and thence, besides souring and spoiling the conversation, is productive of disgusts and, perhaps enmities where you may have occasion for friendship. I had caught it by reading my father's books of dispute about religion. Persons of good sense,

I have since observed, seldom fall into it, except lawyers, university men, and men of all sorts that have been bred at Edinborough.

A question was once, somehow or other, started between Collins and me, of the propriety of educating the female sex in learning, and their abilities for study. He was of opinion that it was improper, and that they were naturally unequal to it. I took the contrary side, perhaps a little for dispute's sake. He was naturally more eloquent, had a ready plenty of words; and sometimes, as I thought, bore me down more by his fluency than by the strength of his reasons. As we parted without settling the point, and were not to see one another again for some time, I sat down to put my arguments in writing, which I copied fair and sent to him. He answered, and I replied. Three or four letters of a side had passed, when my father happened to find my papers and read them. Without entering into the discussion, he took occasion to talk to me about the manner of my writing; observed that, though I had the advantage of my antagonist in correct spelling and pointing (which I ow'd to the printing-house), I fell far short in elegance of expression, in method and in perspicuity, of which he convinced me by several instances. I saw the justice of his remark, and thence grew more attentive to the manner in writing, and determined to endeavor at improvement.

About this time I met with an odd volume of the *Spectator*.[1] It was the third. I had never before seen any of them. I bought it, read it over and over, and was much delighted with it. I thought the writing excellent, and wished, if possible, to imitate it. With this view I took some of the papers, and, making short hints of the sentiment in each sentence, laid them by a few days, and then, without looking at the book, try'd to compleat the papers again, by expressing each hinted sentiment at length, and as fully as it had been expressed before, in any suitable words that should come to hand. Then I compared my *Spectator* with the original, discovered some of my faults, and corrected them.

Source: Benjamin Franklin, *The Autobiography of Benjamin Franklin* (Rockville, MD: Arc Manor, 2008), pp. 15–17.

5.2 SANSOM OCCUM, EXCERPTS FROM *A SHORT NARRATIVE OF MY LIFE* (1768)

Sansom Occum was a Mohegan Indian from Connecticut. By the eighteenth century, the Mohegans had lost their land and with it their way of life. In the 1740s, Occum was educated at the school that would later become Dartmouth College and became a minister to Indians on Long Island. In 1768, he penned a brief autobiography, revealing that in his experience, hard work did not pay off as well as it had for Benjamin Franklin: when a white friend and ally advocated for him with the society for missionaries, asking for more reasonable pay, he was rebuffed.

The Reverend Mr. Buell was so kind as to write in my behalf to the gentlemen of Boston; and he told me they were much Displeased with him, and heard also once again that they blamed me for being Extravagant; I Can't Conceive how these gentlemen would have me Live. I am ready to forgive their Ignorance, and I would wish they had Changed Circumstances with me but one month, that they may know, by experience what my Case really was; but I am now fully convinced, that it was not Ignorance, For I believe it can be proved to the world that these Same Gentlemen gave a young Missionary a Single man, *One Hundred Pounds* for one year; and

---

[1]This was a popular daily published in London from 1711 to 1712.

fifty Pounds for an Interpreter, and thirty Pounds for an Introducer, so it Cost them One Hundred & Eighty Pounds in one Single Year, and they Sent too where there was no Need of a Missionary.

Now you See what difference they made between me and other missionaries; they gave me 180 pounds for 12 Years Service, which they gave for one years Services in another Mission.— In my Service (I speak like a fool, but I am Constrained) I was my own Interpreter. I was both a School master and Minister to the Indians, yea I was their Ear, Eye & Hand, as well as Mouth. I leave it with the World, as wicked as it is, to Judge, whether I ought not to have had half as much, they gave a young man Just mentioned which would have been but 50 pounds a year; and if they ought to have given me that, I am not under obligations to them, I owe them nothing at all; what can be the Reason that they used me after this manner? I can't think of anything, but this as a Poor Indian Boy said, Who was Bound out to an English Family, and he used to Drive Plow for a young man, and he whipt and beat him almost every Day, and the young man found fault with him, and Complained of him to his master and the poor Boy was Called to answer for himself before his master, and he was asked, what it was he did, that he was So Complained of and beat almost every Day. He Said, he did not know, but he Supposed it was because he could not drive any better; but says he, I Drive as well as I know how; and at other Times he Beats me, because he is of a mind to beat me; but says he believes he Beats me for the most of the Time "because I am an Indian."

Source: Colin Calloway, ed., *The World Turned Upside Down: Indian Voices from Early America* (New York: Bedford), p. 61.

5.3 OLAUDAH EQUIANO, EXCERPTS FROM *THE INTERESTING NARRATIVE AND OTHER WRITINGS* (1789)

The late eighteenth-century autobiography of Gustavus Vassa, or Olaudah Equiano, is probably the most famous slave narrative ever published. He claimed to have been born in Africa and brought to America, but scholars have recently demonstrated that it is far more likely that Equiano was American-born and made this claim about himself so as to be able to speak about—and criticize—the slave trade with "authenticity." In any case, having been at sea during the French and Indian War, acting first as a naval officer's personal servant and then as a fighter, he assumed he was to be freed by his master but was disappointed instead.

Our ship having arrived at Portsmouth, we went into the harbour and remained there till the latter end of November, when we heard great talk about peace, and to our very great joy in the beginning of December we had orders to go up to London with our ship to be paid off. We received this news with loud huzzas and every other demonstration of gladness, and nothing but mirth was to be seen throughout every part of the ship. I too was not without my share of the general joy on this occasion. I thought now of nothing but being freed and working for myself, and thereby getting money to enable me to get a good education: for I always had a great desire to be able at least to read and write, and while I was on ship-board I had endeavoured to improve myself in both. While I was in the *Ætna* particularly, the captain's clerk taught me to write, and gave me a smattering of arithmetic as far as the rule of three. There was also one Daniel Queen, about forty years of age, a man very well educated, who messed [that is, ate] with me on board this ship, and he likewise dressed and attended the captain. Fortunately this man soon became very much attached to me and took very great pains to instruct me in many things. He taught me to shave and dress hair a little and also to read in the Bible, explaining many passages to me which I did not comprehend. I was wonderfully surprised to see the laws and rules of my country written almost exactly here, a circumstance which I believe tended to impress our manners and customs more deeply on my memory. I used to tell him of this resemblance, and many a time we have sat up the whole night together at this employment. In short, he was like a father to me, and some even used to call me after his name; they also styled me the black Christian. Indeed I almost loved him with the affection of a son. Many things I have denied myself that he might have them, and when I used to play at marbles or any other game and won a few halfpence, or got any little money, which I sometimes did, for shaving anyone, I used to buy him a little sugar or tobacco, as far as my stock of money would go. He used to say that he and I never should part, and that when our ship was paid off, as I was as free as himself or any other man on board, he would instruct me in his business by which I might gain a good livelihood. This gave me new life and spirits, and my heart burned within me while I thought the time long till I obtained my freedom. For though my master had not promised it to me, yet besides the assurances I had received that he had no right to detain me, he always treated me with the greatest kindness and reposed in me an unbounded confidence; he even paid attention to my morals, and would never suffer me to deceive him or tell lies, of which he used to tell me the consequences; and that if I did so God would not love me; so that from all this tenderness, I had never once supposed, in all my dreams of freedom, that he would think of detaining me any longer than I wished.

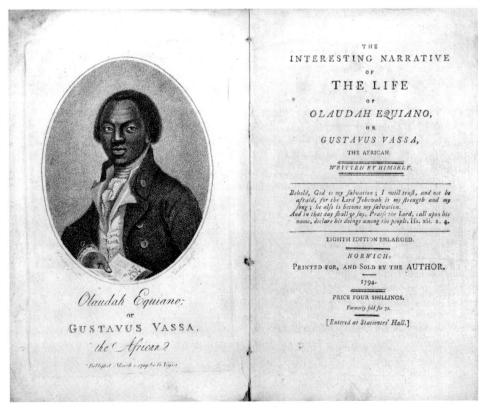

In pursuance of our orders we sailed from Portsmouth for the Thames and arrived at Deptford 10 December, where we cast anchor just as it was high water. The ship was up about half an hour, when my master ordered the barge to be manned, and all in an instant, without having before given me the least reason to suspect anything of the matter, he forced me into the barge, saying I was going to leave him, but he would take care I should not. I was so struck with the unexpectedness of this proceeding that for some time I did not make a reply, only I made an offer to go for my books and chest of clothes, but he swore I should not move out of his sight, and if I did he would cut my throat, at the same time taking his hanger [a short sword]. I began, however, to collect myself, and plucking up courage, I told him I was free and he could not by law serve me so. But this only enraged him the more, and he continued to swear, and said he would soon let me know whether he would or not, and at that instant sprung himself into the barge from the ship to the astonishment and sorrow of all on board. The tide, rather unluckily for me, had just turned downward, so that we quickly fell down the river along with it till we came among some outward-bound West Indiamen, for he was resolved to put me on board the first vessel he could get to receive me. The boat's crew, who pulled against their will, became quite faint, different times, and would have gone ashore, but he would not let them. Some of them strove then to cheer me and told me he could not sell me, which revived me a little, and I still entertained hopes, for as they pulled along he asked some vessels to receive me, but they could not. But just as we had got a little below Gravesend, we came alongside of a ship which was going away the next tide for the West Indies; her name was the *Charming Sally*, Captain James Doran, and my master went on board and agreed with him for me, and in a little time I was sent for into the cabin. When I came there Captain Doran asked me if I knew him; I answered that I did not; "Then," said he, "you are now my slave." I told him my master could not sell me to him, nor to anyone else. "Why," said he, "did not your master buy you?" I confessed he did. "But I have served him," said I, "many years, and he has taken all my wages and prize-money, for I only got one sixpence during the war; besides this I have been baptized, and by the laws of the land no man has a right to sell me." And I added that I had heard a lawyer and others at different times tell my master so. They both then said that those people who told me so were not my friends, but I replied, "It was very extraordinary that other people did not know the law as well as they." Upon this Captain Doran said I talked too much English, and if I did not behave myself well and be quiet he had a method on board to make me. I was too well convinced of his power over me to doubt what he said, and my former sufferings in the slave-ship presenting themselves to my mind, the recollection of them made me shudder. However, before I retired I told them that as I could not get any right among men here I hoped I should hereafter in Heaven, and I immediately left the cabin, filled with resentment and sorrow. The only coat I had with me my master took away with him, and said if my prize-money had been £10,000 he had a right to it all and would have taken it. I had about nine guineas which, during my long seafaring life, I had scraped together from trifling perquisites and little ventures, and I hid it that instant lest my master should take that from me likewise, still hoping that by some means or other I should make my escape to the shore; and indeed some of my old shipmates told me not to despair for they would get me back again, and that as soon as they could get their pay, they would immediately come to Portsmouth to me, where this ship was going: but, alas! all my hopes were baffled and the hour of my deliverance was yet far off. My master, having soon concluded his bargain with the captain, came out of the cabin, and he and his people got into the boat and put off; I followed them with aching eyes as long as I could, and when they were out of sight I threw myself on the deck, while my heart was ready to burst with sorrow and anguish.

Source: Olaudah Equiano, *The Interesting Narrative and Other Writings*, edited by Vincent Carretta (New York: Penguin Books, 1995), pp. 91–94.

5.4 GEORGE WHITEFIELD, ACCOUNT OF A VISIT TO SOUTH CAROLINA (1740)

George Whitefield, the leading preacher of the Great Awakening, maintained a diary in which he recorded his travels to spread the word of the Lord. He edited and published these journals in regular installments so as to reach a wider audience. Though an Englishman by birth, he visited America seven times. This 1740 selection comes from his second trip to the thirteen colonies, which was very successful, in that he drew large crowds and made many converts. Yet in this selection we see that not everyone was inclined to hear Whitefield's message, and that he himself was not always disposed to see all souls as equal.

Tuesday, January 1, 1740. Rode about ten miles, and where we baited, met with one who I had great reason to believe, was a child of God. It grieved me that I could stay no longer, but being in haste, we passed over a half-mile ferry. About sunset, we came to a tavern, five miles within the province of South Carolina. Here I immediately perceived the people were more polite than those we generally met with; but I believe the people of the house wished I had not come to be their guest that night; for, it being New Year's Day, several of the neighbours were met together to divert themselves by dancing country dances. By the advice of my companions, I went in amongst them whilst a woman was dancing a jig. At my first entrance I endeavoured to shew the folly of such entertainments, and to convince her how well pleased the devil was at every step she took. For some time she endeavoured to outbrave me; neither the fiddler nor she desisted; but at last she gave over, and the musician laid aside his instrument. It would have made any one smile to see how the rest of the company, one by one attacked me, and brought, as they thought, arguments to support their wantonness; but Christ triumphed over Satan. All were soon put to silence, and were, for some time, so overawed, that after I had discoursed with them on the nature of baptism, and the necessity of being born again, in order to enjoy the Kingdom of Heaven, I baptized, at their entreaty, one of their children, and prayed afterwards as I was enabled, and as the circumstances of the company required. I and my companions then took a little refreshment; but the people were so bent on their pleasure, that notwithstanding all that had been said, after I had gone to bed, I heard their music and dancing, which made me look back upon my own past follies with shame and confusion of face; for such an one, not long since, was I myself. Lord, for Thy mercies' sake, shew all unhappy formalists of the same favour, and suffer them not to go in such a carnal security till they lift up their eyes in torment! Draw them, O draw them from feeding upon such husks. Let them know what it is to feast upon the fatted calf, even the comforts of the Blessed Spirit. Amen.

Wednesday, Jan. 2. Rose very early, prayed, sung a hymn, and gave a sharp reproof to the dancers, who were very attentive, and took it in good part. At break of day, we mounted our horses, and I think, never had a more pleasant journey. For nearly twenty miles, we rode over a beautiful bay as plain as a terrace walk, and as we passed along were wonderfully delighted to see the porpoises taking their pastime, and heard, as it were, shore resounding to shore the praises of Him Who hath set bounds to the sea that it cannot pass, and hath said, "Here shall your proud waves be stayed." At night we intended to call at a gentleman's house, where we had been recommended, about forty miles distant from our last night's lodging; but the moon being totally eclipsed, we missed the path that turned out of the road, and then thought it most advisable, as we were in the main road, to go on our way, trusting to the Almighty to strengthen both our beasts and us. We had not gone far when we saw a light. Two of my friends went up to it, and found a hut full of negroes; they enquired after the gentleman's house whither we had been directed, but the negroes seemed surprised, and said they knew no such man, and that they were new comers. From these circumstances, one of my friends inferred, that these negroes might be some of those who lately had made an insurrection in the province, and had run away from their masters. When he returned, we were all of his mind, and, therefore, thought it best to mend our pace. Soon after, we saw another great fire near the roadside, and imaging there was another nest of such negroes, we made a circuit into the woods, and one of my friends at a distance observed them dancing round the fire. The moon shining brightly, we soon found our way into the great road again; and after we had gone about a dozen miles, (Expecting to find negroes in every place), we came to a great plantation, the master of which gave us lodging, and our beasts provender. Upon our relating the circumstances of our travels, he satisfied us concerning the negroes, informed us whose they were, and upon what occasion they were in those places in which we found them. This afforded us much comfort, after we had ridden nearly threescore miles, and, as we thought, in great peril of our lives. Blessed be Thy Name, O Lord, for this, and all other Thy mercies, through Jesus Christ!

Thursday, Jan.3. Had a hospitable breakfast; set out late in the morning, passed over a three mile ferry near George Town; and for the ease of our beasts, rode not above nineteen miles the whole day. "A good man," says Solomon, "is merciful to his beast."

Source: William Wale, ed., *Whitefield's Journals* (London: Henry Drane, 1905), pp. 379–381.

5.5 PHYLLIS WHEATLEY, "TO THE UNIVERSITY OF CAMBRIDGE, IN NEW ENGLAND" (1773)

Phyllis Wheatley was brought as a slave from Africa to America in 1761, when she was about eight years old. She was purchased by the wealthy Boston merchant John Wheatley to be a companion to his wife. Wheatley proved to be an excellent student, and they tutored her in English, Latin, history, and Christianity. During this time, the students at Harvard University were becoming increasingly known for their wild and destructive behavior. Here, Wheatley reminds them what people of African descent would do with the education they were being offered if it was given to them. Years later, she would receive her freedom from the Wheatley family.

To the University of Cambridge, in New England

While an intrinsic ardor prompts to write,
The muses promise to assist my pen;
'Twas not long since I left my native shore
The land of errors, and *Egyptian* gloom:
Father of mercy, 'twas thy gracious hand
Brought me in safety from those dark abodes.
      Students, to you 'tis giv'n to scan the heights
Above, to traverse the ethereal space,
And mark the systems of revolving worlds.
Still more, ye sons of science ye receive
The blissful news by messengers from heav'n,
How *Jesus'* blood for your redemption flows.
See him with hands out-stretcht upon the cross;

Source: Library of Congress Rare Book and Special Collections Division
Washington, D.C.

Immense compassion in his bosom glows;
He hears revilers, nor resents their scorn:
What matchless mercy in the Son of God!
When the whole human race by sin had fall'n,
He deign'd to die that they might rise again,
And share with him in the sublimest skies,
Life without death, and glory without end.

    Improve your privileges while they stay,
Ye pupils, and each hour redeem, that bears
Or good or bad report of you to heav'n.
Let sin, that baneful evil to the soul,
By you be shunn'd, nor once remit your guard;
Suppress the deadly serpent in its egg.
Ye blooming plants of human race devine,
An *Ethiop* tells you 'tis your greatest foe;
Its transient sweetness turns to endless pain,
And in immense perdition sinks the soul.

Source: Julian D. Mason, ed., *The Poems of Phyllis Wheatley* (Chapel Hill: University of North Carolina Press, 1989
    [1966]), p. 52.

Conflict in the Empire
1713–1774

COMMON THREADS

What role did the colonies play in imperial conflict? That is, how did they shape that conflict, and how were they shaped by it?

How were Native Americans drawn into imperial conflict? To what extent were they able to shape it for their own purposes?

What did it mean for the American colonies to be peripheral—literally—to the British Empire?

How did the colonists adapt the available political theories to their purposes? What in the American experience made those theories attractive to the colonists?

OUTLINE

HALL

Susannah Willard Johnson
Experiences the Empire

Today the town is Charlestown, New Hampshire, but then it was "No. 4," a small farming village on the northern frontier of Massachusetts. In 1754 Susannah Willard Johnson and her husband, James, lived there, having moved to the frontier during a break in the struggle between Britain and France for North America. At 24, Susannah had been married for seven years and had three children, with another due any day. James, a native of Ireland, had started his life in America as a servant indentured to Susannah's uncle. After working for him for 10 years, James purchased the remainder of his time, married Susannah, and made his way by farming and shopkeeping. He also became a lieutenant in the militia.

The region's Abenaki Indians—Algonquians who were allied with the French and had their own grievances against the encroaching settlers—presented both danger and opportunity. At first the settlers at No. 4 were so frightened that they stayed in the fort. However, Susannah later reported that "hostility at length vanished—the Indians expressed a wish to traffic, the inhabitants laid by their fears. . . ." James Johnson was part of the consumer revolution, selling goods to his fellow settlers and to the Abenakis, who gave him furs in return.

Susannah Johnson described her family's life as "harmony and safety" and "boasted with exultation that I should, with husband, friends, and luxuries, live happy in spite of the fear of savages." By the summer of 1754, however, the rumors of impending warfare with France would make the frontier village a target of France's Abenaki allies.

On August 30, 1754, just before daybreak, a neighbor coming to work for the Johnsons appeared at the door. As the Johnsons opened the door, the neighbor rushed in, followed by 11 Abenaki men. Soon, Susannah said, they were "all over the house, some upstairs, some hauling my sister out of bed, another had hold of me, and one was approaching Mr. Johnson, who stood in the middle of the floor to deliver himself up."

The Abenakis tied up the men, gathered the women and children, and marched the party to the north. On the second day of her captivity, Susannah went into labor. Attended by her sister and husband, she gave birth to a daughter, whom she named Captive. Before they returned home five years later, Susannah and her family were held captive in Canada and sent to England as part of a prisoner exchange.

The French and Indian War had begun on the northern frontier, and the Indians were manipulating it to their advantage. In peacetime they traded furs for manufactured goods, but in wartime they seized British settlers, took them to Canada, and sold them to the French, who either ransomed them back to the British or traded them for prisoners of war. What to others might seem an imperial struggle was to Susannah Johnson a terrifying assault that took her from her home and family. The consumer revolution that gave settlers such as the Johnsons the opportunity to live a good life on the frontier was rooted in a struggle between France and England, two empires competing over both the markets the consumer revolution was creating and the lands it was populating. As families such as the Johnsons pushed at the frontiers, they became actors on a global stage.

The Victory of the British Empire

From 1689 to 1763, Britain and France were at war more than half of the time. These wars gave shape to the eighteenth century and created the international context for the American Revolution in several ways. First, the Revolution grew out of Britain's ineffective efforts to govern the enlarged empire it won from France in 1763. Second, France's support for the colonies in their war against Britain helped secure the colonies' victory. Third, once the colonies secured their independence, they entered a world still torn by conflict between Britain and France.

All of these wars were rooted in a struggle for world dominance between two powerful empires. To a great extent, colonial and imperial objectives coincided. Both Britain and the colonies would benefit from securing the empire's borders and from expanding British markets. Yet the imperial wars also exposed the growing divergence between the political economy of the colonies and that of the mother country. When the growing empire and its wars threatened to increase Britain's power over the colonists, raise their taxes to pay for the empire, and station among them a permanent army, the colonists resisted and finally rebelled.

New War, Old Pattern

England and France were at peace from the end of Queen Anne's War in 1713 (see Chapter 4) until 1739. It was an uneasy peace in the British North American colonies, however. In what is now Maine, New Englanders continued to fight the Abenakis, forcing them into a closer alliance with the French, who were attempting to stabilize relations with the Algonquians. The most common method was by providing "gifts" of trade goods.

France and Spain had also arrived at an uneasy peace in North America. Each had come to an arrangement with the increasingly powerful Comanche empire in the Southwest. When France built its forts along the lower Mississippi valley (see Chapter 4), Spain responded, in 1716, with an outpost in Texas. Both had hoped to expand their empires across the plains but were thwarted by the Comanches, who, like the Iroquois to the east, played the European powers off against each other. By the 1740s, the Comanches had forced both France and Spain to trade with them on advantageous terms, while blocking both from further expansion.

Another round of international warfare broke out in 1739 and lasted nine years. In the War of Jenkins's Ear (1739–1744), Britain attempted to expand into Spanish territories and markets in the Americas. Urged on by merchants, and with the approval of colonists who wanted to eliminate Spain as a rival, Britain found an excuse for declaring war: a ship's captain, Robert Jenkins, turned up in Parliament in 1738 holding in his hand what he claimed was his ear, severed by the Spanish seven years earlier in the Caribbean. Once again, colonists joined in what they hoped would be a glorious international endeavor, only to be disillusioned. In 1741, 3,600 colonists, mostly poor young men lured by the promise of Spanish plunder, joined 5,000 Britons in a failed attack on Cartagena, Colombia. More than half the colonial contingent died.

Another ambitious move against the Spanish Empire failed in 1740. James Oglethorpe and settlers hired by South Carolina, accompanied by Cherokee and Creek allies, failed to seize the Spanish outpost at St. Augustine and left the southern border vulnerable. When Oglethorpe's troops repulsed a Spanish attack in 1742, however, Spain's plan to demolish Georgia and South Carolina and arm their slaves was thwarted.

Just as the War of Jenkins's Ear ended in stalemate, so did King George's War (1744–1748), a conflict between Britain and Austria on one side and France and Prussia on the other over succession to the Austrian throne. A French raid on a fishing village in Nova Scotia met with a huge retaliation by the British. Troops from Massachusetts, supported by the British navy, captured the French fort at Louisbourg. Finally, a joint British-colonial venture had succeeded. But a planned attack on Québec was called off when the British fleet failed to arrive. At war's end, Britain returned Louisbourg to France and warned the colonists that they had to maintain the peace. The British blockade of French ports cut off trade to Canada, including the all-important presents to Indian allies and trade partners. Without these gifts, the French-Indian empire began to crumble.

The Local Impact of Global War

Successive rounds of warfare had a significant impact on politics and society in British North America. Although the colonists identified strongly with the British cause, decades of warfare were a constant drain on the colonial treasury and population.

Wars are expensive. Generally, rates of taxation in colonial America were low, except when wars had to be financed (see Figure 6–1). In a rehearsal for the conflicts that would lead to the American Revolution, the British government complained that the colonists were unwilling to contribute their fair share to the imperial wars. As a rule, colonial legislatures were willing to go only so far in raising taxes to pay for imperial wars or expeditions against Indians. Then they simply issued paper money. Inevitably, the currency depreciated, making even worse the boom-and-bust cycles that war economies always produce.

No colony did more to support the imperial war efforts than Massachusetts, but the result was heightened political conflict at home. Royal governors, eager to please officials in London, pushed the colony to contribute to the imperial wars. As many as one-fifth of the colony's men may have served in the military in the middle of the eighteenth century. In 1747 Boston mobs rioted for three days to resist the Royal Navy's attempt to "impress" (force) men into service, and the local militia refused to restore order. For the first time, Bostonians began to speak about a right to resist tyranny.

Much more than in Europe, civilians in America became victims of war. By the eighteenth century, conventions of "civilized" warfare that held that civilians should be spared broke down in America for two reasons. First, without a transportation system to supply the army, troops often relied on plunder. Second, frontier Indians, adapting their traditional practices of war, routinely attacked villages, seizing captives to replenish their populations and to ransom to the French. Between 1675 and 1763, when frontier settlers such as Susannah Johnson were at risk, Indians took more than 1,600 New England settlers as captives, more than 90 percent during times of war.

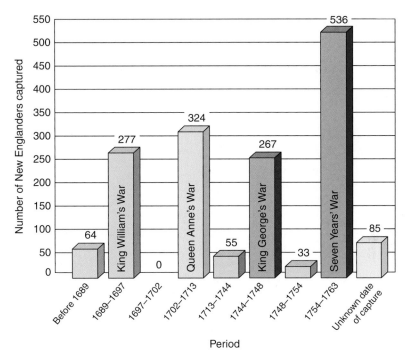

Figure 6–1   New England Captives, 1675–1763 During periods of war, the number of New Englanders taken captive by northern Indians and the French increased dramatically; more than 90 percent of captives were taken during wartime. *Source:* Alden Vaughan, *Roots of American Racism* (New York: Oxford University Press, 1990), p. 31.

Almost half the colonists seized eventually returned home, but, as with Susannah Johnson's son Sylvanus, who had forgotten English entirely, Indian customs "wore off" only "by degree." Other captives died during the arduous march to Canada, sometimes killed by Indians who thought them too weak to survive the journey. Many died of disease, and a few, typically girls between 7 and 15, remained with their captors voluntarily. Historians debate why this was so. Perhaps it was because Puritan culture trained girls to respond without question to those in authority. Or perhaps it was because, after the rigors of a Puritan upbringing, the relative freedom of Indian culture was inviting.

The French Empire Crumbles from Within

In the years after King George's War, a change in French policy offered a small band of Miami Indians the chance to gain an advantage over rivals. In the process, they started a chain of events that led to the French and Indian War.

Although King George's War had ended in a stalemate, it weakened the French position in North America. The costs of war had forced the French to cut back on their presents to allied Algonquian tribes, especially in the Ohio River valley. To raise revenue, the French sharply increased their charges for the lease of trading posts; in turn, traders raised the prices that they charged the Indians for trade goods. These changes significantly weakened the French hold over their Indian allies, creating political instability that was the underlying North American cause of the French and Indian War.

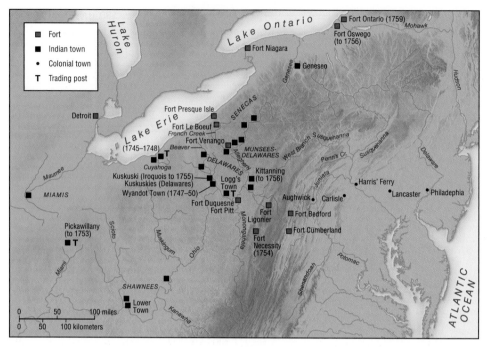

Map 6–1 The Ohio River Valley, 1747–1758 This territory, inhabited by a number of small bands of Indians, was coveted by both the French and the British, not to mention several competing groups of colonial land speculators. The rivalries between the imperial powers, among the Indian bands, and between rival groups of speculators made this region a powder keg. *Source:* Adapted from Michael McConnell, *A Country Between* (Lincoln: University of Nebraska, 1992), pp. 116–117.

The Ohio River valley was home to small, refugee tribes (see Map 6–1). As long as the French provided liberal presents and cheap trade goods, they maintained a loose control. Once that control ended, however, each tribe sought to increase its advantage over the others, at a time when the British recognized the strategic and economic importance of the region.

The temporary power vacuum afforded a small group of Miamis, led by a chieftain called Memeskia, an opportunity to play one group of colonists off another. The chain of events that led to the French and Indian War began in 1748 when Memeskia's group established a new village, Pickawillany, near the head of the Miami River. Memeskia welcomed English traders from Pennsylvania, because their goods were better and cheaper than those of the French. He hoped to trade with the British free of political or military obligations.

Memeskia's move threatened not only the balance of power between Britain and France but also that between Pennsylvania and Virginia. The Pennsylvanians welcomed trade with the Miamis, for it gave them a claim to the western lands that Virginians sought. At the same time, Memeskia used his access to British traders to attract many small bands of followers to his village. Alarmed, the French shifted away from trade to force. In 1749, they sent a small expedition to cow their former Indian allies back into submission. When it failed, they began to raid dissident Indian encampments and planned to establish a fort in the Ohio River valley. With this change in French policy,

Indians faced two options: to gather Indian allies (Memeskia's tactic) or to make alliances with the British (the strategy of an Iroquois chieftain named Tanacharison). Neither route promised real security, but the chaos these bids for advantage created drew the French and British into war.

In 1752, Tanacharison agreed to give Virginia not only the 200,000 acres claimed by the Ohio Company, a group of Virginia speculators, but also all the land between the Susquehanna and Allegheny Rivers (today's Kentucky, West Virginia, and western Pennsylvania). In return, Virginia promised Tanacharison's people trade and protection from their enemies. Memeskia was isolated. With no European or Indian power dominant in the region, conflicts broke out, and the French pried off some of Memeskia's allies and conquered the rest. In a raid on Pickawillany, 250 pro-French Ottawas and Chippewas killed Memeskia. Their village destroyed, the demoralized Miamis returned to the French for protection. For the moment, the French regained power, but by shifting their policy from trade to force, they set a course that would lead to the loss of their North American empire.

The Virginians Ignite a War

Both France and Virginia now claimed the Ohio River valley, and they raced to establish forts to secure their claims. Virginia entrusted the job to a well-connected 21-year-old with almost no qualifications for the post: George Washington. Washington was tied to the powerful Fairfax clan, a British family that owned 5 million acres in Virginia and held a share in the Ohio Company. In the Anglo-American world, advancement came through such linked ties of family and patronage.

In the spring of 1754, the French and Virginians scrambled to see who could build a fort first at the Forks of the Ohio (present-day Pittsburgh). The force that Virginia sent to the region, with Washington second in command, was pathetically small. Although the French army—numbering 1,000—was only 50 miles away, a combined Virginia-Indian band led by Washington attacked and defeated a small French reconnaissance party. The French and Indian War (known in Europe as the Seven Years' War) had begun.

The Virginians had bitten off more than they could chew. Washington's small fort was reinforced by British regulars but was quickly deserted by Indian allies, who recognized it as indefensible. The French overwhelmed the fort, driving Washington and his troops back to Virginia. Although war was not officially declared in Europe until May 1756, fighting soon spread throughout the frontier.

From Local to Imperial War

At the beginning of the war, the advantage was with the French. Although the population in the British colonies greatly outnumbered that of New France, France's population was three times larger than Britain's and its army 10 times the size. More important, the more centralized French state was better prepared to coordinate the massive effort an international war required. The British government, aware that lack of coordination among its colonies could cripple the war effort, in summer 1754 instructed all the colonies north of Virginia to plan for a collective defense and to shore up the alliance with the Six (Iroquois) Nations. Pennsylvania's Benjamin Franklin offered the delegates, who met in Albany, a plan, known as the Albany Plan of Union, which every colony rejected.

The localism of the American colonies made cooperation difficult if not impossible. A deeply ingrained value, localism was suspicious of the centralized European state and its army of professionals.

Britain was now in its fourth war with France in less than a century. It had authorized Virginia's foray into the Ohio River valley and sent two regiments, under the command of General Edward Braddock, to Virginia in late 1754, hoping that the colonists could fight with only a little British assistance. But the disarray continued: colonial soldiers were reluctant to obey an officer from another colony, let alone one from the British army.

With four times as many troops as the British had in North America, superior leadership, and no intercolonial rivalries, the French dominated the first phase of the war, from 1754 through 1757. The British and colonial armies planned to besiege four French forts: Fort Duquesne (Pittsburgh), Fort Niagara (Niagara Falls), Fort St. Frédéric (Crown Point, at the southern end of Lake Champlain), and Fort Beauséjour (Nova Scotia).

Braddock was to attack Fort Duquesne with a combined force of British regulars and colonial troops, but without Indians. He had alienated the regional Indians, who rejoined the French alliance. After a grueling two-month march, on July 9, 1755, Braddock's forces were surprised close to their objective by a French and Indian force. Almost 1,000 British and colonial troops were killed or wounded; Braddock himself died from wounds suffered in the ambush. One of the survivors was George Washington, who had been serving as an unsalaried adjutant to Braddock to learn the art of war.

Two of the other three planned assaults ended in disappointment as well. William Shirley, who became the British commander in chief, led the attack on Fort Niagara himself and assigned Fort St. Frédéric to William Johnson, a Mohawk Valley Indian trader who was soon made superintendent of Indian affairs for the northern colonies. Well suited for leading Iroquois forays against the French, Johnson led a force of about 3,500, including 300 Iroquois. Their advance was stopped by the French and their Native American allies, but with equal casualties on both sides and the capture of the French commander, the British declared victory and elevated Johnson to the nobility. In the winter of 1755–1756 the British built Fort William Henry, and the French, Fort Carillon (which the British renamed Ticonderoga).

Hampered by rough terrain and intercolonial wrangling, Shirley's force never made it to Fort Niagara. The only outright success was at Fort Beauséjour, near the British colony at Nova Scotia. A British-financed expedition of New England volunteers easily seized the fort, and the British evicted 10,000 Acadians (French residents of Nova Scotia) who would not take an oath of loyalty. About 300 ended up in French Louisiana, where their name was abbreviated to "Cajuns."

Both the British and the French expected their colonists to carry most of the load of the war. Their defeats and continued intercolonial rivalries left the British vulnerable and the frontier exposed. The French began a cautious but successful offensive. First, they encouraged Indian raids along the frontier from Maine to South Carolina. Indians swung back to the French because the French appeared less dangerous than the land-hungry British. The price for French friendship, however, was participation in the war against the British. By the fall of 1756, some 3,000 settlers had been killed, and the line of settlement had been pushed back 150 miles in some places.

The French and their Indian allies seized Fort Bull in March 1756 and Fort Oswego several months later. A little over a year later, a massive French force attacked Fort William Henry. This loosely organized army of 8,000 included 1,000 Indian warriors and another 800 converted Algonquians accompanied by their Catholic priests. After a seven-day siege and heavy bombardment, the British commander surrendered on August 9, 1757. Louis-Joseph de Montcalm, the French commander, offered European-style

Braddock's Defeat This detail depicting Braddock's defeat is from a drawing by an engineer with the British army.

DEFEAT and DEATH of GENERAL BRADDOCK in North America.

terms: the British were to return their French and Indian prisoners, keep their personal weapons, and march back to Fort Edward, on the lower Hudson River, promising not to fight the French for 18 months. Historians still debate whether Montcalm knew what was about to take place. The Indians had expected, as was their custom, to be allowed to take plunder and captives. Denied this opportunity, they fell on the British, including the sick, women, and children, as they were evacuating the fort the next morning.

The massacre at Fort William Henry had significant repercussions. Still angry at being denied the spoils of war, Montcalm's Indian allies returned home, taking smallpox with them. The French would never again have the assistance of such a significant number of Indian allies. The British were outraged. The new British commander, Lord Jeffrey Amherst, declared the surrender terms null and void. Later, under his order, Delaware Indians who had been invited to a peace talk were given, ostensibly as presents, blankets that had been infected with smallpox. Historians are not certain whether these blankets were responsible for the outbreak of the disease among local Indians, but that was certainly Amherst's intent.

Problems with British-Colonial Cooperation

The British and the colonists blamed each other for their defeats. There was some truth in their accusations: unwillingness to sacrifice and disastrous infighting among the colonists, and arrogance among the British. These recriminations, more than any side's failing, created problems. The colonists and the British had different expectations about their roles in the war. The colonists were not prepared for the high taxes or sacrifice of liberty that waging an international war required.

Louis-Joseph de Montcalm Americans blamed the French commander for the massacre at Fort William Henry.

The British were dismayed by what they perceived as the colonists' selfishness, as they engaged in profiteering and trading with the enemy. Colonial governments were no more generous. Braddock's expedition to Fort Duquesne was delayed by the colonies' unwillingness to provision his army.

After Braddock's defeat, colonials deserted in droves. The British began recruiting servants and apprentices, angering their masters. Another serious problem was that of quartering soldiers over the winter. Under English law, which did not extend specifically to the colonies, troops in England could be lodged in public buildings rather than private homes. In the colonies, however, there weren't enough buildings in which to house soldiers without resorting to private homes. The residents of Albany took in soldiers only under threat of force. Philadelphians were rescued by the ever-resourceful Franklin, who opened a newly built hospital to the troops. In Charleston, soldiers had to camp outdoors, where they fell victim to disease.

Other problems arose from joint operations. The British army was a disciplined professional fighting force, led by members of the upper classes; service in it was a career. In contrast, colonial soldiers were primarily civilian amateurs, led by members of the middle class from their hometowns. Colonial soldiers believed that they were fighting by contract for a set period of time, for a specific objective, for a set rate of pay, and under a particular officer. If any of the terms were violated, the soldier considered himself free to go home.

The British, however, expected the same discipline from the colonists as they did from their own army. All colonial soldiers operating with regular forces were subject to British martial law, which was cruel and uncompromising. One regular soldier, for example, was sentenced to 1,000 lashes for stealing a keg of beer, which a merciful officer reduced to a mere 900! The British officers were almost unanimous in their condemnation of colonial soldiers. According to Brigadier General James Wolfe, "The Americans are in general the dirtiest most contemptible cowardly dogs that you can conceive."

Yet the colonists certainly believed that they were doing their share. Tax rates were raised sharply, tripling in Virginia in three years, for example. The human contribution was even more impressive. At the height of the war, Massachusetts was raising 7,000 soldiers a year, from a colony of only 50,000 men. Perhaps as many as 3 out of 10 adult men served in the military during the war, and only the Civil War and the Revolution had higher casualty rates.

The British Gain the Advantage

Montcalm's victory at Fort William Henry marked the French high-water mark. After a change of government in 1757, Britain resolved to win the war, as William Pitt became head of the cabinet. His rise to power represented the triumph of the commercial classes and their vision of the empire. Pitt was the first British leader who was as committed to a victory in the Americas as in Europe, believing that the future of the British Empire lay in the extended empire and its trade. Britain's aim in North America now shifted from simply regaining territory to seizing New France itself. Pitt sent 2,000 additional troops, promised 6,000 more, and asked the colonies to raise 20,000 of their own. To support so large an army, Pitt raised taxes on the already heavily taxed British and borrowed heavily, doubling the size of the British debt. He won the cooperation of the colonies by promising that Britain would pay up to half of their costs for fighting the war. As all of this money poured into the colonies, it improved their economies dramatically.

Now the British could take the offensive (see Map 6–2). In a series of great victories, they won Louisbourg on Cape Breton Island in July 1758; then Fort Frontenac in August; and finally, in November, Fort Duquesne, which the British renamed Fort Pitt. The only defeat was at Fort Carillon (called Ticonderoga by the British). There, Susannah Johnson's husband, James, was one of the casualties. The British seized Fort Frontenac, disrupting the supply lines from the French to the Ohio Valley Indians, who shifted their allegiance. The British also moved from a policy of confrontation to one of accommodation. In the Treaty of Easton (1758), 13 Ohio Valley tribes agreed to remain neutral in return for a promise to keep the territory west of the Alleghenies free of settlers. Also, gifts to the Iroquois brought them back into the fold.

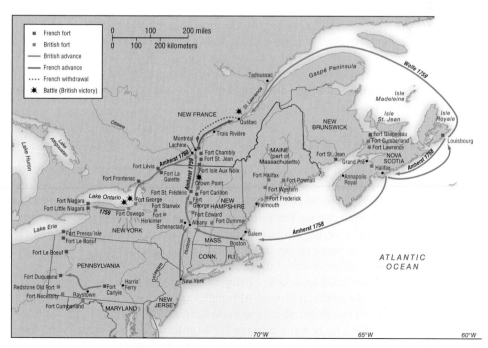

Map 6–2   The Second Phase of the French and Indian War, 1758–1763 This map shows British advances in Pennsylvania, New York, and Canada.

The British were now ready for the final offensive. Historians always argue about when and why a war is "lost": unless an army has been annihilated and the population entirely subjugated, which is rare, when to surrender is always a subjective decision. Political and military leaders must decide when the loss in lives and resources can no longer be justified, and the population must agree that further fighting is pointless. By 1759, some of the French believed that the war was essentially over. Casualties were extremely high, food was in short supply, and inflation was rampant. Most of the Indian allies had deserted the cause, and the French government was unable to match Pitt's spending on the war. It would take two more years of fighting and the loss of thousands more lives before the French surrendered, however.

In the summer of 1759, General James Wolfe took the struggle for North America into the heart of Canada, laying siege to Québec. Québec's position on a bluff high above the St. Lawrence made it almost impregnable, so for months Wolfe bombarded the city and tried to wear down its citizens, terrorizing those who lived on its outskirts by burning crops and houses. In mid-September, Wolfe ordered an assault up the 175-foot cliff below the city. In a battle that lasted only half an hour, his soldiers claimed victory on the Plains of Abraham. Each side suffered casualties of 15 percent, and both Wolfe and his French opponent, Montcalm, were killed. Four days later, New France's oldest permanent settlement surrendered to the British. By the time the British reached Montréal, the French army numbered fewer than 3,000 men.

The Treaty of Paris ended the war in 1763. By then, Britain had also seized the French sugar islands in the Caribbean and, after Spain entered the war on the French side, Havana and the Philippines. Pitt would have continued to fight, but the British public was unwilling to pay more to increase the size of the empire. The French, exhausted by war, surrendered all of Canada except for two small fishing islands in return for the right to hold on to the most valuable sugar islands, the most important part of their American empire. France even gave New Orleans and all of its territory west of the Mississippi to Spain as compensation for losing Florida, which the British claimed (see Map 6–3). (Britain let Spain keep Havana and the Philippines.) Britain staked its future on the mainland of North America, believing correctly that it would ultimately be more valuable than the sugar islands of the Caribbean.

Enforcing the Empire

Even before the French and Indian War, some in the British government urged tighter control over the American colonies. Colonists smuggled and even traded with the enemy throughout the war, and colonial assemblies sometimes impeded the war effort. Pitt had increased Britain's debt to pay for the war, rather than waiting for the colonial assemblies. Now, with the war over, Britain faced a staggering debt of £122,603,336. Moreover, there was a huge new territory to govern, one coveted by speculators and settlers and inhabited by Indian tribes determined to resist encroachment.

The American Revolution grew out of Britain's attempts to draw its American colonies more closely into the imperial system. Although various master plans for reorganizing the empire had been circulated, there had never been an overarching design or a clear set of guidelines. By 1763, there was a new resolve to enforce a vision of the empire and the role of colonies in it. In 1760 a new king, the 22-year-old George III, ascended to the throne upon the death of his grandfather. Reasonably well educated, the young king was

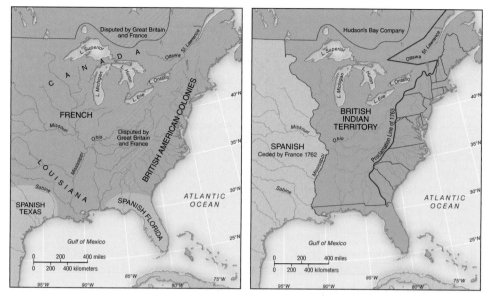

Map 6–3   The North American Colonies Before and After the French and Indian War In the Treaty of Paris in 1763, more American territory was transferred than at any time before or since. *Source:* Helen Hornbeck Tanner, *Atlas of Great Lakes Indian History* (Norman: University of Oklahoma Press, 1987), p. 54.

determined to play a role in government. He changed ministers so frequently that chaos ensued. It is not clear, however, that more enlightened leadership would have prevented the war, for George's ministers pursued a fairly consistent policy toward the colonies. In resisting that policy, the American colonists developed a new and different idea of the purpose of government, one that propelled them to revolution.

Pontiac's Rebellion and Its Aftermath

Because the British had defeated the French and had entered into alliances with the Iroquois and the Ohio Valley Indians, peace in the West should have come easily. The British, however, soon made the same mistake that the French had made when they discontinued presents to their Indian allies 15 years earlier. Thinking they could impose their will on the Indians, the British instead found themselves embroiled in another war.

At the end of the French and Indian War, the western Algonquian tribes hoped the British would follow the practices of the middle ground by mediating their disputes, trading with them at good prices, and giving them presents. Lord Jeffrey Amherst, commanding British forces in North America, cut off the presents, believing them too expensive. He thought that threats of an Indian revolt were exaggerated and was willing to take the risk of war.

The war of 1763 is commonly known as Pontiac's Rebellion, named after the Ottawa chieftain who played a prominent role. It was the first battle in a long, and ultimately unsuccessful, attempt by Indians to keep the region between the Mississippi River and the Alleghenies free of European settlers. The Indians seized every fort except for Pitt, Niagara, and Detroit, and Detroit was under siege for six months (see Map 6–4). Casualties were high: about 2,000 civilians, 400 soldiers, and an unknown number of Indians. Tortures by both sides were horrific, and American colonists took out their aggressions on peaceful or

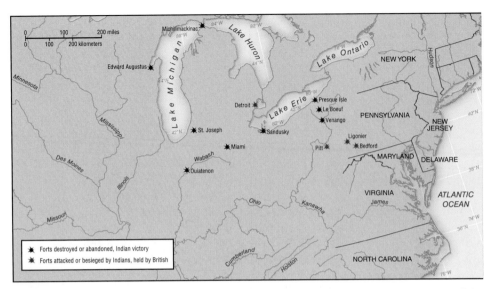

Map 6–4 Pontiac's Rebellion, 1763 The war began when the British abandoned the policy of the middle ground and cut off presents to the western Indians. In their uprising, the Indians destroyed nine British forts and attacked another four before the war ended in a draw. *Source:* Tanner, *Atlas of Great Lakes Indian History*, p. 49.

defenseless Indians. In December 1763, a party of 50 armed men from the Pennsylvania village of Paxton descended on a tiny community of Christian Indians living at Conestoga Manor, eight miles west of Lancaster. They killed and scalped the six people they found— two men, three women, and a child—and burned their houses. Two weeks later, another group of these "Paxton Boys" broke into the county workhouse, where the remainder of the small tribe had been put for their own protection, and killed them, too.

Although colonial leaders decried acts of violence, they did little to prevent or punish them. British officials saw the failure of the colonists to maintain order on the frontier and protect innocent Indians as further proof of the incompetence of colonial govern- ments. Even before Pontiac's Rebellion ended in a draw, the British had decided that peace with the western Indians could be preserved only by keeping colonial settlers and speculators away. The Proclamation of 1763 attempted to confine the colonists to the east of an imaginary line running down the spine of the Alleghenies. George Washington called the proclamation "a temporary expedient to quiet the minds of the Indians" and ignored it. Other Virginia speculators sought to take the territory by force. A pretext came in 1774 when several settlers killed several Indians, and John Logan, a Mingo Indian, sought vengeance for his slain relatives. Rather than resolving this conflict in the ways of the middle ground, Virginia's royal governor sent a force of 2,000 to vanquish the Indians. Although the Virginians' success in Lord Dunmore's War ended Indian claims to Kentucky, Britain was still not ready to permit speculators or settlers to claim the land.

Paying for the Empire: Sugar and Stamps

On the edge of the British Empire, the colonies were important, but not nearly as impor- tant as Britain's domestic concerns. One of George III's highest priorities was to maintain the size of the army. During the French and Indian War, it had doubled, and it was filled with officers loyal to the king. Parliament in 1763 agreed to maintain a huge peacetime army, part of which would be posted in the colonies and West Indies. Colonists feared that the army would enforce customs regulations rather than police the Indians.

This large army, of course, would strain a budget already burdened by a huge war debt. George Grenville, the new prime minister, believed that the colonists should pay a portion of the £225,000 a year that the standing army would cost.

Under Grenville's leadership, Parliament passed four pieces of legislation to force the colonies to contribute to their own upkeep. The Molasses Act of 1733 had established a duty of six cents per gallon, but smugglers paid off customs officials at the rate of one and a half cents a gallon. At Grenville's urging, Parliament passed the Sugar Act (1764), which dropped the duty to three cents but established procedures to make certain it was collected. To discourage smuggling, shippers were required to file elaborate papers each time an item was loaded onto a ship. In addition, accused violators were to be tried in admiralty courts in Nova Scotia, where the burden of proof would be on the defendant and the judgment would be rendered by judges rather than a jury.

To regulate colonial economies in the interest of British creditors, the Currency Act (1764) forbade the issuing of any colonial currency. British merchants had complained that colonists were discharging their debts in depreciated paper money. Moreover, the Sugar Act and the Stamp Act (passed the following year) required that duties and taxes both be paid in specie (silver and gold). The colonists complained that there was not anywhere near as much specie in the colonies as they needed.

The third and most important piece of imperial legislation was the Stamp Act (1765). The first direct tax on the American people, the Stamp Act sought to raise revenue by taxing documents used in court proceedings; papers used in clearing ships from harbors; college diplomas; appointments to public office; bonds, grants, and deeds for mortgages; indentures, leases, contracts, and bills of sale; liquor licenses; playing cards and dice; and pamphlets, newspapers (and the ads in them), and almanacs.

The final piece of legislation, the Quartering Act (1765), required the colonies to house troops in public buildings and provide them with firewood, candles, and drink.

Although the colonists objected to all of these pieces of legislation, the Stamp Act was the most troubling. By taxing newspapers and pamphlets, it foolishly angered printers and editors at a time when newspapers were taking the lead in criticizing the government and were perhaps the most significant public institution in the colonies. The Stamp Act also angered lawyers, for every time a lawyer performed the simplest task of his trade, he would have to buy a stamp. These laws fell hardest on the most affluent and politically active colonists, the merchants, lawyers, and printers. All of these pieces of legislation were an attempt to tie the colonies into a modern, centralized state. As the colonists framed their response to the new laws, they struggled with a question central to American history: Could the people share in the benefits of the modern state—in particular a trade protected by its navy and with borders secured by its army—without the state itself?

The British Empire in Crisis

Colonial resistance to the imperial legislation of 1763 to 1765 was swift and forceful. A coalition of elite leaders and common people, primarily in the cities, worked to

AMERICA AND THE WORLD

Paying for War

For most of human history, the costs of war have worked as a check on war making: a country could not spend any more on warfare than it could pay for. Some countries plundered their neighbors. Others taxed their own people, but there are always absolute limits to how much money can be extracted in this way. Other countries borrowed from foreigners, which put them at the mercy of foreign creditors.

In the seventeenth century, the Dutch figured out a new method of financing government: borrowing money from its own citizens by selling them interest-paying bonds. The government then taxed its people to pay off the bonds and the interest, which enabled it to spread out the costs of war over a long period. The result was higher taxes in peacetime—but no excessive burden during times of war. Those who bought government bonds were literally making an investment in their nation and profiting from its success.

This was the method that Britain used to pay for its rise to power beginning in the eighteenth century. It raised astronomical sums of money: £31 million for King William's War, £51 million for Queen Anne's War, £73 million for the Seven Years' War. And with each war, the government borrowed an increasing portion of the costs.

As Britain's war debt increased—it was up to £122,603,336 at the end of the Seven Years' War—the country had to raise taxes to pay for it. The English were paying higher taxes than any other nation in the world except for the Dutch. In fact, at the time of the French Revolution—caused in part by unacceptably high taxes—the British were taxed at a higher rate than the French. Yet the political mechanisms of taxation were so efficient that the government was able to collect tax revenues with relatively little resistance.

This achievement is remarkable when one considers the relative unfairness of the English tax system. The burden fell on the middle classes, whereas both the poor and the affluent were relatively lightly taxed. There was widespread agreement that the wages and necessities of the poor should be taxed lightly or not at all. Instead, the burden should fall, in theory, on the wealthy. Indeed, in 1690, 47 percent of England's revenues came from taxes on land and other property of the rich, but the powerful landowners refused to pay higher rates. As the need for revenue increased, the proportion of taxes paid by the wealthy fell. By 1763, it was down to 23 percent.

In search of revenue, the English government levied excise and stamp taxes, which fell most heavily on the middle classes. By the end of the Seven Years' War, the public had come close to reaching its limit. Already unhappy with the tax on beer, it objected to one on cider to help finance the last year of war.

Parliament worried that it could not increase taxes on its own people any further, and so it looked for other sources of revenue in other parts of its empire. At just the time that Parliament tried to tax the American colonies to pay for the troops stationed there, it was also stationing more forces in Ireland—and trying, unsuccessfully, to get the Irish parliament to pay for them. When the East India Company conquered the huge Indian state of Bengal, King George III imagined that India's wealth was "the only safe method of extracting this country out of its . . . load of debt." In return for letting the East India Company govern Bengal, the government extracted a fee of £400,000 a year, which the Company demanded from the Bengalis. This crushing tax burden, which coincided with a serious drought, plunged Bengal into a famine that killed 10 million people, a third of the population. With strong traditions of local government, the American colonists and the Irish were better able to resist England's attempts to tax them.

overturn the most objectionable aspects of the new regulations. In 1765, there was almost no thought of revolution, nor would there be for almost 10 years. Instead, the colonists rested their case on the British Constitution: all they wanted were the rights of Englishmen. Although in theory the colonists, as British subjects, were entitled to all of those rights, precisely how the British Constitution applied to colonists had never been clarified. The first phase of opposition, then, was a debate about the British Constitution, with the colonists insisting on their rights and the British government focusing on the colonists' obligations.

An Argument About Rights and Obligations

All along, Britain had maintained its right to regulate the colonies. Precisely what this meant became a matter of dispute after 1763. Did it mean regulation of trade? Taxation? Legislation? When Parliament passed these pieces of legislation, it acknowledged that the empire was a whole, that the parts existed for the benefit of the whole, and that Parliament had the authority to govern for the whole.

Britons were justifiably proud of their Parliament, one of the premier institutions of self-government in the world at the time. In principle, Parliament represented all the elements in society: the king, the aristocrats (in the House of Lords), and the common people (in the House of Commons). It mixed and balanced these three elements of society, which also represented the three possible forms of government—monarchy, rule by the king; aristocracy, rule by hereditary aristocrats; and democracy, rule by the people—thus preventing both tyranny and anarchy and preserving liberty.

The British believed, and American colonists agreed, that their superb government was the product of centuries of struggle. First the aristocrats struggled with the king for more freedom, gaining it in the Magna Carta of 1215, and then the people struggled and won liberty, most recently in the Glorious Revolution of 1688. In this view, liberty was a collective right held by the people against the rulers and a limitation on the power of the monarch. A chief example of public or civil liberty was the right to be taxed only by one's own representatives. Taxes were a free gift of the people that no monarch could demand.

These ideas about the British government can be described as *constitutionalism*. Constitutionalism comprised two elements: the rule of law and the principle of consent, that one could not be subjected to laws or taxation except by duly elected representatives. Both were rights that had been won through struggle with the monarch. In the decade between 1765 and the outbreak of the American Revolution, the colonists worked out their own theory of the place of the colonies in the empire. A consensus formed on the importance of the rule of law and the principle of consent. Those colonists who became revolutionaries never wavered on these two points. In the decade between the Stamp Act and the beginning of the American Revolution, what colonists debated was whether particular pieces of legislation violated these principles and how far colonists should go in resisting those that did.

British officials never denied that the colonists should enjoy the rights of Englishmen. They merely asserted that the colonists were as well represented in Parliament as the majority of Britons. In fact, only 1 out of 10 British men could vote, compared with about 70 percent of American white men. Yet British officials said that all Britons were represented in Parliament, if not "actually," by choosing their own representatives, then by virtual representation, because each member of Parliament was supposed to act on behalf of the entire empire. In Britons' minds, Parliament was supreme, and it had full authority over the colonists. In the decade between the Stamp Act and the beginning of the American Revolution, the controversy turned on only two questions: How forcefully would the British government insist on the supremacy of Parliament? And could colonial radicals put together a broad enough coalition to resist Britain's force when it came?

The Imperial Crisis in Local Context

While newspapers and pamphlets were filled with denunciations of the new imperial legislation, Americans were taking their protests to the streets and to the colonial legislatures. Everywhere, a remarkable cross-class alliance of prosperous merchants and planters and poor people joined to protect what they perceived as their rights from encroachment by British officials.

By the day that the Stamp Act was to go into effect, November 1, 1765, every colony except Georgia had taken steps to ensure that the tax could not be collected. In Virginia, the House of Burgesses took the lead. A young and barely literate lawyer, Patrick Henry, played a key role in the debate on the Virginia Resolves, the four resolutions protesting the Stamp Act that were passed by the burgesses. They asserted that the inhabitants of Virginia brought with them the rights of Englishmen, that Virginia's royal charters confirmed these rights, that taxation by one's own representatives was the only constitutional policy, and that the people of Virginia had never relinquished these rights. In Boston, too, the protest united the elite with poorer colonists. Massachusetts was still reeling from the loss of life and extraordinary expense of the French and Indian War. Imperialists such as Lieutenant Governor Thomas Hutchinson wanted to tie Massachusetts more tightly to the empire. He advocated a consolidation of power, a diminution of popular government (e.g., by reducing the power of the town meeting), making offices that were elective appointive instead, and limiting the freedom of the press.

Boston's public, with its history of radicalism, was ready for a much stronger response to the Stamp Act than the Massachusetts House of Representatives seemed prepared to make. The *Boston Gazette* criticized the House's resolution as a "tame, pusillanimous, daubed, insipid thing." Once word of the more radical Virginia Resolves arrived, the *Gazette* rebuked the weak political leadership again. A group of artisans and printers who called themselves the Sons of Liberty began organizing the opposition, probably in concert with more prominent men who would emerge as leaders of the revolutionary movement, such as James Otis, John Adams, and his cousin Samuel Adams, the Harvard-educated son of a brewer.

In a carefully orchestrated series of mob actions, Bostonians made certain that the Stamp Act would not be enforced. When the militia refused to protect royal officials, including the collector of the stamp tax, the officials took refuge in Castle William in the harbor. Over several days, the mob systematically vandalized the homes of several wealthy government loyalists, including Hutchinson. Although the mob consisted mostly of artisans and poor people, it had the support of Boston's merchant elite, for no one was ever punished. The protest succeeded, and the Stamp Act was never enforced.

Not only did each colony protest against the Stamp Act, but a majority were now ready to act together. In October 1765, delegates from nine colonies met in New York in the Stamp Act Congress to ratify a series of 14 resolutions protesting the Stamp Act on constitutional grounds. At the same time, activists shut down colonial courts so that no stamps could be used, and merchants agreed not to import any British goods until the act was repealed. With 37 percent of British exports then going to the colonies, this was no idle threat (see Figure 6–2).

Facing this opposition, the British partly backed down. George Grenville was replaced by the 35-year-old Marquess of Rockingham, who preferred racehorses to politics. Parliament repealed the Stamp Act but was not prepared to concede the constitutional point, asserting in the Declaratory Act of 1766 that Parliament "had, hath, and of right

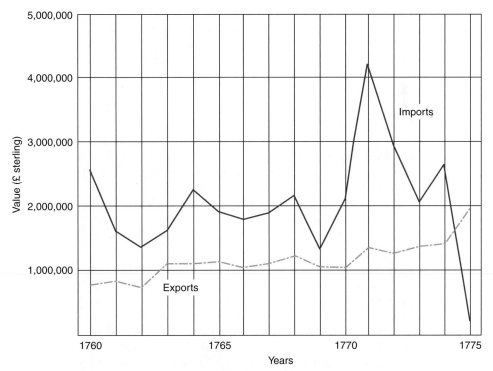

Figure 6–2 **Trade Between England and the Colonies** In the years between 1760 and 1775, colonial exports to England grew slowly but steadily, dropping off only after the beginning of the Revolution. On the other hand, imports from England—which always exceeded exports—rose and fell in response to political conditions. Colonial nonimportation agreements forced drops in imports after the imposition of the Stamp Act and Townshend Duties. But in both cases, imports increased after repeal, and the growth of imports after repeal of the Townshend Duties was dramatic and unprecedented.

ought to have, full power and authority to make laws and statutes . . . to bind the colonies and people of America, subjects of the Crown of Great Britain, in all cases whatsoever."

Contesting the Townshend Duties

Britain gave up on trying to tax the colonies directly, for even some prominent Britons such as William Pitt sided with the colonists on that point. But between 1767 and 1774, those in power still tried to force their vision of empire on the colonies. In response, radical activists and thinkers formed a national opposition and took constitutionalism in new directions. By the time of the American Revolution, they had turned it into a new theory of government.

After a brief return to power by William Pitt, Charles Townshend, a brilliant but erratic man nicknamed "Champagne Charlie," became the third prime minister in as many years. His first act was to punish New York's assembly, which intentionally violated the Quartering Act. The assembly, denied the right to pass any legislation until it complied with the Quartering Act, quickly backed down.

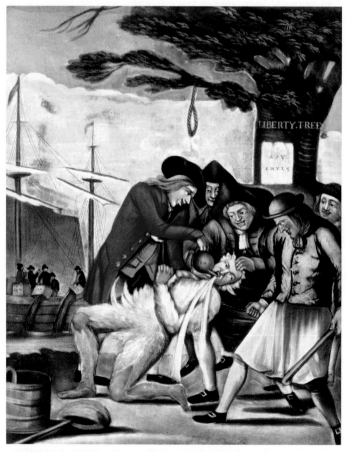

Tarring and Feathering the Customs Officer, 1774 Two Bostonians dress British customs officer John Malcolm in tar and feathers and force him to drink tea, turning him into a "macarony," an effete man who affected the latest fashion.

The colonies refused, however, to comply with the next piece of legislation, the Townshend Revenue Act of 1767, which levied import duties on lead, paint, glass, paper, and tea. Townshend believed that the colonists objected only to taxes within the colonies, "internal taxes," but that they would accept an "external tax," such as an import duty. The revenue would be used to support colonial officials, making them independent of the colonial assemblies that had paid their salaries.

Resistance to the Townshend Act built slowly, as it was hard for colonists to make a case against all duties. Merchants were now complying with the new Revenue Act of 1766, which reduced the duty on molasses. Those colonists most troubled by the first round of imperial legislation, however, were convinced that the Townshend Duties were part of a design for tyranny.

A body of thought known as *republicanism* helped the colonists make sense of British actions. Republicanism was a set of doctrines rooted in the Renaissance that held that power is always dangerous, because "it is natural for Power to be striving to enlarge itself, and to be encroaching upon those that have none." Republicanism supplied constitutionalism with a motive. It explained how a balanced constitution could be transformed into tyranny. Would-be tyrants had access to a variety of tools, including a standing army, whose ultimate purpose was not the protection of the people but their subjection. Tyrants also engaged in corruption, in particular by dispensing patronage positions. So inexorable was the course of power that it took extraordinary virtue for an individual to resist its corruption. Consequently, republican citizens, it was thought, had to be economically independent; the poor were dangerous because they could easily be bought off by would-be tyrants. A secular theory with connections to Puritanism, republicanism asserted that people were naturally weak and that exceptional human effort was required to protect liberty and virtue.

Not only did people have to keep a close eye on power-hungry tyrants, but they also had to look inside themselves. According to republican thought, history demonstrated that republics fell from within when their citizens lost their virtue. The greatest threat to virtue was luxury, an excessive attachment to the fruits of the consumer revolution. When colonists worried that they saw luxury and corruption everywhere, they were criticizing the world that the consumer revolution had created. Although it is understandable why poor people embraced republicanism, it might seem perplexing that wealthy merchants and planters would also strongly denounce "malice, covetousness, and other lusts of man." Yet the legacy of Puritanism was powerful, and even those profiting most from the new order felt ambivalent about its effects on their society. Joining with poorer people in criticizing British officials and accusing them of attempting to undermine colonial liberties helped forge a cross-class alliance.

The colonial legislatures slowly began to protest the duties. Massachusetts's House of Representatives, led by Sam Adams, asked each of the other lower houses in the colonies to join in resisting "infringements of their natural & constitutional Rights because they are not represented in the British Parliament. . . ." When Lord Hillsborough, a hardline secretary of state for the colonies, saw the request, he instructed the colonial governors to dissolve any colonial assembly that received the petition from Massachusetts. Massachusetts refused to rescind it, so Governor Francis Bernard dissolved the legislature. With representative government threatened, those colonial legislatures that had not already approved the Massachusetts petition did so now—and were then dissolved. In response, many legislatures met on their own, as extralegal bodies.

Not only did legislators assert their own authority, but ordinary people did so as well. In each colony, the radicals who called themselves Sons of Liberty organized a nonimportation movement using both coercion and patriotic appeal. Women were actively recruited into the movement, both to encourage household manufacture (an economic activity redefined as a political one) and to refuse British imports. In 1769 women in little Middletown, Massachusetts, wove 20,522 yards of cloth, and throughout the colonies women signed the nonimportation agreements. This politicization of ordinary people horrified conservative British observers. Although there were pockets of defiance, the movement succeeded in cutting imports dramatically. By the time that the Townshend Duties were repealed in 1770, Britain had collected only £21,000 and lost £786,000 in trade.

A Revolution in the Empire

The resistance to the Townshend Duties established a pattern that would be repeated again and again in the years before the Revolution. Each attempt to enforce the empire met with organized colonial opposition, to which the British government responded with a punitive measure. Ostensibly economic regulations such as the Sugar Act, the Townshend Duties, and the subsequent Tea Act, when rejected by the colonies, led to clearly political responses from Britain. Economics and politics became inseparable, as two visions of the empire came into conflict. Britain saw the colonies as a small but integral part of a large empire held together by an increasingly centralized and powerful government. The goal of the empire was to enhance its collective wealth and power, albeit under a system of constitutional government. Although they did not reject the notion of a larger empire outright, the colonists increasingly equated representative government with prosperity, not just for the empire as a whole but for its citizens in the colonies as well. Each round of colonial protest mobilized a larger segment of the population.

"Massacre" in Boston

Years of conflict with royal officials, combined with a growing population of poor and underemployed, had made Boston the most radical and united spot in the colonies. The political leadership had learned how to win popular favor in their ongoing strife with the governor and those who were loyal to him. The repeated attempts of the British government to enforce its legislation increased pressure on Boston and led finally to revolution.

In an attempt to tighten up the collection of customs duties, the British government, now led by Lord North, decided to make an example of John Hancock, Boston's wealthiest merchant and not yet a confirmed radical. In June 1768, customs commissioners seized Hancock's sloop, the *Liberty*, on a technical violation of the Sugar Act and threatened fines totaling £54,000 (most of which would go to the governor and the informer). All charges were dropped, however, after a riot of 2,000 "sturdy boys and men" sent the customs officials once again fleeing to Castle William for protection. Now Hancock was a radical.

After the *Liberty* riot, Governor Bernard called for troops to support the customs commissioners. Rather than restoring order, the arrival of the troops led to further conflict and a year and a half of tension. The Boston Massacre grew out of these tensions.

What angry colonists called a "massacre" was the culmination of months of scuffling between young men and adolescents and soldiers, perhaps inevitable in a town with so many men competing for work. On March 5, 1770, a fracas between a young apprentice and an army officer escalated as a crowd surrounded the officer, insulting him and

Boston Massacre Paul Revere's iconic image of the Boston Massacre (based on Henry Pelham's design) is less an accurate representation of the event than a political statement, depicting the British soldiers as more resolute (and less frightened) and the Bostonians, who had been pelting them with snowballs, as more innocent than they in fact were.

pelting him with snowballs. Someone shouted, "Fire!" and the crowd grew. Seven soldiers came to rescue their terrified colleague, and they too were hit with snowballs and taunts of "Kill them." When one was knocked down, he screamed, "Damn you, fire!" and the soldiers fired on the crowd. Eleven men were wounded, and five were killed. One victim was Crispus Attucks, a 47-year-old free black sailor. The soldiers were later tried, but the only two convicted were later pardoned. The British withdrew their troops from Boston.

As long as the British were willing to back down, more serious conflicts could be avoided. The Boston Massacre was followed by a three-year period of peace. The Townshend Duties had been repealed—except the one on tea, which the colonists could not manufacture themselves—and the nonimportation movement had collapsed. Colonial trade resumed its previous pace, and in 1772, imports from England and Scotland doubled. Colonists were not prepared to deny themselves consumer goods for long. The Quartering Act had expired, and the Currency Act was repealed. As long as Britain allowed the colonists to trade relatively unimpeded, permitted them to govern themselves, and kept the army out of their cities, all could be, if not forgotten, at least silenced.

The Empire Comes Apart

Although the British government was controlled by conservatives who believed the colonists would eventually need to acknowledge Parliament's supremacy, the move that led

The Boston Massacre

On the evening of March 5, 1770, shots rang out in front of the Boston custom house on King Street. The British soldiers who had fired were stunned, and three Bostonians lay dead in the snow. Two others would prove to be mortally injured. The image of the politicized populace of Boston standing up to representatives of the British army and being fired on at point-blank range is a familiar one to all American students; to this day we call the event the Boston Massacre. In this narrative, the people were united in their anger at the arrogance of the British Empire, and the tragic incident only strengthened their determination to make their voices heard.

Recent research has made it clear that the Boston "Massacre" is a misnomer. On the preceding Friday evening, some off-duty British soldiers had come to blows with some local apprentices, and tensions remained high on Monday, March 5. Locals began to taunt and torment a lone British sentry standing guard in front of the custom house. His commanding officer, Captain Thomas Preston, could see what was happening from the main guard station and came to his defense with a relief party, forming a semicircle in front of the building. A larger crowd gathered, with men shouting and daring the soldiers to fire. At length a gun did go off, and in the panic that ensued, the soldiers fired into the crowd.

Whichever element of the story one chooses to emphasize, the moment nevertheless remains an important one in the ongoing creation of American democracy. On one hand, it remains unequivocally true that the British soldiers were an unwelcome presence, a veritable army of occupation. First the Stamp Act and then the Townshend duties had genuinely aroused the ire of a colonial population long accustomed to managing without much assistance from the mother country, and who did not want to be called upon to pay the parent nation's bills. The colonists certainly did not want to host the British army. The young men who demonstrated such belligerence on March 5 were hard-working people who had been hurt by the partial strangulation of the shipyards and port caused by the British presence. Those who died included Crispus Attucks, a former slave who had run away and was supporting himself as a laborer in the city until he could join a ship's crew; Samuel Maverick, an ivory tuner's apprentice; Samuel Grey, a laborer at a rope-making business; James Caldwell, a sailor; and Patrick Carr, a recent Irish immigrant. They and their peers all wanted a provincial point of view to be taken as seriously as the perspective of a Londoner. And as they would have wished, the incident became a rallying point in the build-up to the Revolution.

If, on the other hand, we focus on the lone sentry and the crowd that instigated the violence, we feel far less moved by the political sentiments of the angry Bostonians. Even in this regard, however, the story is an important one, in that it allowed the American political activists to demonstrate that they really were fighting for a more equitable rule of law, not a period of massive upheaval. Thanks to the efforts not only of the British army but also of the

American patriots, the violence did not escalate after that evening. Two well-known lawyers, Josiah Quincy and John Adams, agreed to defend the much maligned British soldiers, despite real risk to their careers. They were successful and Captain Thomas Preston and six of the eight soldiers were acquitted. The two remaining soldiers, whom witnesses were convinced had fired at Attucks and one of the others, were found guilty of manslaughter rather than murder and they were released. It was more than they could have hoped for on the night of March 5. An important precedent had been set.

However one looks at the event dubbed "the Boston Massacre," the conflict and the anger from which it stemmed were both real. The continued suppression of the colonists' voices, through direct or indirect means, would not prove to be possible.

to revolution was more accidental than calculated. The North American colonies were only part of Britain's empire. There were powerful British interests in India, where the British East India Company was on the verge of bankruptcy. Parliament decided to bail out the company, both to rescue its empire in India and to help out influential stockholders. The duty for importing tea into Britain—but not America—was canceled, and Parliament allowed the company to sell directly to Americans through a small number of agents. As a result, the price of tea would drop below that of smuggled Dutch tea. Also, only five men in Massachusetts would be allowed to sell British tea—relatives and friends of the despised Governor Hutchinson. Agents in the other colonies were also well-connected loyalists.

Radicals faced a real challenge, for they realized that once the cheap tea was available, colonists would be unable to resist it. In each port city, activists warned that the Tea Act (1773) was a trick to con colonists into accepting the principle of taxation without representation. In Philadelphia, a mass meeting pronounced anyone who imported the tea "an enemy to his country."

As might be expected, the most spirited resistance came in Boston, where Hutchinson decided the tea would be unloaded and sold—and the duty paid. Sam Adams led extralegal town meetings attended by 5,000 people each (almost one-third of the population of Boston) to pressure Hutchinson to turn the ships away. When Hutchinson refused, Adams reported back to the town meeting, on December 16, 1773: "This meeting can do nothing more to save the country!" Almost as if it were a prearranged signal, the crowd let out a whoop and poured out of the meetinghouse for the wharf. There, about 50 men, their faces darkened and their bodies draped in Indian blankets, boarded three tea-bearing ships, escorted the customs officials ashore, and opened and dumped 340 chests of tea into Boston Harbor: 90,000 pounds, worth £9,000. Perhaps as many as 8,000 Bostonians observed the "tea party." John Adams, never much for riots, was in awe. "There is," he said, "a Dignity, a Majesty, a Sublimity in this last Effort of the Patriots that I greatly admire."

The British government saw only defiance of the law and wanton destruction of property. Parliament passed five bills in the spring of 1774 to punish Boston and

Massachusetts. First, the Boston Port Bill closed the port to all trade until the East India Company was repaid for the dumped tea. Second, the Massachusetts Government Act changed the Charter of 1691. The Council (upper house) would now be appointed by the king, rather than elected by the House; town meetings were forbidden without approval of the governor; the governor would appoint all the provincial judges and sheriffs; and the sheriffs would select juries, who had until then been elected by the voters. Third, the Administration of Justice Act empowered the governor to send to Britain or another colony for trial any official or soldier accused of a capital crime who appeared unlikely to get a fair trial in Massachusetts. Fourth, a new Quartering Act permitted the quartering of troops in private homes. Fifth was the Quebec Act. It assigned to Québec the Ohio River region, which the colonists coveted. In Québec, there was to be no representative government, civil cases would be tried without juries, and the Roman Catholic religion would be tolerated. Together, these acts were known in Britain as the Coercive Acts and in the colonies as the Intolerable Acts (see Table 6–1).

At the same time, General Thomas Gage was appointed governor of Massachusetts and authorized to bring as many troops to Boston as he needed. Boston soon became an armed camp. The Port Act was easily enforced as Gage deployed troops to close the ports of Boston and Charlestown. The Government Act was another matter. Citizens summoned by the sheriff simply refused to serve on juries, and some judges even refused to preside. When Gage called for an election to the legislature, only some towns elected delegates, and a shadow "Massachusetts Provincial Congress" met in Concord in October 1774. The citizens of Massachusetts had taken government into their own hands.

The British had thought that Massachusetts could be isolated, but they underestimated the colonists' attachment to their liberties. The threat to representative government presented by the Intolerable Acts was so clear that the other colonies soon rallied around Massachusetts. In June 1774, the Virginia Burgesses sent out a letter suggesting

Time Line

▼**1718**
French build New Orleans

▼**1720**
French build Louisbourg and Fort Niagara

▼**1731**
French build Fort St. Frédéric

▼**1733**
Molasses Act

▼**1739–1744**
War of Jenkins's Ear

▼**1741**
Attack upon Cartagena fails

▼**1744–1748**
King George's War

▼**1748**
Village of Pickawillany established by Memeskia and his band of Miamis

▼**1749**
French military expedition fails to win back dissident Indians in Ohio Valley

▼**1752**
Tanacharison cedes huge chunk of Ohio Valley to Virginia

▼**1753**
French build small forts near forks of Ohio River

▼**1754**
Albany Plan of Union

▼**1754–1763**
French and Indian War

▼**1755**
Braddock's forces defeated

▼**1757**
British defeated at Fort William Henry, survivors massacred
William Pitt accedes to power in Britain

a meeting of all the colonies. At about the same time, Massachusetts had issued a similar call for a meeting in Philadelphia. These two most radical colonies spurred the others to meet in early September.

The First Continental Congress

Every colony except Georgia sent delegates to the First Continental Congress, which convened on September 5, 1774. Only a few of the delegates had ever met any of their counterparts from the other colonies, so provincial were the colonies. For seven weeks these strangers met in formal sessions and social occasions. Together they laid the foundation for the first national government.

With Massachusetts and Virginia almost ready to take up arms, and the middle colonies favoring conciliation, the greatest challenge was how to achieve unity. Since Massachusetts needed the support of the other colonies, it was ready to abandon any discussion of offensive measures against the British. In return, the Congress ratified the Suffolk Resolves, a set of Massachusetts resolutions that recommended passive resistance to the Intolerable Acts.

The delegates could now consider national action. Hoping to exert economic pressure on Britain, Congress issued a call for a boycott of all imports and exports between the colonies, Britain, and the West Indies. Then the delegates adopted a Declaration of Rights that for the first time expressed as the collective determination of every colony (except Georgia) what had become standard constitutional arguments. The colonists were entitled to all the "rights, liberties, and immunities of free and natural-born subjects" of England. Parliament could regulate trade for the colonies only by the "consent" of the colonies. Parliament could neither tax nor legislate for the colonies. Again and again, the Declaration reiterated the twin principles on which resistance to imperial legislation had been based: consent and the rule of law.

▼**1758**
Treaty of Easton secures neutrality of Ohio Valley tribes in return for territory west of Alleghenies

▼**1759**
British seize Québec

▼**1763**
Treaty of Paris, ending French and Indian War, signed
Pontiac's Rebellion
Proclamation of 1763
Parliament increases size of peacetime army to 20 regiments

▼**1764**
Sugar Act
Currency Act

▼**1765**
Stamp Act
Quartering Act
Stamp Act Congress

▼**1766**
Declaratory Act

▼**1767**
Townshend Revenue Act

▼**1768**
John Hancock's sloop *Liberty* seized

▼**1770**
Boston Massacre

▼**1773**
Tea Act
Boston Tea Party

▼**1774**
Intolerable Acts (known as Coercive Acts in Britain)
Lord Dunmore's War

▼**1775**
First Continental Congress

Table 6-1 Major Events Leading to the Revolutionary War, 1763–1774

1763	Proclamation of 1763	Confines colonists to the east of an imaginary line running down the spine of the Allegheny Mountains.
1764	Sugar Act	Drops duty on molasses to 3 cents/gallon, but institutes procedures to make sure it is collected, such as trial at Admiralty Court (closest is in Nova Scotia), where burden of proof is on defendant and verdict is rendered by judge rather than jury.
1764	Currency Act	Forbids issuing of any colonial currency.
1765	Stamp Act	Places a tax on 15 classes of documents, including newspapers and legal documents; clear objective is to raise revenue.
1765	Quartering Act	Requires colonies to provide housing in public buildings and certain provisions for troops.
1766	Declaratory Act	Repeals Stamp Act, but insists that Parliament retains the right to legislate for the colonies "in all cases whatsoever."
1767	Townshend Revenue Act	Places import duty on lead, paint, glass, paper, and tea; objective is to raise money from the colonies.
1770	Boston Massacre	Several citizens killed by British soldiers whom they had pelted with snowballs; grew out of tensions caused by quartering of four army regiments in Boston to enforce customs regulations.
1773	Tea Act	After Townshend Duties on all items other than tea are removed, British East India Company is given a monopoly on the sale of tea, enabling it to drop price—and cut out middlemen.
1773	Boston Tea Party	To protest Tea Act, Bostonians dump 90,000 pounds of tea into Boston Harbor.
1774	Intolerable Acts	To punish Massachusetts in general and Boston in particular for the "Tea Party": 1. Port of Boston closed until East India Company repaid for dumped tea. 2. King to appoint Massachusetts's Council; town meetings to require written permission of governor; governor will appoint judges and sheriffs, and sheriffs will now select juries. 3. Governor can send officials and soldiers accused of capital crimes out of Massachusetts for their trials. 4. Troops may be quartered in private homes.
1774	Quebec Act	Gives Ohio River valley to Québec; Britain allows Québec to be governed by French tradition and tolerates Catholic religion there.
1774	First Continental Congress	Representatives of 12 colonies meet in Philadelphia and call for a boycott of trade with Britain, adopt a Declaration of Rights, and agree to meet again in a year.

Finally, Congress agreed to reconvene in half a year, on March 10, 1775, unless the Intolerable Acts were repealed. The delegates had achieved consensus on the principles that would shortly form the basis for a new and independent national government.

Conclusion

Within a decade, the British Empire had come apart on its westernmost edge. The stage had been set decades earlier when Britain unintentionally allowed the colonies to develop more self-government and personal freedom than in Britain itself, without requiring them to pay a proportionate share of the costs of empire. As a result, the colonies created their own vision, one that linked democratic government and prosperity. Once Britain decided to knit the colonies more tightly into the empire and impose on them the controls of the centralized state, conflict was inevitable. At the same time, both Britons and Americans revered the same constitution, whose values and protections Americans invoked in their protests. That those protests would end in revolution was by no means a foregone conclusion. Revolution would require two key elements: Britain's unwillingness to compromise on issues of governance, and the ability of colonial radicals to convince moderates that there was no other way. By the end of 1774 that point had almost been reached.

Who, What

Sam Adams 173

Thomas Hutchinson 170

Memeskia 158

William Pitt 163

George Washington 159

Albany Plan of Union 159

Constitutionalism 169

Pontiac's Rebellion 165

Proclamation of 1763 166

Republicanism 173

Review Questions

1. What were the reasons for the conflicts among the British, French, Spanish, and the various Indian tribes on the North American continent?

2. How and why did Britain attempt to reorganize its North American colonial empire?

3. Why did the colonies resist Britain's attempts to reorganize its North American colonial empire?

Critical-Thinking Questions

1. For much of the eighteenth century, Britain and France were at war, involving the American colonies. How did this warfare affect the colonies and their people?

2. What was the series of events that brought Britain and the colonies to the brink of war by 1774? To what extent were they the product of poor leadership? Differing theories of government? Different social experiences?

3. At what point did the American Revolution become unavoidable? Until that point, how might it have been avoided?

**For further review materials and resource information,
please visit www.oup.com/us/oakes**

CHAPTER 6: CONFLICT IN THE EMPIRE, 1713–1774
Primary Sources

6.1 LETTER FROM GEORGE WASHINGTON TO ROBERT DINWIDDE, GOVERNOR OF VIRGINIA (1755)

In 1755, an exhausted and ill George Washington wrote Virginia Governor Robert Dinwiddie describing General Edward Braddock's disastrous attempt to take the French fort at the Forks of the Ohio (the site of modern-day Pittsburgh). Washington describes the chaos of a battle that left the commander and 300 of his soldiers dead and Washington himself with four bullet holes in his coat. The letter also defended the conduct of the Virginia militia, whom the British blamed for the defeat.

Fort Cumberland, July 18, 1755.

. . . We continued our March from Fort Cumberland to Frazier's (which is within 7 Miles of Duquisne) with't meet'g with any extraordinary event, hav'g only a stragler or two picked up by the French Indians. When we came to this place, we were attack'd (very unexpectedly I must own) by abt. 300 French and Ind'ns; Our numbers consisted of abt. 1300 well arm'd Men, chiefly Regular's, who were immediately struck with such a deadly Panick, that nothing but confusion and disobedience of order's prevail'd amongst them: The Officer's in gen'l behav'd with incomparable bravery, for which they greatly suffer'd, there being near 60 kill'd and wound'd. A large proportion, out of the number we had! The Virginian Companies behav'd like Men and died like Soldiers; for I believe out of the 3 Companys that were there that day, scarce 30 were left alive: Captn. Peyrouny and all his Officer's, down to a Corporal, were kill'd; Captn. Polson shar'd almost as hard a Fate, for only one of his Escap'd: In short the dastardly behaviour of the English Soldier's expos'd all those who were inclin'd to do their duty to almost certain Death; and at length, in despight of every effort to the contrary, broke and run as Sheep before the Hounds, leav'g the Artillery, Ammunition, Provisions, and, every individual thing we had with us a prey to the Enemy; and when we endeavour'd to rally them in hopes of regaining our invaluable loss, it was with as much success as if we had attempted to have stop'd the wild Bears of the Mountains. The Genl. was wounded behind in the shoulder, and into the Breast, of w'ch he died three days after; his two Aids de Camp were both wounded, but are in a fair way of Recovery; Colo. Burton and Sir Jno. St. Clair are also wounded, and I hope will get over it; Sir Peter Halket, with many other brave Officers were kill'd in the Field. I luckily escap'd with't a wound tho' I had four Bullets through my Coat and two Horses shot under me. It is suppose that we left 300 or more dead in the Field; about that number we brought of wounded; and it is imagin'd (I believe with great justice too) that two thirds of both [those numbers?] received their shott from our own cowardly English Soldier's who gather'd themselves into a body contrary to orders 10 or 12 deep, wou'd then level, Fire and shoot down the Men before them.

I tremble at the consequences that this defeat may have upon our back settlers, who I suppose will all leave their habitations unless there are proper measures taken for their security.

Source: The Writings of George Washington from the Original Manuscript Sources, 1745–1799. Edited by
John C. Fitzpatrick. Vol. 1.

6.2 PONTIAC'S SPEECH TO THE OTTAWA, POTAWATOMI, AND HURONS (1763)

Pontiac's Rebellion was a military campaign to drive British settlers out of the Ohio Valley and restore the Native way of life in what is known as a religious revitalization movement. Leaders promoted pan-Indian unity and the rejection of European ways of life. In this speech, given to the assembled representatives of the Ottawa, Potawatomi, and Hurons in April 1763, Pontiac tells the story of Neolin ("The Indian"), a prophet from the Delaware tribe who journeyed to the home of the Master of Life to seek his advice. This version of the speech comes from an anonymous French transcription.

After the Indian was seated the Lord said to him: "I am the Master of Life, and since I know what thou desirest to know, and to whom thou wishest to speak, listen well to what I am going to say to thee and to all the Indians: I am He who hath created the heavens and the earth, the trees, lakes, rivers, all man, and all that thou seest and hast seen upon the earth. Because I love you, ye must do what I say and love, and not do what I hate. I do not love that ye should drink to the point of madness, as ye do; and I do not like that ye should fight one another. Ye take two wives, or run after the wives of others; ye do not well, and I hate that. Ye ought to have but one wife, and keep her till death. When ye wish to go to war, ye conjure and resort to the medicine dance, believing that ye speak to me; ye are mistaken—it is to Manitou that ye speak, an evil spirit who prompts you to nothing but wrong, and who listens to you out of ignorance of me.

"This land where ye dwell I have made for you and not for others. Whence comes it that ye permit the Whites upon your lands? Can ye not live without them? I know that those whom ye call the children of your Great Father supply your needs, but if ye were not evil, as ye are, ye could surely do without them. Ye could live as ye did live before knowing them—before those whom ye call your brothers had come upon your lands. Did ye not live by the bow and arrow? Ye had no need of gun or powder, or anything else, and nevertheless ye caught animals to live upon and to dress yourselves up with their skins. But when I saw that ye were given up to evil, I led the wild animals to the depths of the forests so that ye had to depend upon your brothers to feed and shelter you. Ye have only to become good again and do what I wish, and I will send back the animals for your food. I do not forbid you to permit among you the children of your Father; I love them. They know me and pray to me, and I supply their wants and all they give you. But as to those who come to trouble your lands—drive them out, make war upon them. I do not love them at all; they know me not, and are my enemies, and the enemies of your brothers. Send them back to the lands which I have created for them and let them stay there. . . . Tell all the Indians for and in the name of the Master of Life: Do not drink more than once, or at most twice in a day; have only one wife and do not run after the wives of others nor after the girls; do not fight among yourselves; do not 'make medicine' but pray, because in 'making medicine' one talks with the evil spirit; drive off your lands those dogs clothed in red who will do you nothing but harm."

Source: Mary Agnes Burton, ed. *Journal of Pontiac's Conspiracy 1763* (Detroit: Clarence Monroe Burton under the Auspices of the Michigan Society of the Colonial Wars, 1912), pp. 28–32. Available online at http://www.americanjourneys.org/aj-135/print/

6.3 BENJAMIN FRANKLIN, EXCERPTS FROM "A NARRATIVE OF THE LATE MASSACRES" (1764)

The fullest account we have of the Paxton Boys' attacks on the Conestoga Indians comes from Benjamin Franklin, who joined with other civic leaders to persuade a force of 250 men to turn back when they began marching on Philadelphia. Franklin's sympathy for the Natives, who were Christian converts, is evident, as is his contempt for the men who attacked them. Shehaes, mentioned in the excerpt that follows, was an elderly Conestoga who had been present in 1701 when William Penn entered into a treaty with the Indians "and ever since continued a faithful and affectionate Friend to the English."

These Indians were the Remains of a Tribe of the Six Nations, settled at Conestogoe [Conestoga], and thence called Conestogoe Indians. On the first Arrival of the English in Pennsylvania, Messengers from this Tribe came to welcome them, with Presents of Venison, Corn and Skins; and the whole Tribe entered into a Treaty of Friendship with the first Proprietor, William Penn, which was to last "as long as the Sun should shine, or the Waters run in the Rivers." This Treaty has been since frequently renewed, and the Chain brightened, as they express it, from time to time. It has never been violated, on their Part or ours, till now. It has always been observed, that Indians, settled in the Neighbourhood of White People, do not increase, but diminish continually. This Tribe accordingly went on diminishing, till there remained in their Town on the Manor, but 20 Persons, viz. 7 Men, 5 Women, and 8 Children, Boys and Girls . . .

On Wednesday, the 14th of December, 1763, Fifty-seven Men, from some of our Frontier Townships, who had projected the Destruction of this little Common-wealth, came, all well-mounted, and armed with Firelocks, Hangers and Hatchets, having travelled through the Country in the Night, to Conestogoe Manor. There they surrounded the small Village of Indian Huts, and just at Break of Day broke into them all at once. Only three Men, two Women, and a young Boy, were found at home, the rest being out among the neighbouring White People, some to sell the Baskets, Brooms and Bowls they manufactured, and others on other Occasions. These poor defenceless Creatures were immediately fired upon, stabbed and hatcheted to Death! The good Shehaes, among the rest, cut to Pieces in his Bed. All of them were scalped, and otherwise horribly mangled. Then their Huts were set on Fire, and most of them burnt down. When the Troop, pleased with their own Conduct and Bravery, but enraged that any of the poor Indians had escaped the Massacre, rode off, and in small Parties, by different Roads, went home. . . .

The Magistrates of Lancaster sent out to collect the remaining Indians, brought them into the Town for their better Security against any further Attempt, and it is said condoled with them on the Misfortune that had happened, took them by the Hand, comforted and promised them Protection. They were all put into the Workhouse, a strong Building, as the Place of greatest Safety.

When the shocking News arrived in Town, a Proclamation was issued by the Governor, in the following Terms:

"Whereas I have received Information, That on Wednesday, the Fourteenth Day of this Month, a Number of People, armed, and mounted on Horseback, unlawfully assembled together, and went to the Indian Town in the Conestogoe Manor, in Lancaster County, and without the least Reason or Provocation, in cool Blood, barbarously killed six of the Indians settled there, and burnt and destroyed all their Houses and Effects: And whereas so cruel and inhuman an Act, committed in the Heart of this Province on the said Indians, who have lived peaceably and inoffensively among us, during all our late Troubles, and for many Years before, and were justly considered as under the Protection of this Government and its Laws, calls loudly for the vigorous Exertion of the civil Authority, to detect the Offenders, and bring them to condign Punishment."

. . . Notwithstanding this Proclamation, those cruel Men again assembled themselves, and hearing that the remaining fourteen Indians were in the Work-house at Lancaster, they suddenly appeared in that Town, on the 27th of December. Fifty of them, armed as before, dismounting, went directly to the Work-house, and by Violence broke open the Door, and entered with the utmost Fury in their Countenances. When the poor Wretches saw they had no Protection nigh, nor could possibly escape, and being without the least Weapon for Defence, they divided into their little Families, the Children clinging to the Parents; they fell on their Knees, protested their Innocence, declared their Love to the English, and that, in their whole Lives, they had never done them Injury; and in this Posture they all received the Hatchet! Men, Women and little Children—were every one inhumanly murdered!—in cold Blood!

The barbarous Men who committed the atrocious Fact, in Defiance of Government, of all Laws human and divine, and to the eternal Disgrace of their Country and Colour, then mounted their Horses, huzza'd in Triumph, as if they had gained a Victory, and rode off—unmolested!

The Bodies of the Murdered were then brought out and exposed in the Street, till a Hole could be made in the Earth, to receive and cover them.

But the Wickedness cannot be covered, the Guilt will lie on the whole Land, till Justice is done on the Murderers. The Blood of the Innocent will cry to Heaven for Vengeance. . . .

There are some (I am ashamed to hear it) who would extenuate the enormous Wickedness of these Actions, by saying, "The Inhabitants of the Frontiers are exasperated with the Murder of their Relations, by the Enemy Indians, in the present War." It is possible; but though this might justify their going out into the Woods, to seek for those Enemies, and avenge upon them those Murders; it can never justify their turning in to the Heart of the Country, to murder their Friends.

If an Indian injures me, does it follow that I may revenge that Injury on all Indians? It is well known that Indians are of different Tribes, Nations and Languages, as well as the White People. In Europe, if the French, who are White People, should injure the Dutch, are they to revenge it on the English, because they too are White People? The only Crime of these poor Wretches seems to have been, that they had a reddish brown Skin, and black Hair; and some People of that Sort, it seems, had murdered some of our Relations.

Source: "A Narrative of the Late Massacres [January 30, 1764]," Founders Online, National Archives (http://founders .archives.gov/documents/Franklin/01-11-02-0012, ver. 2014-05-09). Source: *The Papers of Benjamin Franklin,* vol. 11, *January 1, through December 31, 1764,* ed. Leonard W. Labaree. New Haven and London: Yale University Press, 1967, p. 42ff.

6.4 A VISITING FRENCHMAN'S ACCOUNT OF PATRICK HENRY'S CAESAR–BRUTUS SPEECH (1765)

Patrick Henry may be best known as the man who said, "Give me liberty or give me death!" His radicalism, however, appeared much earlier than that 1775 speech. As the Virginia House of Burgesses was about to conclude its business in May 1765, Henry introduced a series of resolutions protesting the Stamp Act. He came close to committing treason when he named historic dictators who had been assassinated and suggested King George III might deserve the same fate, but he quickly backed away, pleading "the heat of passion." This description of his speech comes from the travel diary of a Frenchman who was visiting Virginia at the time.

May the 30th. Set out early from half-way house in the chair and broke fast at York[town], arived at Williamsburg at 12, where I saw three negroes hanging at the galous for having robbed Mr. Waltho[w] of 300 pounds. I went immediately to the Assembly which was seting, where I was entertained with very strong debates concerning dutys that the Parlement wants to lay on the America colonys, which they call or stile stamp dutys. Shortly after I came in, one of the members stood up and said he had read that in former time Tarquin and Julius had their Brutus, Charles had his Cromwell, and he did not doubt but some good American would stand up in favour of his Country; but (says he) in a more moderate manner, and was going to continue, when the Speaker of the House rose and, said he, the last that stood up had spoke traison, and [he] was sorey to see that not one of the members of the House was loyal enough to stop him before he had gone so far. Upon which the same member stood up again (his name is Henery) and said that if he had afronted the Speaker or the House, he was ready to ask pardon, and he would shew his loyalty to His Majesty King George the third at the expence of the last drop of his blood; but what he had said must be attributed to the interest of his country's dying liberty which he had at heart, and the heat of passion might have lead him to have said something more than he intended; but, again, if he said anything wrong, he begged the Speaker and the House's pardon. Some other members stood up and backed him, on which that afaire was droped.

May the 31st. I returned to the Assembly to-day, and heard very hot debates stil about the stamp dutys. The whole House was for entering resolves on the records but they differed much with regard [to] the contents or purport thereof. Some were for shewing their resentment to the highest. One of the resolves that these proposed, was that any person that would offer to sustain that the Parlement of England had a right to impose or lay any tax or dutys whatsoever on the American colonys, without the consent of the inhabitants therof, should be looked upon as a traitor, and deemed an enemy to his country: there were some others to the same purpose, and the majority was for entring these resolves; upon which the Governor disolved the Assembly, which hinderd their proceeding.

Source: A visiting Frenchman's account of Patrick Henry's Caesar-Brutus Speech.
        http://www.redhill.org/life/1765_2.html

6.5 PETER OLIVER, EXCERPTS FROM *PETER OLIVER'S ORIGIN & PROGRESS OF THE AMERICAN REBELLION: A TORY VIEW* (1781)

After the failure of the Stamp Act in 1765, the British government tried to raise revenue in the American colonies by taxing imported goods. In response, colonial radicals organized boycotts of British imports, a protest method they called "non-importation." This boycott politicized many aspects of colonial life, from drinking tea to funerals, and involved a broad range of people, such as merchants, farmers, and servants. Peter Oliver, a loyalist from Massachusetts, discussed non-importation in a history of the American Revolution that he wrote in 1781. In this passage his contempt for his fellow Americans, particularly the merchants—"a race of smugglers"—and the "rabble," comes through.

I am now come to the Year 1767, a Year fraught with Occurrences, as extraordinary as 1765, but of a different Texture. Notwithstanding the Warnings that the Colonies had repeatedly given, of their determined Resolution to throw off the Supremacy of the british Parliament, yet the then Ministry chose to make another Trial of Skill, never adverting to the ill Success of former Attempts. They might have known, that the Contest had reach so great an Height, that the Colonists would never descend one Step untill they had first ascended the last Round of the

Ladder…But the Ministry confiding in their own good Intentions, & placing too much Confidence in the Gratitude of the Colonists to the parent State (which by the Way they did not possess a Spark of) . . . they procured a new Act to be passed, laying Duties upon *Tea, Glass, Paper, & Painters Colours.* This Act was not more unreasonable than many other Acts which had been submitted to for many years past, & which, even at this Time, they made no Objection to. But the Colonists had succeeded in their first Experiment of Opposition, & their new Allies in Parliament increased their Importance. . . .

The true Reason of Opposition was this. The Inhabitants of the Colonies were a Race of Smugglers. They carried on an extensive Trade with the *Dutch*, not only in *Holland*, but very greatly with the Dutch Settlements in the *West Indies* & at *Surrinam.* Tea was the objective Part of the Act; & an enormous Quantity of it was consumed on the american Continent; so great, that I have heard a Gentleman of the Custom House in *Boston*, say, that could the Duty be fairly collected, it would amount to £160,000 p. Year, i.e. at 12d p pound. In some of the Colonies, it was notorious that the smuggled Teas were carted through the Streets at Noon Day: whether owing to the Inattention or Connivance of the Custom House Officers, is not difficult to determine.

The Smugglers then, who were the prevailing Part of the Traders in the Capitals of the several Provinces, found it necessary for their Interest, to unite in defeating the Operation of the Act; & *Boston* appeared in the Front of the Battle. Accordingly they beat to Arms, & maneuvered in a new invented Mode. They entered into nonimportation Agreements. A Subscription Paper was handed about, enumerating a great Variety of Articles not to be imported from *England*, which they supposed would muster the Manufacturers in *England* into a national Mob to support their Interests. Among the various prohibited Articles, were *Silks, Velvets, Clocks, Watches, Coaches & Chariots*; & it was highly diverting, to see the names & marks, to the Subscription, of Porters & Washing Women. But every mean & dirty Art was used to compass all their bad Designs. One of those who handed about a Subscription Paper being asked, whether it could be imagined that such Tricks would effectuate their Purposes? He replyed "Yes! It would do to scare them in England:" & perhaps there never was a Nation so easy to be affrighted; witness the preceding Repeal of the Stamp Act.

Nonimportation of British Goods In order to effectuate their Purposes to have this Act repealed also, they formed many Plans of Operation. Associations were convened to prevent the Importation of Goods *from Great Britain*, & to oblige all those who had already sent for them, to reship them after their arrival. This was such an Attack upon the mercantile Interest, that it was necessary to use private evasive Arts to deceive the Vulgar. Accordingly, when the Goods arrived, they were to be in Warehouses, which were to be guarded by a publick Key, at the same Time the Owners of the Stores & Goods had a Key of their Own. This amused the Rabble, whom the Merchants had set to mobbing; & such were the blessed Effects of some of those Merchants Villainy, that Bales & Trucks were disgorged of their Contents & refilled with Shavings, Brickbats, Legs of Bacon & other Things, & shipped for *England*; where some of them were opened on the King's Wharves or Quays, & the Fraud discovered. . . .

Another base Art was used. Under Pretence of Economy, the Faction undertook to regulate Funerals, that there might be less Demand for English Manufactures. It was true indeed that the Custom of wearing expensive Mourning at Funerals, had, for many Years past, been noticed for Extravagance, & had ruined some Families of moderate Fortune; but there had been no Exertions to prevent it; 'till now, the Demagogues & their Mirmidons had taken the Government into their Hands. But what at another Time would have been deemed Economical, was at this Time Spite & Malevolence. One Extreme was exchanged for another.

The Faction deluded their Followers with another Scheme to keep up the Ball of Contention, & to sooth their Hopes of Conquest. They plunged into Manufactures; & like all other Projectors, suffered their Enthusiasm to stop their Ears against the voice of Reason, which warned them of the ill Effects of their Projects. One of their Manufactures was to have been in *Wool . . .* They preached about it & about it; until the Women & Children, both within Doors & without, set their Spinning Wheels a whirling in Defiance of *Great Britain.*

Source: Oliver, Peter, *Peter Oliver's Origin & Progress of the American Rebellion: A Tory View (1781)* (Stanford, CA: Stanford University Press, 1967), pp. 60–64.

6.6 THE INTOLERABLE ACTS (1774)

In response to the 1774 Boston Tea Party, Parliament passed a series of acts to try to bring Massachusetts back under the authority of the British Crown. The acts, which American patriots called the "Intolerable Acts," closed the Boston Harbor, allowed for trials to take place in Great Britain rather than Massachusetts, suspended local elections, and allowed for the quartering of troops on private property. Although the Quebec Act did not directly affect Boston, many patriots were angry that the British government seemed to grant more freedom to the French Catholics living in recently conquered Quebec while simultaneously curtailing political liberty in Massachusetts.

Boston Port Act:

AN ACT to discontinue . . . shipping, of goods, wares, and merchandise, at the town, and within the harbour, of Boston, in the province of Massachuset's Bay, in North America

Whereas dangerous commotions and insurrections have been fomented and raised in the town of Boston, *in the province of* Massachuset's Bay, *in New England, by divers ill affected persons, to the subversion of his Majesty's government, and to the utter destruction of the publick peace, and good order of the said town; in which commotions and insurrections certain valuable cargoes of teas, being the property of the* East India Company, *and on board certain' vessels lying within the bay or harbour of* Boston, *were seized and destroyed: And whereas, in the present condition of the said town and harbour, the commerce of his Majesty's subjects cannot be safely carried on there, nor the customs payable to his Majesty duly collected; and it is therefore expedient that the officers of his Majesty's customs should be forthwith removed from the said town:* . . . be it enacted . . . , That from and after June 1, 1774, it shall not be lawful for any person or persons whatsoever to lade, put, or cause to procure to be laden or put, off or from any quay, wharf, or other place, within the said town of *Boston,* or in or upon any part of the shore of the bay, commonly called *The Harbour of Boston.*

Administration of Justice Act:

AN ACT for or the impartial administration of justice in . . . Massachuset's Bay, in New England

Whereas in his Majesty's province of Massachuset's Bay, in New England, *an attempt hath lately been made to throw off the authority of the parliament of Great Britain over the said province, and an actual and avowed resistance, by open force, to the execution of certain acts of parliament, hath been suffered to take place, uncontrouled and unpunished,* . . . : *and whereas, in the present disordered state of the said province, it is of the utmost importance* . . . *to the reestablishment of lawful authority throughout the same;* be it enacted . . . , That if any inquisition or indictment shall be found, or if any appeal shall be sued or preferred against any person, for murther, or other capital offense, in the province of the Massachuset's Bay, and it shall appear, by information given upon oath to the governor . . . that an indifferent trial cannot be had within the said province, in that case, it shall and may be lawful for the governor . . . , to direct, with the advice and consent of the council, that the inquisition, indictment, or appeal, shall be tried in some other of his Majesty's colonies, or in Great Britain.

Massachusetts Government Act:

AN ACT for the better regulating the government of the province of the Massachuset's Bay, in New England

Whereas the method of electing such counsellors or assistants, to be vested with the several powers, authorities, and privileges, therein mentioned, . . . hath been found to be extremely ill adapted to the plan of government established in the province of the Massachuset's Bay . . . , *and hath . . . for or some time past, been such as had the most manifest tendency to obstruct, and, in great measure, defeat, the execution of the laws; to weaken the attachment of his Majesty's well disposed subjects in the said province to his Majesty's government, and to encourage the ill disposed among them to proceed even to acts of direct resistance to, and defiance of, his Majesty's authority: And it hath accordingly happened, that an open resistance to the execution of the laws hath actually taken place in the town of* Boston, *and the neighbourhood thereof, within the said Province: And whereas it is, under these circumstances, become absolutely necessary, . . . that the said method of annually electing the counsellors or assistants of the said Province should no longer be suffered to continue, . . .* Be it therefore enacted . . . that the council, or court of assistants of the said province for the time being, shall be composed of such of the inhabitants or proprietors of lands within the same as shall be thereunto nominated and appointed by his Majesty.

Quartering Act of 1765:

Whereas doubts have been entertained whether troops can be quartered otherwise than in barracks . . . in such cases, it shall and may be lawful for . . . the officer . . . in command of His Majesty's forces in *North America*, to cause any officers or soldiers in His Majesty's service to be quartered and billeted in such manner as is now directed by law where no barracks are provided by the colonies.

And be it further enacted by the authority aforesaid that, if it shall happen at any time that any officers or soldiers in His Majesty's service shall remain within any of the said colonies without quarters for the space of twenty four hours after such quarters shall have been demanded, it shall and may be lawful for the governor of the province to order and direct such and so many uninhabited houses, outhouses, barns, or other buildings as he shall think necessary to be taken (making a reasonable allowance for the same) and make fit for the reception of such officers and soldiers, and to put and quarter such officers and soldiers therein for such time as he shall think proper.

Quebec Act:

AN ACT for making effectual Provision for the Government of the Province of Quebec, in North America

It is hereby declared, That His Majesty's Subjects professing the Religion of the Church of Rome, of, and in the said Province of *Quebec,* may have, hold, and enjoy, the free Exercise of the Religion of the Church of Rome . . . and that the Clergy of the said Church may hold, receive, and enjoy their accustomed Dues and Rights, with respect to such Persons only as shall profess the said Religion.

Source: http://www.ushistory.org/declaration/related/intolerable.htm

CHAPTER

7

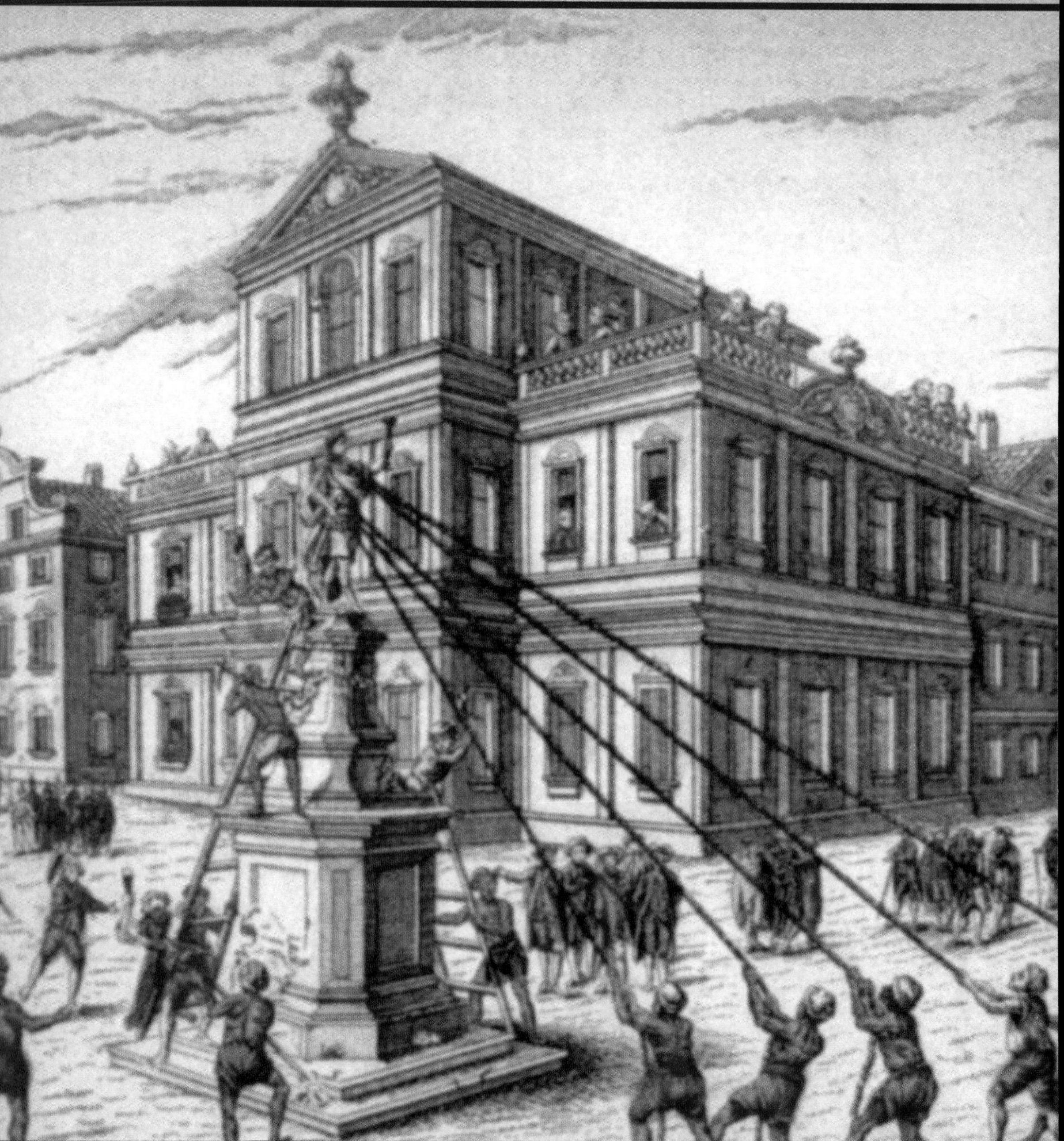

Creating a New Nation

1775-1788

COMMON THREADS

Which political theories did the American colonists use to justify their revolution, and how did they adapt those theories over the course of the next decades in the light of their experiences?

What does Britain's failure to defeat the colonies tell us about the limits of empire?

How did the doctrine of equality take on a life of its own?

To what extent has the conflict between the Federalists and the Antifederalists continued to shape American history?

In which ways was the American Revolution democratic? Not democratic?

James Madison Helps Make a Nation

Why do some people achieve greatness? Perhaps it is not as much a matter of personal qualities as a match between the person and the times, an ability to understand and respond to the needs of the age. There was nothing in James Madison's childhood to suggest that he would become a leader of a revolutionary nation in a revolutionary age.

Madison grew up on the plantation his grandfather and his grandfather's slaves had cleared out of the Virginia Piedmont forest in 1732. Only a few months later, Madison's grandfather was killed by several of those slaves. One of the slaves was executed, but another, a woman named Dido, was given 29 lashes and sent home to work for the widow Madison. Perhaps James had his own grandfather in mind when he wrote later that men are not angels, and that is why government is necessary.

James went north to college, attending Princeton in New Jersey. After his graduation in 1771 at the age of 20, he suffered some sort of breakdown. Back in Virginia, Madison described himself as "too dull and infirm now to look out for any extraordinary things in this world. . . ." Short and slight of build, Madison was convinced that his poor health would lead to an early death. The event that drew this sickly, nervous young man out of his shell was the American Revolution. He became a leader in the nation that he helped create and whose Constitution he helped write. James Madison committed himself to the principles of liberty and order, and he devoted his life to establishing a government that would ensure both. Perhaps more than any other leader at the time, Madison understood how difficult reconciling these two principles would be.

Madison believed that strife and violence were deeply embedded in human nature, and he spent his adult life trying to create a government that would ensure peace without destroying liberty. He helped write the Constitution and then worked for the adoption of the Bill of Rights. His first political battle in Virginia had been on behalf of the Baptists, a dissenting Protestant denomination that demanded religious liberty. Madison was convinced that freedom of conscience was fundamental and that religion must be kept absolutely free from governmental interference. As a political thinker and leader, Madison came to advocate the great liberal principles of his age: the rights of conscience, consent, and property. Believing fervently in both human liberty and the rights of property, he could never reconcile himself either to slavery or to its abolition. He put his faith in the new government, hoping that just as he had learned to live with his own mental and physical disabilities, so the nation would rise above its internal conflicts and inconsistencies.

The War Begins

By the end of 1774, conflict between the colonists and Britain seemed unavoidable. The British government, under the leadership of Lord North and King George III, seemed unwilling to make significant concessions. In the colonies, the radical opponents of British rule dominated politics. Despite these signs, no one anticipated eight years of warfare that would make the colonies a single nation under a centralized government.

The First Battles

Before he became governor of Massachusetts in 1774, General Thomas Gage had a long record of advocating force. He had called for the stationing of troops in Boston in 1768, leading to the Boston Massacre. Even before the Boston Tea Party, he recommended limiting democratic government in Massachusetts. Because he believed that Boston merchants and lawyers were instigating dissent among the poor, he wanted to isolate the colonial Revolutionary elite, by force if necessary.

In the spring of 1775, Gage received orders from England to act decisively against the colonists. He planned to seize the colonists' military supplies, stored at Concord, but alert Bostonians tipped off the patriot leaders once British troops began to march. On the night of April 18, the silversmith Paul Revere and the tanner William Dawes slipped out of Boston on horseback to carry the message that British troops were on the move. Militiamen from several towns began to gather.

The British soldiers arrived at Lexington at daybreak and ordered the militia to surrender, which they refused to do. Exactly what happened next remains unclear. The colonists swore that British soldiers opened fire, saying, "Ye villans [sic], ye Rebels, disperse; Damn you, disperse." The British major insisted that the first shot came from behind a tree. British soldiers lost control and fired, and the colonists returned fire. Eight Americans were killed, most while attempting to flee.

At the same time, the Concord militia had assembled and then pulled back about a mile, allowing the British to enter an almost-deserted town. Fighting broke out when a fire the British troops had set to the Concord liberty pole spread to the courthouse. To protect their town, the militia began marching on the British, who fired when the Americans drew near. In the exchange, three British soldiers were killed and several more injured. The British were forced back across the bridge. The entire battle took two or three minutes (see Map 7–1).

Once news of the fighting at Lexington and Concord spread, militias converged on Boston to evict Gage and his troops. More than 20,000 men soon were encamped in Boston. Gage declared that all the inhabitants of Massachusetts who bore arms were rebels and traitors, although he was willing to pardon everyone but John Hancock and Sam Adams, two leaders of the defiant Provincial Congress. Rather than backing down, the colonists fortified Breed's Hill (next to the more famous Bunker Hill) in Charlestown, overlooking Boston. On June 17, Gage sent 2,400 soldiers to take the hill. The cost was enormous: 1,000 soldiers and 92 officers killed or wounded (compared with 370 casualties among the colonists). The British learned not to make frontal assaults against fortified positions.

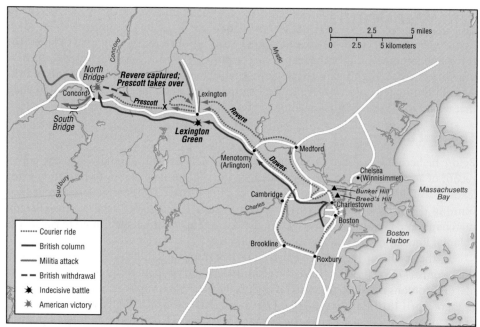

Map 7–1   Battles of Lexington, Concord, and Breed's Hill This map shows the sites of the first battles of the Revolution in and around Boston, along with the routes taken by Paul Revere and William Dawes to warn the colonists of the approach of British troops.

Other New Englanders were also taking matters into their own hands. A group under Benedict Arnold, an ambitious New Haven merchant, and Ethan Allen, the leader of the Vermont Green Mountain Boys, seized the crumbling fort at Ticonderoga on Lake Champlain and other small posts. In these heady days early in the Revolution, many colonists thought that this would be a quick and painless war.

Congress Takes the Lead

When the Second Continental Congress convened in Philadelphia on May 10, its greatest challenge was to maintain consensus. The most radical leaders, such as Sam and John Adams from Massachusetts and Richard Henry Lee from Virginia, were ready for war. However, many leaders, especially in the middle colonies, still hoped that war could be avoided.

Because Congress was an extralegal body, the elected colonial assemblies might easily have rejected its authority. But one after another, they transferred their allegiance from the British government to Congress. Although some moderates hoped for a negotiated settlement with Britain, they were caught between two sides that both anticipated war. The British refused even to acknowledge the petition sent by the First Continental Congress. That refusal, combined with Gage's attack on Breed's Hill, convinced the moderates that military preparations were necessary. Congress voted to create a Continental army and put it under the leadership of Virginia's George Washington. Not only was Washington experienced in military matters and widely respected, but his selection also helped solidify the alliance between New England and the South. Congress decided to attack Canada in the hope that a significant defeat would force the British to accede to American demands. To justify all of these actions, Congress also adopted the Declaration of the Causes and Necessity of Taking Up Arms, a rousing indictment of British "despotism," "perfidy," and "cruel aggression" drafted by Virginia's Thomas Jefferson.

At the same time, to preserve unity with the moderates, the radicals agreed to petition the king one more time. Without making any concessions, the Olive Branch Petition appealed to George's "magnanimity and benevolence." Nevertheless, on August 23, 1775, the king declared the colonists to be in "an open and avowed Rebellion." Although Congress had neither declared war nor asserted independence, the American Revolution had begun.

Military Ardor

Military ardor in the colonies reached its high point between the fall of 1775 and the spring of 1776. Colonists expected war, and they thought it would be quick and glorious. As a consequence, the first enlistments were for a term of only a year. Even if the war was not over by then, Revolutionaries were fearful of creating a permanent standing army.

In the summer of 1775, the Continental army marched on Canada. Victory would have either forced the British to the bargaining table or at least protected New York and New England from assault from the north. The contingent under General Benedict Arnold's command sailed from Newburyport, Massachusetts, to Maine and then marched 350 miles to Québec. In November, after a grueling march, Arnold's forces prepared to assault Québec, joined by troops under General Richard Montgomery, who had just seized Montréal. The battle was a disaster. Half of the 900 Continental soldiers were killed, captured, or wounded, including Montgomery. By the time the expedition retreated to New York in the spring, 5,000 men had been lost. The suffering was extraordinary, but it only increased American resolve.

Declaring Independence

By the beginning of 1776, moderates in Congress who still hoped for a peaceful settlement found themselves squeezed from both directions. The king and Parliament were unyielding, and popular opinion increasingly favored independence. Word arrived from Britain that all American commerce was to be cut off and that the British navy would seize American ships and their cargoes. Britain also began hiring German mercenaries known as Hessians, and Virginia's Governor Dunmore shelled Norfolk from warships. He had already offered freedom to any slaves who would fight for the British. Every prediction the radicals had made seemed to be coming true.

Public opinion also pushed Congress toward a declaration of independence. In January 1776, Thomas Paine, an expatriate English radical in Philadelphia, electrified the public with his pamphlet *Common Sense*, which sold 75,000 copies in a short time. In it, Paine liberated Americans from their ties to the British past so that they could start their government fresh. The idea of a balanced constitution that combined king, nobles, and common people in one government was "farcical," and monarchy was "exceedingly ridiculous." Paine had a message for Congress, too: "The period of debate is closed."

Most members of Congress either desired a declaration of independence or thought it inevitable. Most delegates also agreed that unanimity was more important than speed,

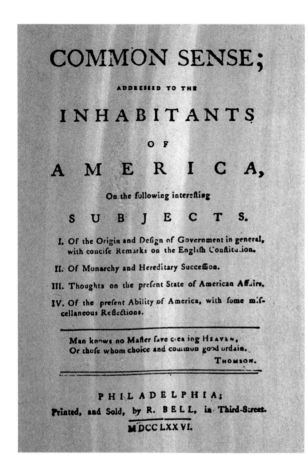

COMMON SENSE;

ADDRESSED TO THE

INHABITANTS

OF

AMERICA,

On the following interesting

SUBJECTS.

I. Of the Origin and Design of Government in general,
with concise Remarks on the English Constitution.

II. Of Monarchy and Hereditary Succession.

III. Thoughts on the present State of American Affairs.

IV. Of the present Ability of America, with some mis-
cellaneous Reflections.

Man knows no Master save creating HEAVEN,
Or those whom choice and common good ordain.
THOMSON.

PHILADELPHIA;
Printed, and Sold, by R. BELL, in Third-Street.
MDCCLXXVI.

Cover of *Common Sense* Thomas Paine's *Common Sense* sold more than 75,000 copies in just a few weeks.

so they waited through the spring of 1776 as, one by one, the state delegations received instructions in favor of independence. Then, under instructions from his colony, on June 7, 1776, Virginia's Richard Henry Lee asked Congress to vote on the resolution that "these United Colonies are, and of right ought to be, free and independent States." A committee of five, including Thomas Jefferson, Benjamin Franklin, and John Adams, was appointed to draft a declaration of independence. Adams asked Jefferson, a 33-year-old Virginia radical who could write stirring prose, to create the first draft. For four days, the delegates debated the draft and took preliminary votes. A clause that accused King George of forcing African slaves on the colonies was deleted. On July 2, the delegates voted unanimously to declare independence.

Many years later Jefferson insisted that there was nothing original about the Declaration of Independence, and he was not entirely wrong. The long list of accusations against King George, which formed the bulk of the Declaration, contained little that was new, and even some of the stirring words in the preamble had been used by the radicals time and again. Moreover, the Revolutionaries borrowed ideas from a number of British and European sources, including constitutionalism, republicanism, Enlightenment thought (see Chapter 6), and millennial Christian thought. The millennial strain in evangelical Protestantism suggested that the 1,000-year reign of Christ might begin soon in America if Americans would repent their sins, seek a spiritual rebirth, and defend their liberties.

However, in a different sense the Declaration of Independence was truly original. Jefferson's achievement was to reformulate familiar principles in a way that made them simple, clear, and applicable to the American situation.

The most important of these principles was human equality, that all people were born with certain fundamental rights. Second, and closely related, was the belief in a universal, common human nature. If all people were the same and had the same rights, then the purpose of government was to protect those rights. Just as people created

LA DESTRUCTION DE LA STATUE ROYALE A NOUVELLE YORCK.

Die Zerstorung der Koniglichen Bild | La Destruction de la Statue royale
Saule zu Neu Yorck | a Nouvelle Yorck

Destruction of Statue of King George Here, a small crowd in New York City pulls down the statue of King George on July 9, 1776, a few days after independence was declared.

government to protect their rights, they could abolish any government that became despotic. Third, government should represent the people.

It was many years, however, before the radical implications of the Declaration became fully evident to the American people. At the moment, more attention was focused on immediate political struggles. The Revolution succeeded because moderates and radicals were able to create effective alliances, reversing the pre-Revolutionary trend toward class and political conflict. To remain leaders of the opposition to Britain, elite Revolutionaries such as John Hancock continually appealed to poorer, more radical people and looked out for these people's interests, as well as their own. The result was a more moderate revolution than it might otherwise have been and a revolution that succeeded. Just as military fervor reached its high point in the spring of 1776, so did political unity, even if there were ongoing struggles over the meaning of the Revolution.

Creating a National Government

Although treated as if it were a legitimate national government, Congress actually had no more authority over the states than the states were willing to give it, and it had none whatsoever over the people. At the same time that Richard Henry Lee presented Congress with his proposal for independence, he also suggested that Congress create a permanent national government, a confederation of the states with a written constitution. John Dickinson, a moderate, was assigned to draft the Articles of Confederation. He sketched out a weak central government with the authority to make treaties, carry out military and foreign affairs, request the states to pay its expenses, and very little else. There was no chief executive, only a Congress in which each state would have one vote.

Term limits were imposed on representatives. Any act of Congress would require 9 votes (of 13), and the Articles would not go into effect until all 13 states had approved them.

With state jealousies strong, it took Congress more than a year to revise and accept a watered-down version of the Articles of Confederation. Not until March 1781, near the end of the war, did the final state ratify the Articles of Confederation, putting them into effect. By then, the weaknesses in a national government with no means of enforcing its regulations were becoming evident.

Creating State Governments

In 1776, all attention was focused on state governments, where the new ideas about liberty, equality, and government were put into practice. Americans were exhilarated by the prospect of creating their own governments. Between 1775 and 1780, each of the 13 states adopted a new written constitution.

Because the Revolutionaries feared concentrations of power, the powers of governors in the new states were sharply limited. In Pennsylvania and Georgia, the position of governor was abolished and replaced with a council. Governors were given term limits or required to run for reelection every year. Because royal governors had appointed cronies to powerful positions, the new governors also were stripped of their power of appointment.

The new state constitutions made the legislatures more democratic. The number of representatives was doubled in South Carolina and New Hampshire and more than tripled in Massachusetts. Many constitutions also imposed either term limits or frequent elections for representatives. As the property qualifications for holding office were lowered, poorer men sat in legislatures alongside richer ones. The admission of more ordinary men into government was one of the greatest changes brought about by the Revolution. Now the elite had to learn to share power and to win the votes of men they had once scorned.

Winning the Revolution

The British entered the war with clear advantages in population, wealth, and power, but with a flawed premise about how to win the war. Britain, arguably the world's most powerful nation, had the mistaken idea that the colonists could be defeated by a swift and effective use of force. It also assumed that Americans loyal to the Crown would support British troops, but they alienated Americans with their actions. Probably no more than one-fifth of the population remained loyal to Britain, but many more shifted loyalties depending on local circumstances. The war ultimately became a struggle for the support of this unpoliticized population.

Competing Strategies

British political objectives shifted during the war. The first goal, based on the belief that resistance was being led by a handful of radical New Englanders, was to punish and isolate Boston. This was the strategy of 1774 and 1775, with the Intolerable Acts and the battles of Lexington, Concord, and Breed's Hill. It failed miserably, due to the faulty assumption that well-trained British regulars were necessarily superior to untrained colonial rustics. However, if the British had a misplaced faith in their invincibility, the Americans had a misplaced faith in their moral superiority; but neither faith could guarantee victory. The result was a long war, as both sides tried to avoid decisive engagements that might prove fatal.

For seven years, the two armies chased each other across the Eastern Seaboard. Neither side had huge armies. Moreover, with no consensus in Britain about the strategic or economic value of the colonies, there was always opposition to the war and a limit to the investment that the British were prepared to make in it. Consequently, every battle presented a significant risk that troops who were lost could not be replaced.

Manpower was also a serious problem for the Americans. It was difficult to recruit enough soldiers into the Continental army. After a defeat in battle or near the end of the year when terms of enlistment were up, men left the army to return home. Any defeat demoralized the public, depressing enlistments. Hence there was limited incentive for the army to risk all in battle.

Early in the war, however, both sides hoped for a decisive victory. After the Americans failed in Québec, the British pursued them back to Ticonderoga on Lake Champlain, where Benedict Arnold's leadership stopped the rout. The war then shifted to southern New York and the middle colonies. Having given up hopes of crushing New England directly, the British planned to isolate the region and defeat the Continental army under George Washington's leadership.

The British also sought to seize all the major American cities, and they did capture Boston, Newport, New York, Philadelphia, Charleston, and Savannah. The capture of these cities, however, did not bring about an American surrender. With 90 percent of Americans living in the countryside, the seizure of a major city did not strike the hoped-for psychological or economic blow.

The British on the Offensive: 1776

Preparing for an offensive in 1776, the new British commander, General William Howe, assembled a huge force on Staten Island: 32,000 soldiers and 13,000 seamen. Some of these soldiers were actually German mercenaries, the Hessians. Anticipating battle and hoping to protect New York, Washington moved his army south to New York (see Map 7–2). He had about 19,000 soldiers, too few for a pitched battle. Half his troops were in Manhattan while the other half, in Brooklyn Heights, dug in to protect Long Island. The British sneaked up behind the Americans in Brooklyn, inflicting heavy casualties, and on August 27, 1776, Washington pulled his remaining forces back into Manhattan. Had the British pursued rapidly, they probably could have crushed Washington's army, but Howe may have been more concerned with winning a peace than a war. After Washington retreated, Howe invited members of the Continental Congress to meet with him privately on Staten Island. He was unable to recognize American independence, which was what the representatives insisted on, so his peace strategy failed.

Still hoping for peace, Howe began pushing Washington back out of Manhattan. Simultaneously, he offered peace to any colonists in the region who would declare their loyalty, and thousands accepted. On November 16, the British forced the Americans out of Manhattan and pursued them to White Plains and then through New Jersey to New Brunswick. The British almost caught Washington twice in New Jersey, but on December 8 the Americans crossed the Delaware at Trenton, taking every boat with them to prevent pursuit. By Christmas Eve, Washington had only 3,000 soldiers, and General Charles Lee, the commander of the other half of the Continental army, had been captured. As Thomas Paine wrote, "These are the times that try men's souls."

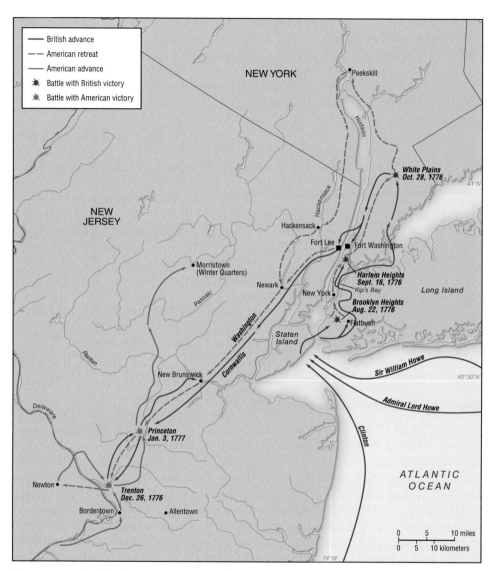

Map 7–2   New York and New Jersey Campaigns, 1776–1777 In the second half of 1776, British troops chased Washington out of New York and across New Jersey. As he would for the remainder of the war, Washington took care never to let the British capture him and his troops, leaving him free to attack at Trenton and Princeton.

Howe had captured New York and New Jersey and was poised to seize Philadelphia (which fell in September 1777). At the end of 1776, the British were close to achieving their objective. Then, on Christmas night, with morale in his army dangerously low, Washington took it across the ice-clogged Delaware and surprised the British garrison at Trenton at dawn, capturing 1,000 Hessian soldiers. About a week later, Washington evaded a British trap and sneaked behind the lines to capture an outpost at Princeton.

These American successes brought another 1,000 troops into the army. More significant, the British decided to concentrate their troops near New Brunswick, fearing the

AMERICA AND THE WORLD
Mercenaries in Global Perspective

In 1776, the Declaration of Independence warned that King George "is, at this time, transporting large armies of foreign mercenaries to complete the works of death, desolation, and tyranny, already begun." It charged that the use of such mercenaries was "scarcely parallelled in the most barbarous ages, and totally unworthy the head of a civilized nation." In fact, the use of mercenaries was the norm, rather than the exception, in eighteenth-century Europe, with some countries renting and others supplying them. Between one-fifth and two-thirds of the British, French, and Prussian armies were foreigners, typically Swiss, Dutch, and various Germans. Wealthy nations could buy other countries' soldiers, thereby protecting their own citizens' freedom.

The practice of using mercenaries had developed several hundred years earlier. Under the feudal system, a lord could command service only for defensive wars. Any lord who wanted to embark on a foreign war would have to pay for soldiers. As the pace of foreign wars increased in the seventeenth century (and feudalism died), so also did the practice of hiring foreign soldiers. Some nations soon became major hirers of mercenaries, and others became sources. John Smith, for example, was a mercenary before he joined the Virginia expedition. He fought for the Dutch against Spain and later for the Austrians against the Turks in Hungary.

Unlike these professional soldiers, less fortunate men were conscripted into their country's service only to be shipped off to fight another nation's war. This was the standard practice in the little German principality of Hesse-Cassel, whose renting of soldiers to other nations generated half of the government's revenues in the middle of the eighteenth century. The government claimed to conscript only "masterless servants and loafers," but as Hesse-Cassel grew dependent on the revenue from its mercenaries, it began to reach into peasant families, seizing their servants and younger sons. Because the law exempted from service men who owned homes, parents tried to give all their sons enough property to keep them out of the army. When inheritance laws were changed to keep parents from dividing their estates, parents began giving their daughters' dowries directly to their sons, sacrificing the girls' prospects for a good match to keep the boys out of the army. In this way, relations between the great nations reached deep into the lives of families.

American colonists rejected the use of mercenaries as "totally unworthy" of a "civilized nation." By the end of the eighteenth century, Enlightenment philosophers had begun to condemn the trade in soldiers—for that is what it was. Under new doctrines of nationalism, men were supposed to fight for patriotism, not for pay, and a nation that hired mercenaries began to seem less than "civilized."

loss of any more garrisons, which were needed to defend the Loyalists. This strategic decision revealed the weakness in the British position and demonstrated why, when victory seemed closest, it was very far away. Without enough troops to overcome the Americans' home advantage, the British needed to ensure that civilians did not aid the Revolutionary War effort. To assure the allegiance of Loyalists, the British had to offer them protection from American reprisals. However, the British were seizing the Americans' goods and property for the war effort. Then, once the garrisons were withdrawn, Loyalists were left alone and vulnerable to the reprisals of the patriots.

The British could control the American countryside only by maintaining troops there, but once the troops were withdrawn, civil warfare would break out. Thus, even though Washington's victories at Trenton and Princeton were small, they exposed the incapacity of the British to defeat the Revolutionaries unless they settled an army of occupation on the Americans, something they were not prepared to do.

A Slow War: 1777–1781

Washington settled in and enlisted soldiers for a long war. Lacking enough soldiers to confront the British head-on, he mostly led the British on chases across the countryside. Maintaining such an army year after year was expensive, but the Americans were unwilling to be taxed at high rates. Continental soldiers who were from the bottom tier of society suffered grievously; at Jockey Hollow, New Jersey, in the winter of 1779–1780, men roasted their own shoes to eat and even devoured their pet dogs.

In 1777, the British political objective was still the same: to isolate New England by seizing the middle colonies. American troops had the advantage in upstate New York by three to one, however, and they defeated the British under General John Burgoyne at Saratoga, stopping the British advance.

The victory at Saratoga convinced the French to enter into a formal alliance, negotiated by Benjamin Franklin, the American envoy. Winning French support was perhaps the major accomplishment of the middle phase of the war: the entry of the French tied down the British in other parts of the world and also brought America more than $8 million in aid.

The British had failed to isolate New England, and it proved impossible to pacify the middle colonies. As a result, the focus shifted from the least loyal section of America, New England, to the most loyal area, the South. British war aims shifted, too, in response to political realities at home. Now the war was needed to protect Loyalists from vengeful patriots.

Seeking to capitalize on internal conflicts and to rally southern Loyalists, the British invaded Georgia in 1778 and South Carolina in 1780. After seizing Charleston and trapping the American commander and thousands of troops, the British ranged out into the countryside, trying to rally the Loyalists and live off the land—the same strategy that had failed in New Jersey.

In the meantime, the Continental army and the militia worked together to wear down the British. The Continental army in the lower South was never large enough for a major battle and was defeated at Camden, South Carolina, in August 1780.

However, as the British marched through South Carolina and North Carolina, they were harassed by bands of irregulars and militia. Each hit depleted the British forces, and each small victory brought more men into the American ranks. This, in fact, became the American strategy as the Continental forces, now commanded in the South by Nathanael

Greene, drew the British, led by Lord Cornwallis, on a wild chase, scoring victories at Cowpens and Kings Mountain.

Finally, Greene met the British at Guilford Court House in North Carolina in March 1781, inflicting heavy losses on the exhausted enemy. The battle was a draw, but Cornwallis, his forces depleted, retreated to Virginia. Greene's army retook almost all of the Deep South.

The cost to South Carolina, however, was enormous. As each side took control, neighbors attacked each other, plundered each other's farms, and carried away each other's slaves. During the Revolution, one-fourth of South Carolina's slaves simply disappeared. Some ran away, some died of disease, some were stolen by whites, and some followed the British, who in June 1780 promised freedom to all rebel-owned slaves who agreed to fight on their side for the rest of the war. Some were actually shipped off to slavery in the West Indies, but many fought with the British. This use of slaves as soldiers, of course, outraged white patriots, but it hardly pleased the Loyalists either. Loyalist slaveholders did not want their way of life undermined. Had the British been willing to wage a war of liberation, freeing all the southern slaves and using them as soldiers, they might have come closer to winning the war. But the British were fighting to preserve social and political order, not to overturn it. The British nonetheless disrupted the slave system significantly, and this disruption was another aspect to the civil war that beset the region for most of the Revolutionary period.

The British southern strategy had failed, but the Americans were not yet ready to win the war. Cornwallis moved on to Virginia in 1781, capturing Richmond, the new capital, and Charlottesville, coming within a few minutes of capturing Thomas Jefferson. Yet the British had been seriously weakened by the war of attrition. George Washington, working closely with the French—who sent a huge fleet into the Chesapeake near Cornwallis's quarters at Yorktown—led most of his forces, accompanied by French troops, to Virginia and laid siege. Trapped, Cornwallis surrendered on October 19, 1781. Although the Treaty of Paris ending the war would not be signed for two more years, the war was effectively over.

Securing a Place in the World

The United States revolted to escape from the British Empire and to turn its back on European power politics. However, to win the war, the new nation had to strike bargains with those same European powers. These alliances and treaties set the stage for America's struggle for a place in the world order.

Early in the war the United States called on Britain's enemies—France, Spain, and Holland—for support, and it played these new allies off against Britain with the cunning of an Old World diplomat. Benjamin Franklin, Congress's envoy to France, now 70, arrived at court in 1776 dressed like a country rustic instead of wearing the expected silks and powdered wig. His appearance was a ruse, intended to make the French think that he was innocent and uncalculating. France entered the war in the hope of breaking up the British Empire and reestablishing itself as the world's most powerful nation. France and Spain both wanted the United States to be independent but small and weak.

The United States wanted to secure its independence, first and foremost, but it had no intention of remaining small or feeble. Americans sought a large chunk of Canada, the territory between the Appalachians and the Mississippi River, and the right to navigate the Mississippi. In return for French and Spanish assistance, the United States

The South Carolina Backcountry

When William Brown settled his family and their slaves at Matthews Bluff on the Savannah River in the South Carolina backcountry in 1769, the land was a fertile swamp teeming with wild animals. These animals had to be subdued before the family could plant a little corn and raise the livestock that provided their living. There was hardly a road worth the name. Until they could erect a log cabin, the family lived in a tent made out of bark. Only six years later, Brown's oldest sons, Bartlett (20) and Tarleton (18), were drafted into the militia. By the time they returned home at the end of the war, the conflict had destroyed everything they had. Like much of the Carolina backcountry, their home had been laid waste as neighbor fought neighbor, Revolutionary against Loyalist.

Once, when campaigning in Georgia, Tarleton Brown was able to return to his home for the night. Around midnight, he heard the dogs barking and then "a loud rap at the door." "Who's there?" he asked. "Several voices together replied 'Friends.'" They said they were on their way home from the militia and wanted a place to spend the night. Suspicious, Brown turned them away, but when they asked for a torch to light their way, he reconsidered; perhaps they really were fellow patriots. So he opened the door a crack, gave them a light, but shut the door quickly. They knocked again, this time asking for water, but Brown had looked through a crack in the logs and seen that they were Tories. He secured the door and told them to leave, but instead "they denounced me, father, and all the family, threatening to visit vengeance upon the whole household, and

with fiendish fury and united strength endeavored to burst the door from its hinges." Failing, they fired their guns through the cracks in the logs, killing Brown's six-year-old brother.

The next time Brown returned home, he knew that his status as a patriot put his family at risk. He and a patriot neighbor thus agreed that if either home were attacked, the other man's family would come to its aid. One night, hearing gunfire, Brown rushed to the neighbor's house, only to find him dead and everything there laid waste. His own family had scattered to the woods.

By this time, Charleston had fallen, and the British army had fanned out, to subdue the rest of the South. Tarleton and his brother Bartlett fled to safety in Virginia. On their way, they passed by the Waxhaw region where British colonel Banastre Tarleton's cavalry had defeated a Revolutionary detachment, massacring the survivors, burning homes, and destroying the local community.

Meanwhile, a band of Loyalists, freed slaves, and allied Indians led by Daniel McGirt moved through Brown's neighborhood, "killing every man he met who had not sworn allegiance to the King." The band killed Brown's father and burned his father's house to the ground. Brown's mother and sisters escaped into the woods.

This was guerilla war, its object to spread terror. Vengeance begat vengeance. When Brown heard what had happened to his family, "my blood boiled within my veins, and my soul thirsted for vengeance." Back in South Carolina, Brown's detachment encountered a Tory. They "gave him his due, and left his body at the disposal of the birds and wild beasts."

Late in the war, Brown contracted smallpox. He returned to his neighborhood to recover, sleeping outdoors, so as not to infect his family. The woman who nursed him turned out to be a Tory "and informed her clan where I was." He had to hide in the woods.

By the time the war was over, much of the backcountry was devastated. Towns were in ruins, farms laid waste, livestock driven off, and many settlers forced to live in the woods. Tarleton Brown had lost almost everything. His mother died soon after, only 47, exhausted by the war. Like much of South Carolina, Brown would have to start all over again.

Surrender of British Army Here, Cornwallis surrenders to Washington.

at first offered only the right to trade, vastly overrating the value in Europe of American trade.

Because America wanted France and Spain to fight for expanded American territory, whereas those countries wanted instead to keep the new nation small, it took three years, until 1778, to negotiate formal treaties. Franklin prodded the French by holding secret truce discussions with a British agent late in 1777 and then leaking reports to well-placed French friends. Although the alliance was an impressive accomplishment, it involved concessions. The Americans promised not to negotiate separately with Britain and to remain France's ally "forever."

The United States broke both promises, the first within a few years and the second in the 1790s. In April 1782, after Cornwallis's surrender at Yorktown but before France and Spain had gained their military objectives, Franklin began peace negotiations with the British. By November, a draft of the treaty had been completed, although Franklin assured the French that nothing would be signed without their consent. The agreement primarily served British and American interests, however. In the Treaty of Paris, signed in 1783, Britain recognized American independence, and the United States acquired the territory between the Appalachians and the Mississippi River and south of the Great Lakes (see Map 7–3).

In the long run Britain probably struck the shrewder bargain. The land it ceded was of little use. The Americans failed to press for commercial concessions, and by the mid-1780s, the British had forbidden Americans to trade directly with Britain or the West Indies. These restrictions seriously damaged the new nation's economy.

Neither France nor Spain gained much from the war. Although Spain won Florida, neither country achieved its other territorial objectives, and France was left with a large debt.

If America's allies were relative losers, so also were Britain's allies, the American Loyalists and Indian tribes that fought with them. The best the British could do for the Loyalists was to secure a commitment of no further reprisals against them and Congress's promise to consider making restitution. The British sold their Indian allies out by transferring their land (the territory between the Appalachians and the Mississippi) to the United States. Although a stunning achievement, the Treaty of Paris also set the stage for future conflicts.

The Challenge of the Revolution

During and after the Revolution, Americans experienced all the upheavals of war: death, profiteering, and inflation, followed by economic depression. Other challenges were also presented by the new Revolutionary ideas about liberty and equality.

Radicals and moderates had compromised for victory, yet significant disagreements resurfaced once the fighting ended. One of the greatest challenges that Americans faced was designing political structures to contain these conflicts. The other great challenge came from the philosophy of revolution itself. Equality implied a transformed society. Followed to its natural conclusion, not only would the transformation lead to prosperity, but it would also necessarily challenge slavery and the subordination of women.

The Departure of the Loyalists

About 15 to 20 percent of the white population had remained loyal to the Crown during the Revolution, along with a majority of the Indians and a minority of slaves. Although sizable in number (almost half a million whites), the Loyalists were never well organized enough to threaten the success of the Revolution.

During the war, partisan fighting was fierce in contested regions such as the Carolinas and New Jersey, but there was relatively little retribution after the war. There were no trials for treason, mass executions, or significant mob actions directed against whites. Nor was there any significant resistance from the Loyalists. Perhaps as many as 80,000

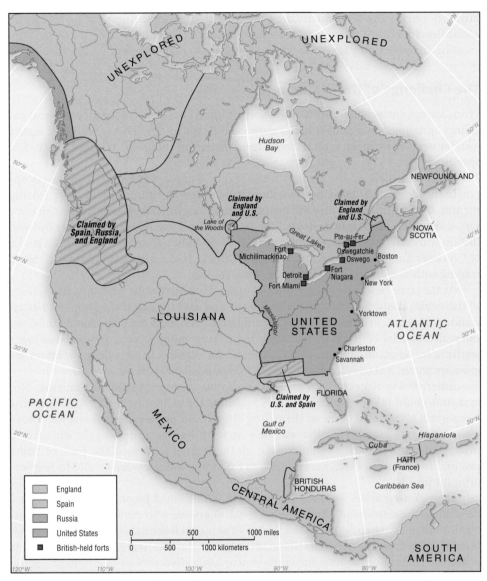

Map 7–3   The Treaty of Paris   The Treaty of Paris confirmed the boundaries of the new United States, north to the Great Lakes, south to Spanish Florida, and west to the Mississippi. But it left the British in several forts west of the Appalachians, forts that they did not abandon until 1797. *Source:* Walter LaFeber, *The American Age*, 2nd ed. (New York: W. W. Norton, 1994), p. 29.

left for Canada, Great Britain, or the West Indies. Among them were thousands of former slaves who had accepted the British offer of freedom.

The white exiles came disproportionately from the top tier of society, and their departure left a void. Confiscated Loyalist property represented a great deal of wealth to be redistributed, and people just below the top rung of society scrambled to take the

Loyalists' places. The departure of the Loyalists enhanced the democratizing tendencies of the Revolution by removing the most conservative element in American society and creating an opportunity for many white Americans to rise to power.

The Challenge of the Economy

Wars disrupt the economy in two ways. First, they interfere with production and exchange, hurting some people and creating opportunity for others. Second, because wars are expensive, they require some combination of increased taxation and deficit spending.

Those who suffered the greatest economic hardships and enjoyed the greatest opportunities from the Revolution were those most deeply involved in the market. During the war, trade with Britain and the British West Indies was cut off, and the British navy seized American ships and destroyed the New England fishing industry. After the war, Britain still excluded American ships from the West Indies. Congress, under the Articles of Confederation, was too weak to negotiate a better trade relationship, and merchants trading with Britain and the West Indies were ruined.

At the same time, other opportunities opened up. Merchants willing to risk seizure of their ships continued the trade with Europe and sold the goods they imported at astronomical prices. Privateering made other merchants rich, as did provisioning the Continental army. In 1779 alone, the army spent $109 million on provisions, fueling a wartime economic boom. The army's demand for supplies drove prices up. Prices for grain increased 200 to 600 percent and, in Maryland, 5,000 percent.

Enterprising Americans with a little capital to invest could rise quickly. Not everyone could take advantage of the Revolutionary economy. In fact, although the Revolution eliminated some of the ruling elite, it did not level social classes. Those who could not profit from the war had to work harder and struggle with rising prices. To meet the army's demand for cloth, women increased the pace of home production. Because there were set prices for cloth, women were unable to reap exorbitant profits.

Skyrocketing prices were hardest on those with limited incomes. While Congress debated price controls and some cities set them, aggrieved citizens sometimes took matters into their own hands. In Boston, a mob of at least a hundred women seized a hogshead of coffee from the merchant Thomas Boylston, who was hoarding it. Such conflicts pitted the community against the entrepreneur and raised serious questions about the purpose of the Revolution: Was it to create opportunities for the individual or to protect the well-being of the community?

After the war, opportunities for profit and prosperity for some increased, whereas a postwar deflation pushed others to misery. Speculation in land and currency offered the fastest ways to become rich. Entrepreneurs bought up paper currency and land patents at a fraction of their worth, counting on the day when they would be redeemed at their face value.

Even before the war ended, there was a clamor for land. Between 1776 and 1790, America's population grew by almost 70 percent, from 2.3 million to 3.9 million, almost all from natural increase. Colonists had long been pushing against the Indians to the west, and by 1783, the Wilderness Road had taken thousands into Kentucky; seven years later, 100,000 people were living in Kentucky and Tennessee.

With the demand for land so great, speculators who could corner huge tracts stood to reap extraordinary profits. Before the Revolution, seven men had secured a patent to 29,350 acres in upstate New York. By the end of the Revolution, three of them were dead; one—a Loyalist—had left the country; and the others were broke or close to it, all victims of the dislocations of war. William Cooper, a small-scale merchant and speculator, bought the patent in a possibly rigged auction for the bargain-basement price of £2,700. Yet his investment was worthless unless Cooper could get others to buy portions of the huge patent from him. After a few months, Cooper sold off thousands of acres not to poor farmers but to speculators who in turn sold farm-sized plots to their own towns-men, turning a profit by increasing the price.

All along the western frontier, farmers rushed to take the new lands, reversing the pre-Revolutionary trend to the cities. With the opening of new regions to the west, America would remain a farming nation for decades more, rather than industrializing rapidly along the rigid class lines of European industrial economies. At the same time, slavery expanded into new territories in the South, ensuring the persistence of inequalities based on race.

Even more than the dislocations of the Revolutionary economy, the financing of the Revolution challenged the American economy. Taxing the population was out of the question, not only because Americans had begun the Revolution precisely to avoid high taxes but also because Congress had no authority to tax. Instead, it simply printed more money. There was no increase in underlying wealth to back up this currency, and the more Congress printed, the less it was worth. By 1780, Congress had printed more than $241 million. In addition, Congress paid for supplies and soldiers' wages with certificates that circulated like money. These certificates put another $95 million into circulation.

The plan was for each state to raise taxes to buy up the Continental currency and remove it from circulation. However, the states were either unable or unwilling to buy up enough currency to maintain its value. Moreover, the states issued their own paper money. Eventually, the states had to tax their inhabitants at rates far higher than had ever been seen before. Collecting taxes was difficult: people could not pay in hard money, and the Continental currency depreciated so rapidly that it was almost worthless (see Figure 7–1).

By April 1777, Continental currency was worth only half its face value, and by April 1781, only half a percent. By the end of the war, some creditors were refusing to accept paper money for debts owed to them, insisting on hard money instead. When trade with Britain resumed, imports increased sharply (because of pent-up demand for consumer goods), while exports fell (because restrictions kept American goods out of British mar-kets). The result was severe deflation and a flood of cheap imports.

The weak central government was almost powerless to address these economic up-heavals. In 1780 it stopped paying the army, which almost led to a mutiny at Newburgh, New York. Congress looked to each state to decide what to do about its debt and which element of its population to serve. Many states showed mercy to debtors. To help pay off debts, some states sold confiscated Loyalist property, whereas others tried to seize Indian lands in the west. Wherever states increased taxes to pay off state debts (as the postwar depression hit), hard-pressed debtors clamored for tax relief. In western Massachusetts, farmers led by Revolutionary War captain Daniel Shays shut down the courts to prevent them from collecting debts. This episode is known as Shays's Rebellion.

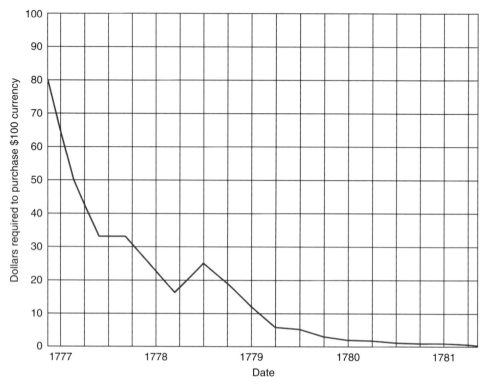

Figure 7–1   Depreciation of Continental Currency, January 1770–April 1781 At the same time that prices were rising, the value of Continental currency was falling dramatically. Between 1777 and 1781, it lost almost all of its value, becoming close to worthless.

Contesting the New Economy

Economic upheaval and popular uprisings against state governments led many Americans to question whether democratic government could survive. The process of rebellion that started in 1765 seemed to be starting again, this time directed against the new republican state governments. Americans now faced the same issue that had led to conflict with Britain: Were they willing to pay for a huge war? Could they avoid the perils of tyranny, on the one hand, and anarchy, on the other? Could they, in short, maintain democratic forms of government?

Shays's Rebellion was simply an extreme form of the protest that occurred in many states. It was an attempt by debtors to force the government to alleviate their economic distress, primarily by shutting down the courts so that their debts could not be collected, but also by passing legislation for the relief of debtors. By 1786, many western Massachusetts farmers had become used to the absence of government, and local courts had been shut down since 1774. Those who put down Shays's Rebellion did so in republican terms, faulting the Shaysites for inadequate virtue.

Such popular uprisings raised serious questions about whether the democratic governments created after the Revolution could contain anarchy. States that faced such uprisings learned that peace could best be preserved by going easy on the rebels. After Shays's Rebellion was put down, John Hancock was elected governor with the support of the Shaysites on a platform of amnesty for the rebels and relief for debtors. As a rule, popular uprisings by economically independent men (as distinguished from those by dependent laborers or slaves) have been punished very lightly in America, which may be a source of American political stability.

The relatively light punishments given to debtor insurgents and the generally inflationary policies of state governments quelled popular unrest, but the postwar depression and the inability of Congress to reopen trade with Britain devastated commerce. The huge national debt went unpaid, leaving numerous creditors holding worthless pieces of paper. Popular unrest had helped debtors but hurt those to whom they owed money. The nationalists, a group of commercial-minded political leaders centered in Congress and including James Madison, Gouverneur Morris, Robert Morris, and Alexander Hamilton, began to make a case for a strong national government that would actively advance commerce and protect private property. These nationalists were, in general, the moderates of the Revolutionary era. Radicals envisioned a weaker central government, a more localized democracy, and a hands-off approach to the economy. Whether these two visions of America could be reconciled was one of the greatest challenges of the Revolution.

Can Women Be Citizens?

The American Revolution raised questions that threatened and in some cases changed the social order. A revolution based on beliefs in human equality and a common human nature brought into question all social relations, including the role of women.

Many women were drawn into the Revolution as consumers. They had eagerly participated in the boycotts of the 1760s and 1770s and had increased home production. Many women identified with the goals of the Revolution and often led riots against merchants suspected of unfair dealings. Women could challenge the Revolutionary governments, as well, when they perceived interference with their rights as consumers and duties as homemakers.

If women were able to extend their traditional economic roles as producers and consumers to support the war effort, there was no consensus on expanding their political roles. Some women pointed out that the right to be taxed only by one's own representatives should apply to them, too. Under the principle of coverture, married women were generally denied the right to own property, but what was the basis for denying the vote to unmarried women who owned property? In 1776, New Jersey extended the vote to unmarried women who met the property qualification (although this right was rescinded in 1807). Although American Revolutionaries were not prepared to let women vote, except in New Jersey, they began to broaden their views of women's intellectual and political capabilities. The state laws that confiscated Loyalists' property, for example, often presumed that married women were capable of making their own political choices. This notion broke with the past, when married women were thought to have no political will separate from that of their husbands.

The Revolution challenged the idea that women lacked independent minds and could not think for themselves. The Enlightenment belief that all human beings had the capacity to reason led to significant improvements in women's education after the war.

Reformers, many of them women, argued that if women appeared ignorant or incapable, it was only because of their inferior education.

Enlightenment ideas about women's intellectual abilities meshed neatly with republican ideas about the need for virtue and liberal ideas about the necessity of consent. If the nation's fate depended on the character of its citizens, both men and women should be able to choose intelligent, upright, patriotic partners. The Revolution also accelerated a trend for people to choose their own marriage partners and marry for love rather than for material interest. If women were to make such choices wisely, they must be educated well.

Yet once again the Revolutionary impulse had its limits. Discussions about women's citizenship and capacities implicitly applied only to prosperous white women. Moreover, almost no one advocated professional education or even knowledge for its own sake for women. Overly intellectual women were ridiculed as "women of masculine minds." Women's education was supposed to make them better wives and mothers and enable them to perform their domestic roles better. Because the family was still the bedrock of the nation, no one was willing to answer a question posed by Abigail Smith Adams in a letter to her husband, John Adams: What recourse was open to women who found that they were treated with "cruelty and indignity" at home?

The ideas of the Revolution presented a powerful challenge to the subordination of women, one that the Revolutionary generation was only partially prepared to meet. Women were recognized as intelligent beings who could make important choices in the market, about their families, and even about their political loyalties. They were partial citizens, and this revealed the limits of Revolutionary doctrines of equality.

The Challenge of Slavery

No institution in America received a greater challenge from the egalitarian ideals of the Revolution than slavery. Although slaves always resisted their enslavement, the world's first organized antislavery movement began before the Revolution with the Pennsylvania Quaker John Woolman, who in 1754 condemned slavery in humanitarian and religious terms. Within a few years, radicals in both the North and the South recognized that the institution was inconsistent with their ideals of freedom.

African American slaves saw immediately that the Revolution offered opportunities for freedom. The rise of egalitarian ideas and wartime disruption enabled thousands of slaves to

Elizabeth Freeman (also known as Mum Bett) Freeman, an enslaved Massachusetts woman, sued for her freedom, contending that Article 1 of the state constitution, which said "all men are born free and equal," made slavery impermissible. In 1781 a local court agreed, and Freeman spent the rest of her long life as a free woman.

claim their freedom. Some used a mix of Christian and Revolutionary principles of liberty to petition for "the natural rights and privileges of freeborn men." Others fought for their liberty by joining the Revolutionary forces; by the end of the war, three-fourths of the Rhode Island regiment and perhaps one-fourth of Washington's troops were black. Many more accepted British offers of freedom to slaves who deserted their masters. Tens of thousands of slaves ran away. This combination of Revolutionary ideals of freedom and African American activism presented a significant challenge to white Americans, and they met it in part. Every state north of Delaware eliminated slavery, either in their constitutions or through gradual emancipation laws. In addition, the Northwest Ordinance of 1787 prohibited slavery in the Northwest Territory (the future states of Ohio, Indiana, Illinois, Michigan, and Wisconsin). In the states of the upper South (Virginia, Maryland, and Delaware) legislatures passed laws making it easier to emancipate slaves.

If slavery was eliminated—sometimes slowly—in the North and questioned in the upper South, it still survived in every state south of New Jersey. Revolutionary ideals made slaveholders uncomfortable. Unwilling to eliminate it, they offered excuses, protesting that abolishing slavery was too difficult or inconvenient. Historians still debate whether the inroads made against slavery were one of the Revolution's greatest successes—or whether the inability to curtail it was its greatest failure.

A New Policy in the West

The new nation faced a major challenge in the West. It had to devise a policy consistent with its interests, rejecting the old colonial models of Britain, France, and Spain. But how would the United States organize the new territory acquired through the war? There was no useful model for new territories and their citizens to become equal members of an expanding, democratic nation.

The Indians' Revolution

At the beginning of the American Revolution, most Indians regarded it as a fight among Englishmen that did not concern them. At the end of the war, all Indians were losers, as land-hungry Americans poured into the region beyond the Appalachians.

By 1776, both the British and the Americans were recruiting Indians. Within a few years, Indians on the frontier were drawn into the struggle, usually on the British side. They feared American moves onto their land; also, only the British could provide the customary "presents" that cemented alliances. Indians struck at American communities all along the frontier.

In retaliation, Washington ordered "the total destruction and devastation" of Iroquois settlements in New York and western Pennsylvania and the capture of "as many prisoners of every age and sex as possible." In 1778, an expedition under General John Sullivan systematically burned 40 Iroquois towns. One chief said that the Americans "put to death all the Women and Children, excepting some of the young Women, whom they carried away for the use of their Soldiers & were afterwards put to death in a more shameful manner." Such brutality undermined American efforts to keep Indian allies.

The End of the Middle Ground

The end of the Revolution brought neither peace nor order. The Indians who had won victories on the frontier were amazed when they learned the British had surrendered and given all of the Indians' land to the Americans. Needing land for settlers more than it needed diplomatic allies, the United States soon abandoned the middle ground (see Chapter 2). No longer able to play one group of Europeans against another, Indian tribes had little leverage.

Western Indians soon found themselves in the midst of a competition among whites for their land. Congress wanted to establish a national claim to Indian lands so it could sell them to pay off the war debt, whereas New York, Pennsylvania, North Carolina, and Virginia all attempted to seize land within their borders. Speculators moved in, knowing they could sell land at an immense profit. At the end of the Revolution, one-third of the men in western Pennsylvania were landless, and they believed that the Revolution's promise of equality entitled them to cheap land. Some of the poorest crossed the Appalachians into Kentucky and Ohio, even during the war, squatting on Indian-owned lands.

Those already on the frontier who both suffered from and inflicted violence maintained a visceral hatred of Indians, sometimes advocating their extermination. These settlers expected government to secure frontier land for them and to protect them from the Indians. Congress and the states moved quickly to force Indians, some with no authority to speak for their tribes, to sign treaties ceding their land.

Such treaties (15 were signed between 1784 and 1796) were almost meaningless. Native Americans refused to honor agreements made under duress and that did not include the customary exchange of gifts, and the states would not recognize another state's claims or those of the national government. Indian leaders were encouraged by the British and the Spanish. The Mohawk leader Joseph Brant took his followers to Ontario. Alexander McGillivray united the Creeks and secured military support from the Spanish in Florida. Not until well into the nineteenth century were American claims to Indian land east of the Mississippi secured and Indian resistance put down.

Settling the West

Establishing effective government in the West was one of the biggest problems the new nation faced. Many frontier regions (in particular Kentucky and the area north of the Ohio River, as well as portions of Vermont and Maine) were claimed by competing groups of speculators. The Articles of Confederation gave Congress limited powers of government in the West, but a national policy was necessary. Just after the Revolution, dissident settlers in New York, Pennsylvania, Kentucky (then part of Virginia), and Tennessee (then part of North Carolina) all hatched plans to create their own states.

Both state governments and nationalists in Congress believed that the Union was in peril. Yet it was difficult to reach a compromise among the competing interests. States wanted Congress to recognize their western claims, whereas states without any claims wanted all of the western lands to be turned over to Congress. Also at issue was which speculators' claims would be upheld, as speculators with dubious claims to the land were selling them to settlers at bargain prices.

The Northwest Ordinance, ratified by Congress on July 13, 1787, was a compromise among these competing interests. Finally realizing that they could not manage vast areas of territory, the large states yielded their claims to Congress. Because Congress validated the claims only of respectable speculators, it made losers not only out of unscrupulous ones but also out of anyone who had bought land from them at cheap prices.

The Northwest Ordinance set out a model of government for the western territories that reflected the liberal political philosophy of nationalists in Congress and established a process for the admission of new states into the nation. Rejecting Britain's colonial model of expansion, it declared that territories would be eligible to apply for statehood once they had 60,000 free inhabitants. There were other important breaks with the past. Slavery was forbidden north of the Ohio River, the first time that a line was drawn barring slaves from a particular region. Trial by jury and habeas corpus were guaranteed, as well as the right to bail and freedom of religion. Cruel and unusual punishments were barred. These were important principles that, except for the provision excluding slavery, would all appear again in the Constitution and Bill of Rights (see Map 7-4).

The Northwest Ordinance was designed to create an orderly world of middle-class farmers who obeyed the law, paid their debts, worshiped as they pleased, and were protected from despotic government and the unruly poor. The ordinance represented the triumph of the moderate Revolutionaries' vision of government.

Creating a New National Government

At the beginning of the Revolution, radicals and moderates had worked together to accomplish common goals. The years of war, however, slowly pulled radicals and moderates apart. Many moderates, particularly those who served in Congress or as officers in the Continental army, became nationalists. They worked with men from other states on national projects and came to think of the states as a threat to the success of the Revolution. Many of the radicals, meanwhile, retained a local, republican perspective. They dreaded a centralized government and feared that the Continental army would become a standing army that might take away their liberties.

This split between moderate nationalists and radical localists culminated in the battle over the Constitution, written by the nationalists to create a stronger central government and resisted by the localists, afraid it would subvert liberty. Almost all the problems that led the nationalists to wish for a stronger national government concerned the economy: paying the war debt, paying the soldiers, and improving commerce. The nationalists were deeply involved in the market economy as merchants, financiers, farmers, and planters. The localists, as a rule, were much less involved in the market and suspicious of those who were. As long as taxes were low and their creditors did not harass them, they were satisfied. The Articles of Confederation provided them all the national government and economy they needed.

A Crippled Congress

Nationalists in Congress soon realized that the national government was powerless to address the most pressing economic questions. By 1779, after printing $200 million in paper money that was dropping in value by the day, Congress had shut down its printing

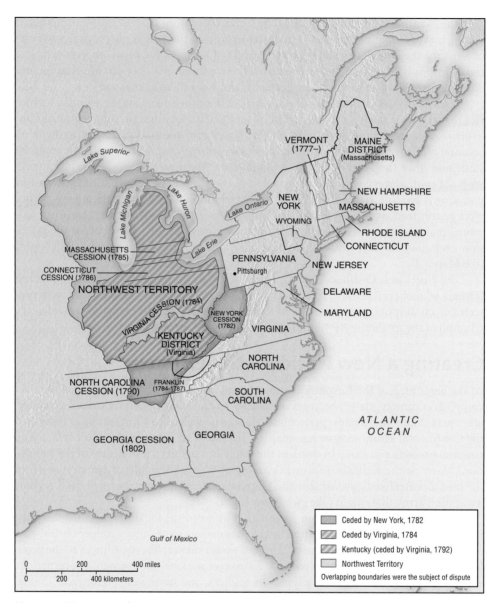

Map 7–4   Western Land Cessions Between 1782 and 1802, eastern states ceded to the national government the territory they claimed in the West. Under the principle established by the Northwest Ordinance, new states were carved out of this territory. Never before had a nation developed such a procedure for bringing in new regions not as colonies but as fully equal states.

presses. It then gave the states the responsibility to provision the army. As legislatures dithered, the unclothed, unfed, and unpaid army threatened mutiny. Congress gave up trying to pay its war debt and passed that back to the states as well. Some states refused. States such as Massachusetts that raised taxes to pay off their portion courted armed upheavals such as Shays's Rebellion.

Congress was powerless to alleviate the economic distress. At the end of the war, British goods flooded in again to meet a consumer demand that seemed insatiable. However, there was no comparable British demand for American exports; in fact, Britain closed its ports to American trade. America could not close its ports to British ships, because the Articles of Confederation denied Congress the authority to regulate commerce. Additional foreign loans were out of the question. Congress could not pay back those it had already taken out. Even western policy, Congress's greatest triumph, presented problems. Once the states had ceded western territory to Congress (leading to the Northwest Ordinance), Congress discovered that it takes an army and a great deal of money to police a territory inhabited by Indians and coveted by land-hungry settlers. Congress lacked that money and could not pay the army it had.

Nationalist attempts to strengthen Congress failed, however, lacking the approval of the states. By the middle of the 1780s, several nationalists abandoned that reform in favor of a new and stronger form of government. James Madison and other nationalists began talking about calling a constitutional convention. But the challenge they faced was how to effect changes that the states did not seem to want.

The road to the Constitutional Convention in Philadelphia in 1787 ran through two earlier meetings. First, in 1785, at Madison's suggestion, commissioners from Virginia and Maryland met at George Washington's home, Mount Vernon, to resolve disputes about navigating the Potomac River. Madison suggested a further meeting of representatives from all the states in Annapolis, Maryland, to build on the accomplishments from Mount Vernon. When only 12 men from five states arrived, they called for another meeting, in Philadelphia, nine months later. In those nine months, Shays's Rebellion and the stalemate in Congress persuaded nationalists to consider strengthening the government. Over the summer of 1787, 55 men from 12 states met in Philadelphia to write one of the most influential documents in the history of the world.

Writing a New Constitution

The men assembled in Philadelphia were primarily moderate nationalists. Committed to the goals of the Revolution, they sought, in Madison's words, "republican remedies" for the problems of republican government. The 55 delegates met for almost four months during the summer of 1787, finally ratifying the Constitution on September 17. They deliberated in secret, in order to talk freely and achieve compromises.

Although there were sharp differences of opinion, there were also wide areas of agreement. Most of the delegates had considerable experience in state and national government. George Washington, a member of Virginia's delegation, was the most widely respected man in the nation. He was elected the presiding officer of the convention.

The delegates were young, with most in their 30s and 40s. No one was more important to the convention than James Madison, just 36. He came with a design for the new government already worked out. Known as the Virginia Plan, it became the outline for the Constitution.

The Virginia Plan was a blueprint for substantial change: a strong central government divided into three branches, executive, legislative (itself with two branches), and judicial, that would check and balance one another; a system of federalism that guaranteed every state a republican government; and proposals for admitting new states and

Table 7–1 Key Provisions of the Articles of Confederation, the Virginia Plan, the New Jersey Plan, and the Constitution

	Articles of Confederation	Virginia Plan	New Jersey Plan	Constitution
Executive	None	Chosen by Congress	Plural; chosen by Congress	President chosen by Electoral College
Congress	One house; one vote per state	Two houses	One house	Two houses
Judiciary	None	Yes	Yes	Yes
Federalism	Limited; each state retains full sovereignty	Yes; Congress can veto state laws	Yes; acts of Congress the "supreme law of the states"	Yes; Constitution the "supreme law of the land"; states guaranteed a republican form of government; Supreme Court to adjudicate disputes between states
Powers of Congress	Conduct diplomacy and wage war; cannot levy taxes or raise army	All powers of Articles of Confederation, plus power to make laws for nation	All powers of Articles of Confederation, plus power to regulate commerce and make states pay taxes	Numerous powers, such as levy taxes, declare war, raise army, regulate commerce, and "make all laws which shall be necessary and proper" for carrying out those powers

amending the Constitution. The only alternative, the New Jersey Plan, was offered on June 15 and quickly rejected. It proposed a single-house legislature, with all states having an equal vote, and a plural executive, chosen by the legislature (see Table 7–1).

The delegates agreed that the new national government would have to be much stronger: Congress would now have the power to collect taxes and duties, to pay the country's debts, to regulate foreign commerce, and to raise armies and pay for them. Once the delegates compromised on a method for choosing the president (by electors chosen in each state) and the length of his term (four years, eligible for reelection), they readily agreed to grant him considerable power to propose legislation, veto bills of Congress (subject to congressional override), conduct diplomacy, and command the armed forces.

The delegates vested judicial authority in the Supreme Court and inferior federal courts and granted them authority over the state constitutions as well. Although the delegates could agree rather easily on the structure and powers of the new government, they argued bitterly anytime the interests of their states seemed in jeopardy. The most difficult issues related to representation: Would the numbers of senators and representatives be based on population or wealth, or would each state have equal numbers? If based on population or wealth, would slaves be counted? Large states generally wanted representation to be based on either population or wealth (they had more of both), whereas northern states did not want slaves to be counted, either as population or as wealth. The conflict between the large and small states was resolved by Roger Sherman's Connecticut (or Great) Compromise: Each state would have an equal number of senators, satisfying the small states. The number of representatives would be based on either population or wealth, satisfying the large states.

The Connecticut Compromise solved the conflict between small and large states, but only by creating another between slave and free states. The South Carolinians were adamant: whether slavery was called population or wealth, the institution must be protected. The argument was fierce, with several delegates threatening to walk out. Finally, the convention compromised. Representation in the House would be based on the entire free population (including women and children, but not Indians) plus three-fifths of the slaves, thus increasing the South's representation. The delegates recognized that the Three-Fifths Compromise was fundamentally illogical, but its acceptance was needed to make the Connecticut Compromise possible.

The Three-Fifths Compromise, or Clause, became the most notorious provision in the Constitution. Although the delegates were careful not to use the word "slave" (instead using bland phrases such as "other persons"), clearly they were establishing a racial line. The convention made two other concessions to slavery. First, it agreed, over Madison's vehement protest, that Congress could not ban the slave trade until 1808 at the earliest. In addition, the Constitution included a fugitive slave clause, which required states to return runaway slaves. The reopening of the slave trade did more to strengthen slavery than the other compromises on slavery. Madison predicted accurately that "twenty years will produce all the mischief that can be apprehended from the liberty to import slaves." Between 1788 and 1808, thousands and thousands of Africans were sold into slavery in the United States.

The nationalists were determined not to leave Philadelphia without a constitution, and they were willing to make whatever compromises seemed necessary. Those compromises were eventually achieved, and the convention adjourned on September 17. The delegates' work was not over, however. Now the Constitution had to be ratified.

Ratifying the Constitution: Politics

There was nothing inevitable about the nation, the Constitution, or the particular form either took. The Constitution was the creation of a small group of men who thought nationally, the Federalists. They then had the difficult task of getting the Constitution ratified by a nation that still thought about government in almost wholly local terms. That the Constitution would be ratified was by no means a given.

The Philadelphia Convention decided that the Constitution would go into effect once nine states had ratified it. They could not bind any states that had not ratified, but the nine signatories could go ahead. Small states were the first to ratify, because they most needed the union. For example, Georgia, the fourth state to ratify, was still in many ways a frontier region, vulnerable to Indian assault, its capital at Augusta an armed camp. The most serious opposition came from the large, powerful states of Massachusetts, New York, and Virginia.

The convention had concluded on September 17, and by December 7, Delaware had already ratified the Constitution. By January 9, 1788, New Jersey, Georgia, and Connecticut followed, with barely any dispute. The Federalists in Pennsylvania forced ratification by using strong-arm tactics. The Federalists in other states learned from this mistake and more willingly made concessions to the Antifederalists (as the opponents of the Constitution were called).

In Massachusetts, as in Pennsylvania, considerable opposition came from the western part of the state among those sympathetic to Shays's Rebellion. In an inspired move that would be used also in Virginia, the Federalists made certain that the Constitution was debated section by section, enabling them to win point by point. And in another key strategic decision, the Federalists agreed that the convention in Massachusetts should propose amendments, not as a condition for ratification but as part of a package that recommended ratification. This concession, which made the Constitution both stronger and more democratic, was critical in winning ratification.

Only three more states were necessary for the Constitution to go into effect. The Federalists postponed or stalled the debate until the states most favorable to the Constitution had ratified it, as it would go into effect once nine states had ratified it. The Virginia ratifying convention was one of the most dramatic and divided. Patrick Henry, who had refused to attend the Philadelphia Convention, saying that he "smelt a rat," spoke in opposition. His impassioned speeches were rebutted by James Madison's careful and knowledgeable remarks. Having worn down the Antifederalists with logic, the Federalists carried the day, and the Constitution was ratified. The Antifederalists agreed to abide by the result, even though there had been threats of armed rebellion. The decision of Antifederalists to accept the Constitution and to participate in the government it created was one of the most important choices made in this era.

In New York, the Federalists stalled debate until news of Virginia's ratification arrived. Then they posed the inevitable question: Ten states had now voted in favor and the Constitution had been ratified; would New York join in or not? New York did, and eventually the Constitution was ratified by all the states. As a condition for ratification, several states had insisted that the first Congress consider a number of amendments. These amendments became the Bill of Rights.

Ratifying the Constitution: Ideas

The Constitution was the product of many compromises, and it did not precisely fit anyone's previous ideas. As the Federalists explained the benefits of the Constitution to skeptical Americans, and as the Antifederalists tried to explain what they thought was

Time Line

▼**1774**
Intolerable Acts

▼**1775**
Battles of Lexington and Concord
Fort Ticonderoga seized
Battle of Breed's Hill
Second Continental Congress convenes
Continental army created, with George Washington in charge
Congress adopts "Declaration of the Causes and Necessity of Taking Up Arms"

George III declares colonists in rebellion
Governor Dunmore offers freedom to Virginia slaves who fight for the British
Continental army attacks Canada

▼**1776**
Thomas Paine writes *Common Sense*
Declaration of Independence
Articles of Confederation drafted
British capture Manhattan

Washington captures Trenton and Princeton
New Jersey Constitution allows unmarried, property-owning women to vote

▼**1777**
British capture Philadelphia
American victory at Saratoga

▼**1778**
French enter into treaty with United States
British conquer Georgia

wrong with it, a new understanding of what American government should be evolved. Despite significant disagreements, this new understanding, which incorporated the Bill of Rights, was sufficiently broad that Antifederalists could join the new government.

Nonetheless, the differences between the Federalists and Antifederalists were profound. As a rule, the Antifederalists were more rural and less involved in the market, came from the western or backwoods regions, and were more likely to be veterans of the militia than of the Continental army. The Antifederalists were, above all, old-line republicans who warned of the dangers to liberty of corruption, tyranny, and enslavement, although now they spoke against the Federalists, not the British.

The Antifederalists believed passionately in the local community. They asserted that republics could survive only in homogeneous communities, where all people had the same interests and values. They believed that too much diversity, whether economic, cultural, ethnic, or religious, destroyed a republic. One Massachusetts Antifederalist criticized the Constitution because it would not allow states to stop immigration so as "to keep their blood pure." Although Antifederalists, like Federalists, generally supported freedom of religion, they also favored the spread of Protestantism as a means of ensuring morality.

At the same time, the Antifederalists were committed to individual rights, and it is to them that the nation is indebted for the Bill of Rights. They retained the republican fear of power, and they did not trust the person they could not see. If government were remote, then it would become oppressive, it would deprive the people of their liberties, and it would tax them. One of the most consistent complaints of the Antifederalists was not so much that taxation would be enacted without representation as that it would be enacted at all. If the national government needed money, let it ask the states for it (a system that failed under the Articles of Confederation). The Antifederalists displayed the same fear of centralized government and hatred of taxation that had led to their revolt against Britain. The Antifederalist contribution to American political thought was a continuing critique of government itself.

Sullivan expedition into New York and Pennsylvania

▼**1779**
Continental troops winter at Jockey Hollow

▼**1780**
British conquer South Carolina

▼**1781**
Articles of Confederation ratified
Battle of Guilford Court House
Cornwallis surrenders

▼**1782**
Franklin begins peace discussions with British

▼**1783**
Treaty of Paris

▼**1785**
Virginia and Maryland commissioners meet at Mount Vernon

▼**1786–1787**
Shays's Rebellion
Meeting at Annapolis

▼**1787**
Northwest Ordinance
Constitutional Convention

▼**1787–1788**
Federalist Papers published
Constitution ratified

The Ratification of the Constitution

In writing the Constitution, the Founding Fathers drew from their knowledge of world history and political theory, but once it was time to turn their new document into an actual government, they were in uncharted territory. Not only was a written Constitution an innovation but so was the process for putting it into effect. The creators of the new United States government were making up the processes of democratic government as they went along.

Approval of the Constitution was by no means assured. Its supporters, the Federalists, made a series of strategic decisions, however, that not only enabled them to prevail but also strengthened the Constitution and enhanced its legitimacy in the process. The first of these decisions was to send the Constitution back to Congress, asking *it* to send the document along to the state legislatures, requesting them to convene ratifying conventions. This tactic was at once democratic and a bit devious. It reflected the Lockean basis of the Constitution: Government is created by the people—the "We the People" of the Constitution's Preamble who "establish this Constitution for the United States of America." But this process broke so sharply from the past that some delegates could not reconcile themselves to it. Maryland's Luther Martin, an Antifederalist, had consistently argued against any representation based upon population. He argued that "the Genl Govt ought to be formed for the States, not for individuals." Nationalists such as James Wilson carried the day with their Lockean understanding: "The Genl Govt is not an assemblage of States, but for the individuals composing them; the *individuals* therefore not the *States*, ought to be represented. . . ." It also brought Congress back into the process, giving the Constitution added legitimacy. At the same time, sending it out to the people for ratification was a bit sly, for had the Convention asked for ratification from the state legislatures, that process would have been slow and difficult, with legislators who were jealous of their states' powers stalling the process; moreover, two-thirds majorities would have been necessary in many states. Had the Constitution been sent to the state legislatures, it is unlikely it would have been adopted.

Consider how close the Pennsylvania assembly came to refusing to call a ratifying convention. The day the assembly was scheduled to vote on whether to issue the call, two Antifederalists intentionally did not show up; without them, the minimum number of necessary members were not present, and no convention could be called. The Federalist Speaker of the House ordered the sergeant-at-arms to bring the two absent legislators to the assembly, which he did, with the assistance of a mob. The Federalists won, but their tactic was considered distasteful.

At each of the state ratifying conventions, the Federalists used different tactics, as the situation seemed to warrant. Especially important to enhancing the legitimacy of the Constitution was the decision to accept amendments to the document. The Convention had defeated with almost no debate a proposal to add a Bill of Rights, but the Antifederalists pushed the idea in the state conventions. In Pennsylvania, Wilson explained the Federalist position: enumerating the rights of the people was downright "dangerous" because it might limit rights to those listed. The Pennsylvania Federalists voted down a proposal for amendments, but their counterparts in Massachusetts, where John Hancock offered amendments as a compromise to "remove the fears and quiet the apprehensions of many of the good people of the commonwealth," were much wiser. They accepted the amendments. At least as important was the form that these amendments would take, not as a condition for ratification, but as a recommendation to the new government. Only Maryland would not attach a list of amendments.

Other decisions were purely tactical. The Federalists were able to get a postponement in New Hampshire, which at that point was unlikely to ratify. They knew that momentum was important and that even one rejection might prove fatal. Then, Maryland and South Carolina ratified, requiring only one more state's approval for the Constitution to go into effect. As it turned out, both New Hampshire and Virginia ratified at almost the same time, unbeknownst to each other.

Democratic government is a combination of procedure and principle. The Federalist proponents of the Constitution were skilled political tacticians who used the processes of government to their own advantage, but they also compromised with their Antifederalist opponents. Their contestation—their arguments, struggles, and compromises—gave meaning to the Constitution and form to the new government of the United States.

Federalists shared many of the beliefs of the Antifederalists, such as individual rights. Hence they readily accepted the Antifederalist proposal to list and protect those rights as amendments to the Constitution. They were also suspicious of government, most agreeing with Thomas Paine that "government even in its best state is but a necessary evil." The separation of powers and elaborate series of checks and balances that the Constitution created, as well as the system of federalism itself, reflects this fear. The Federalists divided power; unlike the Antifederalists, they did not deny it.

Their experience in the market economy, as officers in the Continental army and as members of the national government, provided the Federalists with a different perspective on political economy. They had come to believe that all people were motivated by self-interest. Unlike the Antifederalists, the Federalists were willing to accept self-interest and build a government around it.

The Federalists were convinced that no government could rest entirely on the virtue of its people. The challenge was to build a government out of imperfect human materials that would preserve liberty instead of destroying it. In *The Federalist* No. 10 (one of a series of 85 essays known as the *Federalist Papers*, written by Madison, Hamilton, and John Jay and published anonymously to influence the ratification debate), Madison explained that the causes of conflict "are sown into the nature of man." The only way of eliminating them would be either by "giving to every citizen the same opinions, the same passions, and the same interests" (the Antifederalist solution) or by destroying liberty itself. But "as long as the reason of man continues fallible, and he is at liberty to exercise it, different opinions will be formed." Toleration was the price of liberty and the necessary result of human imperfection.

In the Philadelphia Convention, the Federalists had been so intent on working out compromises and reconciling competing interests that they did not develop a philosophy to explain the profound changes they were proposing. That philosophy emerged from the ratification debates, in which it was met by the alternative philosophy of the Antifederalists. Both these bodies of thought, sometimes in harmony, sometimes in disagreement, constitute the legacy of the Revolution. This dialogue has continued to frame American government from their day until ours.

Conclusion

In rejecting the increasingly centralized British state, the Revolutionaries were clear about what they did not want. Over the course of the Revolution, they began to envision the kind of society and nation that they hoped to create. It would ensure individual liberty and economic opportunity. But this was a vague vision for the future. As the first modern nation created by revolution, the United States was entering uncharted territory. Winning independence from the world's most powerful nation, ratifying the federal Constitution, and planning for the admission of new territories into the federal union were all extraordinary accomplishments, unique in world history.

Yet there were many problems left unresolved. Not only was Britain still occupying forts in the Northwest Territory, but also the European nations were skeptical that the new nation would survive. Although the United States had more than doubled its size, much of the new territory could not be settled because it was inhabited by Indians who refused to recognize America's sovereignty. There were also disagreements among Americans themselves, particularly about the meaning of democracy. How could a nation founded on the principle of liberty practice slavery? How would individual rights be reconciled with the general welfare? Whose economic interests would be served? The American people had begun a great experiment whose outcome was far from assured.

Who, What

Thomas Jefferson 187

Richard Henry Lee 186

Antifederalists 211

Common Sense 187

Coverture 203

Federalists 211

Loyalists 194

Northwest Ordinance 205

Shays's Rebellion 201

Review Questions

1. What was Revolutionary ardor, and why was it highest at the beginning of the war?

2. What were American and British strategies for winning the war? What were the chief challenges the Americans faced in mounting the war, and how did they affect military strategy? What were the constraints on the British in waging a war on American soil?

3. Which Americans believed a stronger central government was needed, and why? What were the compromises they made in writing the Constitution?

4. Describe the political philosophies of the Federalists and Antifederalists.

Critical-Thinking Questions

1. Which group was more democratic, the Federalists or Antifederalists? Or were they democratic (or undemocratic) in different ways?

2. How did Americans respond to the challenges to the social order presented by their doctrine of equality?

3. Assess the relative importance of ideals and economic interests in shaping the history of the period 1775–1787.

For further review materials and resource information, please visit www.oup.com/us/oakes

CHAPTER 7: CREATING A NEW NATION, 1775–1788
Primary Sources

7.1 THOMAS PAINE, *COMMON SENSE* (1776)

In 1775 the political strife between the colonies and Great Britain turned into outright warfare. Nevertheless, many Americans questioned whether the goal of the conflict should be the creation of an independent nation or simply a renegotiation of the colonies' relationship with Great Britain. Thomas Paine's pamphlet *Common Sense*, published in January 1776, helped convince the colonists that monarchy was a corrupt and tyrannical system and that they would be better off independent. The document was widely read and helped shift American public opinion toward revolution.

Of the Origin and Design of Government in General

Some writers have so confounded society with government, as to leave little or no distinction between them; whereas they are not only different, but have different origins. Society is produced by our wants, and government by our wickedness; the former promotes our happiness POSITIVELY by uniting our affections, the latter NEGATIVELY by restraining our vices. The one encourages intercourse, the other creates distinctions. The first a patron, the last a punisher.

Society in every state is a blessing, but government even in its best state is but a necessary evil; in its worst state an intolerable one; for when we suffer, or are exposed to the same miseries BY A GOVERNMENT, which we might expect in a country WITHOUT GOVERNMENT, our calamity is heightened by reflecting that we furnish the means by which we suffer. Government, like dress, is the badge of lost innocence; the palaces of kings are built on the ruins of the bowers of paradise. For were the impulses of conscience clear, uniform, and irresistibly obeyed, man would need no other lawgiver; but that not being the case, he finds it necessary to surrender up a part of his property to furnish means for the protection of the rest; and this he is induced to do by the same prudence which in every other case advises him out of two evils to choose the least. WHEREFORE, security being the true design and end of government, it unanswerably follows, that whatever FORM thereof appears most likely to ensure it to us, with the least expense and greatest benefit, is preferable to all others.

In order to gain a clear and just idea of the design and end of government, let us suppose a small number of persons settled in some sequestered part of the earth, unconnected with the rest, they will then represent the first peopling of any country, or of the world. In this state of natural liberty, society will be their first thought. A thousand motives will excite them thereto, the strength of one man is so unequal to his wants, and his mind so unfitted for perpetual solitude, that he is soon obliged to seek assistance and relief of another, who in his turn requires the same. . . . Thus necessity, like a gravitating power, would soon form our newly arrived emigrants into society, the reciprocal blessings of which, would supersede, and render the obligations of law and government unnecessary while they remained perfectly just to each other; but as nothing but heaven is impregnable to vice, it will unavoidably happen, that in proportion as they surmount the first difficulties of emigration, which bound them together in a common cause, they will begin to relax in their duty and attachment to each other; and this remissness will point out the necessity of establishing some form of government to supply the defect of moral virtue.

Some convenient tree will afford them a State-House, under the branches of which, the whole colony may assemble to deliberate on public matters. It is more than probable that their first laws will have the title only of REGULATIONS, and be enforced by no other penalty than public disesteem. In this first parliament every man, by natural right, will have a seat.

But as the colony increases, the public concerns will increase likewise, and the distance at which the members may be separated, will render it too inconvenient for all of them to meet on every occasion as at first, when their number was small, their habitations near, and the public concerns few and trifling. This will point out the convenience of their consenting to leave the legislative part to be managed by a select number chosen from the whole body, who are supposed to have the same concerns at stake which those who appointed them, and who will act in the same manner as the whole body would act, were they present. If the colony continues increasing, it will become necessary to augment the number of the representatives, and that the interest of every part of the colony may be attended to, it will be found best to divide the whole into convenient parts, each part sending its proper number; and that the ELECTED might never form to themselves an interest separate from the ELECTORS, prudence will point out the propriety of having elections often; because as the ELECTED might by that means return and mix again with the general body of the ELECTORS in a few months, their fidelity to the public will be secured by the prudent reflection of not making a rod for themselves. And as this frequent interchange will establish a common interest with every part of the community, they will mutually and naturally support each other, and on this (not on the unmeaning name of king) depends the STRENGTH OF GOVERNMENT, AND THE HAPPINESS OF THE GOVERNED.

Here then is the origin and rise of government; namely, a mode rendered necessary by the inability of moral virtue to govern the world; here too is the design and end of government, viz. freedom and security. And however our eyes may be dazzled with show, or our ears deceived by sound; however prejudice may warp our wills, or interest darken our understanding, the simple voice of nature and of reason will say, it is right.

Source: Thomas Paine, *Common Sense*, 1776.

7.2 JOSEPH PLUMB MARTIN, EXCERPTS FROM *A NARRATIVE OF SOME OF THE ADVENTURES, DANGERS AND SUFFERINGS OF A REVOLUTIONARY SOLDIER* (1830)

Joseph Plumb Martin was born in western Massachusetts but grew up in his grandparents' home in Connecticut. He joined the army at age 15 under pressure from his friends, eventually serving in both the Connecticut militia and the Continental Army. In the late 1820s, he wrote a memoir. Although he occasionally mentioned politics, he focused on the hunger, cold, and general deprivation experienced by the soldiers, conveying the trauma of warfare. This passage describes conflict along the Delaware River.

Our batteries were nothing more than old spars and timber laid up in parallel lines and filled between with mud and dirt. The British batteries in the course of the day would nearly level our works, and we were, like the beaver, obliged to repair our dams in the night. During the whole night, at intervals of a quarter or half an hour, the enemy would let off all their pieces, and although we had sentinels to watch them and at every flash of their guns to cry, "a shot," upon hearing which everyone endeavored to take care of himself, yet they would ever and anon, in spite of all our precaution, cut up some of us. . . .

It was utterly impossible to lie down to get any rest or sleep on account of the mud, if the enemy's shot would have suffered [allowed] us to do so. Sometime some of the men, when overcome with fatigue and want of sleep, would slip away into the barracks to catch a nap of sleep, but it seldom happened that they all came out again alive. I was in this place a fortnight and can say in sincerity that I never lay down to sleep a minute in all that time. . . . What little provisions we had was cooked by the invalids in our camp and brought to the island in old flour barrels; it was mostly corned beef and hard bread, but it was not much trouble to cook or fetch what we had.

We continued here, suffering cold, hunger and other miseries, till the fourteenth day of November. On that day, at the dawn, we discovered six ships of the line . . . within pistol shot of the fort, on the western side. . . . The soldiers were all ordered to take their posts at the palisadoes, which they were ordered to defend to the last extremity, as it was expected the British would land under the fire of their cannon and attempt to storm the fort. The cannonade was severe, as well it might be, six sixty-four-gun-ships, a thirty-six-gun frigate, a twenty-four-gun ship, a galley and a sloop of six guns, together with six batteries of six guns each and a bomb battery of three mortars, all playing at once upon our poor little fort, if fort it might be called.

Some of our officers endeavored to ascertain how many guns were fired in a minute by the enemy, but it was impossible, the fire was incessant. In the height of the cannonade it was desirable to hoist a signal flag for some of our galleys that were lying above us to come down to our assistance. The officers inquired who would undertake it. As none appeared willing for some time, I was about to offer my services. I considered it no more exposure of my life than it was to remain where I was. The flagstaff was of easy ascent, being an old ship's mast, having shrouds to the ground, and the round top still remaining. While I was still hesitating, a sergeant of the artillery offered himself. He accordingly ascended to the round top, pulled down the flag to affix the signal flag to the halyard, upon which the enemy, thinking we had struck, [surrendered] ceased firing in every direction and cheered. "Up with the flag!" was the cry of our officers in every part of the fort. The flags were accordingly hoisted, and the firing was immediately renewed. The sergeant then came down and had not gone half a rod from the foot of the staff when he was cut in two by a cannon shot. This caused me some serious reflection at the time. He was killed! Had I been at the same business I might have been killed, but it might have been otherwise ordered by Divine Providence, we might have both lived. I a not predestinarian enough to determine it. The enemy's shot cut us up. I saw five artillerists belonging to one gun cut down by a single shot, and I saw men who were stooping to be protected by the works; but not stooping low enough, split like fish to be broiled. . . .

The cannonade continued, directed mostly at the fort, till the dusk of the evening. As soon as it was dark we began to make preparations for evacuating the fort and endeavoring to escape to the Jersey shore. When the firing had in some measure subsided and I could look about me, I found the fort exhibited a picture of desolation. The whole area of the fort was completely ploughed as a field. The buildings of every kind hanging in broken fragments, and the guns all dismounted, and how many of the garrison sent to the world of spirits, I knew not. If ever destruction was complete, it was here. The surviving part of the garrison were now drawn off and such of the stores as could conveniently be taken away were carried to the Jersey shore.

[. . . After evacuating the fort,] we marched a little back into some pitch-pine woods, where we found the rest of the troops that had arrived before us. They had made up some comfortable fires and were enjoying the warmth, and that was all the comfort they had to partake of, except rest, for victuals was out of the question. I wrapped myself up in my blanket and lay down upon the leaves and soon fell asleep and continued so till past noon, when I awoke from the first sound sleep I had for a fortnight. Indeed, I had not laid down in all that time. The little sleep I had obtained was in cat naps, sitting up and leaning against the wall, and I thought myself fortunate if I could do that much. When I awoke I was as crazy as a goose shot through the head.

We left our flag flying when we left the island, and the enemy did not take possession of the fort till late in the morning after we left it.

Source: Joseph Plumb Martin, excerpts from *A Narrative of Some of the Adventures, Dangers and Sufferings of a Revolutionary Soldier; Interspersed with Anecdotes of Incidents That Occurred Within His Own Observation* (Hallowell, ME: Glazier, Masters & Co., 1830), pp. 165–175. http://www.ushistory.org/march/other/martindiary.htm

7.3 LETTER FROM ABIGAIL ADAMS TO JOHN ADAMS (1776)

The American Revolution had a profound impact on the lives of women. Whether they were directly affected by fighting, or struggling to hold down the homefront in the absence of their sons, fathers, husbands, and brothers, women played a vital role in the war years. Abigail Adams's letters to her husband, John, when he was away in Philadelphia at the Continental Congress and, later, serving as a diplomat in France and the Netherlands, captured both the ties of affection and the practical concerns felt by many American women. In addition, Abigail Adams was deeply engaged politically. Note the way that she framed her appeal for women's rights.

I wish you would ever write me a Letter half as long as I write you; and tell me if you may where your Fleet are gone? What sort of Defence Virginia can make against our common Enemy? Whether it is so situated as to make an able Defence? Are not the Gentery Lords and the common people vassals, are they not like the uncivilized Natives Brittain represents us to be? I hope their Riffel Men who have shewen themselves very savage and even Blood thirsty; are not a specimen of the Generality of the people.

I am willing to allow the Colony great merrit for having produced a Washington but they have been shamefully duped by a Dunmore.

I have sometimes been ready to think that the passion for Liberty cannot be Eaquelly Strong in the Breasts of those who have been accustomed to deprive their fellow Creatures of theirs. Of this I am certain that it is not founded upon that generous and christian principal of doing to others as we would that others should do unto us.

Do not you want to see Boston; I am fearfull of the small pox, or I should have been in before this time. I got Mr. Crane to go to our House and see what state it was in. I find it has been occupied by one of the Doctors of a Regiment, very dirty, but no other damage has been done to it. The few things which were left in it are all gone. Cranch has the key which he never deliverd up. I have wrote to him for it and am determined to get it cleand as soon as possible and shut it up. I look upon it a new acquisition of property, a property which one month ago I did not value at a single Shilling, and could with pleasure have seen it in flames.

The Town in General is left in a better state than we expected, more oweing to a percipitate flight than any Regard to the inhabitants, tho some individuals discoverd a sense of honour and justice and have left the rent of the Houses in which they were, for the owners and the furniture unhurt, or if damaged suffecent to make it good.

Others have committed abominable Ravages. The Mansion House of your President is safe and the furniture unhurt whilst both the House and Furniture of the Solisiter General have fallen a prey to their own merciless party. Surely the very Fiends feel a Reverential awe for Virtue and patriotism, whilst they Detest the paricide and traitor.

I feel very differently at the approach of spring to what I did a month ago. We knew not then whether we could plant or sow with safety, whether when we had toild we could reap the fruits of our own industery, whether we could rest in our own Cottages, or whether we should not be driven from the sea coasts to seek shelter in the wilderness, but now we feel as if we might sit under our own vine and eat the good of the land.

I feel a gaieti de Coar [French: gaieté de Cœur, lightness of heart] to which before I was a stranger. I think the Sun looks brighter, the Birds sing more melodiously, and Nature puts on a more chearfull countanance. We feel a temporary peace, and the poor fugitives are returning to their deserted habitations.

Tho we felicitate ourselves, we sympathize with those who are trembling least the Lot of Boston should be theirs. But they cannot be in similar circumstances unless pusilanimity and cowardise should take possession of them. They have time and warning given them to see the Evil and shun it.—I long to hear that you have declared an independency—and by the way in the new Code of Laws which I suppose it will be necessary for you to make I desire you would Remember the Ladies, and be more generous and favourable to them than your ancestors. Do not put such unlimited power into the hands of the Husbands. Remember all Men would be tyrants if they could. If perticuliar care and attention is not paid to the Laidies we are determined to foment a Rebelion, and will not hold ourselves bound by any Laws in which we have no voice, or Representation.

That your Sex are Naturally Tyrannical is a Truth so thoroughly established as to admit of no dispute, but such of you as wish to be happy willingly give up the harsh title of Master for the more tender and endearing one of Friend. Why then, not put it out of the power of the vicious and the Lawless to use us with cruelty and indignity with impunity. Men of Sense in all Ages abhor those customs which treat us only as the vassals of your Sex. Regard us then as Beings placed by providence under your protection and in immitation of the Supreem Being make use of that power only for our happiness.

Source: Letter from Abigail Adams to John Adams, 31 March–5 April 1776 [electronic edition]. *Adams Family Papers: An Electronic Archive.* Massachusetts Historical Society. http://www.masshist.org/digitaladams/

7.4 SLAVE PETITION FOR FREEDOM TO THE MASSACHUSETTS LEGISLATURE (1777)

While many slaveowners supported the Patriot cause without questioning the morality of slavery, the rhetoric of liberty profoundly challenged slavery. This petition for freedom, submitted by a group of eight Massachusetts slaves, failed. Slaves there continued to petition the courts, arguing that slavery was inconsistent with Article I of the Massachusetts Constitution, which declared "all men are born free and equal." In 1781, a local court ruled in favor of Elizabeth Freeman (also known as Mum Bett), and in response to slave Quock Walker's suit in 1783, the Massachusetts Supreme Judicial Court ruled that the Massachusetts Constitution prohibited slavery.

The petition of A Great Number of Blackes detained in a State of slavery in the Bowels of a free & Christian Country Humbly shuwith that your Petitioners apprehend that thay have in Common with all other men a Natural and Unaliable Right to that freedom which the Grat Parent of the Unavers hath Bestowed equalley on all menkind and which they have Never forfuted by any Compact or agreement whatever—but thay wher Unjustly Dragged by the hand of cruel Power from their Derest friends and sum of them Even torn from the Embraces of their tender Parents—from A popolous Pleasant and plentiful contry and in violation of Laws of Nature and off Nations and in defiance of all the tender feelings of humanity Brough hear Either to Be sold Like Beast of Burthen & Like them Condemnd to Slavery for Life— Among A People Profesing the mild Religion of Jesus A people Not Insensible of the Secrets of

Rational Being Nor without spirit to Resent the unjust endeavours of others to Reduce them to a state of Bondage and Subjection your honouer Need not to be informed that A Life of Slavery Like that of your petioners Deprived of Every social privilege of Every thing Requisit to Render Life Tolable is far worse then Nonexistence.

[In Imitat]ion of the Lawdable Example of the Good People of these States your petitiononers have Long and Patiently waited the Evnt of petition after petition By them presented to the Legislative Body of this state and cannot but with Grief Reflect that their Success hath ben but too similar they Cannot but express their Astonishment that It has Never Bin Considred that Every Principle form which Amarica has Acted in the Cours of their unhappy Dificultes with Great Briton Pleads Stronger than A thousand arguments in favowrs of your petioners they therfor humble Beseech your honours to give this petion [petition] its due weight & consideration & cause an act of the Legislatur to be past Wherby they may be Restored to the Enjoyments of that which is the Naturel Right of all men—and their Children who wher Born in this Land of Liberty may not be heald as Slaves after they arrive at the age of twenty one years so may the Inhabitance of this Stats No longer chargeable with the inconsistancey of acting themselves the part which they condem and oppose in others Be prospered in their present Glorious struggle for Liberty and have those Blessing to them, &c.

Prince Hall

Lancaster Hill

Peter Bess

Brister Slenser

Jack Pierpont

Nero Funelo

Newport Sumner

Job Look

Source: Slave Petition for Freedom to the Massachusetts Legislature, 1777. http://www.heritage.org/initiatives/first-principles/primary-sources/slave-petition-for-freedom-to-the-massachusetts-legislature

7.5 PATRICK HENRY, EXCERPT FROM SPEECH TO THE VIRGINIA RATIFYING CONVENTION (1788)

For more than three weeks, delegates to the Virginia Ratifying Convention debated the merits of the proposed Constitution. James Madison, George Wythe, and John Marshall argued passionately for it, while Patrick Henry, George Mason, and James Monroe argued just as passionately against it. Marshall later said, "If I were called upon to say who of all men I have known had the greatest power to convince, I should perhaps say Mr. Madison; while Mr. Henry had without doubt the greatest power to persuade." Here is an excerpt from one of Henry's speeches given on June 7, 1788.

Mr. Henry replied, that it made a deep impression on his mind, and that he verily believed that system would operate as he had said. He then continued: I will exchange that *abominable* word for *requisitions*. Requisitions, which gentlemen affect to despise, have nothing degrading in

them. On this depends our political prosperity. I never will give up that *darling* word *requisi-*
tions: my country may give it up; a majority may wrest it from me, but I will never give it up till
my grave. Requisitions are attended with one singular advantage. They are attended by delib-
eration. They secure to the states the benefit of correcting oppressive errors. If our Assembly
thought requisitions erroneous, if they thought the demand was too great, they might at least
supplicate Congress to reconsider—that it was a little too much. The power of direct taxation
was called by the honorable gentleman the *soul* of the government: another gentleman called
it the *lungs* of the government. We all agree that it is the most important part of the body politic. If the power of raising money be necessary for the general government, it is no less so for
the states. If money be the vitals of Congress, is it not precious for those individuals from
whom it is to be taken? Must I give my soul, my lungs, to Congress? Congress must have our
souls; the state must have our souls. This is dishonorable and disgraceful. These two coordinate, interfering, unlimited powers of harassing the community are unexampled: it is unprecedented in history. They are the visionary projects of modern politicians. Tell me not of
imaginary means, but of reality; this political solecism will never tend to the benefit of the
community. It will be as oppressive in practice as it is absurd in theory. If you part from this,
which the honorable gentleman tells you is the soul of Congress, you will be inevitably ruined.
I tell you, they shall not have the soul of Virginia. They tell us that one collector may collect the
federal and state taxes. The general government being paramount to the state legislatures, if
the sheriff is to collect for both,—his right hand for Congress, his left for the state,—his right
hand being paramount over the left, his collections will go to Congress. We shall have the rest.
Deficiencies in collections will always operate against the states. Congress, being the paramount, supreme power, must not be disappointed. Thus Congress will have an unlimited, unbounded command over the soul of this commonwealth. After satisfying their uncontrolled
demands, what can be left for the states? Not a sufficiency even to defray the expense of their
internal administration. They must therefore glide imperceptibly and gradually out of existence. This, sir, must naturally terminate in a consolidation. If this will do for other people, it
never will do for me.

   If we are to have one representative for every thirty thousand souls, it must be by implication. The Constitution does not positively secure it. Even say it is a natural implication,—
why not give us a right to that proportion in express terms, in language that could not admit
of evasions or subterfuges? If they can use implication for us, they can also use implication
against us. We are giving power; they are getting power; judge, then, on which side the implication will be used! When we once put it in their option to assume constructive power, danger
will follow. Trial by jury, and liberty of the press, are also on this foundation of implication.
If they encroach on these rights, and you give your implication for a plea, you are cast; for
they will be justified by the last part of it, which gives them full power "to make all laws which
shall be necessary and proper to carry their power into execution." Implication is dangerous,
because it is unbounded: if it be admitted at all, and no limits be prescribed, it admits of the
utmost extension. They say that every thing that is not given is retained. The reverse of the
proposition is true by implication. They do not carry their implication so far when they speak
of the {150} general welfare—no implication when the sweeping clause comes. Implication is
only necessary when the existence of privileges is in dispute. The existence of powers is sufficiently established. If we trust our dearest rights to implication, we shall be in a very unhappy situation.

   Implication, in England, has been a source of dissension. There has been a war of implication between the king and people. For a hundred years did the mother country struggle under
the uncertainty of implication. The people insisted that their rights were implied; the monarch
denied the doctrine. The Bill of Rights, in some degree, terminated the dispute. By a bold implication, they said they had a right to bind us in all cases whatsoever. This constructive power
we opposed, and successfully. Thirteen or fourteen years ago, the most important thing that

could be thought of was to exclude the possibility of construction and implication. These, sir, were then deemed perilous. The first thing that was thought of was a bill of rights. We were not satisfied with your constructive, argumentative rights.

Mr. Henry then declared a bill of rights indispensably necessary; that a general positive provision should be inserted in the new system, securing to the states and the people every right which was not conceded to the general government; and that every implication should be done away.

Source: Patrick Henry, excerpt from speech to the Virginia Ratifying Convention, June 7, 1788. http://www.constitution .org/rc/rat_va_06.htm#henry-02

Contested Republic

1789–1800

COMMON THREADS

What were the continuing disagreements about the power of a central government?

What were the conflicting values and ideas of citizenship?

How did the new nation negotiate with the European powers?

What was the status of slavery in the early republic?

Ona Judge Finds Her Freedom

Ona Judge was only 16 when George and Martha Washington brought her to Philadelphia in 1790. She was Martha Washington's slave, the daughter of Betty, an African American seamstress, and Andrew Judge, a white indentured servant who worked as a tailor at Mt. Vernon. According to the law of slavery, because her mother was enslaved, so too was Ona. When Ona was 10, she was brought to live in Mt. Vernon itself, as a playmate for Martha Washington's granddaughter. She was trained as a seamstress and body servant, and in Philadelphia, at the president's house, she worked as Martha Washington's chambermaid. Her older brother, Austin, was a waiter.

When Washington's term was ending, the slaves were told that they would all soon return to Virginia. Martha Washington planned to give Ona Judge to another granddaughter as a wedding present. Judge decided to liberate herself. "Whilst they were packing up to go to Virginia," she later explained, "I was packing to go, I didn't know where; for I knew that if I went back to Virginia, I should never get my liberty. I had friends among the colored people of Philadelphia, had my things carried there beforehand, and left Washington's house while they were eating dinner."

Judge's friends in the free black community hid her until they could find a way to smuggle her out of the city. The Fugitive Slave Act that Washington had signed in 1793 had made it a crime to help a slave escape bondage. Judge sneaked out of Philadelphia aboard a boat bound for Portsmouth, New Hampshire, where, however, it was her bad luck to run into the daughter of the Washingtons' good friend, Senator John Langdon. "Oney!" she called out. "Where in the world have you come from?" The young woman could not understand why anyone would run away "from such an excellent place." "Yes—I know," Judge replied. "But I wanted to be free, misses; wanted to learn to read and write."

Told his slave was in Portsmouth—where slavery was still legal, although unpopular—Washington asked a government official to send Judge back, and to keep it quiet. Neither Washington nor his wife could comprehend why their slave might have left. Washington believed the escape had "been planned by someone who knew what he was about and had the means to defray the expense of it and to entice her off." But when the official met with Judge, she convinced him that she had not been "decoyed away" and that her "only motive for absconding" had been "a thirst for complete freedom." She would "rather suffer death than return to slavery and [be] liable to be sold or given to any other persons."

Washington told the official he was wrong. He was certain that Ona Judge had been seduced, and then abandoned, by a Frenchman and was probably pregnant. He insisted that the official send her back, but the official explained that he did not see how he could do it "without exciting a riot or mob." He even warned the president that increasing numbers of slaves would seek "asylum" in New England and that, "for the good of Society," southerners should consider "the abolition of this species of servitude."

Not even the president could persuade the New Englander to return an escaped slave against her will, so Judge remained in New Hampshire. She married a free black sailor, John Staines, and bore three children. She learned to read and converted to Christianity. Several years later, however, one of Martha Washington's nephews turned up at Judge's house, when her husband was at sea. She told him, "I am free now and choose to remain so." When the nephew told Senator Langdon that he planned to seize Judge by force, the senator passed word to Judge so that she could go into hiding.

As the gospel of liberty spread through the new nation, slaves such as Ona Judge seized their own freedom, and along the way they had help from free blacks and whites both, redefining the meaning of American democracy.

The Struggle to Form a Government

At his presidential inauguration, George Washington confessed that "among all the vicissitudes incident to life, no event could have filled me with greater anxieties" than the news of his election. He was right to worry. Not only was the new nation embarking on an almost unprecedented experiment in democratic government, but the country faced enormous challenges, none greater than proving that a government of the people, by the people, and for the people could work.

Creating a National Government

Although Washington did not take the oath of office until April 30, his term began on March 4, 1789. When he was inaugurated, Congress was already in session. It was not a promising start: only 13 members of the House of Representatives and 8 senators were on hand when the first Congress convened. Yet the new government faced the unprecedented challenge not only of making the new structure work but also of earning the allegiance of the people. Almost every challenge of the 1790s, from economic policy to controlling the borderlands and managing foreign affairs, was, at base, about creating a government strong enough to gain the loyalty of its citizens, but not so strong that, like the British government against which they had rebelled, it alienated them instead.

Among Congress's first tasks was deciding what the president should be called. Believing that the president needed an impressive title to demonstrate that the new nation was "civilized," a Senate committee recommended "His Highness the President of the United States of America, and Protector of the Liberties." But the House argued that the suggestion smacked of aristocratic pretension and in the end insisted simply on "the President of the United States."

Meanwhile, Congress approved official advisors to the president (the cabinet). Washington's first administration reflected both his own close circle of friends and the political clout of the large states. The president was from Virginia, the most populous state, as were his secretary of state, Thomas Jefferson, and his attorney general, Edmund Randolph. For his secretary of the treasury he chose former aide-de-camp Alexander Hamilton of New York. Washington's vice president (John Adams), his secretary of war (Henry Knox), and his postmaster general (Samuel Osgood) were from Massachusetts.

The Constitution had specified the existence of a third branch of government, a federal judiciary, but had not offered much of a blueprint for its structure. Congress might have created a federal system that dominated state courts. Recalling the high-handedness of British courts, however, with the Judiciary Act of 1789 Congress created a federal court system with limited power. Under its first chief justice, John Jay, the Supreme Court remained a minor branch of government.

The States and the Bill of Rights

The Federalists had agreed to let the state ratifying conventions propose amendments to the Constitution, possibly to be added as a bill of rights. Two hundred of these had been suggested. Some Federalists originally opposed the idea of a bill of rights: if the Constitution did not protect liberty and property, no appended list of rights would help. But they agreed to allow Congress to make amendments to the Constitution when several states made it a condition for ratification (see Chapter 7).

Within a month of Washington's inauguration, James Madison, recently elected to the House, set about making good on the promise. Madison never expected to incorporate all 200 of the state proposals in a bill of rights, and he never imagined that he could placate all of the groups critical of the Constitution. But he did believe that adding a bill of rights could secure the Antifederalists' support for the Constitution without harming "the structure and stamina of the Government." This belief guided Madison's selection of proposed amendments. He ignored those that would alter the structure of the central government or strengthen the powers of the states at the expense of the federal government, and he dismissed outright one that would have limited the power of Congress to levy taxes. Instead, he focused on amendments that affirmed human rights within the structure already ratified (although the reference to a "well-regulated Militia" in the Second Amendment and the Third Amendment's restrictions on the quartering of soldiers reflected Americans' profound mistrust of standing national armies). The First Amendment protected citizens against congressional interference with freedom of religion, speech, the press, the right of assembly, and the right of petition. The Fourth Amendment protected the rights of citizens "against unreasonable [government] searches and seizures." The Fifth, Sixth, Seventh, and Eighth Amendments laid down the rights of citizens accused of crimes and established protection from "cruel and unusual punishments." The Ninth affirmed that the Constitution's silence on a specific right of the people "shall not be construed" as a denial of that right, and the Tenth ambiguously reserved all rights not delegated to the new government "to the States respectively, or to the people."

Congress eventually sent twelve amendments to the states for ratification. Two were rejected: one on congressional compensation (adopted in 1992 as the Twenty-seventh Amendment) and one covering representation. The remaining ten amendments were declared in force on December 15, 1791.

Debating the Economy

As Congress deliberated the structure of government, Secretary of the Treasury Alexander Hamilton turned to the problem of financial solvency, the problem that had plagued the Confederation (see Chapter 7). His proposals to strengthen the nation by strengthening the economy soon brought to the fore underlying disagreements about the future of the nation.

Table 8-1 Sources of Federal Revenue, 1790–1799

	Tariffs	Internal Taxes	Other (inc. sale of public lands)
1790–1791	$4,399,000		$10,000
1792	3,443,000	$209,000	17,000
1793	4,255,000	338,000	59,000
1794	4,801,000	274,000	356,000
1795	5,588,000	338,000	188,000
1796	6,568,000	475,000	1,334,000
1797	7,550,000	575,000	563,000
1798	7,106,000	644,000	150,000
1799	6,610,000	779,000	157,000

Source: Curtis P. Nettels, *The Emergence of a National Economy, 1775–1815* (New York: Holt, Rinehart and Winston, 1962), p. 221.

The first challenge was to raise money for current expenses. Hamilton proposed that Congress place a tariff on imported goods and the foreign ships carrying them. The Tariff Act of 1789 passed easily. In the coming years the federal government would depend on tariffs for the vast majority of its funds (see Table 8–1).

The next challenge was how to pay off the debt left over from the Revolution, a total of $79 million that included not only the amounts the government had borrowed from foreign countries and promised to soldiers and suppliers but also the debts owed by state governments. In a plan known as "funding and assumption," Hamilton proposed that the government assume all of the debt and pay it off at full value, even the parts that were in badly depreciated paper money. But rather than paying off the national debt immediately, the government would give creditors new federal bonds that paid interest (which in turn would be paid for by a new federal excise tax on whiskey and other luxuries). In this way, Hamilton thought he could turn the national debt into a "blessing" by making sure that people with money had a literal investment in the success of the nation.

Madison and Jefferson were alarmed, however. Not only had most southern states paid their debts by 1790, but many soldiers and ordinary people had sold off their paper money to speculators at far less than its face value—sometimes as little as 10 percent. The speculators would now reap huge profits. Why should they benefit? At the same time, southerners were also unhappy about the possibility that the nation's capital (temporarily located in New York) might be moved permanently to Philadelphia. They preferred a site in Virginia, closer to the center of the country. At last, representatives struck a compromise: Hamilton got his debt plan, and southerners got the nation's capital.

Hamilton next recommended the creation of a national bank that would ensure a stable currency and enable the government to mobilize capital for development, two activities he considered essential to an expanding commercial economy. The bank would be chartered by Congress to collect, hold, and pay out government receipts; hold the new federal bonds and oversee their payment; and issue currency; and it would be backed up by government bonds.

The bank proposal passed Congress against the opposition of Madison, Jefferson, and other Virginians, who viewed the bank as an extralegal structure to support the interests of merchants and financiers against "the republican interest." Jefferson advised the president to veto the bill on the grounds that the Constitution gave the federal government no expressed authority to create such an institution, a position known as *strict constructionism*. Hamilton countered that every specified power in the Constitution implied "a right to employ all the means requisite . . . to the attainment" of that power. In granting the federal government the responsibility to coin and regulate money, pass and collect taxes, pay debts, and "make all laws which shall be necessary and proper" to these ends, the Constitution implied the power to create a bank. Washington accepted Hamilton's position and signed the bank bill.

Hamilton's final major recommendation to Congress was that the federal government subsidize domestic manufacturing. Jefferson and Madison were now convinced that the republic was being sold out to speculators and financiers. Hamilton had been using a Philadelphia newspaper, John Fenno's *Gazette of the United States*, to promote his views. In October 1791, Jefferson and Madison prevailed on their friend Philip Freneau to come to Philadelphia to establish a newspaper favorable to their position, and Madison began to use Freneau's *National Gazette* to publish essays in which he framed the rationale for the permanent necessity of political parties in a republic. There would always be schemers who placed self-interest above the good of the whole. Parties, according to Madison, arose in a struggle of the true "republican interest" against such dangerous conspirators, a struggle of "good" against "evil." He identified the two groups as "Republicans" and "Anti-Republicans."

Hamilton's efforts to create a strong government based on a commercial economy alienated those such as Madison and Jefferson who believed Hamilton's policies were "subverting step by step the principles of the Constitution." This theme was taken up by the Democratic Republican Societies, groups that had come together in late 1792 and early 1793 to support the French Revolution. They became the nucleus of the first political party, the Democratic Republicans. They believed that the new government was becoming too strong and thus a threat to "liberty and equality." The societies included some common people, but most members were from middling and even prosperous families. Washington blamed the societies for spreading "suspicions, jealousies, and accusations of the whole government."

At the same time, the supporters of Hamilton's policies became known as the Federalists, to suggest their commitment to the new government. At first, most candidates resisted formal party alignment, however, and congressional voting patterns showed little sense of "party" discipline. There were several reasons for this, including the tendency of most citizens (including many partisans themselves) to associate political parties with corruption and a loss of independence. By 1796, the opposing groups coalesced into Democratic Republicans and Federalists, and congressional voting patterns revealed a distinct tendency to vote on one side or the other.

A Society in Transition

The new political parties reflected growing divisions in society itself. The end of the Revolution ushered in a period of explosive growth—in the economy, in population, and in territory. As one American observed, "Population is increasing, new houses building, new lands clearing, new settlements forming, and new manufacture establishing with a rapidity beyond conception." So much change offered both opportunity and danger. Americans responded with both optimism and fear.

A People on the Move

A quarter century of political unrest, compounded by the depression of the 1780s, had stalled the development of the American economy, but once peace was restored, the patterns of growth and development of the mid-eighteenth century resumed. Even with the disruptions of the Revolution, the American population grew at the greatest rate in its entire history in the 1780s, and it continued to double every 20 years, primarily from natural increase. In the 1790s, the United States added 1.4 million people, only 100,000 of whom were immigrants. Many of those immigrants were political refugees, fleeing revolutions in France and Saint-Domingue and political repression in Britain and Ireland. For most of the growing population, native born or refugees, democracy meant opportunity and political freedom. Thirty thousand, however, were enslaved Africans, purchased to enhance their owners' opportunity at the denial of their own.

The United States was overwhelmingly a rural nation and would remain so until well into the nineteenth century. (Ninety-seven percent of its almost 4 million people enumerated in the first census lived in the countryside, most of them on family farms of 50–100 acres.) As the population grew, thousands of families looked for fertile, inexpensive land so that they could continue as farmers. They found it in the hinterlands of established states and in the territories that would become states over the next several decades. Seeking quick revenue, the government sold large tracts of land to speculators and large proprietors, some of whom were federal officials. Alexander Hamilton and Secretary of War Henry Knox were both silent partners in the huge Macomb Purchase in New York. Speculators also bought up land abandoned by Loyalists. William Cooper, for example, purchased—for a suspiciously low price—the huge Otsego, New York, tract that had been owned by William Franklin.

In regions such as frontier Maine, squatters simply occupied the land that such "great proprietors" hoped to sell for a huge profit. Squatters built small cabins, cleared the land, and planted crops, resisting when the legal owners tried to oust them. Such disputes were typically resolved when the squatters purchased the land—but for far less than the speculators had wanted. The population of Kentucky and Tennessee tripled in the 1790s. By 1800, 220,000 people lived in Kentucky, and not a single adult (excluding Native Americans) had been born in the state. At the same time, settlers were trickling into what would become Indiana, Alabama, and Mississippi, and almost 50,000 moved into Ohio. Because land in these territories was still held by Native Americans, conflict was almost inevitable as settlers pressed the new government to secure the land for them.

American cities grew rapidly, too. Philadelphia and New York grew by almost 50 percent between 1789 and 1800. St. Louis, Detroit, Pittsburgh, Cincinnati, Lexington, Cleveland, Nashville, and Louisville all became important regional centers, serving the surrounding populations. As in the farming regions, the rapid influx of population and its youthfulness—two-thirds of the white population was 25 or younger—made it hard to control. Philadelphia had a particularly large number of young people who were on their own. The result was a boisterous culture, particularly among the lower classes. Men and women of all classes took advantage of a more liberal sexual environment. Rates of

The Quilting Frolic What appears to be a cozy domestic scene actually reveals the complexity of urban life in Philadelphia at the time: We see women putting away their work as fashionably dressed guests arrive. The many consumer objects, from the well-stocked cupboard to the plates on the table and the tea set on the tray held by the African American girl, show that the family is prosperous. So too does the presence of African American servants, both with the exaggerated features that were beginning to become racist stereotypes.

adultery and divorce increased, and the proportion of children born outside of marriage doubled. Houses of prostitution flourished, as did taverns such as the one owned by the free African American John York, where "all the loose and idle characters of the city, whether whites, blacks, or mulattoes . . . indulge in riotous mirth and dancing til dawn."

In later decades this growing population would provide the workforce for the industrial revolution, but in the first decades of the new nation, most people worked as farmers.

In spite of their hostility to the growing merchant "monied interest," most farmers sought international as well as local markets for their crops. The principal exports were all farm or plantation products—grains, tobacco, and rice. But without the protection of Britain (which banned Americans from trading with British colonies), Americans struggled to secure old markets and establish new ones, at the same time that the British were dumping manufactured goods into the American market at low prices that undercut American manufacturers. As farm families struggled, much of the burden fell on women, who were required to increase production of cloth, butter, and other marketable goods. Their earnings provided the cash that enabled families to make ends meet or, for the more successful, to expand further into the market.

The depression of the 1780s had hit American merchants especially badly. Some had gone bankrupt, while others had made loans to western farmers who could not repay

Philadelphia

Serving as the nation's capital in the 1790s, Philadelphia was the city where the new doctrines of freedom were given shape, in the new Congress Hall just west of Independence Hall, in humble homes, and in the president's mansion.

Philadelphia was America's biggest city and growing bigger by the day. Between 1780 and 1790, the population grew by more than 50 percent, to 42,520. After the Revolution, European immigrants began to arrive again, and people from the country-side flocked to the city. This rapid growth led to overcrowding, especially for the laboring class. Poor people were renters, living in rooming houses or back alleys, typically in overcrowded wooden buildings. Martin Summers, a laborer, and Henry Birkey, a shoemaker, and their families shared a home—and the annual rent of £18. Tailor William Smith and his wife shared their tiny home—550 square feet—with their three children and two boarders. Mrs. Smith cooked their meals in her fireplace.

Philadelphia was just coming out of the postwar depression. During the depression, even skilled workers had trouble making ends meet, and some, such as shoemaker John Dougherty and his wife Esther and their three children, had to seek poor relief. Other laboring families cut back on their expenses, for example eating more grains and less meat and vegetables and using less firewood. Such economies, of course, weakened them and made them more vulnerable to disease.

As the population increased and land in the center of the city became more valuable, poor people were forced to move to the outskirts of Philadelphia. Wealthier people bought lots in the choicest locations and erected three-story brick houses, 18 feet wide but two or three times as deep, and with separate washhouses, stables, and kitchens.

One of the most splendid homes of the day was the one on Market Street owned by the financier Robert Morris. George Washington had stayed with the Morrises when he attended the Constitutional Convention and liked it so much that when he became president, he rented the house from Morris. By the standards of the day, it was a mansion, two-thirds the size of the White House, which would be built several years later. Even with at least six bedrooms and four servants' rooms, a detached two-story kitchen, an icehouse, a bathhouse, and a stable for 12 horses, it was not large enough for Washington's household. Washington added a two-story bow and rooms for his servants. When the Washingtons took up residence in November, they had with them about 30 people, not only the president and his wife Martha but also her grandchildren, his secretary and the secretary's wife, 3 more male secretaries, 8 African slaves, and about 15 white servants. The president's staff lived and worked in the home. Their office was on the third floor, and people who had business with the president had to walk up two flights of stairs and pass by the private chambers to get to it.

Philadelphia was also home to about 1,600 African Americans, two-thirds of whom were free and who created the nation's first significant free black community. James Oronoko Dexter, one of the leaders

continued

of that community, lived only a few blocks from Independence Hall, on the north side of Fifth Street, between Arch and Race, then on the edge of the city. This was a densely populated neighborhood filled with frame-and-brick homes and workshops of artisans, laborers, and merchants. Dexter's two-story house, which he shared with his wife and family, was described in 1791 as "very plain." Dexter's wife, Sarah, worked as a washerwoman. The center of this community was only two blocks from the president's house.

Philadelphia in the 1790s was a bustling city where people lived and worked in the same buildings, rich and poor living in the same neighborhoods and even the same houses.

them. By 1790, the remaining trade was concentrated in fewer hands. These merchants sought new markets, for example in Asia. Americans took pride in these early ventures. As the *Massachusetts* prepared to sail for Canton in 1790, "parties of people of every rank of society frequently came on board to gratify their curiosity and express their admiration." The voyage, however, was a disaster. The ship was made of rotten wood, and the crew, which lacked proper instruments and expertise both, guessed at latitude and longitude. It took several years for American merchants to establish an international trade, but over the decade they did, and by 1815, they were reexporting (to Europe and the Caribbean) $23 million in goods a year, including such Asian products as pepper, tea, and Chinese porcelain and fabrics. The profits from this trade financed the establishment of American factories several decades later.

In so diverse a country, its population rapidly growing, spreading across hundreds of thousands of square miles and even trading halfway across the world, how were the people to be attached to the nation?

The First Emancipation Movements

Although slavery had existed in America for over 150 years by the time of ratification of the Constitution, its continued existence in the new republic was not a foregone

American Hong in China Each Western nation built its own trading house, or "hong," in Canton. This early-nineteenth-century porcelain bowl shows the American hong with the American flag flying above it.

conclusion. By 1789, many European nations were beginning to reconsider their involvement in the slave trade. Even England, which led all other nations in slave trafficking by the late eighteenth century, outlawed slavery within its borders and by 1783 had begun what would become a 50-year-long drive to abolish both the English slave trade and the ownership of slaves by English subjects abroad (including in the British colonies). Although Napoleon would later resurrect slavery in the French colonies, in 1794 revolutionary France abolished slavery in the nation and all of its colonies.

Could slavery have been abolished in the United States as well? The numbers alone presented a formidable challenge. Roughly 18 percent of the total population of 3.9 million was enslaved, and slavery was a national institution (see Table 8–2). In large areas of Virginia and South Carolina, slaves made up at least half of the population, while in 1789 northerners still owned more than 30,000 slaves (see Map 8–1). New York City had the second-highest number of enslaved people of any city, after Charleston, South Carolina. Northern merchants were active in the overseas slave trade, and countless shippers, merchants, and artisans in the North relied on business ties to the South. Moreover, the Constitution implicitly recognized slavery as a part of the republic in the Three-Fifths Compromise and explicitly protected the slave trade for at least 20 years.

On the other hand, although few were prepared to embrace a racially mixed society, many white Americans considered slavery immoral and contrary to the principles on which their new government had been founded. Almost no one was prepared to make a positive, public defense of the institution. When Ona Judge ran away, George Washington tried to get her back—but out of the public eye.

Many Christian denominations (notably including Quakers, Baptists, and Methodists) spoke out against slavery. None of the first state constitutions specifically recognized slavery, and many central and northern states took steps to outlaw it, either directly in their new state constitutions or in subsequent state supreme court decisions interpreting those constitutions. Vermont, Massachusetts, and New Hampshire enacted state constitutions with broad declarations of rights, although it took a series of court decisions in Massachusetts to apply that declaration to slavery. Pennsylvania had been home to an active abolition movement since at least 1775, when Anthony Benezet organized the Society for the Relief of Free Negroes Unlawfully Held in Bondage. African Americans were important abolitionist voices. In his 1786 Address to the Negroes of the State of New York, Jupiter Hammon, a slave on Long Island and the first published African

Table 8-2 Americans in 1790

Population: 3,979,000					
Northeast		**Northcentral**		**South**	
Whites	1,900,000	Whites	50,000	Whites	1,271,000
African Americans	67,000	African Americans	1,000	African Americans	690,000
Urban	160,000	Urban	0	Urban	42,000
Rural	1,807,000	Rural	51,000	Rural	1,919,000

Free African Americans 58,000

African American slaves 700,000

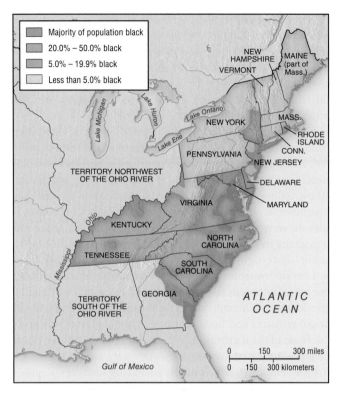

Map 8-1   Distribution of Black Population, 1775 At the founding of the nation, the overwhelming majority of African Americans lived in the South and were enslaved. In parts of the South Atlantic states, African Americans had long outnumbered whites. (Future states here are identified in parentheses.) *Source:* Lester J. Cappon et al., eds., *Atlas of Early American History: The Revolutionary Era, 1760–1790* (Princeton, NJ: Princeton University Press, 1976).

American author, called on slaves to obey their masters, refrain from stealing, and cultivate humility. But he also noted that slaves would be welcomed in heaven (where "we shall find nobody to reproach us for being black, or for being slaves") and advocated gradual emancipation. As Phillis Wheatley (1753–1784), an African American poet, wrote in "On Being Brought from Africa to America," the subject of salvation spoke to the subject of slavery: "Some view our sable race with scornful eye, / 'Their colour is a diabolic die.' / Remember, Christians, Negros, black as Cain, / May be refin'd, and join th' angelic train."

Although the process of emancipation in the North was sometimes slow and often contested, the first steps toward the elimination of slavery had been taken. By 1804, every state north of Delaware had placed slavery on the road to extinction. In the North, free blacks collected in the port cities, where they found employment, the men most often in the maritime trades and the women as domestic servants. The free black population of New York almost doubled in the 1790s, while that of Philadelphia tripled. Once they were able to choose freely where to live, African Americans began establishing their own neighborhoods (such as the one where Ona Judge sought refuge), their own schools, churches, burial grounds, and organizations. Free property-owning African American males enjoyed the right to vote in many northern and even some southern states in the first years of the republic, although few black men had sufficient property to exercise that right.

Even in the South there were signs of a growing opposition to slavery. Virginia, Delaware, and Maryland all passed laws permitting the private manumission of slaves. As a result, the number of free blacks in the upper South tripled between 1790 and 1810. Although the emancipation movement never took hold in the lower South, even there, slave owners were put on the defensive. In the 1790s, many Americans hoped, and even believed, that slavery would gradually be eliminated.

Conflicting Visions of Republican Society

Agreeing on a structure for the new republic had not been easy. It had taken free Americans thirteen years to frame their government: a year to propose the Articles of Confederation, four years to pass them, seven more to fight over them and devise an alternative (the federal Constitution), and two years to ratify it. Even then, many Americans still opposed ratification, and two states (North Carolina and Rhode Island) had not yet ratified the Constitution when George Washington was sworn into office. Moreover, supporters of the Constitution did not necessarily agree on its meanings or on the principles of a republican society.

Still, there was a common ground of beliefs for many white inhabitants of the new republic. Most free Americans thought the success of the republic depended on the character of its citizens, by which they meant the traits that would enable citizens to protect themselves against either would-be tyrants or lawless mobs. For many, these traits included industriousness, independence, and an ability to put self-interest aside for the larger good. Very often, these qualities were associated with certain types of economic life. When people grew too wealthy and used to luxury, many believed, they grew lazy and were willing to support corrupt governments for their own selfish purposes. Poverty, on the other hand, led to desperation, riots, and anarchy.

This consensus obscured real disagreements about the nature of a republic and about who really embodied its key virtues. In 1790, 97 percent of free Americans lived in nuclear households (parents and children) on farms or in rural villages, where they produced much of their own food, clothes, tools, and furnishings. For this great mass of the people, republican virtue was rooted in the land, and particularly in the working freehold farm. In *Letters from an American Farmer* (1782), J. Hector St. John de Crevecoeur had identified the new nation as "a people of cultivators scattered over an immense territory . . . animated with the spirit of an industry that is unfettered and unrestrained, because each person works for himself." Thomas Jefferson echoed this view in his *Notes on the State of Virginia* (1785). He thought that only the independent farmer could achieve true self-reliance, warning that "dependence begets subservience and venality, [and] suffocates the germ of virtue."

This emphasis on labor and the private ownership of land did not mean that rural Americans opposed manufacturing and trade. Farms were tied to villages that were tied to larger markets in the port cities and overseas. Even Jefferson considered overseas trade essential to rural virtue, because it gave Americans access to manufactured goods without the blight of industrialization. As trade with Britain improved and the demand for American agricultural products grew both in Europe and in the plantation slave colonies of the West Indies, rural Americans agreed that a successful new nation required a booming free international trade.

The profits made by large merchants and landowners were another matter. Farmers, small shopkeepers, landless settlers, and craft workers saw the wealth of large merchant families and families with great landed estates as the moral equivalent of theft. "[N]o person can possess property without laboring," farmer and tavern keeper William Manning emphasized, "unless he get it by force or craft, fraud or fortune, out of the earnings of others." Manning viewed this distinction as "the great dividing line" of society.

Unsurprisingly, merchants and landed proprietors saw matters differently. They agreed that republican virtue resided in labor, but they included commercial labor, which opened markets and expanded trade, nurtured invention, taught discipline, and contributed new wealth to society. Alexander Hamilton, the first secretary of the Treasury, was a chief proponent of this view. Hamilton, who was born in the West Indies, was left on his own at the age of 13 when his mother, a shopkeeper, died. His father, who had never married his mother, had abandoned the family earlier. Hamilton then entered the merchant firm of Beekman and Cruger as a clerk, becoming so valuable that Cruger paid for his college education. These experiences taught Hamilton that the merchant class (traders, investors, and financiers who took risks to generate new wealth, new markets, and new ideas) best embodied the qualities needed in republican citizens.

Just as farmers viewed merchants and financiers with distrust, so wealthy merchants and proprietors often regarded Americans of the middling and laboring ranks as their inferiors. Most people were undisciplined and gullible, Hamilton believed. Easily deceived by fanatics and demagogues, they required proper leadership. City elites dismissed their backcountry compatriots as "yahoos" and "clodpoles." To the rich, the rude huts of homesteaders, their barefoot children, and their diets of beans, potatoes, and coarse bread all signaled not the hardships of settlement but rather the laziness of the settlers. The merchants and proprietors especially disliked the casualness with which country people treated debt. Rural people conducted trade in a combination of barter, cash, and promissory notes, with records kept casually and payments constantly renegotiated. Large-scale merchants and proprietors needed timely payment, preferably in hard currency, to pay off their own debts or to make new deals and investments.

Most white Americans denied that hard work produced republican character in slaves. They argued that because slaves could not own the property they produced, slaves' labor could never lead to self-reliance or the stake in the public order essential to citizenship. This view was rife with contradictions. As Thomas Jefferson, himself a slave owner, pointed out in *Notes on the State of Virginia*, slavery undermined the ambition of slave owners. "[I]n a warm climate, no man will labor for himself who can make another labor for him," Jefferson wrote. If slaves were of bad character, simply because of their status as slaves, then surely the institution of slavery was itself unrepublican.

Nevertheless, the unrepublicanism seemed to attach itself to slaves themselves, rather than to the institution. Even as northern states moved to abolish slavery, many expressed concern about the ability of former slaves to adjust to freedom and democracy and suggested that freed slaves should be resettled in the territories or Africa. In the northern states, although some working-class whites socialized freely with African Americans, other Americans refused to work with them. White passengers refused to ride in stagecoaches alongside them, and landlords refused to rent them any but the worst housing. Meanwhile, the Naturalization Act of 1790 restricted naturalized citizenship to "free white persons" (who had resided in the country for two years).

Although free white women were citizens of the nation, women labored under severe legal disabilities and restrictive social prejudices. Under the English common-law principle of coverture, a married woman subsumed her separate legal identity under that of her husband. While some individual women (usually wealthy women with access to special legal measures) did own property in their own names, as a category married women could not own property or wages, could not enter into contracts, and were not the legal guardians of their own children. Most women lost control of their property when they married and took little property other than their own clothing in divorce.

Social prejudice also made it difficult for most women to earn an independent living. Wives and unmarried women continued to ply their skills as midwives, seamstresses, hucksters, grocers, and milliners and in a variety of other trades. But the more lucrative male crafts and professions were closed to them, and most working women struggled to make ends meet.

A growing bias against the idea of female autonomy marked the final years of the eighteenth century. The earlier years of the century were by no means a golden age of female independence, yet age, wealth, and family appear to have mattered as much as gender in delineating individual status. And for a time it seemed that women (especially wealthy white women) might be among the beneficiaries of the Revolutionary spirit. Indeed, New Jersey granted single, property-owning women the right to vote in 1776 (but rescinded it in 1807), and women participated actively in the discussions both of their own new republic and of the French Revolution. In France and in England, women spoke out publicly against restraints on the natural rights of women.

In the wake of the creation of the new republic, however, attitudes toward women grew more conservative. As the *Apollo Magazine* put it in 1795, the exemplary woman married and asked no more than that "Her good man [was] happy and her Infants clean." Ironically, these hardening attitudes may in some ways have resulted from the experiment in democracy itself. In the face of social and political disorder, controlling the conduct of females may have seemed reassuring to some Americans.

The Culture of the Republic

Americans discussed these views, both the agreements and the disagreements, through a variety of practices—written and simply enacted.

Perhaps most important was the circulation of information through newspapers. Although fewer than 20 newspapers were being published in all the British North American colonies in 1760, by 1790 the new republic claimed 106 newspapers, and by 1800 more than 200. Most stories were strictly local, but editors also published official government documents and reprinted articles from other cities, states, and even countries.

The 1790s also saw the beginnings of an American fictional literature. In 1789, William Hill Brown published *The Power of Sympathy*, often considered the first genuinely American novel because some of its content was based on events in Boston. Other novelists also tried to develop distinctly American stories and themes. Actress and author Susanna Rowson wrote the historical novel *Rachel and Reuben* (1798), which imagined the lives of the fictional heirs of Columbus, and Charles Brockden Brown chose the countryside near Philadelphia as the setting for *Wieland* (1798), a tale of religious zealotry and the fallibility of human reason. In Connecticut, a group of poets known as the Hartford Wits produced a series of political satires celebrating New England as the model for national order and self-discipline.

News was easiest to come by in the cities, but a variety of information sources linked city to backcountry and region to region. Copies of periodicals and books found their way into the countryside, and comparatively high literacy rates produced a reading audience that went beyond urban elites. In shops, taverns, and homes, those who could not read listened as stories were read aloud. Where papers did not reach, travelers, peddlers, and preachers brought information and opinion.

In cities, prosperous Americans established salons (where local luminaries, male and female, gathered to discuss politics and culture), museums, libraries, and specialized societies of learning. Many of these reflected Americans' keen sense of themselves as involved in an important historical undertaking. The Philadelphia subscription library, founded in 1731 by Benjamin Franklin and others, became the de facto library of the government until 1800, when the capital moved to Washington, and the Library of Congress was founded.

For every occasion that drew American citizens together, however, there seemed to be another that divided them. Strong attachments to place and great disparities of condition often transformed seemingly shared values and ideas into fodder for sharp conflicts. Many, if not most, Americans felt stronger attachments to the neighborhoods or states where they lived, rather than to the nation as a whole. If anything, the process of ratification had underscored just how many differences remained among Americans. Advocates had won approval only by putting together a different coalition of interests in each state, not by drawing on a uniform set of interests across all the states. Even so, a bare nine states had ratified the document, and virtually all of these had made qualifications.

The localism of American society in 1789 was evident in daily life, as well as in formal politics. Never traveling far from home, ordinary Americans knew little about other parts of the country and tended to view them as quite different, becoming more exotic—and frightening—the greater the distance. Writing from Massachusetts to Philadelphia in 1776, Abigail Adams had asked John whether it was true that in Virginia the "gentery" were "Lords" and "the common people vassals." Travelers often described other parts of the nation as if they were foreign countries. The hard economic times of the era also nursed a suspicion of strangers. Describing these differences as an East-West contrast was also common in the early years of the nation. Rural revolts in the Carolinas in the 1760s and Shays's Rebellion in western Massachusetts in 1786–1787 had underscored the differences between backcountry farmers and eastern commercial elites, differences that settlers experienced as conflicts between "the people" and eastern governments. This sense of division and distrust persisted in the 1790s.

These disagreements ran deep and were not confined to formal politics or to polite discussion and debate. Newspapers often revealed sharp local bias in vituperative debates over the proper direction of republican politics. They were accompanied into the public arena by vitriolic political tracts and single-page "broadsides" that attacked individual politicians. Among these was William Manning's 1798 "Key of Liberty," condemning the predations of the "Few" upon the "Many."

Not all of the arguments took place in print. Wealthy city people met in parlors and salons to discuss the concerns of the day, and common Americans held their arguments outside courthouses and churches, on post office porches, at liveries and craft shops, and in taverns like the one run by William Manning. Travelers, peddlers, and preachers were sources of information and opinion.

The early republic was also an era of school building—primarily academies to prepare sons for professions or university training and daughters to participate in the discussions (if not the formal electoral politics) of republican society. More than 350 academies for females opened between 1790 and 1830. The first incorporated publicly was the Young Ladies' Academy of Philadelphia (1787). Intended for daughters of prosperous families, to educate them in "Reading, Writing, Arithmetic, English, Grammar, Composition, and Geography," its curriculum implicitly argued that women could flourish in a challenging academic environment.

Citizens also formed societies intended to provide relief to the needy. A group of prosperous Philadelphians established an almshouse to care for and house the poor (and to teach them the values of industry) and a penitentiary to reform criminals by isolating them from one another. Jewish organizations founded in New York in the late eighteenth century provided aid for the city's small Jewish community.

In a variety of occupational and manufacturing societies, masters and journeymen furthered their common interests, sometimes against what they perceived as the haughtiness of the merchants. Many of the trades of Philadelphia participated in the Federal Procession of 1789, for example—a sign to the elites that craft workers had their own expectations of the new republic. Promoting a different vision, Alexander Hamilton and his assistant secretary, Tench Coxe, formed the Society for Establishing Useful Manufactures in 1791, a joint-stock corporation meant to demonstrate the economic virtues of cooperation between the private sector and the government.

Securing the Nation

The internal turbulence the United States faced in these years was matched by conflict on the western borders of the nation and in the larger Atlantic community of which the new nation was inextricably a part. Moreover, those conflicts and disagreements about how to resolve them became the major sources of political conflict in the new nation.

Borders and Boundaries

The United States of America had come into formal existence as a republic with the Articles of Confederation in 1781, and its existence had been recognized in the Paris Peace Treaty with Britain in 1783 and again in the ratification of the federal Constitution. Still, much remained unclear, unfinished, and highly contested when George Washington took office in 1789.

On the simplest level, the new republic lacked even clear external borders. Although the Treaty of Paris seemed to describe a very specific territory being ceded from Britain to the United States, things were much less clear on the ground. For example, the treaty set a boundary beginning "from the northwest angle of Nova Scotia, viz., that angle which is formed by a line drawn due north from the source of the St. Croix River to the highlands; along the said highlands which divide those rivers that empty themselves into the river St. Lawrence, from those which fall into the Atlantic Ocean, to the northwesternmost head of Connecticut River; thence down along the middle of that river to the forty-fifth degree of north latitude . . ." across the Great Lakes, down the Mississippi

River, and across the border of New Spain to the Atlantic. But what exact spot marked "the source of the St. Croix River"? Where was the "middle" of the Connecticut River? These were not abstract problems: Britain and the United States would argue for years over present-day Maine, and Spain claimed a sizable chunk of present-day Mississippi and Alabama.

A related problem was that much of the territory America claimed was literally unmapped. When his nation sent him to England to resolve trade and boundary disputes (resulting in Jay's Treaty; see "To the Brink of War"), John Jay was handicapped by a lack of basic geographical knowledge about North America. How could he argue for favorable terms when it was unknown how far north "the Mississippi River extends"?

European empires were not the only ones challenging the territorial integrity of the new nation. There were also a hundred thousand or so Native Americans who lived within the boundaries of the republic, many of them crisscrossing large expanses of hunting and growing grounds in seasonal migrations. The United States had acknowledged the sovereignty of Indian nations in eight treaties before the ratification of the Constitution and again in Article I of the Constitution, granting Congress the power "to regulate commerce with . . . the Indian tribes." But the Native Americans rejected both European American ideas of fixed borders and the specific borders delineated in the Treaty of Paris. Most of the "United States of America" was still Indian land to them— the land of the Shawnee, for example, or of the people of the longhouses, or of the turtle people. Settlers kept moving into these lands, however (see Map 8–2).

Even the states of the new nation disagreed on the division of lands within its borders. Many of the original boundary conflicts had been settled in the 1780s, but Virginia, Georgia, and North Carolina still claimed lands running to the Mississippi River (although North Carolina wanted to cede the land to the United States). Massachusetts, New Hampshire, and New York still fought over present-day Maine. Finally, the attachment of many western settlers to the new nation was so weak that, well into the nineteenth century, some flirted with detaching portions of the West and turning them over to the Spanish or creating another independent nation.

Controlling the Borderlands

For all of its symbolic importance as a source of republican order, the backcountry had so far been marked by constant conflict among owners and settlers and between Indians and Americans. Americans fought with each other over land prices and rights of ownership. In spite of these conflicts, squatters, proprietors, and governments shared the assumption that the land was theirs to fight over. The Treaty of Paris did not acknowledge Indian claims, and treaties promising Indians peace in exchange for land proved illusory (see Chapter 7). By the time Washington took office in 1789, the backcountry was in an uproar. Undisciplined federal troops and state militias roamed western lands in search of a fight, often attacking neutral or sympathetic Indian villages. Betrayed and angry, Indians banded together in loose confederations, retaliating against settlers and striking alliances with the British and Spanish.

By 1789, the Eastern Woodland and Great Lakes nations had been deeply altered by the westward pressure of white settlement. In the North, a group of battered Iroquoian villages traded large tracts of land for promises of security and called on tribes of the Northwest Territory to do the same. However, these peoples refused and effectively shut down settlement north of the Ohio River valley. In the South, the Creeks, trapped

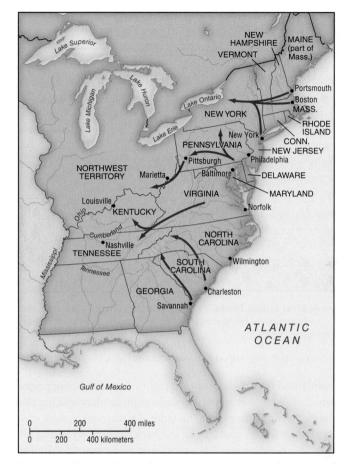

Map 8–2   Western Expansion, 1785–1805 Between the Treaty of Paris (1783) and the Louisiana Purchase (1803), Americans flooded into the territories that lay between the Appalachians and the Mississippi River. Then (as later) migration often followed rivers and valleys into the interior of the continent. *Source:* Gregory Evans Dowd, *A Spirited Resistance: The North American Indian Struggle for Unity, 1745–1815* (Baltimore: Johns Hopkins University Press, 1991), p. 92.

between white settlements and the Native American nations of the Mississippi River valley, allied with militant Cherokees to keep the Georgia, Tennessee, and Kentucky frontiers ablaze with war parties.

Washington had more reasons to worry about the western territories. By 1789, Spain was actively luring United States settlers into New Spain at the foot of the Mississippi River in order to weaken the loyalty of the West to the new United States government. In the Great Lakes region, Britain hung on to the string of forts it had promised to give up in the Treaty of Paris. Many Americans believed that Britain was biding its time to regain control of the lands south of the Great Lakes.

This turmoil took its toll in the East. The inability of the national government to control Native Americans angered states, would-be settlers, and small-business owners.

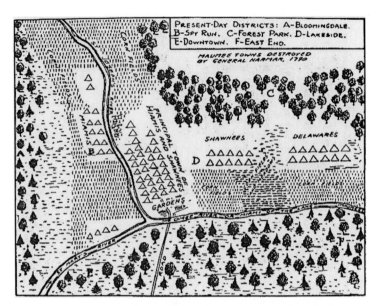

Maumee River Indian Towns This 1790 drawing suggests the complex economic arrangement of the Maumee River Indian towns and the diverse groups that occupied the towns.

Landowners complained that their property rights were not being protected, and small settlers complained of favoritism in land distribution. Understanding that both external relations and the domestic authority of the federal government were at stake, Washington turned immediately to the problem of the backcountry. Working with Secretary of War Henry Knox, Washington sought a more fair and consistent Indian policy, with a preference for "civilizing" Native Americans in order to avoid future conflict. He also used the territories to demonstrate the power of the federal government.

Less than a month after assuming office, Washington submitted to Congress a report by Knox on Indian affairs. Knox argued that the United States should acknowledge a residual Indian "right in the soil" not affected by a treaty between Britain and the United States. That right could be extinguished, he insisted, only by separate dealing with the Indians; he recommended that the United States purchase Indian claims to disputed lands.

In part, Knox and Washington shifted policy in the name of justice, but they also sought to avoid the costs of having to take the Northwest Territory by war. A change in tactics did not mean a change in ultimate goals, however. Although Knox tried to keep white settlers outside treaty boundaries, his policy did not recognize Native Americans' right to refuse to negotiate. Seeking to bolster the authority of the national government, Knox argued that Indian bands were not communities within state borders but rather foreign entities, on the level of nations. Indian relations were therefore properly the business of the federal government. Knox in effect declared Indians aliens on their own lands, using federal policy to define Indians as the ultimate outsiders.

By 1790, continuing troubles in the Northwest Territory convinced Washington to send troops there (see Map 8–3). His first two efforts were dismal failures. In 1790 a combined Native American force led by the Miami war leader Little Turtle routed the United

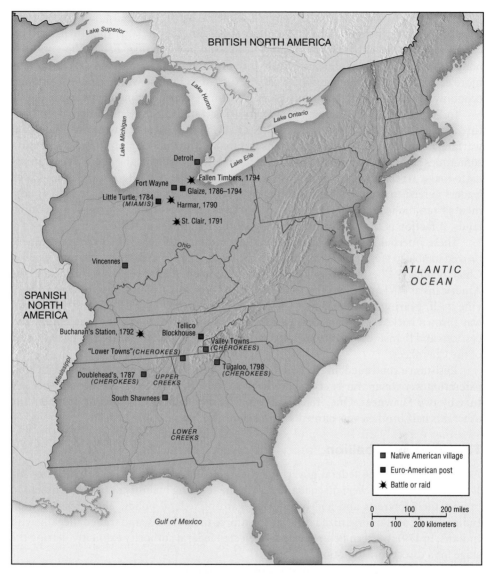

Map 8-3 Major Indian Villages and Indian–US Battle Sites, 1789–1800 During its first decade of existence, the new federal government struggled to assert control over the trans-Appalachian territories, claimed by Native Americans as their homelands and coveted by United States settlers and land speculators.

States Army, led by General Josiah Harmar. The next year a much smaller party crushed the troops of territorial governor general Arthur St. Clair. In 1792, Congress authorized a "strong coercive force" (bigger, better paid, and better trained) and Washington turned to a seasoned infantry officer, Pennsylvanian major general Anthony Wayne. By the time Wayne found the Indians in 1794 at Fallen Timbers, near Lake Erie, his army was more than 3,000 strong. Facing a force of only 400 warriors, Wayne claimed a decisive victory.

According to the Treaty of Greenville, signed August 3, 1795, Indians ceded two-thirds of the later state of Ohio and a piece of present-day Indiana. In return, they received annual federal payments ranging from $500 to $1,000 per band. The annuities bought the United States influence within Indian communities and rendered the Indians more economically dependent. The treaty also tried to impose white ideas of work and economy by offering Indians annuities in the form of farm equipment, cows, and pigs.

Indian efforts at confederacy proved less successful in the South, where deep fractures existed within the Cherokee and Creek nations. Older leaders, wearied by constant warfare, and mixed-heritage populations familiar with white economic and social ways sometimes favored accommodation and entered into agreements they lacked the authority to make. At the Treaty of New York in 1790, Alexander McGillivray and other Creek leaders agreed to exchange lands belonging to the entire Creek nation for annual payments from the federal government and promises of US protection for their remaining lands. A faction of the Cherokee nation signed a similar pact in 1791.

These internal disputes weakened Indian military efforts. When the government proved unable to stop settlers flowing into the future state of Tennessee, younger Creeks, Chickamaugas, Cherokees, and Shawnees repudiated the treaties and attacked the Americans at Buchanan's Station, near Nashville, Tennessee, planning to move on Nashville itself. Fearing reprisals, older Cherokee leaders betrayed the plan, and the assault was thrown back. US Indian commissioners used military victories to coerce new land cessions and to insinuate white customs more deeply into Indian cultures, especially that of the Cherokees.

Resistance continued, in the North and the South, but dreams of a pan-Indian confederation were temporarily stymied. They would be resurrected at the turn of the century by two Shawnees. One, Tenskwatawa, would become an important prophet. The other, his half-brother, was named Tecumseh.

The Whiskey Rebellion

Another threat to the federal government came from western settlers themselves. By 1791, western settlers were disenchanted with the seeming inability of the government to protect their interests and had begun disregarding federal policy. They trespassed on Indian lands, sent unorganized militias to enforce their claims, and traded illegally with Indians. In 1791, western Pennsylvanians rejected federal authority explicitly, setting the stage for a direct confrontation.

The trouble began with the passage of Hamilton's excise tax. Living in a gateway to the Northwest Territory, residents of western Pennsylvania anticipated an economic bonanza from westward migration but were frustrated with the failure of the government to secure safe passage into the Ohio River valley. Hamilton's tax on spirits fueled their simmering anger over the question of republican fairness. Many Americans regarded excise taxes (internal taxes on specific goods) as unfair in principle. This particular tax seemed targeted specifically at western farmers, who found it cheaper to transport their grain in liquid than in bushel form.

Popular protests intensified at each new report of the army's failure in the Northwest Territory (efforts the tax was supposed to fund). Western Pennsylvanians vowed that they would not pay the tax and urged citizens to treat tax collectors with "contempt." Washington took the challenge seriously, and in August 1794 he sent 13,000 troops into western Pennsylvania. Against this show of force, the Whiskey Rebellion fizzled, but the government drove its point (and power) home. Remaining protestors were rounded up; twenty were sent to Philadelphia to face treason charges, and two were sentenced to death. Washington pardoned them both, but he had proven the authority of federal law.

Western Pennsylvanians were not without sympathizers, however. The congressional elections of 1792 were contests between the policies of Alexander Hamilton, on the one hand, and the beliefs of the self-named "republican interest," on the other, over what it meant to be a republican nation and society.

Other Revolutions

Just as the United States was launching its federal republic, France entered the throes of revolution. After years of fiscal mismanagement by the crown, high unemployment, and widespread malnutrition and starvation, the French bourgeoisie began a reform of the monarchy that soon led to wholesale grassroots revolution. In July 1789, just eight weeks after Washington took the oath of office, the people of Paris stormed the Bastille prison in symbolic rejection of the power of the monarchy. The next month the new National Constituent Assembly abolished feudalism and promulgated the Declaration of the Rights of Man and of the Citizen, modeled on the American Declaration of Independence.

Initially, most Americans, including many Federalists, supported the French Revolution. As a part of its long eighteenth-century conflict with Great Britain, France had aided the Americans in their own revolution and had recognized the nation and its diplomats after the war. Americans now saw the efforts of the French people to overthrow monarchy as a reflection of their own struggle against Britain, and they read events in France as a confirmation that the United States would lead the world into a new era of democracy.

By 1793, however, as the Parisian mob grew more violent and moderate politicians lost power, many Americans lost their enthusiasm for the French republic. Although many, Jefferson and Madison among them, remained avid French partisans, others grew convinced that France was spiraling into chaos—which would spread to the United States.

Part of their alarm may have derived from events on the French island colony of Saint-Domingue (present-day Haiti) in the West Indies. In 1791, its free people of color led an insurgency against the white planter class but soon lost control in the face of a full-scale revolution by the island's tens of thousands of slaves. Eventually, under the leadership of former slave François-Dominique Toussaint-Louverture, Saint-Domingue would become the first black republic in the Americas.

Washington's response to the revolution in Saint-Domingue was complicated. He did not support the revolutionaries, especially after the movement for equality for free blacks turned into a slave rebellion. Like other slave owners, Washington feared that supporting the Saint-Dominguans would encourage slave rebellion in the southern United States. Still, he did not want to enter into an alliance with France (which sent soldiers to put down the rebellion), as that might seem hostile to the British. His compromise was to order supplies and ammunition sent directly to the island's white-planter ruling class.

Between France and England

Washington would later summarize his foreign policy goals: "The great rule of conduct for us, in regard to foreign nations, is, in extending our commercial relations, to have with them as little political connexion as possible." The United States wanted to trade freely with every nation, but other nations used trade barriers to protect not only their economic but their political interests as well. Washington and his successors thus found that it was one thing to announce a policy and another to achieve it, particularly when Americans too had loyalties to France or England, two nations that were almost continuously at war from 1793 to 1815.

Washington's efforts to avoid the appearance of pro-French partiality were soon tested. On February 1, 1793, France and Spain declared war on Great Britain and Holland. American sentiments were divided. Many Democratic Republicans (among them Jefferson and Madison) viewed with horror the possibility that America might join with its former colonial master against a fellow republic. Hamiltonians, meanwhile, believed that friendly relations with Britain best served American interests. Searching for a middle ground, President Washington endorsed neutrality.

Then, on May 16, Edmond-Charles Genêt, citizen of France, arrived in Philadelphia, the temporary capital. France had several hopes for the Genêt mission. Genêt was supposed to incite the European colonies in the Americas to revolution. He was also to press the United States for a new treaty allowing French naval forces and privateers to resupply in American ports. France's hopes were not entirely fanciful. The impoverished Washington administration had lent money to the new French government and recognized the Republic as the legitimate government of France.

But the French overestimated American support. Giving preferential treatment to French ships could only strain relations between America and England. Barely able to muster a force to the Northwest, Washington was not about to risk a foreign war or to inflame tensions on western borders. Washington considered Genêt's proposals reckless.

Genêt, however, did not believe that Washington's views represented the sentiments of Americans generally. In Philadelphia, he authorized the refitting of a captured English ship as a French privateer, and he encouraged American settlers in Kentucky to attack the Spanish.

Washington was furious. "Is the Minister of the French Republic to set the Acts of this Government at defiance, with impunity?" he fumed. Issuing a formal Proclamation of Neutrality, Washington disavowed Genêt and demanded that he be recalled. Disappointed by Washington's growing support of Federalist policies, Jefferson resigned as secretary of state.

To the Brink of War

Even without Genêt's provocations, by 1794 tensions with Britain were high. There were already issues left over from the Revolution—debts owed to British creditors, compensation due to southerners whose slaves had been seized, and forts the British still occupied in the Northwest. To these were added new irritants: the British navy was confiscating US merchant ships trading with (and for) the French in the Caribbean and impressing their sailors into the British navy. The Americans wanted compensation. Still, Washington sought to avoid confrontation. Even though the British kept the Americans out of West Indian and Canadian ports, US shipping had been steadily expanding, making it hard to argue that British policies were injurious enough to risk a war. Washington dispatched Chief Justice of the Supreme Court John Jay to England to resolve outstanding issues.

Already at war with France, Britain was ready to reduce tensions with the United States. Although Britain was unwilling to let the United States trade with France, Britain agreed to open West Indies ports to smaller US ships. Both countries agreed that (with some exceptions) their ships would receive equal treatment. They agreed as well to establish arbitration boards to determine compensation for prewar debts and the seized ships, as well as to set the boundary between Canada and the United States. Britain also promised to evacuate its forts in the Northwest by June 1, 1796. Jay, an opponent of slavery, did not try very hard to get compensation for the slaves.

Most Americans knew nothing about Jay's Treaty until after it was approved, for the Senate debated it in secret. When Democratic Republicans learned of its contents and its ratification, they were outraged. They protested the closed deliberations and the failure to gain "neutral rights," the right to trade with Britain's enemies. They feared being drawn closer to Britain, their old enemy, and being pulled from France, the nation's first ally. But positive developments in the West helped the fury to subside. First came news of Anthony Wayne's victory against the Great Lakes tribes at Fallen Timbers. Word followed that Thomas Pinckney had also concluded a treaty with Spain, opening the Mississippi River to US navigation and permitting Americans to use the port at New Orleans. (Pinckney's Treaty also set the boundary between the United States and Florida.) Once the United States made peace with Britain, a weak Spain feared a formal alliance would come next and accepted an American presence in the West as a price for peace.

Wayne's victory and Jay's and Pinckney's negotiations seemed at last to open the territories to settlement (see Map 8–4). Western land prices soared, and the US export

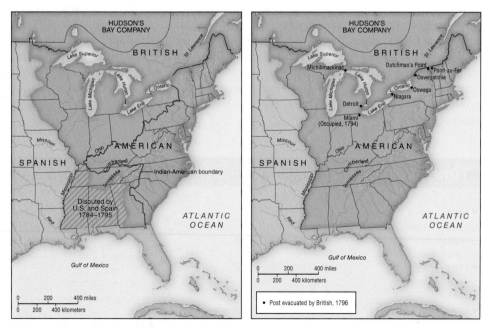

Map 8–4   Extension of United States National Territories, 1783 and 1795 The Treaty of Paris with Great Britain (1783) left the United States' borders with Spain (much of the western and southern boundaries) ambiguous. Those borders were clarified in the Pinckney Treaty with Spain (1795).

trade boomed. By the time opponents in the House of Representatives tried to scuttle Jay's Treaty by denying necessary funds, popular sentiment had shifted to strong support for the treaty as a key to prosperity.

The Administration of John Adams

George Washington, reluctant to serve a second term, had been convinced to do so when Jefferson and Hamilton argued that no one else could bring the republic's fractious politics together. But Washington refused to run for a third term, and in 1796 the nation faced its first contested presidential election.

In his farewell address, published on September 19, 1796, Washington made clear his Federalist concern with social order and personal discipline. Having acknowledged the right of the people to alter their Constitution, he stressed the "duty of every individual to obey the established Government" until it was changed "by an explicit and authentic act of the whole people." Sounding themes that would echo through the first half-century of the republic, he warned against unlawful "combinations and associations" with designs on the rightful "power of the people," an image that, 30 years later, would drive the emergence of Jacksonian democracy.

With Hamilton too controversial to be an effective candidate, Federalists selected Vice President John Adams as their choice. Adams had served in the Continental Congress, been a part of the committee to draft the Declaration of Independence, served as representative to France, helped negotiate the peace treaty, and served two terms as vice president. Thomas Pinckney of South Carolina was their vice-presidential choice. For president, Democratic Republicans supported former secretary of state Thomas Jefferson, along with Madison, the most visible opponent of Hamilton. New Yorker Aaron Burr was intended as vice president.

Although contested, the election of 1796 was not decided by popular majority. State legislatures chose two-fifths of the members of the Electoral College. Moreover, procedures in the Electoral College did not distinguish between votes for the offices of president and vice president. The person who received the most electoral votes became president. The person who received the second-highest number of electoral votes became vice president.

Time Line

▼1781
Articles of Confederation ratified

▼1787–1788
Constitution ratified

▼1789
George Washington inaugurated
Judiciary Act of 1789

Tariff Act of 1789
John Fenno founds *Gazette of the United States*
William Hill Brown publishes *The Power of Sympathy*

▼1790
Alexander Hamilton's Report on the Public Credit
Assumption Act
Naturalization Act

▼1791
Excise tax (including tax on whiskey) passes
First Bank of the United States
Philip Freneau establishes *National Gazette*
Bill of Rights ratified

▼1792–1794
Whiskey Rebellion

This procedure proved dangerously unpredictable in a new age of political parties. Although the Federalist Adams received a majority of electoral votes (71) and became president, the Democratic Republican Jefferson received the second-highest count (68 to Pinckney's 59) and became vice president.

Benjamin Franklin once said that John Adams was "always an honest man, often a wise one, but sometimes, and in some things, absolutely out of his senses." Also cranky, defensive, and self-doubting, he was not the man to negotiate growing party rifts successfully. Against a background of partisan resentment, Adams confronted an increasingly hostile relationship with France. Unsurprisingly, Franco-American relations had been harmed by Jay's Treaty—which seemed to France to ally America with England—and by the French practice of plundering American ships. There was also the issue of Saint-Domingue. By the time John Adams took office, the revolutionaries (now led by former slave Toussaint-Louverture) were seeking to resume trade with the United States as a step toward full independence. The abolitionist Adams had no qualms about supporting the revolutionaries and saw a number of advantages in allying with them. A trade deal with Haiti would further isolate the island from French control, it would help the US economy, and it might prompt Louverture to close his ports to the French privateers attacking US merchant ships. In June 1799, the Adams administration signed a three-way British–US–Saint-Dominguan trade agreement. Although that agreement was unratified when Adams left office, in the last months of his presidency Adams stationed US warships outside Saint-Dominguan ports to help quash an internal rebellion of conservative free people of color wishing to reimpose slavery, while members of his administration discussed with Louverture the form that an independent Saint-Dominguan republican government might assume. None of this pleased France, particularly not after the rise of Napoleon and the resurgence of French imperial ambitions in the late 1790s.

Even before his inauguration on March 4, 1797, Adams thought about sending a special envoy to France to resolve these issues. When Adams's cabinet objected, the president temporarily abandoned the plan. At the end of March, he learned that new American ambassador Charles Pinckney had been kicked out of France because the French government would "no longer recognize or receive" an ambassador from the United

Sedition and the Limits of Dissent

What are the limits of dissent in a democracy? The new American government struggled with this question at the end of the 1790s. By that time, two political parties had developed in a nation that still considered such organized opposition as illegitimate. When the French Revolution became more violent, the parties were driven even further apart. The Federalists feared the spread of French radicalism to the United States, while the Democratic Republicans remained sympathetic to the aims of the Revolution, if not always its tactics.

The debates over the Alien and Sedition Acts reflected the Federalists' fears that the American republic was vulnerable to both external and internal foes. No amount of reasoning by their Democratic Republican opponents could convince them otherwise because they were not even convinced of the other party's loyalty to the United States. Federalist Jonathan Dayton believed that "the time was arrived when we ought to take measures for our own security," and his colleague David Brooks warned that "we have those within our bosom who would give up our country too." When Nathaniel Macon, a Revolutionary War veteran, asked if the Federalists truly thought that "men who had fought and won the Revolution" would now "relinquish the prize to any nation," a Federalist Congressman replied that he had no doubts. Some Federalists imagined tens of thousands of French radicals coming to invade the United States. The Democratic Republicans asked for proof, and Robert Livingston insisted that "we must legislate upon facts, not on surmises; [we] must have evidence, not vague suspicions. . . ." A Federalist Congressman responded, "Because proof is not produced in a fortnight, it does not follow that it will not be produced" at some later time. Then again, "legal proof was one thing, and he did not know that he should ever be able to produce it."

It was in this heated environment that the Sedition Act was passed, making it illegal to "write, print, utter or publish . . . . any false, scandalous and malicious writing against the government of the United States, or either house of the Congress of the United States, or the President . . . with intent to defame [them], or to bring them . . . into contempt or disrepute; or to excite against them . . . the hatred of the good people of the United States." The Democratic Republicans believed it was a political bill, aimed at undermining their party. Indeed, the pattern of prosecutions—against Republican newspaper editors and critics of President John Adams—suggests that they were right. Republican newspapers were either suppressed or put out of business altogether. Pennsylvania editor Thomas Cooper was jailed for listing what he believed to be Adams's chief failures as president, while a mob that included soldiers beat another editor, William Duane, unconscious. Vermont Congressman Matthew Lyon, in the middle of his campaign for reelection in a swing district, was jailed for publishing a letter in a local newspaper that accused Adams of "unbounded thirst for ridiculous pomp, foolish adulation or selfish avarice."

If the goal of the Sedition Act was to insure Adams' reelection, it was a failure. Indeed, some of the prosecutions—for example, of the inebriated New Jersey man who said he hoped the ceremonial cannon welcoming the president to Newark would shoot President Adams "thro' his arse"— now seem ridiculous. But the effect was to shut down a number of newspapers and to make radicalism itself suspect. Although Jefferson won the election, he subsequently distanced himself from former radical allies. And this pattern of questioning the loyalty of opponents would be repeated in years to come.

States. Adams decided to send a mission to France, appointing Elbridge Gerry, John Marshall, and Pinckney.

When the American mission arrived, French foreign minister Talleyrand made clear that he expected a bribe for his willingness to talk. Such arrangements were not uncommon in European politics, but to the starched and wary Adams, the idea was abhorrent. He turned over all documentation of the affair to Congress, identifying Talleyrand's agents by the letters X, Y, and Z.

The so-called XYZ Affair prompted a largely Federalist Congress to suspend commercial ties to France, empower American ships to seize armed French vessels, and expand the nation's military. In what became known as the "Quasi-War" (neither nation formally declared war), between 1798 and 1800 the United States and France skirmished on the seas, with the United States capturing more than 80 French ships. In the Convention of 1800, France and the United States agreed to end these hostilities. France agreed to return captured American ships; the United States assumed Americans' claims against the French for damages in shipping; and the earlier Franco-American Alliance was replaced by mutual most-favored-nation status.

Tensions at Home

The military expansion necessary for this conflict soon created tensions at home. Adams and Congress needed $2 million for it, which they found by imposing a tax on houses, land, and slaves. Each state had a specified portion of the cost to pay. The levy on houses, assessed according to the size of the house, fell especially hard on residents of states with few or no slaves or huge plantation estates and was particularly odious to German immigrants, whom it reminded of harsh taxes exacted by the kings of Germany. When the assessors reached eastern Pennsylvania, settled predominantly by German immigrants, unrest became civil disobedience. Led by John Fries, men of the area raised a small army to chase collectors away, while women poured hot water on the assessors. When the governor tried to have the resisters arrested, Fries's supporters freed them. Adams sent a militia of 1,000 men to capture the leaders. Fries and most of the other leaders were arrested, tried for treason, and sentenced to hang. In the face of strong public sentiment, Adams pardoned the rebels. (This was the second uprising in less than a decade, and in both cases, the rebels were pardoned.)

The Federalists had also used the XYZ Affair and hostilities with France for domestic political purposes. Insisting that pro-French influence endangered the nation, in 1798 Congress passed the Alien and Sedition Acts, aimed at gagging the Democratic

Republican opposition and preventing it from using the war issue to win the 1800 election. The acts required a 14-year naturalization period, the highest at any period in American history, and targeted immigrants, whom the Federalists presumed to be Democratic Republicans. The acts also empowered the president to deport any "suspicious" aliens and established a broad definition of sedition, intended to stop all Democratic Republican criticism of the administration's policies.

The Alien and Sedition Acts backfired against the Federalists. Twenty-five prosecutions were eventually brought under the Sedition Act (all against Democratic Republicans), and 10 men were convicted. The acts were so transparently partisan that individuals convicted under them became martyrs to the Democratic Republican cause. A Vermont congressman who published criticisms of administration policies was reelected even as he served out his four-month jail term. But by targeting those believed to be "radical," especially newspaper editors, and warning immigrants away, the acts silenced the most outspoken opponents of the government.

Although Democratic Republicans insisted that the acts were unconstitutional, they hesitated to challenge them in the Supreme Court, both because the Court was dominated by Federalists and because Democratic Republicans did not want to set a precedent for giving the Supreme Court the power to rule on constitutionality. Instead, Madison and Jefferson encouraged the states to pass resolutions denouncing the Alien and Sedition Acts. Madison, now retired from Congress, authored a set of resolutions in Virginia affirming the rights of states to judge the constitutionality of federal laws. Jefferson, vice president of the United States, framed a more militant set of resolutions for the Kentucky legislature, saying that states might declare federal laws they deemed unconstitutional to be without force within their state boundaries.

Jefferson and Madison expected that other states would support the Virginia and Kentucky resolutions, but they did not. Rather, voters simply returned the Democratic Republicans to power in the election of 1800, and the acts expired in 1801.

Before retiring, the Federalist Congress got off one more shot at the Democratic Republicans. Just as the session expired, Congress passed the Judiciary Act of 1801, which gave John Adams the power to expand the federal judiciary by appointing new judges, justices of the peace, attorneys, clerks, and marshals. He promptly filled these positions with good Federalists and then left office.

Conclusion

After a tumultuous first decade, it was not clear that the United States' experiment in government of, by, and for the people could survive. As the nation grew in size and population, the government struggled to maintain not simply order but, even more, the allegiance of its peoples. Americans had fallen into two rival political parties, with rival visions for the future and rival international attachments. Yet, in the midst of all this turmoil, Americans such as Ona Judge maintained a deep commitment to the principle and, even more, realization of freedom. Out of these conflicts and aspirations, a new nation was being born.

Who, What

Review Questions

1. What were the key elements of Hamilton's fiscal and economic policies?

2. Why did political parties emerge during Washington's administration? How did the two parties differ, and why was the conflict between them so intense?

3. What was the Whiskey Rebellion? How did it reflect larger tensions in the early republic?

Critical-Thinking Questions

1. Why were foreign and domestic affairs so intertwined in the 1790s?

2. How fragile do you think the new nation was? What were the reasons for that fragility?

3. Could slavery have been eliminated in the 1790s?

For further review materials and resource information, please visit www.oup.com/us/oakes

CHAPTER 8: CONTESTED REPUBLIC, 1789–1800
Primary Sources

8.1 ALEXANDER HAMILTON, REPORT ON MANUFACTURES (1791)

Washington's Secretary of the Treasury, Alexander Hamilton, proposed a number of initiatives to strengthen the American economy and make it more like that of the European nations, with a national bank, a funded debt, and increased commerce and manufacturing. In his Report on Manufactures he described the benefits that would come from national support of manufacturing, including increasing the productivity of women and children. He also advocated increased immigration, to provide workers for the growing industries. Jefferson, Madison, and others who organized to oppose Hamilton feared that a shift from agriculture to manufacturing would create a permanent dependent class that would undermine the new republic.

III. As to the additional employment of classes of the community, not ordinarily engaged in the particular business.

This is not among the least valuable of the means, by which manufacturing institutions contribute to augment the general stock of industry and production. In places where those institutions prevail, besides the persons regularly engaged in them, they afford occasional and extra employment to industrious individuals and families, who are willing to devote the leisure resulting from the intermissions of their ordinary pursuits to collateral labours, as a resource of multiplying their acquisitions or [their] enjoyments. The husbandman himself experiences a new source of profit and support from the encreased industry of his wife and daughters; invited and stimulated by the demands of the neighboring manufactories.

Besides this advantage of occasional employment to classes having different occupations, there is another of a nature allied to it [and] of a similar tendency. This is—the employment of persons who would otherwise be idle (and in many cases a burthen on the community), either from the byass of temper, habit, infirmity of body, or some other cause, indisposing, or disqualifying them for the toils of the Country. It is worthy of particular remark, that, in general, women and Children are rendered more useful and the latter more early useful by manufacturing establishments, than they would otherwise be. Of the number of persons employed in the Cotton Manufactories of Great Britain, it is computed that 4/7 nearly are women and children; of whom the greatest proportion are children and many of them of a very tender age.

And thus it appears to be one of the attributes to manufactures, and one of no small consequence, to give occasion to the exertion of a greater quantity of Industry, even by the same number of persons, where they happen to prevail, than would exist, if there were no such establishments.

IV. As to the promoting of emigration from foreign Countries.

Men reluctantly quit one course of occupation and livelihood for another, unless invited to it by very apparent and proximate advantages. Many, who would go from one country to another, if they had a prospect of continuing with more benefit the callings, to which they have been educated, will often not be tempted to change their situation, by the hope of doing better, in some other way. Manufacturers, who listening to the powerful invitations of a better price for their fabrics, or their labour, of greater cheapness of provisions and raw materials, of an exemption from the chief part of the taxes burthens and restraints, which they endure in the old world, of greater personal independence and consequence, under the operation of a more equal government, and of what is far more precious than mere religious toleration—a perfect equality of religious privileges; would probably flock from Europe to the United States to pursue their own trades or professions, if they were once made sensible of the advantages they would enjoy, and were inspired with an assurance of encouragement and employment, will, with difficulty, be induced to transplant themselves, with a view to becoming Cultivators of Land.

If it be true then, that it is the interest of the United States to open every possible [avenue to] emigration from abroad, it affords a weighty argument for the encouragement of manufactures; which for the reasons just assigned, will have the strongest tendency to multiply the inducements to it.

Here is perceived an important resource, not only for extending the population, and with it the useful and productive labour of the country, but likewise for the prosecution of manufactures, without deducting from the number of hands, which might otherwise be drawn to tillage; and even for the indemnification of Agriculture for such as might happen to be diverted from it. Many, whom Manufacturing views would induce to emigrate, would afterwards yield to the temptations, which the particular situation of this Country holds out to Agricultural pursuits. And while Agriculture would in other respects derive many signal and unmingled advantages, from the growth of manufactures, it is a problem whether it would gain or lose, as to the article of the number of persons employed in carrying it on.

V. As to the furnishing greater scope for the diversity of talents and dispositions, which discriminate men from each other.

... The results of human exertion may be immensely increased by diversifying its objects. When all the different kinds of industry obtain in a community, each individual can find his proper element, and can call into activity the whole vigour of his nature. And the community is benefitted by the services of its respective members, in the manner, in which each can serve it with most effect.

If there be anything in a remark often to be met with—namely that there is, in the genius of the people of this country, a peculiar aptitude for mechanic improvements, it would operate as a forcible reason for giving opportunities to the exercise of that species of talent by the propagation of manufactures.

VI. As to the affording a more ample and various field for enterprise.

... The spirit of enterprise, useful and prolific as it is, must necessarily be contracted or expanded in proportion to the simplicity or variety of the occupations and productions, which are to be found in a Society. It must be less in a nation of mere cultivators, than in a nation of cultivators and merchants; less in a nation of cultivators and merchants, than in a nation of cultivators, artificers and merchants.

Source: Alexander Hamilton, "Report on Manufactures," 1791.
http://press-pubs.uchicago.edu/founders/documents/v1ch4s31.html

8.2 GEORGE WASHINGTON, FAREWELL ADDRESS (1796)

After serving two terms as president, George Washington decided to retire, setting a precedent for a two-term limit on the presidency. In his farewell address, he encouraged American citizens to remain vigilant in the defense of their freedom. He warned the nation about the dangers of sectionalism, which he saw emerging between the North, South, and West. He also discouraged the formation of political parties and the addition of "innovations" to the Constitution. Most of the speech, however, focused on the importance of avoiding entanglements with European nations.

Friends and Citizens:

The period for a new election of a citizen to administer the executive government of the United States being not far distant, and the time actually arrived when your thoughts must be employed in designating the person who is to be clothed with that important trust, it appears to me proper, especially as it may conduce to a more distinct expression of the public voice, that I should now apprise you of the resolution I have formed, to decline being considered among the number of those out of whom a choice is to be made. . . .

The impressions with which I first undertook the arduous trust were explained on the proper occasion. In the discharge of this trust, I will only say that I have, with good intentions, contributed towards the organization and administration of the government the best exertions of which a very fallible judgment was capable. Not unconscious in the outset of the inferiority of my qualifications, experience in my own eyes, perhaps still more in the eyes of others, has strengthened the motives to diffidence of myself; and every day the increasing weight of years admonishes me more and more that the shade of retirement is as necessary to me as it will be welcome. Satisfied that if any circumstances have given peculiar value to my services, they were temporary, I have the consolation to believe that, while choice and prudence invite me to quit the political scene, patriotism does not forbid it. . . .

Here, perhaps, I ought to stop. But a solicitude for your welfare, which cannot end but with my life, and the apprehension of danger, natural to that solicitude, urge me, on an occasion like the present, to offer to your solemn contemplation, and to recommend to your frequent review, some sentiments which are the result of much reflection, of no inconsiderable observation, and which appear to me all-important to the permanency of your felicity as a people.

. . . Against the insidious wiles of foreign influence (I conjure you to believe me, fellow-citizens) the jealousy of a free people ought to be constantly awake, since history and experience prove that foreign influence is one of the most baneful foes of republican government. But that jealousy to be useful must be impartial; else it becomes the instrument of the very influence to be avoided, instead of a defense against it. Excessive partiality for one foreign nation and excessive dislike of another cause those whom they actuate to see danger only on one side, and serve to veil and even second the arts of influence on the other. Real patriots who may resist the intrigues of the favorite are liable to become suspected and odious, while its tools and dupes usurp the applause and confidence of the people, to surrender their interests.

The great rule of conduct for us in regard to foreign nations is in extending our commercial relations, to have with them as little political connection as possible. So far as we have already formed engagements, let them be fulfilled with perfect good faith. Here let us stop. Europe has a set of primary interests which to us have none; or a very remote relation. Hence she must be engaged in frequent controversies, the causes of which are essentially foreign to our concerns. Hence, therefore, it must be unwise in us to implicate ourselves by artificial ties in the ordinary vicissitudes of her politics, or the ordinary combinations and collisions of her friendships or enmities.

Our detached and distant situation invites and enables us to pursue a different course. If we remain one people under an efficient government. the period is not far off when we may defy material injury from external annoyance; when we may take such an attitude as will cause the neutrality we may at any time resolve upon to be scrupulously respected; when belligerent nations, under the impossibility of making acquisitions upon us, will not lightly hazard the giving us provocation; when we may choose peace or war, as our interest, guided by justice, shall counsel.

Why forego the advantages of so peculiar a situation? Why quit our own to stand upon foreign ground? Why, by interweaving our destiny with that of any part of Europe, entangle our peace and prosperity in the toils of European ambition, rivalship, interest, humor or caprice?

It is our true policy to steer clear of permanent alliances with any portion of the foreign world; so far, I mean, as we are now at liberty to do it; for let me not be understood as capable of patronizing infidelity to existing engagements. I hold the maxim no less applicable to public than to private affairs, that honesty is always the best policy. I repeat it, therefore, let those engagements be observed in their genuine sense. But, in my opinion, it is unnecessary and would be unwise to extend them. . . .

In offering to you, my countrymen, these counsels of an old and affectionate friend, I dare not hope they will make the strong and lasting impression I could wish; that they will control the usual current of the passions, or prevent our nation from running the course which has hitherto marked the destiny of nations. But, if I may even flatter myself that they may be productive of some partial benefit, some occasional good; that they may now and then recur to moderate the fury of party spirit, to warn against the mischiefs of foreign intrigue, to guard against the impostures of pretended patriotism; this hope will be a full recompense for the solicitude for your welfare, by which they have been dictated.

How far in the discharge of my official duties I have been guided by the principles which have been delineated, the public records and other evidences of my conduct must witness to you and to the world. To myself, the assurance of my own conscience is, that I have at least believed myself to be guided by them.

Source: George Washington, Farewell Address, 1796.

8.3 THE HOUSE OF REPRESENTATIVES, TESTIMONY OF CONGRESSMAN S. SITGREAVES (1798) AND VISUAL DOCUMENT: ENGRAVING, "CONGRESSIONAL PUGILISTS" (1798)

Without strong parties to mediate conflict and with participants thinking the fate of the new nation depended on the outcome, politics in the early republic was passionate, and disagreements sometimes led to outbreaks of violence—in this case, a physical fight between two members of Congress, within the Hall itself. Congressman Matthew Lyon had a history of breaking the rules of parliamentary order. Nevertheless, the 1798 fight between him and Congressman Roger Griswold was politically motivated: Lyon was a Democratic-Republican and Griswold a Federalist. Following are excerpts from the testimony of a Congressman who witnessed the assault.

The Committee of Privileges, to whom was referred a resolution in the following words, to wit: "*Resolved,* That Roger Griswold and Matthew Lyon, members of this House, for riotous and disorderly behavior committed in the House, be expelled therefrom," with instructions to report the evidence, in writing, have, according to the order of the House, proceeded to take the evidence which they herewith report; and they report, further, that it is their opinion that the said resolution be disagreed to.

Mr. Sitgreaves's testimony.

. . . I was in my seat, engaged in writing, when my attention was excited by the sound or report of a heavy blow. I looked to the quarter from whence the sound seemed to proceed, and saw Mr. Lyon, on his feet, in the place where he usually sits, and Mr. Griswold in the area in front of him, beating him over the head and shoulders with a cane or walking stick. Mr. Lyon appeared to be endeavoring at once to evade the blows, and to extricate himself from the chairs and desks of the row in which he stood. He soon was in the area, and Mr. Griswold continued to beat him, keeping him at such a distance that the blows could take effect, until Mr. Lyon turned and fled behind the partition in the rear of the Speaker's chair, whither he was pursued by Mr. Griswold, still beating him. . . . Mr. Lyon [was] holding in his hand the tongs, which he grasped by one leg. Mr. Griswold seized with his left hand the arm by which Mr. Lyon held the tongs, and closed in with him, and shortly afterwards I saw them come to the ground together, Mr. Lyon falling under Mr. Griswold; I then left my place; the members gathered round them, and they continued on the floor for a few moments. Mr. Lyon being still under Mr. Griswold, until they were parted by one member separating their arms and shoulders, while two others seized each one of Mr. Griswold's legs, and in that manner dragged him off. When they were separated, I went to Mr. Griswold, and observing that he had not his cane, advised him to get it again, lest he should be assailed by Mr. Lyon, who was now on his feet. Mr. Griswold . . . went, at my instance, to take a draught of water; . . . I [next] saw both Mr. Griswold and Mr. Lyon in the lobby, but at the distance of six or eight feet from each other. Mr. Lyon held a cane in his hand; and as I hastened towards that end of the room, I was met by the assistant doorkeeper, who handed me Mr. Griswold's cane, and, appearing unwilling to interpose, requested me to give it to him; I did so, and Mr. Griswold immediately advanced apparently to renew the attack on Mr. Lyon, when the Speaker called the House to order; upon which Mr. Griswold directly relinquished his design, turned round, and went to his seat, as I did to mine.

Source: American State Papers: Documents, Legislative and Executive, of the Congress of the United States, 1789–1809, Issue 37, p. 174. http://books.google.com/books?id=pO81AQAAMAAJ&pg=PA174&lpg=PA174&dq=beating+of+matthew+lyon&source=bl&ots=U8QyTLiDU4&sig=vS4-L8ayfZUbljpJmwgIUQoNu28&hl=en&sa=X&ei=87I UVP2gCY6OyAS5xoCgCQ&ved=0CEoQ6AEwCQ#v=onepage&q=beating%20of%20matthew%20lyon&f=false

8.4 UNITED STATES CONGRESS, "AN ACT TO ESTABLISH AN UNIFORM RULE OF NATURALIZATION" (1790) AND AN ACT RESPECTING ALIEN ENEMIES (1798)

The first naturalization policy, established by Congress in 1790, set liberal terms for residency, only two years, but restricted citizenship to persons who were free and white. In 1795, as fear of foreigners increased, the residency period was extended to five years, and then, in 1798, to fourteen years. At the same time the Alien Enemies Act empowered the president, if there were a declared war, to apprehend, confine, or deport any adult male aliens who were natives of the enemy country, while the Alien Friends act enabled him to deport any alien he considered "dangerous to the peace and safety of the United States." Following are two of these pieces of legislation.

United States Congress, "An act to establish an uniform Rule of Naturalization" (March 26, 1790)

Be it enacted by the Senate and House of Representatives of the United States of America, in Congress assembled, That any Alien being a free white person, who shall have resided within the limits and under the jurisdiction of the United States for the term of two years, may be admitted to become a citizen thereof on application to any common law Court of record in any one of the States wherein he shall have resided for the term of one year at least, and making proof to the satisfaction of such Court that he is a person of good character, and taking the oath or affirmation prescribed by law to support the Constitution of the United States, which Oath or Affirmation such Court shall administer, and the Clerk of such Court shall record such Application, and the proceedings thereon; and thereupon such person shall be considered as a Citizen of the United States. And the children of such person so naturalized, dwelling within the United States, being under the age of twenty one years at the time of such naturalization, shall also be considered as citizens of the United States. And the children of citizens of the United States that may be born beyond Sea, or out of the limits of the United States, shall be considered as natural born Citizens: Provided, that the right of citizenship shall not descend to persons whose fathers have never been resident in the United States: Provided also, that no person heretofore proscribed by any States, shall be admitted a citizen as aforesaid, except by an Act of the Legislature of the State in which such person was proscribed.

An Act Respecting Alien Enemies (July 6, 1798)

SECTION 1. *Be it enacted by the Senate and House of Representatives of the United States of America in Congress assembled,* That whenever there shall be a declared war between the United States and any foreign nation or government, or any invasion or predatory incursion shall be perpetrated, attempted, or threatened against the territory of the United States, by any foreign nation or government, and the President of the United States shall make public proclamation of the event, all natives, citizens, denizens, or subjects of the hostile nation or government, being males of the age of fourteen years and upwards, who shall be within the United States, and not actually naturalized, shall be liable to be apprehended, restrained, secured and removed, as alien enemies. . . . Provided, that aliens resident within the United States, who shall become liable as enemies, in the manner aforesaid, and who shall not be chargeable with actual hostility, or other crime against the public safety, shall be allowed, for the recovery, disposal, and removal of their goods and effects, and for their departure, the full time which is, or shall be stipulated by any treaty, where any shall have been between the United States, and the hostile nation or government, of which they shall be natives, citizens, denizens or subjects: and where no such treaty shall have existed, the President of the United States may ascertain and declare such reasonable time as may be consistent with the public safety, and according to the dictates of humanity and national hospitality.

SEC. 2. *And be it further enacted*, That after any proclamation shall be made as aforesaid, it shall be the duty of the several courts of the United States, and of each state, having criminal jurisdiction, and of the several judges and justices of the courts of the United States, and they shall be, and are hereby respectively, authorized upon complaint, against any alien or alien enemies, as aforesaid, who shall be resident and at large within such jurisdiction or district, to the danger of the public peace or safety, and contrary to the tenor or intent of such proclamation, or other regulations which the President of the United States shall and may establish in the premises, to cause such alien or aliens to be duly apprehended and convened before such court, judge or justice; and after a full examination and hearing on such complaint. and sufficient cause therefor appearing, shall and may order such alien or aliens to be removed out of the territory of the United States, or to give sureties of their good behaviour, or to be otherwise restrained, conformably to the proclamation or regulations which shall and may be established as aforesaid, and may imprison, or otherwise secure such alien or aliens, until the order which shall and may be made, as aforesaid, shall be performed.

SEC. 3. *And be it further enacted*, That it shall be the duty of the marshal of the district in which any alien enemy shall be apprehended, who by the President of the United States, or by order of any court, judge or justice, as aforesaid, shall be required to depart, and to be removed, as aforesaid, to provide therefor, and to execute such order, by himself or his deputy, or other discreet person or persons to be employed by him, by causing a removal of such alien out of the territory of the United States; and for such removal the marshal shall have the warrant of the President of the United States, or of the court, judge or justice ordering the same, as the case may be.

Source: United States Congress, "An act to establish an uniform Rule of Naturalization," (March 26, 1790); "An Act Respecting Alien Enemies" (July 6, 1798).

8.5 THE VIRGINIA AND KENTUCKY RESOLUTIONS (1798–1799)

As the Democratic Republicans debated how best to respond to the Alien and Sedition Acts, rumors spread that Thomas Jefferson's home state of Virginia was going to rise in revolution—which Alexander Hamilton seemed ready to put down by force. Jefferson and Madison, however, chose a more moderate path, one with lasting implications for states' rights: They encouraged the states to pass resolutions opposing the Acts, which Virginia and Kentucky did. The 1798 Virginia resolution affirmed the right of states to determine the constitutionality of federal laws, while in 1799 the Kentucky Act went even further, suggesting a state might nullify any federal law it deemed unconstitutional.

Virginia Act

RESOLVED, That the General Assembly of Virginia, doth unequivocally express a firm resolution to maintain and defend the Constitution of the United States, and the Constitution of this State, against every aggression either foreign or domestic, and that they will support the government of the United States in all measures warranted by the former.

. . . That the General Assembly doth also express its deep regret, that a spirit has in sundry instances, been manifested by the federal government, to enlarge its powers by forced constructions of the constitutional charter which defines them; and that implications have appeared of a design to expound certain general phrases (which having been copied from the very limited grant of power, in the former articles of confederation were the less liable to be misconstrued) so as to destroy the meaning and effect, of the particular enumeration which necessarily explains and limits the general phrases; and so as to consolidate the states by degrees, into one sovereignty, the obvious tendency and inevitable consequence of which would be, to transform the present republican system of the United States, into an absolute, or at best a mixed monarchy.

That the General Assembly doth particularly protest against the palpable and alarming infractions of the Constitution, in the two late cases of the "Alien and Sedition Acts" passed at the last session of Congress.

. . . That this state having by its Convention, which ratified the federal Constitution, expressly declared, that among other essential rights, "the Liberty of Conscience and of the Press cannot be cancelled, abridged, restrained, or modified by any authority of the United States," and from its extreme anxiety to guard these rights from every possible attack of sophistry or ambition, having with other states, recommended an amendment for that purpose, which amendment was, in due time, annexed to the Constitution; it would mark a reproachable inconsistency, and criminal degeneracy, if an indifference were now shewn, to the most palpable violation of one of the Rights, thus declared and secured; and to the establishment of a precedent which may be fatal to the other.

That the good people of this commonwealth, having ever felt, and continuing to feel, the most sincere affection for their brethren of the other states; the truest anxiety for establishing and perpetuating the union of all; and the most scrupulous fidelity to that constitution, which is the pledge of mutual friendship, and the instrument of mutual happiness; the General Assembly doth solemnly appeal to the like dispositions of the other states, in confidence that they will concur with this commonwealth in declaring, as it does hereby declare, that the acts aforesaid, are unconstitutional. . . .

That the Governor be desired, to transmit a copy of the foregoing Resolutions to the executive authority of each of the other states, with a request that the same may be communicated to the Legislature thereof; and that a copy be furnished to each of the Senators and Representatives representing this state in the Congress of the United States.

Kentucky Act

. . . RESOLVED, That this commonwealth considers the federal union, upon the terms and for the purposes specified in the late compact, as conducive to the liberty and happiness of the several states: That it does now unequivocally declare its attachment to the Union, and to that compact, agreeable to its obvious and real intention, and will be among the last to seek its dissolution: That if those who administer the general government be permitted to transgress the limits fixed by that compact, by a total disregard to the special delegations of power therein contained, annihilation of the state governments, and the erection upon their ruins, of a general consolidated government, will be the inevitable consequence: That the principle and construction contended for by sundry of the state legislatures, that the general government is the exclusive judge of the extent of the powers delegated to it, stop nothing short of despotism; since the discretion of those who adminster the government, and not the constitution, would be the measure of their powers: That the several states who formed that instrument, being sovereign and independent, have the unquestionable right to judge of its infraction; and that a nullification, by those sovereignties, of all unauthorized acts done under colour of that instrument, is the rightful remedy: That this commonwealth does upon the most deliberate reconsideration declare, that the said alien and sedition laws, are in their opinion, palpable violations of the said constitution; and however cheerfully it may be disposed to surrender its opinion to a majority of its sister states in matters of ordinary or doubtful policy; yet, in momentous regulations like the present, which so vitally wound the best rights of the citizen, it would consider a silent acquiesecence as highly criminal: That although this commonwealth as a party to the federal compact; will bow to the laws of the Union, yet it does at the same time declare, that it will not now, nor ever hereafter, cease to oppose in a constitutional manner, every attempt from what quarter soever offered, to violate that compact:

AND FINALLY, in order that no pretexts or arguments may be drawn from a supposed acquiescence on the part of this commonwealth in the constitutionality of those laws, and be thereby used as precedents for similar future violations of federal compact; this commonwealth does now enter against them, its SOLEMN PROTEST.

Source: Virginia and Kentucky Resolutions, 1798–1799.
    http://avalon.law.yale.edu/18th_century/virres.asp
    http://avalon.law.yale.edu/18th_century/kenres.asp

8.6 EXCERPTS FROM "AN ACT FOR THE GRADUAL ABOLITION OF SLAVERY," IN *LAWS OF THE STATE OF NEW YORK,* 22ND SESSION (1799)

After the Revolution, a number of northern states began to abolish slavery within their borders. State legislatures found themselves balancing carefully the rights of slave owners to their property with the Revolutionary promise of equality. While Massachusetts enacted general emancipation in 1783, most other northern states, including Pennsylvania, New Hampshire, Connecticut, Rhode Island, Vermont, New York, and New Jersey, decided upon a "gradual" method that emancipated slaves on a certain future date, or only emancipated slaves born after a given day. Here is New York's 1799 Act.

Be it enacted . . . That any child born of a slave within this state after the fourth day of July next shall be deemed and adjudged to be born free: Provided nevertheless. That such child shall be the servant of the legal proprietor of his or her mother until such servant, if a male, shall arrive at the age of twenty-eight years, and if a female, at the age of twenty-five years.

And be it further enacted. That such proprietor, his, her or their heirs or assigns, shall be entitled to the service of such child until he or she shall arrive to the age aforesaid, in the same manner as if such child had been bound to service by the overseers of the poor.

And be it further enacted. That every person being an inhabitant of this state who shall be entitled to the service of a child born after the fourth day of July as aforesaid, shall, within nine months after the birth of such child, cause to be delivered to the clerk of the city or town whereof such person shall be an inhabitant, a certificate in writing containing the name and addition of such master or mistress, and the name, age and sex of every child so born, which certificate shall be by the said clerk recorded in a book to be by him for that purpose provided, which record shall be good and sufficient evidence of the age of such child; and the clerk of such city or town shall receive from said person twelve cents for every child so registered . . .

And be it further enacted. That the person entitled to such service may, nevertheless, within one year after the birth of such child, elect to abandon his or her right to such service, by a notification of the same from under his or her hand, and lodged with the clerk of the town or city where the owner of the mother of any such child may reside; in which case every child abandoned as aforesaid shall be considered as paupers of the respective town or city where the proprietor or owner of the mother of such child may reside at the time of its birth; and liable to be bound out by the overseers of the poor on the same terms and conditions that the children of paupers were subject to before the passing of this act.

And be it further enacted. That every child abandoned as aforesaid shall be supported and maintained till bound out by the overseers of the poor as aforesaid, at the expence of this state: Provided however. That the said support does not exceed three dollars and fifty cents per month for each child; and the comptroller is hereby authorized and directed to draw his warrant on the treasurer of this state for the amount of such account, not exceeding the allowance above prescribed. . . . And provided also, That the person so abandoning as aforesaid, shall, at his own expence, support and maintain every such child till it arrives at the age of one year, and every owner omitting to give notice in due form as aforesaid shall be answerable for the maintenance of every such child until the arrival of the respective periods of servitude specified in the first section of this act.

And be it further enacted. That it shall be lawful for the owner of any slave, immediately after the passing of this act, to manumit such slave by a certificate for that purpose under his hand and seal.

Source: "An Act for the Gradual Abolition of Slavery," passed March 29, 1799, in *Laws of the State of New York,*
22nd Session. http://www.rootsweb.ancestry.com/~nycayuga/land/towns/1799abolition.html

A Republic in Transition

1800–1819

Andrew Jackson's America

Andrew Jackson came of age with the new nation. Already fatherless by the age of one, he later lost "everything that was dear" to him—his mother, his two brothers, and his South Carolina home, too—while he "embarked in the struggle for our liberties" during the Revolution. Jackson's hatred of the British, as well as any form of aristocracy, was deep and enduring. By the age of 21, Jackson had tried out a few trades, settling on that of lawyer; bought his first slave; fought his first duel; and made his way to Tennessee, which had been opened up to settlement by the Americans' victory in the Revolution. In this region, a smart and aggressive young man like Jackson could succeed, but he would need land and slaves. Political connections helped individuals secure land, some of which they would then sell to settlers at a higher price, using the profits to buy slaves to grow cotton. Profits from cotton, in turn, would go toward more land and slaves. Jackson quickly began moving up the social and economic ladder in this frontier region, as a lawyer, politician, land speculator, and slave-owning planter. He was aided by his marriage to a well-connected young woman, Rachel Donelson Robards, who, unfortunately, happened also to be married to another man.

Jackson rose quickly in Tennessee, in short order occupying the offices of representative, senator, and judge. He built, lost, and rebuilt a fortune as a land speculator and planter. (The frontier economy was unstable, and after his first reversal, Jackson developed a strong hatred of banks.) More than anything, though, he longed for a military career, both for the glory and for the opportunity to fight those who blocked his countrymen's occupation of fertile southern lands: the British (who had not yet vacated the West), the Spanish (who held Florida), and the Indian tribes who claimed the land. Jackson offered to round up a "thousand brave Tennesseeans" to help William Henry Harrison defeat Tecumseh: "That banditti ought to be swept from the face of the earth."

At the outbreak of the War of 1812, Jackson received a US commission to lead Tennessee volunteers to Louisiana. Then, in 1813, came orders to avenge a horrific attack by the Red Stick faction of the Creek Indians on a group of white settlers and their Creek allies at Fort Mims, near Mobile, Alabama. The influx of settlers onto Indian lands and the political contests among the Spanish, British, and Americans had destabilized the Indian tribes, encouraging the most violent elements in the tribes to fight more moderate members for supremacy. Even before receiving orders, Jackson rallied his volunteers. "Your frontier is threatened with invasion by the savage foe! Already do they advance towards your frontier with their scalping knifes unsheathed, to butcher your wives, your children, and your helpless babes."

Jackson's forces defeated the Red Sticks in a series of battles known as the Creek War. More Indian combatants died in the final battle at Horseshoe Bend than in any other American-Indian battle in US history. To assure an accurate body count, the Tennessee soldiers cut off the tips of the dead Indians' noses—557 of them. With the victory in the Creek War, Jackson secured his reputation, an appointment in the regular US army, and a treaty that ceded 23 million acres to the United States. It covered not only land that had been occupied by the rebellious Red Sticks but also land occupied by the more moderate Creeks, including those who had actually fought *with* Jackson against their tribesmen.

Further triumphs—and controversy—lay ahead. General Jackson and his troops defeated the British in New Orleans in 1815, at the end of the War of 1812. He then assumed command of the US army in the southern territory to defend against Indians and the Spanish. Jackson secured tens of millions more acres by treaties. He also moved against the Spanish and the Seminoles in Florida, perhaps exceeding his orders; secured Florida for the United States; and executed two British agents in the process. Jackson's aggressive measures gained him powerful critics in Washington but made him a hero to other Americans. What cannot be denied is his role in the expansion of the United States and the southern slave-based economy.

Jackson's advance helped people like him: poor whites looking for opportunity. And the most important factors for advancement in the South remained land and slaves. In this way, opportunity for whites came directly at the expense of Native Americans and enslaved African Americans.

A Politics of Transition

In his inaugural address in 1801, Jefferson strove to put the partisan bitterness of the previous decade behind American politics. He asked Americans to come together "in common efforts for the common good" and assured Federalists that he was committed to the rights of the minority. "Let us, then, fellow-citizens, unite with one heart and one mind," he encouraged. In some ways, Jefferson got his wish: over time many of the policies of the Democratic Republicans would so come to resemble the policies of the Federalists that it would seem as if the two parties had grown closer. In the daily battle of national politics, however, the Democratic Republicans and the Federalists seemed not to share any common ground at all.

A Contested Election, an Anxious Nation

As a fractured country approached its second contested presidential election, in 1800, it was not clear that the nation could survive. Virginia had just thwarted a revolt led by a 24-year-old slave named Gabriel. Recruited from taverns and religious meetings around Richmond, as many as 500 or 600 slaves were prepared to assemble outside of Richmond, take the city, and then spread through the countryside, freeing slaves. Inspired by the American, French, and Haitian revolutions, the conspirators hoped to rally "the poor white people" to their cause of liberty. Gabriel planned to spare those who were "friendly to liberty" and the "poor white women who had no slaves." The conspiracy was discovered, however, and 27 African Americans, including Gabriel, were executed. According to white witnesses, all went to their deaths with "a sense of their rights and a contempt of danger." It was a determination, Congressman John Randolph later cautioned, "which, if it becomes general, must deluge the Southern country in blood."

STRUGGLES FOR DEMOCRACY

The Gabriel Revolt

On the evening of August 30, 1800, a torrential rain fell on the city of Richmond, Virginia. Despite the weather, an enslaved man named Gabriel and a number of his companions met to launch a long-planned rebellion, but they agreed the cause was presently hopeless. They postponed the uprising and promised each other to try to get the word out to their fellow slaves. They had to reconstitute the movement quickly, as it was only a matter of time before the plot was discovered. On an agreed-upon date they would set fire to the dockyards and warehouses, and while the white population was distracted, they would rouse the black population to fight for freedom. It was, however, already too late. Someone had given them away. In the ensuing days, some slaves were taken in for questioning and were probably tortured. The authorities had a list of people they wanted to arrest, including Gabriel, who had escaped. Eventually, on September 24, he was captured. By then, the trials of his fellow slaves were already under way. He and over two dozen others were sentenced to death.

Gabriel was born in 1776, as the Declaration of Independence was being read aloud throughout the thirteen colonies. He was the youngest of three sons born to an enslaved couple living on a tobacco plantation in Henrico county. All three children were given Biblical names; Gabriel was named for the angel who visited Mary to tell her she would bear the baby Jesus. Gabriel was exactly the same age as the master's son and almost certainly played with him when they were children. Both boys grew up hearing about the course of the fight for freedom from Britain.

By the 1790s, Gabriel, who was tall and strong, had become a blacksmith and lived at least part of each month in the city of Richmond, where he was hired out to others. He kept some of the money he earned. When he wasn't working, he socialized with both free and enslaved folk. The biggest news of the day was the drama of the Revolution of Saint-Domingue (today's Haiti). A former slave named Toussaint L'Ouverture was leading a successful revolution against the master class. Some of the whites who fled and the black servants and slaves they brought with them landed in Richmond, carrying their tales. Gabriel was intelligent and able to read. He would have been aware that the situation in Saint-Domingue was different from the one in Virginia, for on the island, the black population outnumbered the white, and the French government could not come to the colonists' aid, for they were engulfed in their own revolution. But in Richmond, Gabriel lived in a world in which the black population outmatched the white, albeit by a slim margin, and on the countryside plantations, blacks more dramatically outnumbered whites. He also knew that the election of 1800 was bitterly contested. There was so much rancor between the Federalists and the Republicans that many people spoke of the danger of civil war. Gabriel reasoned that this was the slaves' moment to demand their freedom.

Given that the memory of the American Revolution was still so recent, and the French and Haitian Revolutions still ongoing, many people, even whites, could not help but recognize Gabriel's motivation. Two years later, Thomas Jefferson wrote in a private letter to a friend, "[Slave rebels] are not felons, or common malefactors, but persons guilty of what the safety of society, under actual circumstances, obliges us to treat as a crime, but which their feelings may represent in a far different shape."

Still, few whites were ready to remedy the gaping hole in American logic. Gabriel stood in the tumbril with his hands bound behind his back and was taken to the gallows. The time of freedom for the enslaved had not yet come after all.

Would bloodshed among whites follow? Deeply unpopular, John Adams nonetheless ran for a second term. Thomas Jefferson came out of retirement to oppose him. Each side predicted disaster if the opposition won. The election's uncertain outcome only compounded the sense of danger. The Constitution required the presidency to go to the man with the highest number of electoral votes, but both Jefferson and his running mate, Aaron Burr, received 73 votes. The choice was thrown into the House of Representatives, where Federalists threatened to block Jefferson by supporting Burr. Only after 34 ballots was Jefferson elected, once the Federalists had secured Jefferson's promise to keep Hamilton's financial system.

Democratic Republicans in Office

The peaceful transition of power in 1800 proved that the government could contain intense political conflict. Immediately on gaining office, Democratic Republicans closed the loophole in the Constitution that had led to the electoral stalemate. They quickly passed the legislation that became the Twelfth Amendment (1804), providing for party tickets in national elections. The Democratic Republicans also attempted to reduce the Federalist presence on the Supreme Court by impeaching Associate Supreme Court Justice Samuel Chase. Chase was notorious for his open partisanship during the Sedition Act prosecutions, but it was unclear whether his behavior met the constitutional standard of "Treason, Bribery, and high Crimes and Misdemeanors." In the final vote, Chase was acquitted, and the Supreme Court remained Federalist, five to one. Jefferson's desire for a Democratic Republican Court had to wait.

Before leaving office, the Federalists had tried to pack the courts with Federalists. The Judiciary Act of 1801, passed by the lame-duck Federalist Congress, increased the number of federal judgeships. Adams promptly appointed—and Congress confirmed—loyal Federalists. He also issued commissions for 41 justices of the peace, but they had not yet been acted on when he left office, and Jefferson ordered their appointments withheld. One of those "midnight" appointees, William Marbury, went directly to the Supreme Court, asking it for a "writ of mandamus," a court order compelling the executive to issue the commission. In a landmark decision, Chief Justice John Marshall, speaking for the Federalist-dominated Court, refused—but in a ruling that actually enhanced the Court's power. The provision in the Judiciary Act of 1789 that gave the Supreme Court the power to issue writs of mandamus was unconstitutional. The Constitution had set out the powers of the Supreme Court, and no act of legislation could change them. Marbury was out of luck, but the principle of judicial review (itself nowhere mentioned in the

Constitution) had been established. Henceforth, the Supreme Court would decide whether acts of legislation were constitutional or not. Jefferson had won the battle but lost a very big constitutional war.

Jefferson also set out to reduce the size of the federal government. Working with Secretary of the Treasury Albert Gallatin, he slashed the army budget by half and the navy budget by more than two-thirds. He also supported congressional efforts to reduce the $80 million national debt and to repeal internal taxes, including the hated one on whiskey. By 1807 the national debt had been cut in half.

These efforts at thrift were soon derailed by the politics of overseas commerce. The monarchs of the North African nations of Tunis, Algeria, Morocco, and Tripoli had long sought to dominate shipping on the Mediterranean, seizing the ships and enslaving the crews of those nations that refused to pay tribute. In 1794 Congress appropriated a million dollars to ransom captives and another million to build a navy to protect American shipping. By the end of the decade, tribute and ransoms absorbed 20 percent of the US budget. The conflict was about trade and money, not religion. The 1796 Treaty of Tripoli reassured the Arab nations that "the Government of the United States of America is not, in any sense, founded on the Christian religion" and "has in itself no character of enmity against the laws, religion, or tranquility, of Mussulmen [Muslims]."

Jefferson had long opposed paying tribute. When he became president, he was still convinced that it would be "more economical and more honorable" to go to war than continue paying tribute. He asked Congress for an appropriation for warships and gunboats "to protect our commerce and chastise their insolence—by sinking, burning or destroying their ships and vessels wherever you shall find them."

Results were mixed. Democratic Republicans managed to avoid new internal taxes, and they cut the national debt substantially. They were not, however, able to dismantle Hamilton's economic system, which provided the revenue to finance the country's defense. America's military intervention in the Mediterranean was not particularly successful. The United States signed a second treaty with Tripoli in 1805—and paid $60,000 to ransom prisoners. Payments to the other North African states continued until 1815.

The Louisiana Purchase

Many citizens, including Jefferson himself, had long presumed that white Americans would eventually settle west of the Mississippi River, but Pinckney's Treaty of 1795 (which improved American access to the Mississippi) had removed any need for immediate action.

Napoleon Bonaparte changed all that. By the turn of the century, American-French relations had chilled. Ambitious to establish his own empire in the Americas and determined to prevent further United States expansion, in 1800 Napoleon acquired Louisiana from Spain. Jefferson worried that France would eventually send troops to occupy New Orleans. Hoping to thwart Napoleon, Jefferson secretly sent help to the rebels in Saint-Domingue, pushed Native Americans across the Mississippi, and raised an army. He then dispatched Robert Livingston and James Monroe to France to purchase New Orleans and West Florida, too.

By then, Napoleon had lost 30,000 troops in a failed effort to put down the rebellion in Saint-Domingue. Defeated by the island's former slaves and by infectious disease, Napoleon was ready to unload his American territory. He stunned the American agents by offering to sell not only New Orleans but also the entire Louisiana Territory—883,000 square miles. (The Americans claimed that the purchase included West Florida, but Spain denied selling the territory to France. This issue was not resolved until 1819; see Chapter 10.) On April 12, 1803, the deal was struck. The United States purchased the entire Louisiana Territory for $15 million, or roughly 3.5 cents an acre.

Selling the deal to Congress was another matter. Many Democratic Republicans, including Jefferson himself, questioned whether the territory could be acquired and made part of the United States without a constitutional amendment. Federalists worried about whether the United States could govern so vast a territory or make citizens out of its multiracial, largely foreign populace. Reversing the position they had held when the Federalists were in power, Jeffersonians decided that the "necessary and proper" and "general welfare" clauses of the Constitution provided adequate authority. Using the precedent of the Northwest Ordinance (see Chapter 7), Congress set out a path to statehood, granted citizenship to French and Spanish inhabitants of the territory, and ignored the status of Indians living there. Congress also established a government for Louisiana, which soon passed laws to make Louisiana's practices more American: a Black Code defined slaves as property and instructed free people of color never "to conceive of themselves as equal to whites."

Congress also banned the foreign slave trade in Louisiana, fearing that slaves imported from Saint-Domingue would spread revolution. Louisiana had long been a cauldron of slave unrest. This was probably buttressed by events in revolutionary France and Saint-Domingue and by the arrival in New Orleans in 1810 and 1811 of perhaps 10,000 refugees from the revolution in Saint-Domingue—whites, free people of color, and slaves. Some of them joined the 1811 uprising on the German Coast of the Mississippi led by a Louisiana-born slave of mixed racial background, Charles Deslondes. As many as 300 well-organized slaves marched on New Orleans, burning plantations, destroying crops, and gathering weapons on the way. West of the city, they were met by a planter militia and United States troops. Deslondes and 15 other slaves were captured, tried, and executed, their decapitated heads raised on pikes along the road as a warning to any other slaves thinking of rebellion.

Long before Louisiana belonged to the United States, Jefferson began to plan its exploration. Jefferson appointed his trusted secretary, Captain Meriwether Lewis, and another officer, William Clark, to lead the expedition. Lewis was an ambitious soldier with some experience in the Old Northwest. Clark, who had commanded troops on the Mississippi, was a skilled surveyor and mapmaker. Their mission was to follow the Missouri River, chart the territory as far as the Pacific, and scout opportunities for commerce with the Indians of the northern Missouri River, who traded chiefly with the British.

The expedition left St. Louis on May 14, 1804, on three boats containing 45 men and a dog, firearms, medicines, scientific instruments, tools, flour, and salt. The party traveled first up the Missouri River, closely observed by the Mandans, the Minnetarees, and the Hidatsas, who visited their camps and sent ahead stories of these curious people. In early November, the white men made their winter camp. When the expedition broke camp the following spring, a Shoshone woman, Sacagawea, her French-Canadian trapper husband, and their newly born child left with them. She became an invaluable guide and interpreter. Native women such as Sacagawea and Malinche often served as cultural mediators.

Some encounters with Native Americans were less friendly. Far more dangerous than the Indians, however, were waterfalls and rapids, freezing temperatures and paralyzing snows, accidents, diseases (especially dysentery), and dead-end trails. After a difficult portage across the Rocky Mountains in the fall of 1805, the expedition finally reached the Pacific Ocean on November 7, 1805.

Throughout their journey, Lewis and Clark had represented themselves as the envoys of a great nation with whom the Native Americans should now trade. But they also kept an eye out for future settlements. After their return, in 1806, parts of their journals and letters, including detailed maps and drawings, slowly found their way into print, advertising what Jefferson called America's new "empire for liberty."

Other Americans had other plans for the territory west of the Mississippi. In 1805, former vice president Aaron Burr, who had recently killed Alexander Hamilton in a duel, went to New Orleans, looking for a fresh start. He immediately fell in love with it, and saw, too—or so he later claimed—that the United States might extend its sovereignty to include some of Spanish Mexico, where settlers were unhappy with high taxes and little government attention. By 1806 Burr had raised a force of several thousand men. Convinced that Burr intended treason, and wanting to avoid trouble with Spain, Jefferson ordered his arrest. Burr was brought back to Richmond to stand trial before John Marshall, who happened to be presiding over the federal circuit. Marshall interpreted treason in the narrowest sense possible. "Conspiracy is not treason," he instructed the jury. Burr was acquitted, but he was also disgraced. The incident indicated the government's weakness, when a former vice president could raise his own army for his own purposes, whether treasonous or not.

Embargo

In the fall of 1804, Jefferson's popularity was soaring. Internal taxes had been abolished; the national debt was falling; the United States had (seemingly) stood up to international coercion; and, most amazingly, it had acquired a huge western empire. Jefferson won reelection handily, and the Democratic Republicans took control of both houses of Congress. Faced with the prospect of federal surpluses, Jefferson began to contemplate a future role for the federal government encouraging "the great objects of public education, roads, rivers, canals, and such other objects of public improvement as may be thought proper." But Jefferson's second term had barely begun when his attention was riveted to developments in Europe.

In his first inaugural address, Jefferson had counseled "peace, commerce, and honest friendship with all nations, entangling alliances with none." He remained committed to American neutrality, but by 1805 Napoleon's growing power in France and his expansionistic designs on Europe had complicated this policy. On the one hand, Jefferson knew he might need Napoleon's help to settle the unresolved question of West Florida, still claimed by Spain. On the other hand, France's increasing indifference toward American shipping rights raised the possibility that the United States might need Britain as an ally. Napoleon's victory over Austria in 1805 made France the undisputed master of western Europe. At the same time, English victories over the fleets of France and Spain had made England the undisputed master of the seas. The stalemate had dire consequences for American shipping.

Jefferson's hopes that Britain might respect the neutrality of American ships were dashed in 1805 when Britain again began seizing ships traveling between enemy ports, taking more than 200 American ships in that year alone. Then Napoleon declared a

A Philosophic Cock This 1804 cartoon caricatured Jefferson as a "philosophic cock" courting his slave Sally Hemings. Jefferson's Federalist opponents tried to tarnish his reputation by publicizing his relationship with his slave, but the voters re-elected Jefferson by a decisive margin.

blockade of England and also began confiscating American ships. In June 1807 the British ship *Leopard* stopped the American frigate *Chesapeake* as it left Norfolk, Virginia. The captain of the *Leopard* demanded the right to search the American ship, insisting that it had recruited British deserters for its crew. When he was denied, he fired on the ship, boarded it, and took four men prisoner, leaving the *Chesapeake* to limp home.

Jefferson immediately ordered all British ships out of American waters and demanded reparation for the *Chesapeake*. In secret sessions, Congress passed an act that permitted only those American ships with the president's express approval to sail into foreign ports and prohibiting foreign ships from the American export trade. In effect, the United States had embargoed itself.

It was the most disastrous policy of Jefferson's career. Because enforcement was impossible, wealthy merchants enjoyed the large profits of smuggling. At the same time, small merchants, sailors, and shopkeepers who depended on steady maritime trade were thrown into crisis, and farmers in the South and West had trouble finding overseas trading outlets. As the economy settled into depression in 1808, the remaining Federalists charged that the embargo was helping Napoleon. Adding to American frustration, Napoleon then slyly claimed the right to attack US ships in any continental port because, by Jefferson's own order, they could not be legal carriers.

The ironies of the embargo did not end there. As violations mounted, ever more repressive versions of the embargo were enacted. The final, fifth Embargo Act (signed January 9, 1809) swept away protections against self-incrimination and the right to due process and trampled on the right to trial by jury. By comparison, even the Alien and Sedition Acts looked tame.

As he himself acknowledged, the Embargo Acts represented the failure of Jefferson's agrarian political economy. His dream of a republic of farmers was dead, the victim of the principles of territorial expansion and free trade on which he had based it. Meeting

America's need for manufactured goods solely by "this exuberant commerce," as Jefferson admitted in 1809, "brings us into collision with other powers in every sea, and will force us into every war of the European powers. The converting of this great agricultural country into a . . . mere headquarters for carrying on the commerce of all nations, is too absurd."

The anguish caused by the Embargo Acts exposed long-simmering dissension within Democratic Republican ranks. The most serious rupture came after the Louisiana Purchase. Although Jefferson insisted that West Florida was a part of the Louisiana Purchase, Spain denied ever ceding it to France. Napoleon hedged, but his ministers let it be known that the right price might convince them to lobby the American cause with Spain. Jefferson asked Congress for the money. To Jefferson's most radical critics, this was the Louisiana Purchase all over again—the government exercising powers unauthorized by the Constitution. These critics, led by the Virginian John Randolph, took the name Tertium Quids (the "third something"), neither Federalists nor Democratic Republicans. By 1808, the Quids were threatening open rebellion. To avoid the risk of public brawling, in 1808 party loyalists met in a closed caucus to select Jefferson's successor. They chose James Madison. In the election, Madison captured 122 electoral votes to Federalist Charles C. Pinckney's 47. The Democratic Republicans again won both houses of Congress.

From 1801 until 1829, the federal government would remain under the control of a single party. By itself, that did not challenge Democratic Republican principles. Neither Madison nor Jefferson considered a two-party system necessary to American political life. Both, however, warned against the day when a small cadre of like-minded men would meet in secret to choose the nation's ruler. Democratic Republican ascendancy itself had now come to rest on just such a closed institution. Meanwhile, with American hopes for international prestige now a joke, and with commerce and agriculture in trouble, on March 1, 1809, Jefferson signed a bill repealing the Embargo Act. Three days later, Jefferson left the office he now described as a "splendid misery."

The War of 1812

Facing ruptures in his party serious enough to compel him to accept nomination by the kind of closed and antirepublican institution he himself had once condemned, James Madison took office on March 4, 1809. Madison had stood side by side with Thomas Jefferson on virtually every important political and ideological issue since the founding of the nation. Now he inherited his friend's presidential woes.

Madison and the War

In 1809, with Madison's approval, Congress replaced the embargo with the Non-Intercourse Act, reopening trade with all of Europe except England and France but authorizing the president to resume commerce with whichever of these countries dropped its restrictions and attacks on American shipping. The act set off a series of diplomatic feints by England and France, both pretending to change policies without making actual concessions.

France eventually won the game. In the summer of 1810, Napoleon's ministers officially told Madison that, as of November of that year, France would stop seizing

American ships if Britain would do likewise. Probably correctly, Britain did not believe France would follow through on this policy. But Madison accepted the French declarations, and he altered American Non-Intercourse Act policy to apply to Britain alone.

Still, war might have been averted. A quarter of a century of European wars and Napoleon's continental policy—which closed continental markets to English goods—had taken its toll on Britain's economy. Although far more powerful militarily than the United States, Britain would have been happy to avoid the cost of an additional war. On June 1, 1812, in light of continuing British attacks on American shipping, Madison requested that Congress declare war on Great Britain. He listed several other reasons, including that the British were "impressing" American seamen into service and instigating Indian attacks in the Northwest. On June 4, the House voted to pass a war bill. On June 18, the Senate concurred. Ironically, unaware of events in the United States, England announced that it was revoking its maritime policy against US ships.

The war vote in Congress went largely along party and regional lines. Proponents, led by Henry Clay of Kentucky and John C. Calhoun of South Carolina, mostly hailed from the West and South. Known as the War Hawks, they were fiercely nationalistic and expansionist young men who had come of age since the Revolution. They predicted an easy conquest of Canada—"a mere matter of marching," in Jefferson's words—where they fantasized the people would rise up against British rule. Farmers and planters in the West and South wanted to open up the seas, while western migrants were convinced that Creek and Shawnee resistance was the work of the British, with their forts still along the Great Lakes. New Englanders, however, were adamantly opposed. Shipping was just beginning to recover and their region's prosperity depended on trade with Britain. Even moderate Democratic Republicans were hesitant. They dreaded the cost of the war and doubted that the nation could gear up to take on such a formidable foe.

All of these tensions were reflected in the election of 1812. Maverick Democratic Republican De Witt Clinton rallied Federalist support and ran against Madison. He lost, with 89 electoral votes (to Madison's 128), but with a higher proportion than the Federalists had enjoyed since the election of 1800.

Doubts about America's war readiness were soon justified. An ill-planned attempt to invade Canada in the summer of 1812 failed. Two thousand American troops surrendered at Detroit, and two advances failed when state militiamen insisted they were not required to leave the country to fight. Commodore Oliver Hazard Perry's dramatic victory on Lake Erie, however, led to another attempt on Canada and a victory at the Battle of the Thames, where the Shawnee leader Tecumseh was killed. Demoralized by his death, the Britons' Indian allies withdrew from the war.

A comparable victory eluded Americans in the Atlantic. After initial successes, the tiny American navy was easily overwhelmed by superior British sea power. Americans turned to private schooners and sloops and by the war's end managed to capture more than 1,300 British vessels. Nevertheless, by 1813 the British navy had succeeded in blockading the American coast from the Chesapeake Bay to New Orleans; in the following year, the blockade extended to New England. The British fleet pummeled coastal cities and villages. On August 24, 1814, British troops invaded Washington, burned the Capitol, the White House, the Treasury Building, and the Naval Yard, and terrorized civilians. The entire cabinet, including President James Madison, had already evacuated.

While Washington smoldered, the British turned to Baltimore. Through the night of September 13, its ships fired on Fort McHenry, the island citadel guarding Baltimore's

A VIEW of the BOMBARDMENT of Fort McHenry, near Baltimore, by the British fleet taken from the Observatory under the Command of Admirals Cochrane & Cockburn, on the morning of the 13th Sepr 1814 which lasted 24 hours, & thrown from 1500 to 1800 shells in the Night attempted to land by forcing a passage up the ferry branch but were repulsed with great loss.

Fort McHenry Fort McHenry is best known for its role in the War of 1812, when it successfully defended Baltimore Harbor from an attack by the British navy in Chesapeake Bay. It was this bombardment that inspired Francis Scott Key to write "The Star-Spangled Banner."

harbor. Among the anguished observers was a Washington lawyer by the name of Francis Scott Key. Elated that the United States flag still flew over the fort at dawn, Key quickly scribbled the words that would in 1931 become the lyrics of the national anthem, "The Star-Spangled Banner."

In the Old Southwest, Andrew Jackson used the war to suppress Indian resistance to US settlement. In March 1814, he defeated the Red Stick faction of the Creeks at Horseshoe Bend, forcing them to sign a treaty ceding two-thirds of remaining Creek lands to the United States.

Federalist Response

For a time the war worked in favor of the Federalists. In 1812, they doubled their numbers in Congress. New Englanders actively impeded the war effort. Governors refused to call out their militias, and trade with the enemy was rampant. Then, in October 1814, emboldened Massachusetts Federalists called for a convention of the New England states "to lay the foundation for a radical reform in the National compact." They planned to meet on December 15 in Hartford, Connecticut.

The Federalists meeting in Hartford were divided. Extreme Federalists, arguing that the Union could not be saved, lobbied for a separate New England confederacy that could immediately seek an end to the war. More moderate voices prevailed, and in the end, the convention sought amendments to the Constitution. The Federalists demanded restrictions on the power of Congress to declare war, an end to the Three-Fifths Compromise allowing slaves to be counted for purposes of representation, exclusion of naturalized citizens from elective federal office, and restrictions on the admission of new states. They also sought to limit the number of terms a president could serve and the frequency with which the presidential candidate could be chosen from a given state.

Federalists misjudged their strength and mistimed their efforts. By 1814, a weary Britain was ready to end the war. Emerging as the dominant power in Europe, Britain had little incentive to offer Americans more than simple peace. Signed in Ghent, Belgium, on December 24, 1814, the treaty that ended the War of 1812 was silent on the issues of free trade and impressment that had triggered the war. The Treaty of Ghent also sidestepped boundary disputes between Canada and the United States. British negotiators did agree to remove British troops from the Old Northwest, in effect acknowledging the failure of Indian resistance to white settlement.

Only Andrew Jackson's victory at New Orleans saved Americans from outright humiliation in the war. After the victory at Horseshoe Bend, his troops moved on to New Orleans (see Map 9–1), where a British fleet prepared to take control of the mouth of the Mississippi River. Unaware that two weeks earlier, on January 8, 1815, a peace treaty had

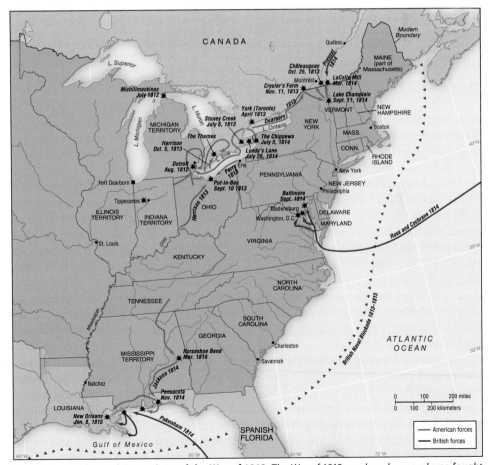

Map 9–1   Battles and Campaigns of the War of 1812 The War of 1812 was largely a naval war, fought along the Atlantic coast, in the Gulf of Mexico, and on the Great Lakes. Several land campaigns proved important, however: the British ground attack that ended in the looting and burning of the capital and Andrew Jackson's trek overland to New Orleans.

been signed in Ghent, 7,500 British regulars stormed Jackson's position. In 30 minutes the battle was over, and, miraculously, the Americans had won and Jackson had become a national hero.

In 1815, the chief political importance of Jackson's victory was the lift it gave to American nationalism and the light it cast on the Federalist Hartford Convention, still meeting in Connecticut. Threatening secession was one thing in a failing war, but quite another in a moment of national triumph. Suddenly, the proceedings at Hartford seemed downright traitorous.

An Economy in Transition

The end of the war ushered in a half century of fundamental economic change and growth. These changes, sometimes called "the market revolution," were reflected in every aspect of society, from religion and politics to family life and everyday values. Paternalistic employment arrangements (apprenticeship, indenturing) gave way to labor contracts and wage labor, and informal transactions to formal contracts. Self-sufficiency declined, while longer-distance market exchange increased. All of these changes were enhanced by improvements in technology and transportation as well as laws to encourage commerce.

International Markets

The economic transformation of the late eighteenth and early nineteenth centuries had many sources. One of the most significant was the gradual revival of overseas commerce at the end of the eighteenth century, much of this supported by conflicts in Europe. As Napoleon tried to spread the French Revolution (and his own power) throughout Europe, Europe remained at war—disrupting agriculture on the Continent and impeding European overseas trade. American shippers happily filled the gap.

This American shipping was of three kinds: export/import (exporting American wheat, rice, indigo, tobacco, and especially cotton to Europe and importing European manufactured goods to growing United States markets); reexport (carrying goods between two foreign ports with an intermediate stop in the United States, often to avoid French and English embargoes on each other's Caribbean colonies); and the simple carrying trade between two foreign ports (as US ships became the main carriers between warring England and France). In addition to farm products and manufactured goods, American ships also carried people: political refugees from France and from Ireland's ill-fated rebellion seeking safety in the new republic and—before 1808, when the slave trade was officially ended—captives from Africa sold into slavery in the Caribbean and the United States.

American shipping tonnage tripled between 1780 and 1810, reaching almost 11 million tons annually. The American share of the traffic between England and the United States grew from 50 percent in 1790 to 95 percent by 1800. The value of the reexport carrying trade also increased from about $500,000 a year in the 1790s to about $60 million a year in 1807. By the first decade of the nineteenth century, American ships were in the harbors of India, the East Indies, China, the Philippines, Japan, and Hawaii and on the Pacific coast of North America and the eastern coast of South America.

The return of overseas trade fed an already rampant inflation (the result of a shortage of gold and silver and a surfeit of local- and state-issued currencies of doubtful values). But it also created many jobs and helped alter the way Americans understood the terms of labor.

Merchants contracted for vessels (built at an astonishing rate), captains hired crews, and teamsters hurried goods to port. Some merchants also invested in port-city manufacturing. They gathered tailors, for example, into large central shops to turn out cheap clothing for sailors or to sell to planters for their slaves—even though the new merchant-manufacturers seldom recognized the traditional obligations of shop master to worker: food, housing, and training. Rather, they tended to hire unattached workers, apprentices, or jobless young men and put them to work at some single, specialized aspect of the craft. Some traditional shop masters became merchants, taking investments in ships to carry their goods to southern and Caribbean markets.

The growth of overseas shipping also spurred the development of business services in the early republic, particularly in port cities. The National Bank of the United States would be reauthorized in 1816. In the meantime, citizens formed insurance companies against the risks of loss in trading and local institutions for pooling capital for investment. By 1810 there were more than 100 banks in the nation. Many of these banks, corporations, and insurance companies operated under special state charters that allowed them to function as legal entities. As the businesses mushroomed, so did new jobs for clerks and lawyers.

In the countryside, farming families shifted from a relatively self-sufficient model of agriculture to more commercially oriented enterprises. Farmers were willing to travel longer distances to sell their goods. Whenever possible, they expanded the size of their holdings. In Delaware, for example, families used the profit from women's dairying activities to finance new land to grow wheat for sale in the cities or in Europe. Farmers, like merchants and shop masters, tried to hedge their bets by reducing their costs and liabilities. They ceased using indentured servants, to whom they would have owed year-round room and board and a freedom bonus at the end of their term, in favor of hiring seasonal wage workers, to whom they had no responsibilities in the off-season.

The most significant boost to American commercial agriculture arose from the late eighteenth-century mechanization of the English textile mills and the resulting increased demand for cotton. The colonies had not been an important source of raw cotton, because the only variety that grew well in most of North America was extremely laborious and time-consuming to clean. Spurred by the new English markets, in 1793 Eli Whitney invented a mechanism that increased the amount of this short-staple cotton that could be cleaned in a day from 1 pound to 50 pounds. Almost at a stroke, Whitney's gin made cotton a viable cash crop for much of the South.

The invention occurred at a critical moment. American indigo was losing market share to indigo from the East Indies. The tobacco trade was in decline. The market for rice was still strong, but rice cultivation required such large investments of land and labor as to exclude most farmers from production. Cotton gave the South a new commodity crop, and one that, unlike rice, could be grown on small farms without significant investment. Between 1790 and 1810, American cotton production increased from 3,000 bales to 178,000 bales a year. Increasingly after 1800, cotton was the largest single US export commodity, making the development of the nation, not merely that of the South, dependent on cotton and its labor system, slavery.

At the same time, the United States banned another kind of international trade: that of enslaved Africans. The Constitution forbade a national ban until 1808, but by 1806 every state except South Carolina, which imported almost 40,000 slaves between 1803 and 1807, had ended the trade. In early 1807 Congress banned the international slave trade as of January 1, 1808, but only after debating one troubling issue: What was to be done with the slaves confiscated from ships that defied the ban? Slavery's opponents thought the slaves should be freed, while the institution's defenders feared the introduction of more free blacks. A compromise left it up to the individual states to decide, which meant that Africans confiscated in the South could be sold into slavery there. Americans could agree that no more Africans should be brought into the United States, but not what to do with those who were already there. The ending of the international slave trade was a significant achievement, but the debate gave signs of trouble to come.

Crossing the Appalachian Mountains

After the Treaty of Greenville opened the Ohio River valley, the expansion of overseas markets fed a pent-up desire for new lands in Tennessee, Kentucky, and the soon-to-be state of Ohio (1803). The Land Ordinance of 1785 had provided for sales to private individuals who could afford sections of 640 acres or more at $1 an acre, but that was far beyond the reach of ordinary citizens. Sales were effectively restricted to speculators. Hoping to find a source of revenue, in 1796 Congress made matters worse by raising the price to $2 an acre.

Finally, in 1800, settlers got some relief. The Land Act of 1800 reduced the size of the minimum parcel from 640 acres to 320 acres. For the first time, buyers were permitted to spread their payments over time. In 1804, the minimum size was decreased to 160 acres and the price reduced from $2.00 to $1.64 an acre. Even though the cost of the land and the journey were still prohibitive for many Americans and easy credit sometimes led to unmanageable debt, lower prices per acre, lower minimums, and the promise of credit opened the West to tens of thousands of settlers.

The unprecedented migration set off by the Treaty of Ghent quickly swelled the population of the trans-Appalachian region. Kentucky grew from 220,955 in 1800 to 564,317 in 1820; Tennessee from 105,602 to 422,823; and Ohio from 42,159 to 581,434. Equally important, settlement led to the organization of new states. After Ohio in 1803, nine years passed before the next new state, Louisiana, entered in 1812. But then the admissions came rapid-fire. Indiana became a state in 1816, Mississippi in 1817, Illinois in 1818, and Alabama in 1819. By then both Missouri and Maine were also eager to join the Union.

The westward migration was a remarkably diverse parade. The earliest arrivals were usually hunters, fur traders, explorers, and surveyors. Wealthy speculators (European and American) sometimes traveled to the backcountry just long enough to buy up the best parcels of land, then scurried home to sell them to investors or migrants. Single men (displaced mechanics, sons of poor farmers, husbands sent ahead to purchase land) trekked along dusty roads, sometimes on horseback, often on foot. Andrew Jackson was one of their number. Families soon followed. Some traveled in wagons, packing food and seed, a few household items, and perhaps a gun, herding a cow or a few pigs alongside. But equally common was the sight of a "man, wife, and five children, with all their household goods thrown in a wheelbarrow . . . walking to Ohio."

The backcountry roiled in "anxiety and confusion," one observer noted, as newcomers raced to claim their share of territorial lands. There were cotton lands in the South and huge expanses for grain in the Old Northwest Territory—and favorable possibilities for transportation. Speculators were eager for huge returns on land investment, and migrants were eager to escape debt and taxes, oppressive jobs, and overworked soil.

Invention and Exploration

Western lands offered the potential for vastly enlarged markets within the United States. Settlers wanted to get their tobacco, wheat, corn, hemp, and cotton to coastal and European customers, and merchants and manufacturers were impatient to get their buttons, shoes, pots, pans, and farm tools to rural stores. Making that connection was still a backbreaking task, and the challenge of figuring out how to connect people to land and products to markets spurred some of the century's most important inventions.

The first improvements in transportation came from locally sponsored toll roads. Although states generally granted a special charter of incorporation for such projects, most of the capital came from local investors expecting to benefit from tolls. New York communities increased their road mileage from 1,000 miles in 1810 to more than 4,000 miles in 1820. To bolster the trade from cities such as Cincinnati, Pennsylvania extended an older highway that ran from Philadelphia to Pittsburgh. But the toll roads proved a poor investment. Only one (a short turnpike in Connecticut) paid profits, whereas many made no money at all.

The most important effect of road building in the post–War of 1812 era was the spur it gave to bridge building. The new bridges (such as one constructed over the Hudson River at Newburgh, New York) dramatically improved the time and cost of transport. They were heavily used and usually turned a good profit.

But it was the application of the steam engine to transportation that made the most dramatic difference. By the end of the War of 1812, the steam engine had begun to attract investors. There were some steam-powered overland rail carriers, but they remained fragmentary until the 1850s and conveyed only passengers, not cargo. The use of steam engines to power boats proved more successful. The technology came together in August 1807 when Robert Fulton and his patron Robert Livingston (Jefferson's minister to France during the Louisiana negotiations) announced the Hudson River trial run of the *North River Steamboat of Clermont*, a 140-foot-long vessel with two steam-driven paddle wheels. Fulton wryly described the trip, 150 miles from New York City to Albany, as "rather more favorable than I had calculated." "I ran it up in thirty-two hours, and down in thirty," he boasted.

Although he had not invented the steamboat, Fulton had demonstrated its practical value for transporting people and goods. By 1817 steamboats were common in the coastal waters of the East and across the Great Lakes, but their most telling impact occurred on the western rivers: the Ohio, the Wabash, the Monongahela, the Cumberland, and especially the Mississippi. In 1809 Livingston and Fulton hired Nicholas Roosevelt to survey the river waters from Pittsburgh to New Orleans, and in 1811 they sent the steamboat *New Orleans* downriver from Pittsburgh. After carrying troops and supplies on the river during the War of 1812, in 1815 steamboats began regular private routes upriver on the Mississippi.

The steamboat powered the market development of the Mississippi River valley. Able to travel upstream as well as down, it knit northern and southern regions together in an integrated economic system, with eastern manufactured goods and passengers

Fulton and Livingston's *North River Steamboat of Clermont* This image shows the steamboat as it approaches Albany, New York, two days after departing New York on August 17, 1807.

flowing upriver into the Ohio River valley and northern grain, livestock, and manufactured goods flowing to downstream markets and out through the Gulf of Mexico, joined in Kentucky, Tennessee, and Mississippi by a swelling cargo of cotton. In 1811 the Mississippi River valley produced some 5 million pounds of cotton. Within two decades it produced 40 times that much, virtually all of it carried downstream to market on steamboats. In 1817 the overland route from Cincinnati to Philadelphia or New York took nearly two months. Freight sent downriver from Cincinnati through New Orleans on steamboats and then by packet boat to Philadelphia took about half the time.

The steamboat soon became a conspicuous and controversial symbol of American economic promise. Not only were steamboats fast and exciting, but they were also relatively inexpensive to own and operate, within the reach of small investors eager to have a chance at making their fortunes. Citing the importance of orderly and reliable service, however, state lawmakers often encouraged large enterprises, awarding monopoly rights to specific prime routes. In 1798, Robert Livingston had gained exclusive rights for 20 years over the waters of the state of New York by vessels propelled by steam, a monopoly he revived and expanded to include Robert Fulton in 1803. Fulton and Livingston failed to obtain sole rights to the Mississippi, but in 1811 they succeeded temporarily in gaining a monopoly on steamboat transportation at the mouth of the river. Their success provoked a storm of protest from competitors, who saw government favoring wealth at the expense of the small entrepreneur. In 1819 the monopoly was withdrawn, but many small operators remained convinced of the state's favoritism toward the wealthy. In fact, few got rich running steamboats on the Mississippi. The twists and hidden snags of the shallow river saw to that. Only in the East, where rivers were deeper and where steamboats became fashionable transportation for wealthy travelers, did investors realize large profits.

Even steamboats were limited by the existing waterways. Since the turn of the century, investors and inventors had sought to enlarge those water routes by linking them artificially with canals, but the early history of canals did not portend great success. By the end of the War of 1812, only about 100 miles of canals existed in the United States (the longest ran 27 miles between the Merrimack River and Boston Harbor). None earned much money.

Thus, when at the end of the war New York City mayor De Witt Clinton proposed building a canal to connect Albany and Buffalo (see Map 9–2), he was thought to have taken leave of his senses. The canal would run 364 miles, making it the longest canal in

Map 9–2   The Development of Regions and of Roads and Canals By 1830 internal development had fostered a growing transportation infrastructure throughout the United States. That development was regional in character, however. In the southern states, where natural waterways ran from deep in the interior to the coast, citizens saw little need to build additional linkages. In the North, where natural waterways seldom ran directly to coastal outlets, investors were far more willing to spend money on internal development, especially canals.

the world. It would require an elaborate system of aqueducts and locks to negotiate a 571-foot rise in elevation and would cost $7 million, the largest investment of the sort in the nation's history. Clinton argued that the canal would "create the greatest inland trade ever witnessed" and would tie the "most fertile and extensive regions of America" to the city of New York, making that city "the granary of the world, the emporium of commerce, the seat of manufactures, the focus of great moneyed operation." In 1817 he convinced the state legislature not only to authorize the project but also to pay for it entirely in state funds, a gamble that amounted to a $5-per-capita levy for the entire population of New York.

Begun on July 4, 1817, the Erie Canal was completed in 1823 and officially opened two years later. At 10:30 on the morning of Wednesday, November 2, 1825, the first boats cleared the final locks and made their way into the Albany basin. Bells pealed, bands played, a huge crowd cheered, and 24 cannons fired successively in a national salute.

Clinton's gamble paid off spectacularly. Passenger boats and transport barges produced revenues high enough for the state to pay for later stages of construction with the profits of early ones. Transportation costs from Buffalo to New York City fell from $100 a ton to about $10 a ton when the canal opened and dropped even lower later on. The Erie Canal set off an explosion of canal building that lasted up to the Civil War, but few later canals duplicated its success.

Early Industrial Society in New England

New Englanders had been experimenting with the idea of water-powered textile mills since the 1780s, when prominent Massachusetts merchants tried to convince the state legislature to support the creation of textile machinery in the United States. In 1790, émigré mechanic Samuel Slater had replicated the English water-powered carding and spinning machines in his mill in Pawtucket, Rhode Island. But Slater lacked the power loom necessary to turn yarn into finished cloth. It took Eli Whitney's invention of the cotton gin in 1793, some industrial sabotage, and the devastating trade losses during the embargo and the War of 1812 to finally propel Americans to devise a power loom and invest seriously in a domestic textile industry. Boston merchant Francis Cabot Lowell pioneered the shift.

A graduate of Harvard with a knack for machine design, Lowell traveled to England to see the loom for himself and surreptitiously to memorize its plan. Back home, working with mechanic Paul Moody, he duplicated the English model in 1814. With a special charter from the Massachusetts legislature, Lowell and his Boston associates (organized as the Boston Manufacturing Company) opened the United States' first fully mechanized textile mill in Waltham, Massachusetts. Within three years the mill had expanded and was paying a whopping 20 percent dividend.

Lowell died in 1817, but under Nathan Appleton's leadership the company (now the Merrimack Manufacturing Corporation) raised more than $8 million to finance a second group of mills in East Chelmsford, Massachusetts. The new mills turned out their first finished cloth in 1823. A sleepy rural village of 200 in 1820, by 1826 East Chelmsford had grown to 2,600 and had incorporated as the city of Lowell, America's first industrial town. The mills relied entirely on the South for their raw cotton. Northern domestic purchase of raw southern cotton grew from 8 million pounds in 1800 to 31.5 million by the end of the war in 1815.

The Waltham system, as Lowell's approach was called, differed from earlier American manufacturing enterprises in several ways. The Waltham mill was the largest industrial undertaking attempted in America up to that time. It housed the full production process, from fiber to finished cloth. It relied on a new organization plan in which a professional managerial rank (separate from the owners) oversaw daily operations. Finally, to cultivate an appearance of benevolence (in contrast to the plight of workers in the English mills), the Waltham system required that employees live on-site in subsidized and supervised housing.

For their workforce, the owners turned to the young rural women from Vermont, New Hampshire, and western Massachusetts. Textiles were traditionally women's work, and power-driven textile machinery was not necessarily identified with either sex. Moreover, female workers were cheaper than men, the result of their long exclusion from customary craft protections and their loss of the right to make contracts if they were married.

In the early years, parents and daughters both saw benefits in mill work for unmarried young women. Presumably, a daughter would leave her family anyway when she married. Having her work in the mills before marriage reduced the number of mouths to be fed at home. The residential system allayed fears that a young woman was compromising her respectability. Matrons supervised company-owned boardinghouses, where operatives lived together in single-sex settings. Strict rules of behavior guided leisure time, and factory bells regulated the workday.

The success of the mills underscored the paradoxes of American slavery and American freedom in the early nineteenth century. In the early years, at least, the women operatives enjoyed a financial and social independence virtually unknown under the parental roof. They lived together under the guidance of a female head of household. They returned home for vacation largely at their own discretion. Many of the young women kept all or most of their pay, enjoying (perhaps for the only time in their lives) a separate disposable income. They developed pride in their work and in their community and began to see themselves as part of a long Yankee history of hard work and independence. All of this was made possible by the fact of slavery in the American South.

The final irony of this contradiction would play out only in the later years of the mills, after employers had cut pay and intensified production. In 1834 and again in 1836, the operatives turned out in defiant strikes—condemning the mill owners for reducing them, "the daughters of freemen," to the condition of slaves.

The Rule of Law and Lawyers

Americans had long emphasized the importance of the written law to the preservation of the republic, but the law became important in new ways in the growing commercial economy. Overseas trade, internal expansion, the buying and selling of land, new inventions—all required complex legal documents and lawyers to draw them up and execute them. The revival of commerce and the work of government converged to make the legal profession attractive. By 1815, lawyers made up about half the members of Congress.

The growing importance of lawyers reflected the growing importance of courts and of the judiciary. Again and again, judicial interpretation reinforced and set the course for market development. When tradition clashed with economic development, judges tended to side with the entrepreneurs. For example, as businesses experimented with the use of water power in manufacturing, they sought to erect dams and millraces that altered the flow of streams. English common law protected the use of waterways undisturbed by alterations upstream. But in 1805, in *Palmer v. Mulligan*, a New York court ruled in favor of the right of development, against customary common-law rights.

On the federal level, the power of the Democratic Republicans (and, later, the Jacksonian Democrats) in the executive and legislative branches was countered by the power of Federalist John Marshall, who was chief justice of the Supreme Court from 1801 until 1835. Between 1805 and 1824, the Marshall Court issued three decisions that brought the Constitution to bear in support of the new market-based economy.

The first, *Dartmouth v. Woodward* (1819), explicitly reinforced the rights of contract. The case concerned an attempt by the New Hampshire legislature to alter the original charter of Dartmouth College, given to the college by King George III in 1769 when the nation was still a set of British colonies. New Hampshire argued that the original charter was not binding on the current state government, but Dartmouth insisted that the charter was in fact a contract, protected under Article VI of the US Constitution, which protected debts and engagements entered into before the Revolution. Acting to ensure the stability of contract in the broadest sense, the Court ruled in Dartmouth's favor.

The case of *McCulloch v. Maryland*, also decided in 1819, upheld the constitutionality of the Second Bank of the United States. The creation of the bank had been one of the successes of the new Democratic Republicans, who had managed to overpower their party's objections to national banks by attracting Federalist votes. The Second Bank had created a number of branches, one of which was in Baltimore. Viewing the presence of the bank within its borders as a threat to its sovereignty, Maryland attempted to assert its authority over the Baltimore branch by taxing it. James W. McCulloch, chief clerk of the branch, refused. Maryland appealed to the Supreme Court, arguing that because the federal government was a creation of the states, its branch institutions could be taxed in the states in which they existed. Marshall's Court unanimously rejected this position. The federal government was superior to the states, the Supreme Court concluded. Because "the power to tax involves the power to destroy," the states could not tax the creations of the federal government, whatever their location. The ruling was a victory for federal power and the Bank both.

Gibbons v. Ogden (1824), the last in Marshall's long line of landmark decisions, concerned a disputed ferryboat monopoly in New York. Having exclusive rights to operate steamboats in the state's waters, Robert Fulton and Robert Livingston had, in turn, "contracted" a part of this right out to Aaron Ogden, giving him a ferry monopoly across the Hudson River from New York to New Jersey. At the same time, however, Thomas Gibbons had obtained a federal license to operate a boat line along a coastal route that came into conflict with Ogden's line. Who controlled these waters and therefore had the right to grant licenses, New York or the federal government? Consistent with its national view of power and development, the Marshall Court found in favor of the federal power. The decision noted that the Constitution had given to Congress (Article I, Section 8) the right "to regulate Commerce with foreign nations, and among the several States." Because the waterways under dispute did not fall clearly within the boundaries of a single state, state power was in this case in conflict with federal power. In such cases, the Marshall Court found, federal power took precedence.

Ways of Life in Flux

Americans at the turn of the century played active roles in the political, social, and economic changes affecting their communities. Those changes grew out of choices some Americans made—to invest in an overseas venture, for example, or to buy new lands in the West to grow wheat or cotton. Their choices affected their own lives and the lives of others and slowly added up to a far more market-driven way of life.

Indian Resistance to American Expansion

Although he expressed benevolence toward Indians, President Jefferson believed that they must give way to American settlement. Not only did the territories represent the supply of land necessary to nurture republican virtues and stabilize republican institutions, but they also provided a western buffer against Britain, France, and Spain. Preferring peaceful American expansion westward, Jefferson fostered a growing Indian dependency on American agents that would, he hoped, lead them to sell off their lands.

Nevertheless, by the turn of the century, that westward migration was devastating native life and culture. As settlers occupied new lands, Indians lost their villages and fields. Thrown back on the fur trade, they overhunted dwindling grounds. By 1800 many of the pelts and skins brought to traders in the Northwest Territory had actually been hunted west of the Mississippi River, and the deer were all but gone in the Southeast. Protestant missionaries urged the Indians to adopt European American religious and social practices, including male-headed households and private ownership of property. Unscrupulous agents bullied Indian nations into signing away their land. When the Indians resisted, the agents made deals with leaders they knew to be of doubtful legitimacy, promising bounties and annuities for territory.

Native Americans resisted these assaults on their autonomy. Seneca communities accepted some missionary aid but refused to abandon their holdings, gender division of labor, and matrilineal households. The southern nations declined Jefferson's promise of new lands in the West and focused on constructing internal institutions Americans might recognize as "civilized." For example, the Cherokees adopted a series of laws that functioned as a constitution, established a congress, and executed individual land titles. Meanwhile, resistance to European American culture also took the form of a broad movement for spiritual revitalization. Ganioda'yo (Handsome Lake), who rose to influence among the Senecas after 1799, preached revival through a synthesis of traditional beliefs and Christianity, but for other groups revitalization meant cleansing themselves of European American practices. Cherokees revived the Green Corn Ceremony, celebrating personal bonds and repudiating material wealth.

This crisis of survival virtually ensured armed confrontation. As early as 1807, William Henry Harrison, governor of the Indiana Territory, heard rumors of "a general combination of the Indians for a war against the United States." Two Shawnee leaders, Tecumseh and his half-brother, Tenskwatawa (known as the Prophet), coalesced the diffuse anger into organized resistance. Tecumseh's struggles against whites in the Old Northwest and in the South helped him build a pan-Indian alliance. After 1805 Tenskwatawa became the leader of a movement that rejected white culture. About 1808, Tecumseh and Tenskwatawa founded a village in present-day Indiana on the banks of the Tippecanoe River. The Prophet remained there while Tecumseh traveled widely, encouraging organized resistance to white settlement.

By 1811, Tecumseh's success alarmed Harrison. That fall, Harrison marched an army toward Tecumseh's village on the Tippecanoe River. Although cautioned by Tecumseh not to be drawn into battle in his absence, on November 7, 1811, the Prophet engaged Harrison's troops and was defeated. The Prophet was discredited, but when war broke out between Britain and the United States the following year, Tecumseh was still able to amass a huge force for the British. He played a decisive role in the British victory at Detroit but was killed in the Battle of the Thames in 1813. Tecumseh's death marked the end of organized Indian resistance east of the Mississippi.

Winners and Losers in the New Economy

For many Americans, the more cash- and contract-based society at the turn of the century offered both new freedom and new wealth. Large merchants who were able to absorb

Tenskwatawa (known as the Prophet) The Shawnee Prophet was about 60 in 1830 when George Catlin painted him holding his "medicine fire" in one hand and sacred beads in the other. Catlin said he "has been a very shrewd and influential man, but circumstances have destroyed him . . . and he now lives respected, but silent and melancholy in his tribe."

the risks of war might realize enormous profits in transatlantic shipping. Owners of shipbuilding and related enterprises benefited from the prolonged boom in American shipping. Farmers able to expand their holdings and take advantage of trade networks thrived in the increasingly commercial environment.

The blessings of these new liberties were mixed. New, unskilled workers took jobs away from journeymen, but they were as quickly fired as hired. Wages fell. Near poverty, journeymen in Philadelphia, New York, and Baltimore began to form mutual aid societies, helping each other and laying the foundations for trade associations. But when they tried to organize for higher wages, they discovered that in the eyes of the law, these assertions of liberty amounted to a conspiracy against the rights of trade. When Philadelphia journeyman shoemakers demanded a bill of higher wages in 1805–1806 (in the first strike in US history), they were arrested and required to pay stiff fines.

But craft masters paid, too. New opportunities in manufacturing lured entrepreneurs and merchants who organized bigger shops, hired cheap workers, and offered cutthroat competition. Initially, the traditional craft masters refused to associate with these new entrepreneurs. By the early 1800s, however, their solidarity eroded. Wanting to take advantage of economic opportunities or to cut costs, shop masters began to hire runaway servants with no questions asked or unskilled workers to whom they had fewer lasting obligations.

Americans described these changing relations of labor and society in the language of the Revolution. Elites fretted that the masses were unfit for republican self-government, whereas workers condemned the older structures of authority as repugnant to a free people. However, local conditions were also sources of new social instability. Apprentices ran away not to express allegiance to Jeffersonianism but to escape cruel masters or to seek higher wages. Masters did not hire untrained workers to affirm republican freedom but to protect profits by cutting costs.

Religion

These were years of ongoing religious upheaval, some of it evidence of a new freedom of belief and some of it expressing a sense of profound personal dislocation.

The new demands for personal liberty focused on religion, as well as work and family, as Americans increasingly objected to paying taxes to support state churches. Anglicanism had been disestablished in the South in the 1780s, replaced by the Protestant Episcopal Church. The Congregational Church was disestablished in New England in 1834, and new denominations began thriving in all regions.

Southerners were drawn especially to new evangelical Christian faiths, principally Methodism and various forms of Baptist practice. In contrast to the more staid and ritual-based Episcopal Church, these sects stressed the personal, emotional nature of religion and the ability of individuals to struggle actively for their own redemption. Methodists rejected what they deemed artificial differences among Christians, pronouncing "[o]ne condition, and only one" required for salvation: "a real desire." Their system of itinerant preaching (preachers traveled among congregations, rather than associating with a single church) enabled the clergy to reach out to the dispersed and the displaced. Emphasizing inner truth, a plain style, and congregational independence, evangelical denominations offered a relatively egalitarian vision of the community of believers that was especially attractive to the poor, to enslaved and free African Americans, and to white women. Some congregations questioned the morality of slaveholding itself.

Even before Congregationalism was fully disestablished, it was plagued by breakaway movements from within and by competition from the evangelical sects. The most important splinter groups were the Unitarian and Universalist movements, which held generally positive views of human nature, embraced universal salvation, and offered an alternative to strict Calvinism. Everywhere, the far greater threat to established religion came from the Methodists and Baptists, who found converts among country folks and city workers.

This widespread religious turmoil was expressed in a series of highly emotional revivals at the turn of the century, sometimes called the Second Great Awakening. These began in Virginia and western New England and spread quickly into newly settled areas of Kentucky and Tennessee. The most famous of these revivals occurred in August 1801, in the tiny rural community of Cane Ridge, Kentucky, where thousands of men, women, and children, black and white, free and enslaved, came to watch and experience mass conversions. Eventually, the awakening spread to all parts of the country and to virtually all faiths. Yet many members of older denominations were displeased that revivals were led by unschooled preachers and encouraged unconventional beliefs and extravagant emotionalism. In 1803 to 1805 these misgivings led to schism, as the "Old Light" members of the Kentucky Synod purged "New Light" revivalists. Where Congregationalists and Presbyterians saw confusion in the revivals, Methodists and Baptists saw converts. In the first years of the nineteenth century, the number of Baptist congregations grew from about 400 to about 2,700, and membership in Methodist churches more than doubled, from 87,000 to 196,000. Eager for new members, Methodists founded the national Sunday School Union and the first denominational publishing house in the United States.

AMERICAN LANDSCAPE

Religion in the Backcountry: Cane Ridge, Kentucky

Barton W. Stone was a Presbyterian minister, but one with a number of reservations about his church. In particular, Stone doubted the key Presbyterian doctrine of original sin, which directed that all humans were born sinful and were unable to act for their own salvation; salvation, orthodox Presbyterians believed, came completely through the grace of God. To Stone, as to a growing number of dissenting Presbyterian ministers, God had given humans a capacity to yearn toward salvation and required fervent belief and longing as a condition for grace. Religion without that longing seemed to Stone lifeless and cold.

Pastor of the Presbyterian Church of Cane Ridge, Kentucky, Stone worried especially about the deadness to God's grace in the people around him in the backcountry. The year was 1801, and many of Stone's congregants and neighbors were transplants from Virginia and Maryland busy settling new farms, slaves newly forced from their families in the East, and drifters fleeing family and community. Most had few church ties and, in Stone's view, little interest in religion.

But by 1801 something was stirring in the backcountry. Prayer meetings scattered throughout Kentucky were drawing thousands of participants: 4,000 at Concord, for example, and 6,000 at Lexington. Stone went to investigate one in Logan for himself—and was amazed at what he found: "Many, very many fell down . . . in an apparently breathless and motionless state," Stone recorded in his journal, their trances broken only "by a deep groan, or piercing shriek, or by a prayer for mercy most fervently uttered." Then they rose up "shouting deliverance . . . men, women and children declaring the wonderful works of God."

Back in Cane Ridge, Stone began organizing a sacramental Communion service to be held in August, sending out invitations by word of mouth across the region. Participants began to arrive on August 6. As one observer noted: "On the first Sabbath of August, was the Sacrament of Kainridge, the congregation of Mr. Stone.—This was the largest meeting of any that I have ever seen: It continued from Friday till Wednesday. About 12,000 persons, 125 waggons, 8 carriages, 900 communicants. . . ." The prayer meetings continued day after day and deep into the night. News of events at Cane Ridge spread "like fire in dry stubble driven by a strong wind." Soon, the roads were jammed "with wagons, carriages, horsemen, and footmen," as "between twenty and thirty thousand" people (women, men, and children, whites and blacks, Methodists, Baptists, Presbyterians, the churched and the unchurched, anguished sinners, and the merely curious) hastened to the scene. Cane Ridge was the climactic event of the western revivals of 1800–1801, but it fed waves of revivals that moved into upstate New York (later dubbed "the burned-over district," for the intensity of its meetings). In the first decades of the nineteenth century, religious enthusiasm flamed brightly in the republic. In one sense, there is no surprise in this. Religion had always played an important role in American history. But why this particular outpouring of fervor, and why just at the turn of the century? And why the Kentucky frontier?

Some of the answers lay in the broader rejection of old Calvinist orthodoxies and hierarchical religious styles. The revival ministers preached a theology of self-striving surely welcome to people gambling everything they owned on their ability to make a better life for themselves in the West. And they preached that message with a directness, intimacy, and spontaneous passion that could not have been in starker contrast to the intimidating formality of most Presbyterian and Congregational churches. Ultimately, the Baptists and Methodists were the chief beneficiaries of this shift. Although Stone was a Presbyterian, he was dismissed from the Kentucky Synod for his nonconformist beliefs shortly after Cane Ridge and went on to help found the nondenominational Christian Restoration movement, which had no formal creed.

Why these revivals caught fire on the Kentucky frontier can be answered by the circumstances of frontier life in 1800 and 1801. The new sects were more willing than the Presbyterians and Congregationalists to send itinerant ministers into the field, wherever people lived. Those preachers often found people newly dislocated from family and friends, excited about their new lives but also isolated and homesick. Christian churches had often supplied sites of solace and community for Americans.

The anxieties of the frontier extended beyond the loss of the familiar. These settlers were part of a torrent of expansion across the Appalachians, advancing into territories still claimed by indigenous people and facing constant resistance from Cherokees, Chickasaws, Shawnees, and others. For European Americans, Christianity had long been a boundary of distinction between themselves and Native Americans and a marker of superiority. And it served that purpose again as migrants grappled with the consequences to others of their new opportunities.

Federalists often viewed this religious upheaval as a sign of the deterioration of both politics and morality, but the linkages were seldom so simple. Neither Jefferson nor Madison, the founding lights of the Democratic Republican Party, embraced evangelical faiths. Moreover, far from signaling a drift toward irreligion, this contentious fragmentation of belief at the turn of the century had the effect of securing the language of religion, especially Protestant Christianity, as an idiom of both identity and exclusion in the new nation. Even as they fought over the correct form of Christian practice, many Americans formulated their visions of the ideal political community in the language of Protestant Christianity and suspected those who disagreed with them not only of bad politics but also of bad faith.

The Problem of Trust in a Changing Society

As old friends headed west for new lands, as young people slipped away from parents or masters, as newcomers swelled the port cities, many Americans began to wonder whom or what they could trust.

Particularly distressing to middling and wealthy Americans were signs that workers and children were forgetting their proper place. The customary discipline of the craft shop seemed to be crumbling. Apprentices demanded better treatment, refused drudgery work, or just ran away. In the larger port cities, unemployed young men gathered on the streets shouting obscenities, frightening children, hassling shopkeepers, and sometimes attacking strangers. Journeymen in Philadelphia and New York demanded better pay and threatened to take their skills elsewhere.

Household society seemed to be falling apart, too. Domestic workers told masters and mistresses that they should now be called "help" instead of "servants." Indentured workers balked at having their lives closely scrutinized. Even children seemed to have found a new "republican" determination to make their own decisions about whom to marry, where to live, and what work to pursue.

To their parents and masters and mistresses, it seemed that the youth and laboring classes were out of control. Indeed, in 1820, half the nation's population was under the age of 16 (compared with 24 percent under 18 in 2010). Parents threatened and cajoled. Masters offered rewards for runaway apprentices. Ministers warned against libertinism (especially young women's fashions, cut too daringly, they thought). Meanwhile, local authorities responded with laws intended to control apprentices and regulate public behavior.

For several reasons, these efforts were largely doomed. The Revolution and its aftermath had changed society. Young people coming of age at the turn of the century had been nurtured on the rhetoric of independence. The market revolution offered them numerous alternatives to older structures of authority. Why should a young person remain on the family farm when there were jobs in nearby towns? Why not just leave the controls of indentures or an apprenticeship? Why languish in Temple, Maine, when New York beckoned?

Rumor and deception thrived everywhere in this landscape. On the brink of war in 1812, one Charles Redheffer told the Philadelphia city government that he had invented

Time Line

▼**1800**
Thomas Jefferson elected
  president

▼**1801**
Judiciary Act of 1801
Cane Ridge (Kentucky) Revival

▼**1803**
Louisiana Purchase
Marbury v. Madison

▼**1804**
Jefferson reelected
Lewis and Clark begin
  exploration of Louisiana

▼**1805**
Palmer v. Mulligan (New York)

▼**1806**
Conspiracy trial of Philadelphia
  journeyman shoemakers

▼**1807**
First Embargo Act
Hudson River trial of Fulton's
  *North River Steamboat of
  Clermont*

▼**1808**
External slave trade becomes
  illegal
Madison elected president

▼**1809**
Non-Intercourse Act

a perpetual motion machine. When the city commissioners discovered that Redheffer was actually powering his machine through a hidden cranking device, rather than simply crying foul, they responded with a hoax of their own. They had a local engineer build a similar but even more cleverly deceptive machine. Redheffer fled Philadelphia for New York City, where he was exposed by Robert Fulton (who had his own interest in debunking the machine).

Meanwhile, the New England countryside was filled with treasure hunters who had heard countless rumors of long-buried riches. Some of these seekers were amateur scientists and historians. Some were charlatans, trying to make a quick buck off gullible visitors. Some were just the down-and-outers of New England's changing economy who still believed in miracles that might turn their fortunes around.

One of these was the treasure seeker Joseph Smith. Smith was born in 1805 to a family of poor farmers in Vermont and grew up in western New York surrounded by economic and religious uncertainty. Although the family moved constantly in a region bursting with development, economic security eluded the Smiths. Perhaps in search of some sense of constancy, Smith was drawn to the religious revivalism that scorched upstate New York, and he believed in direct spiritual revelation. Occasionally Smith and his father used what they claimed were supernatural powers to hire out as guides in what an observer described as "the money digging business." In 1819, however, Joseph Smith's powers of divination took a different turn: he experienced the first of a series of revelations in which he claimed that God had instructed him to found a new church that would teach the true lessons of Jesus Christ. In a second vision a few years later, an angel gave him the location of golden tablets, buried near his home, which described God's intentions for the "latter days" of creation, now approaching. In 1830 Smith published his translation of the ancient writings on the tablets as the Book of Mormon. He formally founded the church now known as the Church of Jesus Christ of Latter-day Saints (or the Mormon Church).

▼**1810**
American cotton production reaches 178,000 bales

▼**1811**
Tecumseh at peak of influence
Battle of Tippecanoe River

▼**1812**
War of 1812 begins
James Madison reelected

▼**1814**
Federalist Hartford Convention
Treaty of Ghent ends War of 1812

Fully steam-powered textile mills established in Waltham, Massachusetts

▼**1815**
Battle of New Orleans

▼**1817**
Work on Erie Canal begun
Steamboats common on Mississippi River

▼**1819**
Panic of 1819
Dartmouth v. Woodward
McCulloch v. Maryland

▼**1824**
Gibbons v. Ogden

▼**1825**
Erie Canal opened

The Panic of 1819

In 1819 Americans learned that the market revolution could produce dream-shattering plunges, as well as exhilarating rises. After he signed the bill chartering the Second Bank of the United States in 1816, James Madison appointed an old political ally, Captain William Jones, as its director. Jones was a poor choice, speculating in bank stock and willing to accept bribes to overlook reckless local practices. By the time he was replaced, bank stock was at an all-time low, and the state banks had glutted the economy with unsecured paper money.

Jones's successor, Langdon Cheves, moved quickly to cut the supply of paper money (too quickly, given that Great Britain was taking the same measures). Cheves began to call in loans and to redeem the bank's holdings of currency issued by the various state banks. Dangerously overextended, the state banks were forced to respond with their own programs of retrenchment. As credit dried up and the value of paper money plummeted, the nation was thrown into depression. Without credit or sufficient circulating money, commodity prices crashed throughout the Atlantic community. The market in cotton, basic to the growing American economy, fell by almost two-thirds. Their mortgages unpaid, farms and businesses failed. And tens of thousands of workers lost their jobs. For three long years, the economy stalled. Visitors to America warned potential immigrants not to come.

Because the branches of the Second Bank of the United States reached far beyond the East Coast, so did the distress of the panic. When the branch in Cincinnati, Ohio, suddenly cashed in the paper money it held from local banks, for example, Cincinnati's booming economy felt the blow, as local banks scurried to collect enough debts to make good on the face value of their paper. Similar shock waves rolled through Kentucky and Tennessee and into the lower South.

Cheves had saved the monetary system of the United States but did not make many friends for the Second Bank. State legislators, who saw the national bank (not runaway local speculation or wildcat state banks) as the villain, scrambled to reduce its power. Fourteen states passed laws preventing the bank from collecting its debts, Kentucky abolished imprisonment for debt, and six states levied heavy taxes on bank branches (a practice soon banned by the Supreme Court in *McCulloch v. Maryland*, discussed earlier). After opening 18 branches in 1817, the Second Bank opened no additional new branches until 1826.

Conclusion

In 1819, Andrew Jackson returned home physically exhausted. He had gone to Washington, where Congress was debating censuring him for his actions in the Seminole War. Henry Clay charged that Jackson's "inhumanity, and cruelty, and ambition" made him no better than the despots of Europe. Jackson's supporters replied, however, that "when at war with a nation which observes no rules . . . the attempt may be made of bringing them to the laws of humanity." Congress could not agree. Nor could the American people. Although crowds cheered Jackson in Baltimore, an important question lingered: After more than a half century of conflict, the United States was finally at peace with both Britain and France, and it had acquired a vast new territory, rapidly filling with an ever-expanding population. As Jackson regained his strength, he and his fellow Americans asked themselves once again what kind of nation they were to be.

Who, What

Review Questions

1. What were the primary challenges facing the Jefferson administration? How well did the administration handle those challenges?

2. What was the market revolution?

3. How did changes in religion help Americans adjust to their rapidly changing world?

Critical-Thinking Questions

1. The War of 1812 was hardly an American victory, yet at its conclusion, the United States was stronger than it had ever been. Why was this so?

2. What challenges did the addition of vast new territories create for the United States, and how did it address them? Why didn't it make colonies out of the new territories?

3. This period saw the development of both cotton plantations in the South and factories in the North. Though seemingly quite different, both were expressions of the market revolution. How so?

For further review materials and resource information, please visit www.oup.com/us/oakes

CHAPTER 9: A REPUBLIC IN TRANSITION, 1800–1819
Primary Sources

9.1 THOMAS JEFFERSON, FIRST INAUGURAL ADDRESS (1801)

The election of 1800 aroused great anxiety for both the Federalists, the party of the incumbent, John Adams, and the Republicans, the party of the challenger, Thomas Jefferson. Each party had feared the takeover of the government by force. The goal of Jefferson's inaugural address was reconciliation and a vigorous statement of his liberal principles, which he presented as if they were the simple truth, with which every American would naturally agree. In this memorable speech, he achieved his goal.

Friends & Fellow Citizens,
Called upon to undertake the duties of the first Executive office of our country, I avail myself of the presence of that portion of my fellow citizens which is here assembled to express my grateful thanks for the favor with which they have been pleased to look towards me, to declare a sincere consciousness that the task is above my talents, and that I approach it with those anxious and awful presentiments which the greatness of the charge, and the weakness of my powers so justly inspire. A rising nation, spread over a wide and fruitful land, traversing all the seas with the rich productions of their industry, engaged in commerce with nations who feel power and forget right, advancing rapidly to destinies beyond the reach of mortal eye; when I contemplate these transcendent objects, and see the honour, the happiness, and the hopes of this beloved country committed to the issue and the auspices of this day, I shrink from the contemplation & humble myself before the magnitude of the undertaking. . . .

During the contest of opinion through which we have past, the animation of discussions and of exertions has sometimes worn an aspect which might impose on strangers unused to think freely, and to speak and to write what they think; but this being now decided by the voice of the nation, announced according to the rules of the constitution all will of course arrange themselves under the will of the law, and unite in common efforts for the common good. All too will bear in mind this sacred principle, that though the will of the majority is in all cases to prevail, that will, to be rightful, must be reasonable; that the minority possess their equal rights, which equal laws must protect, and to violate would be oppression. Let us then, fellow citizens, unite with one heart and one mind, let us restore to social intercourse that harmony and affection without which liberty, and even life itself, are but dreary things. And let us reflect that having banished from our land that religious intolerance under which mankind so long bled and suffered, we have yet gained little if we countenance a political intolerance, as despotic, as wicked, and capable of as bitter and bloody persecutions. During the throes and convulsions of the ancient world, during the agonising spasms of infuriated man, seeking through blood and slaughter his long lost liberty, it was not wonderful that the agitation of the billows should reach even this distant and peaceful shore; that this should be more felt and feared by some and less by others; and should divide opinions as to measures of safety; but every difference of opinion is not a difference of principle. We have called by different names brethren of the same principle. We are all republicans: we are all federalists. If there be any among us who would wish to dissolve this Union, or to change its republican form, let them stand undisturbed as monuments of the safety with which error of opinion may be tolerated, where reason is left free to combat it. I know indeed that some honest men fear that a republican government cannot be strong; that this government is not strong enough. But would the honest patriot, in the full tide of successful experiment, abandon a government which has so far kept us free and firm, on the theoretic and visionary fear, that this government, the world's best hope, may, by possibility, want energy to preserve itself? I trust not. I believe this, on the contrary, the strongest government on earth. I believe it the only one, where every man, at the call of the law, would fly to the standard of the law, and would meet invasions of the public order as his own personal concern.—Sometimes it is said that man cannot be trusted with the government of himself. Can he then be trusted with the government of others? Or have we found angels, in the form of kings, to govern him? Let history answer this question.

Let us then, with courage and confidence, pursue our own federal and republican principles; our attachment to union and representative government. Kindly separated by nature and a wide ocean from the exterminating havoc of one quarter of the globe; too high minded to endure the degradations of the others, possessing a chosen country, with room enough for our descendants to the thousandth and thousandth generation, entertaining a due sense of our equal right to the use of our own faculties, to the acquisitions of our own industry, to honor and confidence from our fellow citizens, resulting not from birth, but from our actions and their sense of them, enlightened by a benign religion, professed indeed and practised in various forms, yet all of them inculcating honesty, truth, temperance, gratitude and the love of man, acknowledging and adoring an overruling providence, which by all its dispensations proves that it delights in the happiness of man here, and his greater happiness hereafter; with all these blessings, what more is necessary to make us a happy and a prosperous people? Still one thing more, fellow citizens, a wise and frugal government, which shall restrain men from injuring one another, shall leave them otherwise free to regulate their own pursuits of industry and improvement, and shall not take from the mouth of labor the bread it has earned. This is the sum of good government; and this is necessary to close the circle of our felicities. . . .

Source: Thomas Jefferson, Inaugural Address, March 4, 1801.

9.2 SAMUEL MITCHILL, ACCOUNT OF AARON BURR'S FAREWELL SPEECH TO THE SENATE (1805)

Aaron Burr had a tumultuous political career, culminating in his election as vice president under Jefferson in 1800. He enjoyed politics and openly campaigned for political offices, which made him a valuable asset in the emerging political party system, but also made him seem untrustworthy to his allies. Jefferson replaced Burr on the ticket in 1804, and his term came to an end in 1805. Before then, in 1804, he blamed Alexander Hamilton for spreading scandalous rumors about him and challenged Hamilton to a duel that left Hamilton dead. Burr evaded prosecution and returned for his final year as vice president and fulfilled his duties of presiding over the Senate. His farewell speech to the Senate is notable for the emotion it evoked; such displays of feeling were thought to demonstrate a refined man's character.

Senate-Chamber, March 2, 1805

This day I have witnessed one of the most affecting scenes of my life. Colonel Burr, whose situation and misfortunes you will know, after having presided in the Senate during almost the whole session, came in, as is customary, and took the chair today. He went on with the public business as usual until about two o'clock. Then, the Senate-chapter happening to be cleared for the purpose of considering some matters of an executive nature, he rose from the chair, and very unexpectedly pronounced to the Senate his farewell address. He did not speak to them, perhaps, longer than twenty minutes or half an hour, but he did it with so much tenderness, knowledge, and concern that it wrought upon the sympathy of the Senators in a very uncommon manner. Every gentleman was silent, not a whisper was heard, and the deepest concern was manifested. When Mr. Burr had concluded he descended from the chair, and in a dignified manner walked to the door, which resounded as he with some force shut it after him. On this the firmness and resolution of many of the Senators gave way, and they burst into tears. There was a solemn and silent weeping for perhaps five minutes.

For my own part, I never experienced any thing of the kind so affecting as this parting scene of the Vice-President from the Senate in which he had sat six years as a Senator and four years as presiding officer. My colleague, General Smith, stout and manly as he is, wept as profusely as I did. He laid his head upon his table and did not recover from his emotion for a quarter of an hour or more. And for myself, though it is more than three hours since Burr went away, I have scarcely recovered my habitual calmness. Several gentlemen came up to me to talk about this extraordinary scene, but I was obliged to turn away and decline all conversation.

I have just received a billet from him and have written an answer to it. He is a most uncommon man, and I regret more deeply than ever the sad series of events which removed him from public usefulness and confidence. The Senate passed a bill to give him the privilege of franking letters and parcels [i.e., sending mail for free] during life, but the House of Representatives refused their assent. The Senate has also passed him unanimously a vote of thanks for the ability, impartiality, and dignity with which he has presided in that body. Burr is one of the best officers that ever presided over a deliberative assembly. Where he is going or how he is to get through with his difficulties I know not.

Source: Samuel Mitchill Describes Aaron Burr's Farewell Speech to the Senate, 1805.
Harper's New Monthly Magazine, vol. 58, New York, 1879, pp. 749–750.

9.3 FELIX GRUNDY, PREDICTIONS ABOUT THE WAR OF 1812

In May 1812, Congress debated President Madison's request that it declare war on Great Britain. While opponents such as Virginia's John Randolph and New York's Harmanus Bleecker argued that the country was utterly unprepared and would suffer defeat, War Hawks such as Tennessee's Felix Grundy thought the only logical next step would be a declaration of war and questioned the patriotism—and manliness—of anyone who disagreed, asking "Are you for your country or against it?"

Mr. BLEECKER: . . . it is said, by the gentleman from South Carolina (Mr. CALHOUN) that war will be declared within sixty days, and by the gentleman from Kentucky (Mr. JOHNSON) that he will vote for a declaration of war within that time. If, sir, this be so; if gentlemen will have the hardihood to plunge the country into a war in its present unprepared state, without an army, without a navy, and without money, and bring upon us the defeat, and disgrace, and ignominy, which must inevitably result, then will the people, whose complaints who now refused to hear, and who are to bear the privations, sufferings, and calamities of the war; whose blood is to be spilled, whose houses are to blaze, whose towns are to be demolished, speak in a tone that shall, and will, and must be heard; they will speak in thunders that will ring the heavens from Maine to Georgia, from the Atlantic to the Mississippi. I rejoice, sir, in the signs of the times; and I wonder that gentlemen are not sensible that the opinion of the people is against their measures.

Mr. GRUNDY: Mr. Speaker . . . I have risen to reply to some of the remarks of the gentleman from Virginia (Mr. RANDOLPH) and the gentleman from New York (Mr. BLEECKER).

Sir, . . . The great body of the people in that quarter, as well as every other, are only waiting to see the constituted authorities of the country lead the way, in an honorable course, in vindication of the nation's rights, and they will be with us. . . . Public opinion condemns delay; it condemns a halfway state of things; it calls for action; it demands a firm and determined course to be taken by the National Legislature, and to be persistent in until foreign nations are compelled to respect our rights. If we change our policy from day to day—if we *talk* of war, and *tamely submit*—then, indeed, public opinion will and ought to be against us. The gentleman from Virginia (Mr. RANDOLPH) has charged the majority in the House with not having made the necessary preparations to place the country in an attitude of defense. I ask that gentleman, are his own skirts clear of this charge? Who have exerted themselves to place the nation in a condition to defend itself against any attack from a foreign enemy? The majority have. Who has thrown every obstacle in the way? The gentleman from Virginia, and those with whom he generally acts on the floor. . . .

. . . The gentleman from Virginia supposes, that with a very few exceptions, the majority in this House are anxious to get out of the scrape into which they have been precipitated. I imagine, that the gentleman did not consult his usual accuracy of expression, when he permitted himself to employ this phraseology. Does the gentleman mean to say, that the majority would surrender the national rights, and tamely submit to the wrongs and insults which have been heaped upon us by Great Britain? If so, he is in a gross error, of which I hope in a few days to see him convinced. But, if he means, that we are anxious to be relieved from our present embarrassments by a just and honorable peace, the sentiment corresponds with the wishes of every friend to his country. War is not desired by any one. Necessity, not choice, has induced us to resort to this last appeal of nations. There is no prospect of an adjustment by amicable negotiation. Shall we then submit, or go on? There is no difficulty in the decision; and I trust, that every member of the majority will do his duty without fear or trembling.

. . . It is a fact much to be lamented, that there exists in this country an organized opposition to the constituted authorities, whose influence is seen and felt on this floor, and whenever an appeal is made to the patriots of the people, its effects are transfused from one extremity of the United States to the other, for the purpose of defeating the measures which are adopted to maintain the honor of the nation. Ye, sire, every exertion has been made to weaken the arm of the Government, by means the most disgraceful. The people have been admonished to withhold their resources from us, in an hour of great public difficulty and danger. Sir, on the eve of a war with a foreign Power, it is surely no subject of contragulation to see a set of men combining together to weaken their own country, and thereby indirectly give an advantage to the enemy. Sir, I venture to predict, that if war is once begun, the difficulties which now present themselves [for paying for the war] will vanish. The distinction of Federalists and Republicans will cease; the united energies of the people will be brought into action; the inquiry will be, are you for your country or against it?

. . . The gentleman from New York admonishes us that if we go to war, we ought to take the hearts of the people with us. Sir, we all know that without this nothing effectual can be done. But is this object to be attained by a variable policy, which is to-day one thing and to-morrow another? No; convince them by a firm and determined conduct of your intentions, and they will go with you in every extremity, against any foreign foe with whom you come in collision. . . .

Source: War Hawk Tennessee Congressman Felix Grundy's Predictions About the War of 1812, Annals of Congress, House of Representatives, 12th Congress, 1st Session, pp. 1406–1411.

9.4 CONSTITUTION OF THE LOWELL FACTORY GIRLS ASSOCIATION (1834)

While women had always contributed to the family economy, the establishment of factories in the early nineteenth century offered a new type of employment, outside the home, for wages. The Lowell textile factories hired women to work in the mills while also providing room and board for their workers, most of whom were young, unmarried women. The "Factory Girls" united to protest some of the conditions in the factory and fight for higher wages, creating the first union for working women in the United States.

PREAMBLE.

Whereas we, the undersigned, residents of Lowell, moved by a love of honest industry and the expectation of a fair and liberal recompence, have left our homes, our relatives and youthful associates, and come hither, and subjected ourselves to all the danger and inconvenience, which necessarily attend young and unprotected females, when among strangers, and in a strange land; and however humble the condition of Factory Girls, (as we are termed,) may seem, we firmly and fearlessly (though we trust with a modesty becoming our sex,) claim for ourselves, that love of moral and intellectual culture, that admiration of, and desire to attain and preserve pure, elevated and refined characters, a true reverence for the divine principle which bids us render to every one his due; a due appreciation of those great and cardinal principles of our government, of justice and humanity, which enjoins on us "to live and let live"—that chivalrous and honorable feeling, which with equal force, forbids us to invade others rights, or suffer others, upon any consideration, to invade ours; and at the same time, that utter abhorence and detestation of whatever is mean, sordid, dishonorable or unjust—all of which, can alone, in our estimation, entitle us to be called the daughters of freemen, or of Republican America.

And, whereas, we believe that those who have preceded us have been, we know that ourselves are, and that our successors are liable to be, assailed in various ways by the wicked and unprincipled, and cheated out of just, legal and constitutional dues, by ungenerous, illiberal and avaricious capitalists,—and convinced that "union is power," and that as the unprincipled consult and advise, that they may the more easily decoy and seduce—and the capitalists that they may the more effectually defraud—we (being the weaker,) claim it to be our undeniable right, to associate and concentrate our power, that we may the more successfully repel their equally base and iniquitous aggressions.

And, whereas, impressed with this belief, and conscious that our cause is a common one, and our conditions similar, we feel it our imperative duty to stand by each other through weal and woe: to administer to each others wants, to prevent each others back-sliding—to comfort each other in sickness, and advise each other in health, to incite each other to the love and attainment of those excellences, which can alone constitute the perfection of female character—unsullied virtue, refined tastes and cultivated intellects—and in a word, do all that in us lies, to make each other worthy ourselves, our country and Creator.

Therefore, for the better attainment of those objects, we associate ourselves together, and mutually pledge to each other, a females irrefragable vow, to stand by, abide by, and be governed by the following

PROVISIONS.

1. It shall be denominated the LOWELL FACTORY GIRLS' ASSOCIATION.
2. Any female of good moral character, and who works in any one of the Mills in this city, may become a member of this Association, by subscribing to this Constitution.

3. The officers of the Association shall be, a President, Vice President, a Recording Secretary, a Corresponding Secretary, a Treasurer, a Collector, and a Prudential Committee, two of whom shall be selected from each Corporation in this city.

4. The officers shall be chosen by the vote of the Association; that is, by the vote of a majority of the members present.

5. The duties of the President, Vice President, Secretaries, Treasurer, and Collector, shall be the same as usually appertain to such offices. The duties of the Prudential Committee shall be to watch over the interests of the Association generally; to recommend to the Association, for their consideration and adoption, such By-Laws and measures as in their opinion the well-being of the Association may require: and also to ascertain the necessities of any of its members, and report the same, as soon as may be, to the Association. And whenever, in the opinion of the Committee, there are necessities so urgent as to require immediate relief, they shall forthwith report the same to the President, who shall immediately draw upon the Treasurer for the sum recommended, and which sum the Committee shall forthwith apply to the relief of the necessitous.

6. The Treasurer and Collector shall be subject to the supervision of the Prudential Committee, to whom they shall be accountable, and to whom they shall give such security for the faithful discharge of their duties, as the Committee shall require.

7. All moneys shall be raised by vote of a majority of the Association, or of the members present, and shall be assessed equally on all the members.

8. All the officers shall hold their office for the term of one year, with the privilege of resigning, and subject to be removed by vote of the Association, for good cause.

9. The Association shall meet once in three months, and may be convened oftener, if occasion require, by the President, upon a petition of twenty of the members first.

10. It shall forever be the policy of the members of this Association, to bestow their patronage, so far as is practicable, upon such persons as befriend, but never upon such as oppose our cause.

11. The Association shall have power to make all necessary By-Laws, which shall be consistent with these Provisions, and such By-Laws, when made, shall be binding upon all the members.

12. Any member may dissolve her connection with the Association, by giving two weeks notice to the Recording Secretary; and any member shall be expelled from the Association by a vote of a majority of the members present, for any immoral conduct or behavior unbecoming respectable and virtuous females . . .

Source: Constitution of the Lowell Factory Girls Association, 1834.

9.5 CHIEF JUSTICE JOHN MARSHALL, MAJORITY OPINION *GIBBONS V. OGDEN* (1824)

In the competition for steamboat traffic on the Hudson River, Aaron Ogden, under a license from inventor Robert Fulton, obtained an injunction from New York courts barring the rival company run by Thomas Gibbons. Daniel Webster argued the case for Gibbons that the state of New York was not allowed to do this. In *Gibbons v. Ogden* (1824), Chief Justice John Marshall writing for a unanimous US Supreme Court struck down New York State's regulation of navigation on the Hudson River as a violation of the Commerce Clause of the Constitution. In so doing, Marshall claimed exclusive jurisdiction over navigable waters for the federal government and simultaneously promoted the development of steamboat traffic on those waters.

Marshall, C.J.: The subject to be regulated is commerce, and our Constitution being, as was aptly said at the bar, one of enumeration, and not of definition, to ascertain the extent of the power, it becomes necessary to settle the meaning of the word. The counsel for the appellee would limit it to traffic, to buying and selling, or the interchange of commodities, and do not admit that it comprehends navigation. This would restrict a general term, applicable to many objects, to one of its significations. Commerce, undoubtedly, is traffic, but it is something more: it is intercourse. It describes the commercial intercourse between nations, and parts of nations, in all its branches, and is regulated by prescribing rules for carrying on that intercourse. The mind can scarcely conceive a system for regulating commerce between nations which shall exclude all laws concerning navigation, which shall be silent on the admission of the vessels of the one nation into the ports of the other, and be confined to prescribing rules for the conduct of individuals in the actual employment of buying and selling or of barter.

If commerce does not include navigation, the government of the Union has no direct power over that subject, and can make no law prescribing what shall constitute American vessels or requiring that they shall be navigated by American seamen. Yet this power has been exercised from the commencement of the government, has been exercised with the consent of all, and has been understood by all to be a commercial regulation. All America understands, and has uniformly understood, the word "commerce" to comprehend navigation. It was so understood, and must have been so understood, when the Constitution was framed. The power over commerce, including navigation, was one of the primary objects for which the people of America adopted their government, and must have been contemplated in forming it. The convention must have used the word in that sense, because all have understood it in that sense, and the attempt to restrict it comes too late. . . .

It is the power to regulate, that is, to prescribe the rule by which commerce is to be governed. This power, like all others vested in Congress, is complete in itself, may be exercised to its utmost extent, and acknowledges no limitations other than are prescribed in the Constitution. These are expressed in plain terms, and do not affect the questions which arise in this case, or which have been discussed at the bar. If, as has always been understood, the sovereignty of Congress, though limited to specified objects, is plenary as to those objects, the power over commerce with foreign nations, and among the several States, is vested in Congress as absolutely as it would be in a single government, having in its Constitution the same restrictions on the exercise of the power as are found in the Constitution of the United States.

Source: Chief Justice John Marshall, "Majority Opinion Gibbons v. Ogden, 1824," in *The Constitutional Decisions of John Marshall*, Volume II, ed. Joseph P. Cotton (New York: G. P. Putnam's Sons, 1905), pp. 41–43, 49.

9.6 LETTER FROM THOMAS JEFFERSON TO WILLIAM HENRY HARRISON (1803)

Thomas Jefferson believed that the strongest foundation for democracy was widespread land ownership, which created independent citizens. Increasing population, however, meant the United States would need more land in order to achieve Jefferson's goal. While president, he wrote a private letter to William Henry Harrison, at the time the governor of the Indiana territory, outlining a peaceful method for acquiring lands from Indian tribes. Jefferson suggested that Harrison encourage Indians to adapt to the American way of life, including gender roles. As they purchased American goods, the Natives would run into debt and sell their excess lands to white settlers. Jefferson thought this the best policy to "promote the interests of the Indians & ourselves."

. . . You will receive herewith an answer to your letter as President of the Convention; and from the Secretary of War you receive from time to time information and instructions as to our Indian affairs. these communications being of the public records are restrained always to particular objects & occasions. but this letter being unofficial, & private, I may with safety give you a more extensive view of our policy respecting the Indians, that you may the better comprehend the parts dealt out to you in detail through the official channel, and observing the system of which they make a part, conduct yourself in unison with it in cases where you are obliged to act without instruction. our system is to live in perpetual peace with the Indians, to cultivate an affectionate attachment from them, by every thing just & liberal which we can do for them within the bounds of reason, and by giving them effectual protection against wrongs from our own people. the decrease of game rendering their subsistence by hunting insufficient, we wish to avow them to agriculture, to spinning & weaving. the latter branches they take up with great readiness, because they fall to the women, who gain by quitting the labours of the field for these which are exercised within doors. when they withdraw themselves to the culture of a small piece of land, they will perceive how useless to them are their extensive forests, and will be willing to pare them off from time to time in exchange for necessaries for their farms & families. to promote this disposition to exchange lands, which they have to spare & we want, for necessaries, for which we have to spare & they want, we shall push our trading houses, and be glad to see the good & influential individuals among them now in debt, because we observe that when these debts get beyond what the individuals can pay, they become willing to lop them off by a cession of lands. at our trading houses too we mean to sell so low as merely to repay us cost and charges so as neither to lessen or enlarge our capital. this is what private traders cannot do, for they must gain; they will consequently retire from the competition, & we shall thus get clear of this pest without giving offence or umbrage to the Indians. in this way our settlements will gradually circumscribe & approach the Indians, & they will in time either incorporate with us as citizens of the U.S. or remove beyond the Mississippi. the former is certainly the termination of their history most happy for themselves, but in the whole course of this, it is essential to cultivate their love. as to their fear, we presume that our strength & their weakness is now so visible that they must see we have only to shut our hand to crush them, & that all our liberalities to them proceed from motives of pure humanity only. should any tribe be fool hardy enough to take up the hatchet at any time, the siezing the whole country of that tribe & driving them across the Mississippi, as the only condition of peace, would be an example to others, and furtherance of our final consolidation.

. . .[In purchasing these lands,] the minds of the [Indian tribe members] should be soothed & conciliated by liberalities and sincere assurances of friendship. perhaps by sending a well qualified character to stay some time in Decoigne's village as if on other business, and to sound him & introduce the subject by degrees to his mind & that of the other heads of families, inculcating the way of conversation all those considerations which prove the advantages they would receive by a cession of these terms, the object might be more easily & effectually obtained than by abruptly proposing it to them at a formal treaty. of the means however of obtaining what we wish you will be the best judge; and I have given you this view of the system which we suppose will best promote the interests of the Indians & ourselves, & finally consolidate our whole country into one nation only, that you may be enabled the better to adapt your means to the object. for these purposes we have given you a general commission for treating. the crisis is pressing. whatever can now be obtained must be obtained quickly. the occupation of New Orleans, hourly expected, by the French, is already felt like a light breeze by the Indians. you know the sentiments they entertain of that nation under the hope of their protection. they will immediately stiffen against cessions of land to us. we had better therefore do at once what can now be done.

I must repeat that this letter is to be considered as private & friendly, & is not to controul [sic] any particular instructions which you may receive through the official channel. you will also perceive how sacredly it must be kept within your own breast, and especially how improper to be understood by the Indians. for their interests & their tranquility it is best they should see only the present page of their history. I pray you to accept assurances of my esteem & high consideration. Th. Jefferson

Source: Thomas Jefferson, personal letter to William Henry Harrison, February 27, 1803. Gilder Lehrman Collection: LC07171. http://www.gilderlehrman.org/collections/ed1b417c-81cc-4c61-8dfc-952041352225?back=/mweb/ search%3Fneedle%3DCulture

Jacksonian Democracy

1820-1840

COMMON THREADS

Why was the Bank of the United States so controversial in the early republic?

How did the market revolution affect wage labor?

What actions and policies of the Democratic Republican presidents, 1800–1824, laid the groundwork for Jackson's breakaway movement?

Did the territorial expansion of the republic require the removal of Native Americans?

OUTLINE

AMERICAN PORTRAIT

Harriet Noble

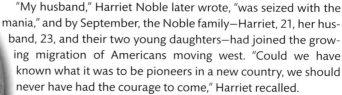

By 1824, the New York backcountry was abuzz with talk of Michigan Territory and the opportunities there for families willing to make the trip. The economy was at last bouncing back from the Panic of 1819. Markets for agriculture, in the East or down the Mississippi River, were reviving. Land prices had declined slightly, and families could buy in for smaller parcels.

"My husband," Harriet Noble later wrote, "was seized with the mania," and by September, the Noble family—Harriet, 21, her husband, 23, and their two young daughters—had joined the growing migration of Americans moving west. "Could we have known what it was to be pioneers in a new country, we should never have had the courage to come," Harriet recalled.

Harriet's husband had already made the journey once that year, with his brother, to scout out land for their families. Now the two families set out. First came a rough trip by wagon over bad roads to Buffalo. Next, after a four-day wait in Buffalo for a steamship that never showed up, a seven-day trip on a schooner across Lake Erie "entirely prostrated with seasickness," Noble recalled. And then, after days of trekking through the Michigan wilderness until "my feet were so swollen I could walk no further," they arrived at Ann Arbor: "some six or seven log huts occupied by as many inmates as could be crowded into them." The Nobles jammed in with the others, so packed that they could not move in the night without stepping on someone's hand or foot. So they survived for a month and a half, until the men managed to put up separate cabins. But

No pictures of Harriet Noble exist, but this one of Ann Allen, who moved to Michigan at the same time, suggests what Noble might have looked like in her 50s.

that winter most of the community fell mysteriously ill. Deciding they had chosen an unhealthful place, the following spring the Nobles moved again, this time to Dexter, 10 miles west. They were fortunate enough to be able to take over a shell of a log cabin abandoned by discouraged settlers before them. That summer and fall, Harriet and her husband worked together to put a roof over their heads and haul stones to set a fireplace. By the second winter, they had a roof, a floor, a fireplace, and a door. Provisions were always scarce. Waiting 15 days for her husband to return from Detroit with supplies, Harriet ran out of flour. "After being without bread three or four days, my little boy, two years old, looked me in the face and said, 'Ma, why don't you make bread; don't you like it? I do.'"

The difficulties continued into the next year: First Harriet and her husband were recurrently ill with fever and barely able to work. As they seemed to be recovering, her husband had his hand "blown to pieces" in a gun accident, permanently disabling him and forcing Harriet to do all the field work, the tending of the animals, and the laying by of wood. Not until the following spring, three years after their arrival, did prospects look up, when Harriet's husband was at last able to travel back east to get a nephew to help with the work.

Harriet Noble and her husband were the kind of Americans Andrew Jackson considered the heart of the democracy—ordinary citizens of modest means willing to risk their resources, even their lives, to gain new opportunities and forge new freedoms. They were the people for whom he and his generation had fought the Revolutionary War. Especially after he lost his first bid for the presidency in what he considered "a corrupt bargain" among the eastern and western elites, Jackson resolved that these Americans must be protected. Of course, settlers were not the only struggling common Americans by 1824. The port cities were awash with wage laborers trying to support themselves and their families on smaller and smaller paychecks. But Jackson was a man of the pre-market revolution era. He distrusted paper money and wages and banks. His was still a world of settlers to be protected against the rich and well connected. Convinced that he alone could provide that protection, he would do this even if it meant forcibly dispossessing tens of thousands of indigenous people, ignoring the decisions of the Supreme Court, threatening to send federal militia against state authorities, and, all in all, claiming for the executive branch of government an expanse of powers so unprecedented that his critics would label him "the tyrant."

A New National Politics

The conclusion of the War of 1812 brought a new confidence to the American government, a bolder foreign policy, and, for a moment, less contentious national politics. By 1816, the party of Jefferson itself was changing. Both Jefferson and party cofounder James Madison had flexed the muscles of the central government before and during the War of 1812. They had both loathed Hamilton's bank, and Madison had happily allowed its charter to expire in 1811. But that was before the war taught him the importance of a central bank for financing war. In 1816 Madison signed the bill to recharter the bank—on the same terms as the first!

Changes in the Democratic Republican Party

In the early nineteenth century the Democratic Republican Party fell under the influence of a new generation of politicians who came of age during the troubled years of the Confederation Congress. Having witnessed the effects of poor transportation and a weak federal military in the War of 1812, they believed that a strong, activist national government might well be the nation's best protection against localism and fragmentation. By the election of 1824, they would identify themselves as National Republicans.

This new brand of Republicanism was epitomized by four men: Henry Clay of Kentucky, John C. Calhoun of South Carolina, and Daniel Webster and John Quincy Adams of Massachusetts. Clay (1777–1852) entered national politics as the champion of the large planters and merchants of Kentucky, who had turned to the federal government for support for projects (especially transportation) they could not win at home. Calhoun (1782–1850) was first a representative and then senator and vice president. Although both Calhoun and South Carolina later became symbols of states' rights sentiment, in the postwar years South Carolinians believed that their international export economy was best served by a strong federal government.

Adams and Webster, both New Englanders, illustrated the compatibility of National Republicanism with the old Federalist views. Webster promoted the interests of New England's banking classes. He was a strong supporter of protective tariffs after the War

Henry Clay Henry Clay was 44 when Charles Bird King painted this portrait in 1821, but he looks much younger. He charmed both women and men. Margaret Bayard Smith said that he had a "power of captivation, which no one who was its object could resist."

of 1812, as Massachusetts merchants shifted from importing to manufacturing. Born in 1767, John Quincy Adams was influenced by his father's Federalist views and was first elected to the Senate in 1800 by the Federalist Massachusetts legislature. Adams broke rank with his party when it opposed the Louisiana Purchase.

Led by Clay, the new nationalists fashioned a vision of a Republican political economy based on individual entrepreneurial and market development (including domestic manufacturing), guided by an active federal government. Not surprisingly, their platform, loosely called the American System, was devised to appeal to local interests and identities. In the West and South, that meant promoting a national subsidy to improve transportation, whereas in the Northeast, it meant a protective tariff for domestic industries. To protect federal credit and stabilize currency and internal credit, they supported a national bank.

The various elements of the American System came before Congress as separate bills after the War of 1812, each with its own supporters. The bills to create the Second Bank of the United States and to increase the national tariffs passed easily and were signed by President Madison. Authorized in 1816, the Second Bank of the United States was chartered for 20 years and located in Philadelphia, with the federal government providing one-fifth of its capital and appointing one-fifth of its directors. The tariff bill was less protective than some nationalists wished.

Transportation subsidies fared less well. Madison was skeptical about the constitutionality of this form of federal intervention. In his annual messages of 1815 and 1816, he urged Congress to initiate a constitutional amendment to clarify federal power in this area. A torn Congress eventually passed a bill creating a federal fund for internal improvements. On his last day in office, Madison vetoed it. In 1818, the federal government opened a section of the National Road, a highway that connected Baltimore to Wheeling,

Virginia (later West Virginia). Otherwise, federal transportation initiatives fell victim to questions of constitutionality and regional jealousies.

James Monroe and National Republicanism

In 1816, Republican James Monroe ran for the presidency against Rufus King, the last Federalist to vie for that office. In the flush of postwar victory and prosperity and in the aftermath of the Hartford Convention, the returns were lopsided in Monroe's favor: 183 electoral votes to King's 34. He was the third Virginian in a row to hold the office.

Monroe's inaugural address sounded many familiar Republican themes: he praised the virtue of the American people and warned against corruption, greed, and the usurpation of power by foes of the republic. But in explaining the "principles" that would guide him in office, Monroe seemed almost to sound Federalist themes. He suggested the need for a more vigorous national defense and a more aggressive foreign policy toward Europe generally. He also recommended federally subsidized internal improvements as necessary for a prosperous, cohesive nation.

In office, Monroe governed with the nationalist bent suggested in his inaugural address. He asked former Federalist John Quincy Adams to be secretary of state (the presumed stepping-stone to the presidency). Together Monroe and Adams moved toward a more assertive foreign policy.

First, the administration arrived at agreements with Britain limiting British and American forces on the Great Lakes and along the 49th parallel to the Rocky Mountains. Then, in 1819, the United States forced Spain to fix definite borders to the Louisiana Purchase. After the purchase, Jefferson had attempted unsuccessfully to buy Florida from Spain. His successor, Madison, had simply declared that West Florida had been a part of the Louisiana Purchase all along. Taking the Florida peninsula had been left for James Monroe, who sent Andrew Jackson to lead a raid into Florida, ostensibly to frighten the Seminoles. When Jackson appeared to exceed his intentionally vague orders, he faced investigation by Congress (see Chapter 9), but he demonstrated that Spain was too weak, both politically and militarily, to hold onto Florida.

Capitulating to American forcefulness, in the Transcontinental Treaty of 1819, Spain ceded all of Florida to the United States in return for the US government's agreement to assume private American claims against Spain of about $5 million. The Transcontinental Treaty also clarified the border between the United States and Spanish Mexico. The United States gave up claims not only to California (which few considered part of the original purchase) but also to Texas (which many did). The boundary gained in return ran in a series of ascending steps from Louisiana to the Pacific, defining the United States as a nation that spanned the continent.

In the 1820s, under Monroe, the United States began to view itself as American, not quasi-European, and as protector of the Americas against Europe. By 1815 a number of former Spanish colonies, including Argentina, Chile, and Venezuela, had revolted, and an independence movement was under way in Mexico. As these new republics won their independence, they turned to the United States for recognition and support, while the absolute monarchies in Europe sought to preserve and extend their territorial empires. France offered to help Spain regain its colonies in South America. Russia reasserted and strengthened its long-standing claims in the Pacific Northwest.

Disavowing any future new territorial ambitions for itself in the Americas, Great Britain offered to make a joint declaration with the United States warning other nations against intruding in the internal affairs of Western Hemisphere countries. An alliance with Britain would have enhanced US diplomatic credibility, but many Americans suspected that Britain would use its position to squeeze the United States out of South American markets.

Secretary of State John Quincy Adams convinced Monroe to refuse the British offer and, instead, to act independently and issue a unilateral statement of support for the new republics. Adams hoped that being identified with this policy would help him shed the pro-British tag that was associated with many New Englanders.

In his annual message to Congress in 1823, Monroe enunciated the policy that has since become known as the Monroe Doctrine. Monroe asserted a special United States relationship with all parts of North and South America, with which, he insisted, "we are of necessity more immediately connected." "We . . . declare," he added, "that we should consider any attempt on their part to extend their system to any portion of this hemisphere as dangerous to our peace and safety." The Monroe Doctrine marked an important milestone in the development of American nationalism and internationalism. The United States asserted not only a new relation (as peer) to the European nations but also a new relation to the Americas. Surveillance over the nations of North and South America would be the domestic right of the United States.

The Missouri Compromise

Yet just as a more assertive nation flexed its muscles, internal divisions threatened to pull it apart. Since the first compromises on slavery at the Constitutional Convention in 1787 (see Chapter 7), it was clear that slavery had the potential to create fierce conflict. For decades, no one was willing to call the institution a positive good, and northerners and southerners both seemed to agree publicly that slavery was unfortunate and in due course it would just fade away. Nonetheless, each time slavery entered national politics—the debate over Louisiana, setting the terms for ending the slave trade (see Chapter 9)—southerners did all they could to protect the institution. Then, as slavery spread to newly acquired territories, northern opponents of the institution saw clearly that, rather than disappearing, as it seemed to be doing in the North, the institution was becoming stronger elsewhere. In the decade after 1810, the number of slaves in the United States increased 30 percent.

In 1819, when Missouri applied for permission to organize as a state, antislavery politicians made their move. In the House debate, New York representative James Tallmadge proposed that Missouri be admitted under two conditions. First, no more slaves were to be brought into the state, and, second, slavery was to be gradually abolished after the state was admitted to the Union. Southerners unanimously opposed the amendment, whereas northerners voted unanimously for it. The more populous North carried the vote. Slavery's defenders warned that such an attack on private property was unconstitutional and would incite "servile war." But slavery's opponents insisted that the institution was both immoral and antirepublican. "You boast of the freedom of your Constitution," Tallmadge told them, "and yet you have slaves in your country."

But when the House bill reached the Senate committee charged with its consideration, the vote was reversed. The Tallmadge amendment died in committee, to be reintroduced in the next session.

By the time Congress reconvened, positions on both sides had hardened. All notions of an antislavery South were now dead. A northern congressman said, "I awoke as from a trance." The struggle over Missouri foreshadowed later congressional debates over slavery and made southerners wary of a strong federal government. As North Carolina senator Nathaniel Macon explained, "If Congress can make canals, they can with more propriety emancipate."

The firestorm over Missouri was finally resolved when Maine applied for statehood as a free state. At that time there were 22 states in the Union, 11 free and 11 slave. Under Speaker of the House Henry Clay's guidance, the bills admitting both states were linked, preserving the balance in the Senate. The compromise also provided that slavery would be permitted in the Arkansas Territory but excluded from the rest of the Louisiana Purchase. The compromise passed narrowly in March of 1820.

Almost immediately, another problem arose when Missouri submitted a state constitution that barred free black people and free persons of mixed heritage from the state. This was a clear violation of Article IV of the Constitution, which provided that citizens of one state should enjoy the rights of citizens in all states. Here was another sign of an emerging sectional division over the issue of black citizenship. In 1821, during the second round of the Missouri crisis, that division was just beginning to show itself, as Henry Clay struggled to engineer a second compromise. Congress allowed Missouri to enter under the proposed constitution, but it demanded that the new state legislature promise never to interpret the clause to mean what it so obviously meant, that Missouri reserved the right to deny free African Americans their constitutional rights. The Missouri territorial legislature made the promise but withheld any power to bind the people of the state to what it said. Finally, in August 1821, President James Monroe greeted Missouri as the 24th state of the Union.

The Election of 1824 and the "Corrupt Bargain"

In the usual order of custom in the young republic, Secretary of State John Quincy Adams would have been Monroe's presumed successor. But by 1824 the Republican Party housed experienced men who considered themselves next in line. In addition to Adams, there were John C. Calhoun (secretary of war), Henry Clay (Speaker of the House), and William H. Crawford of Georgia (secretary of the Treasury, who had suffered a massive stroke in 1823). This group, which called itself the National Republicans, contained some of the nation's most experienced and respected leaders.

And then there was the outlier, Andrew Jackson. In spite of his fame as a war hero, when the Tennessee legislature nominated Jackson for the presidency in 1822, few politicians took the candidacy seriously, given his competition. But by 1824 voting Americans were beginning to pull back from the new expansive Republican vision. As a political unknown, without a legislative record, Jackson was free to run on his image, as a forceful leader and an outsider. An early indication of the storminess of the election came with the Republican nomination. Because James Monroe had not designated a successor, the selection was thrown to the Republican congressional caucus and was expected to benefit Crawford. But this time, the other candidates disowned the caucus as a corrupt and irregular institution so effectively that only 66 of a possible 216 Republican members of Congress even attended. Crawford did get the nod, but its value had been diminished.

In the election, no candidate claimed a majority either of the popular vote or of the Electoral College. The underdog Andrew Jackson came closest, with 43 percent of the popular vote and 99 electoral votes. Next was Adams, with 31 percent of the popular vote and 84 electoral votes. Crawford managed only 41 electoral votes, and Clay came in last with 37. (Calhoun had withdrawn.) See Map 10–1.

The election was thus thrown to the House of Representatives, where members had to select from among the three candidates with the highest electoral count. As the highest vote getter, Jackson was confident at first, but by late December he began to hear rumors "that deep intrigue is on foot." Those rumors were correct. Although Adams did not receive a single popular vote in Kentucky, and although the Kentucky legislature had directed its delegation to vote for Jackson, Clay overrode those instructions and also marshaled support for Adams in other states. Adams received the votes of 13 of the 24 state delegations. Jackson received 7 and Crawford received 4.

Jackson later charged that Adams had bought Clay's support with the promise of the post of secretary of state. Adams did give Clay that job, but Clay had had good reasons for allying himself with Adams. They shared similar political philosophies. In addition, Jackson and Clay vied for the same regional vote. Clay's support for him in 1824 would have helped Jackson build a stronger western base for 1828.

Jackson was furious. His supporters charged that the election had been stolen in a "corrupt bargain" brokered by insiders who debased the virtue of the republic and disregarded the clear will of the electorate.

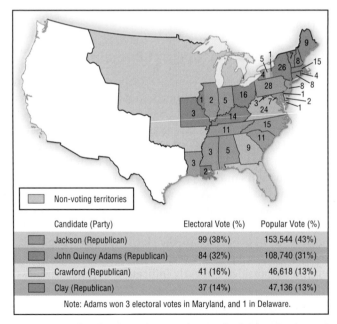

Candidate (Party)	Electoral Vote (%)	Popular Vote (%)
Jackson (Republican)	99 (38%)	153,544 (43%)
John Quincy Adams (Republican)	84 (32%)	108,740 (31%)
Crawford (Republican)	41 (16%)	46,618 (13%)
Clay (Republican)	37 (14%)	47,136 (13%)

Note: Adams won 3 electoral votes in Maryland, and 1 in Delaware.

Map 10–1   The Election of 1824 Almost all of Adams's electoral votes came from the Northeast, while Jackson's were spread through the South, the Midwest, and the Mid-Atlantic.

The Adams Presidency and the Gathering Forces of Democracy

In many respects, Adams's choice of Clay made perfect sense. Since the postwar period both men had shared a commitment to the "American System": the preservation of a national bank, the levying of a national tariff, and the improvement of infrastructure.

Adams continued to support these policies in office, even using his first annual message to Congress in 1825 to lay out a grand vision for federal involvement in the political economy. He called not only for economic projects, such as transportation improvements, but also for the creation of a national university, a national observatory, a naval academy, and an elaborate system of roads and canals supported by federal expenditures. He urged Congress not to be "palsied by the will of our constituents." His opponents railed that this was clear evidence of his intention to benefit the wealthy at the expense of the common people and that this branch of the Republican Party (increasingly identifying itself as the National Republicans) seemed more Federalist than Jeffersonian.

John Quincy Adams was a wise and principled statesman, but he was never able to set an independent agenda for his presidency. He was shadowed by the political battle that began with his election and by his unpopular identification with banking and mercantile interests. Defensive and prickly in public, he did not build strong political alliances, and he misread the gulf developing within the American electorate.

And Jackson's supporters worked hard to discredit Adams, especially on the issue of the tariff. Early on, the federal government had depended on the tariff and on land sales for most of its revenue. By the end of the War of 1812, the importance of the tariff for generating funding had declined, but its role in addressing the growing regional economic differences had increased. The 1816 tariff was protectionist, but only very mildly so, working to give some recognition to the importance of domestic manufactures. But the Panic of 1819, brought on in part by the United States' reliance on world markets, reenergized protectionists: a bill to raise tariffs on the entire list of imported products by 5 percent (even higher for cotton, wool, iron, and glass) failed passage by only one vote. It was broadly supported in the western and middle states and opposed in the South (where it was seen as favoring high-priced New England products), whereas New England split on the issue. But by 1824 New England was committed enough to industrial growth to become solidly pro-tariff. That year, when Congress proposed a tariff that included levies of 35 percent on imported cotton, wool, hemp, and iron, passage was a forgone conclusion.

Passage of the 1824 tariff was ominous for several reasons. First, of course, it was vehemently opposed by the South. Second, neither the North nor the federal government really needed it. In 1824 the federal government reported a surplus of funds, a year when New England manufactures were doing well enough not to need the help. The tariff had become the language of sectionalism, but the underlying conflict was over the power of the federal government. This was not a simple question of nationalism versus localism. Jackson, a nationalist willing to support some level of protective tariff, had even conceded, "It is time we became a little more Americanized." The difference between Adams and Jackson was the question of federal legitimacy. In what actions could the federal government claim the authority of the American people? And in what actions did it overstep that authority? That conflict was now infused with the energy of a rising democratic spirit.

The Social and Political Bases of Jacksonian Democracy

Jacksonian democracy captured the hopes and fears of a rapidly changing country. As settlers such as Harriet Noble and her family looked for opportunity in the West, city dwellers struggled to make a living in the new urban landscape. Anyone who wanted to enter the market—to purchase land or establish a business—needed credit, but in a volatile economy, risk accompanied opportunity. When things went wrong, Americans looked for someone to blame—and for bold politicians to advocate their causes.

Settlers

The migration into the backcountry, set off by the Treaty of Ghent in 1815, continued throughout the 1820s. After Maine in 1820 and Missouri in 1821, no new states entered the Union until Arkansas in 1835. But in the meantime the populations of the new states grew steadily, in some cases doubling and tripling in a single decade: Mississippi grew from 75,448 in 1820 to 136,621 in 1830, Illinois from 55,211 to 157,445, and Indiana from 147,178 to 343,031.

North or South, migrants wanted land. They also wanted easy credit and low prices—but they weren't always convinced that government was their friend in getting these. To be sure, the price of land per acre and the size of the minimum-permitted individual purchase had fallen steadily during the early nineteenth century. The Land Act of 1820 reduced the price to $1.25 per acre for a minimum purchase of 80 acres. In lowering the minimal outlay to $100, however, Congress also eliminated the 1800 provision that had permitted settlers to buy on credit from the government and added the requirement that land that wasn't promptly paid for would go back up for sale. This made small buyers even more dependent on easy credit from local or state banks. There were plenty of these institutions, but state and local bankers were often more interested in putting together big deals with land speculators than in making smaller loans to risky individual settlers. In 1819, when local banks had tried to foreclose on mortgages in arrears, other settlers had formed vigilante committees to intimidate potential buyers and convince the banks that foreclosure was not in their financial interest.

The obstacles to land purchase for ordinary citizens had kept alive the practice of squatting, of claiming land simply by occupying it, demanding that a person's labor on it over time be recognized as a legal claim. As they had in the late eighteenth century, squatters harassed surveyors and ran off sheriff's deputies. Even when a small settler had a legal claim, if the land was good, or the area promising, the settler was likely to have to fight off high-powered lawyers and their clients. Backwoodsmen, squatters, and settlers did not always share the same interests, but probably all would have agreed with William Manning that "no person can possess property without laboring, unless he get it by force or craft," and that "those that labor for a living and those who get one without laboring— or, as they are generally termed, the Few and the Many"— was "the great dividing line" of society.

Free Labor

Settlers were not alone in feeling abandoned to the wiles of the wealthy. Although farm labor would dominate the workforce for decades to come, by the second decade of the

Emigrants Crossing the Appalachians This early nineteenth-century engraving depicts emigrants crossing the Appalachians on their way to Pittsburgh, Pennsylvania. Harriet Noble and her family would have traveled in a similar wagon.

nineteenth century nonfarming wage labor was becoming more common. Especially in the cities of the coasts, growing numbers of people worked for wages in increasingly precarious circumstances. They had been hard hit by the war, and even improved prosperity afterward left many wage workers with barely enough money to meet their own and their families' needs. Like the frustrated settlers, wage workers worried that the new economy was keeping common working people dependent on the rich. Workers had stuck with Jefferson and Madison through the embargo and the War of 1812, but their patience grew thin.

The Panic of 1819 strengthened that skepticism and gave rise to the beginnings of organized protest in the 1820s. Workers turned out in huge numbers to hear critics denounce the growing inequities of American life. Scotswoman Frances Wright, one of the most popular of these speakers, charged that the clergy conspired to keep workers shackled to superstition, inveighed against slavery, and advocated for women's rights.

In addition, workers began to form unions and go out on strike. Printers, weavers, carpenters, tailors, cabinetmakers, masons, stevedores, and workers in other crafts turned out on strike throughout major cities, protesting poor pay and long hours. Strikers argued that the shorter day was essential if they were to have time to refresh themselves, to be with their families, and to obtain the education necessary for newly enfranchised voters. Over time, these separate strikes merged into citywide and regional labor organizations. The first, the Mechanics' Union, was established in Philadelphia in 1827. Pledged to the 10-hour day, the union protested the exhaustion associated with industrialization and the "evils which . . . arise from a depreciation of the intrinsic value of human labor."

Suffrage Reform

At the founding of the nation, suffrage was restricted not just by gender and race but even more on the basis of property ownership and tax payment. Urban craft workers, who often owned little more than their tools and clothing, demanded the vote as the emblem of liberty. "Suffrage," as one editor insisted, "is the first right of a free people."

Territorial expansion also raised the question of suffrage. Settlers who owned little more than the mortgages on their land saw themselves as the chief embodiment of the democratic spirit.

The new, less settled states led in expanding white male suffrage. Vermont entered the Union in 1791 (the first new state after the original 13) with virtually universal white manhood suffrage. The next year, New Hampshire dropped its last qualification, and Kentucky entered the Union without restrictions on adult white males. Tennessee, which became a state in 1796, required that voters own property but did not set a minimum value. Ohio became a state in 1803 without property requirements for voting, and all the six states admitted between 1812 and 1821 entered with universal white male suffrage (see Map 10–2).

In 1817 Connecticut became the first of the older states to abolish all property qualifications for white men. In 1824, when Jackson made his first run for the presidency, only Virginia, Louisiana, and Rhode Island retained any significant restrictions on white

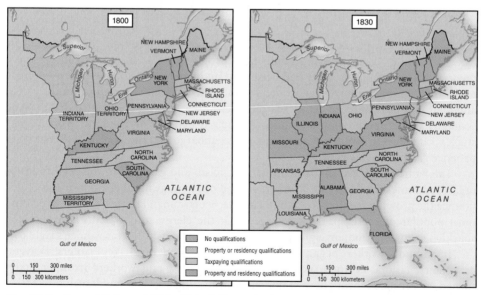

Map 10–2 Toward Universal White Male Suffrage As the western territories organized and entered the Union, they formed a band of states in which there were no property qualifications on white male suffrage, and often minimal taxpaying qualifications. By 1830, Virginia and Connecticut were unusual in the nation for restricting white male suffrage based on both property and tax payment. At the same time, free black males and women lost the vote where they had enjoyed it.

male suffrage, and only 6 of the 24 states retained indirect selection of the delegates to the Electoral College.

The struggle for an expanded male suffrage was fought openly on the landscape of race. As suffrage was extended to all white males, it was withdrawn from African American men in New York, Maryland, Pennsylvania, Connecticut, and New Jersey (where single, propertied women also lost the right to vote). In addition, every new state admitted after 1819 specifically excluded African Americans from the vote. Through suffrage reform, white Americans refashioned the vote as the domain of white citizenship. "The people of this state are for . . . a political community of white persons," one Pennsylvanian asserted bluntly.

The partial exception to this pattern was Rhode Island, where elites blocked universal white male suffrage throughout the 1830s. When, in 1841, white working men called a People's Convention to demand universal white male suffrage, they rejected pleas to include African American men in their demands. Spurned by white working men, African Americans supported the conservative opposition. When state conservatives later broadened the franchise, they repaid African American men for their earlier support by including them.

Opposition to Special Privilege and Secret Societies

Since the nation's founding, one strain of American political rhetoric had focused on corrupt insiders who enjoyed opportunities not available to other citizens. In the early nineteenth century, politics became a symbolic battle of the virtuous "many" against the corrupt "few."

Early in the century, specially chartered corporations became visible symbols of affluence and the target of these suspicions. Created by special acts of state legislatures, these corporations were, theoretically, open to all Americans. However, the charters were granted on a personal basis to people of wealth, power, and reputation who were known to individual legislators. The movement to use charters to promote development accelerated after the War of 1812. States chartered companies to build roads, provide transportation, and establish banks. Local reactions to chartered projects were mixed. Many shared journalist William Leggett's bitterness that "[n]ot a road can be opened, not a bridge can be built, not a canal can be dug, but a charter of exclusive privileges must be granted for the purpose." Some of the specially chartered initiatives, especially banks, provided easy credit to local farmers and workers. When the Panic of 1819 ended that bubble of easy credit, shopkeepers, farmers, and urban workers were devastated. They focused their anger on eastern bankers, especially the Second Bank of the United States, and grew suspicious that the new Republican leadership would increase preferential rules. By 1820 John C. Calhoun noticed the appearance, in "every part of the Union," of "a general mass of disaffection to the Government . . . looking out anywhere for a leader."

Corporations were not the only focus of hard feelings. The old Republican fears of special privilege extended to secret societies that might give their members special access to money and success. In western New York, where the opening of the Erie Canal had ushered in an economic boom and widespread social instability, tensions exploded in a virulent fear of Masons in the late 1820s.

The Masonic movement had originated to counter aristocratic power and protect craft masons, but in the eighteenth century a new Order of Freemasons emerged, made up of urban businessmen, professionals, and politicians who pledged to support one another. By the 1820s the Masons seemed to many working people to embody a dangerous antidemocratic spirit. This distrust was galvanized into popular opposition in 1826 by the mysterious disappearance (and presumed murder) of New Yorker William Morgan, who had written an exposé of the order's purported secret designs on public power. The story spread that Morgan had been abducted to Niagara Falls and then drowned. The outcry against this subversion of justice was magnified by the fact that public officials, including Andrew Jackson and Henry Clay, were also Masons. By 1827 New Yorkers had organized a separate political party to oppose the Masons. The Antimason Party spread from New York into other states, winning local elections in Massachusetts, Pennsylvania, and Vermont. In 1831 Antimasons held the first open presidential nominating convention, choosing William Wirt of Maryland as their candidate. Wirt carried only one state, and the party remained a minor player in national politics. Nevertheless, the battle against cabals illustrated the belief that American party politics was a struggle of common people against the monied aristocracy. This would become a staple of Jacksonian rhetoric.

Southern Slavery

Southern slavery was another base of Jacksonian democracy: Opportunity for southern whites meant the opportunity to own slaves. Between the Revolutionary and the Civil Wars, slave plantations spread across the southern frontier, creating one of the largest slave societies in history, stretching from Delaware to Texas.

Although only a minority of whites owned slaves at any one time, almost all hoped that they might. Moreover, the southern economy rested on slave property. In 1860, the 4 million enslaved Americans were worth $3 billion—representing 19 percent of the wealth of the entire nation.

"Property in Man"

By 1860 southern slaves worked in a variety of different circumstances—in cities, in factories, as skilled artisans, cooks, housekeepers, nurses, and most often as field hands. But what made all of them "slaves," no matter what they did or where they lived, was the fact that they were defined as property, treated as property, and defended as property.

By defining slaves as personal property, the slaveholders gave themselves the freedom to buy and sell their slaves virtually without restraint. To be sure, Congress banned the foreign slave trade in the United States as of 1808 (the earliest date permitted by the Constitution). In anticipation of this action, between 1800 and 1808 slave traffickers delivered and southern planters purchased at least 40,000 Africans into American slavery. But by then a domestic trade in slaves was beginning to flourish, becoming a mainstay of southern slavery until the Civil War.

Slavery had already begun to expand westward when Eli Whitney built the first cotton gin in 1793. Nevertheless, his invention stimulated a boom in cotton production and with it the aggressive expansion of the South into the new cotton lands in the West. In response, eastern slave owners began to enhance their profits by trading in slaves—selling their own excess labor farther south and west to newer farms in Mississippi, Alabama, and western Tennessee and Kentucky. There is little evidence that slaveholders consciously "bred" slaves to increase profits. But there is abundant evidence that slave-holders were aware of the additional profits to be garnered from slave women who bore many children, and many went out of their way to encourage slave reproduction.

The Domestic Slave Trade

Wherever there was slavery, there were slave markets. Between 1790 and 1860, more than 850,000 slaves were forced to migrate south, perhaps as many as one-third by 1820, transported by slave traders. The internal slave trade was often a highly organized business, with firms of 10 or 20 employees (bosses, clerks, guards, agents) in fine offices in Charleston, Richmond, and Baltimore. Professional traders enabled slave owners in the upper South to turn their extra slaves, particularly valuable young people, into a lucrative commodity. Any enslaved person had a 50% chance of being sold. More than the plantation, the slave market reflected the defining feature of slavery as "property in man."

The slave market was a ghastly collision of worlds: for potential buyers, sellers, and onlookers, it was a lively gathering place (like a club or tavern) for white men, whose easy camaraderie stood in stark contrast to the terror of the black people about to be offered for sale. Indeed, the amiability of the market helped potential buyers more easily to see themselves as rational, well-motivated businessmen, rather than purveyors of misery. And yet the truth of the transaction permeated the place—in the audible sobs of mothers and children, in the rough, physical inspections of the naked enslaved people, and in the absence of white females, a powerful silent admission that what was occurring at the slave market was so nakedly brutal as to taint the purity of white women.

Former slave Frederick Douglass, born in Maryland, later described the terror that the threat of being "sold South" struck in the hearts of enslaved African Americans. After his owner died when Douglass was eight or nine years old, the enslaved workers were hustled together to be appraised and allotted—some to be retained by family members, some to be "sold at once to the Georgia traders." "I have no language to express the high excitement and deep anxiety which were felt among us poor slaves during this time," Douglass wrote. "Our fate for life was now to be decided. We had no more voice in that decision than the brutes among whom we were ranked. A single word from the white men was enough—against all our wishes, prayers, and entreaties—to sunder forever the dearest friends, dearest kindred, and strongest ties known to human beings." One in three enslaved children under 14 was separated from at least one parent as a result of westward migration. One in three slave marriages in the upper South was destroyed.

Plantation Slavery

The symbol of the nineteenth-century South was the cotton plantation, a large commercial farm owned and operated by a single white family and worked by a large number of enslaved laborers, toiling up and down plowed rows planting the seed in the spring, hoeing the young plants in the hot summer sun, and picking the sticky cotton balls in the autumn. For good reason this image seemed to capture life in the slave South. Although slavery existed in America long before the cotton boom of the late 1790s, that boom vastly increased the demand for slaves. Cotton was a crop highly suitable to slave economies. It could be grown on large plantations tended by gangs of coerced workers who (thanks to the relatively short height of the cotton plant) could be kept under supervision at all times.

The number of slaves on a plantation varied widely. Of the nearly 4 million enslaved inhabitants of the South in 1860, probably three-quarters lived on plantations with 10 or more slaves. Sugar plantations averaged 30 or more workers. Rice plantations were smaller, but still larger on average than cotton and tobacco farms. The wealthiest families of the South owned hundreds of slaves on several different plantations, often hundreds of miles apart. Owning large tracts of land and large numbers of enslaved workers was the highest symbol of status in the South. Cotton plantations proliferated in the new western lands. Meanwhile, tobacco plantations in Virginia and North Carolina, rice plantations in South Carolina and Georgia, and sugar plantations in Louisiana continued to flourish.

The conditions of slave life varied with the crop. For a slave, there was nothing worse than the harsh life on the sugar plantation. Masters there drove workers hardest, producing the highest rates of sickness and death in the South. The crop cycle for sugar was 13 months or more, which meant that the planting of a new crop overlapped with the harvesting of the old one—producing weeks of almost unbearably intense labor. Because sugar, unlike cotton or tobacco, had to be processed immediately on harvesting, sugar plantations had to have the boiling and pressing machinery to rush the cane immediately into production. For these reasons sugar planters preferred to buy strong adult men. Fewer women meant fewer slave families on sugar plantations. To top it off, this intense exploitation took place in the hottest, swampiest parts of the South. Higher rates of sickness and death combined with lower rates of reproduction meant that sugar planters had to restock their slave labor force frequently with newly purchased slaves. The cost of the sugar presses, plus the cost of buying large numbers of the most expensive slaves—strong young men—meant that only the wealthiest owners could afford to set up sugar plantations. The needs of the sugar parishes of southern Louisiana sustained the Old South's largest slave market, in New Orleans.

Rice cultivation was not quite as lethal, but it was also centered in the sickliest low-country regions of the South—the coastal tidewater regions of South Carolina and Georgia, where rice workers stood ankle deep in mud under the blazing sun in snake-infested, swampland fields. Skilled rice cultivators sometimes operated under a "task" system, in which workers were assigned a specific task for the day and were able to exercise some autonomy over their labor. Over time, however, rice planters shifted to a "gang" labor system more familiar to cotton plantations.

Sugar and rice were restricted by geography to relatively contained coastal regions of the South. The vast majority of slaves worked cultivating cotton and, to a lesser extent, tobacco on farms and plantations in the drier inland regions. Growing seasons for these crops were shorter, and the plantations were more self-sufficient in foodstuffs. As a result, cotton and tobacco slaves were relatively healthy. On large cotton plantations, slaves were more likely to be organized in "gangs," set at repetitive tasks under close supervision. Cotton workers dragged their harvest to the gins that pulled the sticky cotton fibers from their bolls, continuing by the light of torches long after sunset. Tobacco workers were busier in the spring, carefully transplanting young plants and pruning off extra shoots.

Not all plantation slaves were field workers. On tobacco farms, slaves tended the drying leaf. On sugarcane plantations, workshops were needed to wash, chop, and squash the stalks and reduce their juices to sugar. On big cotton and tobacco plantations, as much as one-quarter of the workforce was assigned to domestic service or to crafts

AMERICAN LANDSCAPE

Gowrie: The Story of Profit and Loss on an American Plantation

"**G**owrie" was a plantation, 265 acres of fertile rice fields spread across a large island in the middle of the Savannah River, upstream from Augusta, Georgia, and over the border from South Carolina.

In 1833, Gowrie's land and enslaved labor force of 50 people became the property of Charles Manigault. Manigault had lost half of his paternal inheritance in the volatile markets of the early 1820s. By the end of the decade he was eager not simply to restore his wealth but also to establish his family among the ruling dynasties of the South.

For Manigault, Gowrie was the means to that end—an investment and a profit center, but never his "home." He never lived full time at Gowrie and never built a family seat there, preferring instead the elaborate mansion at Marshlands, his plantation seven miles from Charleston. Manigault ran Gowrie from afar, directing affairs through periodic visits and regular letters of instruction to his resident overseer, while he traveled abroad and enjoyed more cosmopolitan living.

For the enslaved workers who lived there, Gowrie held different meanings. It was, above all, a place of hard, forced labor. Rice cultivation began in the winter months, when slaves burned off the old stubble in 15 fields and leveled and plowed the land. Women seeded the rice between mid-March and early June. Then, "trunk-minders" (aided by the tides of the Savannah River) opened the elaborate irrigation systems to flood the fields. As the seeds grew into young plants, the slaves periodically drained the fields (to allow for weeding and hoeing) and then reflooded them, until the final flooding in mid-July.

The flooding and draining reduced (but did not eliminate) the work of cultivation. However, it created the additional labor of building, repairing, and cleaning ditches, canals, traps, and drains. Men built the systems, while women hauled in the mud to construct earthworks and hauled away the muck that clogged ditches and canals.

But for its laborers Gowrie was also home and it offered slaves a few advantages, however meager, over life on other types of farms. Because of the economics of scale, rice plantations were among the largest in the South and had unusually large slave populations—119 at Gowrie in 1849. The large workforce created a community of kin and friends unknown to slaves on smaller holdings. Moreover, the complexity of the work led some overseers to retain the task system—which provided slaves with a degree of autonomy in their labor. The breaks in the rhythms of cultivation allowed slaves time to plant their own gardens, yielding produce to improve their diets and perhaps some to sell. The slaves were all but forced to do this. Rice planters such as Manigault underfed their workers in the expectation that the slaves themselves would make up for it in their spare time by fishing, raising chickens, tending vegetable gardens, and exchanging their produce among themselves.

Gowrie was a harsh home. Tending muddy or flooded fields was dangerous

continued

and exhausting labor, and accidents were common. Constantly wading in the waters, rice workers were particularly subject to snakebites and to malaria. Being forced out in the unpredictably high tides, hurricanes, and floods to mend dikes and clear canals was part of the dangerous everyday labor on rice plantations. Manigault evidently did little to reduce these dangers. Health decisions were often left up to the overseer (who virtually never called in a doctor) and to a single elderly slave woman (who was hard pressed to care for such a large community).

While Manigault grew spectacularly wealthy, enslaved workers paid the price of a staggeringly high mortality rate, especially among children. None of the six infants who lived at Gowrie when Manigault purchased the estate lived to see adulthood. By January 1835, only half of the original labor force remained alive.

intended to make the plantation more self-sufficient. Although white observers tended to view household servants as fortunate, their lot was not necessarily better than that of field workers. Constantly on call, their workday could last even longer than that of field workers. They were also more vulnerable to the whims and moody outbursts of owners.

More independent than the house slaves were the 5 to 8 percent of the workforce trained for craft work. Men became carpenters, ironworkers, and boatmen. A smaller number of women became spinners, weavers, seamstresses, and dairymaids. Because they worked in separate shops, craft workers often enjoyed a degree of autonomy rare for most slaves.

Other Varieties of Slavery

Although most enslaved African Americans were held on fairly sizable plantations, some slaves worked in other settings. On large plantations that did not always require the work of all the slaves, and on older plantations where the soil was exhausted, planters made part of their income by renting out slaves to other plantations or to small farmers. Other enslaved people were hired out to nonagricultural work. By one estimate, a quarter of all Appalachian slaves were hired out, most to nonagricultural jobs. Other slaves hired themselves out to work in stores, hotels, blacksmitheries, and cotton gin works. Frederick Douglass hired himself out as a skilled caulker on the Baltimore docks.

A smaller number of slaves worked in extractive industries or mills in the South. In Kentucky, Virginia, and West Virginia, for example, slaves toiled in saltworks. White people held virtually all of the supervisory positions, but slaves tended and stirred the boiling kettles of brine and prepared the salt for drying and packing. As the industry grew, it supported an expanding economy in lumber, coal mining, boatbuilding, and shipping (down the Ohio and Mississippi Rivers). Some of these related jobs (cutting lumber, operating boats and ferries, coal—and even gold—mining) were also done by slaves, and some by free workers whose employment depended on a slave-based industry.

Neither slave owning nor plantation farming typified the experiences of southern whites, most of whom lived on small holdings of several hundred acres or less. In 1860, three out of four southern households had no slaves. Some of these "yeoman" farmers hired slaves from nearby planters, a stepping-stone into the slaveholding class for the most successful. They often relied on nearby planters to gin their cotton, sell their crops, or rent them a slave for a brief period of time.

Although most white people did not own slaves, the institution of slavery influenced their material lives and personal values. Slaveholders could afford to buy the best lands near rivers that provided them with ready access to markets. A workforce of millions of unpaid laborers meant that there were fewer stores and businesses in the slave states than in the North. A large number of rivers flowing from inland regions to coastal ports reduced the need for expensive railroads and canals. All of this meant that the southern economy remained less developed than the North's, and this had important consequences for the southern whites who owned no slaves. For subsistence farmers, the relatively underdeveloped slave economy offered some measure of protection. For more ambitious farmers, slavery restricted economic opportunity to the accumulation of land and slaves. Small farmers could hire field slaves from larger planters more cheaply than they could hire free labor, and planters could put a slave to craft work for less than it would cost to hire a free artisan.

Because southern slavery was overwhelmingly agricultural, the South had fewer and smaller cities than the North. Even in the older seacoast states, less than 3 percent of southerners lived in cities. This number included planters taking refuge during the malaria season, slaves in domestic service for the urban professional class, and the free African American population. Traditionally, southern planters looked to Philadelphia and New York for services and luxury goods. When planters sought alternatives to this pattern of external dependence, they looked not to local villages or towns but to their own plantations, reassigning field workers to produce the butter, cheese, and tools they might otherwise have purchased locally. With a few exceptions, the economies of southern cities were based narrowly on the commerce of slaves and cotton.

As ideas about the family became more sentimental in the nineteenth century, prosperous slaveowners adapted these new ideas to the plantation. They tried to convince slavery's critics—and perhaps themselves—that the plantation was like a family presided over by affectionate parents who had only the best interests of their "children" at heart, and, as preposterous as it might seem, that their slaves loved them. The South Carolina planter Henry Hammond explained to a British abolitionist, "We . . . content ourselves with our dear labor under the consoling reflection that what is lost to us is gained to humanity." The more slavery came under attack, the more slave owners insisted, even in the face of powerful evidence to the contrary, that the plantation and its owners were both modern and moral.

But make no mistake: slaves were another part of the master's property and were fiercely defended as such. Because the accumulation of slaves was a source of wealth in its own right, southern reformers argued that the economic interests of the master could dovetail with the benign treatment of his human property. That was the ideal, of course, but planters determined to secure a quick profit provided slaves with as little as possible and used the whip freely. One Mississippi slave owner hired an overseer to "whip up" his slaves, calculating that the harsh treatment would double their productivity. Slavery was a system designed to turn a profit.

Resistance and Creation Among Southern Slaves

For enslaved people, slavery was not merely a system of enforced and often harsh labor. It was also a system of daily survival, practically and emotionally. It was a struggle against arbitrary authority, a monotonous diet, the constant threat of brutal treatment, and the breakup of families and communities. Slavery gave masters so much power over their slaves that the treatment of slaves necessarily varied widely from one owner to another. The slaves themselves spoke of "good masters" and "mean" ones. On any given plantation the impulses of a brutal or a paternalistic master could be offset by an over-seer who might be competent or cruel, or by a mistress who might be kindly or mean-spirited. Particular slaves might be singled out as favorites, others for especially harsh treatment.

Yet most masters and slaves came to an accommodation that allowed the system to function on a day-to-day basis. Plantation routine created norms and expectations. Slaves worked "from sunup to sundown" and ate their predictable meals at predictable hours. Diligent masters set clear expectations for the amount of labor their slaves were to perform and equally clear guidelines for the food, clothing, and shelter provided them, as well as the punishments meted out for infractions of the rules. Slaves in turn came to expect certain "privileges" such as free time—generally Saturday afternoon and Sunday, as well as a yearly holiday at Christmas—and passes to leave the plantation to visit spouses and children on neighboring farms. Arbitrary punishments, cruel overseers, or the withdrawal of privileges could disrupt the smooth operation of the plantation and undermine its profitability.

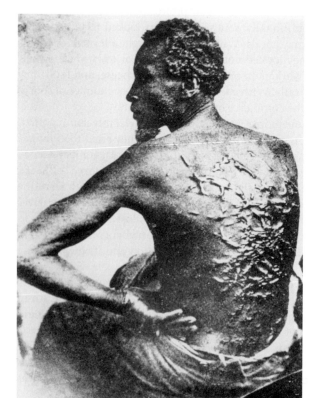

At the same time, slavery vested so much arbitrary power in the master that the system could be defined less by what was routine than by what it allowed. Wanton murder of a slave was illegal, but killing a slave who resisted the master's authority was not. Slaves were maimed and branded often enough that inventors devised special instruments for them, and

Slave with Scars Slave owners used a variety of methods to maintain worker discipline. Some masters enticed their slaves with small privileges in exchange for hard work and cooperation. Many others relied instead on the cruelty of the lash.

owners included descriptions of signs of torture in their advertisements for runaway slaves.

Few slaves escaped the familiar casual humiliations of the system. It was not unusual for enslaved women to bear children whose fathers were free and white. Undoubtedly, some intimate relations between enslaved women and free men were consensual, but most were not. In her memoir *Incidents in the Life of a Slave Girl*, Harriet Jacobs described the limited choices available to female slaves. Jacobs's master began making sexual advances when she was only 15: "[S]hudder[ing] to think of being the mother of children who should be owned by my old tyrant," and hoping to make him so angry that he would sell her, Jacobs entered a sexual relationship with another white man, with whom she eventually bore two children.

Among southern whites, nothing was so fearful as the prospect of outright slave rebellion. Historically, slave rebellions were quite rare and almost never successful. But slave revolts and their rumor periodically shook the white population—the Gabriel rebellion in 1800 and the German Coast uprising a decade later (see Chapter 9), then the Denmark Vesey conspiracy in South Carolina in the 1820s and finally the Nat Turner rebellion in 1831—and southern masters never fully let down their guard. While southern whites feared the prospect of slave rebellion, slave resistance usually took forms other than outright or attempted rebellion. Although masters and mistresses were ready enough to punish slaves without cause, individual slaves also set boundaries on that punishment. In his *Narrative of the Life of Frederick Douglass, An American Slave*, Douglass recalled how he had been rented out to Edward Covey, who whipped Douglass regularly for six months. And then one day Douglass fought back, brawling with Covey for two hours until, exhausted and bleeding, the white man gave up. He never tried to whip Douglass again.

Most forms of resistance were less dramatic than Douglass's act of defiance. Feigned illness or ignorance, carelessness, a slow pace of work—all of these diminished the power of the master or mistress or driver, forcing him or her to adjust to the distinctive tempo or personality of the laborer. Field workers carved out implicit understandings with their masters about at least some of the terms of their labor. For example, task groups finishing early expected to be rewarded with free time and individuals with particular expertise expected deference from drivers, overseers, and even owners. Slaves were also able to accumulate a certain status, based on age or expertise or their place in the slave community, which owners could not ignore altogether.

To focus solely on their acts of resistance, however, is to see unfree African Americans only in relation to the institution of slavery. Albeit with one eye always on survival, enslaved African Americans also established familial and community bonds and cultural traditions. Parenthood often came to slaves unchosen or, if chosen, still under circumstances choreographed by owners (who often tried to arrange partners). Certainly, some slaves—like some free people—were unable to navigate the responsibilities of parenthood successfully. Separated from spouses and children, many slaves never had the chance to try. All these conditions make the record of slave parenting all the more impressive. Parents taught their children to fish and hunt and cook. They praised their children. They told them stories about their grandparents and great-grandparents. White owners felt they were the masters of all their chattel, but African American parents made certain their children understood that, as Jacobs remembered her father's words, "You are my child, and when I call you, you should come immediately, if you have to pass through fire and water."

Enslaved Americans also created communities of custom, both formally and informally. Market women carried produce and handicrafts to county seats and gossiped while they traded with local whites. Men fished and trapped small game. Men and women perfected skills at cooking and storytelling, quilt making and wrestling, and gained reputation and status among their friends. Whites denied legal recognition to slave marriages, but slaves sanctioned their own relationships, combining African ceremonies with European wedding rituals.

As slaves built the economy of the South, they also left a lasting imprint on the culture of southern whites and blacks. Enslaved African Americans began converting to Christianity in the late eighteenth century, and many embraced the religious revivals of the early nineteenth century. Yet as they accepted Christianity, they made it their own. Slave preachers made selective use of Christian themes, emphasizing the story of Moses and the escape from bondage over homilies on the importance of absolute obedience. Newly arrived Africans provided a constant infusion of African religious forms, such as dancing, spiritual singing, chanting, and clapping, as well as distinctly African and Afro-Caribbean religions, such as voodoo. Slave religious practice became both the embodiment and the instrument of self-assertion. The call to "cross over Jordan" in the refrain of many slave songs symbolized the harshness of slave life but perhaps also the singer's intention to escape.

Slavery and National Development

By 1827, when New York finally concluded its long abolition process, few slaves resided in the North and Northwest. But in the North, as in the South, dependency on slavery was not a simple matter of owning or not owning slaves. A free American worker might never see a slave and yet be dependent on the shipping business that carried slave-produced goods or the manufacturing or farming enterprises that supplied planters' needs. An American proud of the country's growth might cherish elaborate shirts and petticoats without ever wondering where the cotton came from. A white American might never have seen a slave and yet believe that there was some natural association of African Americans with servility.

Slavery and Industrialization in the Northeast

As capitalism developed in northwestern Europe and the northern United States, it generated an explosion of commerce that reached across the globe. But instead of spreading freedom, the profits of commerce intensified the various forms of social organization it touched. Commerce made plantation slavery more profitable in the Americas; and it made factory labor more profitable in England and the northern United States. Here was the paradox that would one day bring civil war to the United States: commerce tied two incompatible societies together, one in the South based on slave labor, the other in the North based on free labor.

The seagoing economy of the central and northern coast had long benefited from commercial ties to southern slavery. Yankee ships and crews carried food to the slave islands of the Caribbean and slave-produced commodities to European markets. In the early nineteenth century the northern economy began to develop robustly on its own, whereas the slave economy continued to depend on the northern and European markets for the sale of its cash crops.

In the North, cities such as Philadelphia, New York, and, later, Chicago began to stretch their economic tentacles deep into the surrounding countryside, and northern farms fed a growing army of city factory workers and other wage laborers. Meanwhile, southern cities such as Charleston and New Orleans remained chiefly commercial ports with few signs of the economic development beginning to emancipate northern cities from their long-standing commercial dependence on the southern slave economy.

Boosters of the southern slave economy missed the signs of the North's slowly emerging economic independence because their own cotton economy was thriving. The slaveholders were shipping ever-larger volumes of cash crops to the North—evidence, they thought, of increasing northern commercial dependence on southern slave society. In many ways the slaveholders were right. In the first half of the nineteenth century, merchants in New York and Philadelphia began to specialize in consolidating shiploads of consigned cotton and sending it to England, where agents arranged for sales to English textile manufacturers. Those agents then put together shipments of consumer goods for sale in the United States, often to southern planters. The importance of this commerce to the economy of the North cannot be measured in voyages alone. Every voyage required a ship and a crew. The ships were made in Boston, Salem, Essex, and other New England towns, where local residents were employed in logging or as carpenters, caulkers, or sailmakers and on the rope walks. The crews were mostly New England bred but also came from around the world and included African Americans and Native Americans. Overseas trade also developed the business services of seaport cities. Insurance companies and banks in mid-Atlantic and New England ports catered to southern planters, providing agents for their sales, protecting their goods against the risks of oceanic trade, and holding their debts.

Northerners also benefited from southern consumers. Planters' annual shopping trips to Philadelphia or New York prompted merchants to import expensive English furniture and Chinese porcelain and encouraged tailors, seamstresses, milliners, and glove makers to keep up with the latest European fashions. Peddlers carried household goods into the southern countryside, and northern bookbinders sold religious tracts and prescriptive manuals to southern households. The symbiotic relationship of northern industry and the slave South is nowhere clearer than in the textile mills of early nineteenth-century New England that powered the Industrial Revolution in the North. The desire for such mills was an old story in the republic, but it took slave-produced southern cotton to make that aspiration viable.

The cotton boom proved that commerce can intensify the differences between buyers and sellers. During and after the War of 1812, as the cotton economy was exploding, Francis Cabot Lowell and his associates made large investments in northern textile mills that employed free wage laborers. The profits of the cotton trade also paid for large tracts of land with rivers and falls and eventually supported industrial towns, with all their ancillary commerce, across Rhode Island and Massachusetts. As the textile factories flourished, their commercial ties to the South flourished. In a sense, this was mutual dependency. Northern factory workers needed the cotton slaves produced, and the slaveholders needed northern factories as customers for their cotton. But the cotton trade forged a potentially explosive connection, for it enhanced rather than diminished the differences between northern capitalism and southern slavery.

The many linkages between northern and southern economies led some slaveholders to predict defiantly that the Yankees would never wage war on slavery because they were too dependent on the South. But this was an illusion. What the northerners wanted was cotton, whether it came from Egypt or Alabama, whether it was produced by wage laborers or by slaves. The statistics showing the importance of cotton to America's overseas trade impressed slaveholders. But what those statistics did not show was the far greater volume of trade and commerce within the northern states themselves that was dependent on the development of cities and industry at home rather than oceanic commerce. The textile mills needed the cotton produced by southern slaves, but the mill owners and shoe manufacturers of New England needed even more the northern workers and western farmers who were steadily becoming each other's best customers. By 1860 the South was more dependent on the North than ever, but the North was not nearly as dependent on the South as it had once been.

Slavery and the Laws of the Nation

The men who wrote the Constitution had compromised on the issue of slavery, and it is the nature of compromises to produce ambiguities. After the Constitution was ratified, for example, both New York and New Jersey abolished slavery in their states—completing the process of emancipation in the North. Congress reenacted the Ordinance of 1787, prohibiting the importation of slaves into the Old Northwest and into the federal territories of the Old Southwest. And in 1807, the earliest possible date allowed by the Constitution, Congress prohibited the importation of any more slaves from the Atlantic slave trade. Under the Constitution, the states were now free to abolish slavery on their own, and the federal government assumed the power to regulate and even prohibit slavery in the territories. The Founders' sensibilities were reflected in their deliberate decision to refer to slaves as "persons" rather than property throughout the Constitution.

At the same time, however, the Constitution recognized and even protected slavery from federal interference in the states where it already existed. The Three-Fifths Clause, for example, gave white southerners disproportionate power in the House of Representatives and the Electoral College (in which the number of electors for each state was based on the number of senators and representatives). Article IV gave masters the right to capture and return slaves who ran away: "No person held to service or labour in one state, under the laws thereof, escaping into another, shall, in consequence of any law or regulation therein, be discharged from such service or labour, but shall be delivered up on claim of the party to whom such service or labour may be due." The article avoided the word "slave," but everybody referred to it as the "fugitive slave clause" of the Constitution.

Legal experts and lawmakers agreed that the Constitution prohibited the federal government from interfering with slavery in the states where it existed. But this left several questions unanswered. Did Congress have the power to interfere with slavery in the territories? Could Congress regulate the interstate slave trade? Was the federal government constitutionally obliged to protect the interests of slaveholders on the high seas? And who was responsible for enforcing the fugitive slave clause, the federal government or individual states? In 1793, for example, Congress enacted a fugitive slave law that made it a federal crime to aid an escaping slave. But it left enforcement of the law to the states, and in the North accused runaways were often guaranteed the due process rights of free citizens, much to the dismay of the slaveholders. The slaveholders objected because slaves were, by definition, not citizens. But northerners resented the Three-Fifths Clause for precisely the same reason. In principle, only citizens were supposed to be counted for purposes of representation. By counting as citizens three-fifths of the slave population, the Constitution rewarded southern states with enough extra representatives and Electoral College votes to help ensure the election of a string of presidents from the South. Their support for a limited federal government helped protect slavery from federal interference.

Local and state laws concerning slavery affected the lives of people in all the states. Northern states, for example, passed personal-liberty laws designed to protect free blacks from being kidnapped into slavery by bounty hunters in search of fugitive slaves. These personal-liberty laws made it much harder for masters to enforce the fugitive slave clause of the Constitution. Southern masters deeply resented what they saw as northern-state interference with their rights of property. Conversely, when Charlestonians, fearful of the influence of free black sailors over South Carolina slaves, empowered sheriffs in southern ports to lock up free black sailors, they affected the lives and the employment of men from Boston and Nantucket and New York. The South Carolina Negro Seamen Act of 1822 not only specified the imprisonment of black sailors but also required a bond from their captains to cover the costs of incarceration. Under pressure from a planters' organization, the sheriff of Charleston imprisoned free Jamaican sailor Harry Elkinson. In court, lawyers argued that any treaty that interfered with the power of the state to guard against internal revolution must be unconstitutional. The court rejected this position, but South Carolina continued to enforce the act. By this time, black sailors made up roughly a fifth of northern seamen—a proportion far higher than their presence in the free population. Sailing was an important occupation for them and their families. The act in effect made hiring them a handicap to any captain using South Carolina's ports and jeopardized the sailors' employment. The South Carolina act was later copied by Louisiana, North Carolina, Alabama, Georgia, Florida, and Texas.

Free Black People in a Republic of Slavery

By 1815, some 200,000 African Americans lived as free inhabitants of the United States, most of them in urban areas. Whether they were more than inhabitants—whether they were citizens—varied from state to state and from North to South.

Free blacks faced formidable discrimination in all parts of the country. In the slave South, their very existence was a threat to the system, both in the possibilities of freedom they represented and in the avenues of communication they offered enslaved people. Southern and border states responded by tightening laws permitting individual emancipation, by increasing surveillance of slaves, and by regulating the movement and occupations of free black people. Southern courts increasingly argued that the "taint" of color followed African Americans out of slavery, assuming that free blacks lacked the privileges and immunities of citizens. Free blacks in the South were barred from militias, from the ownership of weapons, and from occupations that might bring them into contact with slaves, such as operating groceries or taverns. What's more, they lived in daily danger of being enslaved, especially as the demand for slaves in the new southern territories increased. It was worth a free black person's life to cultivate ties with the white community, should he or she need authority to ward off the greed of traders. Some border states—including Maryland, New Jersey, and Ohio—barred free blacks from settling within their borders.

Free blacks in the North suffered from similar discriminations, but their conditions varied from state to state. In New England, blacks could vote and send their children to public schools alongside white children. In other states, such as New York, free black men could vote only if they met a property qualification not required of white men. Elsewhere, blacks were barred from voting altogether. Most northern courts assumed that blacks were citizens entitled to own property, to make contracts, to move about freely, and, if accused of crimes, to have a jury trial. But some northern states, particularly along the borders of the South, prohibited free blacks from moving into the state, thus denying them one of the traditional "privileges and immunities" of citizenship. And, as in the South, blacks were often segregated from whites in schools, churches, theaters, cemeteries, hotels, streetcars, ferries, and railways.

In the North and the South, however, the laws were not always a reliable measure of social practice. Often, free blacks and whites interacted every day in ways that defied state statutes. They did business with one another, attended the same churches, and helped one another in times of need. In some southern states the laws restricted free blacks from owning land and houses, but free blacks did so anyway. Periodically, states and localities would require free blacks to be licensed for certain jobs or to carry freedom papers with them at all times, but the laws were only erratically enforced. The threat of enforcement, however, was a constant source of pressure on free black communities across the South.

Within this complicated mosaic of formal and informal discriminations, free African Americans found ways to survive, to earn a living, and, once in a while, to flourish. By the 1820s, the self-help movement founded at the beginning of the republic had yielded many African American mutual-aid and benevolent associations. Organizing was most lively in Philadelphia, where free blacks established more than 40 new societies between 1820 and 1835, but the self-help impulse extended south to Baltimore and Charleston and north to New York and Boston. Although some societies were clearly limited in membership to relatively prosperous free blacks, self-help organizing crossed economic lines: coachmen, porters, barbers, brick makers, sailors, cooks, and washerwomen all formed associations.

The growth of white racial prejudice in the nineteenth century was reflected not simply in the spread of laws discriminating against blacks but also in renewed calls for the abolition of slavery. In 1816, a group including prominent national politicians, northerners, and slave owners formed the American Colonization Society (ACS). Styling itself as a benevolent organization, the Society (whose founders included Andrew Jackson, Francis Scott Key, Daniel Webster, and Henry Clay) determined that because of "unconquerable prejudice resulting from their color," African Americans could succeed only in Africa, which was declared their home (although by 1816 almost all United States slaves had been born in the republic). Made up of wealthy, influential white men, the ACS lobbied Congress for funds. It received $100,000 in 1819 and sent out its first emigrant ship in 1820. Dedicated to removing free African Americans from their native land to Liberia, in Africa, the ACS signaled waning white support for a racially integrated republic.

Jacksonian Democracy in Action

The Democratic campaign of 1828 ushered in a new era of national politics, one that mobilized the public in support of a popular president. To make the point that they were a new breed, Jacksonians began to refer to themselves as "Jacksonian Democrats" (or just "the Democrats").

The Election of 1828

The campaign was personal and vicious. Adams's supporters tarred Jackson as an undisciplined liar and blasphemer. They accused him of having married Rachel Robards before her own divorce was final. Jackson supporters retorted that Adams was a Sabbath breaker, a closet Federalist, and an unprincipled hypocrite who disdained popular government.

Earlier campaigns had been fought primarily on the local level and among a far smaller group of potential voters, but in 1828 New York senator Martin Van Buren coordinated a Democratic national campaign designed to appeal to a mass electorate. Van Buren oversaw the creation of a highly controlled party hierarchy of local and state societies linked to the national organization. He pioneered the use of carefully choreographed demonstrations and converted nonpartisan occasions (such as Fourth of July celebrations) into Democratic rallies. Van Buren also used political imagery to evoke campaign themes. Trading on Jackson's nickname, "Old Hickory" (for the hardest wood in the United States), campaign workers handed out hickory canes at political events. Supporters also used editorials and campaign tracts to describe Jackson as the embodiment of the common man.

When the votes were counted in 1828, Jackson had won a clear majority (see Map 10–3): 56 percent of the popular vote and 178 electoral votes to Adams's 83 electoral votes. Although Adams had retained New England, New Jersey, Delaware, and northern Maryland, Jackson had solidly taken the South and the West, as well as Pennsylvania, most of New York, and even northern Maine.

Jackson was elected by a cross section of voters who identified with his stance as an outsider to, and victim of, eastern elites. Van Buren had put together a coalition of "planters of the South and plain Republicans of the North," actively suppressing the divisive issue of slavery and instead appealing to those who believed that special privilege was denying them their chance of prosperity. He was the candidate of westerners, migrants, settlers, and landowners who opposed eastern banks and congressional land policies, but he also drew support from urban professionals, shopkeepers, laborers, and craftsmen. Jackson claimed the mantle of Jefferson, who also had favored the individual common American and warned against concentrations of economic and political power.

At the same time, the Jacksonians were vague about exactly where the heart of their new democratic movement resided. Structurally, they believed that it evolved from the states, which restrained federal power. At the same time, however, Jackson's strong conviction that he was the people and that his will was indistinguishable from theirs confused matters. The ironic result was a shift of power from the states to the executive during the presidency of the man elected to protect the common man.

The tendency to personalize political struggle characterized Jackson's presidency. He never forgave the National Republicans for publicly questioning the legitimacy of his marriage. Later, he viewed his battle against the Second Bank of the United States in the

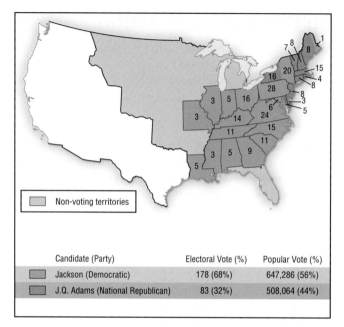

Candidate (Party)	Electoral Vote (%)	Popular Vote (%)
Jackson (Democratic)	178 (68%)	647,286 (56%)
J.Q. Adams (National Republican)	83 (32%)	508,064 (44%)

Map 10–3   The Election of 1828 In 1828, Jackson solidified his hold on the South and Midwest and even made inroads in the Northeast.

same highly personal terms: "The Bank," he informed Van Buren, "is trying to kill me, but I will kill it."

If Jackson understood himself as the embodiment of the people's will, he understood the new Democratic Party as its direct instrument. After personal loyalty to Jackson, party loyalty became the avenue to appointment and the justification for an unprecedented turnover in appointees. The overall results were mixed. Jackson expanded the powers of the presidency, but his conviction that he alone embodied the true virtue of the republic also led to personal pettiness, widespread patronage, and turmoil within his cabinet. His efforts to abolish the Second Bank of the United States created serious hardship for average Americans, and his hostility to Native Americans resulted in widespread death and impoverishment.

The Bank War

The message of the new presidency was clear: reform. Jackson turned his eye on the special privileges and unfair advantages of the rich and well connected. Jackson had long associated this obstacle with Henry Clay, John Quincy Adams, John Calhoun, and the Republican caucus. By 1828 Jackson focused his anger on the Second Bank of the United States.

Jackson hated the bank for all the reasons southerners and westerners did: it was powerful and privileged, and wealthy easterners and foreign investors controlled its private stock. Also, as much as they liked easy credit, most Americans were suspicious of banknotes of all kinds. They had been stung too often by counterfeiters and deadbeats.

But Jackson also had very personal reasons for his opposition. Soon after his first election, Jackson heard rumors that the bank had used its power to buy votes for Adams in 1828. Declaring that the bank threatened "the purity of the right of suffrage," Jackson vowed to oppose it.

Nicholas Biddle, the bank's president, rebuffed Jackson's criticisms. Confident the bank enjoyed broad support, Biddle decided to force the issue before the next presidential election. Although the bank's authorization ran until 1836, on January 6, 1832, Biddle asked Congress to take up renewal early. Jackson may have felt Biddle's behavior to be a personal challenge, because he vetoed it in 1832. "The rich and powerful," he thundered, "too often bend the acts of government to their selfish purposes. . . . [W]hen the laws undertake . . . to make the rich richer, . . . the humble members of society . . . have a right to complain of the injustice of their Government."

The Democrats carried the bank veto proudly into the 1832 election as a contest of "the Democracy and the people, against a corrupt and abandoned aristocracy." The Republicans responded that Jackson's veto showed his tendency toward despotism. The Supreme Court had ruled the national bank constitutional, and Congress had voted to recharter it. Jackson had trammeled the authority of the other branches of government, assuming the sole right to determine the future of the bank.

Dismembering the Bank

Jackson won reelection in 1832, although by a smaller majority than in 1828. By 1833 he was ready to disassemble the Second Bank of the United States. He asked Secretary of the Treasury Louis McLane to select other banks into which the federal government could move its deposits. McLane balked, worried that the selection would be compromised by politics and that the state banks would lose all fiscal restraint. Impatient, Jackson replaced McLane with William J. Duane, and then replaced Duane with Attorney General Roger Taney. On October 1, 1833, the federal government began to distribute its deposits to 22 state banks. By the close of the year, the government deposits had been largely removed.

The deposits had been used to make loans to individuals and corporations around the country. To make the funds available, the Second Bank began furiously calling in loans and foreclosing on debts. In effect, Biddle was repeating the process that triggered the Panic of 1819. In six months he took more than $15 million worth of credit out of the economy.

As recession gripped the nation, the Senate passed an unprecedented resolution censuring Jackson for assuming "authority and power not conferred by the constitution and laws." Jackson's response underscored the new "democratic" politics of the times: "The President," he maintained (and no other branch of government), "is the direct representative of the American people." The expansion of white male suffrage (and the spreading practice of electing members of the Electoral College directly) made Jackson the first president who could claim to be elected directly by the voters. Congress, on the other hand, would soon become the power base of elites.

The first recession passed quickly as state banks tapped their federal deposits to churn out loans, and new wildcat banks took advantage of the glut of paper money. Much of the borrowing went for land sales.

The Specie Act

Correctly, Jackson believed that the excess of paper money in circulation had caused the recession. As soon as conditions improved, he implemented a hard-money policy. In 1833 he had announced that the federal government would no longer accept drafts on the Second Bank in payment of taxes, a move that reduced the value of the bank's notes. In 1834 Jackson declared that the "deposit" banks receiving federal monies could not issue paper drafts for amounts under $5 (later raised to $20), an action that reduced the small-denomination paper in circulation. In July 1836 he had the Treasury Department issue the Specie Circular, which directed land offices to accept only coins or precious metals in payment for western lands. This shut out actual settlers, who could not get together enough gold or silver for their purchases. Meanwhile, the Deposit Act, passed in 1836, expanded the number of "pet banks" to nearly 100 and distributed a federal surplus of more than $5 million to the states, on top of the more than $22 million already deposited in the state banks from the Second Bank of the United States. Underregulated and under local pressure, the state banks could not absorb these funds. They issued loans and printed money that vastly exceeded their assets. When the bubble burst in 1837, the nation faced the worst financial disaster of its young history.

A Policy of Removing Indigenous People

When Jackson looked west, he saw a different sort of problem. For Andrew Jackson, the quintessential "common man" was the western settler, struggling to bring new lands under cultivation and new institutions to life. Pioneers confronted many obstacles in their trek west, but none loomed larger than the resistance of Indian peoples.

Jackson and Native Peoples

The War of 1812 had ended intertribal resistance east of the Mississippi River. By 1828, most of the Great Lakes nations had been pushed out of Ohio, southern Indiana, and Illinois, but the Ojibwa, Winnebago, Sauk, Mesquakie, Kickapoo, and Menominee tribes retained sizable homelands in the region. In the South, in spite of repeated forced cessions, the Chickasaws, Choctaws, Creeks, Cherokees, and Seminoles—the Five "Civilized" Tribes that had adopted American ways—retained ancestral territories.

Jackson's views concerning Native Americans had been settled in the crucible of the Indian wars of the 1790s. "Does not experience teach us that treaties answer no other Purpose than opening an Easy door for the Indians to pass [through to] Butcher our citizens?" he wrote in 1794. Congress should "Punish the Barbarians."

In these views Jackson was no different from many American settlers—some of whom had directly experienced the violence of white incursions into Indian Country, but many of whom formed their ideas long before they ever saw an Indian, basing their preconceptions on inflamed newspaper accounts in the new mass-produced "penny press." Most American settlers saw Indians only in passing. Some of these encounters were surely unnerving, but they were usually of no harm to the settlers. The harm that Indians represented was more basic: they occupied lands recognized as belonging to them in treaties with the federal government. Despite recurrent wars and land cessions, western settlers were no happier with federal initiatives in the 1820s than they had been in the 1790s.

Tension ran especially high in Georgia. There officials complained that the federal government had not kept its promise to remove all Indians from the state, a condition of Georgia's 1802 agreement to cede its western land claims to the federal government. A few Creeks and most of the Cherokee nation remained. In 1826 the federal government pressured the Creeks to give up all but a small strip of their remaining lands in Georgia, but white Georgians were not satisfied. Georgia governor George Michael Troup sent surveyors onto that last piece of Creek land. When President Adams objected to this encroachment on federal treaty powers, Troup threatened to call up the state militia.

The election of Andrew Jackson emboldened Georgians to go after Cherokee land. They invalidated the constitution of the Cherokee nation within Georgia and proclaimed that the Cherokees were subject to the authority of the state of Georgia. When discoveries of gold sent white prospectors surging onto Cherokee land, Georgia refused to stop the trespassers or to protect the Indians. To the contrary, the state passed laws that stripped Cherokees of their rights and their land. Jackson quickly notified the Cherokees that it was his duty, as president, to "sustain the States in the exercise of their rights."

In fact, the states were not exercising their rights. In 1830 the Cherokee nation took the state of Georgia to the Supreme Court, arguing that the Cherokee nation was a "foreign nation in the sense of our constitution and law" and that, as a state, Georgia had no right to pass laws over the inhabitants of a foreign nation. In *Cherokee Nation v. Georgia*, Chief Justice John Marshall agreed that the Cherokees were a distinct political society, but he demurred that they were not a foreign state "in the sense of the constitution, and cannot maintain an action in the courts of the United States." But the following year, *Worcester v. Georgia*, which was not brought by the Cherokee nation, gave Marshall the opportunity to say more. He identified the Cherokee nation as "a distinct community, occupying its own territory, with boundaries accurately described in which the laws of Georgia can have no force, and which the citizens of Georgia have no right to enter but with the assent of the Cherokees themselves or in conformity with treaties and with the acts of Congress." Marshall concluded, "The whole intercourse between the United States and this nation is, by our Constitution and laws, vested in the government of the United States." Georgia had acted unconstitutionally.

Jackson refused to enforce this decision. He had long believed that the best policy would be to remove the Indians entirely from lands sought by settlers. The place he had in mind was across the Mississippi River. Because full-scale removal of the Indians involved shifting populations across state lines and into federal territories, however, it required congressional consent.

The proposed policy was not unopposed. "[I]f, in pursuance of a narrow and selfish policy, we should . . . drive away these remnants of tribes, in such a manner, and under such auspices, as to insure their destruction . . . ," Jeremiah Evarts, secretary of the American Board of Commissioners for Foreign Missions, warned, "then the sentence of an indignant world would be uttered in thunders." In Congress the Native Americans found unexpected allies. To the old Adams men, now led by Henry Clay, "removal" was the policy of states, forced on the federal government. For Congress to pass an act authorizing the policy would mean encouraging states to trample on federal powers.

Van Buren responded by forming a counterlobby, the Board for the Emigration, Preservation, and Improvement of the Aborigines of America, which argued that Indians were ill equipped for contact with white civilization and that removing them was humane. Among the proponents of removal was former president John Quincy Adams. In the end, the bill passed by only five votes and only after four months of debate.

The Removal Act

In 1830 Congress passed and President Jackson signed an act "to provide for an exchange of lands with the Indians residing in any of the states or territories, and for their removal west of the river Mississippi." In one sense, the act only made official and accelerated a policy that Americans had pursued since the founding of the nation. In his State of the Union address that year, Jackson praised the Removal Act as an act of "Philanthropy." He reminded Congress that for generations European Americans had been "leav[ing] the land of their birth to seek new homes in distant regions" and that new lands meant opportunity and liberty. "Doubtless it will be painful to leave the graves of their fathers," he acknowledged of the eastern Indians, "but what do they more than our ancestors did or than our children are now doing?" In fact, leaving "the land of their birth" was for Native Americans not an act of opportunity but rather an eviction from their very identity as a people.

In 1830 the Choctaws were forced from their lands in Mississippi to present-day Oklahoma. The Chickasaws and the Creeks followed in 1832. Then, in 1836, six years after passage of the Removal Act and four years after they had exhausted their judicial options, a small splinter group of the Cherokees (claiming to speak for the whole nation)

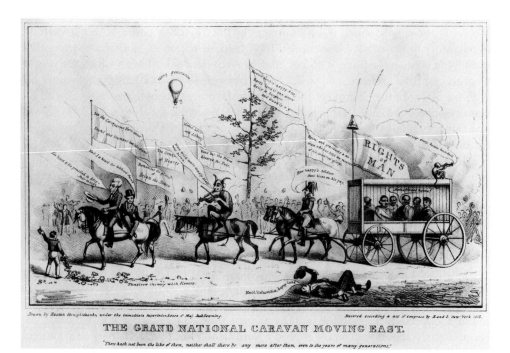

The Grand National Caravan Moving East In this satirical cartoon, Jackson and Van Buren are on the left, followed by the devil, an army officer, and a group of caged Indians, who represent Indian removal. On the ground, a drunken Jacksonian proclaims, "Hail! Columbia, happy land."

at last agreed to removal. The Treaty of New Echota provided that within two years the Cherokees would leave the mountains for Indian Territory, in return for safe passage, $5 million, and food, shelter, equipment, and medicine for a year after their arrival. The Senate ratified the treaty in the spring of 1836. The protreaty Cherokees began to leave almost immediately. The overwhelming majority of Cherokees, who considered the treaty fraudulent, remained in the East.

Three years later, after their unsuccessful appeals to the Supreme Court and after several years of resistance, the Cherokees were removed from their eastern lands. In a forced march that became known as the Trail of Tears, they were driven off their home-lands to Indian Territory in what is now eastern Oklahoma. Most people had delayed leaving until the last moment and had made few preparations for the journey. Many died of disease, malnutrition, dehydration, and exhaustion along the way.

Indians did not accept removal willingly. In 1831, the Sauk and Fox people (de-scended from Native Americans who had earlier been pushed across the Great Lakes region) were forced to relocate once again. In their new lands, however, they began to hear rumors of whites desecrating their former burying grounds. When Indians re-crossed the Mississippi to rebury their dead and harvest produce from their old fields, white farmers and the Illinois militia attacked them. The Sauk and Fox Indians turned to a revered old fighter, Black Hawk, who raised a band of 500 warriors. Attacked by state militiamen, they spent the summer fighting a series of skirmishes called Black Hawk's War. Finally, on August 2, 1832, the exhausted remnants of Black Hawk's band were cornered and massacred by the army.

More successful were the Florida Seminoles, also a diverse community including militant Creek warriors, known as Red Sticks, and runaway slaves. When federal troops arrived to remove the Seminoles in 1832, the Indians resisted with skill and determina-tion. Unfamiliar with the terrain and vulnerable to malaria, the American troops were picked off by both disease and snipers. The war dragged on for seven years. Not until 1842 could President John Tyler proclaim victory.

History, Destiny, and the Remaking of Indian Societies

Beginning with Washington, federal policy had encouraged Indians to adopt American ways of life—a private-property-based agrarian economy in which men worked in the fields and women in the home. At the same time, another strand in American thought held that Native Americans were incapable of change and Native American disposses-sion was inevitable, not only because white Americans were perfectly matched to the land but also because Indians were not. Americans who wanted to seize Indian lands claimed to have tried again and again to help Native Americans survive but considered them incapable of taking full advantage of the land. Ignoring the example of the Five Civilized Tribes, Jackson reflected this view in his 1833 address to Congress. Native Americans, he declared, had "neither the intelligence, the industry, the moral habits, nor the desire of improvement which are essential" to realizing the potential of the land.

This understanding of manifest destiny as entailing the inevitable disappearance of Native Americans made its way into American literature in the 1820s, just as white Americans were considering Indian removal as an official government policy. Its venue was the historical novel. The depiction of Native Americans in antebellum historical novels represented a departure from earlier Indian captivity narratives, which often

Western Comanche in War Dress Comanche culture rewarded risk taking and prowess in war. Warriors made headdresses out of the hair of their captives and the hair of their own wives.

described Indians as almost incapable of human feeling and bent on the violent destruction of European American civilization. Although the historical novels of the 1820s did not romanticize all Native Americans, they did identify among the Indians individuals of high character—of integrity, intelligence, and great sensitivity—but who, significantly, were always doomed to extinction.

Although dispossession was a devastating experience for Native Americans, native societies adapted. The Comanches agreed to make room for removed Indians who would trade with them. Soon the displaced tribes, which had reestablished their agricultural way of life, were trading their crops and government-issued guns and ammunition to the Comanches for their new neighbors' chief commodities, horses and slaves. When they were forced to migrate, the southeastern Indians had brought 5,000 black slaves with them, a workforce they replenished with the enslaved Indians, Mexicans, and Anglo-Americans sold by the Comanches. Ironically, the Indians who were displaced because they supposedly could not adapt took American values and practices with them: representative government, Christianity, and racial slavery. Drawing from their experience, they became middlemen, facilitating the trade between the Comanches to the west and Americans to the east.

As American weapons made their way to the western edge of the Comanche empire, the Spanish became alarmed. They now found that thousands of dollars' worth of gifts no longer purchased the loyalty of the Comanches, who increasingly wanted trade with the wealthier Americans. As Spanish influence in the West waned after Mexico achieved independence in 1821, American traders began moving into the region, at first destabilizing it. By 1840, however, the Comanche Empire had established commercial dominance in the southern plains. Josiah Gregg, an American trader, observed that the Comanches "acknowledge no boundaries, but call themselves the lords of the entire prairies."

The Growth of Sectional Tension

The growing fiscal strains in Jacksonian America were matched by brewing sectional conflict. Americans had not always viewed the differences between the political economies of the North and South as bad. Those regional differences had powered northern industrialization during the War of 1812 and had laid the foundation for the National Republican vision of robust nationalism after the war. But economic expansion brought old differences into open conflict. The immediate catalyst was the tariff, but by 1832 the tariff question had ignited a broader debate over the institution of slavery.

The Sources of Southern Discontent

Despite an apparent victory in the Missouri controversy, many white southerners had felt betrayed by northern criticisms of slavery. Economic and political frustrations in the 1820s nurtured that sense of mistreatment, leading the planter class, which had so far dominated the presidency, to see itself as the victim of the federal government.

White southerners read signs of shifting public attitudes toward slavery. Proslavery advocates in Illinois (where many African Americans were already held in indentures comparable to slavery) were unable to elect a proslavery congressman in 1820. In 1824 Ohio asked Congress to consider a plan for the gradual abolition of slavery throughout the United States. On July 4, 1827, New York completed its long process of gradual emancipation, an occasion celebrated by free African Americans as far south as Virginia. And news from England had it that abolitionist William Wilberforce was likely to get slavery outlawed in the British West Indies.

Most important, though, was the economy. By 1828 cotton prices were only about one-third of their 1815 levels. Many planters and farmers tried to compensate for falling profits by planting more acres, but worn-out fields kept production low. Large eastern planters often sold off slaves, lands, and city houses. Many smaller farmers, dependent on cotton as their cash crop to pay off debts, were forced to sell out. Although the Panic of 1819 hurt northern farms and businesses, most of the Northeast bounced back faster than the South, which focused planter attention on the 1816 protective tariff as a sign of government favoritism. They complained that the tariff was unnaturally driving up the prices of European imports, forcing strapped southerners to purchase expensive northern-made products and driving down southern export sales. "We have no objection to the North being enriched by our riches," one Charleston *Mercury* reporter wrote sarcastically in 1827, "but not from our poverty."

Of the slaveholding states, South Carolina was particularly insecure. Its white residents faced a growing African American majority (the result of white migration west) that heightened fears of slave insurrection.

South Carolina's Protest

Passage of the Tariff of 1828, the "tariff of abominations," led to nullification talk in South Carolina and created a new leader, John C. Calhoun. Like other South Carolinians, Calhoun had been disenchanted by the experiences of the 1820s and was a far less enthusiastic nationalist than he had once been. Yet he retained enough faith in the Democratic Party to believe that Democrats would lower the tariff once in office and would see the injury to southern states from such national laws. To encourage both results, in

1828 Calhoun wrote the *South Carolina Exposition and Protest*, a justification for the theory of nullification, under which states might declare particular federal laws null and void within their borders. Although Calhoun published the pamphlet anonymously (still aspiring to the presidency, he was reluctant to associate himself too openly with the extreme position), he let his authorship be widely known, hoping for the support of radicals in his home state. In the *Exposition*, Calhoun argued that the federal government was the creation of the states. In agreeing to create a federal government, the states had ceded some of their powers, but only conditionally, and always reserving the right to do whatever was necessary to ensure their survival as "distinct political communities." A state had the right to assert its sovereignty in defiance of federal policies that might threaten its distinctive character. It was at such a juncture, Calhoun argued, that the states of the South had arrived in 1828. They had become the "minority" culture, their interests and institutions endangered by "the unrestrained will of a majority." The tariff would gradually drain away the money and the independence of the South, subjecting it to northern tyranny.

Much in America's history supported Calhoun's view. The states had existed before the federal Constitution. Representation at the Constitutional Convention and ratification of the Constitution had been by state, and representation in the federal government continued to be on the basis of states. Moreover, defenders of the theory included Thomas Jefferson and James Madison, in their resolutions opposing the Alien and Sedition Acts.

On the other hand, the Constitution's status as the supreme law of the land rested on the fact that it had been ratified by the *people*, acting through special conventions, not by the state governments, and subsequent suffrage reform had enlarged the popular participation of white men. Moreover, after the debacle of the Hartford Convention, states' rights arguments had the whiff of treason. And Calhoun went further than that convention had: he argued explicitly what the Federalists had dared only hint, that if all else failed, states retained the right to withdraw from the compact.

Among those who viewed the federal government as properly the creation of "the people," not of the states, and who regarded threats to withdraw from the Union as unforgivable, was President Jackson.

The Nullification Crisis

Other southern states, less economically pressed than South Carolina and more optimistic that regional political differences could yet be reconciled, did not rush to endorse the *Exposition*. But two events increased political tensions: a seemingly innocuous Senate debate over western land sales that sharpened the rhetoric over sectional differences, and a slave rebellion in Virginia that came closer than any other to succeeding.

Eager to attract population, westerners had long lobbied for a reduction in the price of federal lands. Southern representatives offered to support the measure if the western states would join in opposing the tariff. When, in December 1829, Senator Samuel A. Foot of Connecticut advocated limiting land sales in the West, South Carolina Senator Robert Y. Hayne accused him of conspiring to keep labor prices low in the East and insinuated that the government was keeping land prices artificially high to build a slush fund "for corruption—fatal to the sovereignty and independence of the states."

Rising to defend his region, Senator Daniel Webster of Massachusetts countered that it was South Carolina, not the Northeast, that was a hotbed of disloyalty, pointing

The Federal Government Responds to Abolitionism

As the election of 1836 approached, Andrew Jackson's Democratic Party had a problem. The rise of the abolitionist movement made slaveholders nervous, and they wanted proof that Jackson's hand-picked successor, Vice President Martin Van Buren, a New Yorker, would protect slavery. Because there was little more that the federal government could do, southerners looked for symbolic gestures. How could the Democratic Party mollify slave owners without losing northern support? By defining abolitionists as the problem.

In 1835 alone, abolitionists mailed 175,000 antislavery tracts to the South. The Charleston, South Carolina, postmaster refused to deliver them. Then a mob of 2,000, one-seventh of the white population of the city, broke into the post office and burned the offending mail, a clear violation of federal law. Rather than enforce it, Jackson's administration tried to "pacify the South" by making it illegal to mail to the South "incendiary publications intended to instigate the slaves to insurrection." It argued that the abolitionists were terrorists, that southerners had the right to suppress free speech to insure "the safety of their people," and the federal government was obligated to protect the South from the distribution of "papers calculated to produce domestic violence."

As unpopular as the abolitionists were, however, Congress refused to pass the law, which smacked too much of nullification. The Post Office Act threatened to punish postmasters who did not deliver the mail, whatever it contained. Nonetheless, south- ern postmasters quietly refused to deliver abolitionist tracts, and no one was ever punished. Such was the uneasy compromise that held the Democratic Party together and preserved civil liberties in the North but not the South: although the law said that abolitionist tracts must be delivered everywhere, slaveholders succeeded in suppressing free speech in the South with a wink and a nod from the North.

Abolitionist men and women responded by exercising another basic civil right, the right to petition. They flooded Congress with petitions asking it to end slavery. South Carolina Representative James Henry Hammond insisted that Congress refuse even to accept the petitions. He "could not sit there and see the rights of the southern people assaulted day after day, by the ignorant fanatics from whom these memorials proceed." Because there was no chance that Congress would abolish slavery, the purpose of Hammond's heated rhetoric was to signal to northern Democrats that southern ones expected complete adherence to their position. The Senate and the House struck a slightly less extreme compromise called the Gag Rule, which prohibited discussion of particular matters (such as slavery), while northern Democrats competed to see who could best satisfy southern demands to brand the abolitionists as dangerous radicals. Senator James Buchanan of Pennsylvania said the abolitionists were "fanatics, led on by foreign incendiaries," while Representative Garret Wall of New Jersey claimed that
continued

STRUGGLES FOR DEMOCRACY *continued*

"we all, North and South, abhor abolition incendiarism," and that "it is the attempt . . . to put the dagger and the torch in the hand of infuriated madmen . . . to involve our fellow-citizens in the horrors of rapine, murder, and a servile war."

The southern Democrats succeeded in the short term, silencing discussion of slavery as much as they could, not only in the South but even in Congress. That was the

price northern Democrats had to pay to maintain their national party. The cost to the civil liberties of slavery's opponents, however, was high. Rights guaranteed to them by the Bill of Rights were effectively suppressed. Their petitions to Congress were put aside, their mail sent to the South left undelivered. When democracy is contested, who gets to enjoy which of its rights is often a matter of struggle.

for evidence to the *Exposition*. The Revolution had been fought by *the American people*, Webster thundered, and *the American people* had created the federal government. Uncannily foreshadowing, Webster evoked the image of "a once glorious union" "rent with civil feuds, or drenched, it may be, in fraternal blood!" Signaling an acceptance of slavery in "the Union as it is," Webster also insisted that "every true American heart" must recommit itself to the founding spirit of the nation: "Liberty and Union, now and forever, one and inseparable."

Although he supported the federal Union, President Jackson did sympathize with southern complaints about the fairness of tariff levels, and he advocated tariff reform. The Tariff of 1832 lowered duties on many goods to 1816 levels, but not on textiles and iron. In this continued protection for the largest northern industries, South Carolinians

Time Line

▼**1793**
Eli Whitney invents cotton gin

▼**1808**
External slave trade becomes illegal

▼**1819**
Missouri applies for statehood

▼**1820**
Missouri Compromise
Maine becomes a state

▼**1821**
Missouri becomes a state

▼**1822**
South Carolina Negro Seamen Act
Denmark Vesey conspiracy

▼**1824**
John Quincy Adams elected president (the "corrupt bargain")

▼**1827**
Antimason Party organized

▼**1828**
Andrew Jackson elected president
Virtually universal white male suffrage
Tariff of 1828 passes
Calhoun writes *South Carolina Exposition and Protest*

saw a defiant reaffirmation of a special relationship between northern interests and the federal government.

By then, the South had been the scene of another slave insurrection. In the summer of 1831 an African American driver and preacher by the name of Nat Turner launched a rebellion in Virginia. The rebellion was put down, and Turner and other conspirators were executed, but unlike earlier plots, this revolt had actually taken place. Inspired by a millennialist fervor, for two days Turner and his followers had effectively controlled parts of southern Virginia, recruiting new allies, executing whites, and freeing slaves. Although the number of active insurrectionists probably never exceeded 70, 57 whites died in the uprising, more than in any previous slave rebellion. Southern whites took their revenge in a monthlong reign of vigilante terror, but the insurrection had left its mark. Southern whites lived in a state of constant fear, convinced that northerners and southern slaves were in league against them. So traumatic was the Turner rebellion that the Virginia legislature debated, but ultimately rejected, a proposal for the gradual abolition of slavery in the state.

In an 1832 convention, South Carolina radicals voted to nullify the tariffs of 1828 and 1832, passing the Ordinance of Nullification by 136 votes to 26 votes. The act forbade the collection of the tariffs within South Carolina. For Jackson, the act of nullification transformed the crisis from a question of regional interests to one of national union. "The laws of the United States must be executed," he declared. "I have no discretionary power on the subject; my duty is emphatically pronounced in the Constitution." He asked Congress for a law specifically affirming his responsibility to compel the collection of the tax in South Carolina, by force of arms if necessary.

Congress rushed to find a compromise. In early 1833 it passed a tariff that gradually reduced duties over the next decade but also passed the law Jackson had requested, known as the Force Bill. Jackson signed both the new tariff law and the Force Bill, a signal to South Carolina that nullification and secession would not be tolerated.

In 1832, with South Carolina virtually alone even among southern states, supporters of nullification had no choice but to withdraw their ordinance. At the same time, they

▼**1830**
Removal Act passes

▼**1831**
Antimason Party holds first open presidential nominating convention
Cherokee Nation v. Georgia
Nat Turner leads rebellion in Virginia

▼**1832**
Worcester v. Georgia
Black Hawk's War
Jackson vetoes act rechartering Second Bank of the United States
Jackson reelected
Tariff of 1832
South Carolina passes Ordinance of Nullification

▼**1833**
Congress passes Force Bill

▼**1836**
Deposit Act expands number of Jackson's "pet banks" and provides for distribution of federal surplus

voted to nullify the Force Bill within the boundaries of South Carolina. Jackson let the gesture pass, and at least for the time being, the constitutional crisis was over.

Conclusion

The Jacksonian consensus was forged from belief in the efficacy of the individual, a distrust of unfair privilege, a commitment to geographic expansionism, and an insistence that slavery be kept out of national politics. Few of these elements were new to Americans, but their meanings had shifted since 1776. The republic was becoming a democracy. But the harmony that seemed to be expressed in the Jacksonian celebration of democracy was misleading. Consensus was always partial, and conflict always present and growing. African Americans and Native Americans were excluded altogether; workers and women were included only contingently. Within 25 years of Jackson's election, workers were in the streets, hundreds of thousands of Americans were petitioning to end slavery, political parties were in chaos, and the nation stood on the brink of civil war.

Who, What

The Monroe Doctrine 288

National Republicanism 285

The "corrupt bargain" 285

Special privilege 295

Antimason Party 296

Frederick Douglass 297

Nat Turner 303

South Carolina Negro Seamen Act 307

American Colonization Society 308

The Second Bank of the United States 286

Black Hawk 315

Nullification 317

Review Questions

1. How did the United States show its self-confidence at the end of the War of 1812?

2. What was the Missouri Compromise?

3. How was slavery generally practiced in the United States?

4. Describe the relationship between southern slavery and northern capitalism.

5. Why did Jackson oppose the *South Carolina Exposition and Protest*? Why didn't other southern states support South Carolina in the nullification crisis?

Critical-Thinking Questions

1. How could the Jacksonians create a coalition between two such different interests as southern planters and northern workers?

2. The Cherokees and the other "civilized" tribes were removed from the Southeast even though they had adopted American customs and forms of government. Why?

3. The Second Bank of the United States and Indian removal were simultaneously symbolic and substantial issues. How was this the case?

4. Compare and contrast how slavery brought the North and South closer together and how it drove the two regions apart. How did the cotton trade enhance rather than diminish the differences between northern capitalism and southern slavery?

For further review materials and resource information, please visit www.oup.com/us/oakes

CHAPTER 10: JACKSONIAN DEMOCRACY, 1820–1840
Primary Sources

10.1 JAMES MONROE, EXCERPTS FROM THE STATE OF THE UNION ADDRESS TO CONGRESS (1823)

In the decades after the American Revolution, many other nations in North and South America declared independence from their European colonizers, first Haiti in 1804, and most countries in Latin America by 1820. International rumors, however, suggested that European powers were interested in regaining old colonies or conquering new ones. The United States, developing its foreign policy, wanted to protect its trading partners in the Americas without becoming entangled in costly wars. In what became known as the "Monroe Doctrine," President James Monroe declared in 1824 that the "Old World" should stop interfering with the "New World."

... In the discussions [with Great Britain and Russia] to which this interest has given rise and in the arrangements by which they may terminate the occasion has been judged proper for asserting, as a principle in which the rights and interests of the United States are involved, that the American continents, by the free and independent condition which they have assumed and maintain, are henceforth not to be considered as subjects for future colonization by any European powers.

It was stated at the commencement of the last session that a great effort was then making in Spain and Portugal to improve the condition of the people of those countries, and that it appeared to be conducted with extraordinary moderation. It need scarcely be remarked that the results have been so far very different from what was then anticipated. Of events in that quarter of the globe, with which we have so much intercourse and from which we derive our origin, we have always been anxious and interested spectators. The citizens of the United States cherish sentiments the most friendly in favor of the liberty and happiness of their fellow-men on that side of the Atlantic. In the wars of the European powers in matters relating to themselves we have never taken any part, nor does it comport with our policy to do so. It is only when our rights are invaded or seriously menaced that we resent injuries or make preparation for our defense. With the movements in this hemisphere we are of necessity more immediately connected, and by causes which must be obvious to all enlightened and impartial observers. The political system of the allied powers is essentially different in this respect from that of America. This difference proceeds from that which exists in their respective Governments; and to the defense of our own, which has been achieved by the loss of so much blood and treasure, and matured by the wisdom of their most enlightened citizens, and under which we have enjoyed unexampled felicity, this whole nation is devoted. We owe it, therefore, to candor and to the amicable relations existing between the United States and those powers to declare that we should consider any attempt on their part to extend their system to any portion of this hemisphere as dangerous to our peace and safety. With the existing colonies or dependencies of any European power we have not interfered and shall not interfere. But with the Governments who have declared their independence and maintain it, and whose independence we have, on great consideration and on just principles, acknowledged, we could not view any interposition for the purpose of oppressing them, or controlling in any other manner their destiny, by any European power in any other light than as the manifestation of an unfriendly disposition toward the United States. In the war between those new Governments and Spain we declared our neutrality at the time of their recognition, and to this we have adhered, and shall continue to adhere, provided no change shall occur which, in the judgment of the competent authorities of this Government, shall make a corresponding change on the part of the United States indispensable to their security.

The late events in Spain and Portugal show that Europe is still unsettled. Of this important fact no stronger proof can be adduced than that the allied powers should have thought it proper, on any principle satisfactory to themselves, to have interposed by force in the internal concerns of Spain. To what extent such interposition may be carried, on the same principle, is a question in which all independent powers whose governments differ from theirs are interested, even those most remote, and surely none of them more so than the United States. Our policy in regard to Europe, which was adopted at an early stage of the wars which have so long agitated that quarter of the globe, nevertheless remains the same, which is, not to interfere in the internal concerns of any of its powers; to consider the government de facto as the legitimate government for us; to cultivate friendly relations with it, and to preserve those relations by a frank, firm, and manly policy, meeting in all instances the just claims of every power, submitting to injuries from none. But in regard to those continents circumstances are eminently and conspicuously different.

It is impossible that the allied powers should extend their political system to any portion of either continent without endangering our peace and happiness; nor can anyone believe that our southern brethren, if left to themselves, would adopt it of their own accord. It is equally impossible, therefore, that we should behold such interposition in any form with indifference. If we look to the comparative strength and resources of Spain and those new Governments, and their distance from each other, it must be obvious that she can never subdue them. It is still the true policy of the United States to leave the parties to themselves, in hope that other powers will pursue the same course. . . .

Source: President James Monroe's annual address to Congress, December 2, 1823.

10.2 DAVID WALKER, EXCERPTS FROM "WALKER'S APPEAL" (1829)

The son of a free black woman and a black slave, David Walker was born a free man in South Carolina. As an adult, he moved to Boston, where he became a successful businessman, an outspoken abolitionist, and a vociferous critic of racial slavery. The following selection comes from "Walker's Appeal," a pamphlet he published in 1829 that encouraged fellow blacks, both slaves and free, to fight racism and slavery. Walker's passionate critique of slavery encouraged people of all races to become more radical in their opposition to slavery.

. . . I therefore ask the whole American people, had I not rather die, or be put to death, than to be a slave to any tyrant, who takes not only my own, but my wife and children's lives by the inches? Yea, would I meet death with avidity far! far! in preference to such *servile submission* to the murderous hands of tyrants. For let no one of us suppose that the refutations which have been written by our white friends are enough—they are *whites*—we are *blacks*. We, and the world wish to see the charges of Mr. Jefferson [in *Notes on Virginia*, 1785] refuted by the blacks *themselves*, according to their chance; for we must remember that what the whites have written respecting this subject, is other men's labours, and did not emanate from the blacks. I know well, that there are some talents and learning among the coloured people of this country, which we have not a chance to develope, in consequence of oppression; but our oppression ought not to hinder us from acquiring all we can. For we will have a chance to develope them by and by. God will not suffer us, always to be oppressed. Our sufferings will come to an *end,* in spite of all the Americans this side of *eternity.* Then we will want all the learning and talents among ourselves, and perhaps more, to govern ourselves.—"Every dog must have its day," the American's is coming to an end.

But let us review Mr. Jefferson's remarks respecting us some further. Comparing our miserable fathers, with the learned philosophers of Greece, he says: "Yet notwithstanding these and other discouraging circumstances among the Romans, their slaves were often their rarest artists. They excelled too, in science, insomuch as to be usually employed as tutors to their master's children; Epictetus, Terence and Phædrus, were slaves,—but they were of the race of whites. It is not their *condition* then, but *nature,* which has produced the distinction." [See *Notes on Virginia,* p. 211.]

See this, my brethren!! Do you believe that this assertion is swallowed by millions of the whites? Do you know that Mr. Jefferson was one of as great characters as ever lived among the whites? See his writings for the world, and public labours for the United States of America. Do you believe that the assertions of such a man, will pass away into oblivion unobserved by this people and the world? If you do you are much mistaken—See how the American people treat us—have we souls in our bodies? Are we men who have any spirits at all? I know that there are many *swell-bellied* fellows among us, whose greatest object is to fill their stomachs. Such I do not mean—I am after those who know and feel, that we are MEN, as well as other people; to them, I say, that unless we try to refute Mr. Jefferson's arguments respecting us, we will only establish them….

Are we MEN!!—I ask you, O my brethren! are we MEN? Did our Creator make us to be slaves to dust and ashes like ourselves? Are they not dying worms as well as we? Have they not to make their appearance before the tribunal of Heaven, to answer for the deeds done in the body, as well as we? Have we any other Master but Jesus Christ alone? Is he not their Master as well as ours?—What right then, have we to obey and call any other Master, but Himself? How we could be so *submissive* to a gang of men, whom we cannot tell whether they are *as good* as ourselves or not, I never could conceive. However, this is shut up with the Lord, and we cannot precisely tell—but I declare, we judge men by their works.

The whites have always been an unjust, jealous, unmerciful, avaricious and blood-thirsty set of beings, always seeking after power and authority. We view them all over the confederacy of Greece, where they were first known to be any thing, (in consequence of education) we see them there, cutting each other's throats—trying to subject each other to wretchedness and misery—to effect which, they used all kinds of deceitful, unfair, and unmerciful means. We view them next in Rome, where the spirit of tyranny and deceit raged still higher. We view them in Gaul, Spain, and in Britain.—In fine, we view them all over Europe, together with what were scattered about in Asia and Africa, as heathens, and we see them acting more like devils than accountable men. But some may ask, did not the blacks of Africa, and the mulattoes of Asia, go on in the same way as did the whites of Europe. I answer, no—they never were half so avaricious, deceitful and unmerciful as the whites, according to their knowledge.

Source: David Walker. *An Appeal to the Coloured Citizens of the World.* Boston: published for the author, 1829, pp. 17–20. http://docsouth.unc.edu/nc/walker/walker.html

---

10.3 RUFUS KING, EXCERPTS FROM *THE SUBSTANCE OF TWO SPEECHES DELIVERED IN THE SENATE OF THE UNITED STATES, ON THE SUBJECT OF THE MISSOURI BILL* (1820) AND WILLIAM PINKNEY, EXCERPTS

FROM HIS RESPONSE ON THE MISSOURI QUESTION (1820)

Politicians and leaders had known since the early days of the nation that slavery would be a divisive and contested issue. Congress had banned the importation of slaves in 1807, while still allowing the slave trade to continue via the internal slave market. Many hoped that the institution would slowly decline into oblivion. The acquisition of new territory, however, along with rising cotton prices, caused new debates over slavery to erupt. In 1820, Congress debated whether or not Missouri could be required to abolish slavery before becoming a state.

Rufus King, New York, February 11 and 14, 1820

The constitution declares, "that Congress shall have power to dispose of, and make all needful rules and regulations respecting the territory and other property of the United States."

. . . The question respecting slavery in the old thirteen states, had been decided and settled before the adoption of the constitution, which grants no power to Congress to interfere with, or to change, what had been so previously settled: the slave states therefore are free to continue or to abolish slavery. . . .

The constitution contains no express provisions respecting slavery in a new state that may be admitted into the union: every regulation upon this subject, belongs to the power whose consent is necessary to the formation and admission of such state. Congress may therefore make it a condition of the admission of a new state, that slavery shall be forever prohibited within the same. We may with the more confidence pronounce this to be the true construction of the constitution, as it has been so amply confirmed by the past decisions of Congress. . . .

The existence of slavery impairs the industry and the power of a nation; and it does so in proportion to the multiplication of its slaves: where the manual labour of a country is performed by slaves, labour dishonours the bands of freemen.

If her labourers be slaves, Missouri may be able to pay money taxes, but will be unable to raise soldiers, or to recruit seamen; and experience seems to have proved that manufactures do not prosper where the artificers are slaves. In case of foreign war or domestic insurrection, misfortunes from which no states are exempt, and against which all should be seasonably prepared, slaves not only do not add to, but diminish the faculty of self defence; instead of increasing the public strength, they lessen it, by the whole number of free persons whose place they occupy, increased by the number of freemen that may be employed as guards over them.

. . . If Missouri, and the other states that may be formed to the west of the river Mississippi, are permitted to introduce and establish slavery, the repose, if not the security, of the union may be endangered; all the states south of the river Ohio and west of Pennsylvania and Delaware, will be peopled with slaves, and the establishment of new states west of the river Mississippi, will serve to extend slavery instead of freedom over that boundless region.

Such increase of the states, whatever other interests it may promote, will be sure to add nothing to the security of the public liberties, and can hardly fail hereafter to require and produce a change in our government. . . .

William Pinkney, Maryland, responds, February 15, 1820

. . . The whole amount of the argument on the other side is, that you may refuse to admit a new State, and that therefore if you admit, you may prescribe the terms.

The answer to that argument is—that even if you can refuse, you can prescribe no terms which are inconsistent with the act you are to do. You can prescribe no conditions which, if carried into effect, would make the new State less a sovereign State than, under the Union as it stands, it would be. You can prescribe no terms which will make the compact of Union between it and the original States essentially different from that compact among the original States. You may admit, or refuse to admit: but if you admit, you must admit a State in the sense of the Constitution—a State with all such sovereignty as belongs to the original parties: and it must be into this Union that you are to admit it, not into a Union of your own dictating, formed out of the existing Union by qualifications and new compacts, altering its character and effect. . .

The truth is, that the restriction has no relation, real or pretended, to the right of making slaves of those who are free, or of introducing slavery where it does not already exist. It applies to those who are admitted to be already slaves, and who (with their posterity) would continue to be slaves if they should remain where they are at present; and to a place where slavery already exists by the local law.

. . . I trust, then, that I shall be forgiven if I suggest that no eccentricity in argument can be more trying to human patience than a formal assertion that . . . a clause commanding Congress to guarantee a republican form of government to [slaveholding] States, as well as to others, authorizes you to determine that slavery and a republican form of government cannot co-exist.

But if a republican government is that in which all the men have a share in the public power, the slaveholding States will not alone retire from the Union. The constitutions of some of the other States do not sanction universal suffrage, or universal eligibility. They require citizenship, and age, and a certain amount of property, to give a title to vote or to be voted for; and they who have not those qualifications are just as much disfranchised . . . as if they were slaves. . . . If it be true that all men in a republican Government must help to wield its power, and be equal in rights, I beg leave to ask . . . and why not all the *women?* . . . If the ultra republican doctrines which have now been broached should ever gain ground among us, I should not be surprised if some romantic reformer, treading in the footsteps of Mrs. Wolstencraft, should propose to repeal our republican law . . . and claim for our wives and daughters a full participation in political power, and to add to it that domestic power which, in some families, as I have heard, is as absolute and unrepublican as any power can be.

Sources: Rufus, King. *The Substance of Two Speeches Delivered in the Senate of the United States, on the Subject of the Missouri Bill.* Philiadelphia: Clark and Raser. Rufus King, Feburary 11 and 14, 1820. http://archive.org/stream/ substanceoftwosp00king/substanceoftwosp00king_djvu.txt

William Pinkney's response from: Johnston, Alexander. *American Eloquence: Studies in American Political History.* New York: G. P. Putnam's Sons, 1896. Available online at http://www.gutenberg.org/files/15392/ 15392-h/15392-h.htm#link2H_4_0006. Additionally: *Annals of Congress,* Senate, 16th Congress, 1st session, pp. 414–415. Available online at http://memory.loc.gov/cgi-bin/ampage?collId=llac&fileName=035/ llac035.db&recNum=203

10.4 ANDREW JACKSON, EXCERPTS FROM BANK VETO MESSAGE (1832) AND VISUAL DOCUMENT: H.R. ROBINSON, "GENERAL JACKSON SLAYING THE MANY HEADED MONSTER" (1836)

In 1832, shortly before the end of President Andrew Jackson's first term, Congress proposed rechartering the Bank of the United States. Jackson vetoed the bill, and he and the Democrats used the veto as an issue in the reelection campaign. As much as any other address to the American people, Jackson's veto message, a brief excerpt of which follows, sets out his vision for the role of government in advancing economic equality and preventing undemocratic concentrations of political and economic power.

To the Senate.

. . . A bank of the United States is in many respects convenient for the Government and useful to the people. Entertaining this opinion, and deeply impressed with the belief that some of the powers and privileges possessed by the existing bank are unauthorized by the Constitution, subversive of the rights of the States, and dangerous to the liberties of the people, I felt it my duty at an early period of my Administration to call the attention of Congress to the practicability of organizing an institution combining all its advantages and obviating these objections. I sincerely regret that in the act before me I can perceive none of those modifications of the bank charter which are necessary, in my opinion, to make it compatible with justice, with sound policy, or with the Constitution of our country.

The present corporate body . . . will have existed at the time this act is intended to take effect twenty years. It enjoys an exclusive privilege of banking under the authority of the General Government, a monopoly of its favor and support, and, as a necessary consequence, almost a monopoly of the foreign and domestic exchange. The powers, privileges, and favors bestowed upon it in the original charter, by increasing the value of the stock far above its par value, operated as a gratuity of many millions to the stockholders. . . .

Every monopoly and all exclusive privileges are granted at the expense of the public, which ought to receive a fair equivalent. The many millions which this act proposes to bestow on the stockholders of the existing bank must come directly or indirectly out of the earnings of the American people. It is due to them, therefore, if their Government sell monopolies and exclusive privileges, that they should at least exact for them as much as they are worth in open market.

. . .

It is to be regretted that the rich and powerful too often bend the acts of government to their selfish purposes. Distinctions in society will always exist under every just government. Equality of talents, of education, or of wealth can not be produced by human institutions. In the full enjoyment of the gifts of Heaven and the fruits of superior industry, economy, and virtue, every man is equally entitled to protection by law; but when the laws undertake to add to these natural and just advantages artificial distinctions, to grant titles, gratuities, and exclusive privileges, to make the rich richer and the potent more powerful, the humble members of society—the farmers, mechanics, and laborers—who have neither the time nor the means of securing like favors to themselves, have a right to complain of the injustice of their Government. There are no necessary evils in government. Its evils exist only in its abuses. If it would confine itself to equal protection, and, as Heaven does its rains, shower its favors alike on the high and the low, the rich and the poor, it would be an unqualified blessing. In the act before me there seems to be a wide and unnecessary departure from these just principles.

Nor is our Government to be maintained or our Union preserved by invasions of the rights and powers of the several States. In thus attempting to make our General Government strong we make it weak. Its true strength consists in leaving individuals and States as much as possible to themselves—in making itself felt, not in its power, but in its beneficence; not in its control, but in its protection; not in binding the States more closely to the center, but leaving each to move unobstructed in its proper orbit.

Experience should teach us wisdom. Most of the difficulties our Government now encounters and most of the dangers which impend over our Union have sprung from an abandonment of the legitimate objects of Government by our national legislation, and the adoption of such principles as are embodied in this act. Many of our rich men have not been content with equal protection and equal benefits, but have besought us to make them richer by act of Congress. By attempting to gratify their desires we have in the results of our legislation arrayed section against section, interest against interest, and man against man, in a fearful commotion which threatens to shake the foundations of our Union. It is time to pause in our career to

GENERAL JACKSON SLAYING THE MANY HEADED MONSTER.

Here, the Second Bank of the United States is depicted as a monster, the mythological many-headed Hydra. The largest of the heads, in the top hat, is that of Nicholas Biddle, the president of the Bank.

Source: Library of Congress Prints and Photographs Division Washington, D.C.

review our principles, and if possible revive that devoted patriotism and spirit of compromise which distinguished the sages of the Revolution and the fathers of our Union. If we can not at once, in justice to interests vested under improvident legislation, make our Government what it ought to be, we can at least take a stand against all new grants of monopolies and exclusive privileges, against any prostitution of our Government to the advancement of the few at the expense of the many, and in favor of compromise and gradual reform in our code of laws and system of political economy.

Source: Andrew Jackson, "Bank Veto, July 10, 1832" in *The Addresses and Messages of the Presidents of the United States, from 1789 to 1839: Together with the Declaration of Independence and Constitution of the United States* (New York: MacLean and Taylor, 1839), pp. 398–399, 409–410.

10.5 ANDREW JACKSON, MESSAGE TO CONGRESS "ON INDIAN REMOVAL" (1830)

As the expansion of cotton planting pushed southern planters westward, their desire for cheap, fertile soil led to increased conflict with indigenous settlements. Some individual states mediated land purchases with resident tribes and policed boundaries, but others terminated native sovereignty. As violence developed, Andrew Jackson's solution was to remove forcibly all tribes from their current states and move them into federally designated Indian territory farther west. In his speech to Congress, Jackson argued that the removal of natives was for their own good.

It gives me pleasure to announce to Congress that the benevolent policy of the Government, steadily pursued for nearly thirty years, in relation to the removal of the Indians beyond the white settlements is approaching to a happy consummation. Two important tribes have accepted the provision made for their removal at the last session of Congress, and it is believed that their example will induce the remaining tribes also to seek the same obvious advantages.

The consequences of a speedy removal will be important to the United States, to individual States, and to the Indians themselves. The pecuniary advantages which it promises to the Government are the least of its recommendations. It puts an end to all possible danger of collision between the authorities of the General and State Governments on account of the Indians. It will place a dense and civilized population in large tracts of country now occupied by a few savage hunters. By opening the whole territory between Tennessee on the north and Louisiana on the south to the settlement of the whites it will incalculably strengthen the south-western frontier and render the adjacent States strong enough to repel future invasions without remote aid. It will relieve the whole State of Mississippi and the western part of Alabama of Indian occupancy, and enable those States to advance rapidly in population, wealth, and power. It will separate the Indians from immediate contact with settlements of whites; free them from the power of the States; enable them to pursue happiness in their own way and under their own rude institutions; will retard the progress of decay, which is lessening their numbers, and perhaps cause them gradually, under the protection of the Government and through the influence of good counsels, to cast off their savage habits and become an interesting, civilized, and Christian community.

What good man would prefer a country covered with forests and ranged by a few thousand savages to our extensive Republic, studded with cities, towns, and prosperous farms embellished with all the improvements which art can devise or industry execute, occupied by more than 12,000,000 happy people, and filled with all the blessings of liberty, civilization and religion?

The present policy of the Government is but a continuation of the same progressive change by a milder process. The tribes which occupied the countries now constituting the Eastern States were annihilated or have melted away to make room for the whites. The waves of population and civilization are rolling to the westward, and we now propose to acquire the countries occupied by the red men of the South and West by a fair exchange, and, at the expense of the United States, to send them to land where their existence may be prolonged and perhaps made perpetual. Doubtless it will be painful to leave the graves of their fathers; but what do they more than our ancestors did or than our children are now doing? To better their condition in an unknown land our forefathers left all that was dear in earthly objects. Our children by thousands yearly leave the land of their birth to seek new homes in distant regions. Does Humanity weep at these painful separations from everything, animate and inanimate, with which the young heart has become entwined? Far from it. It is rather a source of joy that our country affords scope where our young population may range unconstrained in body or in mind, developing the power and facilities of man in their highest perfection. These remove hundreds and almost thousands of miles at their own expense, purchase the lands they occupy, and support themselves at their new homes from the moment of their arrival. Can it be cruel in this Government when, by events which it cannot control, the Indian is made discontented in his ancient home to purchase his lands, to give him a new and extensive territory, to pay the expense of his removal, and support him a year in his new abode? How many thousands of our own people would gladly embrace the opportunity of removing to the West on such conditions! If the offers made to the Indians were extended to them, they would be hailed with gratitude and joy.

And is it supposed that the wandering savage has a stronger attachment to his home than the settled, civilized Christian? Is it more afflicting to him to leave the graves of his fathers than it is to our brothers and children? Rightly considered, the policy of the General Government toward the red man is not only liberal, but generous. He is unwilling to submit to the laws of the States and mingle with their population. To save him from this alternative, or perhaps utter annihilation, the General Government kindly offers him a new home, and proposes to pay the whole expense of his removal and settlement.

Source: President Jackson's Message to Congress "On Indian Removal," December 6, 1830; Records of the United States Senate, 1789–1990; Record Group 46; Records of the United States Senate, 1789–1990; National Archives and Records Administration (NARA).

Reform and Conflict

1820–1848

AMERICAN PORTRAIT

Charles Grandison Finney

Charles Grandison Finney had originally trained in the law, but in 1821 he experienced a calling to the ministry. Although Finney's rejection of the Presbyterian belief in original sin worried his teachers, he developed into a charismatic preacher, and after ordination in 1824 he moved to upstate New York to begin his work. The New York Evangelical Missionary Society of Young Men raised money to send missionaries to new settlements of western Pennsylvania, upstate New York, and Georgia. No one was more successful or controversial than Finney, who became an influential advocate for a dynamic Protestantism based on personal responsibility.

By the 1820s, construction of the Erie Canal was drawing even the most remote farmers closer to East Coast markets and enmeshing them in relations of cash and commerce. Inhabitants of towns and small cities were at the center of the rapidly developing market economy. Some people were troubled by the swirl of development around them. Others were attracted to the way the new economy appeared to reward industry, hard work, and personal ambition.

To this latter audience, Finney preached of the power of human spiritual striving. Instead of the stern God of Calvinism, he offered a God of justice, who spoke to a humankind "just as free as a jury" to accept salvation or not. This theology gave great latitude to human effort, but it also placed a new burden on the sinner. If "a man that was praying week after week for the Holy Spirit . . . could get no answer," Finney insisted, it must be that the man "was praying from false motives," not that God had abandoned him.

Finney enjoyed immediate success in the Genesee Valley of New York. Drawn to his preaching were those most benefiting from the economic boom: the families of merchants and bankers and of grain dealers and mill owners, as well as young, ambitious employees in such businesses. Finneyite Presbyterianism gave individual ambition a new role in the process of salvation, a sign of the human potential for good. For America, Finney claimed a new and optimistic religion based on the power of the individual.

Finney's preaching alarmed the Presbyterian establishment in the East, which feared the emotionalism and unorthodoxy of the revivals and Finney's influence in the new western areas. Among the eastern leaders was Lyman Beecher, pastor of the prestigious Hanover Street Presbyterian Church in Boston. Like many New Englanders of his era, Beecher was convinced that America's future greatness lay in transferring New England culture and its orthodoxy westward. Finney represented a dangerous threat to that orthodoxy. In 1832, Beecher moved his family to the new boomtown of the West, Cincinnati, where he wrote *A Plea for the West*, in which he predicted that the final battle of the Christ and the Antichrist would take place in the American West.

Despite their differences, both Beecher and Finney helped democratize American Christianity as champions of the Second Great Awakening. By emphasizing individual free will and the possibility of salvation through good works, Finney's religious teachings held much broader social and political implications. He railed against the evils of alcohol and tobacco. Women played a large role in his revivals, not only as organizers but also as public speakers—a controversial practice. He was also a fierce opponent of slavery. The revivals of the Second Great Awakening helped lay the groundwork for the reform movements that would characterize much of the early and mid-nineteenth century. In this regard, Charles Finney was emblematic of his day. He went on to become president of Oberlin College, a religious institution that also stood as a bastion of women's rights and antislavery ideals. Many of the listeners Finney inspired would go on to become giants of social and political reform, some of whom were more concerned with the explosive issues of the times than with saving their souls.

Perfectionism and the Theology of Human Striving

There was nothing about the depth of Charles Grandison Finney's faith, or its centrality to his life and identity, to set him apart from many others in early nineteenth-century America. The profound revivals of the turn of the century continued into the 1830s and set the terms in which many people understood themselves and their world. Revitalized religion melded with the Revolutionary tradition to infuse nineteenth-century American democracy with a religious strain and provided a framework—or a variety of frameworks—with which Americans could approach their changing world. Some Americans looked at the changes of the preceding decades and saw a nation on the verge of losing its moral compass. Convinced that the day of final reckoning grew near, they preached doom and withdrew from society into covenanted communities to prepare themselves for the end of time. Others remained hopeful that the nation could yet be redeemed. Some adhered to a Revolutionary egalitarianism; others adopted an evangelical Christian approach, while others crafted wholly new religious traditions. What united all these movements was the belief that change was both necessary and possible. Many reformers believed that it was the responsibility of each individual to work actively to perfect American society. Both reformers and separatists, however, shared the conviction that social life should be modeled on the principles of Protestant Christianity and self-improvement.

Millennialism and Communitarians

Separatist communities were not new to the American spiritual landscape in these years, and they never accounted for more than a minority of the American people. Nevertheless, they enjoyed renewed success in the 1820s. As a group, these religious communitarians sought to create more perfect societies on earth by withdrawing from daily contact with their neighbors and instituting tightly controlled spiritual, social, and economic regimens. Collectively, they revealed the fault lines in a rapidly changing society.

One of the earliest of these religious communities was the United Society of Believers in Christ's Second Appearing, a radical branch of Quakerism dubbed "Shakers" by its critics, for the "[d]ancing, singing, leaping, clapping . . . , groans and sighs" that characterized its services. Shakerism was rooted in the experiences of Ann Lee, a late eighteenth-century English factory worker and lay preacher who believed that she was the second, female embodiment of the Messiah. Lee preached that believers should return to the simplicity and purity of the early Christian church, pooling their worldly resources, withdrawing from the vanities of society, and observing celibacy. The Shakers migrated to North America in 1774 and established their first community near Watervliet, New York. By the turn of the century the Shakers had established a dozen communities in New England and four settlements in Ohio and Kentucky. By the 1830s, membership approached 4,000.

Shaker beliefs required a community based on a "union of faith, of motives, and of interest" of all members. To ensure this perfect unity, Shakers organized themselves into "families" of 30 to 100 members, each of which was supervised by a panel of eight people (two women and two men to oversee spiritual matters, and two men and two women to oversee temporal concerns), guided by a ministry also composed equally of men and women.

Their search for perfection led the Shakers to repudiate the values of contemporary society. They embraced celibacy while rejecting materialism and competitive individualism, allocating individual labor according to the needs of the community. This alternative political and economic arrangement resulted in prosperity and innovation, as Shakers sold their goods to outsiders.

Women appear to have been especially drawn to Shakerism, probably because of the Shaker belief in the spiritual equality of women and men, which was reflected in the organization of the communities, with "sisters" and "female elders" supervising the

Shakers Outsiders labeled members of the United Society of Believers in Christ's Second Appearing "Shakers" after the active twirling and shaking movements that accompanied their services.

women's lives and "brothers" and "male elders" supervising the men's. The practice of celibacy afforded women freedom from the dangers of childbirth.

The largest and most long-lived of the millennial communities of the early nineteenth century was the Church of Jesus Christ of Latter-day Saints, also known as the Mormons, founded by Joseph Smith Jr. in 1830 (see Chapter 9). In addition to traditional Christian doctrine, the Mormon Articles of Faith included a belief "in the literal gathering of Israel and in the restoration of the Ten Tribes; that Zion (the New Jerusalem) will be built upon the American continent; that Christ will reign personally upon the earth; and, that the earth will be renewed and receive its paradisiacal glory."

Smith's preaching attracted rural followers, most of them displaced by the changing antebellum North. To them, Smith preached that it was God's will that they go forth into the wilderness to found the city of Zion, where they would reign over the coming millennium.

The opposition of their neighbors, who considered Mormon beliefs blasphemous, forced the Mormons to leave New York. Smith first moved his followers to Ohio, and then to Missouri. In 1839 a large group moved on to Illinois, founding the city of Nauvoo. By the early 1840s, Smith had begun to preach the doctrine of plural marriage. The Mormon community split, and anti-Mormon outrage flared anew. Smith was arrested

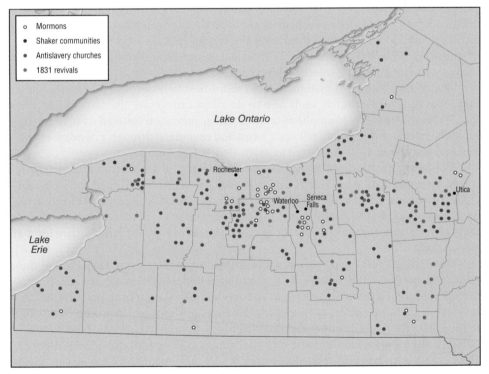

Map 11–1   Revival and Reform Social and economic transformation, religious revival, and social reform movements went hand in hand in the antebellum North. The so-called burned-over district of New York (the region directly served by the Erie Canal) nurtured numerous millennial sects (including Mormons and Shakers), Antimasonry, Finneyite revivals, and antislavery activism, as well as the Seneca Falls Woman's Rights Convention.

and thrown in jail in Carthage, Illinois, where, on June 27, 1844, he was murdered by a mob (allegedly helped by a jail guard supported by leading citizens). In 1847, following Brigham Young, the Mormons left again, reaching the Great Salt Lake in the West. By 1850, hard work, irrigation, and careful cultivation had turned the desert into a garden paradise inhabited by more than 11,000 people.

The success of such communities reflected the dissatisfaction with the gender and economic norms of the wider society. Others, however, focused outward, attempting to change the wider society.

The Benevolent Empire

Separatist millennialists were a relatively minor stream in the floods of religious organizing during the 1820s and 1830s. Far more numerous were the Americans who sought to perfect society by carrying the spirit of reform into their own communities. This massive evangelizing of America took many forms. Itinerant Methodists and Baptists continued to minister to newly settled churches in the backcountry. By the 1820s, however, even such great metropolises as Boston, Philadelphia, and New York became hothouses of evangelism.

The career of Presbyterian minister Ezra Stiles Ely reflects this shift in mainstream religious life. From 1811 to 1813, Ely was a chaplain for the Society for Supporting the Gospel, working with people who lived in public shelters. He led religious services, distributed Bibles, and prayed at the bedsides of the sick and dying, observing firsthand the growing poverty of American cities. After the War of 1812, he worked the shanties and tenements of New York's poor neighborhoods. He increasingly understood his mission to be not merely providing solace but also converting souls.

"Every truly converted man turns from selfishness to benevolence," Charles Finney said, "and benevolence surely leads him to do all he can to save the souls of his fellow man." The new evangelical emphasis on personal agency soon fostered a broad impulse for social reform, expressed in religious terms and organized through a network of charities and associations, often referred to as the Benevolent Empire.

The Benevolent Empire reflected Americans' love of organizing, a tendency observed by Frenchman Alexis de Tocqueville when he visited the United States in 1831–1832. Americans, Tocqueville wrote, "combine to . . . found seminaries, build churches, distribute books, and send missionaries to the antipodes. . . . [I]f they want to proclaim a truth or propagate some feeling by the encouragement of a great example, they form an association."

Local societies linked up into national umbrella groups. Among the largest of these were the American Bible Society (which distributed Bibles in cities and new settlements), the Female Moral Reform Society (devoted to reclaiming women from prostitution), and the American Board of Commissioners for Foreign Missions (which promoted missions in the West). Every major city fostered Bible groups, asylums to help the poor, houses of industry, orphanages, and humane societies, among other charitable organizations. By 1830, evangelicals had also created a Sunday school movement and a movement to prohibit the delivery of mail on the Christian Sabbath.

Benevolent societies combined emotional and rational approaches to reform. The method of the Benevolent Empire was moral suasion. Reformers believed that social change came about not from external rules but rather through the gradual internal awakening of

The American Board of Commissioners for Foreign Missions

The soldiers of the Benevolent Empire did not confine their attention to the United States. In 1810, in the earliest awakenings of the antebellum reform spirit, the General Assembly of Massachusetts (the governing body of the Massachusetts Congregational Church) created the American Board of Commissioners for Foreign Missions, an umbrella organization intended to promote Christian evangelizing in "heathen" lands around the world. The action came at the urging of a group of young Williams College students, who had pledged their lives to the project of "send[ing] the Gospel to the Pagans of Asia, and to the disciples of Mohammed."

Modeled on the London Missionary Society, the ABCFM sent out its first missionaries to Calcutta, India, in 1812, but other groups soon followed—to Hawaii, Turkey, and Palestine in 1819, to China in 1830, and to Africa in 1833. (By then, other Christian denominations in the United States had founded their own foreign missionary branches.) But "foreign" referred to the non-Christianized condition of the target communities, rather than literally to their residence in another country. From very early on the ABCFM sought "to extend the blessing of civilization and Christianity, in all their variety, to the Indian tribes within the limits of the United States." The most famous of these interventions was among the eastern Cherokees, where ABCFM influence encouraged acculturation and, later, voluntary removal.

As with other benevolent enterprises, the efforts of the ABCFM were funded through the donations of a vast network of local societies across the United States (particularly New England). Local supporters sponsored speakers, solicited donations, and produced a stream of pamphlets and letters to the editor on the importance of carrying Christianity to the "ignorant" people of other lands. By mid-century, the foreign missionary movement may well have been the largest of the undertakings of the Benevolent Empire.

The ABCFM, like other Christian missionary enterprises, consistently linked Christianity with United States culture, and its evangelizing focused as much on teaching the mores of western European society as on the Christian gospel. Making the Christian Bible accessible to non-English speakers involved ABCFM agents in educational and translation projects and sometimes in the creation of a written language for a nonliterate culture. ABCFM schools taught American standards of conduct and dress, as well as the English language. Mission hospitals introduced American medicine. The practice of sending married couples meant that missionary communities replicated American norms of domesticity. In 1817 the Board founded its own school, the Foreign Mission School in Cornwall, Connecticut, for educating converts to return to their own lands as missionaries of Christianity and United States civilization.

Even as it intervened in the cultures of other societies, discouraging traditional customs and replacing them with the social *continued* and religious norms of the United States, the ABCFM shaped Americans' views of other parts of the world. Missionaries constantly wrote letters home. In 1821 the ABCFM founded the magazine *Missionary Herald*, which featured the reports of missionaries. The Board also subsidized the publication of missionaries' recollections of their sojourns abroad. These pages came alive with strange and dangerous customs in exotic places, where ignorant people "jabber[ed] in their horrid jargon," worshiped "idol gods," and lived at "the lowest depths of sin and depravity."

American missionaries in Asia sometimes wrote criticisms of other imperial nations, especially Great Britain for its role in creating the Chinese opium trade (although rarely noted was the American participation in that commerce). Occasionally missionaries reflected critically on their own society. Encountering systems of bondage in other cultures, for example, a few ABCFM agents lamented the survival of slavery in the United States.

But the effect of the American mission movement was to portray the non-European world as a lost paradise, awaiting the arrival of its American rescuers. As one missionary to Hawaii wrote, in the non-Christian world even "the fruits and vegetables . . . taste of heathenism."

individual moral purpose through personal contact, testimony, and (where needed) exhortation. Yet the Benevolent Empire soon resembled a bureaucratic corporation.

Founded in 1816 in New York by wealthy Christian men, the American Bible Society illustrates this paradox. The society consisted initially of a volunteer board of managers who hired out the printing of Bibles. By 1832, the society was run by a professional staff in its own building in Manhattan. However, the society still depended on idealistic young ministers as its traveling agents and local volunteer organizations as its community contacts.

As they pursued their good deeds—distributing Bibles or religious tracts, praying with the sick—evangelicals came into intimate contact with the poor and ministered to their material needs. They arranged fuel deliveries and medical care, helped homeless families find lodging, and organized soup kitchens. Both men and women were engaged in the charitable associations of the early nineteenth century, but voluntary reform offered special opportunities for women. Women had already been active in organizing maternal societies to improve their parenting habits and Bible societies to discuss their moral failings. By the second decade of the nineteenth century, women were becoming active in the Sunday school movement and founding orphan asylums, homes for wayward girls, and asylums for "respectable" homeless adults. By the 1830s, women were the acknowledged volunteer backbone of the Benevolent Empire.

The Politics of Slavery

Although to some it seemed as if opposition to slavery suddenly became a national issue when Missouri applied to enter the union in 1819 (see Chapter 10), the issue had simmered under the surface as northern states moved to abolish slavery and the institution became entrenched in the South with the spread of slavery and cotton culture into the Southwest.

Free blacks and a significant number of whites continued to attack slavery as immoral and proposed to abolish it. In the 1820s, new religious perspectives joined with older egalitarian ones and gave rise to a new abolitionist movement that challenged both the institution of slavery and the national political parties. At the same time, a larger group of white people, though far from committed abolitionists, felt uncomfortable supporting the institution, and many northern churchgoers were uneasy with their denominations' acquiescence to slavery. Still, northern mill owners and merchants, tied to the institution, nevertheless shied away from acknowledging that linkage publicly. Religious perspectives did not all lead to antislavery sentiments.

The Antislavery Movement

The Missouri Compromise was a devastating defeat for the opponents of slavery. For decades they had struggled to hold back the expansion of slavery and the growing power of the slaveholders in national politics. Disgusted by the increasing belligerence of proslavery politicians, antislavery northerners had campaigned to stop slavery once and for all, they hoped, by keeping it out of Missouri. But they had failed, and the consequences of their failure were soon apparent. Slavery's defenders had always used racial politics to try to stop antislavery politics, but their successes were limited and local until the 1820s. Impressed by the strength of antislavery sentiment during the Missouri crisis, southerners joined an emerging political coalition that came to be known as the Democratic Party. This coalition started from the premise that slavery would henceforth be excluded from national politics. It worked by demonizing the emerging abolitionist movement. By the late 1820s national antislavery politics was effectively dead, not to reemerge again until the 1850s, when it broke about the national political parties.

Black Abolitionists

With the collapse of antislavery politics, leadership of the movement passed to a small group of articulate abolitionists. Free black leaders in the North led the way. They began to wonder whether the American Colonization Society had become a cover for slaveholders who wanted to forestall abolition by insisting that blacks were unfit for self-government. Colonization, which began as a conservative means of supporting abolition, looked more and more like an effort by slaveholders to rid themselves of the troubling presence of free blacks.

There was another, bigger, problem with colonization. By the 1820s almost all African Americans in the United States were American born. Although some later thought about migrating to Haiti or to Canada, most claimed the United States as their own. They strongly rebuffed the ACS's attempt to recruit them for relocation efforts. Many earlier black efforts had focused understandably on self-help and community building. The emphasis on self-help grew in the wake of the Missouri debates, the organization of the ACS, and the racism of the early nineteenth century. It was a constant refrain from black abolitionists: "Too long have others spoken for us," John Russwurm and Samuel E. Cornish declared in the first issue of the first independent black newspaper, *Freedom's Journal*.

In the 1820s, free blacks began to form their own all-black antislavery groups, beginning in 1826 with the General Colored Association of Massachusetts. Their protest, which drew from the older Revolutionary tradition, was not timid. In 1829 David Walker, an early member of the association, published a pamphlet titled *An Appeal to the Colored Citizens of the World*, calling on blacks to take resistance to slavery into their own hands by armed insurrection, if necessary. Walker's protest, like those of other black antislavery writers in this period, targeted the hypocrisies of white people, but at the same time drew from the Declaration of Independence. Many whites were furious, and southerners put a $3,000 bounty on Walker's head. Walker was undeterred: "Somebody must die in this cause," he added. "I may be doomed to the stake and the fire, or to the scaffold tree, but it is not in me to falter if I can promote the work of emancipation."

Black organizing continued to grow more assertive over the 1830s. Most black abolitionists did not counsel armed insurrection, but a growing number wrote and lectured on slavery and the condition of African Americans in the republic. In 1832 Maria Stewart, a free black woman in Boston, urged African Americans to take their destinies into their own hands. "If they kill us," she said of white opponents, "we shall but die."

These entreaties found responsive audiences. From 1830 until 1835 (and less regularly thereafter), free African Americans met in annual conventions to coordinate antislavery efforts and to secure free African American men "a voice in the disposition of those public resources which we ourselves have helped to earn." This National Negro Convention movement consistently framed its goals in the idiom of "manhood," calling for "the speedy elevation of ourselves and brethren to the scale and standing of men." At the same time, African American women worked to raise funds for the antislavery press and to raise awareness by inviting antislavery speakers to address their societies.

By the 1840s militant abolitionism had grown common in African American communities. In 1841 escaped slave Frederick Douglass delivered his first public abolitionist speech in Nantucket, Massachusetts; four years later he published his moving autobiography about the brutalities of slavery, *Narrative of the Life of Frederick Douglass, An American Slave, Written by Himself*. In 1843 former slave and itinerant preacher Isabella Baumfree changed her name to Sojourner Truth and became a powerful and popular antislavery speaker throughout New England. Also in 1843, Henry Highland Garnet delivered "An Address to the Slaves of the United States of America," in which he called 4 million American slaves to open rebellion: "[A]rise, arise!" he cried. "Strike for your lives and liberties. Now is the day and the hour. . . . Rather die freemen than live to be slaves."

Immediatism

Although always a minority, a growing number of whites in the North began to confront the issue of slavery directly. The most signficant was William Lloyd Garrison, who founded his own abolitionist newspaper, *The Liberator*, in Boston in 1831. In the first issue he announced his absolute rejection of any compromise with slavery: "I will not equivocate—I will not excuse—I will not retreat a single inch—and I will be heard." Garrison's approach was known as immediatism—by which abolitionists meant not the immediate abolition of slavery but the immediate beginning of the process that would lead to slavery's ultimate extinction. In 1831, under Garrison's leadership, the immediatists formed the New England Anti-Slavery Society.

Increasingly inspired by the philosophy of "perfectionism," Garrison and his follow-ers eventually rejected all forms of compromise with slavery, public or personal. They became fierce critics of American religion and even ended up repudiating the Constitu-tion. Few abolitionists went that far. Most were willing to risk contact with the imperfect world. One of these was Theodore Dwight Weld, an early supporter of the Colonization Society. After his conversion in the Finneyite revivals of 1825 and 1826, however, he began to doubt that the Society would ever risk alienating its southern constituency. By the 1830s Weld was a committed abolitionist, and in 1834 he became a full-time antislav-ery organizer.

There were quick converts to the new, energized antislavery movement, especially in urban areas of the Northeast, upstate New York, Pennsylvania, and in western states heavily settled by New Englanders, especially Ohio. Quakers and liberal Congregation-alists were particularly active. Local antislavery societies formed throughout New Eng-land in 1832. By the end of 1833, local and state organizations had grown strong enough to support a national society, the American Anti-Slavery Society, which included six African Americans on its original board. This integration was unparalled in the United States at that time.

The American Anti-Slavery Society dedicated itself to abolishing slavery without compensation for owners and to the admission of African Americans to full citizenship. Society members pledged to pursue their goals through nonviolent moral suasion, ex-horting individuals to undertake voluntary self-reform and the reform of society.

Antiabolition Violence

Although it was nonviolent, moral suasion did not exclude confrontation. In 1835, in the wake of Virginia's unwillingness to take any action against slavery, the Society ratcheted up its challenge to American society, especially the South. The Society dramatically in-creased its publication of antislavery pamphlets from 100,000 to 1 million pieces.

The response, in the North as well as the South, was immediate and fierce, in part orchestrated by the Jackson administration as a tactic to pave the way for Martin Van Buren's election by unifying the Democratic Party around opposition to the abolition-ists, whom it depicted as dangerous radicals (see Chapter 10). In the South, anger and panic turned violent. With the memory of Nat Turner still fresh, slave owners denounced the campaign. Southern communities offered rewards for prominent abolition leaders, dead or alive. Vigilante committees were appointed to police free African American neighborhoods, to patrol waters for runaway slaves, and to search post offices for offend-ing materials. The abolitionists were now outcasts.

Even before the 1835 campaign, northerners who opposed slavery still had reserva-tions about racial equality. In 1833, some whites boycotted a Connecticut school for young women when its principal, Prudence Crandall, admitted two African American scholars. When Crandall admitted an entirely African American student body, white citizens lobbied for laws to bar black students from the state, threatened Crandall, and burned the school to the ground.

The anti-abolitionist campaign led to a new fury in the North. Anti–African Ameri-can and antiabolitionist riots tore through St. Louis, Pittsburgh, Cincinnati, and Phila-delphia, and abolitionist meetings were regularly broken up by mobs. In Boston in 1835, a crowd captured William Lloyd Garrison and dragged him through the streets on a rope. Antiabolitionist mobs also targeted newspapers. Rioters in Alton, Illinois, destroyed abolitionist newspaper editor Elijah Lovejoy's press four times in 1837. In the last attack, they murdered Lovejoy himself.

Abolitionists were undeterred and even began to find more converts. Antiabolition violence suggested to some moderates that proslavery forces would stop at nothing—the flagrant violation of civil rights, the destruction of property, or murder.

Jackson and the Democrats, however, were not prepared to let opponents of slavery rupture their party. In 1835 Jackson asked Congress for measures curtailing antislavery organizing. Congress refused but Jackson prevailed with the use of the "gag rule," passed in 1836 and under which the House of Representatives automatically tabled antislavery petitions, thus assuring that Congress would not discuss the issue of slavery (see Chapter 10). The gag rule was renewed by succeeding Congresses until 1844.

The American Anti-Slavery Society, however, was quick to capitalize on the passage of the gag rule. In July 1836 the society published *An Appeal to the People of the United States*, charging that it violated the right of petition. That summer, female antislavery leaders organized a systematic drive to obtain signatures on antislavery petitions. They traveled across the North, speaking in private parlors and in public halls, and within two years collected some 2 million signatures, more than two-thirds of which were women's.

The petition campaign called attention to the gag rule, to congressional support of slavery, and to the ability of proslavery forces to abridge the rights of all Americans. It also provided moderate northerners with a nonconfrontational avenue of protest. Thanks to a growing awareness of slavery, the American Anti-Slavery Society grew from 225 local auxiliaries in 1835 to more than 1,500 by the end of the decade. Thus, at the same time that national political parties succeeded in keeping slavery out of national politics, the abolitionist movement slowly picked up support in northern cities and towns.

The Emergence of Political Abolitionism

Fearful that the slavery issue would destroy the Union, politicians north and south determined to maintain a political coalition that would prevent a reoccurrence of the kind of crisis that had erupted over the admission of Missouri. The result was a new party system that began with the emergence of the Democrats, led by Andrew Jackson, and later an anti-Jackson coalition eventually known as the Whigs. Democrats and Whigs were both national parties: each had strong northern and southern wings, meaning that both parties were committed to keeping the slavery issue out of national politics.

Hence the focus of antislavery politics shifted to the states. By the mid-1820s, popular clamor had prompted a few northern states to pass laws divorcing them from the national Fugitive Slave Act and making it more difficult for masters to recapture runaway slaves. An 1820 state law made it illegal for Ohio officials to enforce the federal 1793 Fugitive Slave Act and made kidnapping free people of color in Ohio punishable by fines of up to $2,000 and "seven to twenty-one years' imprisonment at hard labor." When proslavery forces tried to scuttle the act in 1826, antislavery workers—black and white—combined to pass another bill that essentially restated the first.

But the emergence of radical abolitionism, and the backlash it provoked, made it seem as though slavery was a threat not simply to the freedom of southern blacks but to the civil rights of northern whites. In defense of slavery, northern speakers were hounded from their lecterns; northern editors were dragged through the streets and murdered. The government even proposed to interrupt the flow of the US mail. The threat slavery posed to northern freedom was the wedge issue that began to push slavery back into national politics.

The lack of support for the petition campaign in Congress led abolitionists to the conclusion that they would have to elect more antislavery men. At first they tried interviewing candidates to sound them out and endorsing only those who expressed satisfactory antislavery views. But it quickly became clear that campaign promises were an unreliable predictor of support for antislavery issues by elected officials. By late 1839 and early 1840 a small group of abolitionists, most of them in New York, decided to launch a political party of their own.

The new interest in electoral politics divided abolitionism. Garrison's growing commitment to perfectionism led him and his followers to object to all forms of government coercion; therefore, they reacted with increasing vehemence against the move into politics. And even among "political abolitionists" there was no clear agreement on the desirability of establishing a third party, what the party should stand for, and whether it should focus on the single issue of slavery or try to broaden its appeal by adopting positions on additional issues. Most abolitionists also flinched at the increasingly aggressive tactics of Garrison's movement and at the visible participation of women and African Americans.

These tensions were palpable in 1840 at the American Anti-Slavery Society's national convention. Participants quickly divided over whether women should participate in deliberations and whether the organization should work to elect abolitionist candidates to office. The Garrisonian branch stacked the convention. When Abby Kelley was elected to a previously all-male committee, anti-Garrisonians walked out. The exodus freed the majority of abolitionists to launch an abolitionist political party. The Liberty Party fielded its first presidential candidate, James Gillespie Birney, in 1840 and again in 1844. Birney had no chance of being elected president, and Liberty Party organizers understood that. Their hope was to gain enough strength in different localities to give antislavery men leverage in swing districts. Though Liberty Party candidates themselves won few elections, they were more successful in many northern localities than Birney's meager presidential votes might otherwise indicate. But the most enduring achievement of the Liberty Party was in its formulation of an antislavery constitutional doctrine and a political platform that went on to become the basis of later electoral success.

Freedom National, Slavery Local

The first premise of the Liberty Party was that freedom was national and slavery merely local. This meant that slavery had no reach beyond the borders of the states where it existed. Everywhere outside those borders—in the western territories, on the high seas, in Washington, DC, and in the free states of the North—the Constitution obliged the federal government to promote freedom and oppose slavery. The Constitution did not allow the federal government to abolish slavery in the states where it already existed, but that did not mean that there could be no national antislavery politics. On the contrary, the federal government could exclude slavery from the western territories, refuse to admit any new slave states, regulate the interstate slave trade, abolish slavery in the nation's capital, and join Great Britain in the suppression of the Atlantic slave trade.

Because political abolitionists had alerted northerners to the disproportionate influence of a "Slave Power" on national politics, they paved the way for a much more successful foray into politics in 1848. By then the War with Mexico had dramatically increased the size of the western territories and many northerners had come to suspect that this was a way of creating more new slave states, increasing the influence of the Slave Power on federal policy. Armed with the same basic principle of "Freedom National, Slavery Local," most of the Liberty Party men joined in a much more successful Free-Soil Party in 1848. This time their candidate, former president Martin Van Buren, garnered a respectable 225,000 votes. The ideological continuity of antislavery politics was provided by Salmon P. Chase, who drafted both the Liberty Party platform of 1844 and the Free-Soil platform of 1848.

Chase did not expect the Free-Soil Party to displace either of the two major parties. Instead, he placed his hopes on a "fusion" with either the Whigs or the Democrats. Over the next four years, successful fusion movements got Chase elected to the Senate from Ohio and Charles Sumner from Massachusetts. But after 1850 both major parties committed themselves more firmly than ever to suppressing all discussion of slavery in national politics. However successful it was in some localities, "fusion" could not be the basis of a successful antislavery political movement.

But neither could the two major parties withstand the pressure of the slavery issue. Over the next several years, the Whig Party collapsed and the Democratic Party split into hostile northern and southern wings. Once that happened, the path was clear for the establishment of a new antislavery party, the Republicans, committed to the same basic principle of "Freedom National, Slavery Local" that had animated political abolitionists for nearly 20 years. With the emergence of abolition as a force in national politics, the era of antebellum reform, drawing from both the Revolutionary and religious traditions, came to fruition and made its mark on American democracy.

Reform and the Urban Classes

Drawing from both the Revolutionary egalitarian tradition and evangelical Christianity, Americans in this era also created organizations to address concerns about secular life, particularly in the cities. There, the market revolution and immigration opened a new rift between the haves and the have-nots.

Wage Dependency and Labor Protest

By 1830, in response to growing markets, master craftsmen had subdivided the production process into smaller, discrete tasks, sending part production (of shoes, hats, or shirts) to outworkers who worked from home and were paid by the number of pieces they completed rather than the hours they worked. In house, employers relied more and more on apprentices or poorly trained helpers, who worked more cheaply than journeymen. As work was subdivided, workers became more interchangeable, and their wages dropped, threatening not only their livelihoods but their belief in democratic equality.

The Panic of 1819 had thrown thousands of people out of work, driving wages down and prices up. The reviving economy of the 1820s did not reverse those trends, which were deepened by depressions in 1829 and 1837. The lives of outwork seamstresses, of whom there were tens of thousands in the eastern cities, were particularly harrowing. Philadelphia philanthropist Mathew Carey estimated the wages of Philadelphia seamstresses at $1.25 a week, but a committee of seamstresses revealed that they were lucky to earn $1.12 a week. After rent, they were left with a little more than a nickel a day for food, clothing, heat, and anything else they needed.

Five Points, New York City Once the site of a thriving community of craft shops and smaller retailers, Five Points had become one of New York City's poorest neighborhoods and, as this drawing suggests, a symbol of urban poverty, immorality, and crime.

By 1830 the urban Northeast was witnessing the damages of wage dependency and the subdivision of labor. In the largest cities, neighborhoods had become stratified by class. The New York neighborhood of Five Points, once a thriving community of master craftsmen and trade shops, by 1829 was home to prostitutes, beggars, public drunks, thieves, and confidence men. High rents crowded whole working families into single unventilated rooms. Many went homeless or threw up shanties.

The organizing begun in the 1820s exploded in the 1830s, both among craft workers and in occupations long excluded from craft recognition. When the Philadelphia Mechanics' Union dissolved, leadership passed to the New England Association of Farmers, Mechanics, and Other Workingmen, founded in 1831 by, among others, Seth Luther. The association used its newspaper, the *New England Artisan*, for worker self-education and organizing.

In February 1831, protest erupted in an unexpected quarter. With wages in sharp decline, over 1,800 tailoresses (women who worked in specific aspects of the tailoring craft) struck the New York garment industry. The tailoresses had been advised not to strike to avoid harsh public censure and to wait for times to improve. Sarah Monroe, the secretary of the union, resisted the advice: "Long have the poor tailoresses of this city borne their oppression in silence, until patience is no longer a virtue—and in my opinion to be silent longer would be a crime." The women drew up a constitution, elected officers, and stayed out on strike for five months.

Deteriorating labor conditions led to protest even in that industrial paradise, Lowell (see Chapter 9). After a decade of rapid expansion, the market stalled in 1834. When prices fell and owners cut wages by 12.5 percent, 800 female operatives walked off their jobs. The protest failed, but two years later, when owners tried to increase the price of company housing, 2,000 operatives went out on strike, forcing owners to rescind the increases. The 1836 victory was fleeting, however. Business was booming, and the owners had a vested interest in keeping the mills open. When business was slow or inventories high, workers would have far less power.

Workers tried to strengthen their position by forming regional and national associations. The most successful national association was the National Trades' Union (NTU), formed in 1834. The NTU survived for a number of years but was unable to effect statewide coordinated actions. In the end, much of its energy went into lobbying for currency reform, worker access to education and free land, and the 10-hour day.

A New Urban Middle Class

If the new working classes turned to Revolutionary principles and collective action to address their status, the new middles classes looked increasingly to revitalized religion and individual responsibility.

Seth Luther framed his criticisms of American industrial society as a struggle between the "producing classes" and the "rich." However, this was not an accurate description. The concept of the "producing classes" was ambiguous, encompassing Americans of many different standards of living and levels of wealth. For Luther, the term meant primarily urban households dependent on wage labor. Luther sometimes distinguished among the "poor," the "rich," and the "middling classes." Americans were proud of their great "middling" ranks of solid farmers and artisans, the bedrock of democracy. But the composition of the category had changed by the 1830s, as had its relation to the group Luther now called the "working classes."

These new middling classes were difficult to define exactly. Like the new working classes, the middling classes were primarily urban based. Middle-class households tended to receive their income as fees and salaries, rather than wages, and their paid workers held jobs that required mental, rather than physical, labor. These included doctors, lawyers, ministers, middle managers, agents, supervisors, tellers, clerks, shopkeepers, editors, writers, and schoolteachers.

The relationship of these urban households of moderate means to the new industrial economy was complicated. On the one hand, they were highly susceptible to catastrophic economic reversal, whether sudden unemployment, business failure, or bad speculation. At the same time, the new middle class was created by and benefited from the industrial transformation. The paid occupations on which middle-class families depended had expanded enormously. These jobs brought annual salaries ranging roughly from $1,000 to $1,500, compared with the $300 to $400 an average working man might earn. Middle-class families also tended to have access to other resources through family, friends, and business connections.

The middle class celebrated the new economy, the expansion of democracy, and the growth of individual opportunity even as it deplored the special privilege of the wealthy. Deeply religious and committed to the doctrines of personal agency, middle-class citizens were churchgoers who both donated to and participated in the causes of the Benevolent Empire.

Individuals who aspired to urban middle-class status began to distinguish them-selves from the urban poor rather than the rich. This was especially evident in their un-derstanding of personal responsibility and material success. In sermons and tracts, children's books, and novels, members of the new middle class described the commercial economy as a test of personal character. Success demonstrated superior individual in-dustriousness and self-discipline; failure signified the opposite. These beliefs took their toll on middle-class families that failed, bringing on social and psychological censure. Nevertheless, middle-class writers continued to hone the idiom of the "common man" into the more class-based language of the "self-made man" of business. From this point of view, the middle class was the repository of moderation in a changing world, the heir of Jefferson's idealized "husbandmen."

Meanwhile, middle-class families struggled to distinguish themselves from the working class. Middle-class parents recoiled from manual labor and urged their sons to become "a rich merchant, or a popular lawyer, or a broker." They expressed a new value for education, even for their daughters. Whereas workers crowded into smaller and smaller homes, the emerging middle class expressed itself in increasingly elaborate residential spaces. The ideal middle-class home, the "cottage," offered a private sitting room for the family and a separate "public" parlor for guests. The parlor was a stage on which the family could proclaim its success through a display of costly furnishings and decorations.

To emphasize their distance from the industrial world, members of the new urban middle class insisted on a "natural" division of temperament and capability between men and women. Although men were required to confront the degradations of labor, women were intended by nature to remain at home to restore the sensibilities of hus-bands and raise children protected from the ravages of industrialization.

This view of women as the primary influence on children represented a dramatic change in attitude. It was, however, largely inaccurate, as many middle-class women pursued paid labor. They took in boarders, did fancy sewing, opened schools, and worked in family-owned businesses. They all worked unpaid at the daily labor of cooking, clean-ing, washing, ironing, preserving food, sewing, and caring for children. Domestic wom-anhood became the primary symbol of middle-class respectability and a bulwark against the contradictions of the new industrial society.

Immigration and Nativism

Facing enormous changes, even economically secure Americans were alert for sources of potential danger. While labor leaders and utopians felt that industrialists were posing that danger, others focused their anxieties on the poor, deemed incapable of self-improvement. Immigrants became natural targets, and especially the Catholic Irish.

In spite of the difficulties facing wage workers, the robust economy drew increasing numbers of immigrants from Europe, 90 percent of whom came from England, Ger-many, or Ireland. The largest group by far was Irish. Plagued by chronic poverty and harsh British rule, almost 60,000 Irish immigrants arrived in the 1820s, 235,000 in the 1830s, and 845,000 during the potato famines of the 1840s. Through most of the period, the Irish accounted for more than one-third of all immigrants.

Their customs and their poverty made Irish immigrants conspicuous. Unable to afford land, they remained crowded in the seaports where they arrived. Desperate, they often had to accept jobs and conditions that native-born workers scorned. With no other place to go, one boss observed, the Irish could "be relied on at the mill all year round."

Not all of the Irish went into mills. Many built roadways, dredged river bottoms, and built canals. Irish women cooked and did laundry for the camps or hired out as domestic workers in middle-class households.

Most of all, the Irish were distinguished by their Catholic religion. By 1830, immigration had virtually doubled the number of Catholics in the country. Not all Catholics were Irish, but many were, making the Irish visible targets of long-standing anti-Catholic prejudices. Anti-Irish stereotypes represented Catholics as given to superstition and unthinking obedience. Funded by the new middle class and supported by Protestant ministers, anti-Catholic newspapers charged the Catholic hierarchy with "tyrannical and unchristian" acts "repugnant to our republican institutions."

By the early 1830s, anti-Catholicism spilled over into street violence. Organizations such as the New York Protestant Association sponsored "public discussions" on the immorality of monks, the greed of priests, and the pope's alleged designs on the American West. The debates deteriorated into small riots. Anti-Catholicism was especially strong in Massachusetts. In 1834, the associated Congregational Clergy of Massachusetts issued a frantic challenge to Protestants to rescue the republic from "the degrading influence of Popery." Sermons and editorials whipped up a frenzy of anti-Catholic fear. The hysteria was aimed at an Ursuline convent in Charlestown, Massachusetts, in which, purportedly, nuns were brainwashing innocent Protestant students. On the night of August 11, 1834, a cheering mob burned the convent to the ground. Anti-Catholicism was beginning to serve as a bond among Americans who otherwise had little in common with one another.

Internal Migration

The constant stream of internal migrants also heightened the sense of turmoil in antebellum American society. Strong internal migration signaled growth and opportunity, but it also produced a steady flow of individuals who seemed to have no settled stake in American society.

Many of these were westward settlers, but many were marginalized rural folks seeking employment in the cities. There was both a push and a pull to this movement. Children were pushed out from farming families whose land could no longer support them.

In the cities, these young people often lived in rented rooms without adult guidance. Young men joined neighborhood fire companies that served as gathering places for fun and sport. Young women navigated the city unescorted. Young people used their earnings to buy the things unavailable in the countryside: new shoes, clothing of the latest cut, hats, and canes. Migrants usually traveled fairly short distances to the nearest large towns and cities and swelled the populations of the midsized cities in which most American manufacturing took place.

At the same time, the constant migration of Americans westward provoked alarm among the eastern, urban middle class. Moralistic observers worried that this migration was draining ambitious, upright citizens from the East Coast, leaving the dregs of society behind. Observers also worried about the influence of the West on future American citizens. The West lacked the institutions that easterners associated with civilization and civic responsibility. There were few schools and churches and too many unattached young men, saloons, and brothels. Moreover, westward migration stood for the materialism and greed that easterners were beginning to worry about. The desire for money drove some families on an almost endless migration. One family, the Shelbys, had made four moves west by 1850, when they ended up in Oregon.

Into this changing land were being born more and more of the nation's young. Once families had begun to pour in, fertility rates in the newly settled areas became far higher than they were in the older, coastal regions. Easterners were alarmed by the specter of a generation of children growing up in the wilderness without proper social constraints. The values of self-reliance, industry, and civic virtue, which only a decade before had seemed to capture the essence of American nationalism, appeared in danger of disappearing.

Self-Reform and Social Regulation

Americans during this era felt both hope and fear that the foundations of American character and democracy were disappearing, but that they could be reclaimed, if only Americans exercised sufficient control, of themselves and others. Faced with deep divisions and seemingly impossible obstacles to an ideal industrial society, reformers began to turn away from broad programs of social perfection to endeavors that centered on self-control and external restraint.

A Culture of Self-Improvement

Answering criticisms from fellow senators that only the rich and well-connected enjoyed the benefits of the new American industrial order, in 1832 Henry Clay rose to defend the entrepreneurial class. "In Kentucky," he asserted, "almost every manufactory known to me is in the hands of enterprising and self-made men, who have acquired whatever wealth they possess by patient and diligent labor." Clay's emphasis on personal enterprise captured a perspective increasingly shared by ambitious Americans by the 1830s. Success or failure was less a matter of external injustice and constraint than of individual striving. Those who truly worked hard—who were industrious and clever and frugal— would succeed. Thus was born the concept of American "individualism," a term coined by the French traveler Alexis de Tocqueville, who visited the United States in 1831–1832, and observed that Americans "are apt to imagine that their whole destiny is in their own hands."

Individualism led directly to a culture of self-improvement among members of the new middle class. The emphasis on self-creation helped to resolve their ambivalence about industrial society: middle-class families had escaped the worst ravages of wage labor not because they were lucky or had some special advantage but because they worked harder.

The culture of self-improvement embraced the body as well. From the 1820s to the 1840s, health reform became a national obsession, as Americans experimented with new diets, clothing, exercise programs, abstinence, and hydropathy, the cleansing of the body through frequent bathing and drinking of water.

Middle-class men and women crowded lectures and devoured writings that espoused the philosophy of self-culture. By 1831 the lyceum movement claimed several thousand local organizations under a national association and sponsored such speakers as the writer Ralph Waldo Emerson, Daniel Webster, and later Abraham Lincoln. Meanwhile, middle-class readers supported a publishing bonanza in novels, periodicals, and tracts devoted to self-improvement.

Lyceum Movement Americans' enormous interest in self-improvement in the antebellum years was reflected in their enthusiasm for public lectures, known as the lyceum movement. This cartoon gently spoofed a lecture by James Pollard Espy, a meteorologist. As the drawing suggests, women were prominent in lyceum audiences.

These publications promoted a variety of images of the self-made American. In his *Leatherstocking Tales*, James Fenimore Cooper celebrated the pioneer. Novels like Catharine Sedgwick's *The Poor Rich Man, and the Rich Poor Man* romanticized urban poverty and suggested that hard work put "true wealth" (virtue) within the reach of even the most humble family.

Although in most cases the myth of the self-made American was decidedly male, it also had important implications for women. On the one hand, it highlighted the importance of childrearing. Periodicals such as the *Ladies Magazine* and *Godey's Lady's Book* and advice books such as Lydia Maria Child's *The Mother at Home* and William Alcott's *The Young Mother* instructed women on the development of the proper mental and moral habits in the young. On the other hand, a generation of female novelists appropriated the themes of self-culture to emphasize female self-reliance. In her 1827 novel *A New-England Tale*, Sedgwick told the story of a young orphan left penniless by an improvident wealthy father and a pampered mother. Jane, the protagonist, learns that hard work builds both economic independence and strength of character and is appropriately rewarded with a prosperous husband, children, and a safe middle-class home.

Some writers mounted a determined assault on the new American political and economic order. Transcendentalists such as Ralph Waldo Emerson, Margaret Fuller, and Henry David Thoreau believed in the power of the independent mind not only to understand the material environment but also to achieve a spiritual wholeness with the world. They saw that, in contemporary America, self-improvement was often cultivated only for immediate material gain. In his essay "Self-Reliance" (1841), Emerson tried to distinguish true independence of mind from slavish rushing after privilege and celebrity.

Temperance

Of the many movements for regulating the body, the largest by far—and the longest lived—was the temperance movement. By the 1840s hundreds of thousands of Americans had taken the pledge to swear off demon rum.

Prior to the nineteenth century, liquor played a central role in the lives of Americans. The Puritans (even ministers) had insisted on having their supply of wine, beer, and hard cider, and in craft shops, workers took rum breaks from their labor.

Some religious groups, especially the Quakers and the Methodists, had opposed the drinking of hard liquor in the eighteenth century, but it was only in 1808, in Saratoga, New York, that the first temperance society was formed. Within the next five years, at least four more temperance societies were established in New England.

In the 1820s, the temperance movement was taken over by evangelicals who saw demon rum as the enemy not just of piety but of the self-control essential to the perfection of society. Evangelists began to depict drinking as a sign of social disorder. In a series of six sermons preached in 1825, Lyman Beecher effectively changed the debate over alcohol. He did not call for absolute abstinence, and he urged his followers to form voluntary associations to drive the demon rum from American society. The following February saw the formation of the American Society for the Promotion of Temperance (ASPT). The ASPT quickly set about organizing local chapters across the country. By 1834 there were at least 5,000 state and local temperance societies.

The Common School Movement and Democracy

By the 1830s, workers, members of the new middle class, and elite philanthropists all identified education as a critical arena for reform. The drive to expand public education, like so many movements of this era, grew out of both hope and fear. As in other reform movements, however, the motives of different groups varied widely.

Since the founding of the nation, educational opportunities for the sons and daughters of prosperous parents had steadily increased. Children from wealthy urban families had private tutors, followed (for boys) by training in private seminaries and academies. By the 1820s, young women from prosperous northern families could choose from a growing number of seminaries. Meanwhile, subscription schools offered basic education to rural children.

These schools were out of reach for working-class children and even much of the growing middle class. Labor reformers linked this lack of schooling directly to the larger process of industrial oppression. In their 1831 constitution, the Working Men's Association of New York placed the demand for "a system of equal, republican education" above every other goal, because education "secures and perpetuates every political right we possess." Only free public education, workers argued, could defy "the siege of aristocracy." At the same time, middle-class fathers in Utica, New York, called for a public school system that would permit children to "keep pace with the age in its improvements" and "calculate their own profits in the world."

Middle-class parents knew that their daughters might not marry or might marry into families that would face financial ruin; they worried that traditional housewifery skills would be of little use to daughters who faced an increasingly complex market culture and new domestic technologies. At the same time, reformers who were concerned that expanded suffrage would introduce volatility into the American electoral process often supported expanded public education as "the great bulwark of republican government," in the words of New York governor De Witt Clinton. If white working men and their sons were to vote, it was important that they first be educated.

This convergence of interests led to a growing demand for more common schools. Nevertheless, broad segments of the public resisted the idea. In Cincinnati, wealthy property owners opposed paying taxes to send poor children to school. Other skeptics considered the whole idea an invasion of their rights as free citizens. States were often left to passing simple enabling legislation such as Pennsylvania's 1834 act that made public schools a local option.

In 1837 the Massachusetts legislature went further, creating a state board of education and appointing educational reformer Horace Mann as its first secretary. Mann addressed the anxieties of more prosperous Americans. On the one hand, he reassured middle-class parents that relying on an extrafamilial institution was both right and natural, given the changing society. On the other hand, he assured them that nothing else need change about the industrial society on which they depended. Only the lack of education barred the poor from prosperity, and benevolence and education would "disarm the poor of their hostility toward the rich."

The commitment to public education did not extend to the education of the small free African American community. Until the 1850s, free African American children were excluded from public common schools, and tax monies were not used to establish schools for them. Education for free black children came almost entirely from the work of the free African American community. In the North, the efforts bore fruit, but in the South, opposition to the education of slaves hardened. In fact, many enslaved and free African American southerners did learn to read and write, but usually surreptitiously.

Penal Reform

In the first years of the republic, with memories of British injustice still fresh, Americans tended to think of crime as a problem of bad laws, not flawed people. Fair laws would nurture good republican character, and good republican citizens would respect laws they had had a hand in passing.

Yet by the 1820s eastern cities were incarcerating thousands of citizens—some for debt but many for robbery, larceny, fraud, vagrancy, and disorderly conduct. Where individuals failed to obey the law, the community must devise some mechanism for its own protection.

The most popular solution from the 1820s on was the establishment of state prison systems, where deviant individuals could be kept apart from the community but could also be rehabilitated. State and city prisons soon began to replace older charity institutions. The two primary models, devised by New York and Pennsylvania, were variants on a single principle: the first step in making prisons places of real reform was to prevent inmates from influencing one another.

The New York version became most widely associated with the penitentiary at Ossining, New York, known as Sing Sing. There, prisoners worked side by side all day but were prevented from talking or even looking at one another. They slept in separate cells. The Pennsylvania model called for absolute isolation of the prisoners.

Visitors often toured these prisons and frequently applauded them, but they also noted the exaggerated hopes that Americans seemed to invest in them. Alexis de Tocqueville observed of American reformers: "They have caught the monomanie of the penitentiary system, which to them seems to remedy for all the evils of society."

Electoral Politics and Moral Reform

Frustrated with the seeming resistance of social problems to moral suasion, reformers turned increasingly to electoral politics for solutions, just as the abolitionists did, but without facing the same national backlash. The effect was to fragment and weaken party organization rather than to consolidate it. The political landscape became littered with specialized and often largely local parties, demonstrating the inability of the major parties to absorb basic social conflicts into their agendas.

Nowhere was possession of the vote more important than among newly enfranchised white male workers. During the struggles of the 1820s and 1830s, laboring people, drawing on the democratic heritage of the Revolution, believed that many of their problems would be remedied only through electoral action. As long as the economic power of employers was backed by laws that oppressed workers (debt laws that imprisoned them, bankruptcy laws that took their property, conspiracy laws that made union organizing illegal), strikes and petitions would never be enough.

By the late 1820s workers had begun to mobilize politically. In 1827 a group of workers in Philadelphia formed the Mechanics' Union of Trade Associations. Within a year that group became the Philadelphia Working Men's Party, a new political party dedicated to "the interests and enlightenment of the working classes." Over the next five years, under various names, the movement spread through most of the nation, becoming strongest in northern cities.

Workers were at a political crossroads. On the one hand, the formation of the Working Men's Party implied that workers were still optimistic that change was possible and that working men thought of themselves as citizens with the right and power to affect the makeup of the republic in such issues as public education, broadened incorporation laws, an end to imprisonment for debt, and banking reform. On the other hand, the organization of a separate political party indicated that workers remained deeply skeptical of the responsiveness of existing parties. Workers were moving toward a distinct identity within the new political economy.

In the winter of 1835–1836 anger at the legal system came to a head. With inflation and unemployment running high, New York City journeymen tailors went out on strike. The leaders of the union were arrested, tried, convicted on conspiracy charges, and fined. The labor press denounced the courts as "the tool of the aristocracy, against the people!" Nearly 30,000 people (the largest crowd in American history to that date) protested the convictions. The protestors resolved to meet the following fall in Utica, New York, to organize a "separate and distinct" political party to represent workers' interests. The 93 "workers, farmers, and mechanics" who met in Utica six months later voted to form the Equal Rights Party.

Labor movements in other states also began to focus on legislative reform. The 10-hour day, a long-standing demand, reemerged in the late 1840s as a central point of labor organizing. Workers in New England supported candidates friendly to the 10-hour day, petitioned legislatures for laws setting work hours, and testified before legislative committees. Female workers testified as well, using their life stories to create sympathy for the cause. It was male workers, however, who had the power to vote representatives out of office.

Other reform movements, ones with roots in the Benevolent Empire, began to focus on electoral strategies. The Female Moral Reform Society, which had long worked to redeem prostitutes from their sins, shifted strategies and began working for the passage of rent laws and property protections for women. This growing emphasis on legal reform grew out of an enhanced sense of connection between the reformer and the recipient of her aid.

Throughout the 1840s, temperance workers turned increasingly toward the passing of state laws. Among some temperance advocates (especially women), the shift was motivated by concern for legal protections for the wives and families of alcoholic men. But the use of legal strategies also expressed a growing belief on the part of middle-class, native-born reformers that alcoholism was a problem of the unruly immigrant working classes. As they identified drinkers as fundamentally different from themselves, temperance workers grew less interested in aiding drinkers directly and more willing to take recourse to legal controls.

Women's Rights

Many of the antebellum reform movements generated widespread controversy and passionate disagreement. But no others touched the central nerve of society like the organized abolition movement after 1830 and the women's rights movement. Race and gender, it seemed to many Americans, were defining their nation and society.

Women and Reform Movements

Women from all classes and ranks in antebellum society were beginning to chafe under cultural and legal restrictions on their full autonomy as Americans. The young women workers who marched at Lowell called themselves "daughters of freemen" and edged closer to claiming an independent status as citizens, as did the tailoresses, who were tired of waiting for chivalry to improve their lot. Educated women and women who worked as authors, editors, and educators participated actively in the public discourse and profoundly influenced public opinion. Were they to be regarded as mere subordinates to fathers and husbands?

For many women, the growing importance of suffrage and electoral tactics to reform movements created a new consciousness of their precarious status. Reform work permitted women to participate in shaping the new democratic order and to perfect skills useful in civic culture. They ran meetings, kept track of money and records, and honed their skills at public speaking. Elite women involved in charities also learned to make use of the new institutions of the market revolution. Because married women could not hold property or make contracts in their own names, most women would have had trouble accumulating the money to fund asylums and schools. But these married women, wives and daughters of wealthy and influential men, could use their social position to obtain donations, endorsements, and even special charters (comparable to those granted to male entrepreneurs) that permitted a group of married women to function legally as males.

Reform women soon learned that there were limits to their authority. Even women who were involved in the mildest of reform activities (e.g., as members of the American Bible Society) were rebuked for "acting out of their appropriate sphere." Women engaged in more controversial activities such as labor reform or abolition work were heckled and hounded by mobs.

Elizabeth Cady Stanton Stanton, one of the founders of the women's rights movement, is pictured here holding her daughter Harriot in 1856.

STRUGGLES FOR DEMOCRACY

The Seneca Falls Convention

"**W**e hold these truths to be self-evident: that all men and women are created equal; that they are endowed by their Creator with certain inalienable rights; that among these are life, liberty, and the pursuit of happiness; that to secure these rights governments are instituted, deriving their just powers from the consent of the governed. . . . " The speaker who first read these words aloud was not a twentieth-century feminist presenting a more "politically correct" version of the Declaration of Independence. The person who wrote and then read these words was Elizabeth Cady Stanton, speaking on a summer day in 1848. She was passionately convinced that the words of the Declaration of Independence were flawed because they did not explicitly apply to everyone.

Weeks before she read those words, Elizabeth Cady Stanton had been chafing under the endless round of household responsibilities that belonged to a wife and mother. Her husband, Henry Stanton, was frequently away from home campaigning against the spread of slavery, and Elizabeth was left at home in Seneca Falls, New York, to care for their family. She kept up with the newspapers and learned that in Europe, revolutionary movements were brewing. One day in July, a Quaker neighbor named Jane Hunt invited her to tea with several other Quaker friends, among them Lucretia Mott, a well-known abolitionist whom Elizabeth had met years before on a trip to England, where she and her husband attended an antislavery conference. Elizabeth poured out her heart to sympathetic ears, and the conversation turned to the need to organize on behalf of women, who were barred from higher education, the right to enter lucrative professions, and in most states, if they were married, the right to own property or keep their children after a divorce. The group decided to hold a convention at the local Wesleyan chapel and see what came of it.

They advertised in local papers and wrote to a number of well-known activists and reformers, including Frederick Douglass. The women were pleased and surprised when about 300 people turned up, including over 40 men on the first day. Walking from her home to the chapel that first morning, the nervous Elizabeth confessed to her sister that she felt like "abandoning all her principles and running away." She had never spoken in public before. During the convention, which took place on July 19 and 20, the women read aloud and debated each section of the document they called their "Declaration of Rights and Sentiments." Only one segment aroused resistance from the otherwise largely sympathetic audience, and that was the demand that women be given the right to vote. Not even all the organizers were in favor of it. Lucretia Mott had warned, "Lizzie, thee will make us ridiculous." But Elizabeth was determined to defend the measure. Frederick Douglass helped immensely. The former slave, nationally known as a speaker and writer, declared that he could not possibly demand the right to vote for himself and his brethren if he did not also ask for it on behalf of all women. All the measures, even the demand for the franchise, were approved by the audience in a vote.

continued

STRUGGLES FOR DEMOCRACY *continued*

Several New York State newspapers covered the convention and the coverage was picked up by many papers around the nation. That was the good news, as far as the organizers were concerned. The bad news was that much of the commentary was negative, even derisive. The women had not been prepared for that. The cause seemed so right and just to them; reform and change were in the air. However, several of the attendees later held conferences of their own in their home communities, and far more people than before began to write about women's issues in various periodicals. The need to end slavery soon became the preeminent cause, and then the Civil War absorbed reformers' energies.

A generation later, however, in the late nineteenth century, women's rights and especially women's suffrage became major national concerns. In some ways, the Seneca Falls convention became mythologized, envisioned as far larger and grander than it really was. Its actual spontaneity was masked when people looked back upon it as a founding moment. But the meeting had certainly constituted an important step in the forging of American democracy. When Elizabeth Cady Stanton died in 1902, she still could not vote, but she was rightly convinced that her daughters would be able to; they had already obtained the college education she herself had hungered for.

In 1837, in her *Essay on Slavery and Abolitionism*, Catharine Beecher attacked female abolitionists for violating the bounds of "rectitude and propriety" and for being motivated by unwomanly "ambition." The same year, the Massachusetts clergy criticized Sarah and Angelina Grimké (members of the southern planter class who were touring the North in the abolitionist cause) for daring to take "the place and tone of man as public reformer."

Time Line

▼1824
Charles Grandison Finney begins preaching in upstate New York

▼1826
American Society for the Promotion of Temperance formed
General Colored Association of Massachusetts formed

▼1827
John Russwurm and Samuel E. Cornish found *Freedom's Journal*

▼1829
David Walker publishes *An Appeal to the Colored Citizens of the World*

▼1830
Joseph Smith founds the Church of Jesus Christ of Latter-day Saints (Mormons)
National Negro Convention movement begins

▼1831
New England Association of Farmers, Mechanics, and Other Workingmen founded

New York Protestant Association founded
Lyceum movement begins
William Lloyd Garrison founds *The Liberator*
New England Anti-Slavery Society founded

▼1831–1832
Alexis de Tocqueville visits United States

▼1832
Maria Stewart lectures in Boston

By the late 1830s women involved in abolition work were subjected to growing criticism from within. Although William Lloyd Garrison remained a staunch ally, other leaders, such as Arthur and Lewis Tappan, believed that outspoken, assertive women were embarrassing the movement. For women who had given years of their labor and had endangered their lives in the cause of abolition, these attacks were galling. Disappointing, too, was the willingness of such men to abandon the old moral-reform strategies, which embraced gender equality. The turn toward electoral reform reduced women to second-class status in the movement. They could still raise money, lobby, and speak, but they could not perform the new essential act of reform, voting.

The Seneca Falls Convention

After the 1840 division of the American Anti-Slavery Society over women's participation, abolitionist women spearheaded a drive for an organized women's rights movement. In Seneca Falls, New York, on July 14, 1848, five women (including the seasoned Quaker abolitionist Lucretia Mott and the much younger Elizabeth Cady Stanton) placed an advertisement in the *Seneca County Courier* stating, "A convention to discuss the social, civil and religious condition and rights of woman will be held in the Wesleyan Chapel, Seneca Falls, New York, on Wednesday and Thursday, the 19th and 20th of July current, commencing at 10 a.m."

The response was overwhelming. On July 19, 300 people (including perhaps 40 men, among them the famous abolitionist Frederick Douglass) showed up. The group debated, voted on, and passed a Declaration of Sentiments (modeled after the Declaration of Independence, and adapting the Revolutionary legacy for a new purpose) and a list of resolutions. They demanded specific social and legal changes for women, including a role in lawmaking, improved property rights, equity in divorce, and access to education and the professions. All of the resolutions passed unanimously but one: a demand for the vote. Even as reform became ever more tied to electoral strategies, some reformers considered suffrage too radical for women.

▼**1833**
American Anti-Slavery Society founded

▼**1834**
Anti-Catholic mob burns Ursuline Convent in Charleston, Massachusetts
Lowell operatives go on strike
National Trades' Union formed
Female Moral Reform Society formed
Anti–African American riots in major cities

▼**1835**
Lyman Beecher publishes *A Plea for the West*
American Anti-Slavery Society begins postal campaign

▼**1836**
Congress passes "gag rule"

▼**1837**
Bread riots in New York City
Massachusetts creates first state board of education; Horace Mann appointed secretary
Abolitionist editor Elijah Lovejoy murdered

▼**1840**
James Gillespie Birney runs for president as first Liberty Party candidate

▼**1848**
Women's rights movement begins at Seneca Falls, New York
Martin Van Buren runs for president on Free Soil Party ticket

Conclusion

When Andrew Jackson took office in 1829, he declared his mission to be "reform." Jackson, of course, meant reform of America's political society and, specifically, personal revenge on the politicians who had earlier denied him the presidency. By the time Jackson left office in 1837, Americans had begun to take the cause of reform into their own hands. For some, it was a purifying mission, returning the nation to its founding promises of justice and equality. For others, it was an impossible task, tearing apart the fabric of the democracy. In the nation's short history, the West had always functioned as the republic's social and cultural release. Soon that symbol of reconciliation and prosperity would become the site of America's insoluble conflicts.

Who, What

Finneyite 326

Lucretia Mott 349

Benevolent Empire 330

American Colonization Society 333

William Lloyd Garrison 334

Lyceum movement 343

Moral suasion 330

Perfectionism 335

Revivals 326

Review Questions

1. What conditions gave rise to labor protest in the 1820s and 1830s? What forms did that protest take?

2. What conditions gave rise to the development of religious communities such as the Shakers?

3. Why did some reformers abandon the tactic of "moral suasion" over time?

4. What does the phrase "Freedom National, Slavery Local" refer to?

Critical-Thinking Questions

1. Antebellum reformers created large organizations to pursue their various goals but also placed a strong emphasis on personal agency and helped shape the image of the "self-made man." How were these two seemingly contradictory ideas able to exist side by side?

2. Did the rise of perfectionism and the Benevolent Empire reflect a new democratic impulse or a desire for social control?

3. Which of the reform movements of this period do you think was most successful? Explain your answer.

4. Compare and contrast the tactics that different abolitionists used to further their cause (for example, speeches, mailings, working within the political system).

What are the strengths and weaknesses of each? Which seems to have been most effective?

5. The reforms of this period had many sources: both hope and fear, and both the Revolutionary commitment to equality and an evangelical Christian commitment to individual and social moral reform. Describe how these trends worked in shaping the era's reform movements.

For further review materials and resource information, please visit www.oup.com/us/oakes

CHAPTER 11: REFORM AND CONFLICT, 1820–1848
Primary Sources

11.1 WILLIAM LLOYD GARRISON, EXCERPT FROM THE FIRST ISSUE OF *THE LIBERATOR* (1831)

William Lloyd Garrison was one of the most dedicated and radical abolitionists of the antebellum period. At a time when most opponents of slavery supported gradual abolition, colonization, and political negotiation, Garrison advocated for immediate and uncompensated emancipation. He considered the Constitution a pro-slavery document and resisted any suggestions for compromise on the issue of slavery. Following is an excerpt from the first edition of Garrison's abolitionist newspaper, *The Liberator*, which he published every week from 1831 to 1865.

During my recent tour for the purpose of exciting the minds of the people by a series of discourses on the subject of slavery, every place that I visited gave fresh evidence of the fact, that a greater revolution in public sentiment was to be effected in the free States—and particularly in New-England—than at the South. I found contempt more bitter, opposition more active, detraction more relentless, prejudice more stubborn, and apathy more frozen, than among slave-owners themselves. Of course, there were individual exceptions to the contrary. This state of things afflicted, but did not dishearten me. I determined, at every hazard, to lift up the standard of emancipation in the eyes of the nation, within sight of Bunker Hill and in the birthplace of liberty. That standard is now unfurled; and long may it float, unhurt by the spoliations of time or the missiles of a desperate foe—yea, till every chain be broken, and every bondman set free! Let Southern oppressors tremble—let their secret abettors tremble—let their Northern apologists tremble—let all the enemies of the persecuted blacks tremble.

I deem the publication of my original Prospectus unnecessary, as it has obtained a wide circulation. The principles therein inculcated will be steadily pursued in this paper, excepting that I shall not array myself as the political partisan of any man. In defending the great cause of human rights, I wish to derive the assistance of all religions and of all parties.

Assenting to the "self-evident truth" maintained in the American Declaration of Independence, "that all men are created equal, and endowed by their Creator with certain inalienable rights—among which are life, liberty and the pursuit of happiness," I shall strenuously contend for the immediate enfranchisement of our slave population. In Park-Street Church, on the Fourth of July, 1829, I unreflectingly assented to the popular but pernicious doctrine of gradual abolition. I seize this moment to make a full and unequivocal recantation, and thus publicly to ask pardon of my God, of my country, and of my brethren the poor slaves, for having uttered a sentiment so full of timidity, injustice, and absurdity. A similar recantation, from my pen, was published in the *Genius of Universal Emancipation* at Baltimore, in September, 1829. My conscience is now satisfied.

I am aware that many object to the severity of my language; but is there not cause for severity? I will be as harsh as truth, and as uncompromising as justice. On this subject, I do not wish to think, or to speak, or write, with moderation. No! no! Tell a man whose house is on fire to give a moderate alarm; tell him to moderately rescue his wife from the hands of the ravisher; tell the mother to gradually extricate her babe from the fire into which it has fallen; —but urge me not to use moderation in a cause like the present. I am in earnest—I will not equivocate—I will not excuse—I will not retreat a single inch—AND I WILL BE HEARD. The apathy of the people is enough to make every statue leap from its pedestal, and to hasten the resurrection of the dead.

It is pretended, that I am retarding the cause of emancipation by the coarseness of my invective and the precipitancy of my measures. The charge is not true. On this question of my influence, —humble as it is, —is felt at this moment to a considerable extent, and shall be felt in coming years—not perniciously, but beneficially—not as a curse, but as a blessing; and posterity will bear testimony that I was right. I desire to thank God, that he enables me to disregard "the fear of man which bringeth a snare," and to speak his truth in its simplicity and power. . . .

Source: Wendell Phillips Garrison, *William Lloyd Garrison, 1805–1879: The Story of His Life, Told by His Children*, vol. I (New York: The Century Company, 1885), pp. 224–226.

11.2 CHARLES DICKENS, EXCERPTS FROM *AMERICAN NOTES FOR GENERAL CIRCULATION* (1842)

Charles Dickens, the English writer and speaker, visited New York City in 1842 and made the following notes on his impression of Broadway and the Five Points district. He published them as *American Notes*. Dickens had already gained fame and fortune as a novelist with such works as *David Copperfield*, *Oliver Twist*, and *Great Expectations*. This travelogue was part of a long tradition of writers making observations about the great American experiment.

This is the place: these narrow ways, diverging to the right and left, and reeking everywhere with dirt and filth. Such lives as are led here, bear the same fruits here as elsewhere. The coarse and bloated faces at the doors, have counterparts at home, and all the wide world over. Debauchery has made the very houses prematurely old. See how the rotten beams are tumbling down, and how the patched and broken windows seem to scowl dimly, like eyes that have been hurt in drunken frays. Many of those pigs live here. Do they ever wonder why their masters walk upright in lieu of going on all-fours? and why they talk instead of grunting?

So far, nearly every house is a low tavern; and on the bar-room walls, are coloured prints of Washington, and Queen Victoria of England, and the American Eagle. Among the pigeon-holes that hold the bottles, are pieces of plate-glass and coloured paper, for there is, in some sort, a taste for decoration, even here. And as seamen frequent these haunts, there are maritime pictures by the dozen: of partings between sailors and their lady-loves, portraits of William, of the ballad, and his Black-Eyed Susan; of Will Watch, the Bold Smuggler; of Paul Jones the Pirate, and the like: on which the painted eyes of Queen Victoria, and of Washington to boot, rest in as strange companionship, as on most of the scenes that are enacted in their wondering presence.

What place is this, to which the squalid street conducts us? A kind of square of leprous houses, some of which are attainable only by crazy wooden stairs without. What lies beyond this tottering flight of steps, that creak beneath our tread? . . . Ascend these pitch-dark stairs, heedful of a false footing on the trembling boards, and grope your way with me into this wolfish den, where neither ray of light nor breath of air, appears to come. . . .

Here too are lanes and alleys, paved with mud knee-deep, underground chambers, where they dance and game; the walls bedecked with rough designs of ships, and forts, and flags, and American eagles out of number: ruined houses, open to the street, whence, through wide gaps in the walls, other ruins loom upon the eye, as though the world of vice and misery had nothing else to show: hideous tenements which take their name from robbery and murder: all that is loathsome, drooping, and decayed is here. . . .

What is this intolerable tolling of great bells, and crashing of wheels, and shouting in the distance? A fire. And what that deep red light in the opposite direction? Another fire. And what these charred and blackened walls we stand before? A dwelling where a fire has been. It was more than hinted, in an official report, not long ago, that some of these conflagrations were not wholly accidental, and that speculation and enterprise found a field of exertion, even in flames: but be this as it may, there was a fire last night, there are two to-night, and you may lay an even wager there will be at least one, to-morrow. So, carrying that with us for our comfort, let us say, Good night, and climb up-stairs to bed.

Source: Charles Dickens, *American Notes for General Circulation* (Paris: Baudry's European Library, 1842), pp. 109–111, 113.

11.3 LOUISA MAY ALCOTT, EXCERPTS FROM *TRANSCENDENTAL WILD OATS* (1873)

Louisa May Alcott, best known as the author of *Little Women* (1868), was also an abolitionist and feminist. Her father was involved in the transcendentalist movement, along with Ralph Waldo Emerson and Henry David Thoreau, and believed that humans could achieve perfection by living in harmony with nature. As a child, Louisa lived for seven months at a transcendentalist commune founded by her father. Although the experiment was short-lived, the community's beliefs influenced her writing career. Years later, she wrote a short story based on her experience at the commune, satirically describing how the idealism of the male leaders created more work for the women.

. . . Thus these modern pilgrims journeyed hopefully out of the old world, to found a new one in the wilderness.

This prospective Eden at present consisted of an old red farm-house, a dilapidated barn, many acres of meadow-land, and a grove. Ten ancient apple-trees were all the "chaste supply" which the place offered as yet; but, in the firm belief that plenteous orchards were soon to be evoked from their inner consciousness, these sanguine founders had christened their domain Fruitlands.

Here Timon Lion intended to found a colony of Latter Day Saints, who, under his patriarchal sway, should regenerate the world and glorify his name for ever. Here Abel Lamb, with the devoutest faith in the high ideal which was to him a living truth, desired to plant a Paradise, where Beauty, Virtue, Justice, and Love might live happily together, without the possibility of a serpent entering in. And here his wife, unconverted but faithful to the end, hoped, after many wanderings over the face of the earth, to find rest for herself and a home for her children.

"There is our new abode," announced the enthusiast, smiling with a satisfaction quite undamped by the drops dripping from his hatbrim, as they turned at length into a cart-path that wound along a steep hillside into a barren looking valley.

"A little difficult of access," observed his practical wife, as she endeavored to keep her various household goods from going overboard with every lurch of the laden ark.

"Like all good things. But those who earnestly desire and patiently seek will soon find us," placidly responded the philosopher from the mud, through which he was now endeavoring to pilot the much-enduring horse.

"Truth lies at the bottom of a well, Sister Hope," said Brother Timon, pausing to detach his small comrade from a gate, whereon she was perched for a clearer gaze into futurity.

"That's the reason we so seldom get at it, I suppose," replied Mrs. Hope, making a vain clutch at the mirror, which a sudden jolt sent flying out of her hands.

The new-comers were welcomed by one of the elect precious,—a regenerate farmer, whose idea of reform consisted chiefly in wearing white cotton raiment and shoes of untanned leather. This costume, with a snowy beard, gave him a venerable, and at the same time a somewhat bridal appearance.

The goods and chattels of the Society not having arrived, the weary family reposed before the fire on blocks of wood, while Brother Moses White regaled them with roasted potatoes, brown bread and water, in two plates, a tin pan, and one mug; his table service being limited. But, having cast the forms and vanities of a depraved world behind them, the elders welcomed hardship with the enthusiasm of new pioneers, and the children heartily enjoyed this foretaste of what they believed was to be a sort of perpetual picnic. . . .

"Every meal should be a sacrament, and the vessels used should be beautiful and symbolical," observed Brother Lamb, mildly, righting the tin pan slipping about on his knees. "I priced a silver service when in town, but it was too costly; so I got some graceful cups and vases of Britannia ware."

"Hardest things in the world to keep bright. Will whiting be allowed in the community?" inquired Sister Hope, with a housewife's interest in labor-saving institutions.

"Such trivial questions will be discussed at a more fitting time," answered Brother Timon, sharply, as he burnt his fingers with a very hot potato. "Neither sugar, molasses, milk, butter, cheese, nor flesh are to be used among us, for nothing is to be admitted which has caused wrong or death to man or beast."

"Our garments are to be linen till we learn to raise our own cotton or some substitute for woollen fabrics," added Brother Abel, blissfully basking in an imaginary future as warm and brilliant as the generous fire before him. . . .

"Haou do you cattle 'ate to treat the ten-acre lot? Ef things ain't 'tended to right smart, we shan't hev no crops," observed the practical patriarch in cotton.

"We shall spade it," replied Abel, in such perfect good faith that Moses said no more, though he indulged in a shake of the head as he glanced at hands that had held nothing heavier than a pen for years. He was a paternal old soul and regarded the younger men as promising boys on a new sort of lark.

. . . "Each member is to perform the work for which experience, strength, and taste best fit him," continued Dictator Lion. "Thus drudgery and disorder will be avoided and harmony prevail. We shall rise at dawn, begin the day by bathing, followed by music, and then a chaste repast of fruit and bread. Each one finds congenial occupation till the meridian meal; when some deep-searching conversation gives rest to the body and development to the mind. Healthful labor again engages us till the last meal, when we assemble in social communion, prolonged till sunset, when we retire to sweet repose, ready for the next day's activity."

"What part of the work do you incline to yourself?" asked Sister Hope, with a humorous glimmer in her keen eyes.

"I shall wait till it is made clear to me. Being in preference to doing is the great aim, and this comes to us rather by a resigned willingness than a wilful activity, which is a check to all divine growth," responded Brother Timon.

"I thought so." And Mrs. Lamb sighed audibly, for during the year he had spent in her family Brother Timon had so faithfully carried out his idea of "being, not doing," that she had found his "divine growth" both an expensive and unsatisfactory process . . .

Source: Louisa May Alcott, "Transcendental Wild Oats: A Chapter from an Unwritten Romance," *The Independent* (New York), vol. 25, no. 1307, December 18, 1873, pp. 1569–1571.

11.4 ALEXIS DE TOCQUEVILLE, EXCERPTS FROM *DEMOCRACY IN AMERICA: VOLUME II* (1840)

Alexis de Tocqueville, a French political scientist and historian who traveled the United States in 1831–1832, published his observations in a two-volume book, *Democracy in America* (Volume 1 was published in 1835 and Volume 2 in 1840). Having been involved in political struggle in his own country, Tocqueville paid keen attention to the workings of democracy in American society. In the following selection, he notes the proclivity of Americans to form groups, perhaps based on his observations of the Anti-Slavery Society, the American Temperance Society, and numerous other reform societies founded in the 1820s and 1830s.

... The political associations that exist in the United States are only a single feature in the midst of the immense assemblage of associations in that country. Americans of all ages, all conditions, and all dispositions constantly form associations. They have not only commercial and manufacturing companies, in which all take part, but associations of a thousand other kinds, religious, moral, serious, futile, general or restricted, enormous or diminutive. The Americans make associations to give entertainments, to found seminaries, to build inns, to construct churches, to diffuse books, to send missionaries to the antipodes; in this manner they found hospitals, prisons, and schools. If it is proposed to inculcate some truth or to foster some feeling by the encouragement of a great example, they form a society. Wherever at the head of some new undertaking you see the government in France, or a man of rank in England, in the United States you will be sure to find an association.

...Thus the most democratic country on the face of the earth is that in which men have, in our time, carried to the highest perfection the art of pursuing in common the object of their common desires and have applied this new science to the greatest number of purposes. Is this the result of accident, or is there in reality any necessary connection between the principle of association and that of equality?

Aristocratic communities always contain, among a multitude of persons who by themselves are powerless, a small number of powerful and wealthy citizens, each of whom can achieve great undertakings single-handed. In aristocratic societies men do not need to combine in order to act, because they are strongly held together. Every wealthy and powerful citizen constitutes the head of a permanent and compulsory association, composed of all those who are dependent upon him or whom he makes subservient to the execution of his designs.

Among democratic nations, on the contrary, all the citizens are independent and feeble; they can do hardly anything by themselves, and none of them can oblige his fellow men to lend him their assistance. They all, therefore, become powerless if they do not learn voluntarily to help one another. If men living in democratic countries had no right and no inclination to associate for political purposes, their independence would be in great jeopardy, but they might long preserve their wealth and their cultivation: whereas if they never acquired the habit of forming associations in ordinary life, civilization itself would be endangered. A people among whom individuals lost the power of achieving great things single-handed, without acquiring the means of producing them by united exertions, would soon relapse into barbarism.

...When the members of an aristocratic community adopt a new opinion or conceive a new sentiment, they give it a station, as it were, beside themselves, upon the lofty platform where they stand; and opinions or sentiments so conspicuous to the eyes of the multitude are easily introduced into the minds or hearts of all around. In democratic countries the governing power alone is naturally in a condition to act in this manner, but it is easy to see that its action is always inadequate, and often dangerous. A government can no more be competent to keep alive and to renew the circulation of opinions and feelings among a great people than to manage all the speculations of productive industry. No sooner does a government attempt to go beyond its political sphere and to enter upon this new track than it exercises, even unintentionally, an insupportable tyranny; for a government can only dictate strict rules, the opinions which it favors are rigidly enforced, and it is never easy to discriminate between its advice and its commands. Worse still will be the case if the government really believes itself interested in preventing all circulation of ideas; it will then stand motionless and oppressed by the heaviness of voluntary torpor. Governments, therefore, should not be the only active powers; associations ought, in democratic nations, to stand in lieu of those powerful private individuals whom the equality of conditions has swept away.

As soon as several of the inhabitants of the United States have taken up an opinion or a feeling which they wish to promote in the world, they look out for mutual assistance; and as soon as they have found one another out, they combine. From that moment they are no longer isolated men, but a power seen from afar, whose actions serve for an example and whose language is listened to. The first time I heard in the United States that a hundred thousand men had bound themselves publicly to abstain from spirituous liquors, it appeared to me more like a joke than a serious engagement, and I did not at once perceive why these temperate citizens could not content themselves with drinking water by their own firesides. I at last understood that these hundred thousand Americans, alarmed by the progress of drunkenness around them, had made up their minds to patronize temperance.

. . . Nothing, in my opinion, is more deserving of our attention than the intellectual and moral associations of America. The political and industrial associations of that country strike us forcibly; but the others elude our observation, or if we discover them, we understand them imperfectly because we have hardly ever seen anything of the kind. It must be acknowledged, however, that they are as necessary to the American people as the former, and perhaps more so. In democratic countries the science of association is the mother of science; the progress of all the rest depends upon the progress it has made.

Among the laws that rule human societies there is one which seems to be more precise and clear than all others. If men are to remain civilized or to become so, the art of associating together must grow and improve in the same ratio in which the equality of conditions is increased.

Source: Alexis de Tocqueville, *Democracy in America: Volume II*, 1840.

11.5 JOHN TAYLOR, ACCOUNT OF THE MURDERS OF JOSEPH AND HYRUM SMITH (1844)

Of the many religious movements that emerged in the antebellum period, the Church of Latter Day Saints has proven to be the most successful. Founder Joseph Smith, Jr., preached the coming of Zion in a utopian vision of America, and led his followers to the town of Nauvoo, Illinois, where their desire to form a theocracy came in conflict with the belief systems of those around them. Eventually, Smith was arrested; a mob then stormed the prison, killing him and his brother. In 1845, a church elder named John Taylor, who had been held in the same jail, described the scene and the seeming complicity of town officials in the attack.

During one of these conversations [in the jailhouse] Dr. Richards remarked: "Brother Joseph, if it is necessary that you die in this matter, and if they will take me in your stead, I will suffer for you." At another time, when conversing about deliverance, I said, "Brother Joseph, if you will permit it, and say the word, I will have you out of this prison in five hours, if the jail has to come down to do it." My idea was to go to Nauvoo, and collect, a force sufficient, as I considered the whole affair a legal farce, and a flagrant outrage upon our liberty and rights. Brother Joseph refused.

Elder Cyrus H. Wheelock came in to see us, and when he was about leaving, drew a small pistol, a six-shooter, from his pocket, remarking at the same time "Would any of you like to have this?" Brother Joseph immediately replied, "Yes, give it to me," whereupon he took the pistol, and put it in his pantaloons pocket.

. . . The report of the governor having gone to Nauvoo without taking the prisoners along with him caused very unpleasant feelings, as we were apprised that we were left to the tender mercies of the Carthage Greys, a company strictly mobocratic, and whom we knew to be our most deadly enemies; and their captain, Esquire (Robert F.) Smith, was a most unprincipled villain. Besides this, all the mob forces, comprising the governor's troops, were dismissed, with the exception of one or two companies, which the governor took with him to Nauvoo. The great part of the mob was liberated, the remainder was our guard.

. . . Soon afterwards I was sitting at one of the front windows of the jail, when I saw a number of men, with painted faces, coming around the corner of the jail, and aiming towards the stairs. The other brethren had seen the same, for, as I went to the door, I found Brother Hyrum Smith and Dr. Richards already leaning against it. They both pressed against the door with their shoulders to prevent its being opened, as the lock and latch were comparatively useless. While in this position, the mob, who had come upstairs and tried to open the door, probably thought it was locked and fired a ball through the keyhole. At this Dr. Richards and Brother Hyrum leaped back from the door, with their faces towards it. Almost instantly another ball passed through the panel of the door, and struck Brother Hyrum on the left side of the nose, entering his face and head. . . . Immediately, when the ball struck him, he fell flat on his back, crying as he fell, "I am a dead man!" He never moved afterwards.

Brother Joseph as he drew nigh to Hyrum, and, leaning over him, exclaimed, "Oh! my poor, dear brother Hyrum!" He, however, instantly arose, and with a firm, quick step, and a determined expression of countenance, approached the door, and pulling the six-shooter left by Brother Wheelock from his pocket, opened the door slightly, and snapped the pistol six successive times. Only three of the barrels, however, were discharged. I afterwards understood that two or three were wounded by these discharges, two of whom, I am informed, died. I had in my hands a large, strong hickory stick, brought there by Brother Markham and left by him, which I had seized as soon as I saw the mob approach; and while Brother Joseph was firing the pistol, I stood close behind him. As soon as he had discharged it he stepped back, and I immediately took his place next to the door, while he occupied the one I had done while he was shooting. . . .

It certainly was a terrible scene. Streams of fire as thick as my arm passed by me as these men fired, and, unarmed as we were, it looked like certain death. . . . Every moment the crowd at the door became more dense, as they were unquestionably pressed on by those in the rear ascending the stairs, until the whole entrance at the door was literally crowded with muskets and rifles, which, with the swearing, shouting, and demoniacal expressions of those outside the door and on the stairs, and the firing of the guns, mingled with their horrid oaths and execrations, made it look like pandemonium let loose, and was, indeed, a fit representation of the horrid deed in which they were engaged.

After parrying the guns for some time, which now protruded farther and farther into the room, and seeing no hope of escape or protection there, as we were now unarmed, it occurred to me that we might have some friends outside. . . . I made a spring for the window which was right in front of the jail door, where the mob was standing, and also exposed to the fire of the Carthage Greys, who were stationed some ten or twelve rods off. . . . As I reached the window, and was on the point of leaping out, I was struck by a ball from the door about midway of my thigh. . . .

It would seem that immediately after my attempt to leap out of the window, Joseph also did the same thing, of which circumstance I have no knowledge only from information. The first thing that I noticed was a cry that he had leaped out of the window. A cessation of firing followed, the mob rushed downstairs, and Dr. Richards went to the window. . . . Soon afterwards Dr. Richards came to me, informed me that the mob had precipitately fled, and at the same time confirmed the worst fears that Joseph was assuredly dead.

Source: John Taylor's Account of the Murder of Joseph and Hyrum Smith at Carthage, Illinois, June 27, 1844.

Manifest Destiny

1836–1848

COMMON THREADS

How did the expansion of slavery in the 1820s and 1830s affect US foreign policy in the 1840s?

How did settlers' preconceptions of other cultures affect their attitudes toward expansion?

How did the Democratic Party change between 1828 and 1848?

Was "manifest destiny" consistent with the Monroe Doctrine of 1823 or a repudiation of it?

How important were the politics of slavery in the 1840s compared with the previous decade and the decade following?

OUTLINE

Elias Boudinot Dies in Oklahoma

On a June day in 1839 near Tahlequah, Oklahoma, Elias Boudinot was building a home for his family. Four men emerged from the nearby woods, looking haunted and hungry. They asked if he had some medicine for a sick comrade of theirs, and he said he could find some at the home of a friend, a quarter of a mile away. He turned to walk with them. Suddenly, one of the men struck him with a hatchet, dealing a mortal blow. This was no ordinary robbery: it was the culmination of years of desperate strain within the Cherokee community, because there was no easy answer to the demands of the United States that they give up their homes in the East and move West.

Elias Boudinot was born Buck Watie, the son of a Georgia Cherokee chief named Oo-watie, in 1805. His father had him tutored by the local Moravian missionaries, and he proved to be so talented that they recommended sending him to a school in Cornwall, Connecticut, for "heathens" from abroad. A wealthy benefactor, Dr. Elias Boudinot, offered to support Buck's education, and the boy took his godfather's name. When the younger Elias Boudinot arrived in Connecticut, he found his new school was home to one Abenaki, two Choctaws, two Chinese, two Malaysians, one Bengalese, one Hindu, several Hawaiians, and a number of other Cherokees, all brought there by missionaries. While in Connecticut, Boudinot also met and fell in love with a local girl named Harriet Gold, who was equally smitten. The town, however, was outraged. After Boudinot was sent home, young Harriet watched from a window while the Christian neighbors who had always professed affection for her burned her and her suitor in effigy. The two stubbornly continued to correspond and were married in 1826.

They lived in the Cherokee capital of New Echota, in Georgia, where Boudinot worked tirelessly in the late 1820s to prevent the forced removal of his people to the West. He worked to educate his people in the new Cherokee syllabary, designed by Cherokee blacksmith George Gist, and he established *The Cherokee Phoenix*, a bilingual newspaper read by locals and international sympathizers alike. The Act of Removal was passed in 1830, but Boudinot, undaunted, helped to further a lawsuit that went all the way to the Supreme Court in 1832. The case was won, but the joy was short-lived; President Andrew Jackson soon made it clear that he had no intention of enforcing the ruling.

By the end of the summer of 1832, Boudinot and two close friends from another chiefly family, the Ridges, began to change their minds about Removal. As they now saw the situation, the Cherokee could wait until they were forced out at gunpoint, or they could negotiate a treaty with good terms—including payment for their land, money for the move, and deeds to new lands in Oklahoma. They decided to fight for their people's survival, rather than for the land. Most Cherokees, however, were not educated in the American legal system and did not see the significance of the Executive's response to the Supreme Court; they adamantly refused to cede their traditional lands. Their spokesperson was tribal chief

John Ross, who was only one-eighth Cherokee, but who prided himself on holding tightly to the views of the people.

On December 29, 1835, twenty tribal leaders met at Boudinot's house and signed a treaty with the US government giving the Cherokee 13.8 million acres in Oklahoma and a payment of $4.5 million. The elder John Ridge is supposed to have remarked, "I have signed my death warrant," because in 1829, while he and others were fighting Removal, he had orchestrated the passage of a tribal law making the sale of Cherokee lands to people outside the nation punishable by death. The treaty signers began to arrange their affairs to move and attempted to convince the Cherokee people that they had no better alternatives. John Ross, on the other hand, continued to advocate staying, and most Cherokees did not go.

In 1838, Boudinot and his children (Harriet died not long after the signing of the treaty) were building new lives in Oklahoma when troops began to turn the Cherokee people out of their homes in Georgia. The survivors of the forced march began to arrive in Indian Territory in early 1839. They were starving and sick, reeling with grief and rage. A group of them met one evening in June and swore to punish those who had willingly given up their people's lands. The next morning, they killed not only Boudinot but also the two Ridges, father and son. They felt powerless, and like people everywhere in such situations, they turned on those they knew best. The real authors of the crimes against them were faceless and far away.

The Decline of Jacksonianism

Andrew Jackson had governed on a philosophy of federalism, in which a strong presidency had been necessary to combat, rather than support, the growth of a powerful central government. He had backed territorial expansion, the powers of individual states, the claims of settlers, and had opposed federal control of those processes as well as Indian sovereignty. By 1836, people in new territories sought admission to the Union, settlers were launching the largest westward migration in the history of the nation, and Jackson's Democratic Party seemed to have reduced the old Republican dynasty (now regrouped as Whigs) to whining observers. But there were costs to Jackson's successes: his hatred of strong central government had thrown the nation's banking system into chaos, his zeal for territorial expansion had helped nurture a strong abolition movement in the North, and his own Democratic Party had grown too diverse to remain stable. Jackson would be succeeded in 1837 by a Democrat known for his political acumen, Martin Van Buren—but the "Little Magician" would lose reelection by a landslide in 1840 and fail again when he ran on a third-party ticket in 1848.

Political Parties in Crisis

The expansion of white male suffrage and the translation of moral-reform agendas into electoral politics energized American politics in the 1830s and 1840s. In 1840, 66 percent of the electorate voted in Massachusetts, 75 percent in Connecticut, and 77 percent in Pennsylvania. Yet the capacity of major political parties to accommodate a wide range of conflicting interests and beliefs was limited.

Increasingly fractured since the election of 1824, the Republican Party had struggled to reorganize in opposition to Andrew Jackson. Jackson's war on the national bank had offered the immediate occasion. Although unable to save the bank, Henry Clay and the anti-Jacksonians narrowly passed a Senate resolution in 1834 censuring Jackson for assuming "authority and power not conferred by the Constitution and the laws." (Jackson had refused to turn over a paper on the bank that he had read to his cabinet.) In the debate before the censure, Clay identified his own anti-Jackson position as "Whiggish" (meant to evoke memories of the English "Whigs" who opposed royal tyranny in the eighteenth century). That label stuck as the name of the new political party.

Former National Republicans in the urban Northeast and upper West made up the bulk of the new Whig Party. Some of these were beginning to doubt the wisdom of uncontrolled territorial expansion, which seemed to promote political corruption, economic disorder, sectional conflict, and the extension of slavery. They feared the disruptive power of wildcat settlers, wage workers, the urban poor, and immigrants. Whigs supported market expansion guided closely by a strong, interventionist central government. They continued to embrace the elements of the earlier "American System": a new national bank, a strong protective tariff, and government-sponsored internal improvements.

By 1834, some former Democrats were also disenchanted with the party of Jackson. Prosperous shopkeepers and middling merchants began to see their own interests as distinct from those of the urban laboring classes and were attracted by the Whig emphasis on discipline and order. Some southerners were still angry over the tariff and the nullification crisis. Some small farmers and shopkeepers wiped out by the depression of 1837 blamed Jackson for their hard times. Workers, who had little trust for the merchant classes at the core of the new Whig Party, tended to form splinter parties or to stay with the Democrats.

Through the 1830s the Whigs were a loose and disorganized opposition. Unable to decide on a single candidate, in 1836 they ran four regional challengers, hoping to deny Van Buren a majority in the Electoral College. The Whig field included William Henry Harrison (governor of Indiana Territory and victor at the Battle of Tippecanoe, nominated by Pennsylvania Antimasons), Senator Hugh Lawson White (Jackson's disenchanted replacement in the Senate, nominated by unhappy Democrats in Tennessee), Senator Daniel Webster (former National Republican and famous orator, nominated by the Massachusetts legislature), and Willie P. Mangum (a protest candidate of the South Carolina Nullifiers).

Jackson's vice president, Martin Van Buren, seemed well positioned for the race. Van Buren was instrumental in creating a successful Democratic coalition, so he was surely the one to hold it together. Van Buren had been constantly at Jackson's side, as secretary of state and as vice president. Few politicians seemed better situated to inherit Jackson's popularity. What was more, Van Buren seemed perhaps uniquely positioned to bridge the growing gulf between northern antislavery and southern proslavery Democrats: his popularity in New York appeared strong enough for him to risk alienating some of the antislavery vote in the effort to gain southern support, a risk he took by publicly declaring himself "the inflexible and uncompromising opponent of any attempt on the part of Congress to abolish slavery in the District of Columbia" or to interfere with slavery "in the states where it exists."

Martin Van Buren One of the most powerful politicians of his time, Martin Van Buren extolled the virtues of party competition. He was also among the first presidents ever to be photographed.

The election was close. Van Buren won part of New England (but not Massachusetts or Vermont). He took his home state of New York, Pennsylvania, Virginia, and North Carolina. And he took Far West states, most of them slave states: Michigan, Illinois (technically free but popularly proslavery, especially in the south), Missouri, Arkansas, Louisiana, Mississippi, and Alabama. He won 58 percent of the electoral vote (after the weighting of the Three-Fifths Compromise in the South) and a bare majority (51 percent) of the popular vote. A shift of fewer than 2,000 votes in Pennsylvania would have denied Van Buren an Electoral College majority and thrown the election to the House of Representatives.

Van Buren and the Legacy of Jackson

In his 1837 inaugural address, Van Buren announced that the nation had arrived at a "singularly happy" condition. Less optimistic, Missourian Thomas Hart Benton observed that in Van Buren's victory "the rising was eclipsed by the setting sun." Benton was closer to the truth. Van Buren's struggle to unite Jackson's party enough to get elected was only the first of the challenges he inherited.

The signs of the Panic of 1837 were already visible when Van Buren was inaugurated that March. Jackson's pet banks had ensured that western land speculation would be built on easy credit. His hard-money measures that had effectively drained the nation of specie did not end the bubble of credit. It simply diverted its source to European financiers, who got higher interest in the United States than in their home countries. When European banks responded to specie shortages in their own countries by increasing interest on deposits and tightening credit, the Europeans called in their American loans. The sudden collapse of credit was exacerbated by crop failures in 1835 and 1837, which put farmers at greater risk for defaulting on their loans and reduced American exports.

As credit evaporated, interest rates rose, paper money depreciated, and debt mounted. The credit-dependent cotton market began to collapse, taking with it several large import-export firms in New York and New Orleans. After years of high inflation, the failures ignited a run on the overextended banks, as depositors tried to hoard their savings before the hard currency was paid out for mercantile debts. "[E]ven during the Embargo, & war that followed," merchant John Perkins Cushing reported in May of 1837, ". . . there was nothing like the complete prostration of commercial credit & confidence that has taken place within the last two months."

A strong federal hand might have stemmed the damage, but Van Buren shared Jackson's view that the federal government should not manage currency. Van Buren's announcement on May 4 that he intended to maintain the Specie Circular in force ensured continued pressure on banks. On May 10, 1837, frightened depositors drained $650,000 from their reserves, and New York City banks closed. Only a show of military force prevented a riot.

Coinciding with large waves of German and Irish immigration, the depression hit the East Coast hard. Wages declined faster than prices. Unemployment was widespread, and losses touched even the prosperous middle classes. Troubled times remained until 1843. While Democrats scrambled to avoid political responsibility, the new Whig Party began to look ahead optimistically to 1840.

Although an additional infusion of federal funds to state banks in 1837 might only have fed the frenzy, Van Buren's decision to delay the scheduled distribution added a new confusion. In an effort to return stability to the nation's monetary system, Van Buren proposed that the Treasury Department establish its own financial institutions to receive, hold, and pay out government funds. The institutions would exist solely to manage government accounts and would not issue paper currency or make loans to business.

The proposal for an independent treasury met with substantial opposition. Predictably, Whigs objected that removing government holdings from circulation would reduce capital investment. But many Democrats also thought the new system would retard growth. The independent treasury did not pass until 1840, enacted as an entirely separate, specie-based system, able neither to receive nor to pay out paper currency.

Van Buren's challenges spilled over from domestic to international crises. Twice, the fears and frustrations of Americans along the Canadian border almost brought the United States and Canada/Great Britain to blows. Americans and Canadians had long argued over who owned the rich timber reserves in the Aroostook Valley on the border of Maine and New Brunswick. When Americans heard rumors in 1838 that Canadian lumberjacks were infiltrating the region and taking trees at will, the Democratic governor of Maine declared that Maine was under invasion and demanded federal protection. Van Buren sent in the army under General Winfield Scott. Aware that the economy could not support a war, he also instructed Scott to offer terms for a truce. If Canada would acknowledge Maine's predominant interest in the valley, the United States would respect existing Canadian settlements pending final disposition of the area.

Meanwhile, Americans along the northern New York border were picking sides in an internal Canadian rebellion against Great Britain (1837–1838). Although the United States was technically neutral, disgruntled unemployed American workers saw the rebels embodying the spirit of the American Revolution and were drawn to support them against wealthy Canadians and the British government. Recruited by the rebels, sympathetic New Yorkers raised funds and offered ships to transport men and arms to Canada. On December 29, 1837, Canadian pro-British troops crossed the river into Schlosser, New York, captured the *Caroline* (owned by American William Wells), towed it out into the middle of the river, and set it afire. A few months later, Americans retaliated by sinking a British ship. The United States and Britain exchanged diplomatic demands until 1840, when Alexander McLeod, a Canadian deputy sheriff, got drunk in a New York tavern and began bragging that he had killed an American during the *Caroline* incident. New York authorities immediately arrested him and local mobs clamored for blood, while Britain protested that McLeod's status was an international matter, beyond New York's jurisdiction, and threatened to break diplomatic relations. Van Buren, fighting for reelection as the anti-big-government Democratic candidate, was not ready to intervene. Only with the election of a Whig president and Congress in 1840 was McLeod released.

The Political Economy of the Trans-Mississippi West

Jackson had embodied the restless energy and assumed right of white Americans to settle ever deeper in the North American continent. Manifest destiny, the belief that white Americans had a providential right to as much of North America as they wanted, had been a core belief and policy since the founding of the republic. It was implicit in the Northwest Ordinance, in scores of Indian treaties, in the Louisiana Purchase, in the Transcontinental Treaty, in the 1824 Monroe Doctrine, and in the Removal Act of 1830. But only in 1845 did the phrase enter the American vocabulary, when journalist John O'Sullivan proclaimed that it is "[o]ur manifest destiny . . . to overspread the continent allotted by Providence for the free development of our yearly multiplying millions." As the United States' treatment of Native Americans had long made clear, the manifest destiny of the nation was for many Americans racial, as well as territorial and political.

Manifest Destiny in Antebellum Culture

On the simplest level, manifest destiny was a political slogan and a crass claim for property, a way of asserting that Americans wanted and would have the continent all the way to the Pacific. But most Americans resisted such a naked statement of their ambitions and framed—and deeply understood—their aspirations in the language of democracy and freedom. This land was intended by Providence as the physical home of a unique national greatness. In antebellum culture, this understanding of the singularity of North America was often articulated through a linked pair of evocative images: first, the image of the awesome power and natural majesty of the American wilderness, and second, the image of the wilderness giving way to an even nobler state of cultivation on the arrival of American settlers.

Both images were evident in antebellum landscape painting, particularly in the work of a group of artists known as the Hudson River school. Like most Americans of the era, the Hudson River painters were influenced by the Romantic movement sweeping Europe, which emphasized the power and beauty of untamed nature. For example, the canvases of Thomas Cole, the leader of the Hudson River school, depicted wilderness bluffs surrounded by ageless forests presumably untouched by American settlers. Ancient trees spiked toward the heavens and wild waterfalls cascaded over crags far above the ground in Cole's *Falls of the Kaaterskill* (1826), with a massive gathering storm that underscores the unchecked power of the American wilderness. In these landscapes, the only human figures are usually Native Americans, additional emblems of the primitive beauty of the scene.

Cole and other Hudson River painters often combined these visual celebrations of the American landscape with images of American settlement. In these latter paintings, the arrival of the European Americans seemed to bring to fruition the innate grandeur of nature. Cole's *Landscape* (1825) suggested this harmonious blending of destinies, as did *West Rock, New Haven* (1849), by Connecticut native Frederick Church. The Hudson River paintings sometimes suggested bittersweet sadness at the passing of the wilderness, even as they celebrated the coming of ordered fields and farm towns.

Antebellum poets and novelists took up the theme of the land as well, also often envisioning it as a shifting scenery in which the majesty of the wilderness seemed merely to await transformation at the hands of American pioneers. James Fenimore Cooper's *Leatherstocking Tales* narrated European American settlement of the New York back-country as a grand myth of manifest destiny, in which settlement tamed the land even as the land itself became the agent through which the newcomers were forged into a new, ennobled society. In *The Last of the Mohicans,* Cooper described the New York back-country of 1757 as "an impervious boundary of forests" torn by dangerous rapids and rugged passes. By 1793, the fictional time of *The Pioneers,* that same landscape had become "a succession of hills" and "narrow, rich cultivated dales" dotted by "beautiful and thriving villages" and "neat and comfortable farms." In the same spirit, poet William Cullen Bryant visited the Illinois plains in the 1830s and saw not an austere landscape but a vision of "gardens" and "fields, boundless and beautiful." The uniting of the national culture and the land was the "manifest destiny" not only of American citizens but also of the land itself.

Jefferson had imagined this relationship of the people to the land chiefly in terms of the yeoman farmer, with the craftsman a secondary "handmaid." In the wake of innovations in travel and machinery design in the early nineteenth century, however, images of trade and manufacturing began to make their way into ideas about the abundance of the land. Americans would unleash the richness of the continent not only through farming but also through commerce. De Witt Clinton's prediction that the Erie Canal would help make New York City the emporium of the world captured this new vision in the politics of trade. Commerce, Clinton insisted in 1819, would not only collapse regional differences but also "increas[e] the stock of human happiness—by establishing the perpetuity of free government—and by extending the empire of improvement, of knowledge, of refinement and of religion. . . ." The American wilderness, first cultivated into a homestead, would become a huge highway for the transportation of goods and culture.

To this image of North America as a transportation network, Americans added the image of North American power harnessed into manufacturing output. The proof of America's greatness lay not only in the riches coaxed from the land but also in the seemingly endless array of manufactured goods. Reviewing an exhibit of goods manufactured in Massachusetts in 1839, one magazine correspondent argued that manufacturing "blended harmoniously together" the interests of all Americans. The enjoyments of abundant market goods did not extend to all people, however.

Texas

By the terms of the 1819 Transcontinental Treaty, the United States had given up claims to Spanish lands south of the 42nd parallel. Nevertheless, within a few years Americans began to enter the region.

Many of these immigrants were specifically invited; some were not. The Spanish saw their northern region as a buffer zone against the Lipan Apaches and Comanche Indians and between New Spain and the United States. After independence, the Mexican government expanded those policies by offering land grants to Americans in return for the promise to bring settlers to bolster the sparse population. The first American to accept the invitation was Stephen F. Austin, who began settling a colony on the banks of the Brazos and Colorado Rivers in 1821. By 1830 there were more than 20,000 Americans (including 1,000 slaves) living in the northeastern province of Mexico, bordering Louisiana.

Conflict between immigrant Americans and residents of Texas—known as Tejanos—was inevitable. Tejanos resented the influx of Americans, who were often awarded lands that already belonged to Tejanos or that included Tejano communities. Tejanos complained that the *empresarios* (American landholders) were "nothing more than money-changing speculators" who had no respect for existing claims and did not control their settlers or squatters who used the American colonies to hide stolen livestock.

Although they were happy to take advantage of the cheap prices Mexico offered, many Americans had never fully acknowledged the right of Mexico to these lands. Viewing the region as the natural next frontier for American plantation agriculture, southerners had denounced the 1819 treaty and lobbied John Quincy Adams and Andrew Jackson to purchase the tract free and clear. By 1839 some Americans were convinced that Texas was destined to become the "land of refuge for the American slaveholders."

The immigrants themselves criticized the Mexican government in the language of republicanism. They objected to high taxes, but then so did everybody. They objected to being required to convert to Catholicism in order to intermarry with Mexicans and control their Mexican wives' property, but those laws were not really enforced. They objected to having to adopt the Spanish language. But beneath these objections were more fundamental issues, including a deep discontent—which many Mexicans shared—with the autocratic Mexican government.

Southerners who moved to Texas had a particular complaint: the Mexican government's inconsistent policies on slavery. Like the young United States, the new and unstable Mexican government took an erratic course, at one point banning slavery altogether, at another point allowing slaves to enter the nation but mandating gradual abolition.

By the mid-1820s, however, the immigrants had developed a cotton economy dependent on slave labor that they were determined to preserve. They regarded Mexican inconsistency and resistance as evidence of betrayal. In 1824 Stephen Austin, never a devoted supporter of slavery, devised regulations for his colony with harsh provisions for slaves who tried to escape or free people who abetted runaways. By 1830 Austin had concluded that "Texas must be a slave country. Circumstances and unavoidable necessity compels it. It is the wish of the people there. . . ." In Austin's view, "the people" included only white US immigrants and others who agreed with their goals.

But slavery was not the major reason for the increasing tension between Texas and the Mexican government. After 1830 the government took steps to stem immigration and put troops on the United States–Mexican border. Immigrants saw these measures as obstructions to their rightful claims. The rise of General Antonio López de Santa Anna provided the occasion for registering their complaints. But when Santa Anna dissolved the Mexican Congress and made himself dictator in 1834, Texans—both Anglo and

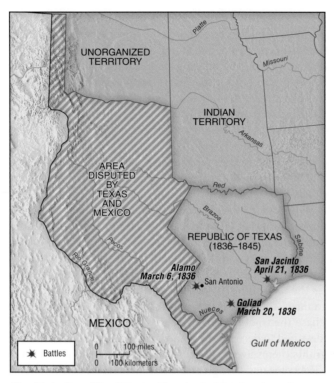

Map 12–1 Republic of Texas After the decisive American victory at San Jacinto that resulted in the independence of Texas, the border dispute between Texas and Mexico continued until it was resolved by the Mexican War a decade later.

Tejano—sharpened their criticisms. Casting themselves as the quintessential republicans, they and residents of several other Mexican states joined in the rebellion. Hoping to secure US statehood, Texas declared itself a sovereign republic on March 2, 1836.

Four days later the huge Mexican army, led by Santa Anna, attacked and wiped out 187 Texas patriots barricaded in a mission called the Alamo. It was a costly and fleeting victory. Santa Anna's army suffered 1,544 casualties and created martyrs for the rebels' cause. Led by Sam Houston, the rebels retreated east, gathering recruits as they went. On April 21 they surprised Mexican troops on the San Jacinto River and scored a huge victory, capturing Santa Anna himself. Bargaining for his life and freedom, Santa Anna declared Texas a free nation (see Map 12–1). Ecstatic Texans drew up a constitution, made Sam Houston their first president, and called for annexation to the United States.

With the nation in economic crisis and his own party bickering over who was responsible, the last thing Van Buren wanted as president was a bitter battle over Texas and slavery. He doubted that the Constitution permitted annexation, which he feared would be construed as meddling in Mexico's internal affairs. Anticipating Texas's application for admission, abolitionists had made opposition to annexation a central issue in their massive petition campaign of 1837–1838, expanding the controversy widely in the North. John Quincy Adams had delivered a stirring speech against annexation in the House, and some senators were publicly denouncing slavery in general and especially in Texas. Southerners had responded with their own states' rights petitions. In the end, Van Buren did not submit Texas's request for statehood to Congress.

Pacific Bound

For most white Americans, however, Texas was not the fulfillment of America's manifest destiny. That goal lay in the rich lands beyond the plains. By the time Van Buren left office, the Mississippi River had become the staging ground for a massive migration west.

The migration began as a trickle of missionaries in the 1830s. In 1831 rumors reached the East of four young Indians who had appeared in St. Louis, exhausted and sick, imploring that religious teachers be sent to their people. Two years later, the Methodist *Christian Advocate and Herald* published a letter from a Wyandot Indian who claimed that western tribes hungered for instruction in Christianity. True or not, such stories enabled missionaries to claim they had been invited into Indian communities. In 1834 the Methodist Missionary Society sent the Reverend Jason Lee west to found a mission in the Willamette Valley of Oregon Territory. Two years later, the American Board of Commissioners for Foreign Missions sent six people (including two women) to settle permanent missions in Oregon.

For their first mission, the board selected Marcus and Narcissa Prentiss Whitman, a doctor and a Sunday school teacher. In 1836, the Whitmans established their mission among the Cayuse Indians near Fort Walla Walla on the Columbia River. Their fellow missionaries Henry and Eliza Hart Spalding founded a mission 125 miles away among the Nez Percés.

At first, the Whitmans seemed to thrive. Marcus Whitman preached and doctored among the Cayuses and taught the men agriculture, and Narcissa taught school and oversaw the operation of the large mission. Over the following decade, however, as white immigration swelled, the Cayuses came to view the missionaries as the cause of the influx of white people and new diseases. In 1847, after a deadly measles epidemic, a Cayuse band attacked the mission, killing Marcus and Narcissa Prentiss Whitman and a number of other white people. But they couldn't stem the rising tide of settlers.

By then, migrants to the West Coast were so numerous that the roads of Iowa "were literally lined with long blue wagons . . . slowly wending their way over the broad prairies," leaving deep, rutted tracks. In the years of heaviest migration, watering holes were so overused and sanitary conditions so poor that the road west became a breeding ground for typhoid, malaria, dysentery, and cholera.

Most of the migrants were farming families of moderate means, pushed out of the Midwest by the hard times of 1837. Men often made the decision to leave with little warning to their families. Sarah Cummins remembered returning home from school one day in Illinois to discover that her father had sold the farm and that "as soon as school closes we are to move." Yet even spur-of-the-moment decisions rarely meant immediate departure for the West. Preparations for the trip took up to half a year, and families could expect to spend another half a year on the trail.

Family Traveling West This rare 1850s photograph shows a family traveling west in a covered wagon.

Travelers funneled through St. Louis, crossed Missouri to rendezvous with wagon trains near St. Joseph or Independence, Missouri, and then followed one of two main routes west (see Map 12–2). The northern route, known as the Oregon Trail, zigzagged northwest roughly parallel to the Rocky Mountains. The Santa Fe Trail headed southwest out of Independence along the Arkansas River through the future state of Kansas before reaching Mexican lands. At Santa Fe, the trail divided, feeding immigrants west along the Old Spanish Trail or south to Chihuahua, Mexico.

Most overland migrants traveled in families, in groups of families, and occasionally in entire communities. If they lacked team animals, families pulled their possessions in two-wheeled handcarts. For the most part, wagons carried supplies, not people. Most migrants walked west. Moreover, wagons broke down, were washed away in river crossings, or had to be emptied to ease the burden on the animals.

Past the plains, wagon trains sometimes went days without finding water or game. Women and men drove the wagons and herded the cattle, collected firewood, and caught small animals for food. When broken equipment or sickness slowed families, the trains were often forced to leave them behind, lest the others not clear the Rocky Mountains before winter. The harrowing dangers of that possibility were immortalized in the story of the ill-fated Donner Party, caught in the Sierra Nevadas by an early winter. For four months the group was trapped by snow, slowly starving. When relief finally arrived in mid-February 1847, "the dead were lying about on the snow, some even unburied, since the living had not strength to bury their dead," according to one survivor. Of the 87 persons snowed in, 42 died. It was not a risk worth taking, even if it meant leaving people behind on the plains.

For migrants who reached the West, the rewards were not always immediately apparent. "My most vivid recollection of that first winter in Oregon," one woman recalled, "is of the weeping skies and of Mother and me also weeping." As soon as they were settled, though, many newcomers proclaimed Oregon "this best country in the world." The climate was hospitable to crops of wheat, flax, and corn and to apple and pear orchards. Lumber was plentiful, and the streams were full of fish. Farther south was California, where, after 1848, rumors of "inexhaustible" gold strikes began to filter north and east.

Nations of the Trans-Mississippi West

American settlers felt they were journeying through national territories. Indigenous communities viewed the settlers as trespassers in Indian Country.

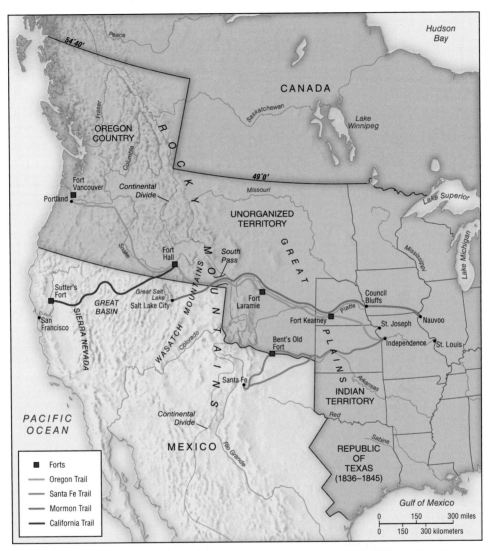

Map 12-2 Major Overland Trails The overland trails to the west started at the Missouri River. The Santa Fe Trail was a conduit for traders and goods to Mexico. The Oregon Trail passed through Wyoming and branched off to California and Oregon.

Most wagon trains departed from Missouri, which meant that settlers first crossed Oklahoma, where Native Americans like Elias Boudinot and the Cherokees had been guaranteed refuge from white intrusion (see Map 12–3). Between Independence, Missouri, and the Rocky Mountains lay the Indian nations of the prairies and Great Plains: the Blackfoot and Crow to the northwest; the Sioux, Pawnee, Arapaho, Shoshone, and Cheyenne, through the northern and central plains; and the Kiowa, Apache, Comanche, and Navajo in the Southwest. Along the Pacific were the Yakima, Chinook, Cayuse, and Nez Percé Indians, and to the south, in California, Pomo, Chumash, Yuma, and many other tribes.

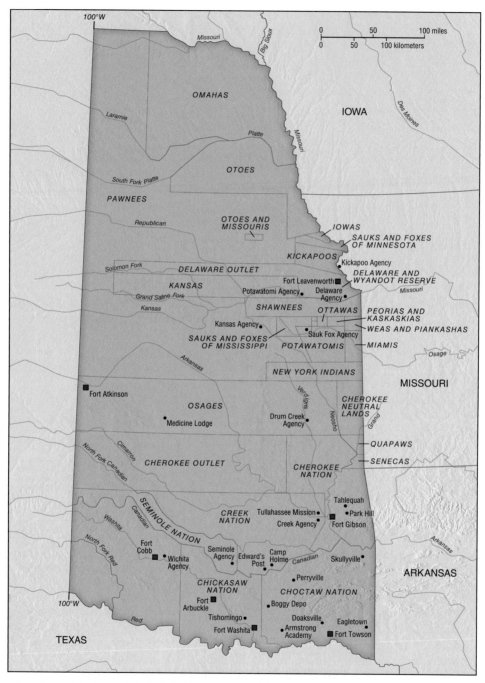

Map 12–3 Major Trans-Mississippi Indian Communities, ca. 1850 Most of the Indians living in the Indian Territories in the 1830s and 1840s had been "removed" from areas east of the Mississippi River. The territories were located west of Arkansas, Missouri, and Iowa. The section to the south (now Oklahoma) was home to Cherokees, Choctaws, Creeks, and Seminoles from the Old Southwest. The northern part (now Kansas and Nebraska) was inhabited by Indians from the Old Northwest.

Because most of this vast territory was part of Mexico, and because Great Britain laid claim to Oregon, crossing to utopia meant transgressing the boundaries of those nations as well.

Penny novelists would depict this contact as a violent confrontation in which war-like Indians massacred well-meaning migrants. In fact, of the more than 250,000 settlers who crossed the plains between 1840 and 1860, fewer than 400 were killed by Native Americans. More deaths were inflicted by white migrants on the Indians.

Prior to massive migration in the 1840s, official US policy toward the Indians had been one of removal, by force or by pressured sale of lands and physical relocation. Even in the 1830s observers saw no evidence that Americans recognized a boundary short of the Pacific Ocean. Alexis de Tocqueville noted that "when it promises these unlucky people a permanent asylum in the West," the US government "is well aware of its inability to guarantee this." By the late 1830s, as the last of the eastern "removals" were completed, federal policy toward Indians began to shift. Removal and resettlement continued to be the primary stated goal, and many western tribes were confined to reservations or moved to Indian Territory.

By the mid-1830s, when white Americans started crossing the Mississippi River in huge numbers, most of these nations had already tasted the effects of expansionism. The Comanches (the largest of the southwestern nations) and the Apaches had been at war with European Americans for several centuries, having fought the Spanish, the Mexicans, and, since the 1820s, both the Mexicans and the US settlers in Texas. All of the Plains Indians, especially the Sioux, Kiowas, and Comanches, had felt the impact of eastern Indians displaced or officially relocated west. The Sioux had been at war for decades with the Indians of the Old Northwest Territory, who were being pushed across the Mississippi River.

For the western Indians, the effects of the migration of the 1840s were social, cultural, and economic. Although the number of deaths from warfare was low, deaths from disease and malnutrition were far higher and took especially high tolls on the children and the old, wiping out both the elders who carried a community's history and collective wisdom and the young people who represented its future. Contact gradually altered the Indians' social organization and gender division of labor. As it became harder to claim and protect planting grounds, tribes shifted to more nomadic ways of life. The relative importance of women's foraging and planting diminished, and the relative importance of men's skills as hunters and warriors increased.

By 1840, the northern grasslands and southern plains supported a complex economy of hunting and foraging. Indians consumed corn, melons, berries, wild sweet potatoes, turnips, and fowl and small game, harvested in a seminomadic way of life and traded through networks. At the center of this economy stood the bison, supplying food and material for clothing, shelter, and trade.

This way of life was threatened as the number of bison declined. Settlers' need for food had only a minor impact on the buffalo. More deadly was their fascination with hunting and killing such a huge creature, regardless of whether they needed its meat and hides. Recreational hunting parties, as well as hunters intent on wiping out the Indians' means of support, took their toll. As early as 1842, the Teton Sioux had complained to federal agents that the heavy migrations were harming their hunting grounds. By 1846 the Sioux were demanding that the US government stem the migrations and prevent the migrants from killing animals indiscriminately. When the government ignored the complaints, the Sioux prevented wagon trains from passing until migrants had paid a toll in money, tobacco, or supplies.

Buffalo Hunt The Plains Indians were extremely adept at hunting buffalo, which served as an integral part of their economic systems. Over the course of the nineteenth century, white encroachments rapidly decimated the buffalo herds and brought the species to the brink of extinction.

In the mid-1840s the energies of the federal government were primarily engaged in Texas, where American nationalists were demanding action against Mexico. In the northern plains, the government constructed a chain of forts intended as quarters for armed rifle units called dragoons, who would, theoretically, protect overland migrants from the Indians. The strategy was not very effective, as Indians continued to exert control over white migration through northern Indian Country.

Slavery and the Political Economy of Expansion

As Americans poured west, expansion became a source of national political controversy. The problem was not the principle of manifest destiny, which few questioned. By the late 1830s, expansion was linked in the public debate with the extension of slavery and raised other problems. Southerners viewed northerners as unfaithful to a 50-year-old compromise ratified in the Constitution. Northerners looked at the spread of slavery into the new Southwest (Louisiana, Mississippi, Alabama, and Arkansas) and worried about the political leverage of a new slave state the size of Texas.

Log Cabins and Hard Cider: The Election of 1840

Approaching the election of 1840, the major parties were in a balancing act. Both hoped to exploit regional differences but without raising the divisive issues associated with slavery. Whigs considered Van Buren vulnerable, both because of the continuing effects of the depression of 1837 and because he was a northerner who seemed to be blocking the annexation of Texas. Henry Clay, leader of the Whigs, also opposed the annexation, but he calculated that southern Democrats would choose a Kentuckian over a New Yorker. Aware of Van Buren's liabilities in the South, Democrats sought to keep slavery out of the debates, although Van Buren was willing to have northerners see him as the alternative to a southern president. A number of northern Whigs were suspicious of Clay's ties to the South.

Van Buren received the Democratic nomination, but in an effort to skirt the explosive sectional issues, the Whigs turned to William Henry Harrison, the hero of the battle of Tippecanoe against Tecumseh's people and an outspoken advocate of cheap western land. Harrison had run strongest against Van Buren in 1836. To bolster the appeal of their slate, for their vice presidential candidate the Whigs chose a former Democrat, John Tyler of Virginia, a strong advocate of states' rights and (at the time) a Clay supporter.

Harrison was a "sentimental" candidate who the Whigs hoped would evoke feelings of military glory and westward expansion. Avoiding tough issues, they crafted a Jackson-like campaign for "Tippecanoe and Tyler, too." When Harrison was derided as a country bumpkin content with sitting on his porch drinking cider, the Whigs took up the image with gusto. In the "Log Cabin and Hard Cider Campaign," the Whigs celebrated Harrison as a simple man of the people (like Jackson). In fact, Harrison was from a wealthy old Virginia family, but he could be linked to the West, and, as Daniel Webster observed, Harrison's main appeal was the vague "hope of a better time."

The turnout was large, and the popular results were close, but the Electoral College was a different story. Harrison, who had taken every large state but Virginia, triumphed with 234 electoral votes to Van Buren's 60. The Democrats held New Hampshire, Illinois, Missouri, Arkansas, Alabama, Virginia, and South Carolina.

And Tyler, Too

Whig jubilation at their presidential victory was short-lived. Harrison fell ill shortly after his inauguration and died on April 4, 1841, the first president to die in office. Harrison was followed in office by his vice president, John Tyler, whom most observers assumed would serve as a caretaker president until the next general election. He soon proved them wrong, succeeding to the full stature and authority of the presidency.

Tyler's ascendancy threw the Whig Party into chaos, for once in office he reverted to his Democratic roots. Much about Tyler was reminiscent of Jackson. He opposed the American System and favored slavery and the annexation of Texas, and he was willing to use the full power of the executive to enforce those views. Unlike Jackson, Tyler strongly advocated extreme southern states' rights positions.

Tyler's attention was first drawn to diplomatic troubles with Britain. In 1841 the slave crew of the US ship *Creole*, en route from Virginia to New Orleans, had seized control of the vessel and forced it into the port of Nassau, where, by British law, the crew was freed. To no avail, white southerners demanded the return of the crew. Meanwhile, northern anti-British feeling flared over the question of the Oregon Territory, a vaguely defined expanse between northern California and Alaska that Britain and the United States had agreed in 1818 to occupy jointly. By 1842, reports of the North American Pacific Coast as a "storehouse of wealth in all its forests, furs, and fisheries" had stirred both immigration and the American desire to claim the Oregon Territory.

In 1842 US secretary of state Webster and British emissary Ashburton concluded the Webster-Ashburton Treaty, which drew a boundary between the United States and Canada from Maine to the Rocky Mountains (Oregon was left undivided), established terms of extradition between the two nations, and created a joint effort to restrict the international slave trade. Great Britain also agreed not to interfere with foreign vessels.

Tyler's success in foreign relations was overshadowed by his 1841 break with his own party. Led by Henry Clay, Whigs in Congress passed legislation that embodied their platform, including tariff bills, a national bank bill, and a bill to distribute federal surpluses to states. Tyler vetoed almost every initiative. He denounced federal distribution as inappropriate when the federal government was in deficit. At last, in 1842, congressional Whigs offered lower tariff increases and detached the tariff from the question of distribution. Needing federal funds, Tyler signed the bill. Tyler supported the repeal of the independent treasury, a Whig goal, but this, too, proved a bitter victory for the Whigs, because Tyler vetoed the national bank with which the Whigs wanted to replace the independent treasury.

Tyler was soon a president without a party. As early as January 1843, there were calls in the House of Representatives for his impeachment. That year, when Tyler vetoed the bill rechartering the national bank, his entire cabinet resigned, except Webster.

"His Accidency," as opponents dubbed Tyler, proved resilient. Tyler interpreted Democratic gains in the 1842 elections as support for his positions, particularly on the national bank. Urged on by extreme states' rights advocates in Virginia and South Carolina, Tyler took up the cause of the annexation of Texas. After Daniel Webster resigned from the cabinet, Tyler fell almost entirely under the influence of southerners committed to Texas.

Texas did all it could to press for annexation. It allowed Great Britain to serve as an intermediary in Texas's efforts to win official recognition from Mexico and hinted that, as an independent republic, Texas might abolish slavery. The idea of an alliance between Texas and Great Britain reawakened old anti-British sentiments, and the prospect of a non–slave republic so nearby filled southerners with dread.

Seeking to capitalize on these anxieties, in 1843 President Tyler secretly opened negotiations with Texas for admission to the Union, expecting to justify the treaty as necessary protection against British influence. In 1844, Tyler submitted a treaty of annexation to Congress. He hoped that potential opposition would be countered by expansionist interests. He was wrong. Even before the treaty was submitted, John Quincy Adams and 12 other Whigs denounced it as constitutionally unauthorized and warned that it would bring the nation to "dissolution." Abolitionists labeled the move a naked power grab by slave owners. Even moderate northerners worried that annexing Texas would cause war with Mexico, without yielding the North any tangible gains. Some southerners worried that Texas would compete with the depleted cotton and sugar lands of the South.

By then, other election-year dramas were afoot. John Calhoun still longed for the presidency and felt he had a good chance against Tyler, another southerner, if he could deny Van Buren the Democratic nomination. To that end, Calhoun wrote a note to the British minister that the US goal in Texas was to protect slavery against British abolitionists. As Calhoun hoped, the note became public. The explicit association of Texas and slavery drove Van Buren away from endorsing the treaty, weakening his position in the South. An overwhelmingly sectional vote defeated the treaty in Congress, but Calhoun believed a Democratic victory in 1844 would revive it.

Occupy Oregon, Annex Texas

By the fall of 1844 the American political party system was in disarray. Harrison's impressive victory in 1840 had not signaled a broad endorsement of Clay or the American System, any more than Van Buren's victory in 1836 had signaled a strong hard-money, antibank sentiment. To the contrary, between 1836 and 1844 the party system seemed most successful at polarizing American interests, which were already diverging economically (see Table 12–1).

Nowhere was that state of affairs more evident than in the 1844 Democratic convention in Baltimore. Van Buren's supporters believed the party owed him the nomination, yet his liabilities were legion. In the South, proslavery, proannexation Democrats led by Calhoun were vowing to have "a slaveholder for President next time regardless of the man." Andrew Jackson was disappointed with Van Buren's refusal to endorse annexation and encouraged former Tennessee governor James K. Polk to run. In the North, workers and entrepreneurs hard hit by years of deflation were disenchanted with Van Buren. His supporters were unable to block a convention rule requiring a candidate to receive a two-thirds vote to secure the nomination. Van Buren could not marshal that level of support, but neither could Tyler, Calhoun, or Lewis Cass, a compromise candidate. Finally, on the eighth ballot the convention fell back on Jackson's choice, James Polk. Tyler accepted renomination by a renegade group of supporters who styled themselves Democratic Republicans.

The 1844 Democratic Party ran on the platform of manifest destiny, calling for "the reoccupation of Oregon and the reannexation of Texas." It was an odd formulation, given that the United States had several times officially denied possession of Texas and had yet to occupy Oregon fully. The platform went even further on Oregon. Although the US claim to Oregon had never extended beyond the 49th parallel, the Democrats now declared their willingness to go to war to gain the entire region ("Fifty-four forty or fight!"). Their strategy incorporated war fears over Texas into a broader assertion of national destiny.

Meanwhile, in 1844 Henry Clay secured the Whig nomination. Clay was certain that opposition to the extension of slavery was strong enough to block a Texas-Oregon compromise and that Americans would not support a war with Mexico. Clay ran

Table 12-1 Personal Income Per Capita by Region: Percentages of United States Average

	1840	1860	1880
United States	100	100	100
Northeast	135	139	141
North Central	68	68	98
South	76	72	51
West	—	—	190

Source: Richard A. Easterlin, "Regional Income Trends, 1840–1950," in *American Economic History* ed. Seymour E. Harris (New York: McGraw-Hill, 1961), p. 528.

Table 12-2 The Liberty Party Swings an Election

Candidate	Party	Actual Vote in New York	National Electoral Vote	If Liberty Voters Had Voted Whig	Projected Electoral Vote
Polk	Democratic	237,588	170	237,588	134
Clay	Whig	232,482	105	248,294	141
Birney	Liberty	15,812	0	—	—

primarily as a supporter of the American System as the necessary means for stabilizing economic growth.

The election results suggested a nation teetering on the edge of political division. Polk, annexation, and manifest destiny won, but by only 38,000 of more than 2.5 million votes cast. More striking, James G. Birney of Ohio, the candidate of the new, explicitly antislavery Liberty Party, drew 62,000 votes, most of them taken from Clay. Had Birney not run, the election might have been a dead heat (see Table 12–2).

Both Tyler and Congress read the election as a referendum on the Democratic platform and specifically on Texas. Early in 1845, with Tyler still in office, a bill approving annexation passed the House. To move it through the Whig-dominated Senate, Senator Robert Walker of Mississippi suggested that the Senate version include the option of negotiating a whole new treaty. Only days away from the presidency, Polk was said to favor this approach, and Whigs thought a revised treaty might get them out of a politically costly position. The Senate approved the amended treaty. The Whigs expected Tyler to concede the decision to the incoming president, but in the last hours of his presidency he sent notice to Texas that (contingent on its own agreement) the republic was annexed to the United States of America. Mexico immediately severed relations with the United States.

War with Mexico

The annexation of Texas was the ostensible cause of the outbreak of war with Mexico in April 1846, but not the only cause. In Polk's eyes, the annexation of Texas was a piece of a larger acquisition: not only Oregon but also present-day New Mexico, Arizona, and California. Polk would have been happy to make these acquisitions peacefully, but he was willing to go to war.

Polk took a two-track approach to foreign relations. In December 1845 he announced his decision to withdraw from negotiations over Oregon, and he called on Congress to terminate the United States–Great Britain Convention of Joint Occupancy. Compromise would be an abandonment of American "territorial rights . . . and the national honour," he insisted, and would be unthinkable. Beyond the combative rhetoric, Polk informed his advisers that he was prepared to hear a compromise offer from England. When one came, proposing a boundary at the 49th parallel, Polk submitted it to Congress. By June 1846 the deal had been struck.

In Oregon, Polk threatened war but quickly accepted peace. However, what Polk really wanted in the Mexican borderlands, Thomas Hart Benton claimed, was "a little war," big enough to justify grabbing the Southwest but not so big as to break the budget. Texas provided the excuse.

AMERICA AND THE WORLD

Lt. Rankin Dilworth in the War with Mexico

Rankin Dilworth was only 18 years old when he entered the United States Military Academy at West Point. By the time he applied to the academy, his mother had been widowed twice, and Dilworth may well have seen the army as his one opportunity to get ahead in life. He was apparently an average cadet, graduating in the middle of his class in 1844, one year behind Ulysses S. Grant, future general of the Union army and president of the United States. But in 1844 neither Grant nor Dilworth was contemplating duty in a civil war. If Dilworth had his sights fixed on anything, it was surely the West, where American territorial ambitions were creating countless opportunities for military advancement.

By the spring of 1846, those opportunities were near at hand. Barracked outside of St. Louis, Dilworth's company was ordered to southern Texas, where hostilities had already broken out between United States troops and the Mexican army. They traveled by boat down the Mississippi and across the Gulf of Mexico to Matamoros, Mexico. From there, they marched up the Rio Grande to Carmargo, Texas, where Dilworth's unit joined with American forces under General Zachary Taylor. From Carmargo, the combined unit proceeded to Monterrey. From April 28 to September 19, 1846, Dilworth kept an almost daily record of that journey.

The diary suggests that, officer or not, Dilworth was shadowed by nostalgia for home. Viewing a beautiful church in Reynosa made him wonder "if I will ever go to church again where I hear the English language spoken." That night, he dreamed he was in church at home "without a thought of camps or bivouacs, with smiling happy faces around me." Awakened by the call to guard duty, "in an instant," he wrote, "I found myself on the hot sandy plaza of Reynosa, many, many miles from those I love."

Still, Dilworth found much to occupy his attention in the journey south. He took a keen interest in Mexico. Waxing romantic, he compared Mexico to "a magnificent flower garden" dotted with plots of "limes, oranges, lemons, [and] pomegranates." He admired young Mexican women, one of whom he declared "the handsomest female that I have seen since I parted with E. M. M." (his sweetheart back home). Dilworth's descriptions sometimes betrayed the flippant cultural superiority so much a part of American expansionism of the 1840s. "The inhabitants present all shades from pure Indian to the white person," he wrote on one occasion. "Their intelligence is in the same scale."

Dilworth's diary also recorded the daily, and sometimes needless, hardships that would eventually make the campaign infamous in army annals. Swollen with untrained volunteers and newly trained officers (like Dilworth himself), the Mexican campaign was a tutorial in bad luck and bad judgment. Dilworth wrote about tents that collapsed in violent rainstorms, marches through mud so thick that it added 10 pounds to the weight of each boot, and temperatures so hot that soldiers died of heat prostration. He wrote of arrogant and inept officers who could not even march their troops in the right direction. On September 19 near Monterrey, Dilworth

continued

AMERICA AND THE WORLD *continued*

encountered an old friend in a different unit. The friend asked Dilworth if he had "heard the 'Elephant' groan," an expression used by the troops to express bitterness and disappointment. Dilworth did not record his reply. Nor did he add any further entries in the diary. On September 21, General Taylor ordered an assault on Monterrey, dividing his small band into two groups to attack the city from opposite sides. The western troops won with relative ease, but the eastern forces lost their way in thick cane fields before being caught in deadly Mexican crossfire. Along the city's narrow streets, they were easy targets for sharpshooters. Remarkably, inch by inch, house by house, Taylor's troops carried the day. On September 24, 1846, Mexican general Pedro de Ampudía offered surrender.

None of this mattered to Rankin Dilworth. During the first day's assault a "twelve-pounder cannon ball" had torn off one of his legs. On September 27, at 24 years of age, he died. His family was unable to pay the costs of having his body returned to Ohio. Lieutenant Rankin Dilworth was buried in Monterrey, Mexico.

As a condition of his surrender and release, the Mexican general Santa Anna had agreed to the Rio Grande as the boundary between Texas and Mexico, a boundary that would have run northward to include present-day New Mexico as well as western Texas. The Mexican government had instead drawn the border at the Nueces River, recognizing only about half the territory claimed by Texans. Polk intended to set the boundary at the Rio Grande, and he may have intended to secure not only the disputed Texas territory but also large portions of northern Mexico.

Polk once again played a double game. As late as September, he appealed for a peaceful resolution. That month, he dispatched former Louisiana congressman John Slidell to Mexico to offer to purchase New Mexico and Texas for $30 million. The Mexican government refused to receive Slidell.

Meanwhile, Polk prepared for war. In the spring of 1845 he had sent 1,500 soldiers, under the command of General Zachary Taylor, allegedly to protect Texas against a possible invasion by Mexico. When Texas approved union with the United States, Polk reinforced Taylor's troops and ordered them to approach the Rio Grande, while also sending an army under Stephen Kearny into the northern part of the disputed territory. In August 1846, Kearny occupied Santa Fe. At the same time, Polk ordered the US squadron in the Pacific closer to the California coast and directed the US consul in California, Thomas Larkin, to encourage local disaffection with the Mexican government. When American settlers in the Sonoma Valley staged a rebellion in June and July, the representatives of the United States claimed California. Kearny later crossed into California to solidify the claim.

By then, Polk's brinkmanship on the Rio Grande had produced results. Mexican troops had crossed the river to drive out Taylor's force, and American soldiers had been killed and wounded. In May 1846, Congress declared that "a state of war exists" between the two nations.

Nebel, Storming of Chapultepec—Quitman's Attack.

Chapultepec Carl Nebel's depiction of the American attack on the Chapultepec fort, near Mexico City, during the Mexican-American War, September 13, 1847.

The United States entered the war unprepared. Although 100,000 volunteers signed up, at the outbreak of hostilities the United States Army had only 7,500 troops. Perhaps Polk shared the expansionist view of Mexico as a "miserable, inefficient" nation. Mexico (and New Spain before it) had always been less interested in its northern provinces than in other parts of the nation. Moreover, after a coup, the Mexican government was unstable. With California guarded by John C. Frémont and the naval squadron, the United States could bring its military power to bear on Mexico City.

Finding the right leader proved tricky. Taylor, the obvious choice, was a popular Whig. Polk finally settled on Winfield Scott, who also harbored Whig ambitions. In the late winter of 1847, a squadron of 200 ships conveyed Scott's army of 10,000 soldiers to Veracruz, which surrendered in April. Scott's troops fought their way to the outskirts of Mexico City, which fell after six days on September 14 (see Map 12–4).

For all the success of the American campaign, support for the war steadily eroded. From the beginning, the war raised the question of slavery. Northern Democrats saw the war as a transparent ploy to extend slavery. Antislavery activists spoke out against the war, and opposition grew as stories of US military atrocities filtered back east.

In spite of the unpopularity of the war, a defeated Mexico was so weak that Polk thought of extracting greater concessions. His minister in Mexico, Nicholas P. Trist, opposed this proposal, however. In 1848 Trist negotiated the Treaty of Guadalupe Hidalgo, recognizing the Rio Grande as the border of Texas and granting the United States the territory encompassed in the present states of New Mexico, Arizona, Colorado, Utah, and Wyoming, as well as California. In return, the United States paid Mexico $15 million and assumed war claims of American citizens against Mexico. The Senate approved the treaty on March 10, 1848. The following May 25, Mexico concurred.

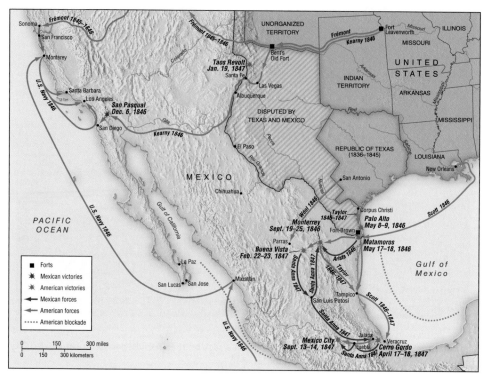

Map 12–4 Mexican War General Zachary Taylor's victories in northern Mexico established the Rio Grande as the boundary between Texas and Mexico. Stephen Kearny's expedition secured control of New Mexico. General Winfield Scott's invasion by sea at Veracruz and his occupation of Mexico ended the war.

Although Polk's presidency was dominated by the war with Mexico, the tariff and the independent treasury haunted domestic politics. In each case, Polk was victorious. Like Jackson, Polk opposed protective tariffs, which he saw as benefiting industrialists at the expense of farmers and republican values. Although Whigs in Congress pushed for higher tariffs to support domestic manufacturing, the 1846 tariff eliminated flat duties and reduced overall levels. Also like Jackson, Polk opposed the national bank. In 1846 he persuaded Congress to reinstate Van Buren's independent treasury to handle the federal government's financial transactions. Meanwhile, he vetoed Whig attempts to enact legislation supporting internal improvements.

Time Line

▼**1834**
First missionaries arrive in
   Oregon Territory

▼**1836**
Martin Van Buren elected
   president
Whig Party runs candidates for
   president
Texas declares independence

▼**1838**
"Aroostook" War
Anti-Slavery Petition campaign
   at height

▼**1839**
Assassination of Elias Boudinot
   and John Ridge

▼**1840**
Independent Treasury Bill
Large-scale overland migration
   to West Coast begins
Whig candidate William Henry
   Harrison elected president

STRUGGLES FOR DEMOCRACY

Mexicans in California Lose Their Rights

Many liberal-minded, educated people in the United States were against the Mexican-American war. They feared the spread of slavery and found the war to be an unjust effort to strip others of their property. Some of this thinking made its way into the 1848 Treaty of Guadalupe Hidalgo, which ended the war, and promised to deliver justice to Mexicans living in the territory that would henceforth be part of the United States. Article 8 of the treaty stipulated that Mexicans living in the territories ceded to the United States had one year to declare that they preferred Mexican citizenship; otherwise they would become US citizens. Article 9 of the treaty stated that Mexicans would be "maintained and protected in the free enjoyment of their liberty and property." Unfortunately, in the decades that followed, different states and courts interpreted the treaty in a wide range of ways.

In California, the discovery of gold in 1848 created a situation in which white North American settlers became eager to see the treaty overturned, and Mexicans were hard pressed to defend their lands. Many were driven away by mobs, and

when the Mexican ambassador complained, he was told that the affected Mexicans must be new arrivals, not people who had been living there for generations. Of course, in this time of warfare against the indigenous people of the West, "Californios," who were primarily of Native American rather than Spanish descent, received no protection at all: the California state constitutional convention explicitly denied them US citizenship.

In 1851, in an effort to ameliorate the chaotic situation in California, Congress passed the Land Act. The legislation created a Board of Land Commissioners whose job was to adjudicate the validity of Mexican land claims in California. Those who had been granted land by Spain or Mexico were required to present documentation upholding their claims within two years. If they did not, their present holdings would pass into the public domain. The Commissioners were instructed to respect the Treaty of Guadalupe Hidalgo, Spanish and Mexican law, and any relevant previous US Supreme Court cases. The Committee received *continued*

▼**1841**
John Tyler succeeds Harrison in
   office
Creole Mutiny

▼**1842**
Webster-Ashburton Treaty

▼**1844**
James Polk is elected president

▼**1845**
The United States annexes Texas

▼**1846**
The United States declares war
   on Mexico

▼**1848**
Treaty of Guadalupe Hidalgo
Teton Sioux attempt to tax
   white settlers passing
   through their lands

STRUGGLES FOR DEMOCRACY *continued*

813 claims and approved 604 of them. Among the successful claimants, however, it was not uncommon to find families who then had to turn around and sell the land they had just been awarded in order to pay the court costs. This was especially true where squatter settlers had brought multiple suits against them from which they had to defend themselves.

The unsuccessful claimants tended to be poorer Californios whose titles had never been formalized but who simply had an understanding for generations either with a local plantation owner or the Church. However, some of those who lost their lands were not poor people with informal claims. One famous example eventually resulted in the 1889 Supreme Court case *Botiller vs. Dominguez*. Dominga Dominguez, a wealthy woman from the San Fernando Valley, had perfect title to her lands, given to her family in a grant from the Mexican government dated 1835. Unfortunately, she ignored the political events happening around her and failed to turn in her claim before the two-year deadline. A Frenchman named Brigido Botiller led a group of squatters in a suit to claim her lands. The California State Supreme Court supported the dignified widow, ruling that by the terms of the Treaty Guadalupe Hidalgo, doña Dominga should not have felt pressured to turn in papers according to a bureaucratic deadline imposed later.

Botiller and the squatters, who were still ranching there as unwelcome neighbors, were not prepared to give up. They brought their suit to the Supreme Court. As the years wore on, many Americans became less interested in promoting justice in connection with the Treaty of Guadalupe Hidalgo and more interested in furthering the connection between government and business. In 1889, the Supreme Court reversed the state court's decision and awarded the Dominguez lands to Botiller and his cohort. The Court reasoned that it would be dangerous to open the door to any other Mexican Americans who had perfect title but had lost their land years ago either because they had failed to present on time or due to some other technicality. *Botiller vs. Dominguez* became a landmark case; henceforth, Mexican Americans tended to lose the cases that had been dragging on in the court system ever since the war. Many became deeply embittered and lost their faith in the American democratic system.

Jackson and Polk shared a broad understanding of politics and the use of political machinery. Like Jackson, Polk framed policy battles as battles between good and evil, between individual opportunity and elite finance and capital. At the same time, also like Jackson, Polk exercised executive power as the tool of the people's will. He was convinced that the president, not the legislature (Whig controlled, by his final years in office), represented the people's will. Before he left office, virtually every important item on his political agenda had been accomplished. Lost in that flush of victory was the steady erosion of popular support for the Democratic Party.

Conclusion

The removal of the Indians was intended to create space for white settlers, but in reality, it created new problems for the country. What exactly was to be done with the lands in the West? The war with Mexico revealed just how far apart the North and South had grown. By 1848, the northern states were deeply committed to a society based on free labor. The southern states, meanwhile, had grown ever more committed to slavery. The Mexican War signaled the beginning of an era in which differences between the North and South would seem undeniable and intractable—and symbolized in the West.

In 1848, Henry David Thoreau spoke to an audience in Concord, Massachusetts, about his refusal to pay poll taxes, which he said supported the institution of slavery and its expansion in the war with Mexico. Thoreau declared himself ready to separate from his government—indeed, to see the Union itself destroyed—rather than support the United States in the West. "How does it become a man to behave toward this American government today?" he asked. "I answer, that he cannot without disgrace be associated with it. I cannot for an instant recognize that political organization as my government which is the slave's government also."

Who, What

Elias Boudinot 356

Indian Territory 368

Henry Clay 373

Tejanos 363

John Tyler 371

Panic of 1837 359

Manifest destiny 361

Republic of Texas 364

James Fenimore Cooper 362

Hudson River School 361

Review Questions

1. What caused the decline of Jacksonianism?

2. How did most Americans express their enthusiasm for westward migration?

3. Why were the annexation of Texas and later the invasion of Mexico so controversial?

Critical-Thinking Questions

1. Support for American expansion was often expressed in the language of freedom and civilization. But was there also a racial component to "manifest destiny"?

2. Did the territorial additions of the 1840s represent a departure (in method or intent) from earlier acquisitions?

3. How and why did the Democratic Party change between 1828 and 1848?

For further review materials and resource information, please visit www.oup.com/us/oakes

CHAPTER 12: MANIFEST DESTINY, 1836–1848
Primary Sources

12.1 CHIEF JOHN ROSS, THE PETITION AND MEMORIAL OF THE DELEGATES AND REPRESENTATIVES OF THE CHEROKEE NATION (1840)

Cherokee Chief John Ross led the faction of his people who refused to leave their homeland even after President Andrew Jackson refused to enforce a Supreme Court decision which stated that Indians had a right to exercise sovereignty over their native lands. In 1838 the Cherokee people moved from Georgia to Oklahoma in the forced march known as the Trail of Tears. Once they arrived in the west, they starved. In 1840, Chief Ross went to Washington in a desperate attempt to gain some financial and legal concessions after the fact.

To the Senate and House of Representatives
Washington City, Febry. 28th, 1840

The Petition and Memorial of the undersigned Delegates and representatives of the Cherokee Nation, respectfully shows and represents: That the present position of the Cherokee Nation, and the events which have taken place since its cause was humbly submitted two years ago to Congress, are of a character to call for deep and immediate attention.

Your memorialists [that is, petitioners] have no desire, at this juncture, to dwell on the harrowing causes of the removal of the great mass of their people from their native and cultivated country east of the Mississippi, to the wilderness of the west; the history of that capture is notorious, and that its agonies mitigated is owing to the considerateness of the stronger, in not demanding of an entire people to say they had acknowledged what it was known they had disavowed; and to the permission humanely accorded to their leading men of personally supervising the compelled removal.

Your memorialists would here respectfully observe, that when it was found indispensable, under all the circumstances, to change the mode at first contemplated for effecting the transit in question, those of your memorialists who were intrusted with the charge of reconciling their countrymen to it, and of conducting them to their destination, encountered difficulties in the task, of which it may be almost impossible for your honorable bodies to form any imagination. Many were the stern minds they had to alter, who even when convinced of the hopelessness of retaining their inheritance they held so sacred, could only be persuaded not to die defending it, by a very slowly inspired reliance on promises that their consenting to remove would ensure peace and freedom to their children in a new and permanent home.

For the success of those of your Memorialists, and others of their fellow citizens, who performed this difficult office, it was fortunate that they were encouraged to assure their indignant, reluctant, and incredulous countrymen, that they would at length live unmolested in a region where their inspiriting national principle of self-government by the power of the majority was no more to be rendered inoperative; where they were to enjoy their own laws, and to be fore ever secured in the glorious privilege of feeling that they were men.

The Cherokee Nation was removed, though, on their first capture by the troops of the American republic, estates, large and small, were, upon the instant, seized and sold to any sordid adventurer, at large commissions to the auctioneers, and next to nothing for the owners; though, in the sudden and forced gathering of the people into separate masses by those troops, children were abruptly severed from doting parents who never met them more; though even the young husband was doomed to know that his wife, whom he was not permitted to protect, nor even to behold, had to pause before the rough soldiers, on the road to a military camp, and under these maddening circumstances, hear the first cry of her infant; though vast multitudes of both sexes and of all ages, were until then habituated to domestic comforts, were sickened by the wretchedness and unwholesomeness of being congregated in open fields, and crowded in Tents during the most scorching heat of summer, and thousands of those nearest and dearest to many of us at length sunk into miserable graves. Yes, though all these aggravations clustered around us on every side, still the drooping Cherokees were cheered on finding their armed captors eventually withdrawn and their conduct into exile transferred to persons among themselves in whom they could confide. The welcome change was hailed by them as the harbinger of a realization of the promise that the United States would secure to them else-where, that national independence, that exemption from intrusive meddlers, from prying and lying tale-bearers, and from military protection of the few, to overawe the many, from which the ill-starred peculiarities of their previous position had forever debarred them in the home whence they had departed. A few of their compatriots found themselves circumscribed by the chase by the advancing change in the modes of life, not only all around but within their native country, and that these few sought hunting grounds in the far west. The place they chose was at that time the property of Spain.[1] It passed into the hands of the United States, from whom, when the policy was arising to remove the Indians, our Mother Country east of the Mississippi purchased it, that her absent children might not be disturbed. Thus began the nucleus around which successive emigrants gathered, until at length its boundaries were outstretched by treaty for all Cherokees who might thenceforward follow. At the time the entire nation bent its course toward the region in question, about (as nearly as can be ascertained) one sixth of this whole population was already established there and this one sixth was generally designated as the western Cherokees. These facts will be well remembered by your honorable bodies; and your memorialists only state them to render their story more distinct.

The Cherokee Nation was removed . . . [Here follows a summary of all the efforts the relocated Cherokees had made between the 1838 removal and the present both to obtain aid from their western brethren, and to obtain that which was promised them by the US government, all to no avail.]

Your memorialists mostly humbly represent, that, if some mode of settling the concerns of the Cherokees with the United states is not presently adopted, their people will be reduced to ruin and despair; and it is their ardent hope that your honorable bodies will assist them to prevent such a result as all must deprecate, and not permit any pretence, however plausibly urged, to exclude us [chiefs] from being heard in the name of our people. The greater portion of them will presently be without goods; as the period of supplying the new Emigrants with rations is just expiring. They have no means. They have not so much as the implements of husbandry [that is, agricultural tools], and their arms which were taken from them some years ago, having never been restored, as promised, they cannot supply themselves with game. The existing relations between us and the United States are so ambiguous and capable of such opposite constructions, that even an obligation which is assumed, to preserve peace and to prevent intestine commotion, is, at this very moment, so exercised as to create the very evils it professes to remedy, and to defeat the very principle of recognizing the power of the majority

---

[1]They are referring to today's Arkansas and eastern Oklahoma. These people are still known as the Western Band of Cherokee.

which the Cherokees are instructed to consider as the principle of the Unites States in their dealings regarding them. We ask that these ambiguities may be cleared away. When our eastern country was lately taken from us without the consent of the majority, and the great mass of our people captured, they said that it was hard, but they were the weaker, and would not resist. They were doubted, but not a hand was raised, and now, those who have survived are in the West. We have done our part. We have given up all. What has been done by the United States? Nothing. Notwithstanding these things, have we yet acted towards the Unites States otherwise than with the meekest spirit of endurance. No one can say we ever did. We implore the great Republic to remember this in our favour and will then echo in its praise the benison [blessing] of the Saviour God himself, "Blessed are the peacemakers."

Your memorialists therefor humbly state that having full powers from the Cherokee people, to bring all questions between them and the United States to a close, they have been waiting for some time in Washington for the purpose;

1st Of obtaining indemnification for the country which has been taken away from them east of the Mississippi, and for the loss of private property and of injuries sustained in their forced removal:

2nd Of establishing a satisfactory definition of the tenure under which they are to hold their lands in the west:

3rd Of procuring some specific stipulations of the relations, which are to exist between them and the United States:

And 4th Of bringing the balance yet due for the expenses of their recent Emigration under General [Winfield] Scott to an immediate settlement:

And your memorialists throw themselves on the humanity and justice of your honorable bodies, as the only resource now left for the arrangement of these momentous affairs, to open the door for their relief, by such action as the wisdom of your honorable bodies may devise and the circumstances of our case urgently demand, and your memorialists will ever pray.

John Ross

John Looney (X)

E. Hicks

Archibald Campbell (X)

Joseph M. Lynch

Edward Gunter

Looney Price

George Hicks

Source: Gary Moulton, ed., *The Papers of John Ross, Volume II, 1840–1866* (Norman: University of Oklahoma Press, 1985), pp. 6–17.

12.2 VISUAL DOCUMENT: THOMAS COLE, *LANDSCAPE* (1825); FREDERIC EDWIN CHURCH, *NIAGARA FALLS* (1857); LOUIS RÉMY MIGNOT, *LANDSCAPE IN ECUADOR* (1859)

In 1825 a New York City magazine reviewed the work of a young painter named Thomas Cole, who had hiked the Adirondacks and created works celebrating the beauty of the world he encountered. Soon a number of artists were producing sublime landscape paintings of the region. At first they were called "the Hudson River school" in gentle mockery, but soon the term's use changed. A second generation of Hudson River school painters worked in the same style but traveled all over North and South America for inspiration. They shared a belief that America's natural world revealed the hemisphere's greatness.

Source: Thomas Cole, *Landscape* (1825). Bequest of Mrs. Kate L. Dunwoody.

Source: Frederic Edwin Church, *Niagara Fall*s (1857). Granger, NYC —

Source: Louis Rémy Mignot, *Landscape in Ecuador* (1859). Purchased with funds from gifts by the American Credit Corporation in memory of Guy T. Carswell, and various donors, by exchange.

12.3 LYDIA ALLEN RUDD, ACCOUNT OF WESTWARD JOURNEY (1852)

Lydia and Harry Rudd, Oregon Trail emigrants, had lost a baby girl named Margaret before they decided to go west and file for land in Oregon under the Donation Act. What especially interested Lydia was the fact that the Act allowed both husbands and wives to file for land claims. They went in 1852, together with two friends, whom Lydia identifies in her diary only as Henry and Mary. They were part of a larger wagon train that frequently purchased goods and services from local Indians.

May 6 1852 Left the Missouri river for our long journey across the wild uncultivated plains and unhabited except by the red man. As we left the river bottom and ascended the bluffs the view from them was handsome! In front of us as far as vision could reach extended the green hills covered with fine grass. . . . Behind us lay the Missouri with its muddy water hurrying past as if in great haste to reach some destined point ahead all unheeding the impatient emigrants on the opposite shore at the ferrying which arrived faster than they could be conveyed over. About half a miles down the river lay a steamboat stuck fast on a sandbar. Still farther down lay the busy village of St. Joseph looking us a good bye and reminding us that we were leaving all signs of civilised life for the present. But with good courage and not one sigh of regret I mounted my pony (whose name by the way is Samy) and rode slowly on. In going some two miles, the scene changed from bright sunshine to drenching showers of rain this was not quite agreeable for in spite of our good blankets and intentions otherwise we got some wet. The rain detained us so that we have not made but ten miles today. . . .

May 7 I found myself this morning with a severe headache from the effects of yesterday's rain. . .

    There is a toll bridge across this stream kept by the Indians. The toll for our team in total was six bits. We have had some calls this evening from the Indians. We gave them something to eat and they left. Some of them [had] on no shirt only a blanket, whiles others were ornamented in Indian style with their faces painted in spots and stripes feathers and fur on their heads beeds on their neck brass rings on their wrists and arms and in their ears armed with rifles and spears.

May 8 . . . We have come about 12 miles and were obliged to camp in the open prairie without any wood. Mary and myself collected some dry weeds and grass and made a little fire and cooked some meat and the last of our supply of eggs with these and some hard bread with water we made our supper.

May 9 . . . We passed a new made grave today . . . a man from Ohio. We also met a man that was going back: he had buried his Wife this morning She died from the effects of measels we have come ten miles today encamped on a small stream called Vermillion creek Wood and water plenty. Their [sic] are as many as fifty waggons on this stream and some thousand head of stock It looks like a village the tents and waggons extend as much as a mile. . . .

    Some are singing some talking and some laughing and the cattle are adding their mite by shaking their bells and grunt[ing]. Mosquitoes are intruding their unwelcome presence. Harry says that I must not sit here any longer writing but go to bed for I will not want to get up early in the morning to get breakfast.

May 10 I got up this morning and got breakfast and before sunrise we had eat in spite of Harry's prophecies to the contrary. . . .

May 11 We had a very heavy fog this morning which cleared up about noon. Our men are not any of them very well this morning. We passed another grave to day which was made this morning. The board stated that he died of cholera. He was from Indiana. We met several that had taken the back track for the states homesick I presume let them go. We have passed through a handsome country and have encamped on the Nimehaw river, the most beautiful spot that ever I saw in my life. I would like to live here. As far as the eye can reach either way lay handsome rolling prairies, not a stone a tree nor a bush even nothing but grass and flowers meets the eye until you reach the valley of the river which is as level as the house floor and about half a mile wide, where on the bank of the stream for two or three rods wide is one of the heaviest belts of timber I ever saw covered with thick foliage so thick that you could not get a glimpse of the stream through it. You can see this belt of timber for three or four miles from the hills on both sides winding through the prairie like some huge snake. We have traveled twelve miles . . .

May 12 . . . Our men not much better.

May 13 . . . Henry has been no better today. Soon after we stopped to night a man came along with a wheel barrow going to California: he is a dutchmann. He wheels his provisions and clothing all day and then stops where night overtakes him sleeps on the ground in the open air. He eats raw meat and bread for his supper. I think that he will get tired wheeling his way through the world by the time he gets to California.

May 14 Just after we started this morning we passed four men dig[g]ing a grave. They were packers. The man that had died was taken sick yesterday noon and died last night. They called it cholera morbus. The corpse lay on the ground a few feet from where they were dig[g]ing. The grave it was a sad sight. . . .

On the bank of the stream waiting to cross, stood a dray with five men harnessed to it bound for California. They must be some of the persevering kind I think. Wanting to go to California more than I do. . . . We passed three more graves this afternoon. . . .

Sept. 5 Traveled eighteen miles today encamped on a slough of powder river poor camp not much grass water nor wood. I am almost dead tonight. I have been sick two or three days with the bowel complaint and am much worse tonight.

Sept. 6 We have not been able to leave this miserable place today. I am not as well as yesterday and no physician to be had. We got a little medicine from a train tonight that has checked the disease some, the first thing that has done me any good.

Sept. 7 . . . I am some better today so much so that they ventured to move me this for the sake of a better camp. Mrs. Girtman is also sick with the same disease. Our cattle are most all of them ailing—there are two more that we expect will die every day. . . .

Oct. 8 started early this morning without any breakfast for the very good reason that we had nothing to eat still three miles from the falls safely landed about eight o'clock tired hungry and with a severe cold from last nights exposure something like civilization here in the shape of three or four houses there is an excuse here for a railroad of a mile and half on which to convey bag[g]age below the falls where they can again take water for the steamboat landing. Harry packed our bag[g]age down the railroad and the rest of us walked the car is drawn across the railroad by a mule and they will car[r]y no persons but sick. We again hired an Indian with his canoe to take us from the falls to the steamboat landing ar[r]ived about sundown a great many emigrants waiting for a chance to leave the steamboat and several flat boats lying ready to start out in the morning encamped on the shore for the night.

October 9-October 13 . . .

October 14 . . . I am so anxious to get some place to stop and settle that my patience is not worth much.

October 15–18 . . .

October 19 . . . We have had a very bad day today for traveling it has rained nearly all the time and it has rained very hard some of the time and we have had a miserable road the rain has made the hills very slippery and had to get up and down we have made but eleven miles of travel encamped on the prairie no water for our stock and not much for ourselves.

October 21 . . .

October 22 . . . Traveled three miles this morning and reached the village of Salem it is quite a pretty town a much handsomer place than Oregon City and larger. . . .

I am afraid that we shall be obliged to pack from here the rest of our journey and it will be a wet job another wet rainy day I am afraid that the rain will make us all sick. I am already begin to feel the affects of it by a bad cold.

October 23 . . . We cannot get any wagon to take us on our journey and are obliged to pack the rest of the way Mr. Clark and wife have found a house to live in and employment for the winter and they will stop here in Salem It took us until nearly noon to get our packs fixed for packing went about two miles and it rained so fast that we were obliged to stop got our dinner and supper in one meal cooked in a small cabin ignorant people but kind started again just.

October 24–25 . . . October 26 . . . we reached Burlington about two o'clock. There is one store one blacksmith shop and three or four dwelling houses. We encamped close by found Mr. Donals in his store an old acquaintance of my husband's. I do not know what we shall yet conclude on doing for the winter. There is no house in town that we can get to winter in. We shall probably stay here tomorrow and by the time know what we are to do for a while at least.

October 27 . . . Our men have been looking around for a house and employment and have been successful for which I feel very thankful. Harry has gone into copartnership with Mr. Donals in the mercantile business and we are to live in the back part of the store for this winter. Henry and Mary are going into Mr. D—house on his farm for the winter one mile from here. Mr. D—will also find him employment if he wants. I expect that we shall not make a claim after all our trouble in getting here on purpose for one. I shall have to be poor and dependent on a man my life time.

Source: Lillian Schlissel, ed., *Women's Diaries of the Westward Journey* (New York: Schocken Books, 1982), pp. 188–197.

12.4 JOHN O'SULLIVAN, "ANNEXATION" (1845)

John O'Sullivan was a newspaper columnist and editor writing in the 1840s. In the summer of 1845, in the pages of *The United States Magazine and Democratic Review*, he was the first to use the phrase "manifest destiny" in connection with America's westward expansion. No one responded, but a piece he wrote a few months later in December for the *New York Morning News* was more widely read, and the term caught on. O'Sullivan was an influential Democrat, and at first, the term was only used derisively by Republicans. In fact, it did not become popular until late in the nineteenth century when the United States launched its career of imperialism.

It is now time for the opposition to the Annexation of Texas to cease, all further agitation of the waters of bitterness and strife, at least in connexion with this question,—even though it may perhaps be required of us as a necessary condition of the freedom of our institutions, that we must live on for ever in a state of unpausing struggle and excitement upon some subject of party division or other. But, in regard to Texas, enough has now been given to party. It is time for the common duty of Patriotism to the Country to succeed;—or if this claim will not be recognized, it is at least time for common sense to acquiesce with decent grace in the inevitable and the irrevocable.

Texas is now ours. Already, before these words are written, her Convention has undoubtedly ratified the acceptance, by her Congress, of our proffered invitation into the Union; and made the requisite changes in her already republican form of constitution to adapt it to its future federal relations. Her star and her stripe may already be said to have taken their place in the glorious blazon of our common nationality; and the sweep of our eagle's wing already includes within its circuit the wide extent of her fair and fertile land. She is no longer to us a mere geographical space—a certain combination of coast, plain, mountain, valley, forest and stream. She is no longer to us a mere country on the map. She comes within the dear and sacred designation of Our Country; no longer a *"pays,"* she is a part of *"la patrie"*; and that which is at once a sentiment and a virtue, Patriotism, already begins to thrill for her too within the national heart. It is time then that all should cease to treat her as alien, and even adverse—cease to denounce and vilify all and everything connected with her accession—cease to thwart and oppose the remaining steps for its consummation; or where such efforts are felt to be unavailing, at least to embitter the hour of reception by all the most ungracious frowns of aversion and words of unwelcome. There has been enough of all this. It has had its fitting day during the period when, in common with every other possible question of practical policy that can arise, it unfortunately became one of the leading topics of party division, of presidential electioneering. But that period has passed, and with it let its prejudices and its passions, its discords and its denunciations, pass away too. The next session of Congress will see the representatives of the new young State in their places in both our halls of national legislation, side by side with those of the old Thirteen. Let their reception into "the family" be frank, kindly, and cheerful, as befits such an occasion, as comports not less with our own self-respect than patriotic duty towards them. Ill betide those foul birds that delight to file their own nest, and disgust the ear with perpetual discord of ill-omened croak.

Why, were other reasoning wanting, in favor of now elevating this question of the reception of Texas into the Union, out of the lower region of our past party dissensions, up to its proper level of a high and broad nationality, it surely is to be found, found abundantly, in the manner in which other nations have undertaken to intrude themselves into it, between us and the proper parties to the case, in a spirit of hostile interference against us, for the avowed object of thwarting our policy and hampering our power, limiting our greatness and checking the fulfillment of our manifest destiny to overspread the continent allotted by Providence for the free development of our yearly multiplying millions. This we have seen done by England, our old rival and enemy; and by France, strangely coupled with her against us, under the influence of the Anglicism strongly tinging the policy of her present prime minister, Guizot. The zealous activity with which this effort to defeat us was pushed by the representatives of those governments, together with the character of intrigue accompanying it, fully constituted that case of foreign interference, which Mr. Clay himself declared should, and would unite us all in maintaining the common cause of our country against foreigner and the foe. We are only astonished that this effect has not been more fully and strongly produced, and that the burst of indignation against this unauthorized, insolent and hostile interference against us, has not been more general even among the party before opposed to Annexation, and has not rallied the national spirit and national pride unanimously upon that policy. We are very sure that if Mr. Clay himself were now to add another letter to his former Texas correspondence, he would express this sentiment, and carry out the idea already strongly stated in one of them, in a manner which would tax all the powers of blushing belonging to some of his party adherents.

It is wholly untrue, and unjust to ourselves, the pretence that the Annexation has been a measure of spoliation, unrightful and unrighteous—of military conquest under forms of peace and law—of territorial aggrandizement at the expense of justice, and justice due by a double sanctity to the weak. This view of the question is wholly unfounded, and has been before so amply refuted in these pages, as well as in a thousand other modes, that we shall not again dwell upon it. The independence of Texas was complete and absolute. It was an independence, not only in fact, but of right. No obligation of duty towards Mexico tended in the least degree to restrain our right to effect the desired recovery of the fair province once our own—whatever motives of policy might have prompted a more deferential consideration of her feelings and her pride, as involved in the question. If Texas became peopled with an American population; it was by no contrivance of our government, but on the express invitation of that of Mexico herself; accompanied with such guaranties of State independence, and the maintenance of a federal system analogous to our own, as constituted a compact fully justifying the strongest measures of redress on the part of those afterwards deceived in this guaranty, and sought to be enslaved under the yoke imposed by its violation. She was released, rightfully and absolutely released, from all Mexican allegiance, or duty of cohesion to the Mexican political body, by the acts and fault of Mexico herself, and Mexico alone. There never was a clearer case. It was not revolution; it was resistance to revolution: and resistance under such circumstances as left independence the necessary resulting state, caused by the abandonment of those with whom her former federal association had existed. What then can be more preposterous than all this clamor by Mexico and the Mexican interest, against Annexation, as a violation of any rights of hers, any duties of ours?

We would not be understood as approving in all its features the expediency or propriety of the mode in which the measure, rightful and wise as it is in itself, has been carried into effect. Its history has been a sad tissue of diplomatic blundering. How much better it might have been managed—how much more smoothly, satisfactorily, and successfully! Instead of our present relations with Mexico—instead of the serious risks which have been run, and those plausibilities of opprobrium which we have had to combat, not without great difficulty, nor with entire success—instead of the difficulties which now throng the path to a satisfactory settlement of all our unsettled questions with Mexico—Texas might, by a more judicious and conciliatory diplomacy, have been as securely in the Union as she is now—her boundaries defined—California probably ours—and Mexico and ourselves united by closer ties than ever; of mutual friendship and mutual support in resistance to the intrusion of European interference in the affairs of the American republics. All this might have been, we little doubt, already secured, had counsels less violent, less rude, less one-sided, less eager in precipitation from motives widely foreign to the national question, presided over the earlier stages of its history. We cannot too deeply regret the mismanagement which has disfigured the history of this question; and especially the neglect of the means which would have been so easy of satisfying even the unreasonable pretensions and the excited pride and passion of Mexico. The singular result has been produced, that while our neighbor has, in truth, no real right to blame or complain—when all the wrong is on her side, and there has been on ours a degree of delay and forbearance, in deference to her pretensions, which is to be paralleled by few precedents in the history of other nations—we have yet laid ourselves open to a great deal of denunciation hard to repel, and impossible to silence; and all history will carry it down as a certain fact, that Mexico would have declared war against us, and would have waged it seriously, if she had not been prevented by that very weakness which should have constituted her best defence.

We plead guilty to a degree of sensitive annoyance—for the sake of the honor of our country, and its estimation in the public opinion of the world—which does not find even in satisfied conscience full consolation for the very necessity of seeking consolation there. And it is for this state of things that we hold responsible that gratuitous mismanagement—wholly apart from the main substantial rights and merits of the question, to which alone it is to be ascribed; and which had its origin in its earlier stages, before the accession of Mr. Calhoun to the department of State.

California probably, will next fall away from the loose adhesion which, in such a country as Mexico, holds a remote province in a slight equivocal kind of dependence on the metropolis. Imbecile and distracted, Mexico never can exert any real governmental authority over such a country. The impotence of the one and the distance of the other, must make the relation one of virtual independence; unless, by stunting the province of all natural growth, and forbidding that immigration which can alone develop its capabilities and fulfil the purposes of its creation, tyranny may retain a military dominion, which is no government in the legitimate sense of the term. In the case of California this is now impossible. The Anglo-Saxon foot is already on its borders. Already the advance guard of the irresistible army of Anglo-Saxon emigration has begun to pour down upon it, armed with the plough and the rifle, and marking its trail with schools and colleges, courts and representative halls, mills and meeting-houses. A population will soon be in actual occupation of California, over which it will be idle for Mexico to dream of dominion. They will necessarily become independent. All this without agency of our government, without responsibility of our people—in the natural flow of events, the spontaneous working of principles, and the adaptation of the tendencies and wants of the human race to the elemental circumstances in the midst of which they find themselves placed. And they will have a right to independence—to self-government—to the possession of the homes conquered from the wilderness by their own labors and dangers, sufferings and sacrifices—a better and a truer right than the artificial tide of sovereignty in Mexico, a thousand miles distant, inheriting from Spain a title good only against those who have none better. Their right to independence will be the natural right of self-government belonging to any community strong enough to maintain it—distinct in position, origin and character, and free from any mutual obligations of membership of a common political body, binding it to others by the duty of loyalty and compact of public faith. This will be their title to independence; and by this title, there can be no doubt that the population now fast streaming down upon California will both assert and maintain that independence. Whether they will then attach themselves to our Union or not, is not to be predicted with any certainty. Unless the projected railroad across the continent to the Pacific be carried into effect, perhaps they may not; though even in that case, the day is not distant when the Empires of the Atlantic and Pacific would again flow together into one, as soon as their inland border should approach each other. But that great work, colossal as appears the plan on its first suggestion, cannot remain long unbuilt. Its necessity for this very purpose of binding and holding together in its iron clasp our fast-settling Pacific region with that of the Mississippi valley—the natural facility of the route—the ease with which any amount of labor for the construction can be drawn in from the overcrowded populations of Europe, to be paid in the lands made valuable by the progress of the work itself—and its immense utility to the commerce of the world with the whole eastern Asia, alone almost sufficient for the support of such a road—these coast of considerations give assurance that the day cannot be distant which shall witness the conveyance of the representatives from Oregon and California to Washington within less time than a few years ago was devoted to a similar journey by those from Ohio; while the magnetic telegraph will enable the editors of the "San Francisco Union," the "Astoria Evening Post," or the "Nootka Morning News," to set up in type the first half of the President's Inaugural before the echoes of the latter half shall have died away beneath the lofty porch of the Capitol, as spoken from his lips.

Away, then, with all idle French talk of *balances of power* on the American Continent. There is no growth in Spanish America! Whatever progress of population there may be in the British Canadas, is only for their own early severance of their present colonial relation to the little island three thousand miles across the Atlantic; soon to be followed by Annexation, and destined to swell the still accumulating momentum of our progress. And whosoever may hold the balance, though they should cast into the opposite scale all the bayonets and cannon, not only of France and England, but of Europe entire, how would it kick the beam against the simple, solid weight of the two hundred and fifty, or three hundred millions—and American millions—destined to gather beneath the flutter of the stripes and stars, in the fast hastening year of the Lord 1845!

Source: John O'Sullivan, "Annexation," *United States Magazine and Democratic Review* 17, no. 1 (July–August 1845): 5–10.

The Politics of Slavery

1848-1860

COMMON THREADS

In previous chapters you read about the development of the American economy and the expansion of slavery. Notice the ways in which these developments became sources of tension between the North and South during the 1850s.

The conflict between Whigs and Democrats during the 1830s and 1840s is sometimes called "the first party system." How did this change in the 1850s?

Do you think that by 1860 the Civil War was "irrepressible"?

AMERICAN PORTRAIT

Frederick Douglass

Frederick Douglass denounced the war with Mexico as "disgraceful, cruel, and iniqui-tous." Northern support for what he saw as a slaveholders' war reinforced Douglass's conviction that the US Constitution had created an unholy union of liberty and slavery. The only solution was for New England to secede. "The Union must be dis-solved," Douglass wrote, "or New England is lost and swallowed up by the slave-power of the country."

Douglass had been urging disunion for several years, ever since he became the most compelling antislavery voice in America. His authority derived from his extraordinary intelli-gence, his exceptional skill as a public speaker, and above all from his personal experience. Frederick Douglass was not simply an abolitionist; he was also the most famous runaway slave in America.

He was born Frederick Augustus Washington Bailey in Talbot County, Maryland, in 1818. At the age of seven he was sent to Baltimore, where he became a skilled caulker in the ship-yards. There he hired out his labor, paying his master three dollars each week and keeping the rest himself. He grew to resent the ar-rangement, and for the rest of his life he would associate freedom with the right to earn a living. When his master ended their arrangement and demanded that the slave hand over all his earnings, Frederick planned his escape.

On May 3, 1838, he dressed as a sailor and boarded a northbound train using bor-rowed papers. By September he was calling himself Frederick Douglass and was living and working in New Bedford, Massachusetts. He began attending antislavery meetings. He subscribed to William Lloyd Garrison's fiery abolitionist newspaper, *The Liberator*. In 1841 he was invited to speak during an abolitionist convention and stunned his listeners with an eloquent recital of his experience as a slave. Garrison was in the audience, and he invited Douglass to speak for the American Anti-Slavery Society. For the next several years Doug-lass was a leading spokesman for the Garrisonian wing of the abolitionist movement.

The Garrisonians felt that the Constitution was hopelessly corrupted by its compro-mises with slavery. They saw no point in pursuing political reforms, advocating instead the separation of the North from the South. The Garrisonians rejected all violent efforts to overthrow slavery, including slave rebellion, in favor of moral persuasion of their oppo-nents. Frederick Douglass initially believed all of these things.

The Mexican War was a turning point for Douglass. By the late 1840s, he saw growing numbers of northerners join the Free-Soil Party, fighting the expansion of slavery, and wondered why this could not become a political coalition against slavery itself. During the 1850s Douglass moved further from the Garrisonians: he openly supported slave rebellion, realized that political action was necessary to eliminate slavery, and came to doubt the wisdom of dismissing the Constitution as a proslavery document.

Douglass moved closer to mainstream northern politics because antislavery sentiment had reentered the mainstream. Since the 1820s, the major parties had studiously avoided the topic of slavery. But the issue had taken on a life of its own. With Texas's annexation and the Mexican War, many northern Whigs and Democrats committed themselves against slavery's further expansion—a position known as "free soil." In 1848 a Free-Soil Party drew thousands of votes. With the collapse of the Jacksonian party system in the mid-1850s, a new Republican Party took the free-soil position. Although the party was by no means favorable to immediate abolition and far less committed to equal civil rights than abolitionists were, it treated the Constitution as an antislavery document, with every ambiguous provision read in favor of freedom. At its most radical extreme, such a party even made room for abolitionists like Frederick Douglass.

The Political Economy of Freedom and Slavery

The politics of slavery reemerged at a moment of tremendous economic growth. As the depression of the 1840s lifted, the American zeal for internal improvements revived. The canals built between 1800 and 1830 were widened during the 1840s and 1850s. Steamboats raced upriver as flatboats carried cheap freight down. Trains were redesigned to have more power to climb hills and looser joints to go around sharp curves. Double tracks were laid to permit train traffic in both directions at the same time. New passenger cars carried more customers by putting them in rows of seats rather than separate compartments. States and towns lent money to help railroads build and own long-distance through lines. Starting in 1850, the national government endowed companies like the Mobile and Ohio and the Illinois Central Railroads with millions of acres in land grants in order to expand business. As a result, railroad construction boomed. In the twenty years leading up to the Civil War, mileage rose from 3,000 to 31,000—more than the rest of the world combined. No less spectacular was the rapid adoption of the telegraph. Invented by Samuel F. B. Morse in 1844, the telegraph made virtually instantaneous communication possible across oceans and continents. By 1860, there were 50,000 miles of telegraph wire in America. The first transcontinental line was completed in 1861.

These developments might have inhibited the growth of sectionalism. An efficient transportation and communication network helped integrate the United States into a single national market. But the economic growth of the North created especially strong ties between the East and the West. Turnpikes, canals, and especially railroads tended to run east and west, linking northeastern cities to the western frontier; few, however, crossed the Mason-Dixon line to link the northern and southern economies (see Map 13–1). By the 1850s the differences between the North and the South overwhelmed the connections that bound them together.

A Changing Economy in the North

The 1850s were booming years for northern farmers, now connected firmly to the national market. Whereas it used to take two months to ship meat and grains from the Midwest to the East Coast in 1810, it now took less than a week. Railroads could carry a ton of wheat for a nickel a mile and a ton of coal for half that much. They could bring a half million bushels of wheat to Chicago in twelve hours. Because of the dramatic reduction in transportation costs, northern farmers could devote more time and effort to

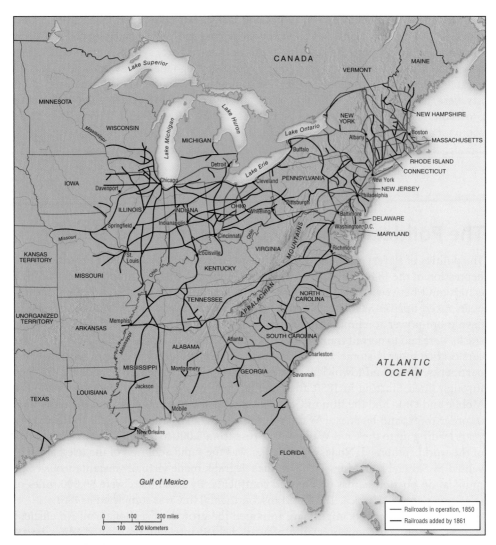

Map 13-1   Railroad Expansion This map shows that there were two distinct patterns of railroad development in the United States. In the North, rail lines connected the western states to the Eastern Seaboard. In the South, railroads tied the inland plantation districts to the coastal ports. Few lines connected the North to the South.

producing crops for sale rather than for subsistence at home. Thanks also to inventions like the steel plow, seed drills, and the McCormick reaper, northern farmers increased their production four times over between 1820 and 1860.

Farmers found expanding markets because more Americans were living in cities and working for wages, producing little of their own food, clothing, or shelter. Yet so productive was American agriculture that it required fewer farmers to supply a growing population. Between 1820 and 1860, the workforce engaged in agriculture dropped from 75 to 57 percent. Wage labor in the North grew too fast for native-born workers to fill the demand. In the mid-1840s the number of Europeans coming to the United States jumped

City of Broad Shoulders and Broader Implications: Chicago

Any town planner in 1811 would have rated Chicago the one location least likely to succeed. A trading post set in Potawatomie Indian country in a swamp on the edge of an unnavigable river that never reached the shallow edge of Lake Michigan, it had nothing to recommend it, even after easterners turned it into a village. Unpaved roads turned into rivers of mud in wet weather. "No Bottom Here. Shortest Road to China," one hotel sign warned. Yet, by the start of the Civil War, it had become formidable.

Eastern money, public and private, made Chicago into a brawny western metropolis. A New York real estate promoter, William Ogden, came west to sell marshland and stayed to make it worth selling. Laying streets and parceling out property into lots was only the beginning. Residents needed access to eastern markets both for what they made and what they bought. With Ogden's backing, a canal opened a waterway from the Chicago River to Lake Michigan. The US government forced the Potawatomie to swap their lands for soil on the high plains west of Missouri and drove them forth at gunpoint. A harbor was dredged out. Later, the state financed a canal linking the city west to the Mississippi River. To entice immigrants, Ogden helped found a medical college and a city horticultural society. He ran a steamship line and built a brewery. By 1837, the community had grown large enough for a city charter. Ogden became its first mayor.

Most of all, Ogden grasped railroads' potential for developing the prairie west

and enriching Chicago. Nearly 3,000 miles of track fed into the city by the mid-1850s. Within a generation, they had absorbed most of the trade from the Dakotas to Kansas City. Salesmen fanned out from the high plains to the upper south, taking orders from storekeepers and local merchants, enough to keep 500 Chicago factories at work full-time. Wisconsin's forests ended up in Chicago lumberyards before spreading across the treeless plains as boards for frame houses. Cincinnati, famed as "Porkopolis" for its hog butchering, could not match Chicago's sway in the corn belt. By the 1860s, tens of thousands of hogs were shipped to "Packingtown's" slaughterhouses to be killed, cured, and sold.

After struggling for years to sell his reapers in the east, Cyrus McCormick headed to Chicago with $300 in his pocket. He never regretted it. His factory sold 1,000 machines in 1851 and 23,000 six years later. Farmers once able to harvest only two acres a day now could do twelve. Instead of raising corn, they could put in wheat, which sold for twice as much per bushel. Prairie land where stock had grazed turned into prime real estate, and nowhere more so than around Chicago, where railroads could haul the reapers in and haul the grain out. By 1853, Chicago shipped out 6 million bushels of grain every year; by 1856, 21 million.

Not surprisingly, the West's most famous figure, Stephen A. Douglas, made Chicago his home. No place better suited the go-ahead spirit that he represented. But

continued

AMERICAN LANDSCAPE *continued*

Chicago did not just epitomize the West's vitality. It showed how steep the odds were against the South sharing the territories, whatever the fate of Kansas. The city's growth helped fill Illinois with northerners, Douglas among them. It bound white settlers' fortunes to northeastern markets, rather than to those of the Mississippi River cities and southern outlets. Ogden became the first president of the Union Pacific Railroad, tying Chicago to the west coast. When Republicans nominated a presidential candidate in 1860, fittingly, they held their convention in Chicago.

OUTWARD BOUND.
The Quay of Dublin.

Contemplating Emigration to America In this 1854 caricature, an impoverished Irishman on the Dublin docks contemplates booking passage to America in hopes of economic prosperity.

sharply, and 3 million arrived in the decade between 1845 and 1854. More than two-thirds were Irish or German, many of them Roman Catholic. By 1855 a larger proportion of Americans was foreign born than at any other time in the nation's history.

Many immigrants, especially the Irish, came to America impoverished, and they congregated in the growing cities and factory towns of the North. By 1860, immigrants made up more than one-third of the residents in northern cities with populations of at least 10,000. These newcomers became wage laborers in numbers that far outstripped their proportions in the population. Men worked in unskilled jobs on the docks, at construction sites, or on railroads and canals and in the coal mines and iron foundries of Pennsylvania. Women worked as seamstresses, laundresses, or domestic servants. In the textile mills and shoe factories of New England, Irish families worked together.

As industrial production increased, businesses opened large downtown stores to sell their goods. Between 1859 and 1862, for example, A. T. Stewart built a huge dry goods store covering a full square block in lower Manhattan. The financial needs of these enterprises were met by an expanding number of banks, insurance companies, and accounting firms that employed armies of white-collar workers.

Economic growth in the North during the 1850s rested on important social changes. A rural society became more urban. Industry was complementing agriculture as a driving economic force. Wage laborers were supplementing small farmers and craftsmen. A Protestant nation saw its first great wave of Catholic immigrants. Machines made it possible for one person to cultivate more acres than ever before. A political economy based on new sources of wealth and new forms of work was being born.

The Slave Economy

It made sense for the wealthy South Carolina planter James Henry Hammond to declare in 1858, "Cotton is king." Recovering from the doldrums of the 1840s, cotton prices held steady while slave prices soared. Southern states threw themselves into railroad construction, building a substantial network. Steamboats plied the South's rivers. Telegraph wires sped news of cotton prices from New York to New Orleans and deep into the plantation belt. Slavery was thriving. So why shouldn't Hammond boast?

The South had changed in many ways during the previous century. It had expanded across half the continent (see Map 13–2). Cotton had become its most profitable crop. The Atlantic slave trade was over, and a native-born, largely Christian slave population had grown up. There were important signs of social change, especially in the upper South. The immigrant workers Frederick Douglass met on the Baltimore docks faced the same process of economic development as the dockworkers of New England. The steady sale of slaves from the upper to the lower South reduced the influence of slaveholders in Maryland, Kentucky, and Delaware. Indeed, among whites across the South the proportion of slaveholding families had been declining for decades, from one in three in 1830 to one in four by 1860.

The expansion of slavery fostered commerce, but the benefits were spread unevenly. Slaveholders prospered the most. By 1860, they ranked among America's wealthiest classes. Wealth enabled slaveholders to monopolize the best lands, eliminating opportunity for small landowners. As a result, farmers without slaves were much poorer than their northern counterparts.

Status in the South rested on owning land and slaves, not investing in industry. So while the South as a whole boasted of industrial growth, it fell further behind the North every year, especially below the border states. Most industry was extractive (coal mining or lumbering) or processed agricultural goods for market. The South had just 6 percent of the nation's cotton-manufacturing capacity. Lowell, Massachusetts, had more cotton spindles than fifteen slave states put together. New York City had as much banking capital as the whole South. Together, those limits explained why the surge of immigrants built the North and West rather than the South, and why by 1860 the states north of the Ohio River had 9 million people—more than the white population in the slave states. They also explained why the inventions transforming America—the sewing machine, the telegraph, reapers, harvesters, and circular saws—all came out of the North. Cyrus McCormick's "Virginia reaper" found few takers in Virginia; he found his buyers in the Midwest. Year by year those changes meant a North growing faster than the South, not just in wealth but in numbers and political power.

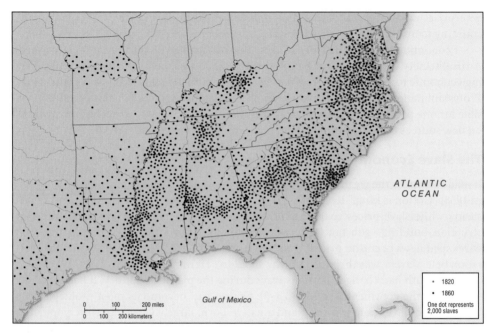

Map 13-2   Slavery's Expansion The westward expansion of the slave economy created political turmoil from 1820 until the Civil War. Sustained by an extensive internal slave trade that sold thousands of humans each year, slavery's expansion represented one of the greatest forced migrations in history.

The Importance of the West

Both the North and the South coveted western lands. By 1850 many northerners believed that slavery, if allowed to expand into the West, would deprive free laborers of an important source of prosperity and independence. But slaveholders had come to believe that their prosperity depended on the spread of the slave economy into the West.

To white southerners, territorial expansion constituted progress. The westward movement of the southern frontier demonstrated the continued strength of the slave economy. Halting that movement would undermine southern prosperity. It was an affront to the moral decency of white southerners, an obstacle to their economic vitality. But above all else it was an infringement on the slaveholders' inalienable rights of property, which included the constitutional right to carry their property with them wherever they saw fit. So argued slavery's defenders with increasing vehemence in the 1850s. For northerners, the West was essential to prosperity. The public lands of the West "are the great regulator of the relations of Labor and Capital," Horace Greeley explained, "the safety valve of our industrial and social engine." In fact, moving west to buy land and begin farming required resources most wage laborers lacked. For small farmers, however, the West remained a rich promise, and every landowner was one less potential competitor for a wage-earner's job. Not surprisingly, slavery's westward expansion stirred up deep anxiety in the North.

As free farmers saw it, slavery jeopardized their own prospects out west. Slaveholders were "settlers with means," bringing their wealth and their slave laborers with them. They easily bought up the best lands, usually river bottoms with the most productive soil and the readiest access to markets. Slaves provided a cheap means of clearing land, building homes, and raising profitable crops. Farmers without slaves could not compete because hired labor was scarce on the frontier. Farm families depended on their own efforts, plus whatever help neighbors could spare. Because the size of free farms was restricted by the amount of labor a family could perform, excluding slavery resulted in more settlers sharing the best lands.

Slavery Becomes a Political Issue

Westward expansion forced the issue of slavery back into the political mainstream in the late 1840s. On the national level, Whigs and Democrats had avoided stirring up debates over slavery, but the Mexican War made it hard to maintain that silence. For nearly 15 years, national politics would focus on one crucial question: Should Congress restrict the movement of slavery into the West? Behind that question lay a larger moral issue, the wrong and the right of "property in man."

Wilmot Introduces His Proviso

On August 8, 1846, Democratic congressman David Wilmot of Pennsylvania attached to an appropriations bill an amendment banning slavery from all the territories acquired in the war with Mexico. Slavery was illegal there already under Mexican law. The Wilmot Proviso wanted it to stay that way, to preserve the land for free white settlement. "The negro race already occupy enough of this fair continent," Wilmot argued; "let us keep what remains for ourselves and our children."

Reintroduced regularly, the proviso never passed Congress. Nevertheless, it roused furious debate and paralyzed action concerning the conquered territories. Antislavery northerners favored a Congressional ban. South Carolina Senator John C. Calhoun's southern followers denied that Congress could bar slavery from the territories and unsuccessfully tried to open Oregon to slaveholding. Calhoun himself favored giving the North and the South veto power over any legislation affecting the other, with two presidents, one northern and one southern, as a last bulwark. In between, moderates talked of extending the Missouri Compromise's dividing line to the Pacific or "noninterference" coupled with "popular sovereignty": letting western settlers work out for themselves whether they would permit slavery.

With tempers rising, both parties finessed the issue during the 1848 presidential contest. Democrats nominated Senator Lewis Cass of Michigan, a "noninterference" man and a hearty supporter of expansion southward into Central America. Whigs ran General Zachary Taylor, known for his victories in Mexico, a professional soldier who may never have voted in his life. Antislavery men, both Whig and Democrat alike, formed the Free-Soil Party and nominated former President Martin Van Buren. Favoring the institution's limitation, not its abolition, the movement made little headway outside of New England and got only 14 percent of the northern vote. But thousands in the mainstream organizations shared a distaste for slavery, and Taylor's presidential victory settled nothing.

Even as Congress deadlocked, westward settlement increased the pressure for a decision. In California, the discovery of gold in the Sierra foothills brought a rush of settlers. "Argonauts," as the gold-seekers were called, crammed whaling ships and sailed around South America or through Panama's fever-infested swamps to the west coast. Traveling associations like the Buckeye Rovers chartered wagon trains. Most prospectors endured a hard, monotonous life and had unrealistic hopes. Few struck it rich. One success story, however, was Levi Strauss, who made a fortune making pants for miners from tent-cloth called "levis," or blue jeans. Philip Armour made $4,000 digging ditches, used his savings to open a butcher shop and ended up in Chicago, one of the biggest meat-packers in America. California's Anglo population soared. San Francisco swelled from 3,000 to 20,000 people by the end of 1849, and in gold country, mining towns sprang from nothing, with names like Whiskey Bar, Gouge Eye, and Mad Mule Gulch. Many newcomers discovered the real wealth in the frost-free climate and rich soil of the central valley. They came to stay—so many in fact that within a year California was ready to bypass territorial status entirely and apply for statehood. If admitted under its proposed free-state constitution, California would close off the richest, most promising part of the Mexican cession to slavery.

By early 1850, California's admission and continuing debate over the Wilmot Proviso had created an even more divided Congress. In the House, northerners called for ending slavery in Washington, DC, and free soil in the new territories. Texas claimed broad boundaries, taking in much of New Mexico and legalizing slavery there. It was ready to fight local authorities or even United States troops to get its way. Fistfights and threats of disunion became commonplace. As a political amateur, President Taylor offered no leadership.

A Compromise Without Compromises

Called out of retirement, Senator Henry Clay of Kentucky proposed a solution: let all the flashpoints in the slavery debate be settled together. In a series of eight resolutions, he tried to balance northern and southern interests. California would be admitted as a free state, but the rest of the Mexican cession would be organized into territories with no mandate for freedom. Whether they could forbid slavery while still territories or needed to wait until applying for statehood was left unclear. Texas was denied its full geographical scope and, in return, the national government would assume its $10 million debt. The District of Columbia's slave trade was abolished, but not slavery itself. Finally, a new fugitive slave law would strengthen national power to retrieve runaway slaves. Clay's "Omnibus," as critics called it, met with immediate opposition at both ends of the political spectrum. Even though dying of tuberculosis, Calhoun was carried into the Senate to oppose any deal admitting California as a free state or giving less than an explicit guarantee to allow slaveholding throughout the Mexican cession. Senator William H. Seward of New York protested the North being forced to give concessions to get what was rightfully theirs, a free California. God and nature, he insisted, demanded that Congress keep the cession slave-free. As a firm nationalist, President Taylor opposed the "Omnibus" and insisted on admitting California unconditionally and promised, if Texas defied national authority, to lead forces against the Texans himself.

Northern and Southern centrists rallied to Clay's side. Appealing for harmony, Daniel Webster of Massachusetts spoke in favor of compromise. "Cotton Whigs," textile manufacturers, merchants relying on the southern trade, and conservatives fearful of agitation warned that the Union itself stood in peril from the controversies of slavery. On the Democratic side, Senator Stephen A. Douglas of Illinois rounded up support for compromise. At the same time, the forces against compromise weakened. Calhoun died in March of 1850, and no southern rights figure matched his influence. In July, President Taylor's sudden death put Millard Fillmore, a supporter of compromise in the White House. Even so, the "Omnibus" failed to win approval because free soil supporters would not vote for certain provisions, and southern rights supporters balked at others. Exhausted and ill, Clay quit Washington, leaving Douglas to carry the package through, piece by piece, as five separate bills designed to win different majorities. Referred to as the Compromise of 1850, the combined set of bills promised to banish the issue of slavery for good. A southern-rights convention at Nashville that had seemed to threaten secession fizzled and both parties embraced the Compromise as a "finality." Free-Soil leaders and southern "fire-eaters," or extremists, however, swore that the day of reckoning had only been put off.

The Fugitive Slave Act Provokes a Crisis

The one great exception to acquiescence in the Compromise of 1850 was the new Fugitive Slave Law. It took jurisdiction over fugitive slave cases away from northern courts and gave it to federal commissioners. Any northerner could be forced into helping catch alleged runaways; to refuse was a federal crime. Accused blacks had no right to a jury trial or a lawyer and a federally appointed commissioner would be responsible for determining their status.

Slaves who had run away years earlier now risked arrest and reenslavement. Freeborn blacks had no legal protection if an unscrupulous slave catcher identified them as a runaway, which happened. Vulnerable African Americans fled further north, out West, or into Canada, but they were not guaranteed safety. Like some abolitionists, Frederick Douglass advocated violent resistance. "A half dozen or more dead kidnappers carried down South," he contended, "would cool the ardor of Southern gentlemen." For many northern communities, slavery's evils were no longer something remote, easy to ignore. In Christiana, Pennsylvania, antislavery demonstrators killed a slave owner who tried to take back a fugitive slave. Crowds saved one accused slave in Syracuse, New York; authorities had to call out the militia to enforce another slave's return from Boston.

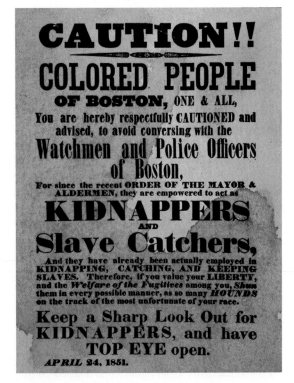

Poster Warning of Fugitive Slave Act The Fugitive Slave Act met strong resistance in many parts of the North. This Boston poster captures the atmosphere of fear and civil disobedience that gripped the city following the Compromise of 1850. It warns all blacks, free or fugitive, to be on the lookout for slave catchers.

Appalled by the new law, Harriet Beecher Stowe published *Uncle Tom's Cabin* in 1852. In time, the book was published in dozens of languages. Theater-goers watched Eliza flee slave-catching bloodhounds over ice floes and Simon Legree lay a murderous whip to Uncle Tom, his Christian slave. The sensational success of Stowe's antislavery novel showed how deep northern misgivings had become about the institution's spread. So did the "personal liberty laws" passed in many northern states to protect the rights of the accused. Although these statutes did not prevent one single slave from being remanded south, white southerners were incensed and insulted.

The Election of 1852 and the Decline of the Whig Party

In 1852, both the Democratic Party and the Whig Party endorsed the Compromise of 1850 as a finality, and both went out of their way to endorse a candidate who was not directly connected to it. The Whigs rejected Fillmore and Webster, both of whom had endorsed and enforced the law, and chose instead another war hero, this time General Winfield Scott. Democrats chose then-governor of New Hampshire, Franklin Pierce. Southerners deserted Scott in droves, not because of his own views—like Pierce, he favored the Compromise—but because of his friends, free-soil Whigs like Seward. Every new western state meant a likely new Democratic stronghold, and, it seemed, every new Catholic immigrant a new Democratic voter. The party's old issues—a national bank and a protective tariff—no longer inspired anyone, but no practical new issues replaced them. Pompous and aristocratic, Scott had none of Taylor's appeal and his attempts to reach foreign-born voters offended Protestant Whigs. The outcome was a landslide for Pierce (see Figure 13–1). He carried 254 electoral votes to Scott's 42 and won every state but four. Severely weakened, the Whigs were unable to meet the two political challenges that soon altered national politics: the issue of slavery and hostility toward immigrants, also known as nativism.

Nativism and the Origins of the Republican Party

The calm of the early 1850s did not last. By the middle of the decade, two forces, nativism—the fear of foreigners and Catholics—and a revived slavery issue had undone the Jacksonian party system. These challenges also brought on a fresh sectional crisis. But this time, there would be no rescue. With the deaths of statesmen Henry Clay and Daniel Webster in 1852, the spirit of compromise and the foundation of trust between the North and South also seemed to have perished.

The Nativist Attack on Immigration

The swell of immigration in the late 1840s intensified fears of foreign and Catholic influence in the United States. Nativism appealed to shopkeepers, independent craftsmen, and clerks, people for whom the Protestant ethic of steadiness and sobriety was a scriptural injunction. They disdained a working class of Irish and German immigrants who drank heavily, lived in squalor, and lacked economic independence. Worst of all from the Whigs' point of view, many of them, Irish Catholics especially, voted Democratic.

The Democrats' appeal to Irish Catholics was double-edged. On the one hand, the party's populist rhetoric attracted immigrants stung by the snobbery of Yankee Whigs. At the same time, Irish Americans heaped contempt on African Americans with whom

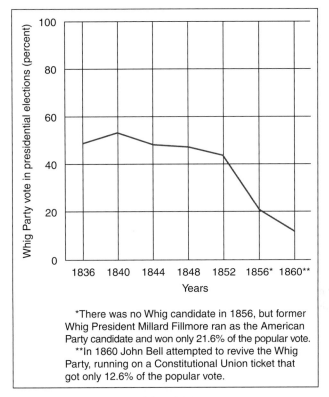

Figure 13.1   The Decline of the Whig Party

they competed for jobs and housing. Democrats cultivated this sentiment, warning that abolition would flood the North with cheap black labor. In fact, free black workers found immigrants replacing them, and the foreign-born had advantages that most African Americans lacked, including the right to vote.

Antislavery and nativist sentiments often blended. In Catholicism, critics saw the same authoritarianism, ignorance, and rejection of "modern" values, like individualism and progress, that they saw in slavery. The basis for this stereotype was the conservatism of the Catholic Church in the early 1850s. The pope expressed contempt for "progress," and the Vatican had condemned the liberal revolutions sweeping Europe in 1848. But alarmists went beyond the facts to imagine Catholic conspiracies against American liberty. Lurid tales depicted monks as debauchers, with nuns delivering illegitimate children that they strangled, baptized, and buried in convent cellars.

By 1854, nativists and anti-Catholics had organized. Secret societies spread, often called "Know-Nothings" because when asked about it, members claimed to "know nothing." Taking over local party organizations and endorsing candidates, the Know-Nothings carried the mayor's offices in San Francisco and Philadelphia, swept Massachusetts, from the governor's office to the state legislature, and across the country, it elected congressmen. Temperance reformers voted Know-Nothing to close the saloons, conservative Whigs to affirm their support for the Union and compromise, and antislavery activists to punish the Democrats for bowing to the South's will. Voters joined the new "American Party" to toss the old politicians out; old politicians joined to ride the movement into office. With so many cross-purposes, the movement rose overnight and perished almost as fast. Among the forces unleashing the Know-Nothing movement was the one that ended up destroying it: the fight over the expansion of slavery into the western territories.

The Kansas-Nebraska Act Revives the Slavery Issue

Advocates of westward expansion dreamed of a transcontinental railroad. Build it, Senator Thomas Hart Benton predicted, and "emigrants would flock upon it as pigeons to their roosts, tear open the bosom of the virgin soil, and spring into existence the long line of farms and houses, of towns and villages, of orchards, fields, and gardens, . . . of noisy shops, clattering mills and thundering forges, and all that civilization affords to enliven the wild domain from the Mississippi to the Pacific." However, west of Missouri, ungoverned prairie barred the way. Indian tribes lived there, but white settlement required a territorial government. As head of the Committee on Territories, Stephen A. Douglas had a special interest in its passage, particularly if Chicago could tap the Pacific trade that a transcontinental railroad promised. That was where southern interests complicated things. In 1853, the House of Representatives passed a bill organizing the Nebraska Territory. As that ground stood north of the Missouri Compromise line, it remained closed to slavery. Southerners killed the bill in the Senate. The next year Stephen Douglas reintroduced it, this time dividing the territory into two, Kansas and Nebraska, and leaving the slavery question in both territories to popular sovereignty.

Douglas's proposal roused, in his words, "a hell of a storm." To win southern congressional support, Douglas had to add a provision repealing the Missouri Compromise of 1820 outright. In doing so, he took away the one concession that the North had won in 1820, just at the point when it had any value. He also revived the slavery issue that both parties had insisted was buried for good (see Map 13–3).

Fierce, bitter debate erupted. Douglas and most Democrats argued that "popular sovereignty" carried the ideal of letting the people rule one step further. Climate and nature, they contended, had made slavery impossible on the prairies. Freedom would win out, without the humiliating legal restriction imposed on slaveholders to carry their property with them. Whig and Democratic opponents responded that the territories' fate was not their concern alone but the nation's, and that only the nation could decide. Not just in Kansas but in the whole Louisiana Purchase, that decision had been for freedom, and must remain so. Southerners argued that Congress had no constitutional right to ban slavery in any territory; northerners pointed out that it had done just that since the 1780s. Administration pressure forced many northern Democrats into line, and together with a nearly solid southern vote from both parties, that was enough to carry the Kansas-Nebraska bill.

Rarely had any bill done such damage. That fall, between the Know-Nothings and Republicans, Democrats lost the House. With northern Whigs against the bill and southern Whigs nearly united for it, the party had broken beyond repair. Along with thousands of northern Democrats and the Free-Soilers, antislavery Whigs gradually formed a new organization, the Republican Party, dedicated not just to restoring the Missouri Compromise restriction, but outlawing slavery everywhere that national law was sovereign, from the territories to the high seas. "We have tried compromises with slavery," one editor wrote; "they have been violated in the basest manner. . . . Now and henceforth the interests of freedom ought not—shall not—be bartered, under any pretense." Over the next two years, a purely sectional party came into being in the North to fight the "Nebrascals" and a one-party cotton South solidified, to hold off the "Black Republicans."

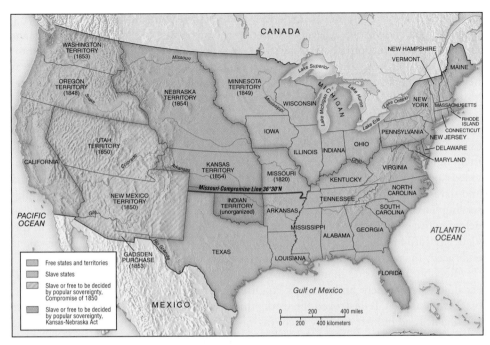

Map 13-3 The Kansas-Nebraska Act of 1854 Stephen Douglas's Kansas-Nebraska Act carved the Kansas Territory out of the larger Nebraska Territory. Because Missouri was already a slave state, the map indicates that slaveholders could move west and settle in Kansas. But because Kansas lay north of the 1820 Missouri Compromise line, many northerners wanted slavery restricted from the territory.

Conservative Whigs built the American Party as an alternative to sectional extremism, and in 1856, they ran Millard Fillmore for president. But the intensity of the slavery issue cut deep into the American Party's appeal. Across the South, most Whigs found no safety for slavery outside of Democratic ranks. Many northern Know-Nothings decided that slavery posed a more immediate threat to liberty than immigration.

Among the Whig converts was Abraham Lincoln, Douglas's longtime political rival in Illinois. Lincoln followed Douglas around the state, demanding the restoration of the Missouri Compromise. In Peoria, on October 16, 1854, Lincoln gave a speech summing up his arguments against slavery and had it published. He pronounced slavery "a great moral wrong," insisted on the humanity of blacks, and denounced the dehumanization of slaves. Blacks were human beings, not property, Lincoln argued, and like all human beings freedom was their natural condition. With this remarkable speech, Lincoln emerged as one of the state's leading antislavery politicians.

The Labor Problem and the Politics of Slavery

As sectional politics took hold, all sides had to ask themselves: what did slavery mean for labor? To what extent did it make America prosperous?

For Democrats, southern prosperity underlay northern security. Slavery meant cheap sugar for the worker's tea and employment for cotton millhands. A "Black Republican" victory, northern Democrats contended, would flood the North with emancipated slaves, "side by side in competition with white men." Worse, it would disrupt the Union, an economic disaster beyond calculation. Ending slavery meant black men marrying white women and voting. Allegedly, different races could not live on equal terms. One must dominate. Freedom, then, meant race war, and no one would be spared. The promise of equality in the Declaration of Independence, Stephen A. Douglas insisted, was never meant to cover an "inferior race." The interests of northern workers therefore required the preservation of southern slavery within the Union.

Southern spokesmen insisted that blacks did not respond to the incentives of free labor the way whites did and that whites, in turn, could not work efficiently in hot climates such as the South. Slavery solved this dual problem. Only force made blacks work productively in an otherwise unproductive climate. At the same time, the southern labor system provided a poor white man with the opportunity to rise up the social ladder by acquiring land and slaves "as soon as his savings will admit." Southern Democrats hailed slavery for preserving the economic independence of free whites in terms reminiscent of the Republican defense of wage labor as a stepping stone to self-employment. Slave property was, in this view, a reward for the same virtues of thrift and industry that Yankees thought they alone embraced. The proof, slaveholders argued, was the booming, expanding slave economy.

Republicans insisted that that prosperity was an illusion, enjoyed by the large planters at non-slaveholders' and society's expense. Slavery degraded all labor, white as well as black, they argued. It destroyed the work ethic by withholding from slaves any incentive to diligence and industry and by encouraging a disdain for hard work and self-discipline among the masters. By stifling the economic progress of the South, slavery was said to deny opportunities to poor whites as well. With an inefficient workforce and an aristocratic ruling class, the South could never meet its economic potential. It "was as poor as a half-starved rat," one congressman jeered, "—the fences of old Virginia are tumbling down, her church steps were overgrown with moss—her school houses without windows or chimneys, and her fields thrown open as tired land grown over with the mullen and the thistle." Unpaid slave labor suppressed the wages of free workers in the South and made toil unrespectable. Artisans and day laborers were sneered at and called "mudsills," persons of the lowest social level. In contrast, Republicans depicted the North as a society where labor was free and hard work rewarded. The Protestant virtues of thrift, sobriety, and diligence were cultivated, opportunities for upward mobility were many, and progress was manifest. All that progress was at risk, however, the moment cheap slave labor came in competition with white farmers or mechanics.

That, Republicans cried, was just what the "Slave Power," or the southern aristocracy, intended. Using their political influence, the "lords of the lash" had carried America far from the founders' intention, of slavery confined and moved toward extinction. From Florida to Texas and the Mexican cession, northern Democrats did slavery's bidding and were allowing the institution to spread across a continent. Conspirators meant to force it on one territory today, all territories tomorrow, and perhaps the free states the day after—unless a united North cried halt.

Any party of former Whigs, Free-Soilers, and Democrats strained to find common ground on older issues, like a high tariff (which Whigs advocated) or a homestead act providing free farms out west (which Democrats favored). But when it came to the question of broadening free blacks' rights up north, radicals and conservatives hardly found any common ground at all.

Between the aims of making the territories exclusively free soil and abolishing slavery in the states, a vast gap remained. Republicans were as likely to call for modifying the

Fugitive Slave Law as repealing it. Not all of them ruled out admitting new slave states to Congress, if their inhabitants insisted. More moderate Republicans talked of encouraging free blacks to emigrate abroad and offering compensation to states willing to end slavery. Many wanted to keep the territories all white as well as all free. Emancipation would require a much broader antislavery agenda than most Republicans were prepared to endorse openly. But all Republicans agreed that slavery's advance must be stopped. The institution must be confined to the states and, if possible, expunged wherever national authority governed. Manifest Destiny, as an engine for spreading the slave economy, must go no further. And all in the long run wanted to see the institution set on the road to its ultimate extinction. Keeping it out of the territories and extinguishing the illegal Atlantic slave trade would be easy first steps. Time and westward settlement with free labor would break the "Slave Power's" political influence and eventually an isolated South would rid itself of slavery.

"Bleeding Kansas"

Under the terms of the Kansas-Nebraska Act, the people in Kansas would determine whether their territory would enter the Union as a slave state or a free state. Elections for the territorial legislature were set for March 1855. Hoping to secure an antislavery victory, the New England Emigrant Aid Company tried to recruit settlers opposed to slavery. Few appeared, but thousands of armed Missourians did. "There are eleven hundred coming over from Platte County to vote," boasted Senator David R. Atchison, the unofficial leader of the proslavery forces, "and if that ain't enough we can send five thousand— enough to kill every God-damned abolitionist in the territory." When the polls opened, they crossed into Kansas, drove voters from the polls at gunpoint, and elected a proslavery legislature. The new "Border Ruffian" government quickly enacted a slave code. To question slavery became a felony, to protect fugitive slaves a capital offense. A new oath prevented most antislavery settlers from voting. Recognizing the territorial government as legitimate, President Pierce used the military to support it.

Free-state settlers repudiated the proslavery government. In January 1856, they took a revolutionary step. Without authorization from Washington, they elected a governor and legislature of their own. With a proslavery government in Lecompton and an antislavery one in Topeka, violence ensued. Arms poured in for both sides. Even Harriet Beecher Stowe's brother, the celebrated antislavery minister Henry Ward Beecher, helped pay for guns. As he explained, Border Ruffians had no more use for Bibles than buffalo did. A rifle had "more moral power" than a thousand Good Books—and before long, Kansas had plenty of "Beecher's Bibles." Sheriffs and federal marshals, backed by "border ruffians" from Missouri, tried several times to enter the town of Lawrence (see Struggles for Democracy: The Settling and Unsettling of Kansas) to arrest free-staters. On May 21, 1856, proslavery forces took the town, destroyed two printing presses, and burned the Free State Hotel to the ground. Although little blood was shed, northern newspapers treated the "sack of Lawrence" as proof of proslavery barbarism.

Three days after the sack of Lawrence, John Brown raided Pottawatomie Creek to mete out revenge. Brown was an awesome and in many ways a frightening man, a religious zealot convinced it was his personal mission to cleanse the nation of the sin of slavery. The wrath of God, not moral persuasion or political organization, was Brown's solution to the problem of slavery. Along with seven men armed with swords, Brown called proslavery settlers from their cabins. Some were shot, others hacked to death. In all, the civil war in Kansas may have cost 200 lives.

AMERICA AND THE WORLD

Slavery as a Foreign Policy

If not for the revival of the slavery issue, Franklin Pierce's administration might have revived Manifest Destiny and pushed into the Caribbean. If all of Pierce's expansionist efforts were southward into land fit for plantations and slaves, this was no accident. Southerners and their northern sympathizers dominated Pierce's cabinet, and he appointed slaveholders to crucial diplomatic posts.

Pierce sent a South Carolinian, James Gadsden, to Mexico with instructions to spend up to $50 million to acquire a large portion of northern Mexico. Mexico's leader resisted the extravagant offer. Gadsden returned with a treaty giving the United States just enough territory for a transcontinental railroad across the southern tier of the nation. Most northern senators balked at even that. For the first time in American history, Congress rejected land ceded to the United States. The Gadsden Purchase ended up with only a small piece of land for $10 million on the southern border of the United States.

The expansionist Pierce fared even worse in Cuba. He appointed Pierre Soulé,

a Louisianan, as minister to Spain. Soulé was instructed to negotiate the purchase of Cuba, with the understanding that if Spain refused to sell he should encourage the Cubans to rebel. To Soulé the Spanish government offered an extraordinary response. It proposed to free millions of Cuban slaves and arm them for the defense of the island against a possible American invasion. The United States responded with the Ostend Manifesto, which declared that Cuba was "naturally" a part of the United States and urged Spain to accept an offer of $120 million for the island. If Spain refused, the United States would "wrest" the island by force.

The Ostend Manifesto was issued in 1854 on the heels of the Kansas-Nebraska Act. Free-Soilers saw it as an extension of the "Slave Power" conspiracy. Southerners were not merely attempting to make slavery national; they were taking it overseas as well. Tainted by its association with slavery, expansionism lost much of its northern following for good.

Blood flowed in Congress, too. Prompted by the national government's support for the Lecompton government, antislavery senator Charles Sumner of Massachusetts delivered a two-day diatribe exposing the proslavery "Crime Against Kansas" in scathing, often personal language, some of it directed at South Carolina senator Andrew Butler. Two days later, Congressman Preston S. Brooks, a cousin of Butler's, delivered a powerful response—but not in words. Using a cane, he bludgeoned Sumner senseless on the Senate floor and continued striking him until the cane splintered. The senator's injuries kept him out of the chamber for more than three years. Across the South rose an almost universal chorus of approval. Many suggested the same treatment for other northern critics. Brooks was reelected unanimously, and admirers sent him a cane inscribed, "Hit him again." Even northerners embarrassed by Sumner's personality were shocked. "If the North submits to be gagged and disarmed, it is unworthy to be free," an Ohio

STRUGGLES FOR DEMOCRACY

The Settling and Unsettling of Kansas

Late in 1854, a journalist touring Kansas marveled at the soil. "So high and thick is the grass in many places that a man would be lost sight of in walking through it," he wrote home. "Not a sterile spot could be seen." Soil once dismissed as part of the "Great American Desert" was a garden that northerners and southerners alike longed to possess. And, the reporter argued, they had just as much right to frame their own institutions as to set down their farms. "Popular sovereignty" embraced the democratic notion that people were capable of making their own laws, and that the best government was the one shaped by inhabitants on the ground.

The problem came in defining who those people were. Did the first few hundred settlers have the right to set the rules for the thousands yet to come, as Missourians did in the territories' first elections before the tide of non-slaveholding emigrants arrived? Did popular sovereignty allow residents to form their own government, without an enabling act from Congress, as "Free Staters" did? And how much closer to real democracy was a territory in which every important official from governor to judge was chosen from Washington rather than elected? Beyond regulating slavery, Douglas's "popular sovereignty" gave Kansas no new right that other territories did not enjoy.

All these complexities lay in the future. Still, the reporter missed the biggest contradiction to popular sovereignty, and one that should have been obvious at the time. He did not tread across unsettled land. It belonged to Delaware and Shawnee Indians. One set of settlers could only define their destiny by displacing another set, almost as recently arrived. Thirty years before, Osage and Kansas Indians had owned the land west of Missouri. Superintendents of Indian Affairs with army backing had strong-armed them into surrendering their land for eastern tribes to settle. For some this was their second dislocation. Not all came willingly. The Potawatomi tribe from the Lake Michigan area later called their journey the "Trail of Death." A white minister recorded the trip's horrors. "On Sunday, September 16, I came in sight of my Christians, under a burning noonday sun, amidst clouds of dust, marching in a line, surrounded by soldiers who were hurrying their steps," he wrote. "Nearly all the children, weakened by the heat, had fallen into a state of complete languor and depression. I baptized several who were newly-born—happy Christians, who with their first step passed from earthly exile to the heavenly sojourn." The newcomers' one comfort was that these lands would be theirs "forever."

"Forever" lasted until 1854. Over the next twenty years, the US government and railroad companies cajoled, bribed, bullied, and swindled Indians out of their domains. Squatters raced into Indian territory to stake claims, expecting that the government would give them valid title—as it generally did. The Ottawa gave up most of their land in return for the promise of citizenship and a university, built from the proceeds of land sales. Before the university could be finished, however, they were evicted from what acreage they had and thrust out of Kansas entirely. Quarrel as *continued* they might over control of Kansas, leaders on both sides of the slavery debate shared the same willingness to use their political power to get some of the choicest sites for themselves. Both sides would remember John Brown's raid on Pottawatomie Creek. Neither recalled or cared for the much greater toll that the Browns and their enemies both took on the tribe that had given the place its name.

congressman wrote. As a result of the so-called Sumner-Brooks affair, "Bully" Brooks and free speech became Republican bywords, alongside free soil, free labor, and free men.

A New Political Party Takes Shape

The election of 1856 presented Americans with a clear choice. A candidate's position on the Kansas-Nebraska Act betrayed a widening circle of convictions—about slavery's expansion, about the relative value of wage labor and slave labor, and about the morality of human property itself. At stake was the fundamental conflict over whether freedom or slavery would be "national" policy. In the past the Whigs and Democrats had avoided sectional issues by running candidates who appealed to both the North and the South. In 1856 a new major party, the Republicans, appealed exclusively to northern voters.

The First Sectional Election

As antislavery brought onetime Whigs, Free-Soilers, and Democrats together, a new Republican Party organized to contest the White House itself. Its first presidential candidate was John C. Frémont, "the Pathfinder" credited with liberating California from Mexico. The Democrats faced a more daunting challenge: to find a candidate unassociated with Kansas-Nebraska, but ready to accept its essential principles. They turned to James Buchanan of Pennsylvania, whose record of long public service made him a welcome contrast to Pierce's inexperience. Pledging "noninterference by Congress with slavery," the Democratic platform kept the principle of popular sovereignty alive without actually endorsing it. Up north, Democrats could insist that this let settlers keep slavery out if they chose. Down south, Democrats claimed that only a state constitution could do that. But everywhere, they agreed that as the only national party left, they alone could save the Union. If Republicans won, southern states would secede.

The Republicans did not succeed in the short run. In 1856, Buchanan won five northern states and all but one of the slave states, winning 45 percent of the popular vote and 174 electoral votes. Frémont swept the upper North and Ohio, winning 114 electoral votes (see Map 13–4). Still, no sectional party had ever done as well as the Republicans did. They far outpaced Fillmore's American party, which vanished quickly after the election. All the antislavery party needed four years hence would be to pick up Pennsylvania and either Illinois or Indiana.

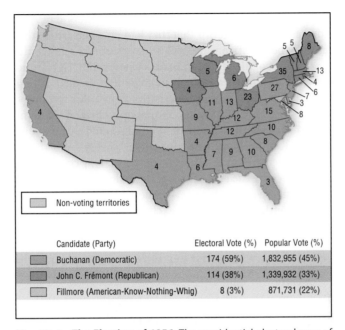

Candidate (Party)	Electoral Vote (%)	Popular Vote (%)
Buchanan (Democratic)	174 (59%)	1,832,955 (45%)
John C. Frémont (Republican)	114 (38%)	1,339,932 (33%)
Fillmore (American-Know-Nothing-Whig)	8 (3%)	871,731 (22%)

Map 13-4   The Election of 1856 The presidential electoral map of 1856 reveals the growing sectional division. Although he lost the election, the Republican Frémont won a string of victories across the upper North and lost narrowly in Pennsylvania, Indiana, and Illinois. By winning those states four years later, the openly antislavery Abraham Lincoln could be elected president by simply winning the North.

The Dred Scott Decision

In 1857, James Buchanan was inaugurated as president. His efforts to silence the slavery issue proved a disastrous failure. When he left office in 1861, his party was in disarray, a Republican had been elected his successor, and the Union had collapsed.

Within days of the inauguration, the Supreme Court, dominated by southern Democrats, issued one of the most controversial decisions in American history. The case stretched back to 1833, when John Emerson, an army surgeon from Missouri, was assigned to Fort Armstrong, Illinois, and took a slave named Dred Scott with him. Emerson spent two years in Illinois and two more years at Fort Snelling in Wisconsin Territory (now Minnesota). Slavery was illegal in Illinois and Wisconsin Territory. Back in Missouri in 1846, Scott sued his owners, claiming that several years of residence on free soil made him legally free. After losing his suit in 1854, Scott appealed to the US Supreme Court. By then two questions stood out: First, was Dred Scott a citizen, such that his suit had standing in a court of law? Second, did the laws of the free state of Illinois or the free territory of Wisconsin prevail over the master's property right?

The justices could have upheld the lower court's decision against Scott. But instead the majority decided, with some clandestine nudges from Buchanan, to render a sweeping decision covering some of the most explosive issues of the day.

The majority decision against Scott did not create the uproar. The problem was Chief Justice Roger Taney's provocative and partisan opinion. Taney argued, first, that Dred

Scott was not a citizen because he was black and in the Founders' day, African Americans had "been regarded as . . . so far inferior that they had no rights which the white man was bound to respect." Not being citizens in 1787, Taney reasoned, they could not be citizens ever. In fact, every state recognized that free blacks had certain rights, and at the time the Constitution was drafted, most states had no color line in their voting requirements. Second, Taney ruled that slaves were property, like any other property, and declared, equally inaccurately, that the Constitution "expressly" affirmed the right of property in slaves. Dred Scott's residence in Wisconsin Territory could not make him a free man, because the Missouri Compromise, which excluded slavery from the territory, was an unconstitutional infringement on the right of property. Nor could his residence in Illinois make Scott free, because the right of property included the right of "sojourn."

Taney's decision effectively made slavery national and freedom merely local. Neither Congress nor western settlers could legally exclude slavery from the territories. Accepting the Dred Scott decision as the law of the land, Stephen A. Douglas could only square it with his popular sovereignty idea by what later came to be called the Freeport Doctrine: the people of a territory still could shut slavery out, simply by refusing to pass the laws necessary to protect it. That way no master would dare go there with his human property.

The Lecompton Constitution Splits the Democratic Party

When the Court undermined popular sovereignty as a viable political position, it contributed to the sectional division of the Democratic Party. But the cause of the final Democratic rupture was again Kansas. There, a rigged convention in Lecompton drew up a proslavery constitution and, contrary to custom, refused to submit it to the voters. When Buchanan tried to have Kansas admitted as a slave state, Stephen A. Douglas of Illinois broke with the Administration to insist on popular sovereignty. In the House, Republicans and northern Democrats forced a free election. Kansas overwhelmingly rejected the Lecompton constitution and with it immediate statehood.

Douglas's fight could not save his party from a rout across the North in the 1858 congressional elections. Douglas had to fight for his own reelection. In a series of national debates, he and his opponent, Abraham Lincoln, mapped out the lines dividing Democrats from Republicans: Should the slavery issue be left to a territory's inhabitants or was it Congress's business? Did "Slave Power" threaten freedom not just in Kansas but nationally? How far did the Dred Scott decision bind policy making? The Illinois legislature did return Douglas to the Senate, but his battle against Lecompton and his Freeport Doctrine had turned southern Democrats into implacable enemies. Kansas had been their best chance to spread slavery. With that lost, they built on the Dred Scott decision to insist that slavery be given formal national protection, legal and military, in every territory until it reached statehood.

The "Irrepressible" Conflict

As the 1860 elections approached, the business of Congress was again stalled by the bitter division over slavery. So deep were the divisions that the House of Representatives was unable to elect a speaker for months. Major legislation foundered, with northerners on one side and southerners on the other.

For years the conflict between the North and the South over slavery was said to be "irreconcilable." Frederick Douglass often said that Liberty and Slavery were at war with one another and that there could be no peace until one or the other was vanquished, until either slavery or freedom was the law everywhere in the land. George Fitzhugh, the most extreme proslavery theorist, had long argued the same thing. By the late 1850s, such talk had drifted into the mainstream. Southern politicians began to claim that the slave states were no longer safe within the Union, and a few "fire-eaters" began making plans for bringing on the breakup. In Illinois, Abraham Lincoln opened his 1858 race for the US Senate with a speech declaring that "a house divided against itself cannot stand." The most famous expression of this sentiment came in a speech by William Seward in 1858. The division over slavery, he said, "is an irrepressible conflict between opposing and enduring forces, and it means that the United States must and will, sooner or later, become either entirely a slaveholding nation, or entirely a free-labor nation."

If by that Seward meant that the two societies' ambitions were incompatible, he had a point. Slaveholders' economy, society, and political power rested on their property rights in slaves. That being true, nothing must undermine it. A society that silenced any criticism of slavery clamped down harder than ever. Northern newspapers were banned and antislavery religious groups like Quakers and Mennonites were driven out. In some states, lawmakers called for expelling free blacks or requiring them to choose a master. More than ever, the Democratic Party in the South was the voice of the slaveholding class, and for them all the government programs that might speed on emigration westward by free laborers constituted a threat to slavery's spread. On most matters, southern Democrats were staunch advocates of states' rights. They opposed protective tariffs and, to western Democrats' irritation, federal support for internal improvements (railroads, canals, turnpikes) or free homesteads. But on slavery issues, it was they who insisted on expanded national authority, both to protect slavery in the territories and to retrieve fugitive slaves. Taney himself was looking for an opportunity for a new ruling, declaring that no state had the right to keep slaves out and that slave property must be recognized everywhere.

The conviction that slavery must grow or die had other effects, too. By the late 1850s, southerners were backing private armies, "filibusters," to seize fresh land for slavery in Latin American countries. They actually landed invading forces in Nicaragua, and members of the expedition came home as heroes. Southern polemicists asserted not only that slavery was right for blacks, but natural for all inferiors, white ones included, and called for reopening the African slave trade so that more people could afford the cost of becoming a slave owner.

At the same time, it made perfect sense for northerners to defend the superiority of free labor. Their own way of life, and the prosperity of their economy, rested on the principle that no human being could rightfully own another. The aggressive expansion of slavery and the disproportionate power of the slaveholders in national politics seemed to threaten freedom everywhere. They, no less than southerners, felt beset.

Still, if the conflict between the North and South was irrepressible, that did not mean that civil war was inevitable. Neither Seward nor Lincoln thought so; Seward saw the day when southern states, of their own free will, would embrace freedom. Instead, the slide from dissension to armed conflict began in late 1859.

The Retreat from Union

In the South, the retreat from unionism was a reaction to John Brown's raid on Harpers Ferry. Brown's death was greeted as a martyr's execution in much of the North, leading many southerners to conclude that a union of the North and the South was no longer viable. In 1860, with the election of Abraham Lincoln, the North ceased compromising with slavery for the sake of maintaining the Union.

John Brown's War Against Slavery

In the fall of 1858, John Brown reemerged to launch another battle in his private war against slavery. By the late 1850s, Brown had concocted a plan to invade Virginia and free the slaves. Friends told Brown his plan was unworkable. Frederick Douglass advised him to give it up. But Brown found financial support from a group of well-connected Bostonians dazzled by his appeal to action rather than words. Brown rented a farm in Maryland, near the town of Harpers Ferry in western Virginia, where a small federal arsenal was located. He apparently planned to capture the arsenal and distribute the guns to local slaves, inciting a rebellion. On the evening of October 16, 1859, Brown and 18 followers crossed the Potomac River with a wagonload of guns and seized the armory. Brown ordered his men to scour the countryside to liberate slaves and take slaveholders prisoner. They found Colonel Lewis Washington, a member of the first president's family, and took him back to Harpers Ferry as a hostage. Mission accomplished, Brown sat back and waited for the slaves to rise.

The slaves did not rise, but the military did. Marines were sent from Washington, DC, led by Lieutenant Colonel Robert E. Lee and his assistant, Lieutenant J. E. B. Stuart, later to become leading Confederate generals. On the morning after Brown seized Harpers Ferry, the militia surrounded the arsenal. The next day Stuart ordered Brown to surrender, and when Brown refused, 12 marines charged in with bayonets. Two of Brown's men and one marine were killed, and Brown was wounded. The rebellion was over in less than two days.

The entire raid was "absurd," Abraham Lincoln later said. "It was not a slave insurrection," he added. "It was an attempt by white men to get up a revolt among slaves, in which the slaves refused to participate." The condemnation of Brown by northerners and the embarrassment of Brown's supporters initially calmed southern outrage. Over the next weeks, however, northern opinion changed. Brown's eloquent statements and dignified behavior in prison, at his trial, and on the gallows moved many northerners to extraordinary demonstrations of sympathy. On December 2, the day Brown was hanged, northern churches tolled their bells. Militia companies fired salutes. Public buildings across the North were draped in black. Although mainstream politicians disavowed Brown and his raid, and mass meetings in every major city denounced antislavery agitation in any and every form, white southerners were shocked to see John Brown become a hero even to some northerners. The *Baltimore Sun* said the South could not "live under a government, the majority of whose subjects or citizens regard John Brown as a martyr and a Christian hero, rather than a murderer and robber." Over the next year, rumors ran wild across the South of would-be Browns, abolitionist infiltrators out to poison wells, burn cities, and raise bloody slave rebellions. Northerners were mobbed, driven from town, beaten, and lynched. One black barber fled for his life before a furious Tennessee crowd, convinced that he was the infamous Frederick Douglass, arrived for unspeakable purposes. In the end, though, it was not John Brown's raid that brought on disunion. It was the election of Abraham Lincoln.

Northerners Elect a President

In February 1860, as the nation's focus shifted from John Brown to the coming presidential election, Abraham Lincoln traveled to New York to address influential eastern Republicans, doubtful of a backwoods figure's fitness for national office. Speaking in the newly opened Cooper Institute, Lincoln grounded Republican doctrine in the Founders' own opposition to slavery and to its spread. Under the Constitution, slaves were seen as persons, not property, and Congress had never doubted its power to regulate the institution where state and local law did not prevail. Denying any wish to harm slavery in the states, the candidate treated its ban from the territories as a restoration, not a revolution.

Both conservative and radical, Lincoln's Cooper Union address vaulted him to the front of eligible Republican presidential nominees. Any one of them would need a united North in November in order to win the presidency. There was no chance of carrying a single slave state. But then, by 1860, even supporters of popular sovereignty like Douglas faced bitter opposition there. Candidates from the South stood almost as poor a chance up north. As a result, the party system was torn four ways, rather than two. In the slave states two southerners strove against each other, and in the free states, two northerners—both from Illinois. All had to cope with the same issues: What, if anything, should be done about slavery? And how best could the Union itself be saved?

When the Democrats met in Charleston, South Carolina, in April 1860, southern delegations insisted that the platform endorse a federal slave code, using national authority to protect slavery in every territory. Any such program would be political suicide up north, dooming the ticket, and northern delegates supporting Stephen A. Douglas knew it. When they insisted on reaffirming popular sovereignty, 49 southern delegates walked out. With too few members left to nominate a presidential candidate successfully, the party adjourned and reconvened in Baltimore in June. There, southerners staged another walkout, this time nominating a presidential candidate of their own, Vice President John C. Breckinridge, on a slave-code platform. The remaining delegates had had enough. They nominated Douglas, the only Democrat with any chance of carrying a single northern state.

To add to the complications, former Whigs and conservatives created a Constitutional Union ticket headed by Senator John Bell of Tennessee. Most onlookers assumed that Republicans would pick the affable and long-experienced Senator William H. Seward of New York. But Seward's "irrepressible conflict" remarks gave him a radical reputation, too hot to carry Pennsylvania, Indiana, or Illinois. The party needed all three. Nativists thought him too cozy with immigrants, especially Catholic ones. New Yorkers recoiled at the hard-eyed political racketeers around him, like Thurlow Weed, "King of the Lobby." Compared to Seward, Lincoln seemed moderate, clean, and refreshingly unpolitical: he had served just one two-year term in Congress. If anybody could carry Illinois against Douglas, he could. So Lincoln was nominated, not because he was the party's best option, but because he could win.

Lincoln's appeal went far beyond his Cooper Institute address. Born in Kentucky, raised in a log cabin, he had all the homespun qualities that Americans liked to associate with the frontier. Posters celebrated him as the self-made man, splitting rails or running a flatboat down the Mississippi. Sloganeers hailed "Honest Abe," a refreshing contrast to the crooked politicians infesting Washington, in Buchanan's

Lincoln-Hamlin Presidential Campaign, 1860 Abraham Lincoln and Hannibal Hamlin as the Republican Party candidates for President and Vice President on a lithograph campaign poster.

administration particularly. Republicanism meant free homesteads for western farmers, a government-funded railroad across the prairies, and a higher tariff desired by Pennsylvania. There never was any question about Lincoln's conviction that slavery was immoral, that the entire slave system should be placed "in the course of ultimate extinction." Shutting slavery out of all the western territories was the one issue on which neither he nor his party would compromise, and doing so, leading southerners warned, would put the institution in mortal danger.

Threats came from fire-eaters that if Lincoln won, their states would depart from the Union. Republicans refused to believe them because they had heard those threats too often before. Breckinridge and Bell protested that their supporters, mostly southern, all cherished the Union. Only Douglas warned that the country faced a mortal peril. So alarmed was he that he broke the political rules of the day and campaigned, "not to ask

Time Line

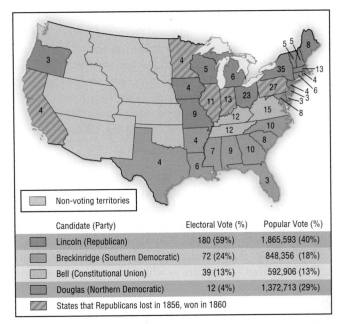

Candidate (Party)	Electoral Vote (%)	Popular Vote (%)
Lincoln (Republican)	180 (59%)	1,865,593 (40%)
Breckinridge (Southern Democratic)	72 (24%)	848,356 (18%)
Bell (Constitutional Union)	39 (13%)	592,906 (13%)
Douglas (Northern Democratic)	12 (4%)	1,372,713 (29%)

Non-voting territories

States that Republicans lost in 1856, won in 1860

Map 13-5   The Election of 1860 By 1860, no presidential candidate could appeal to voters in both the North and the South. By then, the northern population had grown so rapidly that a united North could elect Lincoln to the presidency without any southern support.

for your votes for the Presidency," he told his audiences, "but to make an appeal to you on behalf of the Union."

Even without Democrats split between Douglas and Breckinridge, Lincoln would have won. He took barely 39% of the vote, with Douglas in second place. Only in the border South could Republicans mount a campaign or cast a ballot and live, and even there, they took only a few thousand votes. Breckinridge carried eleven slave states, with the richer plantation counties favoring John Bell, the Constitutional Union candidate. But Lincoln's majorities across the North gave him an electoral landslide, winning every state but one. Missouri alone favored Douglas (see Map 13–5).

▼**1856**
"Bleeding Kansas"
Sumner-Brooks affair
James Buchanan elected
    president

▼**1857**
Dred Scott decision
Lecompton constitution in
    Kansas reopens slavery
    controversy

▼**1858**
Lincoln-Douglas debates

▼**1859**
John Brown's raid on Harpers
    Ferry

▼**1860**
Abraham Lincoln elected first
    Republican president

Republicans had not carried the Senate. They had lost seats in the House. The Supreme Court remained in proslavery hands; and Democrats were sure to gain two years hence, when united against a common enemy. All the same, antislavery forces felt doubly vindicated: not only did the Republican victory demonstrate the free-soil platform's wide appeal, but it also suggested that political power was shifting as a dynamic economy based on free labor outpaced slave society. The future, they knew, belonged to them. In their own way, some white southerners agreed. They concluded that no matter what assurances Lincoln gave them, slavery had no future in the Union.

Conclusion

Frederick Douglass had doubts about Lincoln but sincerely hoped that the Republicans would win the 1860 elections. "Slavery is the issue—the single bone of contention between all parties and sections," he insisted. Slavery and freedom had guided the nation along two diverging pathways. The North was developing an urban, industrial economy based on the productive energy of wage labor. In the South, a prosperous slave economy depended on a system of commercialized agriculture in which laborers were commodities as much as the cash crops they produced. The political tensions arising from these differences finally pushed the nation into civil war. And as the war progressed, the same fundamental differences would shape the destiny of the Union and Confederate forces.

Who, What

John Brown 399

Stephen Douglas 396

Frederick Douglass 384

John C. Frémont 402

Abraham Lincoln 397

Charles Sumner 400

Roger Taney 403

"Bleeding Kansas" 399

Compromise of 1850 393

The Dred Scott decision 403

Fugitive Slave Act 393

Harpers Ferry 406

Know-Nothing 395

Ostend Manifesto 400

Popular sovereignty 391

Wilmot Proviso 391

Review Questions

1. What were the major differences between the northern and southern economies by the 1850s?

2. How did the war with Mexico provoke a conflict over slavery?

3. What did the Republican Party stand for?

4. What was the Kansas-Nebraska Act and why was it so important?

5. What were the major issues in the Lincoln-Douglas debates?

Critical-Thinking Questions

1. Was the slavery battle primarily a conflict between two different economic systems, or was it more of a moral issue?

2. Which congressional action in this period did the most to push the nation toward civil war (the Wilmot Proviso, the Compromise of 1850, the Kansas-Nebraska Act, the debate over the Lecompton Constitution)? Explain your answer.

3. How did developments that first appeared to be victories for the South end up benefiting the antislavery cause in the long run?

4. Violence played a role in the debate over slavery even before the first shots of the Civil War. In your opinion, was John Brown's violent crusade justified? Why or why not?

For further review materials and resource information, please visit www.oup.com/us/oakes

CHAPTER 13: THE POLITICS OF SLAVERY, 1848–1860

Primary Sources

13.1 CHARLES SUMNER, "THE CRIME AGAINST KANSAS" (1856) AND VISUAL DOCUMENT: J. L. MAGEE, "SOUTHERN CHIVALRY—ARGUMENT VS. CLUB'S" (1856)

On May 19 and 20, 1856, Republican Senator Charles Sumner of Massachusetts delivered a formal oration about the disturbances in Kansas Territory. "The Crime Against Kansas," as he entitled the speech, laid out the conspiracy he saw by proslavery interests to force free white settlers there to accept slavery. He also used his remarks to single out Senator Andrew P. Butler of South Carolina, whose earlier remarks had accused Sumner's party of being sectional and fanatical and had warned that keeping slaveholders out of the territories would be grounds for secession. Two days later, on May 22, Butler's kinsman, Congressman Preston S. Brooks, a Democrat from South Carolina, caned Sumner insensible.

The wickedness which I now begin to expose is immeasurably aggravated by the motive which prompted it. Not in any common lust for power did this uncommon tragedy have its origin. It is the rape of a virgin Territory, compelling it to the hateful embrace of Slavery; and it may be clearly traced to a depraved longing for a new slave State, the hideous offspring of such a crime, in the hope of adding to the power of slavery in the National Government. Yes, Sir, when the whole world, alike Christian and Turk, is rising up to condemn this wrong, making it a hissing to the nations, here in our Republic, *force*—aye, Sir, FORCE,—is openly employed in compelling Kansas to this pollution, and all for the sake of political power. There is the simple fact, which you will vainly attempt to deny, but which in itself presents an essential wickedness that makes other public crimes seem like public virtues.

This enormity, vast beyond comparison, swells to dimensions of crime which the imagination toils in vain to grasp, when it is understood that for this purpose are hazarded the horrors of intestine feud, not only in this distant Territory, but everywhere throughout the country. The muster has begun. The strife is no longer local but national. Even now, while I speak, portents lower in the horizon, threatening to darken the land, which already palpitates with the mutterings of civil war. The fury of the propagandists, and the calm determination of their opponents, are diffused from the distant Territory over wide-spread communities, and the whole country, in all its extent, marshalling hostile divisions, and foreshadowing a conflict which, unless happily averted by the triumph of Freedom, will become war,—fratricidal, parricidal war,—with an accumulated wickedness beyond that of any war in human annals, justly provoking the avenging judgment of Providence and the avenging Pen of History, and constituting a strife such as was pictured by the Roman historian, more than *foreign*, more than *social*, more than *civil*, being something compounded of all these, and in itself more than war. . . .

Before entering upon the argument, I must say something of a general character, particularly in response to what has fallen from Senators who have raised themselves to eminence on this floor in championship of human wrong; I mean the Senator from South Carolina, [Mr. BUTLER], and the Senator from Illinois, [Mr. DOUGLAS], who, though unlike as Don Quixote and Sancho Panza, yet, like this couple, sally forth together in the same adventure. I regret much to miss the elder Senator from his seat; but the cause, against which he has run a tilt with such ebullition of animosity, demands that the opportunity of exposing him should not be lost; and it is for the cause that I speak. The Senator from South Carolina has read many books of chivalry, and believes himself a chivalrous knight, with sentiments of honor and courage. Of course he has chosen a mistress to whom he has made his vows, and who, though ugly to others, is always lovely to him; though polluted in the sight of the world, is chaste in his sight—I mean the harlot, Slavery. For her his tongue is always profuse in words. Let her be impeached in character, or any proposition be made to shut her out from the extension of her wantonness, and no extravagance of manner or hardihood of assertion is too great for this Senator . . . The asserted rights of Slavery, which shock equality of all kinds, are cloaked by a fantastic claim of equality. If the Slave States cannot enjoy what, in mockery of the great fathers of the Republic, he misnames Equality under the Constitution,—in other words, the full power in the National Territories to compel fellow-men to unpaid toil, to separate husband and wife, and to sell little children at the auction-block,—then, Sir, the chivalric Senator will conduct the State of South Carolina out of the Union! Heroic knight! Exalted Senator! A second Moses come for a second exodus!

Not content with this poor menace, which we have been twice told was "measured," the Senator, in the unrestrained chivalry of his nature, has undertaken to apply opprobrious words to those who differ from him on this floor. He calls them "sectional and fanatical"; and resistance to the usurpation of Kansas he denounces as "an uncalculated fanaticism.". . . He is the uncompromising, unblushing representative on this floor of a flagrant *sectionalism*, now domineering over the Republic,—and yet, with a ludicrous ignorance of his own position, unable to see himself as others see him, or with an effrontery which even his white head ought not to protect from rebuke, he applies to those here who resist his *sectionalism* the very epithet which designates himself. The men who strive to bring back the Government to its original policy, when Freedom and not Slavery was national, while Slavery and not Freedom was sectional, he arraigns as *sectional*. This will not do. It involves too great a perversion of terms. I tell that Senator that it is to himself, and to the "organization" of which he is the "committed advocate," that this epithet belongs. I now fasten it upon them. For myself, I care little for names; but since the question is raised here, I affirm that the Republican party of the Union is in no just sense *sectional*, but, more than any other party, *national*,—and that it now goes forth to dislodge from the high places that tyrannical sectionalism of which the Senator from South Carolina is one of the maddest zealots.

Source: Charles Sumner, "The Crime Against Kansas, May 19th–20th, 1856." From *Charles Sumner: His Complete Works* (Boston: Lee and Shepard, 1900), vol. 5, pp. 140–146.

SOUTHERN CHIVALRY — ARGUMENT versus CLUB'S.

13.2 JOHN GREENLEAF WHITTIER, "THE HASCHISH" (1854)

New England's great Quaker poet, John Greenleaf Whittier, wrote on many subjects, but before and during the war, he also turned his pen to fervent antislavery appeals and critiques of the North's complicity in that system of human bondage. His poem "The Haschish" compared the hallucinogenic drugs of the East to the self-deluding qualities that profits from the sale of cotton had given to public figures. Its references incidentally suggest the arcane knowledge about Middle Eastern society that poets assumed the general reading public enjoyed.

Of all that Orient lands can vaunt
Of marvels with our own competing,
The strangest is the Haschish plant,
And what will follow on its eating.

What pictures to the taster rise,
Of Dervish or of Almeh dances!
Of Eblis, or of Paradise,
Set all aglow with Houri glances!

The poppy visions of Cathay,
The heavy beer-trance of the Suabian;
The wizard lights and demon play
Of nights Walpurgis and Arabian!

The Mullah and the Christian dog
Change place in mad metempsychosis;
The muezzin climbs the synagogue,
The Rabbi shakes his beard at Moses!

The Arab by his desert well
Sits choosing from some Caliph's daughters,
And hears his single camel's bell
Sound welcome to his regal quarter.

The Koran's reader makes complaint
Of Shitan dancing on and off it;
The robber offers alms, the saint
Drinks Tokay and blasphemes the Prophet.

Such scenes that Eastern plant awakes;
But we have one ordained to beat it,
The Haschish of the West, which makes
Or fools or knaves of all who eat it.

The preacher eats, and straight appears
His Bible in a new translation;
Its angels negro overseers,
And Heaven itself a snug plantation!

The man of peace, about whose dreams
The sweet millennial angels cluster,
Tastes the mad weed, and plots and schemes,
A raving Cuban filibuster!

The noisiest Democrat, with ease,
It turns to Slavery's parish beadle;
The shrewdest statesman eats and sees
Due southward point the polar needle.

The Judge partakes, and sits erelong
Upon his bench a railing blackguard;
Decides off-hand that right is wrong,
And reads the ten commandments backward.

O potent plant! So rare a taste
Has never Turk or Gentoo gotten;
The hempen Haschish of the East
Is powerless to our Western Cotton!

Source: John Greenleaf Whittier, *The Complete Poetical Works of John Greenleaf Whittier* (Boston: Houghton, Osgood & Company, 1879), pp. 201–202.

13.3 FRITHJOF MEIDELL, ACCOUNT OF LIFE ON THE PRAIRIES (1855)

Frithjof Meidell came from Norway in the mid-1850s and wrote home about the boom in the American West. His account affords a glimpse not only into the excitement and bewilderment of an immigrant's life but also of the dynamism of the Old Northwest, where railroad construction over the prewar decade added as many miles of track as in all 15 slave states. That energy and development help explain the Confederacy's failure to match the Union in the means and material needed to carry on a long war.

SPRINGFIELD, ILL., August 7, 1855

DEAR MOTHER:

I received Hansine's letter a couple of days ago and was indeed glad to hear that all of you are getting along so well. The same is true of Christian and me; both of us are feeling fine. I have tried many a ruse to get him to write home, but all in vain. A real porker, that fellow! You must thank Hansine ever so much for her letter. It was very interesting. I sent her a letter about two months ago by a man from Arendal who was returning home. Likely she has received it by now. I must admit that I felt quite flattered by her praise of my epistles, and least of all did I expect that Ditmar would find anything in them worthy of printer's ink. But there you see: do not judge a tramp by his rags.

How pleased I should be if I could only secure copies of Aftenbladet from time to time. Could not this be arranged? In the Norwegian paper, Emiigranten, which is published in Wisconsin, I find many articles from Aftenbladet. In the same paper I also see that you now have both railroad and telegraph. Hurrah for old Norway!

How is the railroad getting along? Here in America it is the railroads which build up the whole country. Because of them the farmers get wider markets and higher prices for their products. They seem to put new life into everything. Even the old apple woman sets off at a dogtrot when she hears the whistle, since she wants to sell her apples to the passengers. Every ten miles along the railways there are stations which soon grow up into towns. "Soon" did I say? I should have said "immediately" because it is really remarkable how rapidly the stations are transformed into little towns. I can but compare it with the building of Aladdin's castle by means of his wonderful lamp, only that things move still faster here, since it is not necessary to sit and rub a rusty old oil lantern. Here you can buy houses all ready to be placed on the freight car, and in half a day's time they can be nailed together.

Since I have nothing else to write about this time, I shall attempt to describe how these towns spring up. First—that is, after the two old log houses that stand one on each side of the tracks—first, I say, the railroad company builds a depot. Next a speculator buys the surrounding one hundred acres and lays it out in lots, streets, and a market place. Then he graces the prospective town with the name of an early president or a famous general—or probably his own name—holds an auction, and realizes many hundred per cent on his investment. A young wagonmaker who has just completed his apprenticeship hears about the station, that it is beautifully located in a rich farming country, is blessed with good water, and, most important of all, that it has no wagonmaker. Making a hasty resolution, he buys the barest necessities for setting up in his profession, hurries off to the place, rents one of the old log houses, and is soon at work. One absolute necessity he still lacks, however: a sign, of course, which is the most important part of a man's equipment here in America. The next day he hears that there is a tramp painter aboard the train; he gets him off, puts him to work, and the very next day the farmers are surprised to see a monstrous sign straddling the roof of the old log house. The sign is an immediate success, for the farmers rush to the shop and order wagons, wheels, and the like. The poor man is overwhelmed with more work than he can handle for ever so long. He is about to regret that sign notion of his, but suddenly he has another idea. He accepts every order, and no sooner are the customers away than he seizes his pen and writes to the editors of three different newspapers that three good apprentices can secure steady work with high wages in the "flourishing town of L." Within two days he has help enough, and the work goes "like a song."

The train stops again and off steps a blacksmith who went broke in one of the larger towns. He saunters over to the wagonmaker's shop as unconcerned as if he only wished to light his cigar. In a casual way he inquires about the neighborhood and wonders what its prospects are, without indicating that he intends to settle there—by no means! But the wagoner, with his keen Yankee nose, soon smells a rat and starts boosting the place with all his might. This inspires the smith with ecstasy; he thereupon starts to jump around and make sledge-hammer motions with his arms. Off he goes and rents the other log house and nails a horseshoe over the door as a sign. The horseshoe, to be sure, cannot be seen any great distance, but the smith has a remedy for this, and he starts to hammer and pound away at his anvil so the farmers for miles around can hear the echoes. They immediately flock to his door, and there is work enough for the blacksmith. Within a short week a carpenter, a tailor, and a shoemaker also arrive in town. The wagoner orders a house from the carpenter and rents the second story to the tailor and the shoemaker. Soon the blacksmith also builds a house, and things progress with giant strides toward the bigger and better.

Again the train stops. This time two young fellows jump off, gaze about, and go over to have a chat with the blacksmith. One of them is a doctor, the other a lawyer. Both of them rent rooms from the blacksmith and start business.

Once more the locomotive stops. But—what's this that comes out? Be patient! Just let it come closer. It is nothing more nor less than a mustachioed, velvet-frocked German with an old, overworked hurdy-gurdy strapped to his back. On the hurdy-gurdy perches a measly little monkey dressed in red. The German goes over to the blacksmith shop and begins to crank his music box while the monkey smokes tobacco, dances a polka, and grinds coffee. But the German receives no encouragement for his art, nor does the monkey—except some rusty nails which the smith tosses to him. The artist realizes that his audience is very unappreciative and the poor man's face is overcast with sorrow. Then he looks about inquiringly as if searching for something and steps up to the doctor to ask if there is a restaurant in town. On receiving a negative reply, his face brightens up again and after a short conversation with the doctor and lawyer, he steams off with the next train and jumps off at the first big town, where he sells his hurdy-gurdy and monkey and buys a barrel of whisky, another barrel of biscuits, two large cheeses, tobacco, cigars, and sausages—miles of them. Thereupon he engages a painter to make an appropriate sign, and in three days he is again back in the new town. Now he rents the blacksmith's old log house and rigs it up as a shop. Soon the sign swings over the door, the whisky barrel is already half empty, and the sausages are dispatched by the yard. But how could it be otherwise? Our clever German calls them egyptische Brautewurste, an irresistible name, nicht wahr? And what of the sign? Polz tausend noch einmal. In the center rests a large barrel adorned with the magic word Lagerbier. On one side of the barrel is a large cheese and on the other a necklace of sausages. Between these German Valhalla delicacies we read in large yellow letters, Wirtschaftshaus zur deutschen Republik, by Carl Klor. Fortune smiles upon the German innkeeper.

His best customers are the railroad workers, most of whom are Irishmen. They discovered the shop one Sunday afternoon while it was closed. But fortunately there were two Germans in the crowd who were attracted by the sign and interpreted its mysteries to the Irishmen, who at once burst into frenzies of joy and started to dance about to the accompaniment of war whoops. Then they stuck their thumbs into their mouths and pulled them out with thuds like the uncorking of bottles, after which they hammered at the door. The German immediately opened both his mouth and his door and commenced to murder the English language and to tap whisky. He is now well on his way to become a capitalist, because these fellows have tremendous capacities and swallow a quart of fire water without batting an eye. I believe I must have mentioned them before. They consist mostly of the worst riffraff of Europe, to whom America is a promised land where you earn a dollar a day and are not hanged for stealing. When these roughnecks get together it is a pretty dull party unless there are a couple of fights and someone gets a good "hiding." As you go along a railway under construction it is easy to detect the places where they have had their frolics by the torn-up sod, the tufts of hair, the broken bottles, pipes, pants buttons, blood, and so forth, which they have left behind them. I imagine that if the most brutish hog in the world could express himself he would do it something like these fellows.

But to get back to my town again. The German, the blacksmith, and the tailor do a rushing business. The train stops again, and this time it is a printer who makes his appearance. He gets in touch with the doctor and lawyer; an old printing press is for sale in the next town; they buy it, and with this new event we can really say that the town has "arrived." Some little trouble there is, to be sure, concerning the political affiliations of the paper, because it develops that the lawyer is a Democrat, the doctor an Abolitionist, and the printer a Whig. But a compromise is soon reached and the new paper announces itself as "independent." The lawyer volunteers to write the editorials, while the doctor promises a wealth of death announcements, and the German and the blacksmith undertake to fill the rest of the paper with advertisements. Within a few years the town is very large. The wagonmaker owns practically one-half of it. The German deals only in wholesale. The lawyer is mayor of the town, and the blacksmith does nothing but smoke cigars, for he is now a man of affluence.

Source: Frithjof Meidell, "The Birth and Growth of a Railroad Town," 1855, in *Norwegian-American Studies and Records* (Northfield, MN: 1936), vol. 9, pp. 48–53, quoted in William Benton, publ., *The Annals of America. Volume 8, 1850–1857: A House Dividing* (Chicago: Encyclopedia Britannica, Inc., 1968), pp. 349–352.

13.4 JAMES H. HAMMOND, "SPEECH ON THE ADMISSION OF KANSAS" (1858)

A South Carolina lawyer and editor who married into money, James Henry Hammond ended up as successful in politics as he had in planting. The legislature elected him governor twice; he served in the House and then in the Senate. Although he was by no means one of the "fire-eater" extremists in the state, he earned that reputation up north in his taunting reply to a speech by Senator William Seward of New York in March 1858.

No, you dare not make war on cotton. No power on earth dares to make war upon it. Cotton is king. Until lately the Bank of England was king; but she tried to put her screws as usual, the fall before the last, upon the cotton crop, and was utterly vanquished. The last power has been conquered. Who can doubt, that has looked at recent events, that cotton is supreme? When the abuse of credit had destroyed credit and annihilated confidence; when thousands of the strongest commercial houses in the world were coming down, and hundreds of millions of dollars of supposed property evaporating in thin air; when you came to a dead lock, and revolutions were threatened, what brought you up? Fortunately for you it was the commencement of the cotton season, and we have poured in upon you one million six hundred thousand bales of cotton just at the crisis to save you from destruction. That cotton, but for the bursting of your speculative bubbles in the North, which produced the whole of this convulsion, would have brought us $100,000,000. We have sold it for $65,000,000, and saved you. Thirty-five million dollars we, the slaveholders of the South, have put into the charity box for your magnificent financiers, your "cotton lords," your "merchant princes."

But, sir, the greatest strength of the South arises from the harmony of her political and social institutions. This harmony gives her a frame of society, the best in the world, and an extent of political freedom, combined with entire security, such as no other people ever enjoyed upon the face of the earth. Society precedes government; creates it, and ought to control it; but as far as we can look back in historic times we find the case different; for government is no sooner created than it becomes too strong for society, and shapes and moulds, as well as controls it. In later centuries the progress of civilization and of intelligence has made the divergence so great as to produce civil wars and revolutions; and it is nothing now but the want of harmony between governments and societies which occasions all the uneasiness and trouble and terror that we see abroad. It was this that brought on the American Revolution. We threw off a Government not adapted to our social system, and made one for ourselves. The question is, how far have we succeeded? The South, so far as that is concerned, is satisfied, harmonious, and prosperous, but demands to be let alone.

In all social systems there must be a class to do the menial duties, to perform the drudgery of life. That is, a class requiring but a low order of intellect and but little skill. Its requisites are vigor, docility, fidelity. Such a class you must have, or you would not have that other class which leads progress, civilization, and refinement. It constitutes the very mud-sill of society and of political government; and you might as well attempt to build a house in the air, as to build either the one or the other, except on this mud-sill. Fortunately for the South, she found a race adapted to that purpose to her hand. A race inferior to her own, but eminently qualified in temper, in vigor, in docility, in capacity to stand the climate, to answer all her purposes. We use them for our purpose, and call them slaves. We found them slaves by the common "consent of mankind," which, according to Cicero, "*lex naturae est.*" The highest proof of what is Nature's law. We are old-fashioned at the South yet; slave is a word discarded now by "ears polite;" I will not characterize that class at the North by that term; but you have it; it is there; it is everywhere; it is eternal.

The Senator from New York said yesterday that the whole world had abolished slavery. Aye, the *name*, but not the *thing*; all the powers of the earth cannot abolish that. God only can do it when he repeals the fiat, "the poor ye always have with you"; for the man who lives by daily labor, and scarcely lives at that, and who has to put out his labor in the market, and take the best he can get for it; in short, your whole hireling class of manual laborers and "operatives," as you call them, are essentially slaves. The difference between us is, that our slaves are hired for life and well compensated; there is no starvation, no begging, no want of employment among our people, and not too much employment either. Yours are hired by the day, not cared for, and scantily compensated, which may be proved in the most painful manner, at any hour in any street in any of your large towns. Why, you meet more beggars in one day in any single street of the city of New York, than you would meet in a lifetime in the whole South. We do not think that whites should be slaves either by law or necessity. Our slaves are black, of another and inferior race. The *status* in which we have placed them is an elevation. They are elevated from the condition in which God first created them, by being made our slaves. None of that race on the whole face of the globe can be compared with the slaves of the South. They are happy, content, unaspiring, and utterly incapable, from intellectual weakness, ever to give us any trouble by their aspirations. Yours are white, of your own race; you are brothers of one blood. They are your equals in natural endowment of intellect, and they feel galled by their degradation. Our slaves do not vote. We give them no political power. Yours do vote, and, being the majority, they are the depositaries of all your political power. If they knew the tremendous secret, that the ballot-box is stronger than "an army with banners," and could combine, where would you be? Your society would be reconstructed, your government overthrown, your property divided, not as they have mistakenly attempted to initiate such proceedings by meeting in parks, with arms in their hands, but by the quiet process of the ballot-box. You have been making war upon us to our very hearthstones. How would you like for us to send lecturers and agitators North, to teach these people this, to aid in combining and to lead them?

Mr. [Henry] Wilson [of Massachusetts] and others: Send them along.

Mr. Hammond: You say send them along. There is no need of that. Your people are awaking. They are coming here. They are thundering at our doors for homesteads, one hundred and sixty acres of land for nothing, and Southern Senators are supporting them. Nay, they are assembling, as I have said, with arms in their hands, and demanding work at $1,000 a year for six hours a day. Have you heard that the ghosts of Mendoza and Torquemada are stalking in the streets of your great cities? That the inquisition is at hand? There is afloat a fearful rumor that there have been consultations for Vigilance Committees. You know what that means.

Transient and temporary causes have thus far been your preservation. The great West has been open to your surplus population, and your hordes of semibarbarian immigrants, who are crowding in year by year. They make a great movement, and you call it progress. Whither? It is progress; but it is progress towards Vigilance Committees. The South have sustained you in a great measure. You are our factors. You fetch and carry for us. One hundred and fifty million dollars of our money passes annually through your hands. Much of it sticks; all of it assists to keep your machinery together and in motion. Suppose we were to discharge you; suppose we were to take our business out of your hands;—we should consign you to anarchy and poverty. You complain of the rule of the South; that has been another cause that has preserved you. We have kept the Government conservative to the great purposes of the Constitution. We have placed it, and kept it, upon the Constitution; and that has been the cause of your peace and prosperity. The Senator from New York says that that is about to be at an end; that you intend to take the Government from us; that it will pass from our hands into yours. Perhaps what he says is true; it may be; but do not forget—it can never be forgotten—it is written on the brightest page of human history—that we, the slaveholders of the South, took our country in her infancy, and, after ruling her for sixty out of the seventy years of her existence, we surrendered her to you without a stain upon her honor, boundless in prosperity, incalculable in her strength, the wonder and the admiration of the world. Time will show what you will make of her; but no time can diminish our glory or your responsibility.

Source: "Speech on the Admission of Kansas," U.S. Senate, March 4, 1858, in *Selections from the Letters and Speeches of the Hon. James H. Hammond, of South Carolina* (New York: John F. Trow & Co., 1866), pp. 317–322, from *Congressional Globe*, 35th Congress 1st session, 961–992.

A War for Union and Emancipation

1861–1865

COMMON THREADS

What made parts of the South leave the Union?

In what ways did the military strategies of the Union and Confederacy reflect the differences between the two regions?

What was the relationship between emancipation and war?

Why did the Confederacy lose the Civil War? Why did the Union win?

What happened to the slaves who were freed by the war?

OUTLINE

AMERICAN PORTRAIT

Laura M. Towne and the Sea Island Invasion

Late in 1861, Union gunboats took control of the flat marshy Sea Islands off the South Carolina coast near Port Royal. Plantation owners fled at the first gunfire, leaving behind 10,000 African Americans, who were slaves no longer. Union commanders wanted to put them to work making cotton for northern mills. Thus began the "Port Royal experiment," in which former slaves worked land abandoned by plantation owners. The program proved that African Americans worked hard and well in freedom. But northern missionaries, who had come south to spread the Gospel, wrote home of multitudes of ill-clothed, ill-fed, and ill-housed African Americans. They needed as much care for their bodies as their souls. Among the volunteers that a Philadelphia relief committee sent in the spring of 1862 to aid the former slaves was Laura Towne.

Born in 1825 in Pittsburgh and trained as a teacher and in homeopathic medicine, Laura Towne was a firm abolitionist. For Towne, the war offered a chance not only to save the Union but also to give it a second chance to live up to its ideals. It was not just men's work but women's as well, and in that war, Towne enlisted, as it turned out, for life. At first working as a healer, Towne and her close friend Ellen Murray began teaching in a plantation mansion. By New England standards, former slaves lacked all self-discipline. "They had no idea of sitting still, of giving attention, of ceasing to talk aloud," she wrote. "They got up by the dozen, made their curtsies, and walked off to the neighboring field for blackberries, coming back to their seats with a curtsy when they were ready. They evidently did not understand me, and I could not understand them, and after two hours and a half of effort I was thoroughly exhausted." But Towne and Murray also found the community eager and able to learn. Classes moved into a prefabricated schoolhouse, and the Penn School was established as a school for freed slaves. It would last well into the next century and Towne would teach there until she died in 1901.

Towne was just one among many "Yankee school marms" who came south during or after the war. Northern congregations paid their wages, which were paltry at best; Towne lived off her small inheritance. Even before the war ended, benevolent associations in Boston, Philadelphia, and New York were raising money to feed and clothe southerners of both races. Towne spent much of her time distributing supplies to the destitute and visiting the sick. Like many northerners, she became an unofficial adviser to freed people, a moral counselor, and a public health officer. A more perfect Union, to her, meant giving former slaves a freedom worth keeping. That meant more than fostering the Penn School's mission as the only institution for black secondary education in South Carolina and one of the foremost training centers for black teachers. It meant imparting Christianity, devotion to the nation, and an understanding of its history as Republicans had always defined it, a belief in racial equality and cleanliness, both moral and physical.

Laura Towne's career shows one of the many ways in which the Civil War depended on women's actions as well as men's, and how the Civil War's original goal of restoring the nation would change. Towne's work also serves as a reminder that no battlefield settlement could create the more perfect Union that reformers envisioned. Towne exemplified that very radicalism that Confederates had feared from the start, in a North where none of the boundaries confining women's roles or those of African Americans would stand fast for long.

Liberty and Union

The four-month period between Lincoln's election and his inauguration must have seemed the longest and worst interval Americans had ever known. Within six weeks, South Carolina dissolved its connection to the Union. Scarcely two months later, it became part of a new nation, stretching from the Atlantic to the Rio Grande. Cheering crowds waved palmetto leaves and set off fireworks to celebrate the parting. Military companies paraded. "We are divorced, North and South, because we have hated each other so," a senator's wife wrote. Cooler heads did not join the celebration. They knew that this divorce would be contested bitterly. "They have . . . set a blazing torch to the temple of Constitutional liberty," a Carolinian warned his compatriots, "and, please God, we shall have no more peace forever." What followed would be a war more horrible than the celebrating crowds dreamed, with results more tremendous than most Americans expected. Why, then, did so many white southerners feel secession was necessary? And what made so many Americans accept war rather than a disunited country?

For secessionists, a Republican presidency seemed the last in a long line of insults against slavery, but also the first move in a conspiracy against their liberty, specifically the right to hold slaves. Far from betraying the American Revolution, they claimed to follow its example. They, too, were breaking free from would-be tyrants to protect a social system dependent on slave labor. Secessionists warned that Republican rule meant slave insurrections, laws keeping slave owners from selling their property across state lines, a welcome mat put out to every runaway come north, and a Supreme Court packed with antislavery zealots. Republicanism would encourage every southern critic of slavery, now cowed into silence and kept from voting his opinions. It would make thousands of new ones among non-slaveholders. In time, the west would furnish enough free states to amend the Constitution. Then slavery would end everywhere. Set free, African Americans would set off a war of races, with the blessing of northern fanatics. If slaveholders craved safety, they must part the Union at once, before the shackles were laid on their limbs.

For most northerners, the Union had become too intertwined with American liberty to surrender. Taught to see America as a lighthouse of liberty in a world of tyranny, they warned that if a government based on the consent of the governed perished, it would carry "the last best hope" for oppressed peoples throughout the world with it. As one state after the other seceded, all doubt about what to do vanished. Retiring president Buchanan may have been weak and indecisive, but he shared a universal northern belief that no state had the right to secede and that the Confederate government had no legal standing. Each day brought another abject surrender to insurrectionary forces: Fort Pulaski on the Savannah River, military installations in Texas, the arsenal in Augusta. Northerners cried that each retreat must be the last. Long before the government called for a single volunteer, communities across the North were raising military companies. When Buchanan sent an abortive relief mission to save Fort Sumter in Charleston Harbor, the whole North applauded him. Northerners blamed the slaveholding elite for the war, telling themselves that most white southerners had been stampeded out of a Union they still loved. Most Democrats would have welcomed, and most Republicans accepted, a reunion leaving slavery intact in states that had it. But a growing number of Unionists were prepared to destroy slavery if the Union could be saved no other way. And, abolitionists and the more radical Republicans insisted there was no other way.

The Deep South Secedes

South Carolina's secession on December 20, 1860, added momentum to the secession movement in its neighbors and across the Gulf. Dissenting voices, denounced as cowards and "submissionists," often took their lives in their hands by standing in public opinion's way. Within weeks, Mississippi, Florida, Alabama, Georgia, Louisiana, and Texas announced their separation (see Map 14–1). Meeting in Montgomery, Alabama, in early February 1861, secessionists drafted a basic charter for their new government, the Confederate States of America. They selected as president an experienced administrator and planter, Senator Jefferson Davis of Mississippi.

The Confederate constitution differed from the US Constitution in only a few provisions, but these were key. The Confederate chief executive served a single, six-year term and had a line-item veto. More important, while the constitution emphasized the states' "sovereign and independent character," it wrote slavery's protection into fundamental law. The new nation's "cornerstone" was "the great truth that the negro is not equal to the white man," Confederate vice president Alexander Stephens announced, "that slavery, subordination to the superior race, is his natural and normal condition." Optimists spoke of a republic spreading to the California coast and possibly even the ultimate absorption of states north of the Ohio River.

The Upper South Makes Its Choice

Then, as quickly as it had begun, the secession movement stalled. Even in the lower South many whites, among them Texas governor Sam Houston, had seen no immediate threat in Lincoln's election. In Louisiana, the secessionists had just barely won. Elsewhere farmers in counties where slavery was comparatively rare had shown much less enthusiasm for leaving the Union. Many had been "cooperationists," wanting the whole South to secede as one, or making their later support for secession conditional on some northern overt act. In the more heavily white states of the upper South, where robust two-party systems survived, outright Unionists joined cooperationists in opposing hasty action.

Lincoln and many Republicans hoped that if they moved cautiously they could keep the upper South in the Union and thereby derail the secession movement. But cooperationism made a shaky foundation for a rebuilt Union, particularly when so many of its supporters opposed any government action enforcing its laws in Confederate territory, which was viewed as coercion, and insisted on northern concessions as the price of future loyalty.

Democrats and upper South Unionists generally hoped to halt secession permanently with one last deal, a series of constitutional amendments proposed by Kentucky

Map 14–1   The Secession of the Southern States   The South seceded in two stages. During the "secession winter" of 1860–1861, the lower South states seceded in reaction to the election of Abraham Lincoln. The following spring, the upper South seceded in response to Lincoln's attempt to resupply Fort Sumter. The border slave states of Maryland, Delaware, Kentucky, and Missouri never left the Union.

senator John J. Crittenden. The Crittenden Compromise would have restored the Missouri Compromise line and guaranteed federal protection of slavery south of that line in all territories currently held or later acquired by the United States. It would have barred Congress from abolishing slavery in Washington, DC, and from regulating the interstate slave trade. Finally, it called for the compensation of masters unable to recover fugitive slaves from the North.

Republicans balked. They were ready to promise enforcement of the Fugitive Slave Law and willing to consider admitting New Mexico as a slave state, or even an amendment protecting slavery in the states from federal interference. But they refused to surrender the program on which they had won. Lincoln would not agree to let slavery spread. As opponents warned, a South able to extort concessions on threats of breaking up the Union would not stop there. Every crisis would bring new demands, under the same threat. What, then, would government by the consent of the governed be worth? Seceding states dismissed the compromise, too; they had no intention of returning for so little.

Even "cooperationists" insisted that the southern states had a right to secede and should do so if the federal authorities took any steps against those states that had already seceded. With eight of the fifteen states still in the Union on March 4, 1861, Lincoln's inaugural address stressed that he would make no aggressive move. "We are not enemies, but friends," he pleaded. "We must not be enemies." It took him a little over a month to realize that war was unavoidable. His best hope of holding onto any of the wavering states depended on how it began—and which side began it. So while the government would not try to retake federal installations already lost, it would not surrender those it still held, Fort Pickens in Pensacola, Florida, or Fort Sumter in Charleston Harbor, South Carolina. In April, Lincoln announced plans to resupply Fort Sumter with nonmilitary provisions. With demands that it prove its authority, Jefferson Davis's government faced pressures from the opposite side. "Unless you sprinkle blood in the face of the Southern people," a friend warned him, "they will be back in the old Union in less than ten days." Before the Union expedition could arrive, on April 12, 1861, Confederates opened fire on the fort. After more than a day of bombardment, the Union commander surrendered.

On April 15, Lincoln responded, calling on the states for 75,000 ninety-day volunteers to put down an insurrection by a pretended government in the South. For much of the upper South, this constituted the "coercion" they had warned against. Virginia seceded at once. Within two months Arkansas, Tennessee, and North Carolina did the same. Most cooperationists became loyal Confederates and many enlisted.

But Lincoln's decision paid off. Four slave states (Kentucky, Maryland, Delaware, and Missouri) remained in the Union, providing tens of thousands of federal soldiers. In the mountains of western North Carolina and eastern Tennessee, unionist sentiment persisted, and here, too, loyalists crossed fighting lines to enlist with the Union. Among the Virginians who put their country ahead of their state were Generals Winfield Scott and George H. Thomas and Admiral David Farragut. The western third of Virginia not only voted overwhelmingly against secession, it seceded from the Old Dominion itself to form a separate state government. In 1863 the state of West Virginia entered the Union, having abolished slavery. That split gave the Union most of the best-developed cities in the South (St. Louis, Louisville, and Baltimore), most of its manufacturing capacity, much of its population—and left the Confederacy with a far less defensible border. By firing on the flag, Confederate forces also guaranteed that in the North, both the Democrat and Republican parties would enter the war united in purpose. As Stephen A. Douglas put it, there could only be two parties now: patriots and traitors. Asked how many men were coming from Massachusetts, one volunteer had a ready answer: "All of us." The West, a reporter wrote, was "one great Eagle-scream."

Civilians Demand a Total War

Both sides filled their armies almost instantly. Not wanting to lie, boys eager to enlist, yet below the minimum age requirement, would write the number 18 on a piece of paper that they then put in their shoe, so that they could tell officers, "I am *over* 'eighteen'"— which, in a technical sense, they were. As Lincoln's proclamation revealed, many Americans assumed a quick, exhilarating war with one battle deciding things. Neither side was prepared for battle though. The navy ranged from measly (Federal) to nonexistent (Confederate). Neither army had a general staff or accurate topographical maps. With only two armories, the United States could not supply enough working rifles for its forces. Half of its older model muskets could not even be fired. Recruits marching to their barracks found their quarters sitting before them as piles of lumber, waiting to be built. Commanders on both sides strove heroically to put the first rudiments of discipline into men wearing kilts, coonskin caps, and peacetime attitudes. Civilians on both sides demanded speedy action. "Forward to Richmond!" cried Horace Greeley, echoing northern sentiment for a swift capture of the new Confederate capital.

The first test of strength came on July 21, 1861, near a creek called Bull Run at the town of Manassas Junction, Virginia, 25 miles from Washington. Everyone knew the battle was coming. Spectators with picnic baskets followed the Union army out of Washington to watch from the surrounding hillsides. Undertrained, untested troops fought blindly. Told to "yell like furies," Confederate soldiers on the charge did, and the "Rebel yell" caused as much alarm as their bayonets. The arrival of General Joseph Johnston's Confederate reinforcements, not well-laid strategy nor strength of will, sent the Union troops running. The winners were too disorganized to follow up on their victory. Many of them had been withdrawing already, sure that the fight had been lost. Thereafter, both sides realized that this would be no 90-day war. On the Union side, it must depend on a well-trained army of three-year volunteers, and among Confederates, on soldiers "for the duration."

What Were Soldiers Fighting For?

Recruits came, kept on coming, and even on the losing side, stuck by it to the bitterest end. For Confederate soldiers, the will to fight had unique aspects. They battled quite literally to protect their soil, homes, and families in ways that had no parallel for Union men outside the border South. Most recruits took for granted that they were fighting to preserve slavery. Slaveholders and their sons were far more likely than yeomen to tie the institution to the Confederacy's reason for being. Troops from areas where slavery was relatively unimportant, like parts of North Carolina, were less enthusiastic about the war than were troops from South Carolina, where slaves outnumbered free whites. Still, nonslaveholders made up a majority of Confederate troops. They, too, felt that they had a stake in the institution. Small farmers cherished the rights of property as much as large planters. Many shared in plantations' prosperity and most looked to the day when they might own a slave themselves. In most Confederate minds, white equality depended on black inferiority. To end the institution was to degrade all but the aristocracy and bring on the horrors of race war.

The similarities between the opposing forces' motives were just as important as the differences. The "spirit of 1776" loomed large in the letters and diaries of Confederate soldiers. They saw themselves fighting to preserve the rights and liberties that their forefathers had won from Great Britain. Federal troops, too, thought themselves the exclusive protectors of America's revolutionary heritage and the country's mission as a "beacon of hope to the nations of the world." They fought in defense of northern society in general. Like southerners, they predicted that defeat would make them "perfect slaves" of the winner. On both sides, soldiers' fervor drew on the feeling in the communities they had left behind. With neighbors shouldering arms alongside them, a recruit knew that any faint-heartedness on his part would be reported home. If his community backed the war, desertion would disgrace his family. War only intensified enlisted men's commitment to the cause and to those who had endured the hardships and the perils alongside them. Moving into enemy territory only confirmed beliefs that each side had about the other being a different people and an inferior civilization.

"Yank" (North) and "Reb" (South) came to respect each other's courage and grudgingly admitted the sincerity of their beliefs, but fighting each other only deepened their

STRUGGLES FOR DEMOCRACY

The Citizen Soldier Learns a Profession

Many a Union commander envied his Confederate counterpart. To hear them tell it, Confederate recruits, coming from a society where deference taught inferiors their place, possessed unquestioning obedience to orders and were skilled at riding, shooting, and drill. Yankee boys, by contrast, were pathologically individualistic—at times almost ungovernable. Democracy had made them so, and that northern notion that any man was just as good as any other, no matter what official rank he held.

In reality, most enlistees on both sides were wholly unready for war and determined to give total subordination to nobody. West Point guaranteed the professional army a top-flight set of officers and engineers, but enlisted men almost never rose beyond private. Just about any job in civilian life paid better than seven dollars a month and got more respect. Every town had private militia companies formed by their members and setting their own rules for themselves, but most of them never saw action off the parade ground, unless they created it themselves in the local saloon after dismissal. They put on a fine show during holiday processions, each regiment designing its own uniforms. As forces poured into Harpers Ferry, John Brown could hardly have complained about the lack of local color. The Richmond Volunteers wore gray, the Valley Continentals yellow, the troops from Alexandria showed up in cerulean, and those from southwestern Virginia in crimson. Militia elected their own officers and obeyed them when they felt like it. During the Black Hawk War, Abraham Lincoln found that out while commanding a company. At his very first order, the men chorused, "Go to hell!" and their bold attacks on the whiskey supply got Lincoln court-martialed for his inability to control his men.

Both armies depended almost entirely on untrained volunteers, enthusiastic about everything but drill. They addressed officers by their first names, or less complimentary terms. At the first battle of Bull Run, there was no uniformity of uniforms, with so many volunteers having come from militia units that chose their wardrobe for themselves. Federal troops wearing West Point gray joined others in army blue against Confederates in blue. The Confederate stars and bars looked confusingly like the Stars and Stripes, but other companies carried banners with stars or pelicans. An Irish force bore a green flag with a golden harp. Convinced that the cunning Yankees would attack disguised as Rebels, some Confederates took no chance and fired at anybody wearing the same color uniform as theirs. One charge dissipated when the attackers took a break to feed off nearby berry bushes.

Given the varying levels of individuality and lack of respect for authority, Confederate and Union commanders needed time to whip their unpromising troops into shape and establish a degree of conformity. Experience and special military boards weeded out some of the most unfit officers. Constant drill trained volunteers to load, fire, and withdraw as one. By 1862, soldiers on both sides had become efficient killing machines, ready to march even toward near-certain death. Ordered against entrenchments at Cold Harbor, Union soldiers obeyed silently; but they wrote their names on paper scraps and pinned them to their shirts, so that when the shooting ceased, their bodies could be identified.

All the same, this remained a democratic war, dependent on the people's consent, even that of enlistees. Lincoln's generals included not just West Point professionals but politicians, Democratic and Republican, whose influence with members of their party made them dangerous to dismiss. As for the soldiers, they continued to think like civilians, if on a lethal holiday. Nearly all of them would muster out eagerly at war's end, some of them before the official dismissal came. And in 1864, still in the service, the Union volunteers voted for president the same as ever, except in one particular. Most of them, even onetime Democrats, cast their ballots for Lincoln.

sense that their own side was in the right. Union soldiers accused Confederates of shelling hospitals, stripping the battlefield dead, bayoneting the wounded, and collecting enemies' skulls as souvenirs. Confederates knew for a fact that "the base and amorous race of Puritans" degraded women and fraternized with blacks. Riding across a battlefield littered with "decapitated bodies and mutilated remains of all kinds," an artilleryman's heart warmed to see "glorious heaps of Yankee dead."

If Union soldiers blamed slavery for the war, few of them started out aiming for its destruction. That came only as the cost of saving the nation mounted and their own bitterness against the enemy and commitment to the cause intensified. By the end of the conflict, most northern soldiers believed that to restore the Union and destroy the Confederacy they would have to abolish slavery as well.

Mobilizing for War

A long war required very different things from both sides than a brief test of strength. By the end of the war, approximately 2.1 million men had served in the Union armed forces and another 900,000 in the Confederacy. To raise and sustain such numbers was an immense political and social problem. To feed, clothe, and arm them was an equally immense technological problem. To pay for such armed forces was an immense economic problem. The Civil War became a test of the competing economies of the North and the South (see Figure 14–1).

The Military Scorecard

In an even fight, Confederates declared, Federal soldiers stood no chance. "Just throw three or four shells among those blue-bellied Yankees and they'll scatter like sheep," a North Carolinian predicted. They learned differently soon enough, but on both sides a myth took hold that Southerners made better natural soldiers. Unlike northern city boys, they had been virtually born in the saddle with a musket grafted to their hand. When it came to shooting accurately, riding, or taking orders, they would have a distinct advantage. There was some truth in the stereotyping. More southerners had gone to

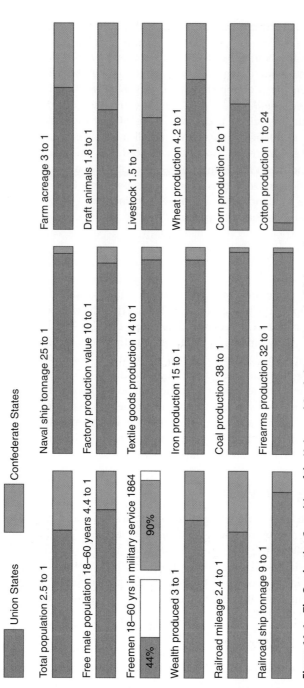

Union States

Confederate States

Total population 2.5 to 1

Free male population 18–60 years 4.4 to 1

Freemen 18–60 yrs in military service 1864

44%   90%

Wealth produced 3 to 1

Railroad mileage 2.4 to 1

Railroad ship tonnage 9 to 1

Naval ship tonnage 25 to 1

Factory production value 10 to 1

Textile goods production 14 to 1

Iron production 15 to 1

Coal production 38 to 1

Firearms production 32 to 1

Farm acreage 3 to 1

Draft animals 1.8 to 1

Livestock 1.5 to 1

Wheat production 4.2 to 1

Corn production 2 to 1

Cotton production 1 to 24

Figure 14-1   The Productive Capacities of the Union and Confederacy Not only did the northern economy dwarf the South's industrial capacity, it also outpaced southern agricultural production in everything but cotton.

military academies, and their West Point officers brought skill and discipline to the Confederate army that the Union's West Pointer alumni struggled to match.

According to secessionists, slavery provided another advantage. Slave labor manned the arms factories and the Tredegar Iron Works, dug lead for bullets, did teamster duty and built the entrenchments that Confederates stood behind. Every black field hand raising food crops freed a white man for military service. Every working slave allowed another southerner to shoulder a gun.

The South saw its greatest advantage in being able to play defense. To win, it did not need to strike the North, destroy the Union army, or wipe out the North's industrial capacity. It simply had to hold its ground. With sources of supply close at hand and a friendly civilian population to support them, the Confederacy could do more with less. The Federal army needed to subdue and then occupy a domain twice the size of the thirteen original colonies, costing it manpower every step that it advanced. Whatever it needed, its longer supply lines must bring along. One hundred thousand men required 2,500 wagons for their goods. Every day the Federals had to replace 500 horses. In eight months, one army's cavalry had to be completely remounted twice. Defenders had interior lines of supply: that is, they had to carry soldiers and supplies a shorter distance to the periphery than attackers would to bolster their campaign.

None of these advantages worked as well as Confederates expected, however. Most northern recruits came from the countryside. Those unfamiliar with horses or muskets learned quickly enough. The advantage of interior supply lines only applied if both sides had the same ability to move reinforcements from one place to another—if, say, the railroads and vessels to carry materials had been just as available. The South lagged far

Tredegar Iron Works in Richmond, Virginia, 1865 This was the South's largest industrial plant. Because the South lagged so far behind the North in industrial capacity, protecting the Tredegar works was essential to the Confederate war effort.

behind in both. Interior supply lines gave no help at all if the front ranged over thousands of miles and the enemy had the manpower to field multiple armies and thus strike possibly two or three places at once.

Under such conditions, a purely defensive war plan was bound to fail. Morale on both sides required an aggressive strategy, even if the attacker lost more than the defender. A static defense almost always meant a war of maneuver and retreat, giving up southern soil. Fighting lines could surge back, but the slave economy in once-taken land was ruined for good. The Confederacy's best chance would be an "offensive-defensive," letting the Federals advance and then choosing where and how to fight them. As for using slaves, Union leadership pointed its forces in one inescapable direction. "Arrest the hoe in the hands of the Negro," Frederick Douglass admonished, "and you smite rebellion in the very seat of its life."

Nonetheless, the challenge facing the Union was a daunting one. General Winfield Scott's proposal of a blockade, slowly strangling the insurgent South like an anaconda wrapping a victim in its folds, might take years to show results. The North did not have years to spare. Every day the Confederacy survived would add to its legitimacy and the chance of foreign recognition. The "anaconda" strategy, as Lincoln soon realized, must be supplemented by a comprehensive approach. Controlling the Mississippi River would cut the Confederacy in two and prevent west and east from reinforcing or supplying each other. Taking out its ports and few manufacturing centers would remove its capacity to make war. To overcome the advantages of interior supply lines, the Union must field many armies, advancing simultaneously on different fronts. Federal forces must be constantly on the offensive on soil unfamiliar to them and amid an unfriendly white population. They would need unprecedented logistical support to move more goods, and to transport them farther and faster than ever before.

Although challenging, the task was not impossible. The Union not only had means enough to fight three armies at one time, but two *wars*, the second being an intermittent conflict against Indian tribes in the territories. Federal troops broke the Cherokee armies enlisted on the Confederate side; after the war, the government confiscated tribal land in punishment—as well as Cherokee slaves. Minnesota Sioux enraged by treaty-breaking raided farms, murdered hundreds, and emptied twenty counties of white settlers before the army suppressed them. Condemned by military courts, thirty-eight Indians died on the gallows on Christmas Eve, 1862. Troops in the Southwest slaughtered the Navajo sheep herds, leveled their orchards, and marched the tribespeople into government reservations. In 1864, Colorado territorial soldiers under Colonel John Chivington descended on a village at Sand Creek, butchering some 400 Arapahoe and Cheyenne. Reprisals along the frontier forced the US Cavalry's engagement, but none of these conflicts set back the Union war effort.

Union Naval Supremacy

The Union's war effort began at the water's edge. By the end of the war, the Union had built one of the largest and most modern navies in the world, not to be matched in American history until World War II. As the Union navy grew, it shut off commerce from Norfolk to the Rio Grande by establishing a blockade. Blockade runners made their way through it, but with less success every year. One out of ten were taken in 1861 and one out of four two years later. By early 1862, the Union army could bolster the fleet with footholds in North Carolina and Georgia, again thanks to the navy's ability to carry troops where needed. Indeed, in taking river towns like New Orleans and Memphis, the credit belonged to admirals like David Farragut and Andrew Foote. When army-navy communications broke down, as they did in efforts to take Charleston in 1863 and in the Red River campaign in upstate Louisiana a year later, they resulted in fiasco.

In an attempt to thwart Union naval supremacy, the Confederates developed a formidable new weapon designed to bust the blockade. Refitting an old Union ship, the *Merrimack*, the Confederates fastened thick iron plates on the hull. No cannonball or shell could pierce it. Rechristened the *Virginia*, on March 8, 1862 the ironclad ship steamed into Union-controlled waters at Hampton Roads, Virginia, and wrought havoc on helpless Federal vessels. But that night the Union's own ironclad, the *Monitor*, arrived from New York. For most of the next day the "battle of the ironclads" raged, with neither vessel dominating. In reality, the threat that the *Virginia* posed was an illusion because ironclads could not navigate the deep waters where blockade ships waited. After the battle, the *Virginia* slipped up the James River to help defend Richmond. Two months later, the Confederates destroyed it to keep it from capture. The Union, on the other hand, turned out fifty more "monitors," in an effort to increase their naval supremacy.

King Cotton's Failed Diplomacy

The conviction that commerce ruled the world came naturally to the leaders of southern slave society. At the start of the war, Confederate strategists believed they could bring their enemies to heel by starving them of cotton. By keeping their most valuable cash crop from the market, they would bring northern industry to its knees and force England to recognize Confederate independence.

Southerners, however, assumed wrong. They overestimated England's dependence on American cotton and underestimated the strength of Britain's economic ties to the North. With their eyes fixed on European dangers, British leaders had no intention of risking an American war by breaking the Union blockade or granting the Confederacy diplomatic recognition, not even when three in every four cotton-mill workers had lost their jobs or been put on part-time employment. Egypt, India, even Brazil, could help satisfy Britain's needs. Union demand kept flax and woolen manufactories going full-blast, and England did a thriving business in saltpeter, which the North needed for making gunpowder.

Union diplomats like Charles Francis Adams, minister to Great Britain, worked hard to cut off the flow of ships built in British ports as blockade runners or privateers for the Confederates. Late in 1861, a Union navy captain waylaid a British ship, the *Trent*, in Havana, Cuba, and arrested two Confederate commissioners heading for Europe. A gust of anger rose across the Atlantic. Hastily, the Union administration let both men go and disclaimed any responsibility for the seizure. The commissioners got a hero's welcome, but not the foreign recognition of the Confederate government that they had come for. By the time the Confederacy started shipping cotton again in 1863, it had much less to offer. Thanks to the blockade, the 1 million bales of cotton that the Confederacy exported in the last three years of the war were miniscule in comparison to the 10 million they had shipped out in the last three years of peace.

The Political Economy of Total War

Total war required a total commitment of government resources and, for both sides, a broad expansion of authority from what Americans had experienced during peacetime. For all its homage to the idea of states' rights, even the Confederacy built a command economy of unprecedented size.

In the North, unhindered by southern opposition, a Republican Congress pushed through several measures to speed up economic development. The Morrill "War Tariff" raised needed revenue but also raised a wall against foreign competition with American industry. The Morrill Land-Grant College Act aided the establishment of "agricultural and mechanic" institutions, among which would be the nation's largest state university systems. A Homestead Act provided 160 acres of public land free to actual settlers. The Pacific Railroad Act issued a charter and gave money and 100 million acres in land to the Union Pacific and Central Pacific railroads to build a transcontinental line from the Missouri River to California—the first of several endowed and a seven-year task that required 20,000 workers.

To pay for the war, Congress augmented the Morrill tariff with taxes on liquor and tobacco, license taxes on almost every profession, stamp taxes, inheritance and property taxes, and the country's first progressive income tax. It also gave the Treasury authority to issue bonds. With skilled marketing by Jay Cooke's banking house, $2 billion of them were sold. The government also printed over $400 million in paper money, "greenbacks," to meet expenses. A Legal Tender Act declared them good for all debts and payments. In 1863, Congress set up a system for creating nationally chartered banks, empowered to issue bank notes as currency.

Confederate plans to finance the war worked less well. The Richmond government also passed an income tax but found it unenforceable. It levied a property tax and left the states to collect it; the states didn't. With planters objecting to any tax code that fell on them and European investors refusing to lend the new nation any money, the Confederate Congress left the Treasury no option but to grind out $1.5 billion in paper currency. Shinplasters, small-denomination notes, could be found in 250 different varieties, one southerner complained, "and not one dime in silver to be seen." Prices climbed at 10 percent per month. Eventually, Confederate dollars fell to one-hundredth of its face value. To supply the army, the government had to commandeer farmers' crops, mules, hogs, and horses and pay them in worthless currency.

Filling the Ranks—and the Jails

As the war dragged on, volunteering lagged. State governments offered bounties for new enlistees, but by April 1862, the Confederacy had to introduce conscription, compulsory enlistment for military service, covering all males from ages 18 to 35. Five months later, it was extended it to age 45. The Union imposed the draft in early 1863. In each case, conscription stirred deep resentments. Northern draftees could buy their way out of service by paying a $300 commutation fee—a year's income for a day laborer—or hiring someone to enlist in their place. Confederate soldiers fumed when their government unilaterally extended conscription. The southern statute contained a "planter's exemption" freeing one white male from service entirely for every twenty slaves that served. Plantation overseers and planters' sons benefitted as a result of this law. The "twenty-Negro law" incensed small farmers, who complained that the Civil War was a "rich man's war but a poor man's fight." In the North, among those drafted, only 7 percent actually served. Employers bought exemptions to keep their labor supply and draft-insurance societies marketed policies that would hire substitutes. In some working-class districts, 98 percent of eligible men paid their way out of service. But that pay helped subsidize the bounty system, where potential draftees enlisted for as much as $1,000 in state, local, and national incentives.

To carry on the war, the Union and Confederate governments arrested people without warrant and jailed without trial. To crush armed rebellion and dissent, the Confederate army arrested Unionists and executed guerillas after a military court-martial. In the first month of the war, Lincoln secured Maryland by suspending the writ of habeas corpus, by which an accused had the right to release unless specific charges were preferred, and by putting suspected secessionists under lock and key at Fort McHenry. Later, the War Department's provost-marshals rounded up draft resisters. Federal authorities locked up several newspaper editors and even a few judges for discouraging enlistments. Unionist mob violence put antiwar papers out of business, with soldiers smashing the presses and strewing the type in the streets. One speech denouncing federal tyranny led to former Ohio Congressman Clement Vallandigham being arrested, tried by military tribunal, and exiled across Confederate lines. None of these actions suppressed free speech much, however. Most of the thousands of arrests took place near the battlefront, in the border South, and few political prisoners stayed behind bars for long. In the case of *Ex parte Milligan* (1866) the Supreme Court declared military trials illegal where civil courts were open—well after the war was over. Further from the danger zone, Lincoln's critics felt free to accuse him of despotism, call for his assassination, and inform readers that he actually was African American himself.

Sinews of War

At the start of the war, the Union had twice as many railroads per square mile as the Confederacy. It made 97 percent of the country's firearms and more than 90 percent of its boots, shoes, cloth, and pig iron. The South could raise more than enough food to feed its armies and civilian population; it just couldn't deliver it. Its rail system, never as comprehensive as the Union's, started off inadequate and only became more so as the war continued. Rails wore out. Locomotives broke down. Nobody could afford to replace them, nor could anyone in the South make them. With food rotting in warehouses, Confederate soldiers made the Commissary-General "the most cussed and vilified man in the Confederacy," but that did not fill their rucksacks.

Only in firepower did the Confederacy hold its own to the war's end. As head of the Ordnance Bureau that handled the supply of arms and ammunition, Josiah Gorgas proved a wizard of improvisation. From Europe came Enfield rifles, while at home small foundries and armories sprang up. Church bells were melted down for bronze to forge cannons, distilleries gave up their copper to manufacture rifle percussion caps, and Confederates combed battlefields for lead to make new bullets.

Union supplies started out almost as badly. Contractors produced cloth for uniforms so poor that it tore to rags in a heavy rain and shoes barely a week old fell apart, giving the term "shoddy" its present meaning. Thanks to Quartermaster-General Montgomery Meigs, uniforms improved dramatically, even as Confederate ones wore into shreds and patches. Stoves, ambulances, underwear, carts, forage for animals—Meigs came up with them all. In terms of infrastructural strength, the United States Military Railroads agency took over captured southern railroads, refitted them, ran them, and built new ones. By 1865, it was the largest single railroad company in the world, with 419 engines and 2,105 miles of track.

Soldiers on both sides grumbled about food. They talked about beef so full of maggots that they ran it away before cooks could desecrate it and "hardtack" crackers that had to be softened with musket butts before being eaten; others preferred to crumble them into the soup, thus allowing the weevils that managed to infiltrate it to float to the surface and properly cook. As the state of Confederate provisions worsened, however, Union diets improved. Salt pork, dried beans, "hardtack" crackers, and coffee "strong enough to float an iron wedge" were varied with potatoes, fresh meat, dried apples, and molasses. From Gail Borden's plant, cans of condensed milk by the thousands made their way to the front. Canneries sprouted up to provide tinned vegetables. By 1865, the Union army was the best supplied and best fed in the world. As a result, there was less sickness and, among the wounded, higher recovery rates.

The Union had one more intangible asset: its president. Lincoln's homespun humor and lack of polish made many underestimate him, though they usually liked him. Soldiers' nicknames suggested that he was as common as if he were family: "Old Abe," "Uncle Abe," and "Father Abraham." Indeed, the most famous mascot of the war was a Wisconsin regiment's bald eagle, "Old Abe" (who, name aside, was actually a female). Intimates glimpsed anguish behind the laughter and sharp instincts about how far public opinion would let him go. No one thought him a statesman, but he was what the war needed: a flexible politician with a gift for expressing ideas in clear, familiar language and an ability to grasp the larger picture. Patient and self-effacing, Lincoln had the ability to get along with Congress and his Cabinet of prima donnas that Jefferson Davis lacked. Lincoln's first Secretary of War, an unscrupulous, incompetent hack, was forced out, so Lincoln chose one of Buchanan's former Cabinet officers, Edwin M. Stanton. Stanton was a rude, hot-tempered bully and his contempt for Lincoln was no secret. But Lincoln saw Stanton's ruthlessness, aggressiveness, and administrative skill as what the war effort needed. When it came to policy, radicals like Senator Charles Sumner lamented how slowly the president struck blows at slavery, but they knew that the door was always open for them to make their case. Sometimes they convinced themselves that it was their words that had converted him. If Lincoln grew in office, abolitionist Wendell Phillips once said, it was "because they had watered him." When Lincoln lay dying, Sumner and Stanton were among those grieving at his bedside, and it was Stanton who pronounced the epitaph: "Now he belongs to the ages."

The Civil War as Social Revolution

By 1862 the North and the South had built up powerful military machines. At the same time, the North's war aims were shifting to include universal emancipation and the destruction of the southern social system. In the earliest months of the war, Republicans in Congress and the Lincoln administration adopted the view that emancipation was a military necessity, but they restricted emancipation to slaves coming voluntarily into Union lines. Within a year they would shift to a policy of universal emancipation as part of an emerging policy of "hard war," with the seizure or destruction of anything of military value to the enemy. Throughout the South, a civil war erupted within the Civil War.

Union Victories in the West

Across the Appalachians, the Union's war went very well. Confederate forces were driven out of Missouri and, at the battle of Pea Ridge, much of Arkansas, too. A Texas expedition to conquer New Mexico was beaten; only a straggling remnant made it home. Kentucky had tried not to join either side, but when a Confederate army entered the state to secure a vital railroad line, the legislature invited the Union army to repel the invasion. By Christmas 1861, Kentucky was under firm Union control.

Early in February 1862, with the help of naval officer Andrew Foote's gunboats, the Union army under Ulysses S. Grant eliminated the Confederacy's main defenses in central Tennessee by putting its two major rivers in Federal hands. Half-underwater and indefensible, Fort Henry on the Tennessee River fell easily. Ten days later, Grant besieged and took Fort Donelson on the Cumberland River (see Map 14–2). Confederate General Simon Buckner's surrender at Fort Donelson cost the Confederacy not just command of a vital waterway; an entire 13,000-man army was taken prisoner. With control of the two rivers, Federal armies could move as far upriver as Alabama. The Confederate government had to evacuate Nashville, and Lincoln appointed a military governor, Senator Andrew Johnson.

Shambling and soft-spoken, Ulysses S. Grant was a modest man. Slow to complain or make excuses, he was quick to spot an opening on the battlefield and quicker still to take advantage of it. Most of all, he learned from his mistakes. His initiative in moving ahead while superiors spent energy pulling rank on each other made him a northern hero.

However, Grant still had much to learn. Eight weeks after Fort Donelson fell, General Albert Sidney Johnston caught Grant's troops off guard in the woods and fields near Shiloh Church in southern Tennessee. Before the Confederate attack on April 6, Union defenses crumpled into a melee. Ordered to the rear, one wounded soldier reappeared, "Cap'n, give me a gun," he told his company commander, "—this blamed fight ain't got any rear." Where Federal lines held, they bought time for retreating soldiers to reform a line. Throughout the day the Union army was forced steadily backward, almost to the Tennessee River's edge before finding a place to hold. The following morning, Grant led a counterattack that retook all the lost ground. Johnston himself had been killed, the highest-ranking general to lose his life in the war. When the Confederates finally retreated, the two armies had suffered an astounding 23,741 casualties. Grant's victory gave the Union secure control of the upper Mississippi River as far south as Memphis; and Memphis fell in June.

With Confederate forces busy at Shiloh, New Orleans had few defenses beyond two forts on the Mississippi River 75 miles south of the city. It took six days of Yankee bombardment before Union commander David Farragut attempted to break through. In the middle of the night of April 24, his fleet pushed upriver through a blaze of burning rafts and Confederate gunfire that lit up the sky. Within a few days the Confederates evacuated both forts, and New Orleans fell to Union forces. Union victories in the West gave rise to northern optimism that war would be over by summer.

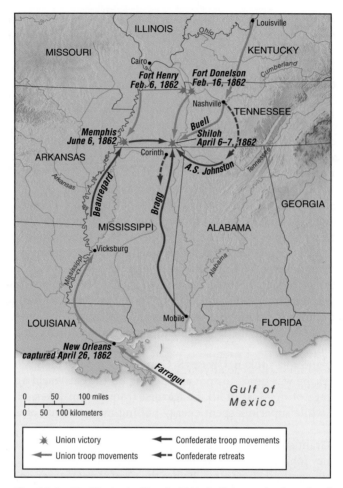

Map 14–2   The War in the West in 1862 As Union armies floundered in the East, northern troops in the West won a decisive series of battles. Here the nature of the war changed. First, General Ulysses S. Grant demanded "unconditional surrender" of the southern troops at Forts Henry and Donelson. Then a bloody battle at Shiloh foreshadowed the increasing brutality of the war. Finally, the western theater produced two of the Union's most effective generals, Grant and William Tecumseh Sherman, and its greatest naval victory, David Farragut's stunning capture of New Orleans.

Richmond Is a Hard Road to Travel

From the beginning, Union strategists trusted that taking the Confederate capital, Richmond, would end the war. That was what Lincoln expected from George B. McClellan as commander of the Army of the Potomac. A crackerjack administrator, with panache and charm, "Little Mac" built a disciplined professional force, restoring troop morale. Most soldiers idolized him and believed that only he could lead them to victory. In fact,

McClellan loved his army too much to use it. Exaggerating the size of his opponents' forces, demanding more troops before he would take the offensive, he treated Lincoln's suggestions with contempt.

As the president's pressure intensified in the spring of 1862, McClellan worked out an elaborate strategy to surround the Confederate army in northern Virginia. Four hundred ships would land 112,000 men south and east of Richmond at Fortress Monroe, on the peninsula between the York and James Rivers. Moving speedily, he could take the Confederate capital before any serious force could stand in his way. But "little Mac" did not move speedily. He dug in at Yorktown and besieged the enemy outposts there. Confederates quickly learned to play to McClellan's fear that he was outnumbered. They moved small numbers of soldiers back and forth to make him think there were more enemy troops than there really were. By the time the enemy slipped away in early May, the Union had lost its head start on Confederate forces under General Joseph E. Johnston.

As the Army of the Potomac inched its way to within five miles of Richmond, it was Johnston's Confederates who struck at Seven Pines on May 31. Both sides took heavy losses. Johnston himself was wounded and replaced by Robert E. Lee, who had the gallantry and reserve of a model southern gentleman. So highly did the military establishment rate Lee that they offered him a Union command before he took his stand with Virginia. The general had no taste for Johnston's war of maneuver and strategic retreat. Daring and aggressive where McClellan was cautious and methodical, Lee not only halted the Union advance in late June at the Seven Days' battle, but also broke McClellan's will to do anything but withdraw south to Harrison's Landing, where the navy could supply his men. Richmond was saved. When "little Mac" found excuses not to take the initiative, Lincoln cobbled together a separate army, under General John Pope, and sent him to take the offensive alone. All swagger and bluster, Pope made no friends among McClellan's officer corps, and he wholly underestimated his adversary. At the second battle of Bull Run (August 29–30), Lee and Stonewall Jackson sent him reeling.

Mistakenly thinking that it would take weeks for Federal forces to regroup, Lee pushed across the Potomac into Maryland. There he assumed Confederate sympathizers would rally to his side, perhaps carrying the state—and with it Washington, DC—out of Union hands. The recruits never came, and with McClellan back in charge, the Army of the Potomac recovered instantly. Before long, Lee's forces were on the run. They were cornered with the Potomac River at their back at Sharpsburg, beside Antietam Creek, on September 17 (see Map 14–3).

McClellan's forces heavily outnumbered Lee's, which had been divided and needed time to reunite. The Union general knew it; a copy of Confederate troop dispositions had fallen into his hands. With that, "Little Mac" vowed, "if I cannot whip Bobby Lee, I will be willing to go home." But when the moment came, McClellan hesitated and temporized. Once engaged, he threw his troops into the fray in waves, keeping tens of thousands in reserve. The delay gave Confederate reinforcements time to arrive. The bloodiest single day in the war ended with nothing gained, but Lee's losses were too great, and he retreated back into Virginia, making it a Union victory. The point was not to send Lee's army back to Virginia but to eliminate it. To Lincoln's exasperation, McClellan made no attempt to destroy the withdrawing army then or later.

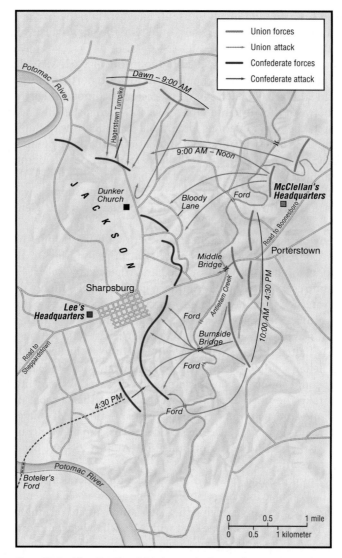

Map 14–3 The Battle of Antietam In September 1862, southern general Robert E. Lee led the Confederacy's first invasion of the North. He was stopped at Sharpsburg, Maryland, by Union troops under the command of George B. McClellan. Antietam was the bloodiest single day of the war, but it was an important turning point for the North. It gave Lincoln the victory he was waiting for to announce the preliminary Emancipation Proclamation.

Lee's advance had been part of a larger Confederate strategy to convince the Union that the war was unwinnable and the European powers that insurgents had formed a nation fit to be recognized. As he moved north, Confederate General Braxton Bragg's army had pushed up from Tennessee into Kentucky, carrying arms for the uprising that would join the commonwealth's fortune with its southern neighbors. No uprising happened. Confederates took the cities of Lexington and Frankfort. They even had time to swear in a Confederate governor before Union forces arrived and forced their retreat. The battle of Perryville stopped the offensive. "Both sides claim the victory—both whipped," a private remarked. Bragg withdrew, with Union forces in leisurely pursuit. The two failed invasions made European recognition unlikelier than ever. They also gave Lincoln the chance to transform the war momentously.

A New Birth of Freedom

Masters could not keep war news from their slaves. House servants passed whites' conversations on to field hands. Literate slaves read newspapers aloud to those who could not read. The "grapevine telegraph," as slaves called it, spread word of military events widely. All told the same story: while the Union claimed to be fighting only to bring the states back to their allegiance, this was really a war to end slavery. By leaving Confederate soil, runaways made themselves free.

Lincoln's inauguration set off a trickle of escapees. As the war began, the trickle grew. Masters under a flag of truce approached Union lines, demanding their slaves be returned under the Fugitive Slave Law. They might not obey Yankee laws, but Yankees were obligated to do so. When three runaways reached Fortress Monroe in Virginia, Union commander Benjamin F. Butler, a hard-nosed Massachusetts lawyer, refused to return them. According to his logic, if he returned them, they would have helped build enemy fortifications. That made them "contraband," property used for war-making purposes. Under the laws of war, belligerents could confiscate contraband goods. The label stuck, and so did the policy. The Administration wired Butler its approval. Two months later, Congress passed the First Confiscation Act, declaring that any slaves used to support the Rebellion were forfeit. The War Department officially added that the "contrabands" did not become *Union* property; they became free. Union commanders could not coax slaves away from their owners or keep runaways not used in war work, but most blacks who reached Federal camps were taken in, with no questions asked. Loyal owners came, asking for their return, often successfully, but increasingly they found it an unhealthy pastime. Eventually, Congress forbade Union troops' use as slave catchers. All these steps constituted the beginnings of "military emancipation."

Meanwhile, Republicans continued to surround the South with a "cordon of freedom." In April 1862, Congress abolished slavery in the District of Columbia and compensated masters for their loss. Two months later it banned the institution from the territories. The Lincoln administration began aggressively prosecuting illegal slave traders, even as Secretary of State William Seward negotiated a treaty with Great Britain to help its suppression of the Atlantic slave trade.

Limiting slavery did not kill it. Deplore the institution though he might, Lincoln had neither the power nor did he wish to force emancipation on the border South. Unionists there depended on unfree labor as much as ever. The last thing the Administration needed was to alienate states vital to the war effort. "Mr. Lincoln would *like* to have God on his side," abolitionists taunted, "but he *must* have Kentucky." Instead, Lincoln tried to ease the transition to free labor. He urged lawmakers to offer incentives to the four border states still in the Union to end slavery gradually, selling their slaves to the federal government. To allay white fears of a free black population in their midst, Lincoln encouraged

Escaping Slaves Designated "contrabands" of war, these Virginia slaves are escaping to Union lines in August 1862. The Lincoln administration took office with a promise not to interfere with southern slavery, but runaways like those pictured here helped push the Union toward a policy of emancipation.

efforts to create an African American homeland in the Caribbean, to which emancipated slaves could go. In theory, between military emancipation and gradual state abolition, slavery might be confined to the Confederate South and thereby be wounded beyond recovery. But neither of the president's strategies led anywhere. Blacks had no intention of leaving their homeland to colonize an alien shore, and every border state rejected Lincoln's plan indignantly.

Neither long-range proposal could remove the enemy's power to make war. As battlefield casualties mounted that spring, the Republican demand for more aggressive blows against Confederate slavery grew louder. In July 1862, Congress passed a Second Confiscation Act. Slaves of disloyal masters in Union-occupied portions of the Confederacy were declared free, and the president was authorized to issue a proclamation doing the same in all unoccupied areas still in rebellion.

Lincoln was ready to do just that. A few days after signing the bill, he arrived at a cabinet meeting on July 22, 1862, with an Emancipation Proclamation. But Secretary of State William Seward warned the president against issuing it yet. Recent military losses in Virginia would make the proclamation seem like an act of desperation. Lincoln agreed to shelve it until the Union had won a battle. Antietam gave him his chance. On September 22, Lincoln issued a preliminary proclamation announcing the emancipation of slaves in areas still in rebellion 100 days later. On New Year's Day, 1863, Lincoln signed his Emancipation Proclamation. Under its terms, the 830,000 slaves in Union-held territory remained in bondage—for the moment. But with the Proclamation, soldiers for the first time could encourage slaves to quit their masters and promise them freedom in return; and every step the army trod turned slave soil into free ground.

Confederate President Jefferson Davis pronounced Lincoln's proclamation the most despicable act "in the history of guilty man." Abolitionists and free blacks rejoiced and celebrated Proclamation Day at gatherings across the North. Other northerners, particularly Democrats, protested making slavery's destruction a war aim. Most Union soldiers shared the mindset of one Illinois volunteer. He and his comrades liked "the Negro no better now than we did then," he allowed, "but we hate his master worse and I tell you when Old Abe carries out his Proclamation he kills this Rebellion and not before."

The Turn of the Tide—Gettysburg and Vicksburg

In vain, Lincoln sought an eastern commander matching the boldness of Lee and Jackson. Weary of McClellan's excuses and delays, Lincoln dismissed him and put Ambrose Burnside at the head of the Army of the Potomac. On December 13, 1862, Burnside threw his forces against Lee's well-entrenched army behind Fredericksburg, Virginia. A terrible, futile slaughter followed. To make matters worse, Burnside moved his men upriver to find a way behind Lee's lines in deep winter. So many soldiers became sick and died in the "Mud March" that the offensive was cancelled. One sufferer spoke for all his fellow soldiers when he complained that thanks to that winter's mishaps, "patriotism has oozed out through the pores." Only "the thought of their families," another wrote, "keeps them from suicide."

With the Army nearly dissolved, Lincoln gave command to "Fighting Joe" Hooker, brave, cocky, and hard-drinking, who may have saved the Army. He restored its morale, improved its food and housing, and imposed discipline. He made the Union cavalry the Confederates' match. One of his officers devised the lights-out bugle call known as "Taps." But in May 1863, moving against Confederate forces, Hooker lost his nerve at Chancellorsville. Lee and Jackson not only bluffed him into yielding the initiative, but in a daring move, they smashed the far end of his lines. With all the fight drained from him, Hooker ordered a retreat, but Lee's victory came at high cost. General Stonewall Jackson was among the thousands killed.

Hoping to deal a fatal blow to the Union's will to fight or at least supply his troops off the fat of the land, Lee crossed the Potomac in June and headed north. Seizing livestock, shoes, and kidnapping free blacks to sell as slaves, Confederates may have aimed to take Harrisburg or Baltimore. The Union army, however, now under General George Meade, caught up with them first, on July 1, in southern Pennsylvania (see Map 14–4) for what proved to be a decisive battle. Pushed south of Gettysburg that first day, Union forces made their stand on a line of hills. They chose their ground well. Confederate forces could neither flank nor dislodge them. On the third day of fighting, Lee gambled on an all-out drive on his enemy's center at Cemetery Ridge. That charge across nearly a mile of open ground broke against Union lines, at such cost of life that Lee had to retreat to Virginia. With more than a third of his force lost, his army would never recover. To Lincoln's perplexity, Meade's exhausted forces were unable to cut off the enemy's escape.

Even as Lee forded the Potomac River, the Confederacy lost its last important bastion along the Mississippi River. After months of effort and a prolonged siege, Grant

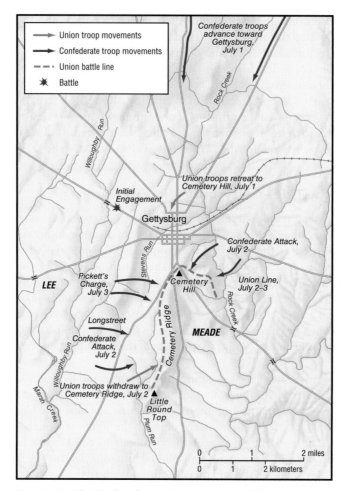

Map 14–4   The Battle of Gettysburg, July 1–3, 1863 In three extraordinary days in Gettysburg, Pennsylvania, the Union army turned back Lee's second invasion of the North. The Union victory, combined with equally important successes in the West at the same time, turned the tide of the war in the North's favor. At the dedication of a military cemetery at Gettysburg a few months later, Lincoln articulated his most profound justification for waging war against the South.

starved Vicksburg into surrender, taking an entire 30,000-man army prisoner. When Port Hudson gave up soon after, the entire river fell into Union hands. Midwesterners could ship their crops out, federal troops landed anywhere along either shore, and Confederate forces in the west were helpless to aid their eastern comrades. Much of Mississippi and nearly two thirds of Tennessee were irretrievably lost.

Despite his disappointment with Meade's failure to pursue and destroy the Army of Northern Virginia, Lincoln grasped the significance of the Union victories. In November, he dedicated a military cemetery at the Gettysburg battlefield. There he

Gettysburg—The Aftermath The bodies of dead soldiers litter the battlefield at Gettysburg. Shortly thereafter, workers rushed to bury the corpses in time for the dedication of the battlefield as a military cemetery. Lincoln's powerful address promised "a new birth of freedom—and that government of the people, by the people, for the people, shall not perish from the earth."

articulated a profound justification of the Union war effort. The Civil War, Lincoln said, had become a great test of democracy and of the principle of human equality. The soldiers who died at Gettysburg had dedicated their lives to those principles, the president noted. It remained only "for us the living" to similarly "resolve that these dead shall not have died in vain—that this nation, under God, shall have a new birth of freedom—and that government of the people, by the people, for the people, shall not perish from the earth."

Emancipation in Practice

That new birth of freedom showed itself clearest in the breakdown of slavery. By the time Lincoln issued the Emancipation Proclamation on January 1, 1863, the Union had been freeing slaves and slaves had been freeing themselves for more than a year, but the pace quickened at once. Instead of entering Union lines by the hundreds, "contrabands" arrived by the thousands. Commanders built sprawling camps across the South to house them. With food and shelter often lacking at first and epidemics in abundance, newcomers often fell sick. Some died and a few made their way back home again. Gradually, the army improved conditions. Across the Potomac from Washington, DC, the Arlington estate formerly owned by Robert E. Lee's family housed "Freedman's Village," a model camp with a school, hospital, and cemetery that would later become Arlington National Cemetery. Most of the camps proved to be way stations on the route to other destinations. Some freed people headed north to work Midwestern fields. Far more moved to Union-occupied plantation country to work as contract labor raising the cotton that northern mills required.

Young black men had another option: they could don the blue uniform of the Union. African Americans had served in the American Revolution and the War of 1812, but the army had refused their services. Now it welcomed them. By war's end, 186,000 African American men had signed up, with 134,411 recruited in the South. That equated to about one Union soldier in ten. After initial doubts, Lincoln quickly discovered their worth. "The bare sight of 50,000 armed and drilled black soldiers upon the banks of the Mississippi," he said in March 1863, "would end the rebellion at once." He was wrong, but their numbers tipped the balance of northern and southern forces decisively in favor of the Union army, contributing to the Confederate disadvantage.

Black soldiers suffered unequal treatment in the army. At first, they received less pay than whites: ten dollars a month with three deducted for their clothing, rather than thirteen with a clothing allowance included. They fought under white commissioned officers almost exclusively. Some Federal soldiers never got used to serving with African Americans. One general let them spearhead a hopeless charge, explaining, "we may as well get rid of them one time as another." Confederates were likelier to kill them than take prisoners, and enslaved many that they captured. Still, for African Americans, fighting for their race's emancipation was exhilarating. Northerners were moved at the courage they showed before the entrenchments of Port Hudson and Fort Wagner, where two in every five were killed or wounded. "A shell would explode and clear a space of twenty feet," a survivor recalled, and "our men would close up again." Black soldiers were an edifying spectacle for those still enslaved, but to white southerners, their worst nightmare had come true. Confederate prisoners confessed "it was the hardest stroke that there cause has received. . . . Not a few of them [said] that they would rather fight two Regiments of White Soldiers than one of Niggers. Rebel Citizens fear them more than they would fear

Company E, 4th United States Colored Infantry, at Fort Lincoln, Washington, DC, 1865 African Americans serving in the Union army symbolized the revolutionary turn the Civil War took with emancipation as the policy of the North. Despite overwhelming loss of life by the African American troops, their bravery impressed many northerners and helped change white attitudes about the goals of the Civil War.

Indians." By the end of the war, fifteen black soldiers and eight sailors were awarded the Congressional Medal of Honor.

The War at Home

African American troops could not end the rebellion "at once," as Lincoln hoped. The war persisted for two more years, and as body counts rose and hardships mounted, civilians in the North and the South began to register their discontent.

The "Butcher's Bill"

Bad generalship cost some lives, but the new technology of war did much more. Instead of the old smoothbore musket, soldiers carried rifled muskets; instead of the round ball that guns once fired, they shot a grooved, oblong bullet, the Minie Ball, that could be pushed down the barrel loose and spun out tight. Those two innovations made muskets more accurate and powerful enough to kill at half a mile, rather than the 100-yard range they had had up until then. The old charge across an open field became far more lethal, and against defenders behind walls or standing in trenches, suicidal. "It was not war, it was *murder*," one general commented after a failed assault on Union positions at Malvern Hill. More than half the Confederate generals were wounded or killed. Two days at Shiloh cost as many casualties as in the country's last three major wars combined. Over 50,000 were killed or wounded at Gettysburg, 35,000 at Chickamauga, and nearly 25,000 at Murfreesboro. In every encounter the "butcher's bill," as newspapers called it, was agonizingly high.

Disease, however, killed far more soldiers than combat. Crowded into camps, recruits fell prey to every contagious disease: measles, mumps, and influenza. Malaria and dysentery were also major killers. Soldiers gave diarrhea joking names like "the Richmond Quick-Step," but it often debilitated and sometimes killed. Unacquainted with germ theory or the need for sterilization, overworked medics found themselves overstretched in tending to the wounded while the battle raged. Injured men might lie on the field for five days before help reached them. A bone-shattering bullet wound carried almost certain infection and probably gangrene as the flesh rotted—invariably fatal. Only immediate amputation could save a life, usually with no anesthetic stronger than whiskey and no surgical tool but a lumberman's saw. Many patients died.

Despite the circumstances, medical conditions improved, more in the North than in the South. At the war's outbreak, the Union had 98 medical officers and the Confederacy had 24. Four years later, 15,000 surgeons tended the armies and over 350 general hospitals handled their care. Many women volunteered their services as nurses. The United States Sanitary Commission, a private organization led by men but inspired by Elizabeth Blackwell, the first woman physician in America, and staffed by thousands of other women, supplied meals and lodging for convalescent soldiers. It sent commissioners to regimental camps to advise them about drainage and keeping the water supply clean. General McClellan is credited with setting up the first ambulance corps to carry the wounded from the field, which became a model for other nations. These medical reforms improved conditions notably. In the Mexican war, disease killed seven

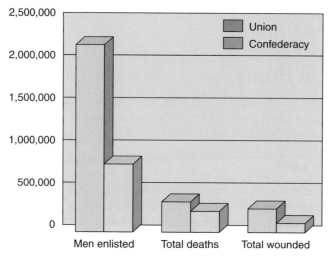

Figure 14–2   Casualties of War

soldiers for every one killed in fighting. In the Civil War, the ratio was two to one (see Figure 14–2).

Discontent on Both Sides

The longer the war went on, the louder criticism grew on either side, and military setbacks gave it real urgency. In the North, Democrats splintered. Some War Democrats like Senator Andrew Johnson of Tennessee and General Benjamin Butler supported the Administration, emancipation included. Most members of the party blamed Republicans for not making the compromises that would have prevented a war. When Lincoln claimed the right to suspend the writ of habeas corpus and institute a draft, Democrats protested bitterly. Every new power the government took carried the country further from the "farmer's republic" that Thomas Jefferson had made, based on liberty and local control. Copperheads, as Peace Democrats were known, went further. In Lincoln they saw a would-be tyrant, in his government a plundering expedition, and in emancipation a deliberate strategy to prolong the war indefinitely while privileged interests lined their pockets at farmers' expense. War, Copperheads argued, only deepened the bitterness between Americans. Negotiation alone could restore the Union. In the 1862 off-year elections, Democrats made gains in Congress and carried Midwestern legislatures. There, enemies of the war threatened to withhold troops.

With inflation outpacing their wages and blacks competing for their jobs, day laborers and unskilled workers resented a draft that the rich could pay their way out of; in their view, unprivileged whites were forced to die in order to make blacks free. Riots erupted in Boston and other cities, the worst of which took place in New York City on July 13, 1863, and lasted four days. Protestors wrecked recruiting stations and draft offices. As the disorder continued, the crowd's composition changed and so did its targets. Mobs went after well-dressed "$300 men" (in reference to the $300 commutation fee men could pay to avoid conscription). They smashed the job-destroying, grain-loading elevators. Irish Catholics burned Protestant churches and missions. Only newly invented Gatling machine guns saved Horace Greeley's New York *Tribune* building from attack. Blaming blacks for the war, whites beat or killed any that crossed their path. At least 12 African Americans were lynched and the Colored Orphan Asylum went up in flames. Troops had to be called in to quell the New York City draft riots. By the time order was restored, over 100 people had died, 74 of them rioters.

In the Confederacy, hardships deepened as the war went on. Due to lack of funds, rural schools and many colleges closed. Short on usable paper, newspapers cut their size or printed on whatever was handy, including wallpaper. The 80 percent inflation rate that the Union suffered over the course of the war was manageable compared to the Confederacy's 9,000 percent increase, which was not. With flour selling for $425 a barrel, potatoes for $25 a bushel, and a ham for $350, once-affluent people just barely scraped by, and poorer ones faced real want. The prosperity of the profiteers only made the contrast more glaring. With wheat scarce for bakeries and abundant for distilleries, angry women led food riots in Richmond and Mobile, taking army supplies for themselves. Women wrote desperate letters to their husbands and sons in the Confederate armies, begging them to come home and rescue their families from the threat of starvation. Soldiers "cannot be expected to fight for the government that permits their wives and children to starve," one officer warned.

For the most part, however, they did fight. Ill-equipped and beleaguered, Confederate troops signed up willingly when their enlistments ran out. "No amount of poverty seems to shake their faith," a Union general marveled. Most whites blamed the North for their sufferings, and Lincoln's emancipation policy only reinforced their belief that their very lives depended on victory. Some, Jefferson Davis and Robert E. Lee among them, took the cause so to heart that by early 1865 they were prepared to arm slaves and promise them their freedom if they would "fight for their homes and country."

Even so, the Confederate government faced intense, often crippling criticism. Southerners protested every infringement on states' rights. Planters seethed when authorities burned private stores of cotton and impressed slaves into service without payment. Farmers despaired, as their own army raided the countryside, collecting fodder, mules, and crops for the war effort. It left behind fistfuls of documents acknowledging debt not worth the paper they were printed on. When, faced with swelling resistance, Davis suspended the writ of habeas corpus, the same cries of tyranny that greeted Lincoln rose against Confederate authority.

Conscription and centralization stoked fierce conflict and several state governors, in particular Joseph E. Brown of Georgia and Zebulon Vance of North Carolina, took matters into their own hands. Brown and Vance were loyal Confederates. They mobilized the state's power to relieve civilian want, and like most states, taxed property and slaves to do it, but their complaints gave the Confederate president endless headaches. Jefferson Davis received more blame than he deserved for Confederate failures, while Lee got the credit for its successes. With no robust two-party system like the North's to compel discipline, Congress bickered, dithered, and undermined Cabinet officials' credibility. As a result, Davis went through four secretaries of state, six secretaries of war, and five attorneys-general in four years.

Draft resistance in the Confederacy went beyond anything the Union had experienced. In eastern Tennessee, one newspaper reported that of over 25,000 conscripts enrolled, only 6,000 showed up at roll call. In Alabama, the governor confessed enforcement of the conscript law "a humbug and a farce." Nor did the North face any resistance movement openly supporting the other side. In the mountains of eastern Tennessee and western North Carolina, where hostility to the Confederacy was widespread, savage guerrilla warfare erupted. Partisan bands burned bridges and bushwhacked Confederate cavalry sent to hunt down deserters.

Union Victory at Terrible Cost

A crippled Confederacy nonetheless sought desperately to maintain itself. At the same time, northern society seemed stronger than ever. Amidst the most ferocious fighting ever witnessed on North American soil, the commander in chief ran for reelection to the presidency and won.

Grant Takes Command

During the summer of 1863, Union forces under William S. Rosecrans pushed Braxton Bragg's Confederate troops out of central Tennessee. Bragg retreated east to Chattanooga, a critical rail terminal. On September 19 the two armies met at Chickamauga Creek. The name, meaning "River of Death," earned its name over the next two bloody days, before Union forces were routed, nearly destroyed, and penned up in Chattanooga. Put in charge of all the Union's western armies, Grant opened supply routes to feed a starving army and in November launched an attack on Bragg's defensive line along the crest of Missionary Ridge. Thrown off the high ground, Confederates had no defensible position left in Tennessee. They were pushed into Georgia, with most of the cotton kingdom west of that virtually out of the fight.

In Grant, Lincoln saw the indomitable spirit he had been looking for. In March 1864 he gave the general charge of the entire Union army. Grant decided on a coordinated strategy, national in scope: heading the Army of the Potomac, he would confront Lee's Army of Northern Virginia while William T. Sherman took on Joseph E. Johnston's troops in Georgia. If he could not beat his opponent, he could keep him from reinforcing Johnston's army.

No Turning Back: Hard War in an Election Year

The "Overland campaign" that spring was like nothing Americans had ever seen, with hard marching and fighting every day. Grant and Lee's forces first collided on May 5 and 6, 1864, in the thick woods and clearings near Chancellorsville. Appropriately called the Wilderness, the terrain made it difficult to see for any distance and impossible for armies to maintain strict lines. Entire brigades got lost. In some places, shellfire set the woods aflame and wounded men burned to death. Two days of fighting cost the Union 17,000 casualties and the Confederates 11,000.

Grant, however, did not withdraw. With smoke still rising from the Wilderness, he turned his forces south, trying to get between Lee's army and Richmond. Only then could he make the Confederate army fight on ground of the Union's own choosing. He did not move fast enough though. When Lee got to Spotsylvania Court House first, a fresh battle ended in 18,000 Union and 12,000 Confederate casualties. The culmination in a campaign of pursuit and assault came on June 3 just outside Richmond when the

Army of the Potomac broke against Confederate defenses near Cold Harbor. Bodies piled on top of bodies; 7,000 Union men were killed or wounded, most in the first 60 minutes of fighting. The armies moved south yet again, but when Lee secured the rail link at Petersburg (critical to the defense of Richmond), Grant settled in for a prolonged siege. More than 50,000 Union men were killed or wounded. Lee's forces had lost fewer, but he had fewer to spare. He understood that with his army pinned down, defeat was only a matter of time. Still, it was not yet destroyed and Richmond stood untaken. As far as civilians could tell, the war was at a standoff, and the presidential election barely four months away.

That was one peril that the Confederate war effort did not have to face. Jefferson Davis had a six-year term and no need to submit his program to the people to be voted up or voted down. Regular elections and a robust, competitive two-party system complicated the Union's conduct of the war. It was not by chance that Lee's first advance north came just before the 1862 elections, when a Confederate victory might persuade northern voters that Lincoln's war was unwinnable, nor that his second in 1863 came when Union reverses might have elected antiwar Democrats in Ohio and Pennsylvania. The longer Grant took, the deeper northern voters would plunge into despair and the more likely it was they would demand a change.

By late summer, Democrats could almost taste victory. That August, they nominated George McClellan for president. The Chicago platform denounced Lincoln for usurping power and violating Americans' cherished liberties. Confederates deluded themselves that a McClellan victory meant recognition of their independence. Pronouncing the war a failure, delegates favored an armistice and opening negotiations with the Confederacy, but only as a means of saving the Union. (McClellan quickly disowned the peace plank and Jefferson Davis made kindling of it when he announced that Confederate independence was non-negotiable). In the campaign that followed, Democrats argued that by insisting on emancipation, Lincoln, "the Widow-Maker of the Nineteenth Century," had needlessly prolonged the war. McClellan's supporters made clear that they favored "the Union as it was and the Constitution as it is."

Despite such sentiments, the defeatism and frustration of summer began breaking even before Democratic delegates trooped home. In late August, David Farragut's Union navy took Mobile Bay, the last major Confederate outlet on the Gulf coast. Soon after, Confederate forces withdrew from Atlanta, and Sherman marched in. To cut off Lee's supplies, Grant ordered the destruction of the rich farmland in the Shenandoah Valley. When Jubal Early's forces tried a counterattack, General Philip Sheridan scattered their army. By Election Day, Union victory seemed months away. McClellan won 45 percent of the vote, but his cohorts carried just three states.

Atlanta to Appomattox

A week after Lincoln's reelection, Sherman's men burned half of Atlanta and headed southeast toward the coast destroying anything that could help the Confederate war effort: cotton gins, mills, bridges, and crops, effectively destroying the slave economy. By bringing the war home to civilians, Sherman meant to show them that the war was lost, that no force could stand in the Union army's way. Confederate general John Bell Hood unsuccessfully tried to draw Sherman back by marching his forces into Tennessee. In doing so, he showed the comparative humanity of an approach that tried to end

AMERICAN LANDSCAPE

"Burnwell": Sherman's March from the Sea and the Long-Term Cost of Devastation

Any southerner who thought William Tecumseh Sherman's troops had done their worst in Georgia learned differently when they moved into South Carolina. There, every house was fair game. Lone chimneys, "Sherman's sentinels," stood on emptied landscapes. Iron rails, heated in a fire of railroad ties, were twisted around telegraph poles to make "Sherman's hairpins." "How shall I let you know where I am" a cavalry officer asked the general. "Oh," he was told, "just burn a barn or something." The town of Barnwell, after the army passed through, was nicknamed "Burnwell." If Confederates started the fire that burned Columbia, and, as Sherman later protested, "God Almighty sent the wind," Sherman's men fed the blaze. Here, if anywhere, total war reached its utter fulfillment.

Where the Confederacy's enemies did not wreck it, its friends did. At war's end, Charleston was, in one traveler's words, "a city of ruins, of desolation, of vacated houses, of widowed women, of rotting wharves, of deserted warehouses, of weed-wild houses, of miles of grass-grown streets, of acres of pitiful and voiceful barrenness." The blockade brought the decay. Parting Confederates started the fire that caused the ruins. They did the same in Richmond. The South had lost most of its railroad cars and engines. Depots were gone, along with trestles and bridges. Farmers had lost their fences because one army or the other had needed firewood, but they could take bitter comfort in knowing that the cattle would not get out for

they had been commandeered, too. No longer did southern banks need to operate on reserves of nearly worthless Confederate bonds and paper: the surrender made them completely worthless.

That story of a proud civilization, gone with the wind, became a lasting myth, but that was all it was. Within a year, an Atlanta bustling and booming more than ever rose out of the embers Sherman had left. Within two years, every railroad was running again and some were raising money to expand. Many planters, sure that slavery's fall had ruined them, discovered that they could get along almost as well or even better on freed peoples' labor, so much so that many persuaded themselves that slavery had been a burden on them and they gloried in throwing it off. By 1880, the South grew more cotton than ever before the war, and by 1900 it was home to thriving iron and textile industries as well.

Sherman's march illustrated not just the concept of hard war, but its limits. The wholesale slaughter of civilians, the free rein given to rape and other atrocities, commonplace in the next century, had no place on either side—against white people. Against Indians or Hispanics out west or southern blacks, soldiers threw off restraints. Many ex-slaves following Sherman's troops through Georgia died, some from neglect, others killed almost casually. For all the general's infamy, white southerners had it easy compared to the western Indians he turned his wrath against after Appomattox. Contemporaries knew Sherman as outspoken in his sympathy for the people he had defeated. Not surprisingly, fifteen years after the burning of Atlanta, civic leaders threw a banquet in his honor. He received a hearty welcome even if, as the city's leading editor, Henry Grady would quip, he had been "a mite careless about fire."

the war by destroying property rather than manpower. However, his attack on Union forces at Franklin cost him most of his army and an equally ill-judged assault on General George Thomas's defenses at Nashville almost wiped the Army of Tennessee from existence.

By then, Sherman had reached Savannah, presenting it to Lincoln as a Christmas present. With the new year, his army headed north into the state that Union soldiers blamed for the war. Unlike Georgia, nothing in South Carolina was spared. Plundering freely, taking life rarely, his army crossed into North Carolina before spring and with virtually no resistance.

By March 1865, Grant had cut off Petersburg's last supply lines. With his army dwindling, rife with desertion, Lee had to retreat. Richmond was left defenseless on April 2,

Atlanta in Ruins Much of Atlanta lay in ruins after General Sherman captured and burned the city. The northern general had made a conscious decision to make war "hell" by destroying the property of the southern civilians who supported the war.

1865. The Confederate government fled and Grant's forces pursued Lee's. Cornered near Appomattox Court House and facing a fight against hopeless odds, Lee accepted Grant's terms of an unconditional surrender. Joseph F. Johnston's army in North Carolina would not surrender to Sherman until a fortnight later, but Appomattox meant the real end of the war.

From Emancipation to Abolition

By the end of the war, military emancipation had freed approximately half a million of the South's 4 million slaves. Lincoln and the Republicans believed that those slaves "practically" freed by the war could never be re-enslaved, but the fate of the vast majority still in service remained unclear. Under intense pressure from Washington, six states had abolished slavery, but they could always reinstate it. Slavery remained legal in the rest of the states, including Kentucky and Delaware. If the institution survived the war, the plantations would simply restock themselves with laborers, just as they had after the American Revolution. A legal challenge to Lincoln's power to set anyone free by military authority was a virtual certainty, and the slave owners might even win.

For all these reasons, by 1864 Republicans concluded that only a constitutional amendment could end slavery for good. War Democrats helped carry it through the Senate, but it fell short of the required two-thirds in the House. With the Republican platform endorsing the Thirteenth Amendment, the election gave voters a chance not only to pass on Lincoln but on abolition. His landslide victory gave the Administration momentum; and persuasion, pressure, and patronage helped round up the Democratic support it needed. On January 30, 1865, the House passed the Thirteenth Amendment, which formally abolished slavery. Northern states ratified it at once, and so did several southern ones. That December, Secretary of State Seward announced the Amendment's ratification.

Time Line

▼1860
South Carolina secedes

▼1861
Lower South secedes
Abraham Lincoln inaugurated
First shots fired at Fort Sumter
Upper South secedes, Border South remains
Union declares runaway slaves "contraband"
First battle of Bull Run

McClellan takes command of Army of the Potomac
First Confiscation Act
Trent affair

▼1862
Battles of Fort Henry and Fort Donelson
"Battle of the ironclads"
Battle of Shiloh
Union capture of New Orleans
Slavery abolished in Washington, DC

Homestead Act
Confederacy establishes military draft
Peninsula campaign
Slavery prohibited in western territories
Second Confiscation Act passed by northern Congress
Second battle of Bull Run
Battle of Antietam
Preliminary Emancipation Proclamation
Battle of Fredericksburg

The Meaning of the Civil War

Despite wartime inflation and terrible loss of life, the Civil War years had only strengthened the North's economy. Mechanization allowed northern farmers to increase wheat production, despite losing one-third of the farm labor force to the army. Huge orders for military rations propelled the growth of the canned-food industry. The railroad boom of the 1850s persisted. By contrast, the slave economy was crushed. Much of the South lay in ruins. Thousands of miles of railroad track had been destroyed. One-third of the livestock had been killed; one-fourth of the young white men were dead. In 1860 the North and the South had identical per capita incomes and nearly identical per capita wealth. By 1870 the North was 50 percent wealthier than the South.

The redistribution of political power was equally dramatic. Until 1860, slaveholders and their allies had controlled the Supreme Court, dominated the presidency, and exercised disproportionate influence in Congress. For the rest of the century, every elected president but one had a Union war record. Most justices, Speakers of the House, and all the commanders in the army and navy came from Union states. Until 1861, most people referred to the United States itself as the Union, something more than a federation of sovereignties, but less than a consolidated entity.

Some 750,000 men—maybe as many as 850,000—died during the Civil War. If anything beyond preserving the Union justified such loss, abolition did. In the sacrifices Lincoln glimpsed dimly the divine will, not on the Union's side, but on freedom's, and the war as a chastisement not just of the South but of all Americans for the wrong that slavery had done. "Fondly do we hope, fervently do we pray, that this mighty scourge of war may speedily pass away," he told his listeners. "Yet, if God wills that it continue until all the wealth piled by the bondsman's two hundred and fifty years of unrequited toil shall be sunk, and until every drop of blood drawn with the lash shall be paid by another drawn with the sword, as was said three thousand years ago, so still it must be said 'the judgments of the Lord are true and righteous altogether.'"

▼**1863**
Emancipation Proclamation
Union establishes military draft
Battle of Chancellorsville
Battle of Gettysburg
Vicksburg surrenders
New York City draft riots
Battle of Chickamauga
Gettysburg Address

▼**1864**
Wilderness campaign
Battle of Cold Harbor
Siege of Petersburg begins
Sherman captures Atlanta
Philip Sheridan raids
    Shenandoah Valley
Lincoln reelected
Sherman burns Atlanta and
    marches to the sea
Battles of Franklin and Nashville

▼**1864–1865**
Sherman's march through the
    Carolinas

▼**1865**
House of Representatives
    approves Thirteenth
    Amendment
Lincoln's second inauguration
Lee surrenders to Grant at
    Appomattox
Lincoln assassinated

Conclusion

The president who had led the nation through the Civil War would not oversee the nation's reconstruction. On the evening of April 14, 1865, actor John Wilkes Booth, believing that he was rescuing America from tyranny and "nigger equality," assassinated Abraham Lincoln at Ford's Theater in Washington, DC. Only luck and misgivings kept his co-conspirators from murdering other top government figures as well. Lincoln had puzzled over how to bind the nation anew, but he and Congress had not yet agreed on any particular plan. Would the Union simply be restored as swiftly as possible? Or would the South be refashioned, continuing the revolution begun during the Civil War? Upon Lincoln's death, those questions remained unanswered. That would come as the freed people in the South pressed to expand the meaning of that undelivered "new birth of freedom."

Who, What

Jefferson Davis 416

Ulysses S. Grant 429

Robert E. Lee 431

Abraham Lincoln 420

George B. McClellan 430

William T. Sherman 442

Antietam 431

Appomattox 443

Arlington 437

Blockade 424

Bull Run 419

Conscription 426

Contrabands 433

Cooperationism 416

Draft riots 441

Fort Sumter 416

Gettysburg 435

Hard war 429

King Cotton diplomacy 425

Secession 415

Vicksburg 435

Review Questions

1. What reasons did white southerners give for seceding?

2. What were the relative military advantages of the Union and the Confederacy at the beginning of the war?

3. What made emancipation a "military necessity"?

4. How much antiwar sentiment was there in the Union and the Confederacy?

Critical-Thinking Questions

1. What role did the different economic systems of the free and slave states play in the Civil War?

2. Both the Union and Confederacy suspended civil liberties during the conflict. In your opinion, did the stakes of the war justify such measures? Explain your answer.

3. What were the military merits of Sherman's "hard war" in Georgia and South Carolina? Did the nature of the conflict warrant such a course of action?

For further review materials and resource information, please visit www.oup.com/us/oakes

CHAPTER 14: A WAR FOR UNION AND EMANCIPATION, 1861–1865
Primary Sources

14.1 DANIEL DECATUR EMMETT, "DIXIE" (1850s)

In April 1859, Bryant's Minstrels first performed the song "Dixie" before a New York audience. Its authorship remains disputed. Blackface performer Daniel Decatur Emmett, known also for the songs "Old Dan Tucker" and "Jordan Is a Hard Road to Travel," claimed authorship, but recent scholars think that he may have lifted it from a black acquaintance in his native Ohio. Whoever deserved the credit, "Dixie" swept the country, later becoming the unofficial marching hymn of the Confederacy. When crowds came to the White House to celebrate the war's end, Lincoln asked the band to play it "as our lawful prize."

Oh, I wish I was in de land ob cotton,
Old times dar am not forgotten.
    Look away, look away, look away, Dixie Land!
In Dixie Land, where I was born in,
Early on one frosty mornin'.
    Look away, look away, look away Dixie Land!

Chorus: Den I wish I was in Dixie,
    Hooray! Hooray!
In Dixie Land I'll take my stan',
To lib an' die in Dixie.
    Away, away,
Away down south in Dixie!
    Away, away,
Aaway down south in Dixie!

Dar's buckwheat cakes an' Injun batter,
Makes you fat, or a little fatter.
    Look away, look away, look away, Dixie Land!
Den hoe it down and scratch your grabble,
To Dixie's Land I'm bound to trabble,
    Look away, look away, look away, Dixie Land!

Chorus: Den I wish I was in Dixie,
    Hooray! Hooray!
In Dixie Land I'll take my stan',
To lib an' die in Dixie.
    Away, away,
Away down south in Dixie!
    Away, away,
Away down south in Dixie!

Source: Atlantic Monthly, February 1862, quoted in Henry Steele Commager, ed., *The Blue and the Gray: The Story of the Civil War as Told by Participants* (Indianapolis: Bobbs-Merrill, 1950), vol.1, pp. 561–563, 571–573.

14.2 JULIA WARD HOWE, "THE BATTLE HYMN OF THE REPUBLIC" (1862)

Julia Ward Howe, wife of antislavery reformer Samuel Gridley Howe, came up with "The Battle Hymn of the Republic" after touring an army camp near Washington, DC. The minister accompanying her suggested "some good words" for the tune of "John Brown's Body." That night, "the long lines of the desired poem began to twine themselves in my mind," she wrote. The *Atlantic Monthly* paid her $4 for the submission, which became one of the most celebrated war hymns of the Union.

Mine eyes have seen the glory of the coming of the Lord
He is trampling out the vintage where the grapes of wrath are stored,
He has loosed the fateful lightening of His terrible swift sword
His truth is marching on.

Glory! Glory! Hallelujah!
Glory! Glory! Hallelujah!
Glory! Glory! Hallelujah!
His truth is marching on.

I have seen Him in the watch-fires of a hundred circling camps
They have builded Him an altar in the evening dews and damps
I can read His righteous sentence by the dim and flaring lamps
His day is marching on.

Glory! Glory! Hallelujah!
Glory! Glory! Hallelujah!
Glory! Glory! Hallelujah!
His truth is marching on.

I have read a fiery gospel writ in burnish'd rows of steel,
"As ye deal with my contemners, So with you my grace shall deal;"
Let the Hero, born of woman, crush the serpent with his heel
Since God is marching on.

Glory! Glory! Hallelujah!
Glory! Glory! Hallelujah!
Glory! Glory! Hallelujah!
His truth is marching on.

He has sounded forth the trumpet that shall never call retreat
He is sifting out the hearts of men before His judgment-seat
Oh, be swift, my soul, to answer Him! be jubilant, my feet!
Our God is marching on.

Glory! Glory! Hallelujah!
Glory! Glory! Hallelujah!
Glory! Glory! Hallelujah!
His truth is marching on.

In the beauty of the lilies Christ was born across the sea,
With a glory in His bosom that transfigures you and me:
As He died to make men holy, let us die to make men free,
While God is marching on.

Glory! Glory! Hallelujah!
Glory! Glory! Hallelujah!
Glory! Glory! Hallelujah!
His truth is marching on.

Source: *Atlantic Monthly*, February 1862, quoted in Henry Steele Commager, ed., *The Blue and the Gray: The Story of the Civil War as Told by Participants* (Indianapolis: Bobbs-Merrill, 1950), vol. 1, pp. 561–563, 571–573.

14.3 WALT WHITMAN, "THE GREAT ARMY OF THE SICK" (1863)

The journalist and poet Walt Whitman served as a hospital nurse during the Civil War. What he saw in the hospitals horrified him, and his account about conditions in 1863, lurid as it is, was less appalling than those he withheld from the public. Like most newspaper writers, he needed to moderate his truthfulness with a delicacy that would not offend readers. As a supporter of the war, he also may have reflected that detailing its horrors would only create defeatism among those who knew the truth.

WASHINGTON, Monday, Feb. 23, 1863.

The military hospitals, convalescent camps, &c. in Washington and its neighborhood sometimes contain over fifty thousand sick and wounded men. Every form of wound, (the mere sight of some of them having been known to make a tolerably hardy visitor faint away,) every kind of malady, like a long procession, with typhoid fever and diarrhœa at the head as leaders, are here in steady motion. The soldier's hospital! how many sleepless nights how many woman's tears, how many long and aching hours and days of suspense, from every one of the Middle, Eastern and Western States, have concentrated here! Our own New-York, in the form of hundreds and thousands of her young men, may consider herself here—Pennsylvania, Ohio, Indiana and all the West and Northwest the same—and all the New-England States the same.

Upon a few of these hospitals I have been almost daily calling as a missionary, on my own account, for the sustenance and consolation of some of the most needy cases of sick and dying men, for the last two months. One has much to learn in order to do good in these places. Great tact is required. These are not like other hospitals. By far the greatest proportion (I should say five-sixths) of the patients are American young men, intelligent, of independent spirit, tender feelings, used to a hardy and healthy life; largely the farmers are represented by their sons—largely the mechanics and workingmen of the cities. Then they are *soldiers*. All these points must be borne in mind.

People through our Northern cities have little or no idea of the great and prominent feature which these military hospitals and convalescent camps make in and around Washington. There are not merely two or three or a dozen, but some fifty of them, of different degrees of capacity. Some have a thousand and more patients. The newspapers here find it necessary to print every day a directory of the hospitals; a long list, something like what a directory of the churches would be in New-York, Philadelphia or Boston.

Barracks Adopted by Government

The Government, (which really tries, I think, to do the best and quickest it can for these sad necessities,) is gradually settling down to adopt the plan of placing the hospitals in clusters of one-story wooden barracks, with their accompanying tents and sheds for cooking and all needed purposes. Taking all things into consideration, no doubt these are best adapted to the purpose; better than using churches and large public buildings like the Patent Office. These sheds now adopted are long, one-story edifices, sometimes ranged along in a row, with their heads to the street, and numbered either alphabetically, Wards A, or B, C, D and so on; or Wards 1, 2, 3, &c. The middle one will be marked by a flagstaff, and is the office of the establishment, with rooms for the Ward Surgeons, &c. One of these sheds or wards, will contain sixty cots—sometimes, on an emergency, they move them close together, and crowd in more. Some of the barracks are larger, with, of course more inmates. Frequently, there are tents, more comfortable here than one might think, whatever they may be down in the army.

Each ward has a Ward-master, and generally a nurse for every ten or twelve men. A Ward Surgeon has, generally, two wards—although this varies. Some of the wards have a woman nurse—the Armory-square wards have some very good ones. The one in Ward E is one of the best.

The Patent Office

A few weeks ago the vast area of the second story of that noblest of Washington buildings, the Patent Office, was crowded close with rows of sick, badly wounded and dying soldiers. They were placed in three very large apartments. I went there several times. It was a strange, solemn and, with all its features of suffering and death, a sort of fascinating sight. I went sometimes at night, to soothe and relieve particular cases; some, I found, needed a little cheering up and friendly consolation at that time, for they went to sleep better afterward. Two of the immense apartments are filled with high and ponderous glass cases, crowded with models in miniature of every kind of utensil, machine or invention, it ever entered into the mind of man to conceive; and with curiosities and foreign presents. Between these cases were lateral openings, perhaps eight feet wide, and quite deep, and in these were placed many of the sick; besides a great long double row of them up and down through the middle of the hall. Many of them were very bad cases, wounds and amputations. Then there was a gallery running above the hall, in which there were beds also. It was, indeed, a curious scene at night, when lit up. The glass cases, the beds, the sick, the gallery above and the marble pavement under foot—the suffering, and the fortitude to bear it in various degrees—occasionally, from some, the groan that could not be repressed—sometimes a poor fellow dying, with emaciated face and glassy eye, the nurse by his side, the doctor also there, but no friend, no relative—such were the sights but lately in the Patent Office. The wounded have since been removed from there, and it is now vacant again.

Of course, there are among these thousands of prostrated soldiers in hospital here, all sorts of individual cases. On recurring to my note-book, I am puzzled which cases to select to illustrate the average of these young men and their experiences. I may here say, too, in general terms, that I could not wish for more candor and manliness, among all their sufferings, than I find among them.

Case of J. A. H., of Company C, Twenty-Ninth Massachusetts

Take this case in Ward 6, Campbell Hospital—a young man from Plymouth Country, Massachusetts; a farmer's son, aged about 20 or 21, a soldierly American young fellow, but with sensitive and tender feelings. Most of December and January last, he lay very low, and for quite a while I never expected he would recover. He had become prostrated with an obstinate diarrhœa; his stomach would hardly keep the least thing down, he was vomiting half the time. But that was hardly the worst of it. Let me tell his story—it is but one of thousands.

He had been some time sick with his regiment in the field, in front, but did his duty as long as he could—was in the battle of Fredericksburgh—soon after was put in the regimental hospital. He kept getting worse—could not eat anything they had there—the doctor told him nothing could be done for him there—the poor fellow had fever also—received (perhaps it could not be helped) little or no attention—lay on the ground getting worse. Toward the latter part of December, very much enfeebled, he was sent up from the front, from Falmouth Station, in an open platform car; (such as hogs are transported upon north,) and dumped with a crowd of others on the boat at Aquia Creek, falling down like a rag where they deposited him, too weak and sick to sit up or help himself at all. No one spoke to him, or assisted him—he had nothing to eat or drink—was used (amid the great crowds of sick) either with perfect indifference, or, as in two or three instances, with heartless brutality.

On the boat, when night came and the air grew chilly, he tried a long time to undo the blankets he had in his knapsack, but was too feeble. He asked one of the employees, who was moving around deck, for a moment's assistance, to get the blankets. The man asked him back if he could not get them himself? He answered no, he had been trying for more than half an hour, and found himself too weak. The man rejoined, he might then go without them, and walked off. So H. lay, chilled and damp, on deck all night, without anything under or over him, while two good blankets were within reach. It caused him a great injury—nearly cost him his life.

Arrived at Washington, he was brought ashore and again left on the wharf, or above it, amid the great crowds, as before, without any nourishment—not a drink for his parched mouth—no kind hand offered to cover his face from the forenoon sun. Conveyed at last some two miles by ambulance to the hospital, and assigned a bed, (bed 47, ward 6, Campbell Hospital, January and February, 1863,) he fell down exhausted upon the bed; but the Ward-master (he has since been changed) came to him with a growling order to get up—the rules, he said, permitted no man to lie down in that way with his old clothes on—he must sit up—must first go to the bath-room, be washed, and have his clothes completely changed. (A very good rule, properly applied.) He was taken to the bath-room and scrubbed well with cold water. The attendants, callous for a while, were soon alarmed, for suddenly the half-frozen and lifeless body fell limpsy in their hands, and they hurried it back to the cot, plainly insensible, perhaps dying.

Poor boy! the long train of exhaustion, deprivation, rudeness, no food, no friendly word or deed, but all kinds of upstart airs, and impudent, unfeeling speeches and deeds, from all kinds of small officials, (and some big ones,) cutting like razors into that sensitive heart, had at last done the job. He now lay, at times out of his head, but quite silent, asking nothing of anyone, for some days, with death getting a closer and surer grip upon him—he cared not, or rather he welcomed death. His heart was broken. He felt the struggle to keep up any longer to be useless. God, the world, humanity—all had abandoned him. It would feel so good to shut his eyes forever on the cruel things around him and toward him.

As luck would have it, at this time, I found him. I was passing down Ward No. 6 one day, about dusk (4th of January, I think,) and noticed his glassy eyes with a look of despair and hopelessness, sunk low in his thin pallid-brown young face. One learns to divine quickly in the hospital, and as I stopped by him and spoke some commonplace remark, (to which he made no reply,) I saw as I looked that it was a case for ministering to the affections first, and other nourishment and medicines afterward. I sat down by him without any fuss—talked a little—soon saw that it did him good—led him to talk a little himself—got him somewhat interested—wrote a letter for him to his folks in Massachusetts, (to L. H. CAMPBELL, Plymouth County,)—soothed him down as I saw he was getting a little too much agitated, and tears in his eyes—gave him some small gifts, and told him I should come again soon. (He has told me since that this little visit, at that hour, just saved him—a day more, and it would have been perhaps too late.)

Of course I did not forget him, for he was a young fellow to interest any one. He remained very sick—vomiting much every day, frequent diarrhœa, and also something like bronchitis, the doctor said. For a while I visited him almost every day—cheered him up—took him some little gifts, and gave him small sums of money, (he relished a drink of new milk, when it was brought through the ward for sale.) For a couple of weeks his condition was uncertain—sometimes I thought there was no chance for him at all. But of late he is doing better—is up and dressed, and goes around more and more (Feb. 21) every day. He will not die, but will recover.

The other evening, passing through the ward, he called me—he wanted to say a few words, particular. I sat down by his side on the cot, in the dimness of the long ward, with the wounded soldiers there in their beds, ranging up and down. H. told me I had saved his life. He was in the deepest earnest about it. It was one of those things that repay a soldiers' hospital missionary a thousand-fold—one of the hours he never forgets.

The Field Is Large, the Reapers Few

A benevolent person with the right qualities and tact, cannot perhaps make a better investment of himself, at present, anywhere upon the varied surface of the whole of this big world, than in these same military hospitals, among such thousands of most interesting young men. The army is very young—and so much more American than I supposed. Reader, how can I describe to you the mute appealing look that rolls and moves from many a manly eye, from many a sick cot, following you as you walk slowly down one of these wards? To see these, and to be incapable of responding to them, except in a few cases, (so very few compared to the whole of the suffering men,) is enough to make one's heart crack. I go through in some cases cheering up the men; distributing now and then little sums of money—and regularly, letter-paper and envelopes, oranges, tobacco, jellies, &c., &c.

Official Airs and Harshness

Many things invite comment, and some of them sharp criticism, in these hospitals. The Government, as I said, is anxious and liberal in its practice toward its sick; but the work has to be left, in its personal application to the men, to hundreds of officials of one grade or another about the hospitals, who are sometimes entirely lacking in the right qualities. There are tyrants and shysters in all positions, and especially those dressed in subordinate authority. Some of the ward doctors are careless, rude, capricious, needlessly strict. One I found who prohibited the men from all enlivening amusements; I found him sending men to the guard-house for the most trifling offence. In general, perhaps, the officials—especially the new ones, with their straps or badges—put on too many airs. Of all places in the world, the hospitals of American young men and soldiers, wounded in the volunteer service of their country, ought to be exempt from mere conventional military airs and etiquette of shoulder-straps. But they are not exempt.

Source: Walt Whitman, "The Great Army of the Sick," from the *New York Times*, February 26, 1863, reprinted in Louis P. Masur, ed., *The Real War Will Never Get in the Books*, pp. 258–262, and elsewhere.

14.4 THOMAS BUCKNER, "A THRILLING NARRATIVE FROM THE LIPS OF THE SUFFERERS OF THE LATE DETROIT RIOT" (1863)

In northern cities, opposition to the war and resentment of the draft roused working-class whites to take out their anger against African Americans, who they blamed for the prolonged fighting. One incident took place on March 6, 1863, in Detroit. Later that spring, Thomas Buckner collected and published the reports of eyewitnesses and victims.

Preface by Thomas Buckner

The present state of affairs in relation to the colored people is one of great perplexity, and is not only so on account of the South but also in the North.

There certainly is something mysterious about them. On the one hand, they are being mobbed, and everything that is sacred to a people to make a country or home dear are denied them in many of the large Northern cities. And, on the other hand, they are marching off to the call of the government as if they were sharing all the blessings of the most favored citizens!

And it is equally mysterious to see the bitter opposition that a class of men professing loyalty to the government of the United States should have against the colored soldier going out and facing the cannon's mouth in defense of a government that appears to be unable to give them any protection from the rage of the Rebels in the South or their enemies in the North.

But one thing the colored man knows, that the class of men of the same politics as those South are doing the mobbing North; so they are not only ready to suffer but to die in the cause that promises over 3 million of their race liberty.

Whatever, therefore, our treatment may be so far as the rage of the enemies of freedom may be, whatever, through cowardice, a ruthless mob of such men may inflict upon our people, they will not be deterred from the duty they owe to their God, themselves, and posterity, to do all they possibly can to undo the heavy burdens and let the oppressed go free! At the first blast the clarion of emancipation may give to call them forth in the irrepressible conflict, though their houses be sacked, their wives and children turned out-of-doors naked and destitute, they too well know that the way to glory is the way of suffering: therefore they desire rather to bear a good part in the battlefield rather than to be always exposed to such outrages as slavery entails on any class it has in its dominion.

Report by Thomas Buckner

The mob, in its first appearance to me, was a parcel of fellows running up Lafayette Street after two or three colored men. They then returned back, and in a short time I saw a tremendous crowd coming up Croghan Street on drays, wagons, and foot, with kegs of beer on their wagons, and rushed for the prison. Here they crowded thick and heavy. After this, while I was standing on the corner with half a dozen other gentlemen, a rifle ball came whistling over our heads, after which we heard several shots, but only one ball passing us. In a short time after this there came one fellow down, saying, "I am shot in the thigh." And another came with his finger partly shot off. A few minutes after that another ruffian came down, saying: "If we are got to be killed up for niggers then we will kill every nigger in this town."

A very little while after this we could hear them speaking up near the jail, and appeared to be drinking, but I was unable to hear what they said. This done, they gave a most fiendish yell and started down Beaubien Street. On reaching Croghan Street, a couple of houses west on Beaubien Street, they commenced throwing, and before they reached my residence, clubs, brick, and missiles of every description flew like hail. Myself and several others were standing on the sidewalk but were compelled to hasten in and close our doors, while the mob passed my house with their clubs and bricks flying into my windows and doors, sweeping out light and sash!

They then approached my door in large numbers, where I stood with my gun and another friend with an axe, but on seeing us, they fell back. They approached four times determined to enter my door, but I raised my gun at each time and they fell back. In the meantime, part of the mob passed on down Beaubien Street. After the principal part had passed, I rushed up my stairs looking to see what they were doing and heard the shattering of windows and slashing of boards. In a few moments I saw them at Whitney Reynolds', a few doors below Lafayette Street. Mr. R. is a cooper; had his shop and residence on the same lot and was the largest colored coopering establishment in the city, employing a number of hands regular.

I could see from the windows men striking with axe, spade, clubs, etc., just as you could see men thrashing wheat. A sight the most revolting, to see innocent men, women, and children, all without respect to age or sex, being pounded in the most brutal manner.

Sickened with the sight, I sat down in deep solicitude in relation to what the night would bring forth; for to human appearance it seemed as if Satan was loose, and his children were free to do whatever he might direct without fear of the city authority.

Source: Thomas Buckner, "A Thrilling Narrative from the Lips of the Sufferers of the Late Detroit Riot" (1863), quoted in William Benton, publ., *The Annals of America. Volume 9, 1858–1865: The Crisis of the Union* (Chicago: Encyclopedia Britannica, Inc., 1968), pp. 467–471.

14.5 HENRY CLAY WORK, "KINGDOM COMING" (1862)

As the Union navy approached South Carolina's Sea Islands in late 1861, planters abandoned their estates and fled. The overturning of the social order inspired this song by northerner Henry Clay Work, a white man and popular songwriter of the Civil War era. Phrased in the comic dialect put into blacks' mouths by minstrel-show performers, it seemed to mock the freed people, but the final verse could be read as giving it a more revolutionary message, of blacks taking it into their hands to keep or take freedom, once they had been given the chance to have it.

Say, darkeys, hab you seen de massa,
Wid de muff-stash on his face,
Go long de road some time dis mornin',
Like he gwine to leab de place?
He seen a smokle, way up de ribber,
Whar de Linkum gumboats lay;
He took his hat, an' lef berry sudden,
An' I spec he's run away!

Chorus:
De massa run? Ha, ha!
De darkey stay? Ho, ho!
It mus' be now de kingdom comin',
An' de year ob Jubilo!

He six foot one way, two foot tudder,
An' he weigh tree hundred pound.
His coat so big, he couldn't pay de tailor
An' it won't go half way round.
He drill so much dey call him Cap'an,
And he get so drefful tanned,
I spec he try an' fool dem yankees
For to tink he's contraband.

De darkeys feel so lonesome libing
In de log-house on de lawn,
Dey move dar tings to massa's parlor
For to keep it while he's gone.
Dar's wine an' cider in de kitchen,
An' de darkeys dey'll hab some;
I spose dey'll all be confiscated
When de Linkum sojers come.

De oberseer he made us trubbel,
An' he dribe us round a spell;
We lock him up in de smoke-house cellar,
Wid de key trown in de well.
De whip is lost, de hand-cuff's broken,
But de massa'll hab his pay.
He's ole enough, big enough, ought to known better
Dan to went an' run away.

Source: "Kingdom Coming," from Louis A. Banks, ed., *Immortal Songs of Camp and Field* (Cleveland, OH: 1899), pp. 140–144, quoted in William Benton, publ., *The Annals of America. Volume 9, 1858–1865: The Crisis of the Union* (Chicago: Encyclopedia Britannica, Inc., 1968), pp. 400–401.

14.6 ABRAHAM LINCOLN, SECOND INAUGURAL ADDRESS (1865)

On March 4, 1865, at the start of his second term, President Lincoln gave what remains the shortest inaugural address in history. In it, he strove to explain how a merciful God could have allowed so cruel a war and how, from the first, the saving of the Union had been bound up with the destruction of slavery.

Fellow-Countrymen:

At this second appearing to take the oath of the presidential office there is less occasion for an extended address than there was at the first. Then a statement, somewhat in detail, of a course to be pursued, seemed fitting and proper. Now, at the expiration of four years, during which public declarations have been constantly called forth on every point and phase of the great contest which still absorbs the attention, and engrosses the energies of the nation, little that is new could be presented. The progress of our arms, upon which all else chiefly depends, is as well known to the public as to myself; and it is, I trust, reasonably satisfactory and encouraging to all. With high hope for the future, no prediction in regard to it is ventured.

On the occasion corresponding to this four years ago, all thoughts were anxiously directed to an impending civil war. All dreaded it—all sought to avert it. While the inaugural address was being delivered from this place, devoted altogether to *saving* the Union without war, urgent agents were in the city seeking to *destroy* it without war—seeking to dissolve the Union and divide effects, by negotiation. Both parties deprecated war, but one of them would *make* war rather than let the nation survive; and the other would *accept* war rather than let it perish. And the war came.

One-eighth of the whole population were colored slaves, not distributed generally over the Union, but localized in the Southern part of it. These slaves constituted a peculiar and powerful interest. All knew that this interest was, somehow, the cause of the war. To strengthen, perpetuate, and extend this interest was the object for which the insurgents would rend the

Union, even by war; while the government claimed no right to do more than to restrict the territorial enlargement of it. Neither party expected for the war, the magnitude, or the duration, which it has already attained. Neither anticipated that the *cause* of the conflict might cease with, or even before, the conflict itself should cease. Each looked for an easier triumph, and a result less fundamental and astounding. Both read the same Bible, and pray to the same God; and each invokes His aid against the other. It may seem strange that any men should dare to ask a just God's assistance in wringing their bread from the sweat of other men's faces; but let us judge not that we be not judged. The prayers of both could not be answered; that of neither has been answered fully. The Almighty has His own purposes. "Woe unto the world because of offences! for it must needs be that offences come; but woe to that man by whom the offence cometh!" If we shall suppose that American Slavery is one of those offences which, in the providence of God, must needs come, but which, having continued through His appointed time, He now wills to remove, and that He gives to both North and South this terrible war as the woe due to those by whom the offence came, shall we discern therein any departure from those divine attributes which the believers in a Living God always ascribe to Him? Fondly do we hope—fervently do we pray—that this mighty scourge of war may speedily pass away. Yet, if God wills that it continue, until all the wealth piled by the bond-man's two hundred and fifty years of unrequited toil shall be sunk, and until every drop of blood drawn with the lash shall be paid by another drawn with the sword, as was said three thousand years ago, so still it must be said "the judgments of the Lord are true and righteous altogether."

With malice toward none; with charity for all; with firmness in the right as God gives us to see the right, let us strive on to finish the work we are in; to bind up the nation's wounds; to care for him who shall have borne the battle, and for his widow and his orphan—to do all which may achieve and cherish a just, and a lasting peace, among ourselves, and with all nations.

Source: Abraham Lincoln, "Second Inaugural Address," from Roy P. Basler, ed., *The Collected Works of Abraham Lincoln* (New Brunswick, NJ: Rutgers University Press, 1953), vol. 8, pp. 332–333.

Reconstructing a Nation

1865–1877

AMERICAN PORTRAIT

John Dennett Visits a Freedmen's Bureau Court

John Richard Dennett arrived in Liberty, Virginia, on August 17, 1865, on a tour of the South reporting for the magazine *The Nation*. The editors wanted accurate weekly accounts of conditions in the recently defeated Confederate states, and Dennett was the kind of man they could trust: a Harvard graduate, a firm believer in the sanctity of the Union, and a member of the class of elite Yankees who thought of themselves as the "best men" the country had to offer.

At Liberty, Dennett was accompanied by a Freedmen's Bureau agent. The Freedmen's Bureau was a branch of the US Army established by Congress to assist the freed people. Dennett and the agent went to the courthouse because one of the Freedmen's Bureau's functions was to adjudicate disputes between the freed people and southern whites.

The first case was that of an old white farmer who complained that two blacks who worked on his farm were "roamin' about and refusin' to work." He wanted the agent to help find the men and bring them back. Both men had wives and children living on his farm and eating his corn, the old man complained. "Have you been paying any wages?" the Freedmen's Bureau agent asked. "Well, they get what the other niggers get," the farmer answered. "I a'n't payin' great wages this year." There was not much the agent could do, but one of his soldiers volunteered to go and tell the blacks that "they ought to be at home supporting their wives and children."

A well-to-do planter came in to see if he could fire the blacks who had been working on his plantation since the beginning of the year. The planter complained the workers were unmanageable now that he could no longer punish them. The sergeant warned the planter not to beat his workers as if they were still slaves. In that case, the planter responded, "Will the Government take them off our hands?" The agent suspected that the planter was looking for a way to discharge his laborers at the end of the growing season but before they had been paid. "If they've worked on your crops all the year so far," the agent told the planter, "I guess they've got a claim on you to keep them a while longer."

Next came a "good-looking mulatto man" representing a number of African Americans worried that they would be forced to sign five-year contracts with their employers. "No, it a'n't true," the agent said. They also wanted to know if they could rent or buy land to work for themselves. "Yes, rent or buy," the agent said. But with no horses, mules, or ploughs, the former slaves wanted to know "if the Government would help us out after we get the land." The agent had no help to offer, except for a note from the bureau authorizing them to rent or buy their own farms.

The last case involved a field hand who came to complain that his master was beating him with a stick. The agent told the field hand to go back to work. "Don't be sassy, don't be lazy when you've got work to do; and I guess he won't trouble you." The field hand left but came back a minute later and asked for a letter to his master "enjoining him to keep the peace, as he feared the man would shoot him, he having on two or three occasions threatened to do so."

Most of the cases Dennett witnessed centered on labor relations, which often spilled over into other matters, including the family lives of former slaves, their civil rights, and their ability to buy land. The freed people preferred to work their own land but lacked the resources to rent or buy farms. Black workers and white owners who negotiated wage contracts had trouble figuring out each other's rights and responsibilities. The former masters clung to all their old authority that they could. Freed people wanted as much autonomy as possible.

The Freedmen's Bureau was in the middle of these conflicts. Most agents tried to ensure that freed people were paid for their labor and were not brutalized as they had been as slaves. Southern whites resented this intrusion, and their resentment reached sympathetic politicians in Washington, DC. The Freedmen's Bureau became a lightning rod for the political conflicts of the Reconstruction period.

Conditions in the South elicited sharply different responses from lawmakers in Washington. At one extreme was President Andrew Johnson, who believed in small government and a speedy readmission of the southern states and looked on the Freedmen's Bureau with suspicion. At the other extreme were radical Republicans, who believed that the federal government should redistribute confiscated land to the former slaves, guarantee their civil rights, give African American men the vote, and take it away from those whites not loyal to the United States during the war. In between were moderate Republicans who at first tried to work with the president. But as reports of violence and the abusive treatment of the freed people reached Washington, Republicans shifted in more radical directions.

It went back and forth this way: policy makers in Washington responded to events in the South, and events in the South were shaped in turn by policies from Washington. What John Dennett saw in Liberty, Virginia, was a good example of this. The Freedmen's Bureau agent listened to the requests of former masters and slaves, his responses shaped by the policies established in Washington. But those policies were, in turn, affected by reports on Southern conditions sent back by agents like him and by journalists like Dennett. From this interaction the politics of Reconstruction, and with it a "New South," slowly emerged.

Wartime Reconstruction

Even as emancipation began, the US government began experimenting with reconstructing the Union. The two goals merged: by creating new, loyal southern states and making their abolition of slavery a condition for reunion, Lincoln could enact emancipation there without court challenge. Through a generous policy of pardons, he could encourage Confederates to make their peace with the Union, speeding the war's end.

Despite the chorus of cries for hanging Jefferson Davis from a sour-apple tree, few northerners wanted to pursue bloody punishments for the million Confederate soldiers who were technically guilty of treason. In the end, Confederate generals went home unharmed to become lawyers, businessmen, and planters; General Robert E. Lee became a college president. No civil leader was hanged for treason, not even Jefferson Davis. Two years after his arrest, he walked out of prison, bailed out by northerners like editor Horace Greeley. In later years, former Confederates became senators, governors, and federal judges. Months before the war ended, northerners were raising money to rebuild the southern economy and feed its destitute people. What the North wanted was not vengeance, but guarantees of lasting loyalty and a meaningful freedom. Questions arose with no easy answers: What did it take to reunite America? Should it be restored, or reconstructed, and if the latter, how drastically? How far could yesterday's enemies be trusted? What did freedom mean, and what rights should the "freed people" enjoy? In reconstructing society, how far did the government's power go?

The Meaning of Freedom

"We was glad to be set free," a former slave remembered years afterward. "I didn't know what it would be like. It was just like opening the door and lettin' the bird fly out. He might starve, or freeze, or be killed pretty soon but he just felt good because he was free." Blacks' departure came as a terrible shock to masters lulled into believing that their "servants" appreciated their treatment. Some former slave owners persuaded themselves that they were the real gainers of slavery's abolition. "I was glad and thankful—on my own account—when slavery ended and I ceased to belong, body and soul, to my negroes," a Virginia woman later insisted. Forced to do their own cooking or washing, other mistresses fumed at blacks' ingratitude. In fact, many African Americans left, not out of unkindness, but simply to prove that they could get along on their own. White fears that blacks, once free, would murder their masters proved groundless.

Leaving the plantation was the first step in a long journey for African Americans. Many took to the roads, some of them returning to their old homes near the coasts, from which masters had evacuated as Union armies approached. Others went searching for family members, separated from them during slavery. For twenty years, black newspapers carried advertisements, appealing for news of a husband or wife long since lost. Those who had not been separated went out of their way to have their marriages secured by law. That way, their children could be made legitimate and their vows made permanent. Once married, men sought sharecropping contracts that allowed their families to live with them on plantations. Because black women across the South had become what the law called "domestic dependents," husbands could refuse employers their wives' services and keep them home. In fact, freedwomen were likelier to work outside the home than white women. They tended the family garden, raised children, hired out as domestics, and, as cotton prices fell, shared the work of hoeing and picking in the fields just so the family could make ends meet.

The end of slavery meant many things to freed people. It meant that they could move about their neighborhoods without passes, and that they did not have to step aside to let whites pass them on the street. They could own dogs or carry canes, which had always been the master's exclusive privilege. They could dress as they pleased or choose their own names, including, for the first time, a surname.

Freedom liberated African Americans from the white minister's take on Christianity. No longer were large portions of the Bible closed off to them. Most southern blacks withdrew from white churches and established their own congregations, particularly in the Methodist and Baptist faith. In time, the church emerged as a central institution in the southern black community, the meeting place, social center, and source of comfort that larger society denied them. A dozen years after the war, South Carolina had a thousand ministers of the African Methodist Episcopal Church alone.

To read the Gospel, however, freed people needed schooling. One former slave remembered his master's parting words on this matter: "Charles, you is a free man they say, but Ah tells you now, you is still a slave and if you lives to be a hundred you'll STILL be a slave, 'cause you got no education, and education is what makes a man free!" Even before the war ended, northern teachers poured into the South to set up schools. When the fighting stopped, the US Army helped recruit and organize thousands of northern women as teachers, but they could never send enough. Old and young spared what time they had from work, paying teachers in eggs or produce when coin was scarce. Black classes met wherever they could: in mule stables and cotton houses, even the slave pen in New Orleans, where the old auction block became a globe stand. Due to a lack of schoolbooks, they read dictionaries and almanacs. On meager resources, hundreds of thousands of southern blacks learned to read and write over the course of the next generation. The first black colleges would be founded in the postwar years, including Hampton Institute in Virginia and Howard University in Washington, DC. The American Missionary Association established seven, among them Atlanta and Fisk Universities.

Finally, freedom allowed freed people to congregate, to celebrate the Fourth of July or Emancipation Day, or to petition for equal rights before the law. Memorial Day may have begun with blacks' gathering to honor the Union dead whose sacrifices had helped make them free.

Experiments with Free Labor

Many whites insisted that blacks would never work in freedom and foresaw a South ruined forever. Freed people proved just the opposite though. When Union troops landed on the Sea Islands off South Carolina in November, 1861, the slaveholders fled, leaving behind between 5,000 and 10,000 slaves. Within months the abandoned plantations of the Sea Islands were being reorganized. Eventually black families were given small plots of their own land to cultivate, and in return for their labor they received a "share" of the year's crop. When the masters returned after the war to reclaim their lands, the labor system had already proven itself. Much modified, it would form the basis for the arrangement known as "sharecropping."

The sugar and cotton plantations around New Orleans provided another opportunity to shape the future of free labor. When the Union army came to occupy New Orleans in 1862, the tens of thousands of field hands on these plantations were no longer slaves, but the landowners still held possession of the land. Unlike the Sea Islands, these plantations could not be broken up. And sugar plantations could not be effectively organized into small sharecropping units.

Hoping to stem the flow of black refugees to Union lines and cut the loss of black lives in the contraband camps, Union general Nathaniel Banks issued stringent regulations to put the freed people back to work quickly in Louisiana. At the time, Banks was the commander of the Department of the Gulf during the occupation of New Orleans and his policy, known as the Banks Plan, required freed people to sign yearlong contracts to work on their former plantations. Workers would be paid either 5 percent of the proceeds of the crop or three dollars per month. The former masters would provide food and shelter, and African American workers were forbidden to leave the plantations without permission. Established planters welcomed the plan, but many critics protested that Banks had simply replaced one form of slavery with another; however, most freed people knew the difference and accepted the work conditions. The Banks Plan became the model for plantations throughout the lower Mississippi Valley.

Understandably, freed people wanted land of their own. Only then could they avoid working for their old masters on any terms. "The labor of these people had for two hundred years cleared away the forests and produced crops that brought millions of dollars annually," H. C. Bruce explained. "It does seem to me that a Christian Nation would, at least, have given them one year's support, 40 acres of land and a mule each." As the war ended, many African Americans expected the government's help in becoming landowners. Union general William Tecumseh Sherman heard an appeal from freed people on the Sea Islands. "The way we can best take care of ourselves is to have land," they argued, "and turn it out and till it by our own labor." Convinced, Sherman issued Special Field Order No. 15 granting captured land to the freed people. By June, 400,000 acres had been distributed to 40,000 former slaves.

Lincoln's Ten Percent Plan Versus the Wade-Davis Bill

Lincoln moved to shape a postwar South based on free labor and to replace military control, Banks's included, with new civil governments. However, wartime Reconstruction had to take Confederate resistance into account. Any terms the President set would need to attract as much white southern support as it could and hold out an inducement to those at war with the United States to return to their old loyalties. In December 1863 Lincoln issued a Proclamation of Amnesty and Reconstruction, offering a full pardon and the restoration of civil rights to all those who swore loyalty to the Union, excluding only a few high-ranking Confederate military and political leaders. When the number of loyal whites in a former Confederate state reached 10 percent of the 1860 voting population, they could organize a new state constitution and government. But Lincoln's "Ten Per Cent Plan" also required that the state abolish slavery, just as Congress had demanded before admitting West Virginia to the Union earlier in the year. Attempts to establish a loyal government foundered, but circumstances in Louisiana proved more promising. Under General Banks's guidance, Free State whites met in New Orleans in 1864 and produced a new state constitution abolishing slavery.

By that time, however, radical Unionists were expecting more. Propertied and well educated, the free black community in New Orleans pleaded that without equal rights to education and the vote, mere freedom would not be enough. Impressed by their argument, Lincoln hinted to Louisiana authorities that he would welcome steps opening the vote for at least some blacks. The hints were ignored.

Black spokesmen found a friendlier audience among radical Republicans in Congress, among them Thaddeus Stevens of Pennsylvania and Charles Sumner of Massachusetts. Believing that justice required giving at least some blacks the vote and setting a more rigorous standard of loyalty for white southerners than Lincoln's plan offered, they shared a much wider concern that any new government must rest on statutory law, not presidential proclamations and military commanders' decrees. They were not at all prepared to treat Lincoln's "loyal" states as fit to return to Congress—not when so much of Louisiana and

Arkansas remained in Confederate hands and was excluded from the new constitution-making—not when a speckling of enclaves pretended to speak for the state of Virginia.

As doubts grew about Louisiana's Reconstruction, Congress edged away from Lincoln's program. In mid-1864, Senator Benjamin F. Wade of Ohio and Congressman Henry Winter Davis of Maryland proposed a different plan, requiring a majority of a state's white voters to swear allegiance to the Union before reconstruction could begin. Slavery must also be abolished and full equality before the law must be granted to African Americans. Lincoln pocket-vetoed the Wade-Davis bill to protect the governments that were already under way toward reform. However, he could not make Congress admit a single one of his newly reconstructed states.

Congress did not leave matters there. In March 1865, the Republicans established the Bureau of Refugees, Freedmen, and Abandoned Lands, commonly known as the Freedmen's Bureau. In the area of labor relations, the Bureau sometimes sided with landowners against the interests of the freed people. But it also provided immediate relief for thousands of people of both races. Indeed, of more than 18 million rations distributed over three years, more than 5 million went to whites in need. The Bureau joined with northern religious groups in creating some 4,000 black schools. It ran charity hospitals and provided medical services. Freed people came to Bureau agents for justice when white-dominated courts denied it and took counsel when labor contracts were to be negotiated. Some agents sided instinctively with the former masters. Most courted white hostility by protecting freed people from violence, settling their complaints, advising them on labor contracts, and seeing that employers paid as promised.

The Freedmen's Bureau also became involved in the politics of land redistribution and controlled the disposition of 850,000 acres of confiscated and abandoned Confederate lands. In July 1865, General Oliver Otis Howard, the head of the Bureau, directed his agents to rent the land to the freed people in 40-acre plots that they could eventually purchase. Many agents believed that to reeducate them in the values of thrift and hard work, the freed people should be encouraged to save money and buy land for themselves. A Freedman's Savings Bank helped many do just that.

Moderate and radical Republicans alike were determined to press for more than a nominal freedom for blacks. Equally important, Congress made it clear that it would insist on being consulted in any Reconstruction policy.

Presidential Reconstruction, 1865–1867

Andrew Johnson took office in April 1865 as a great unknown. Born in a log cabin and too poor to attend school, he began his career on a tailor's bench where he had shown grit and enterprise. In time he had risen to moderate wealth in the eastern Tennessee hill country, enough to own slaves, but he never forgot his humble beginnings. Before the war, he had defended slavery and the common man, called for taxpayer-supported public schools, and free homesteads. A courageous Union Democrat in wartime, he had run roughshod over Tennessee Confederates as military governor. He hated treason and the rich planters that he blamed for the war. Johnson deserved much of the credit for Tennessee abolishing slavery; however, he alarmed some radicals along the way who found more pardons than penalties in his policies. Convinced that a lasting reunion of the states could only come by earning white southerners' good will and determined to see the Thirteenth Amendment ratified quickly, the president started Reconstruction six months before Congress convened and left it entirely in white hands. In doing so, he offended not only the radicals favoring a color-blind suffrage but also the moderates who believed that Reconstruction must be done by law and not executive order.

The Political Economy of Contract Labor

Presidential Reconstruction began in late May 1865, when President Johnson offered amnesty and the restoration of property to white southerners who swore an oath of loyalty to the Union, excluding only high-ranking Confederate military and political leaders and very rich planters. He named provisional governors in seven seceded states and told them to organize constitutional conventions. For readmission to the Union and restoration of their full privileges, conventions must adopt the Thirteenth Amendment, void their secession ordinances, and repudiate their Confederate war debt. Most of the constitutional conventions met the president's conditions, though with some grumbling and a lot of legal quibbling. Many made it clear that they still thought the South had been right all along. They only bowed to military force. "We have for breakfast salt-fish, fried potatoes, and treason," a lodger at a Virginia boarding house wrote. "Fried potatoes, treason, and salt-fish for dinner. At supper the fare is slightly varied, and we have treason, salt-fish, fried potatoes, and a little more treason."

Elections under these new constitutions would then choose civil governments to replace provisional authority. Only white men covered by the amnesty proclamation or subsequent pardons could vote, but by September Johnson was signing pardons wholesale. Secessionists flocked to the elections that followed the conventions. Freshly pardoned Confederates won some of the most prominent offices, former Confederate vice president Alexander Stephens among them.

White southerners welcomed Johnson's leniency. Once pardoned, they petitioned for restoration of their confiscated or abandoned properties. In September 1865 Johnson ordered the Freedmen's Bureau to return the lands to their former owners. By late 1865 former slaves were being forced off the 40-acre plots that the government agency had given them.

No sooner did conservative legislatures meet than they fashioned "Black Codes" defining, or rather confining, blacks' new freedom. Some states ordered different punishments: fines for whites and whipping or sale for black offenders. Elsewhere, lawmakers forbade freed people from renting land, owning guns, or buying liquor. Vagrancy laws gave police wide discretion to collar any black and subject him or her to forced labor, sometimes for an old master. Apprenticeship statutes let the courts take away any black child without parents' consent and bind him or her out to years of unpaid labor. Blacks were allowed to testify only in certain cases. They were taxed to pay for white schools, but the Johnsonian state governments provided them with none of their own.

Landowners gave their black employees as little as they could. With the legal machinery backing them up, they forced them into labor contracts that stipulated what they could do with their private time. One planter required his black workers to "go by his direction the same as in slavery time." Others landowners denied them the right to leave the plantation without their "master's" consent. Some arrangements allotted as little as a tenth of the crop in wages and many employers found an excuse to turn their field hands off unpaid as soon as the crop was in. It was no wonder that contract labor seemed to many freedmen slavery under a new name, or that thousands refused to sign any terms at the year's end.

Freedman's Labor Contract Many freed blacks were forced into labor contracts like this one in the early years of Reconstruction. Harsh working conditions and reports of white landowners refusing to pay agreed-upon wages prompted many to argue that contract labor was little different from slavery.

Resistance to Presidential Reconstruction

An undercurrent of violence underlay conservative control. In North Carolina, a resident wrote, the Negro was "sneered at by all and informed daily yes hourly that he is incompetent to care for himself—that his race is now doomed to perish from off the face of the Earth—that he will not work—that he is a thief by nature[,] that he lies more easily and naturally than an honest man breathes." Blacks were assaulted for not showing proper deference to whites, for disputing the terms of labor contracts, or for failing to meet the standards that white employers demanded. Black churches were burnt, rebuilt, and burnt again. A Freedmen's Bureau agent in Kentucky classified the incidents in just a few counties: twenty-three "cases of severe and inhuman beating and whipping of men; four of beating and shooting; two of robbing and shooting; three of robbing; five men shot and killed; two shot and wounded; four beaten to death; one beaten and roasted; three women assaulted and ravished; four women beaten, two women tied up and whipped until insensible; two men and their families beaten and driven from their homes, and their property destroyed; two instances of burning of dwellings and one of the inmates shot." White witnesses refused to acknowledge what they knew to be true, white judges dismissed cases involving black defendants, and white juries invariably acquitted the offenders. If Johnson expressed content with the speedy restoration of loyalty in the South, a growing chorus of complaints from freed people and Unionists down South told a different story.

Congress Clashes with the President

Troubled by presidential Reconstruction's failings, a Republican Congress refused to readmit former Confederate states without investigation. A Joint Committee on Reconstruction was formed to examine their loyalty and the safety of white and black Unionists' rights. At the same time, moderate Republicans also wanted to establish a program for readmission that Johnson would support. By expanding the power of the Freedmen's Bureau and proposing a Civil Rights bill, they thought they had the makings of a compromise.

The first extended the Bureau's life, strengthened its powers, and permitted it to set up courts that allowed black testimony. The second overturned the Dred Scott decision by granting United States citizenship to American men regardless of race. This marked the first time that the federal government intervened in states' rights to guarantee due process and basic civil rights.

Freedmen's Bureau Poster Led by President Andrew Johnson, attacks on the Freedmen's Bureau became more and more openly racist in late 1865 and 1866. This Democratic Party broadside was circulated during the 1866 election.

To Republicans' amazement, Johnson vetoed both bills and in terms that made no compromise possible. Hinting that Congress had no right to reconstruct until the southern states were readmitted and doubting blacks' fitness to enjoy the same civil rights as whites, the president declared reconstruction completed. Unable to override the Freedmen's Bureau bill veto, Congress did pass the Civil Rights bill, which served as the foundation for section one of the Fourteenth Amendment, and later that summer a new Freedmen's Bureau bill.

Origins of the Fourteenth Amendment

During the spring of 1866, the Joint Committee on Reconstruction proposed a Fourteenth Amendment to the Constitution, outlining the conditions that Republicans thought were essential for a just and lasting peace. Provisions guaranteed payment of the national debt and prevented payment of the Confederate one. Confederates who had held public office before the war were barred from office until Congress removed their disabilities. Replacing the Constitution's three-fifths clause, which allowed slaves to be counted as three-fifths of a human being for the purpose of taxation and representation, representation in Congress would now be based on a state's voting population. If freed blacks entitled southern states to additional House seats, that representation entitled blacks to the right to vote (see Table 15-1). "Happy will our disappointment be if this dry

Table 15-1 Reconstruction Amendments, 1865–1870

Amendment	Main Provisions	Congressional Passage (two-thirds majority in each house required)	Ratification Process (three-quarters of all states including ex-Confederate states required)
13	Slavery prohibited in United States	January 1865	December 1865 (27 states, including 8 southern states)
14	1. National citizenship for all men and women born in the United States	June 1866	Rejected by 12 southern and border states, February 1867
	2. State representation in Congress reduced proportionally to number of voters disenfranchised		Radicals make readmission of southern states hinge on ratification
	3. Former high-ranking Confederates denied right to hold office		Ratified July 1868
	4. Confederate debt repudiated		
15	Denial of franchise because of race, color, or past servitude explicitly prohibited	February 1869	Ratification required for readmission of Virginia, Texas, Mississippi, Georgia. Ratified March 1870

stalk shall bud and blossom into Impartial Suffrage," one radical wrote, doubtfully. Even if it did not, the South would return to Congress weaker in strength than it had left. But the crucial provision wrote civil rights guarantees into fundamental law, guaranteeing citizenship to all males born in the United States.

Deserted by the party that had elected him, Johnson fought on. He launched the National Union movement, a bipartisan coalition of conservatives whose goal was to defeat Republicans at the midterm elections. A railroad tour from Chicago and back to Washington allowed him to make his case to the American people. However, the National Union movement fizzled; hardly any Republican thought the proposed Amendment presented unfair terms for a defeated South. Johnson's "Swing Around the Circle" tour ended in crowds trading insults with the president.

Two incidents confirmed northern fears that presidential Reconstruction had left southern Unionists defenseless. On May 1, 1866, after two drivers—one black, one white—had a traffic accident, Memphis police arrested the black driver. A group of black veterans tried to prevent the arrest and, as a result, a white crowd gathered and began rioting in the streets. Over the next three days, white mobs burned hundreds of homes, destroyed churches, and attacked black schools. Five black women were raped, and nearly fifty people, all but two of them black, were killed.

Three months later, violence of an explicitly political dimension broke out in New Orleans. Alarmed at former Confederates' return to power in Louisiana, "Free Staters" sought to recall the state's 1864 constitutional convention. They may have meant to open voting rights to some blacks or cut "rebels" out, but they never got the chance. On July 30,

1866, when a few dozen delegates assembled at Mechanics Institute, white mobs set on the convention's supporters, who were mostly black. Led by police and firemen, many of them Confederate veterans, rioters opened fire on a black parade and broke into the convention hall. "The floor was covered with blood," one victim remembered, "and in walking downstairs the blood splashed under the soles of my boots." Blacks trying to surrender were gunned down. By the time the attackers dispersed, 34 blacks and 3 white supporters had been killed, and another 100 had been injured.

Congressional Reconstruction

The elections of 1866 became a referendum on whether Johnson's policies had gone far enough to assure the permanent safety of the Union. But they also posed competing visions of what American democracy should mean. For President Johnson, "democracy" meant government by local majorities, which often meant white supremacy. For African Americans and a growing number of Republicans in Congress, genuine democracy demanded a firm foundation of equal civil and political rights. The sweep that followed brought in an even more solidly Republican Congress than before and doomed presidential Reconstruction. Congressional Reconstruction would be far different. It was an extraordinary series of events, second only to emancipation in its impact on the history of the United States.

The South Remade

Republicans had agreed on the Fourteenth Amendment's provisions as a final settlement of the war's issues. Southern states that ratified it would be readmitted, whether they enfranchised blacks or not. Tennessee ratified the amendment and was readmitted to Congress immediately. But in the remaining southern states, conservatives rejected the amendment by wide margins, and with the president's encouragement. As unpunished assaults on Unionists and freed people continued, Congress lost patience. In the short run, the army could keep order, but a long-term solution was needed. Moderate Republicans came to agree with radicals: only by putting loyal men, regardless of race, in charge could a loyal, just South come into being. The only other alternative would be an open-ended national commitment to rule the South by force.

Although they were far from what radical Republicans had hoped for, in March 1867, Congress passed two Reconstruction Acts. Leaving the Johnsonian state governments in office, the acts declared them provisional and their officeholders subject to removal if they hamstrung the Reconstruction process. Ten ex-Confederate states were divided into five military districts and placed under army supervision (see Map 15–1). The army would register voters, both white and black, except for the comparatively small number disqualified by the not-yet-ratified Fourteenth Amendment. To regain congressional representation, each state must call a constitutional convention and draw up a new constitution providing for equal civil and political rights. Voters then must ratify it, and the newly elected governments must adopt the Fourteenth Amendment. Military oversight would end as civil authority replaced it. Thus, most white southern men had a say in constructing the new political order, and when those states were readmitted, they were granted the same rights as others. For all the laws' limits, remaking state governments and requiring a broader male suffrage promised a Radical Reconstruction indeed.

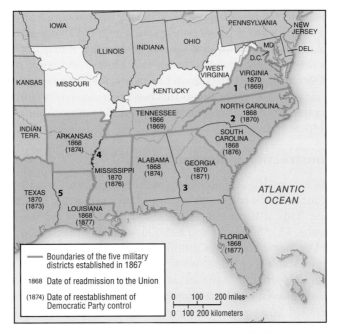

Map 15–1   Reconstruction and Redemption By 1870 Congress had readmitted every southern state to the Union. In most cases the Republican Party retained control of the "reconstructed" state governments for only a few years.

The Impeachment and Trial of Andrew Johnson

Johnson could not stop Congressional Reconstruction. But he could temper it. Battling now to protect the executive's powers, Johnson shared Democrats' fears that Congress had veered far from the Constitution, placing military authority above civil authority and overturning what he saw as the natural order of society, where blacks were kept in subordination.

In vain, radical Republicans called for Johnson's impeachment. Instead, Congress tried to restrain him by law. The Tenure of Office Act kept the president from removing officials who had been appointed in his administration with Senate confirmation. Another law required that every presidential order to the military pass through General Ulysses S. Grant. Johnson could still dismiss district commanders (and did when they interpreted their powers differently than he did), but as long as Grant headed the army and Edwin M. Stanton the War Department, Republicans felt that they had safeguarded the Reconstruction Acts against a potential coup.

Provoked by these challenges to his authority, Johnson issued interpretations of the Reconstruction Acts to permit wider conservative registration, forcing Congress into special session to revise the law with a Third Reconstruction Act. He issued broader amnesty proclamations for former Confederates, forced the dismissal of Republican officers, and, abiding by the Tenure of Office Act, suspended Stanton in August 1867. When the Senate reinstated him the following winter, Johnson ordered him ejected. "What good did your moderation do you?" radical Republican Thaddeus Stevens taunted moderates. "If you don't kill the beast, he will kill you." With the law seemingly broken, the House impeached Johnson.

The expected removal never happened. Rejecting Stevens's argument that presidential obstruction was enough for conviction, senators required an intentional violation of law. The Tenure of Office Act's wording was so unclear that it may not have applied to Stanton. When the president promised to restrain himself and selected a successor to Stanton that moderates trusted, the impeachment process lost momentum. In May, the Senate fell a single vote short of the two-thirds needed to convict. Within a month, Congress had readmitted seven southern states, thus limiting Johnson's power to thwart Reconstruction in those states.

Radical Reconstruction in the South

With the help of Union Leagues, auxiliaries of the Republican Party whose goal was to mobilize and educate black voters, and with military protection against conservative violence in place, Radical Reconstruction transformed the cotton South dramatically. Within six months, 735,000 blacks and 635,000 whites had registered to vote. Blacks formed electoral majorities in South Carolina, Florida, Mississippi, Alabama, and Louisiana and in most states they found white support in the so-called scalawags, white Southerners who supported Reconstruction and Republican policies. Wartime Unionists, hill farmers neglected by planter-dominated governments, debtors seeking relief, development-minded businessmen seeking a new, more diversified South, and even some Confederate leaders and planters all welcomed Radical Reconstruction. Carpetbaggers, northerners who had come south to farm, invest, preach, or teach, were few in numbers, but they took a front rank among the leaders in black-majority states.

Starting in the fall of 1867, ten states called constitutional conventions, heavily Republican and predominantly, but not exclusively, white. The results of these conventions, so-called Black and Tan constitutions, guaranteed a color-blind right to suffrage, mandated public school systems, and overhauled the tax structure. They also included a right to bear arms in their bills of rights. Only a few states shut any Confederates out of the vote, and most of those that did removed the electoral disabilities before a year was out.

Achievements and Failures of Radical Government

Later caricatured as a dire era of "bayonet" and "negro rule," Radical Reconstruction was neither. The Republican governments won in fairer elections and with greater turnouts than any that the South had known up until that time. Republican leadership remained overwhelmingly white and, for the most part, southern born. While some 700 blacks served in state legislatures, only in South Carolina and possibly Louisiana did they ever outnumber whites. No state elected a black governor, while only sixteen blacks served in Congress, two of whom were senators. Still, the contrast between what had been and what would follow as a result of Reconstruction was revolutionary. These Reconstruction legislatures were more representative of their constituents than most legislatures in nineteenth-century America (see Figure 15–1). While some African American officeholders were indeed illiterate, former slaves who did not own land, a disproportionate number came from the tiny prewar free African American elite of ministers, teachers, and small business owners. Freed people also filled hundreds of county offices. They served as sheriffs, bailiffs, judges, and jurors, offering the promise, at least, of a fair hearing in court for black defendants and litigants. Sharing power locally meant a greater chance for black communities to share in the benefits of public expenditures.

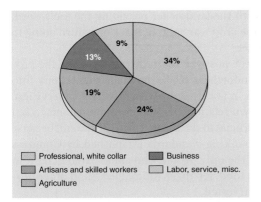

Professional, white collar

Artisans and skilled workers

Agriculture

Business

Labor, service, misc.

Figure 15–1 Occupations of African American Officeholders During Reconstruction Although former slaves were underrepresented among black officeholders, the Reconstruction governments were among the most broadly representative legislatures in US history.

Radical Members One of the greatest achievements of congressional Reconstruction was the election of a significant number of African Americans to public office.

Republican rule delivered on its promises. The whipping post and debtor's prison vanished. The new governments funded insane asylums, roads, and prisons. Homestead exemptions protected debtors' real estate, and lien laws gave tenant farmers more control over the crops they grew and awarded artisans a first right to their employer's assets. The right of married women to hold property in their own name was expanded. Across the Deep South, laws took on racial discrimination on streetcars and railroad lines, mandating equal treatment. Most important, most Reconstruction governments built or extended access to the free public school system to African Americans. Underfunded and segregated, those schools nonetheless boosted literacy rates, especially among freed people.

The Political Economy of Sharecropping

Radical Reconstruction made it easier for the former slaves to negotiate the terms of their labor contracts. Workers with grievances had a better chance of securing justice, as southern Republicans became sheriffs, justices of the peace, and county clerks, and as southern courts allowed blacks to serve as witnesses and sit on juries.

The strongest card in the hands of the freed people was a shortage of agricultural workers in the South. After emancipation, thousands of blacks sought opportunities in towns and cities or in the North. And even though most blacks remained in the South as farmers, they reduced their working hours in several ways. Black women still worked the fields, but they spent more time nursing their infants and caring for their children. And the children went to school when they were able. The resulting labor shortage forced white landlords to renegotiate their labor arrangements with the freed people.

The contract labor system that had developed during the war and under presidential Reconstruction was replaced with a variety of regional arrangements. On the Louisiana sugar plantations, the freed people became wage laborers. But in tobacco and cotton regions, where most freed people lived, a new system of labor called sharecropping developed. Under this system, an agricultural worker and his family typically agreed to work for one year on a particular plot of land, with the landowner providing the tools, seed, and work animals. At the end of the year, the crop was split, perhaps one-third going to the sharecropper and two-thirds to the owner.

Sharecropping shaped the economy of the postwar South by transforming the production and marketing of cash crops. Landowners broke up their plantations into family-sized plots, worked by sharecroppers in family units with no direct supervision. Each sharecropping family established its own relationship with local merchants to sell crops and buy supplies. Merchants became crucial to the southern credit system, because most southern banks could not meet the banking standards established by Congress during the Civil War. Storekeepers, usually the only people who could extend credit to sharecroppers, provided sharecroppers with food, fertilizer, animal feed, and other provisions during the year until the crop was harvested.

These developments had important consequences for white small farmers. More merchants fanned out into up-country areas inhabited mostly by ordinary whites, areas now served by railroads sponsored by the Reconstruction legislatures. With merchants offering credit and railroads offering transportation, small farmers started to produce cash crops. Thus, Reconstruction accelerated the process by which southern yeomen abandoned self-sufficient farming in favor of cash crops.

Sharecropping spread quickly among black farmers in the cotton South. By 1880, 80 percent of cotton farms had fewer than 50 acres, and the majority of those farms were operated by sharecroppers (see Maps 15–2 and 15–3). Sharecropping had several

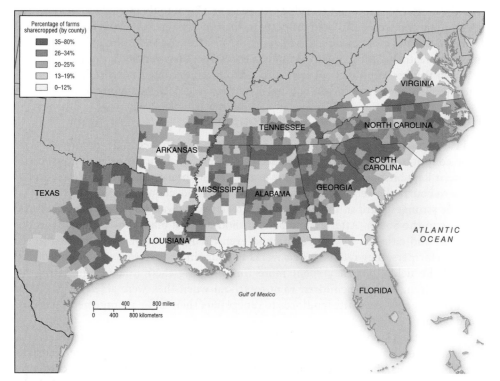

Map 15–2   Sharecropping By 1880 the sharecropping system had spread across the South. It was most common in the inland areas, where primarily cotton and tobacco plantations existed before the Civil War.

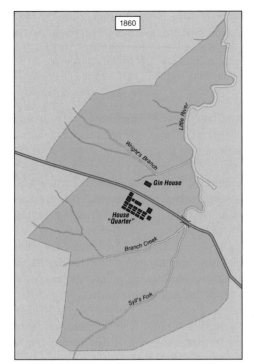
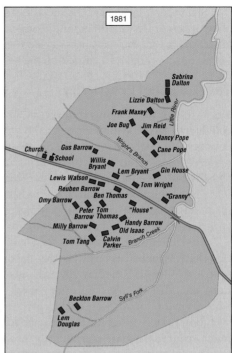

Map 15-3   The Effect of Sharecropping in the South: The Barrow Plantation in Oglethorpe County, Georgia Sharecropping cut large estates into small landholdings worked by sharecroppers and tenants, changing the landscape of the South.

advantages for landlords. It reduced their risk when cotton prices were low and encouraged workers to increase production without costly supervision. Further, if sharecroppers changed jobs before the crop was harvested, they lost a whole year's pay. But there were also advantages for the workers. For freed people with no hope of owning their own farms, sharecropping at least rewarded their hard work. The bigger the crop, the more they earned. It gave them more independence than contract labor.

Sharecropping also allowed the freed people to work in families rather than in gangs. Freedom alone had rearranged the powers of men, women, and children within the families of former slaves. Parents gained new control over their children. They could send sons and daughters to school or put them to work. Successful parents could give their children an important head start in life. Similarly, African American husbands gained new powers.

The marriage laws of the mid-nineteenth century that defined the husband as the head of the household were irrelevant to slaves, because their marriages had no legal standing. With emancipation, these patriarchal assumptions of American family law shaped the lives of freed men and women. Once married, women often found that their property belonged to their husbands. The sharecropping system further assumed that as head of the household the husband made the economic decisions for the entire family. Men signed most labor contracts, and most contracts assumed that the husband would take his family to work with him.

Sharecropping shaped the social system of the postwar South. It influenced the balance of power between men and women. It established the balance of power between landowners and sharecroppers. It tied the southern economy to agriculture, in particular to cotton production, impeding the region's overall economic development.

The Gospel of Prosperity

Only a diversified economy could break the planters' hold over a black labor force; railroads could lower farmers' shipping costs and tap the South's coal and iron resources. Economic development might even give the South an independence worth having: it was no longer required to look north for its investment capital or finished goods. A program that made all classes prosper seemed ready-made to recruit more whites for a party and push racial issues into the background. Republicans preached a "gospel of prosperity" that would use government aid to build a richer South and benefit ordinary white southerners. Reconstruction governments committed the states' credit and funds to building its industrial base.

The strategy had big drawbacks. Diverting scarce resources to railroads and corporations left less for black constituencies' needs, especially school systems. Investors hesitated to invest in bonds issued by governments at risk of violent overthrow. Hungry corporations hounded the legislature for favors and made bribery their clinching argument. State-owned railroads were sold to private firms for a song—and a payoff. States already spending heavily to repair the damage of the war and to build new state services on a much-reduced tax base obligated themselves for millions more. As taxes soared, white farmers became increasingly receptive to Democratic claims that they were being robbed, their money wasted by swag-grabbing outsiders and ignorant black upstarts in office. The passage of civil rights bills, ending discrimination in public transportation, only alienated former scalawags further and stirred conservatives to bring the stay-at-homes to the polls. Everywhere, Republicans were split over how far to trust former Confederates. That division lost Virginia and Tennessee to the "Redeemers," conservative white Democrats, in 1869. In Arkansas, two Republicans claimed the governorship in 1872, and two years later they raised armies to fight it out. The "Brooks-Baxter war" ended with the Democrat-backed contestant winning and a new constitution that put both Republicans out for good.

Republicans' policy failures alone did not destroy them. Terrorism and economic pressure did. Everywhere planters used their power to keep black tenants from voting. White radicals found themselves shunned by society. They were denied credit or employment unless they left politics. As early as 1867, secret organizations were arising, bent on Reconstruction's overthrow and the restoration of white dominance, which, effectively, meant bringing Democrats into power by threats, beatings, and killings. From the Carolinas to Texas, the Ku Klux Klan and similar organizations shot Republican lawmakers and burned black schools and churches. Teachers, party organizers, and white wartime Unionists all fell victim. Politically active blacks were threatened, driven from their homes, whipped, or shot. Their wives were raped and their homes plundered while Democratic newspapers defamed the victims. Intimidated juries dared not convict, and sheriffs dared not arrest. In Arkansas, Texas, and Tennessee, Republican governors mustered a white militia and broke the terrorist movement. Elsewhere they found themselves powerless or outgunned. Terrorism carried North Carolina, Alabama, and Georgia for the Democrats in 1870, crippling Reconstruction in the first state and effectively ending it in the other two. By 1872, Redeemers had regained control of the whole upper and border South. After that, they rigged the election laws to curb the black vote and put any Republican comeback out of reach.

Reconstructing America's Foreign Policy

As the Civil War approached, slavery's expansionists tainted Manifest Destiny for everyone but Democrats. Republicans had no intention of spreading an empire of the unfree. Spreading the republic's bounds would only spread liberty. It could overthrow the puppet state that the French emperor Napoleon III had installed in Mexico. It might even give black southerners a place free of race prejudice where they could fulfill their potential. Secretary of State William Seward dreamed of all North America, perhaps even most of the Caribbean, as one vast federation; Senator Charles Sumner suggested that the United States ease Canada into the Union.

Nothing of the kind happened. The Johnson administration helped force France to withdraw its troops from Mexico, but unbacked, Maximilian's regime collapsed. Seward's biggest success came in 1867, in purchasing Alaska from Russia. A few months later, however, the Senate rejected a treaty buying the Virgin Islands from Denmark and held off on leasing a naval base in Santo Domingo. A treaty with Colombia giving the United States exclusive rights to build a canal across the Isthmus of Panama came to nothing. Canadians showed no interest in joining the Union, and instead forged a union of their own separate provinces.

Not all the wealth of the West Indies could carry the United States beyond trade to the taking of territory. Slavery's end killed most of the zest for annexing Cuba. When a rebellion broke out there in 1868, Congress did nothing about it. Similar inhibitions led the Senate to reject Grant's annexation treaty with Santo Domingo in 1870. Sumner's opposition doomed the treaty, and ironically, himself: as a result, Grant and Fish forced the Senate to depose him from his chairmanship.

Reconstruction had not been meant to work that way. Instead of being able to defend themselves, Reconstruction governments found themselves desperately dependent on national support. But that support had been dissipating ever since the passage of the Reconstruction Acts.

The Retreat from Republican Radicalism

A series of makeshift laws and improvisations, Congressional Reconstruction had stirred misgivings among moderate Republicans who were fearful of stretching the Constitution too far and uneasy with using the expanded authority that war had given them in peacetime. New steps, such as confiscating planters' property, say, or a nationally funded school system, were out of the question. Even the Freedmen's Bureau was cut back and, except for education, closed down completely when reconstructed states were readmitted to Congress. Public backlash against radicalism gave Democrats heavy gains in the 1867 elections. In order to survive, Reconstruction had to consolidate its gains and leave the new state governments to fulfill its promises.

Republicans Become the Party of Moderation

By then, the 1868 presidential campaign was under way. Running the war hero General Ulysses S. Grant for president, Republicans could offer a candidate who was above politics. His slogan, "Let Us Have Peace," emphasized that the party meant to restore the Union, rather than advance radicalism. The platform endorsed Congressional Reconstruction and defended black voting in the South, but insisted that states not covered by Reconstruction should decide the issue of suffrage for themselves. Positioning themselves as protectors of the war's accomplishments came all the more easily after Democrats nominated former New York governor Horatio Seymour on a platform declaring the Reconstruction Acts as illegal, null and void. Their fiercest spokesmen swore that if Democrats won, they would overturn the newly elected southern governments and install white conservative ones. Voiding those governments would invalidate the Fourteenth Amendment, ratified by southern legislatures; some partisans even argued that every measure passed since southern congressmen walked out in 1861 had no legal force. Bondholders, fearful that Democrats would turn their national securities into waste paper or pay them in depreciated "greenbacks," thought Grant the safer choice, even without Republicans' shouting that Seymour's election would reward traitors and bring on civil war again.

Northern voters got a taste of what Democratic rule would mean in an epidemic of violence across the South. Riots and massacres in Louisiana and Georgia kept Republicans from voting and carried both states for Seymour. In the North, the outrages may have been decisive in electing Grant. Carrying the electoral college by a huge margin, he won the popular vote more narrowly with just 53 percent, and then only because of a heavy black turnout in his favor.

Reconstructing the North

Although Reconstruction was aimed primarily at the South, the North was affected as well, especially by the struggle over the black vote. The transformation of the North was an important chapter in the history of Reconstruction.

The Fifteenth Amendment and Nationwide African American Suffrage

Segregated into separate facilities or excluded entirely, denied the right to vote in nearly every state outside of New England, blacks in wartime fought to end discrimination in the North. Biracial efforts chipped away at many states' discriminatory "Black Laws" and the Fourteenth Amendment eliminated the rest nationwide. Streetcar lines in some cities stopped running separate cars, black testimony was admitted on the same terms as white, and in a few northern communities, black children began attending white schools. Ending the color bar on voting and jury service proved to be more difficult: when impartial suffrage went on the ballot, most northern states voted against it (though most Republicans favored it and Congress mandated it in the territories and the District of Columbia).

The shocking electoral violence of 1868 persuaded Republicans that equal suffrage in the South needed permanent protection. In 1869 Congress added a Fifteenth Amendment to the Constitution forbidding the use of "race, color, or previous condition of servitude" as a bar to suffrage in the North as well as the South. For those states not yet readmitted to the Union (Virginia, Mississippi, and Texas), it made ratification of the amendment an additional condition. On March 30, 1870, the Fifteenth Amendment became part of the Constitution.

As terrorism mounted, Congress legislated to protect a free, fair vote. The most important, the 1871 "Ku Klux" Act, gave the US government the power to suppress the Klan, even suspending the writ of habeas corpus. Grant moved cautiously, however, because the newly created Justice Department lacked both funds and personnel. Still, thousands of arrests and hundreds of convictions ended the Klan, restoring peace in time for the 1872 presidential elections.

Revolutionary as it was, the Fifteenth Amendment had serious limitations that would weaken its impact later. As the Supreme Court would note, it did not confer a right to vote on anybody. It simply limited the grounds on which it could be denied. States could impose property or taxpaying qualifications or a literacy test if they pleased, as long as the restrictions made no distinction on the basis of race. They could set up residency requirements or limit the vote to naturalized citizens, or to men.

Women and Suffrage

The issue of black voting added to tensions among northern radicals. Feminists and abolitionists had worked together in the struggle for emancipation, but signs of trouble appeared as early as May 1863 at the convention of the Woman's National Loyal League in New York City. The League had been organized to assist in defeating the slave South. One of the convention's resolutions declared that "there never can be a true peace in this Republic until the civil and political rights of all citizens of African descent and all women are practically established." For some delegates, this went too far. They argued that it was inappropriate to inject the issue of women's rights into the struggle to restore the Union.

With the war's end, the radical crusade for black suffrage intensified debate among reformers. Elizabeth Cady Stanton and others pointed out the injustice of letting "Patrick and Sambo and Hans and Yung Tung" vote while propertied, educated women were denied suffrage. The Fourteenth Amendment, by privileging male inhabitants' right to vote explicitly, appalled Stanton, and the Fifteenth Amendment's failure to address gender discrimination at the polls only confirmed her suspicion that what one abolitionist called "the Negro's hour" would never give way to one for women. Friendly to women's suffrage though they were, abolitionists like Frederick Douglass and suffragists like Lucy Stone argued that the critical issue was the protection of the freed people. "When women, because they are women, are dragged from their homes and hung upon lamp-posts," Douglass reminded an audience, "when their children are torn from their arms and their brains dashed to the pavement; when they are the objects of insult and outrage at every turn; when they are in danger of having their homes burnt down over their heads; when their children are not allowed to enter schools; then they will have an urgency to obtain the ballot." In 1869, radical and abolitionist allies parted ways. The women's suffrage movement divided into rival organizations, Stanton's National Woman Suffrage Association and Stone's American Woman Suffrage Association.

Some radicals, Charles Sumner among them, favored women's suffrage, but most Republicans did not. The territories of Wyoming and Utah enfranchised women. Elsewhere, lawmakers let women participate in school-board elections, but voting reform went no further. Most states refused even to put the issue on the ballot. When they did so, it was voted down. Denying women's appeal that as citizens they were entitled to vote, the Supreme Court declared that the Fourteenth Amendment's right of citizenship did not carry that right with it.

The Rise and Fall of the National Labor Union

Inspired by the radicalism of the Civil War and Reconstruction, industrial workers across the North organized dozens of craft unions, Eight-Hour Leagues, and working-men's associations, all designed to protect northern workers who were overworked and underpaid. They called strikes, initiated consumer boycotts, and formed consumer co-operatives. In 1867 and 1868, workers in New York and Massachusetts campaigned to enact laws restricting the workday to eight hours. Soon, workers began electing their own candidates to state legislatures.

Founded in 1866, the National Labor Union (NLU) was the first significant postwar effort to organize all "working people" into a national union. William Sylvis, an iron molder, founded the NLU and became its president in 1868. He denied any "harmony of interests" between workers and capitalists. On the contrary, every wage earner was at war with every capitalist, whose "profits" robbed working people of the fruits of their labor.

Under Sylvis's direction, the NLU advocated a wide range of political reforms, not just bread-and-butter issues. Sylvis believed that through organization American work-ers could take the "first step toward competence and independence." He argued for a doubling of the average worker's wages. He supported voting rights for blacks and women. Nevertheless, after a miserable showing in the elections of 1872, the NLU fell apart. By then, Reconstruction in the South was facing serious challenges.

The End of Reconstruction

Events outside the South helped speed Reconstruction's collapse. Reform-oriented Re-publicans felt alarm at the spread of political corruption after the war. Convinced, too, that full reconciliation must come, now that the war's goals had been met, they broke with the party and abandoned their support for federal intervention in southern affairs. Additionally, a depression took voters' minds off Reconstruction issues. By 1876 "Re-demption" had carried white Democrats to power in all but a few southern states. Yet a hotly disputed presidential election and divided power would doom even those.

Corruption Is the Fashion

Never before had corruption loomed so large in the United States. With more money to spend, more favors to give, and more functions to perform, both state and federal govern-ments found themselves besieged by supplicants, and officeholders found opportunities to turn a dishonest penny where none had existed before. In New York City, infamous state senator William M. Tweed used the Tammany Hall political machine to steal tens of mil-lions of dollars. Senators bought their seats in Kansas and South Carolina, while Tennessee congressmen sold appointments to West Point. The Standard Oil Company allegedly con-trolled Pennsylvania's legislature. As Henry Clay Warmoth, the governor of Louisiana put it, corruption was "the fashion." He, incidentally, was very fashionable himself.

With an honest but credulous chief executive, Grant's administration became noto-riously corrupt. Customs collectors shook down merchants and used their employees to manage party conventions. With help from Administration insiders, the notorious

STRUGGLES FOR DEMOCRACY

An Incident at Coushatta, August 1874

If biracial democracy had a chance anywhere in Reconstruction Louisiana, it was upstate in Red River parish. With African Americans outnumbering whites more than two to one, majority rule meant Republican government. As in so many other black counties, whites held the choicest offices: sheriff, tax collector, and mayor of the parish seat in Coushatta. A Vermont-born Union veteran, Marshall Harvey Twitchell, represented Red River in the state senate. Most of the wealth and nearly all the property stayed in native white hands, just as it had before the war. Blacks continued to raise and harvest the cotton on other people's land.

Nevertheless, Reconstruction made a difference for African Americans. They elected members of their own race to the police jury that did most of the parish's day-to-day governing. Several justices of the peace who handled minor civil cases were black. Farmers, field hands, and day laborers performed jury duty. What freed people wanted most, however, was what white conservatives had long denied them, a functioning public school system. Twitchell saw that they got one, with separate schools for whites and blacks. So prosperous was Red River under "Negro rule," Twitchell bragged, that it was evident to "the most perfect stranger."

Having the most votes was not enough, however. All the influential newspapers and nearly all the property and firepower in Red River parish remained with the Democrats. When hard times hit, Republicans' enemies organized rifle clubs and a White League, which acted as the military arm of the Democratic Party. Unlike the Ku Klux Klan, it operated in the open and without disguises. By mid-1874, death threats against Republican officials were being posted on the streets of Coushatta. "Your fate is sealed," one letter warned judges. "Nothing but your blood will appease us." Alarmed, the police jury resigned and white Republicans left the parish.

That August, White Leaguers pretended to have uncovered a black plot to slaughter white residents. On that excuse, they arrested several dozen black Republican leaders and all the white parish officers. To save their lives, the officials resigned. The vigilantes promised them an armed escort out of the parish, but instead, it led them into an ambush. Mounted gunmen from the neighboring parish killed six prisoners. Later they rode into Coushatta and hanged two of the captured blacks as well. Absent on political business, Twitchell alone survived. When he returned in 1876, an unknown gunman shot him, costing him both arms. From then on, Republican majorities counted for nothing. Democrats did the voting and governing and thus radical Reconstruction's gains melted away.

Coushatta's fate was Louisiana's. White Leaguers overthrew the governor in September 1874. Federal intervention restored him, but it could not save local Republican governments like Red River's. "The State government has no power outside of the United States Army . . . no power at all," an officer confessed. "The White League is the only power in the State."

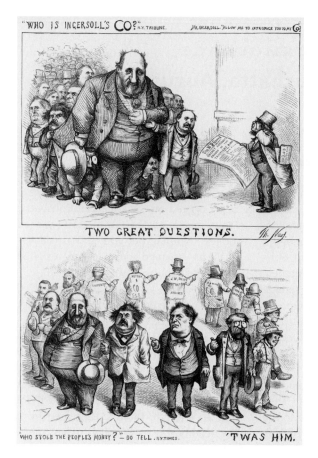

William M. Tweed The boss of New York's notoriously corrupt "Tweed Ring" was parodied by the great cartoonist Thomas Nast. His portrayal of the bloated public official became an enduring symbol of governmental corruption.

speculators Jay Gould and Jim Fisk tried to corner the nation's gold supply and brought on a brief, ruinous panic on Wall Street. Grant's private secretary was even exposed as a member of the "Whiskey Ring," a group of distillers and revenue agents who cheated the government out of millions of dollars in taxes. Charges of making money swindling the Indians forced the Secretary of Interior out of office. Months later, the Secretary of War quit when investigators traced kickbacks to his wife. Having overcharged the government for supplies while building the Union Pacific Railroad, the fraudulent Credit Mobilier contracting firm shared mammoth profits with nearly a dozen top congressmen. The Republican platform, one critic snarled, was just a conjugation of the verb "to steal."

Southern corruption reflected national patterns. In the worst states, both parties stole, bribed, and profited. But in the South, Democrats blamed such action on ignorant black voters and non-landowning white Republicans. Shifting the issue from equal rights to honest government, they insisted that clean, cheap government, run by society's natural leaders (white and well-heeled), would benefit all races. Every scandal discredited Republican rule further, including the many upright and talented leaders, both black and white, that fought against corruption. This helped galvanize the opposition, destroying Republican hopes of attracting white voters and weakening support for Reconstruction. By 1875, northerners assumed the worst of any carpetbagger, even one fighting to cut taxes and block cheats.

Liberal Republicans Revolt

Voicing widely held concerns, a small, influential group of northern Republican intellectuals, editors, and activists challenged a political system that, in their view, rested on greed, selfishness, partisanship, and politicians' keeping war hatreds alive. Known as "liberal Republicans," they viewed bosses and political machines, which were out to loot the treasury, and special interests as detrimental to good government. They were weary of railroads receiving land grants, of steamship lines receiving subsidies, and government clerkships that were given to cronies. Decrying corruption and disenchanted with Reconstruction, they called for reform: a lower tariff, a stable currency system based on gold, a merit-based civil service system for appointments to office, and full, universal amnesty for former Confederates.

When Democrats announced a "New Departure," accepting the three constitutional amendments, liberal Republicans took them at their word. Despairing of preventing Grant's renomination, they nominated the eccentric, reform-minded editor Horace Greeley for president in 1872. The platform promised to end all political disabilities and reconcile North and South, in essence by ending all federal intervention on black southerners' behalf. Desperate to win, Democrats endorsed the editor, their lifelong enemy, but thousands stayed home on election day rather than vote for him. Having cut the tariff and restored the office-holding rights of all but a handful of ex-Confederates, Republicans won many reformers back. Greeley lost in a landslide and died in a sanitarium less than a month later.

Grant's reelection bought Reconstruction time, but it could not do more than that. Northerners, even Republican ones, became increasingly alarmed every time the national government used its power to act on behalf of Reconstruction governments and deal with issues that should be handled by local authorities. As a result, the president found it increasingly hard to justify intervening on the behalf of black voters.

"Redeeming" the South

In September 1873, America's premier financial institution, Jay Cooke & Company, went bankrupt after overextending itself on investments in the Northern Pacific Railroad. Within weeks, hundreds of banks and thousands of businesses failed. The country sank into a depression that lasted five years. Unemployment rose to 14 percent as corporations slashed wages. Bitter strikes in textile plants, coal fields, and on the railroad lines ended in failure and violence. As America turned its attention to issues of corruption, labor unrest, and economic depression, Reconstruction took a backseat.

Between the corruption scandals buffeting the Grant administration and the economic crisis, northern voters' interest in Reconstruction plummeted. Those who had favored government intervention to keep "Rebels" from coming to power no longer saw the need. Former Confederates stood by the flag as earnestly as Unionists. In the 1874 elections, Democrats made a dramatic comeback. For the first time since 1859, they carried the House, guaranteeing a deadlocked Congress. Outgoing Republicans made one last advance, passing Charles Sumner's civil rights bill, which outlawed discrimination in public places. The law left segregated schools and cemeteries alone, and most southern establishments ignored even those provisions that did pass. But with Congress's adjournment in March 1875, Republicans no longer had any chance of bolstering Reconstruction with legislation, or even funding an army big enough to protect a fair vote at the polls.

Supreme Court rulings made implementing Reconstruction legislation harder still. In the 1873 *Slaughterhouse* cases, a majority decided that the Fourteenth Amendment's protection of equal rights under the law covered only those rights associated with national citizenship. Rights affiliated with state citizenship—for example, the right to butcher cattle when a Louisiana state law gave a monopoly to one particular firm—could only be upheld by the state. In 1876, the justices whittled down the national government's power to protect black voters from intimidation and violence or even their right to bear arms and hold public meetings. In *Hall v. DeCuir* (1878), the Supreme Court invalidated a Louisiana law prohibiting racial segregation on public transportation. In the Civil Rights Cases of 1883, the Supreme Court declared that the Fourteenth Amendment did not cover discriminatory practices by private persons.

Even before the 1874 elections, southern Reconstruction was collapsing. As the number of white Republicans fell, the number of black Republicans holding office in the South increased. But the persistence of black officeholders only reinforced the Democrats' determination to "redeem" their states from Republican rule. Blaming hard times on "carpetbagger" corruption and high taxes, conservatives mobilized voters across the South. They formed taxpayers' leagues and armed themselves in White Leagues, paramilitary groups whose goal was to remove Republicans from office and prevent freedmen from voting. Even without much killing, crude appeals to white supremacy and harsh economic pressure forced most scalawags to drop out of politics, making it easier to draw a sharp color line. Paramilitaries were then able to apply violence and intimidation to keep blacks from the polls. By the fall of 1874, they were overthrowing local governments in Mississippi and Louisiana. In 1874, White Leagues took over the streets in New Orleans and briefly ousted the governor. Terrorism helped "redeem" Alabama that November, among other places.

That left two securely Republican states, both with considerable black majorities: South Carolina and Mississippi. In 1875, Democrats "redeemed" the latter in the most blatant show of force yet. Governor Adelbert Ames begged for help from Grant and was told to look to his own resources first. The election that followed was as quiet as White League shotguns could make it. In the end, enough blacks were kept from the polls and enough scalawags voted their racial prejudices to hand power to the Democrats. Within months they forced Ames's resignation. In 1876, South Carolina whites adopted what became known as the "Mississippi Plan" with an even more open commitment to violent overthrow of the Republican majority. Mounted, armed men broke up Republican

Time Line

▼1863
Lincoln's Proclamation of Amnesty and Reconstruction

▼1864
Wade-Davis Bill

▼1865
Thirteenth Amendment adopted and ratified
Freedmen's Bureau established
Confederate armies surrender
Lincoln assassinated; Andrew Johnson becomes president

Johnson creates provisional governments in the South; new civil governments begin
Joint Committee on Reconstruction established by Congress

▼1866
Congress renews Freedmen's Bureau; Johnson vetoes it
Civil Rights Act vetoed by Johnson; Congress overrides veto
Congress passes Fourteenth Amendment

New Orleans and Memphis massacres
Republicans sweep midterm elections

▼1867
First, Second, and Third Reconstruction Acts passed
Tenure of Office Act

▼1868
Johnson fires Secretary of War Stanton
House of Representatives impeaches Johnson

rallies. In Hamburg, white paramilitaries put the local black militia under siege and, after their surrender, killed seven of them. "We write to tell you that our people are being shot down like dogs, and no matter what democrats may say," one South Carolinian wrote the president, "unless you help us our folks will not dare go to the polls." In Louisiana, Redeemer violence may have been worse still.

The Twice-Stolen Election of 1876

Amidst a serious economic depression, and with an electorate tired of Reconstruction, the Democrats stood a good chance of winning the presidency in 1876. The Democratic candidate, New York governor Samuel J. Tilden, had won a reputation for fighting thieves in his own party. On election night, Tilden won 250,000 more votes than his Republican opponent, Ohio governor Rutherford B. Hayes (see Map 15–4). But Republican "returning boards" in three southern states—Florida, South Carolina, and Louisiana—counted Hayes in and gave him a one-electoral vote victory.

Democrats swore that they had been cheated out of the presidency, though even without white violence and manipulation, Hayes probably would have won not just in the three disputed states but elsewhere in the South. Both houses of Congress deadlocked on counting the electoral votes. Cries of "Tilden or Blood" rang through the air. In the end, both sides compromised by choosing a special electoral commission to settle the matter. In an eight-to-seven vote, it awarded Hayes every disputed state. House Democrats could not stop "His Fraudulency" from being sworn in, but their southern members, cutting the best deal they could, agreed to drop their obstruction in return for assurances that Hayes would not aid in the survival of the last two Reconstruction governments. A month after taking office, Hayes withdrew the regiments guarding Republican statehouses in South Carolina and Louisiana; by that time Redeemer Democrats had full control of the states anyway. This order marked Reconstruction's symbolic end. Hereafter, the president would emphasize goodwill between the North and South and trust Redeemers' promises to protect black rights—a trust that was speedily betrayed.

Senate trial of Johnson ends in
    acquittal
Fourteenth Amendment ratified
Waves of Klan violence sweep
    cotton south
Ulysses S. Grant elected
    president

▼1869
Congress passes Fifteenth
    Amendment

▼1870
Fifteenth Amendment ratified

▼1872
"Liberal Republican" revolt
Grant reelected

▼1873
Financial "panic" sets off
    depression

▼1875
"Mississippi Plan" succeeds
Civil Rights Act enacted

▼1876
Disputed presidential election
    of Rutherford B. Hayes and
    Samuel J. Tilden

▼1877
Electoral commission names
    Rutherford B. Hayes
    president
Last Reconstruction
    governments collapse

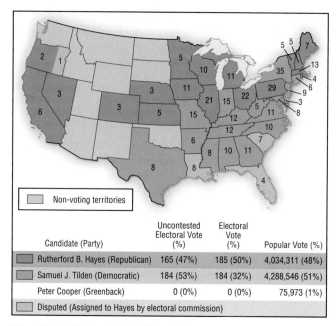

Candidate (Party)	Uncontested Electoral Vote (%)	Electoral Vote (%)	Popular Vote (%)
Rutherford B. Hayes (Republican)	165 (47%)	185 (50%)	4,034,311 (48%)
Samuel J. Tilden (Democratic)	184 (53%)	184 (32%)	4,288,546 (51%)
Peter Cooper (Greenback)	0 (0%)	0 (0%)	75,973 (1%)
Disputed (Assigned to Hayes by electoral commission)			

Map 15–4   The Presidential Election, 1876 In 1876 the Democratic presidential candidate, Samuel Tilden, won the popular vote but was denied the presidency because the Republicans who controlled Congress chose to interpret voting irregularities in Louisiana, South Carolina, Oregon, and Florida in a way that gave their candidate, Rutherford B. Hayes, all of the disputed electoral votes.

Conclusion

Inspired by a vision of society based on equal rights and free labor, Republicans expected emancipation to transform the South. Freed from the shackles of the slave power, the region might yet become a shining example of democracy and prosperity. Twenty years later, events seemed to mock that promise. The South was scarcely more industrial than before the war and, as far as former slaves were concerned, far from completely free. Cotton, sugar, rice, and tobacco still defined the South's economy far more than the hoped-for mines and mills. Only a small fraction of freed people had become landowners, and most of them would never escape poverty and dependence on propertied whites. After the Panic of 1873, sharecropping eliminated most blacks' hope of real economic independence. As fears of a new rebellion dimmed, Republicans lost their zeal for federal intervention in the South. Republican state authorities could not save themselves, much less their black constituents. Chastened by Reconstruction's defects, Americans began to turn their attention to the new problems of urban, industrial America.

Even so, the achievements of Reconstruction were monumental. Across the South, African Americans carved out a space in which their families could live more freely than before. Black and white men elected to office some of the most democratic state legislatures of the nineteenth century. Thousands of black workers had escaped a stifling contract-labor system for the comparatively wider autonomy of sharecropping. Hundreds of thousands of former slaves learned to read and write and were able to worship in churches of their own making. Most important, Reconstruction added three important amendments to the Constitution that transformed civil rights and electoral laws throughout the nation. For the first time, the protections in the Bill of Rights would apply not just against national encroachment but that of the states as well. As a result of those changes in fundamental law, Reconstruction, then, was not so much a promise broken as one waiting to be fulfilled.

Who, What

Nathaniel Banks 455

John Dennett 452

Ulysses S. Grant 463

Horace Greeley 454

Oliver Otis Howard 457

Andrew Johnson 453

Elizabeth Cady Stanton 471

William Sylvis 472

Black Codes 458

Fifteenth Amendment 470

Fourteenth Amendment 460

Freedmen's Bureau 452

"Liberal Republicans" 474

National Labor Union 472

Redemption 472

Sharecropping 454

Ten Percent Plan 456

Tenure of Office Act 463

Review Questions

1. What made congressional Reconstruction "radical"?

2. How did conditions for the readmission of states into the Union change over time?

3. How did Reconstruction change the South?

4. How did Reconstruction change the North?

5. What were the major factors that brought Reconstruction to an end?

Critical-Thinking Questions

1. Compare and contrast wartime Reconstruction, presidential Reconstruction, and congressional (radical) Reconstruction. What were the key differences between the three phases?

2. How critical was the failure of land redistribution for blacks? Was sharecropping an acceptable substitute for achieving economic freedom? Why or why not?

3. In what ways did the tactics of white supremacists in this period end up hurting their own cause?

For further review materials and resource information, please visit www.oup.com/us/oakes

CHAPTER 15: RECONSTRUCTING A NATION, 1865–1877
Primary Sources

15.1 PETROLEUM V. NASBY [DAVID ROSS LOCKE], *A PLATFORM FOR NORTHERN DEMOCRATS* (1865)

David Ross Locke, the editor of the *Toledo Blade*, made his fortune under another name: Petroleum V. Nasby, a fictional postmaster and sometimes pastor, whose letters gave a Republican spoof of what Copperhead Democrats believed. Bad spelling was a common way of signaling to readers that a piece was meant to be humorous, though Locke also meant to show that Nasby's ideas were not only vicious and absurd but founded on a virtually illiterate ignorance.

Saint's Rest (wich is in the Stait uv Noo Jersey), June the 23d, 1865

These is the dark days uv the dimokrasy. The misforchoons that befell our armies in front uv Richmond, the fall uv our capital, follered by the surrender uv our armies to Grant and Sherman, hez hurt us. Our leaders are either pinin in loathsome dunguns, incarseratid by the hevin-defyin, man-destroyin, tyrannical edix uv our late lamented President, or are baskin in the free air uv Italy and Canady. We hev no way uv keepin our voters together. Opposin the war won't do no good, for before the next elecshun the heft uv our voters will hev diskiverd that the war is over. The fear uv drafts may do suthin in some parts uv Pennsylvany and suthern Illinoy, for sum time yuit, but that can't be depended on.

But we hev wun resource for a ishoo—ther will alluz be a dimokrasy so long as ther's a nigger.

Ther is a uncompromising dislike to the nigger in the mind uv a ginooine dimekrat. The Spanish bullfighter, when he wants to inflame the bull to extra cavortin, waves a red flag afore him. When yoo desire a dimekrat to froth at the mouth, yoo will find a black face will anser the purpose. Therefore, the nigger is, today, our best and only holt. Let us use him.

For the guidance uv the faithful, I shel lay down a few plain rools to be observed, in order to make the most uv the capital we hev:

1. Alluz assert that the nigger will never be able to take care uv hisself, but will alluz be a public burden. He may, possibly, give us the lie by goin to work. In sich a emergency, the dooty uv every dimekrat is plane. He must not be allowed to work. Associashens must be organized, pledged to neither give him employment, to work with him, to work for anyone who will give him work, or patronize any wun who duz. (I wood sejest that sich uv us ez hev bin forchoonit enuff to git credit, pay a trifle on account, so ez to make our patronage worth suthin.) This course, rigidly and persistently follered, will drive the best uv em to stealin, and the balance to the poorhouses, provin wat we hev alluz claimed, that they are a idle and vishus race. Think, my brethren, wat a inspirin effeck our poorhouses and jails full uv niggers wood hev on the people! My sole expands ez I contemplate the deliteful vision.

2. Likewise assert that the nigger will come North, and take all the good places, throwin all our skilled mechanics out uv work by underbiddin uv em. This mite be open to two objecshuns, to-wit: It crosses slitely rool the 1, and white men mite say, ef there's jist enuff labor for wat's here, why not perhibit furriners from comin? I anser: It's the biznis uv the voter to reconcile the contraicshun—he may believe either or both. Ez to the second objeckshun, wher is the Dimekrat who coodent be underbid, and stand it even to starvashen, ef the underbiddin wux dun by a man uv the proud Caukashen race? And wher is the Dimekrat so lost to manhjood ez not to drink blood, ef the same underbiddin is dun by a nigger? The starving for work ain't the question—it's the color uv the cause uv the starvashen that makes the difference.

Nigger equality may be worked agin to advantage. All men, without distincshun uv sex, are fond uv flatrin theirselves that somebody's lower down in the scale uv humanity than they is. Ef 'twan't for niggers, what wood the dimokrasy do for sumbody to look down upon? It's also shoor to enlist wun style uv wimmen on our sides. In times gone by, I've notist gushin virgins uv forty-five, full sixteen hands high and tough ez wire, holdin aloft banners onto which wuz inscrib'd – "Save us from Nigger Equality." Yoo see it soothed em to hev a chase uv advertising, 1st, That they wuz frail, helplis critters; and, 2d, That, anshent and tough ez they wuz, some wun wuz still goin for em.

Ef ther ain't no niggers, central commities must furnish em. A half dozen will do for a ordinary county, ef they're hustled along with energy. Ef they won't steal, the central commities must do it theirselves. Show yer niggers in a township in the morning, an the same nite rob the clothes-lines and hen-roosts. Ever willin to sacrifice myself for the cause, I volunteer to do this latter dooty in six populous counties.

These ijees, ef follered, will, no doubt, keep us together until our enemies split, when we will reap the reward uv our constancy and fidelity. May the Lord hasten the day.

Petroleum V. Nasby
Lait Paster uv the Church uv the Noo Dispensashun

Source: David Ross Locke/Petroleum V. Nasby, *A Platform for Northern Democrats*, from Locke, *The Struggles, Social, Financial and Political of Petroleum V. Nasby* (Boston, 1888), quoted in William Benton, publ., *The Annals of America. Volume 9, 1858–1865: The Crisis of the Union* (Chicago: Encyclopedia Britannica, Inc., 1968), pp. 597–598.

15.2 MISSISSIPPI BLACK CODE (1865)

Faced with the speedy emancipation of nearly half of Mississippi's population, the first all-white postwar legislature set out to define what rights blacks should enjoy in freedom. Some of the most basic were guaranteed, including the right to marry and hold property, and to testify under certain limited circumstances. Others were denied, among them the right to vote, sit on juries, hold office, or intermarry with whites. Most controversially, the Apprentice and Vagrancy Laws created a structure, color-blind in its outward workings, that effectively allowed white authorities to commandeer blacks and force them into involuntary labor or even to sell their labor to white bidders at auction.

Apprentice Law

Section 1. *Be it enacted by the legislature of the state of Mississippi*, that it shall be the duty of all sheriffs, justices of the peace, and other civil officers of the several counties in this state to report to the Probate courts of their respective counties semiannually, at the January and July terms of said courts, all freedmen, free Negroes, and mulattoes under the age of eighteen within their respective counties, beats, or districts who are orphans, or whose parent or parents have not the means, or who refuse to provide for and support said minors; and thereupon it shall be the duty of said Probate Court to order the clerk of said court to apprentice said minors to some competent and suitable person, on such terms as the court my direct, having a particular care to the interest of said minors:

Provided, that the former owner of said minors shall have the preference when, in the opinion of the court, he or she shall be a suitable person for that purpose.

Section 2. *Be it further enacted*, that the said court shall be fully satisfied that the person or persons to whom said minor shall be apprenticed shall be a suitable person to have the charge and care of said minor and fully to protect the interest of said minor. The said court shall require the said master or mistress to execute bond and security, payable to the state of Mississippi, conditioned that he or she shall furnish said minor with sufficient food and clothing; to treat said minor humanely; furnish medical attention in case of sickness; teach or cause to be taught him or her to read and write, if under fifteen years old; and will conform to any law that may be hereafter passed for the regulation of the duties and relation of master and apprentice:

Provided, that said apprentice shall be bound by indenture, in case of males until they are twenty-one years old, and in case of females until they are eighteen years old.

Section 3. *Be it further enacted*, that in the management and control of said apprentices, said master or mistress shall have power to inflict such moderate corporeal chastisement as a father or guardian is allowed to inflict on his or her child or ward in common law:

Provided, that in no case shall cruel or inhuman punishment be inflicted.

Section 4. *Be it further enacted*, that if any apprentice shall leave the employment of his or her master or mistress without his or her consent, said master or mistress may pursue and recapture said apprentice and bring him or her before any justice of the peace of the county, whose duty it shall be to remand said apprentice to the service of his or her master or mistress; and in the event of a refusal on the part of said apprentice so to return, then said justice shall commit said apprentice to the jail of said county, on failure to give bond, until the next term of the country court; and it shall be the duty of said court, at the first term thereafter, to investigate said case; and if the court shall be of opinion that said apprentice left the employment of his or her master or mistress without good cause, to order him or her to be punished, as provided for the punishment of hired freedmen, as may be from time to time provided for by law, for desertion, until he or she shall agree to return to his or her master or mistress:

Provided, that the court may grant continuances, as in other cases; and provided, further, that if the court shall believe that said apprentice had good cause to quit his said master or mistress, the court shall discharge said apprentice from said indenture and also enter a judgment against the master or mistress for not more than $100, for the use and benefit of said apprentice, to be collected on execution, as in other cases.

Section 5. *Be it further enacted*, that if any person entice away any apprentice from his or her master or mistress, or shall knowingly employ an apprentice, or furnish him or her food or clothing, without the written consent of his or her master or mistress, or shall sell or give said apprentice ardent spirits, without such consent, said person so offending shall be deemed guilty of a high misdemeanor, and shall, on conviction thereof before the county court, be punished as provided for the punishment of persons enticing from their employer hired freedmen, free Negroes, or mulattoes.

Section 6. *Be it further enacted*, that it shall be the duty of all civil officers of their respective counties to report any minors within their respective counties to said Probate Court who are subject to be apprenticed under the provisions of this act, from time to time, as the facts may come to their knowledge; and it shall be the duty of said court, from time to time, as said minors shall be reported to them or otherwise come to their knowledge, to apprentice said minors as hereinbefore provided.

Section 7. *Be it further enacted*, that in case the master or mistress of any apprentice shall desire, he or she shall have the privilege to summon his or her said apprentice to the Probate Court, and thereupon, with the approval of the court, he or she shall be released from all liability as master of said apprentice, and his said bond shall be canceled, and it shall be the duty of the court forthwith to reapprentice said minor; and in the event any master of an apprentice shall die before the close of the term of service of said apprentice, it shall be the duty of the court to give the preference in reapprenticing said minor to the widow, or other member of said master's family:

Provided, that said widow or other member of said family shall be a suitable person for that purpose.

Section 8. *Be it further enacted*, that in case any master or mistress of any apprentice, bound to him or her under this act shall be about to remove or shall have removed to any other state of the United States by the laws of which such apprentice may be an inhabitant thereof, the Probate Court of the proper county may authorize the removal of such apprentice to such state upon the said master or mistress entering into bond, with security, in a penalty to be fixed by the judge, conditioned that said master or mistress will, upon such removal, comply with the laws of such state in such cases:

Provided, that said master shall be cited to attend the court at which such order is proposed to be made and shall have a right to resist the same by next friend, or otherwise.

Section 9. *Be it further enacted*, that it shall be lawful for any freedman, free Negro, or mulatto, having a minor child or children to apprentice the said minor child or children, as provided for by this act.

Section 10. *Be it further enacted*, that in all cases where the age of the freedman, free Negro, or mulatto cannot be ascertained by record testimony, the judge of the county court shall fix the age.

Vagrancy Law

Section 1. *Be it enacted by the legislature of the state of Mississippi*, that all rogues and vagabonds, idle and dissipated persons, beggars, jugglers, or persons practising unlawful games or plays, runaways, common drunkards, common nightwalkers, pilferers, lewd, wanton, or lascivious persons, in speech or behavior, common railers and brawlers, persons who neglect their calling or employment, misspend what they earn, or do not provide for the support of themselves or their families or dependents, and all other idle and disorderly persons, including all who neglect all lawful business, or habitually misspend their time by frequenting houses of ill-fame, gaming houses, or tippling shops, shall be deemed and considered vagrants under the provisions of this act; and, on conviction thereof shall be fined not exceeding $100, with all accruing costs, and be imprisoned at the discretion of the court not exceeding ten days.

Section 2. *Be it further enacted,* that all freedmen, free Negroes, and mulattoes in this state over the age of eighteen years found on the second Monday in January 1966, or thereafter, with no lawful employment or business, or found unlawfully assembling themselves together either in the day or nighttime, and all white persons so assembling with freedmen, free Negroes, or mulattoes, or usually associating with freedmen, free Negroes, or mulattoes on terms of equality, or living in adultery or fornication with a freedwoman, free Negro, or mulatto, shall be deemed vagrants; and, on conviction thereof, shall be fined in the sum of not exceeding, in the case of a freedman, free Negro, or mulatto, $50, and a white man, $200, and imprisoned at the discretion of the court, the free Negro not exceeding ten days, and the white man not exceeding six months.

Section 3. *Be it further enacted,* that all justices of the peace, mayors, and aldermen of incorporated towns and cities of the several counties in this state shall have jurisdiction to try all questions of vagrancy in their respective towns, counties, and cities; and it is hereby made their duty, whenever they shall ascertain that any person or persons in their respective towns, counties, and cities are violating any of the provisions of this act, to have said party or parties arrested and brought before them and immediately investigate said charge; and, on conviction, punish said party or parties as provided for herein. And it is hereby made the duty of all sheriffs, constables, town constables, city marshals, and all like officers to report to some officer having jurisdiction all violations of any of the provisions of this act; and it shall be the duty of the county courts to inquire if any officers have neglected any of the duties required by this act; and in case any officer shall fail or neglect any duty herein, it shall be the duty of the county court to fine said officer, upon conviction, not exceeding $100, to be paid into the county treasury for county purposes.

Section 4. *Be it further enacted,* that keepers of gaming houses, houses of prostitution, all prostitutes, public or private, and all persons who derive their chief support in employments that militate against good morals or against laws shall be deemed and held to be vagrants.

Section 5. *Be it further enacted,* that all fines and forfeitures collected under the provisions of this act shall be paid into the county treasury for general county purposes; and in case any freedman, free Negro, or mulatto shall fail for five days after the imposition of any fine or forfeiture upon him or her for violation of any of the provisions of this act to pay the same, that it shall be, and is hereby made, the duty of the sheriff of the proper county to hire out said freedman, free Negro, or mulatto to any person who will, for the shortest period of service, pay said fine or forfeiture and all costs:

Provided, a preference shall be given to the employer, if there be one, in which case the employer shall be entitled to deduct and retain the amount so paid from the wages of such freedman, free Negro, or mulatto then due or to become due; and in case such freedman, free Negro, or mulatto cannot be hired out he or she may be dealt with as a pauper.

Section 6. *Be it further enacted,* that the same duties and liabilities existing among white persons of this state shall attach to freedmen, free Negroes, and mulattoes to support their indigent families and all colored paupers; and that, in order to secure a support for such indigent freedmen, free Negroes, and mulattoes, it shall be lawful, and it is hereby made the duty of the boards of county police of each county in this state, to levy a poll or capitation tax on each and every freedman, free Negro, or mulatto, between the ages of eighteen and sixty years, not to exceed the sum of $1 annually, to each person so taxed, which tax, when collected, shall be paid into the county treasurer's hands and constitute a fund to be called the Freedman's Pauper Fund, which shall be applied by the commissioners of the poor for the maintenance of the poor of the freedmen, free Negroes and mulattoes of this state, under such regulations as may be established by the boards of county police, in the respective counties of this state.

Section 7. *Be it further enacted,* that if any freedman, free Negro, or mulatto shall fail or refuse to pay any tax levied according to the provisions of the 6th Section of this act, it shall be prima facie evidence of vagrancy, and it shall be the duty of the sheriff to arrest such freedman, free Negro, or mulatto, or such person refusing or neglecting to pay such tax, and proceed at once to hire, for the shortest time, such delinquent taxpayer to anyone who will pay the said tax, with accruing costs, giving preference to the employer, if there be one.

Section 8. *Be it further enacted,* that any person feeling himself or herself aggrieved by the judgment of any justice of the peace, mayor, or alderman in cases arising under this act may, within five days, appeal to the next term of the county court of the proper county, upon giving bond and security in a sum not less than $25 nor more than $150, conditioned to appear and prosecute said appeal, and abide by the judgment of the county court, and said appeal shall be tried *de novo* in the county court, and the decision of said court shall be final.

Source: Mississippi Black Code, 1865, from *Laws of the State of Mississippi, Passed at a Regular Session of the Mississippi Legislature* (Jackson, 1866), pp. 82–93, 165–167, quoted in William Benton, publ., *The Annals of America. Volume 9, 1858–1865: The Crisis of the Union* (Chicago: Encyclopedia Britannica, Inc., 1968), pp. 628–634.

15.3 SHARECROPPING CONTRACT BETWEEN ALONZO T. MIAL AND FENNER POWELL (1886)

For Republicans, the essence of "free labor" was the *contract*, the notion that either a governing figure and his people, or a wealthy man and those who labored for him, both had to subscribe voluntarily to an explicit agreement outlining their mutual responsibilities in order for their relationship to be binding. Unfortunately, after the war, southern blacks freed from slavery but without land sometimes had little choice but to sign stringent labor contracts with landlords, who were often former slave owners. A system emerged known as sharecropping. The tenant, or "cropper," would sign an annual contract to work a plot of land in return for a share of the crop. The following is a sharecropping contract from 1886, between a landlord named A. T. Mial and a sharecropper named Fenner Powell.

This contract made and entered into between A. T. Mial of one part and Fenner Powell of the other part both of the County of Wake and state of North Carolina—

Witnesseth—That the Said Fenner Powell hath bargained and agreed with the Said Mial to work as a cropper for the year 1886 on Said Mial's land on the land now occupied by Said Powell on the west Side of Poplar Creek and a point on the east Side of Said Creek and both South and North of the Mial road, leading to Raleigh, That the said Fenner Powell agrees to work faithfully and diligently without any unnecessary loss of time, to do all manner of work on Said farm as may be directed by Said Mial, And to be respectful in manners and deportment to Said Mial. And the Said Mial agrees on his part to furnish mule and feed for the same and all plantation tools and Seed to plant the crop free of charge, and to give the said Powell One half of all crops raised and housed by Said Powell on Said land except the cotton seed. The Said Mial agrees to advance as provisions to Said Powell fifty pound of bacon and two sacks of meal per month and occasionally some flour to be paid out of his the Said Powell's part of the crop or from any other advance that may be made to Said Powell by Said Mial. As witness our hands and seals this the 16th day of January A.D. 1886.

Source: Contract between Alonzo T. Mial and Fenner Powell, January 1886, in Roger Ransom and Richard Sutch, *One Kind of Freedom: The Economic Consequences of Emancipation* (New York: Cambridge University Press, 1977), p. 91.

15.4 JOSEPH FARLEY, AN ACCOUNT OF RECONSTRUCTION

Joseph Farley, born in 1843 in Virginia, ran away and joined the Union army. Later he was given a pension. "At that time I never thought about dying," he remembers. "I never thought about anybody shooting me; I just thought about shooting them." Interviewed in 1930 by a black student from Fisk University, he gave a rambling account, from which the postwar material has been excerpted. As with all distant recollections, Farley's may have been affected by the lapse of time and the person conducting the interview.

It was a long, long time before everything got quiet after the war. On Franklin Street here I saw once 100 Ku Klux Klans, with long robes and faces covered. You don't know anything of them. They were going down here a piece to hang a man. There were about 600 of us soldiers, so we followed them to protect the man. The Klan knew this, and passed on by the house and went on back to town and never did bother the man.

One time a colored soldier married a white woman over here at Fort Bruce. The man belonged to my company. His name was Sergeant Cook. About twenty of the soldiers went to the wedding, and they had about five or six white men who said he couldn't marry this woman. Old Dr. Taylor . . . came over to marry them. He stood near me and I told him to go on and marry this couple or else someone here would die. He looked around and saw all these soldiers and he knew about us and that we meant for him to do as he had been told. He married them and we guarded our hack over to the war boat on the Cumberland. They went over to Nashville and lived there. They had a daughter whose name was Mrs. Gnatt. When they married was in 1866. Mrs. Gnatt could tell you her father was named Cyrus Cook. Guess you know you can't do that now, no sir; you just can't do that now. At one time a colored man could ride anywhere he wanted to, but now he can't do it. I am one of the first voters of Montgomery County. They told me at one time that I was not to come to the polls or I would be met by 600 men on horses. So about six or eight hundred of us armed and went to the polls with our bayonets. That man that had told me that did not show up. So we voted, and voted for whom we wanted. At that time the Rebels who rebelled against this country could not vote and they said that these Negroes shouldn't vote but we showed them. Of course, they came down and stood and looked at us but they didn't bother us. We went there armed and prepared for fighting so that if they started anything, there would be trouble. When they mustered me out from the army, I brought my gun from Nashville right here to Clarksville and kept it twenty-five years. Finally I let an old soldier have it.

When I first came here we had no teachers here but white teachers. They would call the roll same as calling the roll for soldiers. They taught school in the churches before they had school houses. They used to go to school at night and work all day. Clarence C. White's father, Will White, was the first teacher or principal of the school here in Clarksville.

. . . .

When the War was over some of the colored returned to their white folks, but I didn't want to be under the white folks again. I was glad to get out. Once, for fifteen years here, I run a saloon and livery stable. One time I worked on a boat. When I was on my first boat, one time I went to vote. A white man told me that if I voted Republican he would fire me, so I told him to fire me then. I just told him he could fire me right now for I didn't want to work anyway. I went on and voted the Republican ticket, and they told me they liked my principle and I could go on and go to work.

I still got my discharge from way back in 1866. I keeps it and I mean to keep it as long as I live. I am proud of it.

Source: Rawick, George P. Rawick, ed. *The American Slave: A Composite Autobiography. Volume 18. Unwritten History of Slavery (Fisk University)* (Westport, CT: Greenwood, 1972), pp. 121–128.

15.5 EXCERPT FROM THE TESTIMONY OF GADSDEN STEEL FROM PROCEEDINGS IN THE KU KLUX TRIALS AT COLUMBIA, S.C. IN THE UNITED STATES CIRCUIT COURT, NOVEMBER TERM (1871)

Gadsden Steel, a black South Carolinian from York County, appeared as a witness before the joint congressional committee investigating terrorism in the Deep South. South Carolina's governor had created a state militia, most of whose members were black. Among the targets of Ku Klux Klan violence were African Americans who voted Republican (that is, Radical), but particularly those who had enlisted. Any freed person who owned firearms risked midnight attack or confiscation of his weapons. Fearing for his safety, Steel moved to North Carolina after the attack.

Q. Were you a voter in York County?

A. Yes, sir.

Q. Vote at the last election?

A. Yes, sir.

Q. Are you twenty-one years of age?

A. Twenty-six.

Q. What ticket did you vote?

A. Voted the Radical ticket.

Q. Vote for Mr. Wallace?

A. Yes, sir.

Q. Now, tell the jury about the Ku Klux coming to your house last March, on the night that Jim Williams was killed; what they said and did and what you said, and all about it.

A. They came to my house on a Monday night. . . .

Q. Very well, tell what occurred.

A. They came to my house about ten o'clock, and I was in bed at that time; and I was asleep, and my wife she heard them before I did, and she shook me and woke me up, and told me she heard a mighty riding and walking, and said I had better get up, she thought it was Ku Klux. I jumped up, and put on my pantaloons, and stepped to the door, and looked out, and very close to the door I seen the men, and I stepped right back into the house; so when they knocked the door open they couldn't see me; and they came in and called for me to give up my gun, and I says I has no gun; and when I spoke they all grabbed me, and taken me out into the yard.

Q. What sort of looking people were they?

A. They was all disguised, as far as I could see—they was all disguised, and struck me three licks over the head, and jobbed the blood out of me, right forninst my eye, with a pistol; and four of them walked around to Mr. Moore's; and, when they started off, one touched the other, and said let's go around, and see this man, and then the crowd that had me taken me to Mr. Moore's, and asked Mr. Moore if I had a gun; and he said no, not that he knew of; and they asked me if I had a pistol, and he said no; they asked if I belonged to that company; he said no.

Q. What company?

A. Jim Williams' company; asked him was I a bad boy, and run about into any devilment; he said no; I was a very fine boy, as far as he knew; they asked how I voted; he said I voted the Radical ticket; they says, "There, G—d d—n you, I'll kill you for that"; they took me on out in the lane, and says, "come out and talk to Number 6"; they locked arms with me, and one took me by the collar, and put a gun agin me, and marched me out to Number 6; when I went out there, he was sitting on his horse; I walked up to him; he bowed his head down to me, (illustrating with a very low bow), and says, "How do you do," and horned me in the breast with his horns; had horns on the head about so long, (indicating about two feet;) I jumped back from him, and they punched me, and said, "Stand up to him, G—d d—n you, and talk to him." I told them I would do so; he told me that he wanted me to tell him who had guns.

Q. Who said that?

A. No. 6; I told him I knew a heap that had guns, but hadn't them now; they had done give them up; well, says he, ain't Jim Williams got the guns? I says I heard folks say that he has them, but I do not know whether he has them or not. Then he says to me: "We want you to go and show ups to where his house is; if you don't show us to where his house is we will kill you;" and then one looked up to the moon and says: "Don't tarry here too long with this d—n n--; we have to get back to hell before daybreak. It won't do to tarry here too long." Says he, "get on." There was a man standing to the right of me with his beast; his head was turned from me; I stepped around and got on behind him and rode on around until they turned towards the school house, about sixty yards down the road, and he asked me did I want to go, and I told him no. Says I, the fix I am in, if you don't do anything to me, may kill me. I hadn't nothing on but a shirt, pantaloons and drawers. They started in a lope then, and he hollowed to No. 6 that he could not keep up, that I was too heavy. Says he, "this God damned n—is too heavy." No. 6 hollows back to him, "let him down," and he rode close enough to the fence so that I could get down, and I stepped off; says he, "you go home and go to bed, and if you are not there when we come along, we will kill you the next time we call on you; we are going to kill Williams, and we are going to kill all these damned n—s that votes the Radical ticket; run, God damn you, run." I ran into the yard, and I heard somebody talking near the store, and I slipped up beside the palings, and it was Dr. Love and Andy Lindsey tallying, and Love seen me, and says, "Gadsden, did they hurt you?" "No," says I, "not much; they punched the blood out in two places, and knocked me two or three times about the head, but they did not hurt me very much." Says he, "you go to bed and I don't think they will trouble you very much." I went home and put on my clothes . . . and I waked the others up, and we all went out into the old field and laid there until the chickens crowed for day, and went back to Mr. Moore's, near the house, and lay there till clear daylight, and I goes into the yard there, and Mr. Moore came to me and looked over my face and seen where they had punched the blood out of me, and says then for me to go on to my work and make myself easy, that they should not come and bother me any more; I never seen any more of them after that.

Q. Now, what time the next day did you learn that Jim Williams was dead?

A. It was about 8 o'clock, when I heard of it.

Q. Did you go down near him?

A. No, sir; I didn't go. I was busy employed, and didn't go. I didn't quit my work to go. I was working at the mill, and some come there to the mill very early that morning and told it. . . .

Q. Jim Williams was killed that night, was he?

A. Yes, sir. He was killed that night.

Source: *Proceedings in the Ku Klux Trials at Columbia, S. C., in the United States Circuit Court, November Term, 1871* (Columbia House, 1872) quoted in Paul M. Angle, *The American Reader From Columbus to Today* (New York: Rand McNally & Company, 1958), pp. 349–352.

Historical Documents

The Declaration of Independence

When in the course of human events, it becomes necessary for one people to dissolve the political bands which have connected them with another, and to assume, among the powers of the earth, the separate and equal station to which the Laws of Nature and of Nature's God entitle them, a decent respect to the opinions of mankind requires that they should declare the causes which impel them to the separation.

We hold these truths to be self-evident, that all men are created equal, that they are endowed by their Creator with certain unalienable Rights, that among these are life, liberty and the pursuit of happiness. That to secure these rights, governments are instituted among men, deriving their just powers from the consent of the governed; that whenever any form of government becomes destructive of these ends, it is the right of the people to alter or to abolish it, and to institute new Government, laying its foundation on such principles and organizing its powers in such form, as to them shall seem most likely to effect their safety and happiness. Prudence, indeed, will dictate that Governments long established should not be changed for light and transient causes; and, accordingly, all experience hath shown, that mankind are more disposed to suffer, while evils are sufferable, than to right themselves by abolishing the forms to which they are accustomed. But when a long train of abuses and usurpations, pursuing invariably the same object evinces a design to reduce them under absolute despotism, it is their right, it is their duty, to throw off such government, and to provide new guards for their future security. Such has been the patient sufferance of these colonies; and such is now the necessity which constrains them to alter their former systems of government. The history of the present King of Great Britain is a history of repeated injuries and usurpations, all having in direct object the establishment of an absolute tyranny over these States. To prove this, let facts be submitted to a candid world:

He has refused his assent to laws, the most wholesome and necessary for the public good.

He has forbidden his governors to pass laws of immediate and pressing importance, unless suspended in their operation till his assent should be obtained; and, when so suspended, he has utterly neglected to attend to them.

He has refused to pass other laws for the accommodation of large districts of people, unless those people would relinquish the right of representation in the legislature, a right inestimable to them and formidable to tyrants only.

He has called together legislative bodies at places unusual, uncomfortable, and distant from the depository of their public records, for the sole purpose of fatiguing them into compliance with his measures.

He has dissolved representative houses repeatedly, for opposing with manly firmness his invasions on the rights of the people.

He has refused for a long time, after such dissolutions, to cause others to be elected; whereby the legislative powers, incapable of annihilation, have returned to the People at large for their exercise; the State remaining in the mean time exposed to all the dangers of invasion from without, and convulsions within.

He has endeavored to prevent the population of these States; for that purpose obstructing the laws for naturalization of foreigners; refusing to pass others to encourage their migrations hither, and raising the conditions of new appropriations of lands.

He has obstructed the administration of justice, by refusing his assent to laws for establishing judiciary powers.

He has made judges dependent on his will alone, for the tenure of their offices, and the amount and payment of their salaries.

He has erected a multitude of new offices, and sent hither swarms of officers to harass our people, and eat out their substance.

He has kept among us, in times of peace, standing armies without the consent of our legislatures.

He has affected to render the Military independent of, and superior to, the civil power.

He has combined with others to subject us to a jurisdiction foreign to our constitution and unacknowledged by our laws; giving his assent to their acts of pretended legislation:

For quartering large bodies of armed troops among us;

For protecting them, by a mock trial, from punishment for any murders which they should commit on the inhabitants of these States;

For cutting off our trade with all parts of the world;

For imposing taxes on us without our Consent;

For depriving us, in many cases, of the benefits of Trial by Jury;

For transporting us beyond Seas to be tried for pretended offences;

For abolishing the free System of English Laws in a neighbouring Province, establishing therein an Arbitrary government, and enlarging its Boundaries so as to render it at once an example and fit instrument for introducing the same absolute rule into these colonies;

For taking away our charters, abolishing our most valuable laws, and altering fundamentally the forms of our governments;

For suspending our own legislatures, and declaring themselves invested with power to legislate for us in all cases whatsoever.

He has abdicated government here, by declaring us out of his protection and waging war against us.

He has plundered our seas, ravaged our coasts, burnt our towns, and destroyed the lives of our people.

He is at this time transporting large armies of foreign mercenaries to complete the works of death, desolation and tyranny, already begun with circumstances of cruelty and perfidy scarcely paralleled in the most barbarous ages, and totally unworthy the head of a civilized nation.

He has constrained our fellow citizens taken captive on the high seas to bear arms against their country, to become the executioners of their friends and brethren, or to fall themselves by their hands.

He has excited domestic insurrections amongst us, and has endeavored to bring on the inhabitants of our frontiers, the merciless Indian savages, whose known rule of warfare, is an undistinguished destruction of all ages, sexes and conditions.

In every stage of these oppressions we have petitioned for redress in the most humble terms; our repeated petitions have been answered only by repeated injury. A prince whose character is thus marked by every act which may define a tyrant, is unfit to be the ruler of a free people.

Nor have we been wanting in attentions to our British brethren. We have warned them from time to time of attempts by their legislature to extend an unwarrantable jurisdiction over us. We have reminded them of the circumstances of our emigration and settlement here. We have appealed to their native justice and magnanimity, and we have conjured them by the ties of our common kindred to disavow these usurpations, which, would inevitably interrupt our connections and correspondence. They, too, have been deaf to the voice of justice and of consanguinity. We must, therefore, acquiesce in the necessity, which denounces our separation, and hold them, as we hold the rest of mankind, enemies in war, in peace friends.

We, therefore, the representatives of the United States of America, in general Congress, assembled, appealing to the Supreme Judge of the world for the rectitude of our intentions, do, in the name, and by the authority of the good people of these colonies, solemnly publish and declare, that these united colonies are, and of right ought to be free and independent states; that they are absolved from all allegiance to the British Crown, and that all political connection between them and the state of Great Britain, is and ought to be totally dissolved; and that, as free and independent states, they have full power to levy war, conclude peace, contract alliances, establish commerce, and to do all other acts and things which independent states may of right do. And for the support of this declaration, with a firm reliance on the protection of Divine Providence, we mutually pledge to each other our lives, our fortunes and our sacred honor.

The Constitution of the United States of America

We the People of the United States, in Order to form a more perfect Union, establish Justice, insure domestic Tranquility, provide for the common defence, promote the general Welfare, and secure the Blessings of Liberty to ourselves and our Posterity, do ordain and establish this Constitution for the United States of America.

Article I
Section 1

All legislative Powers herein granted shall be vested in a Congress of the United States, which shall consist of a Senate and House of Representatives.

Section 2

The House of Representatives shall be composed of Members chosen every second Year by the People of the several States, and the Electors in each State shall have the Qualifications requisite for Electors of the most numerous Branch of the State Legislature.

No Person shall be a Representative who shall not have attained to the Age of twenty five Years, and been seven Years a Citizen of the United States, and who shall not, when elected, be an Inhabitant of that State in which he shall be chosen.

Representatives and direct Taxes shall be apportioned among the several States which may be included within this Union, according to their respective Numbers, which shall be determined by adding to the whole Number of free Persons, including those bound to

Service for a Term of Years, and excluding Indians not taxed, three fifths of all other Persons. The actual Enumeration shall be made within three Years after the first Meeting of the Congress of the United States, and within every subsequent Term of ten Years, in such Manner as they shall by Law direct. The Number of Representatives shall not exceed one for every thirty Thousand, but each State shall have at Least one Representative; and until such enumeration shall be made, the State of New Hampshire shall be entitled to choose three, Massachusetts eight, Rhode-Island and Providence Plantations one, Connecticut five, New York six, New Jersey four, Pennsylvania eight, Delaware one, Maryland six, Virginia ten, North Carolina five, South Carolina five, and Georgia three.

When vacancies happen in the Representation from any State, the Executive Authority thereof shall issue Writs of Election to fill such Vacancies.

The House of Representatives shall choose their Speaker and other Officers; and shall have the sole Power of Impeachment.

Section 3

The Senate of the United States shall be composed of two Senators from each State, chosen by the Legislature thereof for six Years; and each Senator shall have one Vote.

Immediately after they shall be assembled in Consequence of the first Election, they shall be divided as equally as may be into three Classes. The Seats of the Senators of the first Class shall be vacated at the Expiration of the second Year, of the second Class at the Expiration of the fourth Year, and of the third Class at the Expiration of the sixth Year, so that one third may be chosen every second Year; and if Vacancies happen by Resignation, or otherwise, during the Recess of the Legislature of any State, the Executive thereof may make temporary Appointments until the next Meeting of the Legislature, which shall then fill such Vacancies.

No Person shall be a Senator who shall not have attained to the Age of thirty Years, and been nine Years a Citizen of the United States, and who shall not, when elected, be an Inhabitant of that State for which he shall be chosen.

The Vice President of the United States shall be President of the Senate, but shall have no Vote, unless they be equally divided.

The Senate shall choose their other Officers, and also a President pro tempore, in the Absence of the Vice President, or when he shall exercise the Office of President of the United States.

The Senate shall have the sole Power to try all Impeachments. When sitting for that Purpose, they shall be on Oath or Affirmation. When the President of the United States is tried, the Chief Justice shall preside: And no Person shall be convicted without the Concurrence of two thirds of the Members present.

Judgment in Cases of Impeachment shall not extend further than to removal from Office, and disqualification to hold and enjoy any Office of honor, Trust or Profit under the United States: but the Party convicted shall nevertheless be liable and subject to Indictment, Trial, Judgment and Punishment, according to Law.

Section 4

The Times, Places and Manner of holding Elections for Senators and Representatives, shall be prescribed in each State by the Legislature thereof; but the Congress may at any time by Law make or alter such Regulations, except as to the Places of chusing Senators.

The Congress shall assemble at least once in every Year, and such Meeting shall be on the first Monday in December, unless they shall by Law appoint a different Day.

Section 5

Each House shall be the Judge of the Elections, Returns and Qualifications of its own Members, and a Majority of each shall constitute a Quorum to do Business; but a smaller Number may adjourn from day to day, and may be authorized to compel the Attendance of absent Members, in such Manner, and under such Penalties as each House may provide.

Each House may determine the Rules of its Proceedings, punish its Members for disorderly Behaviour, and, with the Concurrence of two thirds, expel a Member.

Each House shall keep a Journal of its Proceedings, and from time to time publish the same, excepting such Parts as may in their Judgment require Secrecy; and the Yeas and Nays of the Members of either House on any question shall, at the Desire of one fifth of those Present, be entered on the Journal.

Neither House, during the Session of Congress, shall, without the Consent of the other, adjourn for more than three days, nor to any other Place than that in which the two Houses shall be sitting.

Section 6

The Senators and Representatives shall receive a Compensation for their Services, to be ascertained by Law, and paid out of the Treasury of the United States. They shall in all Cases, except Treason, Felony and Breach of the Peace, be privileged from Arrest during their Attendance at the Session of their respective Houses, and in going to and returning from the same; and for any Speech or Debate in either House, they shall not be questioned in any other Place.

No Senator or Representative shall, during the Time for which he was elected, be appointed to any civil Office under the Authority of the United States, which shall have been created, or the Emoluments whereof shall have been increased during such time; and no Person holding any Office under the United States, shall be a Member of either House during his Continuance in Office.

Section 7

All Bills for raising Revenue shall originate in the House of Representatives; but the Senate may propose or concur with Amendments as on other Bills.

Every Bill which shall have passed the House of Representatives and the Senate, shall, before it become a Law, be presented to the President of the United States: If he approve he shall sign it, but if not he shall return it, with his Objections to that House in which it shall have originated, who shall enter the Objections at large on their Journal, and proceed to reconsider it. If after such Reconsideration two thirds of that House shall agree to pass the Bill, it shall be sent, together with the Objections, to the other House, by which it shall likewise be reconsidered, and if approved by two thirds of that House, it shall become a Law. But in all such Cases the Votes of both Houses shall be determined by yeas and Nays, and the Names of the Persons voting for and against the Bill shall be entered on the Journal of each House respectively. If any Bill shall not be returned by the President within ten Days (Sundays excepted) after it shall have been presented to him, the Same shall be a Law, in like Manner as if he had signed it, unless the Congress by their Adjournment prevent its Return, in which Case it shall not be a Law.

Every Order, Resolution, or Vote to which the Concurrence of the Senate and House of Representatives may be necessary (except on a question of Adjournment) shall be presented to the President of the United States; and before the Same shall take Effect, shall be approved by him, or being disapproved by him, shall be repassed by two thirds of the Senate and House of Representatives, according to the Rules and Limitations prescribed in the Case of a Bill.

Section 8

The Congress shall have Power

To lay and collect Taxes, Duties, Imposts and Excises, to pay the Debts and provide for the common Defence and general Welfare of the United States; but all Duties, Imposts and Excises shall be uniform throughout the United States;

To borrow Money on the credit of the United States;

To regulate Commerce with foreign Nations, and among the several States, and with the Indian Tribes;

To establish an uniform Rule of Naturalization, and uniform Laws on the subject of Bankruptcies throughout the United States;

To coin Money, regulate the Value thereof, and of foreign Coin, and fix the Standard of Weights and Measures;

To provide for the Punishment of counterfeiting the Securities and current Coin of the United States;

To establish Post Offices and post Roads;

To promote the Progress of Science and useful Arts, by securing for limited Times to Authors and Inventors the exclusive Right to their respective Writings and Discoveries;

To constitute Tribunals inferior to the supreme Court;

To define and punish Piracies and Felonies committed on the high Seas, and Offences against the Law of Nations;

To declare War, grant Letters of Marque and Reprisal, and make Rules concerning Captures on Land and Water;

To raise and support Armies, but no Appropriation of Money to that Use shall be for a longer Term than two Years;

To provide and maintain a Navy;

To make Rules for the Government and Regulation of the land and naval Forces;

To provide for calling forth the Militia to execute the Laws of the Union, suppress Insurrections and repel Invasions;

To provide for organizing, arming, and disciplining the Militia, and for governing such Part of them as may be employed in the Service of the United States, reserving to the States respectively, the Appointment of the Officers, and the Authority of training the Militia according to the discipline prescribed by Congress;

To exercise exclusive Legislation in all Cases whatsoever, over such District (not exceeding ten Miles square) as may, by Cession of particular States, and the Acceptance of

Congress, become the Seat of the Government of the United States, and to exercise like Authority over all Places purchased by the Consent of the Legislature of the State in which the Same shall be, for the Erection of Forts, Magazines, Arsenals, dock-Yards, and other needful Buildings;—And

To make all Laws which shall be necessary and proper for carrying into Execution the foregoing Powers, and all other Powers vested by this Constitution in the Government of the United States, or in any Department or Officer thereof.

Section 9

The Migration or Importation of such Persons as any of the States now existing shall think proper to admit, shall not be prohibited by the Congress prior to the Year one thousand eight hundred and eight, but a Tax or duty may be imposed on such Importation, not exceeding ten dollars for each Person.

The Privilege of the Writ of Habeas Corpus shall not be suspended, unless when in Cases of Rebellion or Invasion the public Safety may require it.

No Bill of Attainder or ex post facto Law shall be passed.

No Capitation, or other direct, Tax shall be laid, unless in Proportion to the Census or enumeration herein before directed to be taken.

No Tax or Duty shall be laid on Articles exported from any State.

No Preference shall be given by any Regulation of Commerce or Revenue to the Ports of one State over those of another; nor shall Vessels bound to, or from, one State, be obliged to enter, clear, or pay Duties in another.

No Money shall be drawn from the Treasury, but in Consequence of Appropriations made by Law; and a regular Statement and Account of the Receipts and Expenditures of all public Money shall be published from time to time.

No Title of Nobility shall be granted by the United States: And no Person holding any Office of Profit or Trust under them, shall, without the Consent of the Congress, accept of any present, Emolument, Office, or Title, of any kind whatever, from any King, Prince, or foreign State.

Section 10

No State shall enter into any Treaty, Alliance, or Confederation; grant Letters of Marque and Reprisal; coin Money; emit Bills of Credit; make any Thing but gold and silver Coin a Tender in Payment of Debts; pass any Bill of Attainder, ex post facto Law, or Law impairing the Obligation of Contracts, or grant any Title of Nobility.

No State shall, without the Consent of the Congress, lay any Imposts or Duties on Imports or Exports, except what may be absolutely necessary for executing it's inspection Laws: and the net Produce of all Duties and Imposts, laid by any State on Imports or Exports, shall be for the Use of the Treasury of the United States; and all such Laws shall be subject to the Revision and Control of the Congress.

No State shall, without the Consent of Congress, lay any Duty of Tonnage, keep Troops, or Ships of War in time of Peace, enter into any Agreement or Compact with another State, or with a foreign Power, or engage in War, unless actually invaded, or in such imminent Danger as will not admit of delay.

Article II
Section 1

The executive Power shall be vested in a President of the United States of America. He shall hold his Office during the Term of four Years, and, together with the Vice President, chosen for the same Term, be elected, as follows:

Each State shall appoint, in such Manner as the Legislature thereof may direct, a Number of Electors, equal to the whole Number of Senators and Representatives to which the State may be entitled in the Congress: but no Senator or Representative, or Person holding an Office of Trust or Profit under the United States, shall be appointed an Elector.

The Electors shall meet in their respective States, and vote by Ballot for two Persons, of whom one at least shall not be an Inhabitant of the same State with themselves. And they shall make a List of all the Persons voted for, and of the Number of Votes for each; which List they shall sign and certify, and transmit sealed to the Seat of the Government of the United States, directed to the President of the Senate. The President of the Senate shall, in the Presence of the Senate and House of Representatives, open all the Certificates, and the Votes shall then be counted. The Person having the greatest Number of Votes shall be the President, if such Number be a Majority of the whole Number of Electors appointed; and if there be more than one who have such Majority, and have an equal Number of Votes, then the House of Representatives shall immediately choose by Ballot one of them for President; and if no Person have a Majority, then from the five highest on the List the said House shall in like Manner choose the President. But in choosing the President, the Votes shall be taken by States, the Representation from each State having one Vote; A quorum for this purpose shall consist of a Member or Members from two thirds of the States, and a Majority of all the States shall be necessary to a Choice. In every Case, after the Choice of the President, the Person having the greatest Number of Votes of the Electors shall be the Vice President. But if there should remain two or more who have equal Votes, the Senate shall choose from them by Ballot the Vice President.

The Congress may determine the Time of choosing the Electors, and the Day on which they shall give their Votes; which Day shall be the same throughout the United States.

No Person except a natural born Citizen, or a Citizen of the United States, at the time of the Adoption of this Constitution, shall be eligible to the Office of President; neither shall any Person be eligible to that Office who shall not have attained to the Age of thirty five Years, and been fourteen Years a Resident within the United States.

In Case of the Removal of the President from Office, or of his Death, Resignation, or Inability to discharge the Powers and Duties of the said Office, the Same shall devolve on the Vice President, and the Congress may by Law provide for the Case of Removal, Death, Resignation or Inability, both of the President and Vice President, declaring what Officer shall then act as President, and such Officer shall act accordingly, until the Disability be removed, or a President shall be elected.

The President shall, at stated Times, receive for his Services, a Compensation, which shall neither be increased nor diminished during the Period for which he shall have been elected, and he shall not receive within that Period any other Emolument from the United States, or any of them.

Before he enter on the Execution of his Office, he shall take the following Oath or Affirmation:—"I do solemnly swear (or affirm) that I will faithfully execute the Office of President of the United States, and will to the best of my Ability, preserve, protect and defend the Constitution of the United States."

Section 2

The President shall be Commander in Chief of the Army and Navy of the United States, and of the Militia of the several States, when called into the actual Service of the United States; he may require the Opinion, in writing, of the principal Officer in each of the executive Departments, upon any Subject relating to the Duties of their respective Offices, and he shall have Power to grant Reprieves and Pardons for Offences against the United States, except in Cases of Impeachment.

He shall have Power, by and with the Advice and Consent of the Senate, to make Treaties, provided two thirds of the Senators present concur; and he shall nominate, and by and with the Advice and Consent of the Senate, shall appoint Ambassadors, other public Ministers and Consuls, Judges of the supreme Court, and all other Officers of the United States, whose Appointments are not herein otherwise provided for, and which shall be established by Law: but the Congress may by Law vest the Appointment of such inferior Officers, as they think proper, in the President alone, in the Courts of Law, or in the Heads of Departments.

The President shall have Power to fill up all Vacancies that may happen during the Recess of the Senate, by granting Commissions which shall expire at the End of their next Session.

Section 3

He shall from time to time give to the Congress Information of the State of the Union, and recommend to their Consideration such Measures as he shall judge necessary and expedient; he may, on extraordinary Occasions, convene both Houses, or either of them, and in Case of Disagreement between them, with Respect to the Time of Adjournment, he may adjourn them to such Time as he shall think proper; he shall receive Ambassadors and other public Ministers; he shall take Care that the Laws be faithfully executed, and shall Commission all the Officers of the United States.

Section 4

The President, Vice President and all civil Officers of the United States, shall be removed from Office on Impeachment for, and Conviction of, Treason, Bribery, or other high Crimes and Misdemeanors.

Article III
Section 1

The judicial Power of the United States shall be vested in one supreme Court, and in such inferior Courts as the Congress may from time to time ordain and establish. The Judges, both of the supreme and inferior Courts, shall hold their Offices during good Behaviour, and shall, at stated Times, receive for their Services a Compensation, which shall not be diminished during their Continuance in Office.

Section 2

The judicial Power shall extend to all Cases, in Law and Equity, arising under this Constitution, the Laws of the United States, and Treaties made, or which shall be made, under their Authority;—to all Cases affecting Ambassadors, other public Ministers and Consuls;—to all Cases of admiralty and maritime Jurisdiction;—to Controversies to which the United States shall be a Party;—to Controversies between two or more States;—between a State and Citizens of another State;—between Citizens of different States;—between Citizens of the same State claiming Lands under Grants of different States, and between a State, or the Citizens thereof, and foreign States, Citizens or Subjects.

In all Cases affecting Ambassadors, other public Ministers and Consuls, and those in which a State shall be Party, the supreme Court shall have original Jurisdiction. In all the other Cases before mentioned, the supreme Court shall have appellate Jurisdiction, both as to Law and Fact, with such Exceptions, and under such Regulations as the Congress shall make.

The Trial of all Crimes, except in Cases of Impeachment, shall be by Jury; and such Trial shall be held in the State where the said Crimes shall have been committed; but when not committed within any State, the Trial shall be at such Place or Places as the Congress may by Law have directed.

Section 3

Treason against the United States, shall consist only in levying War against them, or in adhering to their Enemies, giving them Aid and Comfort. No Person shall be convicted of Treason unless on the Testimony of two Witnesses to the same overt Act, or on Confession in open Court.

The Congress shall have Power to declare the Punishment of Treason, but no Attainder of Treason shall work Corruption of Blood, or Forfeiture except during the Life of the Person attainted.

Article IV
Section 1

Full Faith and Credit shall be given in each State to the public Acts, Records, and judicial Proceedings of every other State. And the Congress may by general Laws prescribe the Manner in which such Acts, Records and Proceedings shall be proved, and the Effect thereof.

Section 2

The Citizens of each State shall be entitled to all Privileges and Immunities of Citizens in the several States.

A Person charged in any State with Treason, Felony, or other Crime, who shall flee from Justice, and be found in another State, shall on Demand of the executive Authority of the State from which he fled, be delivered up, to be removed to the State having Jurisdiction of the Crime.

No Person held to Service or Labour in one State, under the Laws thereof, escaping into another, shall, in Consequence of any Law or Regulation therein, be discharged from such Service or Labour, but shall be delivered up on Claim of the Party to whom such Service or Labour may be due.

Section 3

New States may be admitted by the Congress into this Union; but no new State shall be formed or erected within the Jurisdiction of any other State; nor any State be formed by the Junction of two or more States, or Parts of States, without the Consent of the Legislatures of the States concerned as well as of the Congress.

The Congress shall have Power to dispose of and make all needful Rules and Regulations respecting the Territory or other Property belonging to the United States; and nothing in this Constitution shall be so construed as to Prejudice any Claims of the United States, or of any particular State.

Section 4

The United States shall guarantee to every State in this Union a Republican Form of Government, and shall protect each of them against Invasion; and on Application of the Legislature, or of the Executive (when the Legislature cannot be convened), against domestic Violence.

Article V

The Congress, whenever two thirds of both Houses shall deem it necessary, shall propose Amendments to this Constitution, or, on the Application of the Legislatures of two thirds of the several States, shall call a Convention for proposing Amendments, which, in either Case, shall be valid to all Intents and Purposes, as Part of this Constitution, when ratified by the Legislatures of three fourths of the several States, or by Conventions in three fourths thereof, as the one or the other Mode of Ratification may be proposed by the Congress; Provided that no Amendment which may be made prior to the Year One thousand eight hundred and eight shall in any Manner affect the first and fourth Clauses in the Ninth Section of the first Article; and that no State, without its Consent, shall be deprived of its equal Suffrage in the Senate.

Article VI

All Debts contracted and Engagements entered into, before the Adoption of this Constitution, shall be as valid against the United States under this Constitution, as under the Confederation.

This Constitution, and the Laws of the United States which shall be made in Pursuance thereof; and all Treaties made, or which shall be made, under the Authority of the United States, shall be the supreme Law of the Land; and the Judges in every State shall be bound thereby, any Thing in the Constitution or Laws of any State to the Contrary notwithstanding.

The Senators and Representatives before mentioned, and the Members of the several State Legislatures, and all executive and judicial Officers, both of the United States and of the several States, shall be bound by Oath or Affirmation, to support this Constitution; but no religious Test shall ever be required as a Qualification to any Office or public Trust under the United States.

Article VII

The Ratification of the Conventions of nine States, shall be sufficient for the Establishment of this Constitution between the States so ratifying the Same.

The Word, "the," being interlined between the seventh and eighth Lines of the first Page, the Word "Thirty" being partly written on an Erazure in the fifteenth Line of the first Page, The Words "is tried" being interlined between the thirty second and thirty third Lines of the first Page and the Word "the" being interlined between the forty third and forty fourth Lines of the second Page.

Attest William Jackson Secretary

Done in Convention by the Unanimous Consent of the States present the Seventeenth Day of September in the Year of our Lord one thousand seven hundred and Eighty seven and of the Independence of the United States of America the Twelfth In witness whereof We have hereunto subscribed our Names,

G°. Washington
Presidt and deputy from Virginia

Delaware
Geo: Read
Gunning Bedford jun
John Dickinson
Richard Bassett
Jaco: Broom

Maryland
James McHenry
Dan of St Thos. Jenifer
Danl. Carroll

Virginia
John Blair
James Madison Jr.

North Carolina
Wm. Blount
Richd. Dobbs Spaight
Hu Williamson

South Carolina
J. Rutledge
Charles Cotesworth Pinckney
Charles Pinckney
Pierce Butler

Georgia
William Few
Abr Baldwin

New Hampshire
John Langdon
Nicholas Gilman

Massachusetts
Nathaniel Gorham
Rufus King

Connecticut
Wm. Saml. Johnson
Roger Sherman

New York
Alexander Hamilton

New Jersey
Wil: Livingston
David Brearley
Wm. Paterson
Jona: Dayton

Pennsylvania
B Franklin
Thomas Mifflin
Robt. Morris
Geo. Clymer
Thos. FitzSimons
Jared Ingersoll
James Wilson
Gouv Morris

Articles

In addition to, and Amendment of the Constitution of the United States of America, proposed by Congress, and ratified by the Legislatures of the several States, pursuant to the fifth Article of the original Constitution.

(The first ten amendments to the U.S. Constitution were ratified December 15, 1791, and form what is known as the "Bill of Rights.")

AMENDMENT I

Congress shall make no law respecting an establishment of religion, or prohibiting the free exercise thereof; or abridging the freedom of speech, or of the press; or the right of the people peaceably to assemble, and to petition the Government for a redress of grievances.

AMENDMENT II

A well regulated Militia, being necessary to the security of a free State, the right of the people to keep and bear Arms, shall not be infringed.

AMENDMENT III

No Soldier shall, in time of peace be quartered in any house, without the consent of the Owner, nor in time of war, but in a manner to be prescribed by law.

AMENDMENT IV

The right of the people to be secure in their persons, houses, papers, and effects, against unreasonable searches and seizures, shall not be violated, and no Warrants shall issue, but upon probable cause, supported by Oath or affirmation, and particularly describing the place to be searched, and the persons or things to be seized.

AMENDMENT V

No person shall be held to answer for a capital, or otherwise infamous crime, unless on a presentment or indictment of a Grand Jury, except in cases arising in the land or naval forces, or in the Militia, when in actual service in time of War or public danger; nor shall any person be subject for the same offence to be twice put in jeopardy of life or limb; nor shall be compelled in any criminal case to be a witness against himself, nor be deprived of life, liberty, or property, without due process of law; nor shall private property be taken for public use, without just compensation.

AMENDMENT VI

In all criminal prosecutions, the accused shall enjoy the right to a speedy and public trial, by an impartial jury of the State and district wherein the crime shall have been committed, which district shall have been previously ascertained by law, and to be informed of the nature and cause of the accusation; to be confronted with the witnesses against him; to have compulsory process for obtaining witnesses in his favor, and to have the Assistance of Counsel for his defence.

AMENDMENT VII

In Suits at common law, where the value in controversy shall exceed twenty dollars, the right of trial by jury shall be preserved, and no fact tried by a jury, shall be otherwise re-examined in any Court of the United States, than according to the rules of the common law.

AMENDMENT VIII

Excessive bail shall not be required, nor excessive fines imposed, nor cruel and unusual punishments inflicted.

AMENDMENT IX

The enumeration in the Constitution, of certain rights, shall not be construed to deny or disparage others retained by the people.

AMENDMENT X

The powers not delegated to the United States by the Constitution, nor prohibited by it to the States, are reserved to the States respectively, or to the people.

AMENDMENT XI

Passed by Congress March 4, 1794. Ratified February 7, 1795.

Note: Article III, Section 2, of the Constitution was modified by Amendment XI.

The Judicial power of the United States shall not be construed to extend to any suit in law or equity, commenced or prosecuted against one of the United States by Citizens of another State, or by Citizens or Subjects of any Foreign State.

AMENDMENT XII

Passed by Congress December 9, 1803. Ratified June 15, 1804.

Note: A portion of Article II, Section 1, of the Constitution was superseded by the Twelfth Amendment.

The Electors shall meet in their respective states and vote by ballot for President and Vice-President, one of whom, at least, shall not be an inhabitant of the same state with themselves; they shall name in their ballots the person voted for as President, and in distinct ballots the person voted for as Vice-President, and they shall make distinct lists of all persons voted for as President, and of all persons voted for as Vice-President, and of the number of votes for each, which lists they shall sign and certify, and transmit sealed to the seat of the government of the United States, directed to the President of the Senate;—the President of the Senate shall, in the presence of the Senate and House of Representatives, open all the certificates and the votes shall then be counted;—The person having the greatest number of votes for President, shall be the President, if such number be a majority of the whole number of Electors appointed; and if no person have such majority, then from the persons having the highest numbers not exceeding three on the list of those voted for as President, the House of Representatives shall choose immediately, by ballot, the President. But in choosing the President, the votes shall be taken by states, the representation from each state having one vote; a quorum for this purpose shall consist of a member or members from two-thirds of the states, and a majority of all the states shall be necessary to a choice. [And if the House of Representatives shall not choose a President whenever the right of choice shall devolve upon them, before the fourth day of March next following, then the Vice-President shall act as President, as in case of the death or other constitutional disability of the President.—]* The person having the greatest number of votes as Vice-President, shall be the Vice-President, if such number be a majority of the whole number of Electors appointed, and if no person have a majority, then from the two highest numbers on the list, the Senate shall choose the Vice-President; a quorum for the purpose shall consist of two-thirds of the whole number of Senators, and a majority of the whole number shall be necessary to a choice. But no person constitutionally ineligible to the office of President shall be eligible to that of Vice-President of the United States.

*Superseded by Section 3 of the Twentieth Amendment.

AMENDMENT XIII

Passed by Congress January 31, 1865. Ratified December 6, 1865.

Note: A portion of Article IV, Section 2, of the Constitution was superseded by the Thirteenth Amendment.

Section 1

Neither slavery nor involuntary servitude, except as a punishment for crime whereof the party shall have been duly convicted, shall exist within the United States, or any place subject to their jurisdiction.

Section 2

Congress shall have power to enforce this article by appropriate legislation.

AMENDMENT XIV

Passed by Congress June 13, 1866. Ratified July 9, 1868.

Note: Article I, Section 2, of the Constitution was modified by Section 2 of the Fourteenth Amendment.

Section 1

All persons born or naturalized in the United States, and subject to the jurisdiction thereof, are citizens of the United States and of the State wherein they reside. No State shall make or enforce any law which shall abridge the privileges or immunities of citizens of the United States; nor shall any State deprive any person of life, liberty, or property, without due process of law; nor deny to any person within its jurisdiction the equal protection of the laws.

Section 2

Representatives shall be apportioned among the several States according to their respective numbers, counting the whole number of persons in each State, excluding Indians not taxed. But when the right to vote at any election for the choice of electors for President and Vice-President of the United States, Representatives in Congress, the Executive and Judicial officers of a State, or the members of the Legislature thereof, is denied to any of the male inhabitants of such State, being twenty-one years of age,* and citizens of the United States, or in any way abridged, except for participation in rebellion, or other crime, the basis of representation therein shall be reduced in the proportion which the number of such male citizens shall bear to the whole number of male citizens twenty-one years of age in such State.

Section 3

No person shall be a Senator or Representative in Congress, or elector of President and Vice-President, or hold any office, civil or military, under the United States, or under any State, who, having previously taken an oath, as a member of Congress, or as an officer of the United States, or as a member of any State legislature, or as an executive or judicial officer of any State, to support the Constitution of the United States, shall have engaged in insurrection or rebellion against the same, or given aid or comfort to the enemies thereof. But Congress may by a vote of two-thirds of each House, remove such disability.

Section 4

The validity of the public debt of the United States, authorized by law, including debts incurred for payment of pensions and bounties for services in suppressing insurrection or rebellion, shall not be questioned. But neither the United States nor any State shall assume or pay any debt or obligation incurred in aid of insurrection or rebellion against the United States, or any claim for the loss or emancipation of any slave; but all such debts, obligations and claims shall be held illegal and void.

Section 5

The Congress shall have the power to enforce, by appropriate legislation, the provisions of this article.

*Changed by Section 1 of the Twenty-sixth Amendment.

AMENDMENT XV

Passed by Congress February 26, 1869. Ratified February 3, 1870.

Section 1

The right of citizens of the United States to vote shall not be denied or abridged by the United States or by any State on account of race, color, or previous condition of servitude.

Section 2

The Congress shall have the power to enforce this article by appropriate legislation.

AMENDMENT XVI

Passed by Congress July 2, 1909. Ratified February 3, 1913.

Note: Article I, Section 9, of the Constitution was modified by Amendment XVI.

The Congress shall have power to lay and collect taxes on incomes, from whatever source derived, without apportionment among the several States, and without regard to any census or enumeration.

AMENDMENT XVII

Passed by Congress May 13, 1912. Ratified April 8, 1913.

Note: Article I, Section 3, of the Constitution was modified by the Seventeenth Amendment.

The Senate of the United States shall be composed of two Senators from each State, elected by the people thereof, for six years; and each Senator shall have one vote. The electors in each State shall have the qualifications requisite for electors of the most numerous branch of the State legislatures.

When vacancies happen in the representation of any State in the Senate, the executive authority of such State shall issue writs of election to fill such vacancies: Provided, That the legislature of any State may empower the executive thereof to make temporary appointments until the people fill the vacancies by election as the legislature may direct.

This amendment shall not be so construed as to affect the election or term of any Senator chosen before it becomes valid as part of the Constitution.

AMENDMENT XVIII

Passed by Congress December 18, 1917. Ratified January 16, 1919. Repealed by Amendment XXI.

Section 1

After one year from the ratification of this article the manufacture, sale, or transportation of intoxicating liquors within, the importation thereof into, or the exportation thereof from the United States and all territory subject to the jurisdiction thereof for beverage purposes is hereby prohibited.

Section 2

The Congress and the several States shall have concurrent power to enforce this article by appropriate legislation.

Section 3

This article shall be inoperative unless it shall have been ratified as an amendment to the Constitution by the legislatures of the several States, as provided in the Constitution, within seven years from the date of the submission hereof to the States by the Congress.

AMENDMENT XIX

Passed by Congress June 4, 1919. Ratified August 18, 1920.

The right of citizens of the United States to vote shall not be denied or abridged by the United States or by any State on account of sex.

Congress shall have power to enforce this article by appropriate legislation.

AMENDMENT XX

Passed by Congress March 2, 1932. Ratified January 23, 1933.

Note: Article I, Section 4, of the Constitution was modified by Section 2 of this amendment. In addition, a portion of the Twelfth Amendment was superseded by Section 3.

Section 1

The terms of the President and the Vice President shall end at noon on the 20th day of January, and the terms of Senators and Representatives at noon on the 3d day of January, of the years in which such terms would have ended if this article had not been ratified; and the terms of their successors shall then begin.

Section 2

The Congress shall assemble at least once in every year, and such meeting shall begin at noon on the 3d day of January, unless they shall by law appoint a different day.

Section 3

If, at the time fixed for the beginning of the term of the President, the President elect shall have died, the Vice President elect shall become President. If a President shall not have been chosen before the time fixed for the beginning of his term, or if the President elect shall have failed to qualify, then the Vice President elect shall act as President until a President shall have qualified; and the Congress may by law provide for the case wherein neither a President elect nor a Vice President shall have qualified, declaring who shall then act as President, or the manner in which one who is to act shall be selected, and such person shall act accordingly until a President or Vice President shall have qualified.

Section 4

The Congress may by law provide for the case of the death of any of the persons from whom the House of Representatives may choose a President whenever the right of choice shall have devolved upon them, and for the case of the death of any of the persons from whom the Senate may choose a Vice President whenever the right of choice shall have devolved upon them.

Section 5

Sections 1 and 2 shall take effect on the 15th day of October following the ratification of this article.

Section 6

This article shall be inoperative unless it shall have been ratified as an amendment to the Constitution by the legislatures of three-fourths of the several States within seven years from the date of its submission.

AMENDMENT XXI

Passed by Congress February 20, 1933. Ratified December 5, 1933.

Section 1

The eighteenth article of amendment to the Constitution of the United States is hereby repealed.

Section 2

The transportation or importation into any State, Territory, or Possession of the United States for delivery or use therein of intoxicating liquors, in violation of the laws thereof, is hereby prohibited.

Section 3

This article shall be inoperative unless it shall have been ratified as an amendment to the Constitution by conventions in the several States, as provided in the Constitution, within seven years from the date of the submission hereof to the States by the Congress.

AMENDMENT XXII

Passed by Congress March 21, 1947. Ratified February 27, 1951.

Section 1

No person shall be elected to the office of the President more than twice, and no person who has held the office of President, or acted as President, for more than two years of a term to which some other person was elected President shall be elected to the office of President more than once. But this Article shall not apply to any person holding the office of President when this Article was proposed by Congress, and shall not prevent any person who may be holding the office of President, or acting as President, during the term within which this Article becomes operative from holding the office of President or acting as President during the remainder of such term.

Section 2

This article shall be inoperative unless it shall have been ratified as an amendment to the Constitution by the legislatures of three-fourths of the several States within seven years from the date of its submission to the States by the Congress.

AMENDMENT XXIII

Passed by Congress June 16, 1960. Ratified March 29, 1961.

Section 1

The District constituting the seat of Government of the United States shall appoint in such manner as Congress may direct:

A number of electors of President and Vice President equal to the whole number of Senators and Representatives in Congress to which the District would be entitled if it were a State, but in no event more than the least populous State; they shall be in addition to those appointed by the States, but they shall be considered, for the purposes of the election of President and Vice President, to be electors appointed by a State; and they shall meet in the District and perform such duties as provided by the twelfth article of amendment.

Section 2

The Congress shall have power to enforce this article by appropriate legislation.

AMENDMENT XXIV

Passed by Congress August 27, 1962. Ratified January 23, 1964.

Section 1

The right of citizens of the United States to vote in any primary or other election for President or Vice President, for electors for President or Vice President, or for Senator or Representative in Congress, shall not be denied or abridged by the United States or any State by reason of failure to pay poll tax or other tax.

Section 2

The Congress shall have power to enforce this article by appropriate legislation.

AMENDMENT XXV

Passed by Congress July 6, 1965. Ratified February 10, 1967.

Note: Article II, Section 1, of the Constitution was affected by the Twenty-fifth Amendment.

Section 1

In case of the removal of the President from office or of his death or resignation, the Vice President shall become President.

Section 2

Whenever there is a vacancy in the office of the Vice President, the President shall nominate a Vice President who shall take office upon confirmation by a majority vote of both Houses of Congress.

Section 3

Whenever the President transmits to the President pro tempore of the Senate and the Speaker of the House of Representatives his written declaration that he is unable to discharge the powers and duties of his office, and until he transmits to them a written declaration to the contrary, such powers and duties shall be discharged by the Vice President as Acting President.

Section 4

Whenever the Vice President and a majority of either the principal officers of the executive departments or of such other body as Congress may by law provide, transmit to the President pro tempore of the Senate and the Speaker of the House of Representatives their written declaration that the President is unable to discharge the powers and duties of his office, the Vice President shall immediately assume the powers and duties of the office as Acting President.

Thereafter, when the President transmits to the President pro tempore of the Senate and the Speaker of the House of Representatives his written declaration that no inability exists, he shall resume the powers and duties of his office unless the Vice President and a majority of either the principal officers of the executive department or of such other body as Congress may by law provide, transmit within four days to the President pro tempore of the Senate and the Speaker of the House of Representatives their written declaration that the President is unable to discharge the powers and duties of his office. Thereupon Congress shall decide the issue, assembling within forty-eight hours for that purpose if not in session. If the Congress, within twenty-one days after receipt of the latter written declaration, or, if Congress is not in session, within twenty-one days after Congress is required to assemble, determines by two-thirds vote of both Houses that the President is unable to discharge the powers and duties of his office, the Vice President shall continue to discharge the same as Acting President; otherwise, the President shall resume the powers and duties of his office.

AMENDMENT XXVI

Passed by Congress March 23, 1971. Ratified July 1, 1971.

Note: Amendment XIV, Section 2, of the Constitution was modified by Section 1 of the Twenty-sixth Amendment.

Section 1

The right of citizens of the United States, who are eighteen years of age or older, to vote shall not be denied or abridged by the United States or by any State on account of age.

Section 2

The Congress shall have power to enforce this article by appropriate legislation.

AMENDMENT XXVII

Originally proposed Sept. 25, 1789. Ratified May 7, 1992.

No law, varying the compensation for the services of the Senators and Representatives, shall take effect, until an election of representatives shall have intervened.

Lincoln's Gettysburg Address

Four score and seven years ago our fathers brought forth on this continent, a new nation, conceived in Liberty, and dedicated to the proposition that all men are created equal.

Now we are engaged in a great civil war, testing whether that nation, or any nation so conceived and so dedicated, can long endure. We are met on a great battle-field of that war. We have come to dedicate a portion of that field, as a final resting place for those who here gave their lives that that nation might live. It is altogether fitting and proper that we should do this.

But, in a larger sense, we can not dedicate—we can not consecrate—we can not hallow—this ground. The brave men, living and dead, who struggled here, have consecrated it, far above our poor power to add or detract. The world will little note, nor long remember what we say here, but it can never forget what they did here. It is for us the living, rather, to be dedicated here to the unfinished work which they who fought here have thus far so nobly advanced. It is rather for us to be here dedicated to the great task remaining before us—that from these honored dead we take increased devotion to that cause for which they gave the last full measure of devotion—that we here highly resolve that these dead shall not have died in vain—that this nation, under God, shall have a new birth of freedom—and that government of the people, by the people, for the people, shall not perish from the earth.

Historical Facts and Data
US Presidents and Vice Presidents

Table App B-1 Presidents and Vice Presidents

	President	Vice President	Political Party	Term
1	George Washington	John Adams	No Party Designation	1789–1797
2	John Adams	Thomas Jefferson	Federalist	1797–1801
3	Thomas Jefferson	Aaron Burr George Clinton	Democratic Republican	1801–1809
4	James Madison	George Clinton Elbridge Gerry	Democratic Republican	1809–1817
5	James Monroe	Daniel D. Tompkins	Democratic Republican	1817–1825
6	John Quincy Adams	John C. Calhoun	Democratic Republican	1825–1829
7	Andrew Jackson	John C. Calhoun Martin Van Buren	Democratic	1829–1837
8	Martin Van Buren	Richard M. Johnson	Democratic	1837–1841
9	William Henry Harrison	John Tyler	Whig	1841
10	John Tyler	None	Whig	1841–1845
11	James Knox Polk	George M. Dallas	Democratic	1845–1849
12	Zachary Taylor	Millard Fillmore	Whig	1849–1850
13	Millard Fillmore	None	Whig	1850–1853
14	Franklin Pierce	William R. King	Democratic	1853–1857
15	James Buchanan	John C. Breckinridge	Democratic	1857–1861
16	Abraham Lincoln	Hannibal Hamlin Andrew Johnson	Union	1861–1865
17	Andrew Johnson	None	Union	1865–1869
18	Ulysses Simpson Grant	Schuyler Colfax Henry Wilson	Republican	1869–1877
19	Rutherford Birchard Hayes	William A. Wheeler	Republican	1877–1881
20	James Abram Garfield	Chester Alan Arthur	Republican	1881
21	Chester Alan Arthur	None	Republican	1881–1885
22	Stephen Grover Cleveland	Thomas Hendricks	Democratic	1885–1889
23	Benjamin Harrison	Levi P. Morton	Republican	1889–1893

continued

Table App B-1 *continued*

	President	Vice President	Political Party	Term
24	Stephen Grover Cleveland	Adlai E. Stevenson	Democratic	1893–1897
25	William McKinley	Garret A. Hobart Theodore Roosevelt	Republican	1897–1901
26	Theodore Roosevelt	Charles W. Fairbanks	Republican	1901–1909
27	William Howard Taft	James S. Sherman	Republican	1909–1913
28	Woodrow Wilson	Thomas R. Marshall	Democratic	1913–1921
29	Warren Gamaliel Harding	Calvin Coolidge	Republican	1921–1923
30	Calvin Coolidge	Charles G. Dawes	Republican	1923–1929
31	Herbert Clark Hoover	Charles Curtis	Republican	1929–1933
32	Franklin Delano Roosevelt	John Nance Garner Henry A. Wallace Harry S. Truman	Democratic	1933–1945
33	Harry S. Truman	Alben W. Barkley	Democratic	1945–1953
34	Dwight David Eisenhower	Richard Milhous Nixon	Republican	1953–1961
35	John Fitzgerald Kennedy	Lyndon Baines Johnson	Democratic	1961–1963
36	Lyndon Baines Johnson	Hubert Horatio Humphrey	Democratic	1963–1969
37	Richard Milhous Nixon	Spiro T. Agnew Gerald Rudolph Ford	Republican	1969–1974
38	Gerald Rudolph Ford	Nelson Rockefeller	Republican	1974–1977
39	James Earl Carter Jr.	Walter Mondale	Democratic	1977–1981
40	Ronald Wilson Reagan	George Herbert Walker Bush	Republican	1981–1989
41	George Herbert Walker Bush	J. Danforth Quayle	Republican	1989–1993
42	William Jefferson Clinton	Albert Gore Jr.	Democratic	1993–2001
43	George Walker Bush	Richard Cheney	Republican	2001–2009
44	Barack Hussein Obama	Joseph Biden	Democratic	2009–

Admission of States into the Union

Table App B-2 Admission of States into the Union

	State	Date of Admission		State	Date of Admission
1	Delaware	December 7, 1787	26	Michigan	January 26, 1837
2	Pennsylvania	December 12, 1787	27	Florida	March 3, 1845
3	New Jersey	December 18, 1787	28	Texas	December 29, 1845
4	Georgia	January 2, 1788	29	Iowa	December 28, 1846
5	Connecticut	January 9, 1788	30	Wisconsin	May 29, 1848
6	Massachusetts	February 6, 1788	31	California	September 9, 1850
7	Maryland	April 28, 1788	32	Minnesota	May 11, 1858
8	South Carolina	May 23, 1788	33	Oregon	February 14, 1859
9	New Hampshire	June 21, 1788	34	Kansas	January 29, 1861
10	Virginia	June 25, 1788	35	West Virginia	June 20, 1863
11	New York	July 26, 1788	36	Nevada	October 31, 1864
12	North Carolina	November 21, 1789	37	Nebraska	March 1, 1867
13	Rhode Island	May 29, 1790	38	Colorado	August 1, 1876
14	Vermont	March 4, 1791	39	North Dakota	November 2, 1889
15	Kentucky	June 1, 1792	40	South Dakota	November 2, 1889
16	Tennessee	June 1, 1796	41	Montana	November 8, 1889
17	Ohio	March 1, 1803	42	Washington	November 11, 1889
18	Louisiana	April 30, 1812	43	Idaho	July 3, 1890
19	Indiana	December 11, 1816	44	Wyoming	July 10, 1890
20	Mississippi	December 10, 1817	45	Utah	January 4, 1896
21	Illinois	December 3, 1818	46	Oklahoma	November 16, 1907
22	Alabama	December 14, 1819	47	New Mexico	January 6, 1912
23	Maine	March 15, 1820	48	Arizona	February 14, 1912
24	Missouri	August 10, 1821	49	Alaska	January 3, 1959
25	Arkansas	June 15, 1836	50	Hawaii	August 21, 1959

Antinomianism   The belief that moral law was not binding on true Christians. The opposite of Arminianism, antinomianism held that good works would not count in the afterlife. Justification, or entrance to heaven, was by faith alone. *See* Calvinism.

Arminianism   Religious doctrine developed by the Dutch theologian Jacobus Arminius that argued that men and women had free will and suggested that hence they would earn their way into heaven by good works.

Armistice   A cessation of hostilities by agreement among the opposing sides; a cease-fire.

Associationalism   President Herbert Hoover's preferred method of responding to the Depression. Rather than have the government directly involve itself in the economy, Hoover hoped to use the government to encourage associations of businessmen to cooperate voluntarily to meet the crisis.

Autarky   At the height of the world depression, industrial powers sought to isolate their economies within self-contained spheres, generally governed by national (or imperial) economic planning. Japan's Co-Prosperity Sphere, the Soviet Union, and the British Empire each comprised a more or less closed economic unit.

Benevolent Empire   The loosely affiliated network of charitable reform associations that emerged (especially in urban areas) in response to the widespread revivalism of the early nineteenth century.

Berdache   In Indian societies, a man who dressed and adopted the mannerisms of women and had sex only with other men. In Native American culture, the berdache, half man and half woman, symbolized cosmic harmony.

Blockade   A military tactic used in both land and naval warfare by which a location is sealed off to prevent goods or people from entering or leaving.

Budget deficit   The failure of tax revenues to pay for annual federal spending on military, welfare, and other programs. The resulting budget deficits forced Washington to borrow money to cover its costs. The growing budget deficits were controversial, in part because the government's borrowing increased both its long-term debt and the amount of money it had to spend each year to pay for the interest on loans.

Busing   The controversial court-ordered practice of sending children by bus to public schools outside their neighborhoods in order to promote racial integration in the schools.

Calvinism   Religious doctrine developed by the theologian John Calvin that argued that God alone determines who will receive salvation and, hence, men and women cannot earn their own salvation or even be certain about their final destinies.

Carpetbagger   A derogatory term referring to northern whites who moved to the South after the Civil War. Stereotyped as corrupt and unprincipled, "carpetbaggers" were in fact a diverse group motivated by a variety of interests and beliefs.

Charter colony   Settlement established by a trading company or other group of private entrepreneurs who received from the king a grant of land and the right to govern it.

The charter colonies included Virginia, Plymouth, Massachusetts Bay, Rhode Island, and Connecticut.

City busting   As late as the 1930s, President Roosevelt and most Americans regarded attacking civilians from the air as an atrocity, but during World War II cities became a primary target for U.S. warplanes. The inaccuracy of bombing, combined with racism and the belief that Japanese and German actions justified retaliation, led American air commanders to follow a policy of systematically destroying urban areas, particularly in Japan.

Communist   Member of the Communist Party or follower of the doctrines of Karl Marx. The term (or accusation) was applied more broadly in the twentieth century to brand labor unionists, progressives, civil rights workers, and other reformers as agents of a foreign ideology.

Communitarians   Individuals who supported and/or took up residence in separate communities created to embody improved plans of social, religious, and/or economic life.

Commutation   The controversial policy of allowing potential draftees to pay for a replacement to serve in the army. The policy was adopted by both the Union and Confederate governments during the Civil War, and in both cases opposition to commutation was so intense that the policy was abandoned.

Consent   One of the key principles of liberalism, which held that people could not be subject to laws to which they had not given their consent. This principle is reflected in both the Declaration of Independence and the preamble to the Constitution, which begins with the famous words "We the people of the United States, in order to form a more perfect union."

Conspiracy theory   A belief that history is shaped intentionally by unseen powers. Conspiracy theory lay behind the McCarthy anti-Communism hearings, which assumed that American society and government had been infiltrated by countless Communist spies.

Constitutionalism   A loose body of thought that developed in Britain and the colonies and was used by the colonists to justify the Revolution by claiming that it was in accord with the principles of the British Constitution. Constitutionalism had two main elements. One was the rule of law, and the other the principle of consent, that one cannot be subject to laws or taxation except by duly elected representatives. Both were rights that had been won through struggle with the monarch. Constitutionalism also refers to the tendency in American politics, particularly in the early nineteenth century, to transpose all political questions into constitutional ones.

Consumer revolution   A slow and steady increase over the course of the eighteenth century in the demand for, and purchase of, consumer goods. The consumer revolution of the eighteenth century was closely related to the Industrial Revolution.

Consumerism   An ideology that defined the purchase of goods and services as both an expression of individual identity and essential to the national economy. Increasingly powerful by the 1920s and dominant by the 1950s, consumerism urged people to find happiness in the pursuit of leisure and pleasure more than in the work ethic.

Containment   The basic U.S. strategy for fighting the cold war. As used by diplomat George Kennan in a 1947 magazine essay, "containment" referred to the combination of diplomatic, economic, and military programs necessary to hold back Soviet expansionism after World War II.

Contraband of war   In its general sense, contraband of war was property seized from an enemy. But early in the Civil War the term was applied to slaves running to Union lines as a way of preventing owners from reclaiming them. The policy effectively nullified the fugitive slave clause of the US Constitution. It was a first critical step in a process that would lead to a federal emancipation policy the following year.

Cooperationists   Those southerners who opposed immediate secession after the election of Abraham Lincoln in 1860. Cooperationists argued instead that secessionists should wait to see if the new president was willing to "cooperate" with the South's demands.

Copperhead   A northerner who sympathized with the South during the Civil War.

Crop lien   The first right to the proceeds of a harvested crop, given by farmers to their creditors. At the beginning of the growing season, farmers paid on credit for seeds, supplies, and food to get them through the year. They repaid these debts when the crop was sold.

Deindustrialization   The reverse of industrialization, as factory shutdowns decreased the size of the manufacturing sector. Plant closings began to plague the American economy in the 1970s, prompting fears that the nation would lose its industrial base.

Democratic Republicans   One of the two parties to make up the first American party system. Following the fiscal and political views of Jefferson and Madison, Democratic Republicans generally advocated a weak federal government and opposed federal intervention in the economy of the nation.

Détente   This French term for the relaxation of tensions was used to describe the central foreign policy innovation of the Nixon administration—a new, less confrontational relationship with Communism. In addition to opening a dialogue with the People's Republic of China, Nixon sought a more stable, less confrontational relationship with the Soviet Union.

Diffusion   The controversial theory that the problem of slavery would be resolved if the slave economy was allowed to expand, or "diffuse," into the western territories. Southerners developed this theory as early as the 1800s in response to northerners who hoped to restrict slavery's expansion.

Disfranchisement   The act of depriving a person or group of voting rights. In the nineteenth century the right to vote was popularly known as the franchise. The Fourteenth Amendment of the Constitution affirmed the right of adult male citizens to vote, but state-imposed restrictions and taxes deprived large numbers of Americans—particularly African Americans—of the vote from the 1890s until the passage of the Voting Rights Act of 1964.

Domestic patriarchy   The practice of defining the family by the husband and father, and wives and children as his domestic dependents. Upon marriage a wife's property became her husband's, and children owed obedience and labor to the family until they reached adulthood. In combination with an exclusive male suffrage, domestic patriarchy described the political as well as the social system that prevailed among free Americans until the twentieth century.

Downsizing   American corporations' layoffs of both blue- and white-collar workers in an attempt to become more efficient and competitive. Downsizing was one of the factors that made Americans uneasy about the economy in the 1990s, despite the impressive surge in the stock market.

Dust Bowl   Across much of the Great Plains, decades of wasteful farming practices combined with several years of drought in the early 1930s to produce a series of massive dust storms that blew the topsoil across hundreds of miles. The area in Texas and Oklahoma affected by these storms became known as the Dust Bowl.

E-commerce   Short for "electronic commerce," this was the term for the Internet-based buying and selling that was one of the key hopes for the computer-driven postindustrial economy. The promise of e-commerce was still unfulfilled by the start of the twenty-first century.

Encomienda   A system of labor developed by the Spanish in the New World in which Spanish settlers (*encomenderos*) compelled groups of Native Americans to work for them. The encomendero owned neither the land nor the Indians who worked for him, but had the unlimited right to compel a particular group of Indians to work for him. This system was unique to the New World; nothing precisely like it had existed in Europe or elsewhere.

"Establishment"   The elite of mainly Ivy League–educated, Anglo-Saxon, Protestant, male, liberal northeasterners that supposedly dominated Wall Street and Washington after World War II. The Establishment's support for corporations, activist government, and containment engendered hostility from opposite poles of the political spectrum—from conservatives and Republicans like Richard Nixon at one end and from the New Left and the Movement at the other. Although many of the post–World War II leaders of the United States did tend to share common origins and ideologies, this elite was never as powerful, self-conscious, or unified as its opponents believed.

Eugenics   The practice of attempting to solve social problems through the control of human reproduction. Drawing on the authority of evolutionary biology, eugenists enjoyed considerable influence in the United States, especially on issues of corrections and public health, from the turn of the century through World War II. Applications of this pseudoscience included the identification of "born" criminals by physical characteristics and "better baby" contests at county fairs.

Farmers' Alliance   A group organized in the late nineteenth century to help farmers pool their knowledge and resources. By 1890 it had entered politics, endorsing candidates and building the political connections in the South and West that would lead to the Populist Party.

Federalists   One of the two political parties to make up the first American party system. Following the fiscal and political policies proposed by Alexander Hamilton, Federalists generally advocated the importance of a strong federal government, including federal intervention in the economy of the new nation.

Feminism   An ideology insisting on the fundamental equality of women and men. The feminists of the 1960s differed over how to achieve that equality: while liberal feminists mostly demanded equal rights for women in the workplace and in politics, radical feminists more thoroughly condemned the capitalist system and male oppression and demanded equality in both private and public life.

Feudalism   A social and political system that developed in Europe in the Middle Ages under which powerful lords offered less powerful noblemen protection in return for their loyalty. Feudalism also included the economic system of manorialism, under which dependent serfs worked on the manors controlled by those lords.

Fire-eaters   Militant southerners who pushed for secession in the 1850s.

Flexible response   The defense doctrine of the Kennedy and Johnson administrations. Abandoning the Eisenhower administration's heavy emphasis on nuclear weapons, flexible response stressed the buildup of the nation's conventional and special forces so that the president had a range of military options in response to Communist aggression.

Front   Early twentieth-century mechanized wars were fought along a battle line or "front" separating opposing sides. By World War II, tactical innovations—blitzkrieg, parachute troops, gliders, and amphibious landings—complicated warfare by breaking through, disrupting, or bypassing the front. The front thus became a more fluid boundary than the fortified trench lines of World War I. The term also acquired a political meaning, particularly for labor and the left. A coalition of parties supporting (or opposing) an agreed-upon line could be called a "popular front."

Galveston Plan   A system of municipal government by appointed commissioners, each with responsibility for a utility or service. After a hurricane devastated Galveston, Texas, in 1900, unelected commissioners temporarily took charge to oversee relief and rebuilding efforts.

Gentility   A term without precise meaning that represented all that was polite, civilized, refined, and fashionable. It was everything that vulgarity was not. Because the term had no precise meaning, it was always subject to negotiation, striving, and anxiety as Americans, beginning in the eighteenth century, tried to show others that they were genteel through their manners, their appearance, and their styles of life.

Glass ceiling   The invisible barrier of discrimination that prevented female white-collar workers from rising to top executive positions in corporations.

Globalization   This term first came into use during the 1980s to describe the web of technological, economic, military, political, and cultural developments binding people and nations ever more tightly together. America had been defined by its relationship to the world for centuries, but the coining of the term *globalization* reflected the emergence of closer international ties.

Great Society   President Lyndon Johnson's ambitious legislative program embodying the vision of the activist new liberalism of the 1960s. Enacted from 1965 to 1968, the Great Society sought to wipe out poverty, end segregation, and enhance the quality of life for all Americans.

Greenbackers   Those who advocated currency inflation by keeping the type of money printed during the Civil War, known as "greenbacks," in circulation.

Gridlock   The political traffic jam that tied up the federal government in the late 1980s and the 1990s. Gridlock developed from the inability of either major party to control both the presidency and Congress for any extended period of time. More fundamentally, gridlock reflected the inability of any party or president to win a popular mandate for a bold legislative program.

Horizontal integration   More commonly known as "monopoly." An industry was "horizontally integrated" when a single company took control of virtually the entire market for a specific product. John D. Rockefeller's Standard Oil came close to doing this.

Humanism   A Renaissance intellectual movement that focused on the intellectual and artistic achievements of humankind. Under the patronage of Queen Isabel, Spain became a center of European humanism.

Immediatism   The variant antislavery sentiment that demanded immediate (as opposed to gradual) personal and federal action against the institution of slavery. This approach was most closely associated with William Lloyd Garrison and is dated from the publication of Garrison's newspaper, *The Liberator*, in January 1831.

Imperialism A process of extending dominion over territories beyond the national boundaries of a state. In the eighteenth century, Britain extended imperial control over North America through settlement, but in the 1890s, imperial influence was generally exercised through indirect rule. Subject peoples generally retained some local autonomy while the imperial power controlled commerce and defense. Few Americans went to the Philippines as settlers, but many passed through as tourists, missionaries, traders, and soldiers.

Individualism The social and political philosophy celebrating the central importance of the individual human being in society. Insisting on the rights of the individual in relationship to the group, individualism was one of the intellectual bases of capitalism and democracy. The resurgent individualism of the 1920s, with its emphasis on each American's freedom and fulfillment, was a critical element of the decade's emergent consumerism and Republican dominance.

Industrious revolution Beginning in the late seventeenth century in western Europe and extending to the North American colonies in the eighteenth century, a fundamental change in the way people worked, as they worked harder and organized their households to produce goods that could be sold, so they could have money to pay for the new consumer goods they wanted.

Information economy The post-industrial economy, gradually emerging in the mid- and late-twentieth century, in which sophisticated communications, computing, biomedical technology, and services took the place of manufacturing.

Initiative, recall, and referendum First proposed by the People's Party's Omaha Platform (1892), along with the direct election of senators and the secret ballot, as measures to subject corporate capitalism to democratic controls. Progressives, chiefly in western and midwestern states, favored them as a check on the power of state officials. The initiative allows legislation to be proposed by petition. The recall allows voters to remove public officials, and the referendum places new laws or constitutional amendments on the ballot for the direct approval of the voters.

Interest group An association whose members organize to exert political pressure on officials or the public. Unlike political parties, whose platforms and slates cover nearly every issue and office, an interest group focuses on a narrower list of concerns reflecting the shared outlook of its members. With the decline of popular politics around the turn of the twentieth century, business, religious, agricultural, women's, professional, neighborhood, and reform associations created a new form of political participation.

Isolationist Between World War I and World War II, the United States refused to join the League of Nations, scaled back its military commitments abroad, and sought to maintain its independence of action in foreign affairs. These policies were called isolationist, although some historians prefer the term "independent internationalist," in recognition of the United States' continuing global influence. In the late 1930s, isolationists favored policies aimed at distancing the United States from European affairs and building a national defense based on air power and hemispheric security.

Jim Crow laws Statutes discriminating against nonwhite Americans, particularly in the South. The term specifically refers to regulations excluding blacks from public facilities or compelling them to use ones separate from those allotted to whites.

Joint-stock company A form of business organization that was a forerunner to the modern corporation. The joint-stock company was used to raise both capital and labor for New World ventures. Shareholders contributed either capital or their labor for a period of years.

Judicial nationalism The use of the judiciary to assert the primacy of the national government over state and local government and the legal principle of contract over principles of local custom.

Keynesian economics The theory, named after the English economist John Maynard Keynes, that advocated the use of "countercyclical" fiscal policy. This meant that during good times the government should pay down the debt, so that during bad times, it could afford to stimulate the economy with deficit spending.

Knights of Labor The first national federation of trade unions, led by Terence V. Powderly. The Knights grew to its fullest size in the mid-1880s before a steep decline. The federation was based on the premise of a common interest of all producers (for example, farmers and industrial workers), and it supported reform as well as united action by workers.

Liberalism A body of political thought that traces its origins to John Locke and whose chief principles are consent, freedom of conscience, and property. Liberalism held that people could not be governed except by their own consent and that the purpose of government was to protect people as well as their property.

Linked economic development A form of economic development that ties together a variety of enterprises so that development in one stimulates development in others, for example, those that provide raw materials, parts, or transportation.

Longhorn cattle Rangy, tough, resourceful cattle found on the southern Great Plains. They were ideal for long cattle drives like those along the Abilene Trail.

Lyceum movement A voluntary adult-education movement that swept New England and the Mid-Atlantic states in the early and mid-nineteenth century, credited in large part to the efforts of Josiah Holbrook. Lyceum organizations hosted educational lectures in towns and cities. Lecturers included such prominent speakers as Ralph Waldo Emerson, Mark Twain, and Abraham Lincoln.

Manifest destiny A term first coined in 1845 by journalist John O'Sullivan to express the belief, widespread among antebellum Americans, that the United States was destined to expand across the North American continent to the Pacific and had an irrefutable right to the lands absorbed in this expansion. This belief was frequently justified on the grounds of claims to political and racial superiority.

Market revolution The term used to designate the period of the early nineteenth century, roughly 1815–1830, during which internal dependence on cash markets and wages became widespread.

Mass production A system of efficient, high-volume manufacturing based on division of labor into repetitive tasks, simplification, and standardization of parts, increasing use of specialized machinery, and careful supervision. Emerging since the nineteenth century, mass production reached a critical stage of development with Henry Ford's introduction of the moving assembly line at his Highland Park automobile factory. Mass production drove the prosperity of the 1920s and helped make consumerism possible.

Massive resistance The rallying cry of southern segregationists who pledged to oppose the integration of the schools ordered by the Supreme Court in *Brown v. Board of*

Education in 1954. The tactics of massive resistance included legislation, demonstrations, and violence.

Massive retaliation   The defense doctrine of the Eisenhower administration which promised "instant, massive retaliation" with nuclear weapons in response to Soviet aggression.

McCarthyism   The hunt for Communist subversion in the United States in the first years of the cold war. Democrats, in particular, used the term, a reference to the sometimes disreputable tactics of Republican Senator Joseph R. McCarthy of Wisconsin, in order to question the legitimacy of the conservative anti-Communist crusade.

Mercantilism   An economic theory developed in early-modern Europe to explain and guide the growth of European nation-states. Its goal was to strengthen the state by making the economy serve its interests. According to the theory of mercantilism, the world's wealth, measured in gold and silver, was fixed; that is, it could never be increased. As a result, each nation's chief economic objective must be to secure as much of the world's wealth as possible. One nation's gain was necessarily another's loss. Colonies played an important part in the theory of mercantilism. Their role was to serve as sources of raw materials and as markets for manufactured goods for the mother country alone.

Middle ground   The region between European and Indian settlements in North America that was neither fully European nor fully Indian, but rather a new world created out of two different traditions. The middle ground came into being every time Europeans and Indians met, needed each other, and could not (or would not) achieve what they wanted through use of force.

Millennialism   A strain of Protestant belief that holds that history will end with the thousand-year reign of Christ (the millennium). Some Americans saw the Great Awakening, the French and Indian War, and the Revolution as signs that the millennium was about to begin in America, and this belief infused Revolutionary thought with an element of optimism. Millennialism was also one aspect of a broad drive for social perfection in nineteenth-century America.

Minstrel show   Form of popular entertainment in the nineteenth century, with black performers or white ones pretending to be black. Minstrel shows included music, comedy acts, and drama.

Modern Republicanism   President Dwight Eisenhower's middle-of-the-road legislative program of the 1950s. Reflecting traditional Republican faith in limited government and balanced budgets, Modern Republicanism still left alone such liberal programs as Social Security and farm subsidies.

Modernization   The process by which developing countries in the third world were to become more like the United States—i.e., capitalist, independent, and anti-Communist. Confidence about the prospects for modernization was one of the cornerstones of liberal foreign policy in the 1960s.

Moral suasion   The strategy of using persuasion (as opposed to legal coercion) to convince individuals to alter their behavior. In the antebellum years, moral suasion generally implied an appeal to religious values.

Mugwump   Name applied to liberal reformers in the late nineteenth century. Unattached to either major party, Mugwumps would endorse any candidate supportive of civil service reform, a secret ballot, and honest government.

Mutual aid societies   Organizations through which people of relatively meager means pooled their resources for emergencies. Usually, individuals paid small amounts in dues and were able to borrow large amounts in times of need. In the early nineteenth century, mutual aid societies were especially common among workers in free African American communities.

National Republicans   Over the first 20 years of the nineteenth century, the Republican Party gradually abandoned its Jeffersonian animosity toward an activist federal government and industrial development and became a strong proponent of both of these positions. Embodied in the American system, these new views were fully captured in the party's designation of itself as National Republicans by 1824.

Nativism   A bias against anyone not born in the United States and in favor of native-born Americans. This attitude assumes the superior culture and political virtue of white Americans of Anglo-Saxon descent, or of individuals assumed to have that lineage. During the period 1820–1850, Irish immigrants became the particular targets of nativist attitudes.

Neoconservatism   Form of conservative ideology that advocated the aggressive promotion of democracy abroad by the United States in order to make a better and more secure world. Emerging in the 1970s and 1980s, neoconservative ideas influenced the foreign policy of President George W. Bush.

New conservatism   The resurgent conservative ideology of the 1950s and 1960s reiterated the old conservatism's faith in individual freedom and liberal government and added an aggressive, anti-Communist defense policy.

New Federalism   Conservative policy of President Richard Nixon intended to limit the federal government by returning revenue and control to state and local government.

New Left   The radical student movement that emerged in opposition to the new liberalism in the 1960s. The New Left condemned the cold war and corporate power and called for the creation of a true "participatory democracy" in the United States. Placing its faith in the radical potential of young, middle-class students, the New Left differed from the "old left" of the late nineteenth and early twentieth centuries, which believed workers would lead the way to socialism.

New Right   The conservative movement that swept Ronald Reagan into power in 1980 and sustained his presidency. The New Right was much like the new conservatism of the 1950s and 1960s, but with greater emphasis on social issues such as abortion.

Nickelodeon   The first venue for motion pictures, a machine that showed a movie (lasting several minutes) for a nickel. Galleries with dozens of such machines, and the first movie theaters, came to be called "nickelodeons" as a result.

Omaha Platform   The Populist Party's program endorsed at the party's national convention in Omaha in 1892. Among its planks were government ownership of railroads and telegraph lines, the direct election of senators, a subtreasury system, and an expansion of the money supply.

Patriotism   Love of country. Ways of declaring and displaying national devotion underwent a change from the nineteenth to the twentieth centuries. Whereas politicians were once unblushingly called patriotic, after World War I the title was appropriated to describe the sacrifices of war veterans. Patriotic spectacle in the form of public oration and electoral rallies gave way to military-style commemorations of Armistice Day and the nation's martial heritage.

Patronage   *See* spoils system.

Political economy   Traditionally, the study of the connections between economics and politics. In this text, political economy refers to the relationships between the economy, politics, and the daily lives of ordinary people. Use of the term underscores the importance of the economy in shaping American life and the importance of politics in shaping the economy. However, the economy and politics did not simply shape, but were in turn shaped by, the lives and cultural values of ordinary men and women.

Political machine   An organization controlling a party, usually dominated by a "boss" and held together by loyalty and the distribution of rewards to those who had done the organization service.

Political virtue   In the political thought of the early republic, the personal qualities required in citizens if the republic was to survive.

Popular sovereignty   A solution to the slavery controversy espoused by leading northern Democrats in the 1850s. It held that the inhabitants of western territories should be free to decide for themselves whether or not they wanted to have slavery. In principle, popular sovereignty would prevent Congress from either enforcing or restricting slavery's expansion into the western territories.

Populism   The ideology of the People's (Populist) party in the 1890s, opposing the eastern economic elites and favoring government action to help producers in general and farmers in particular.

Postindustrial economy   The service- and computer-based economy that was succeeding the industrial economy, which had been dominated by manufacturing, at the end of the twentieth century.

Principle of judicial review   The principle of law that recognizes in the judiciary the power to review and rule on the constitutionality of laws. First established in *Marbury v. Madison* (1803) under Chief Justice John Marshall.

Producers ideology   The belief that all those who lived by producing goods shared a common political identity in opposition to those who lived off financial speculation, rent, or interest.

Proprietary colony   Colony established by a royal grant to an individual or family. The proprietary colonies included Maryland, New York, New Jersey, Pennsylvania, and the Carolinas.

Public opinion   Not quite democracy or consent, public opinion was a way of understanding the influence of the citizenry on political calculations. It emerged in the eighteenth century, when it was defined as a crucial source of a government's legitimacy. It was associated with the emergence of a press and a literate public free to discuss, and to question, government policy. In the twentieth century, Freudian psychology and the new mass media encouraged a view of the public as both fickle and powerful. Whereas the popular will (a nineteenth-century concept) was steady and rooted in national traditions, public opinion was variable and based on attitudes that could be aroused or manipulated by advertising.

Realism   A major artistic movement of the late nineteenth century that embraced writers, painters, critics, and photographers. Realists strove to avoid sentimentality and to depict life "realistically."

Reconquista   Literally "reconquest." Between the eleventh and the fifteenth centuries, Christian nobles in Spain and Portugal fought to eject Muslim conquerors who had come from North Africa in the seventh and eighth centuries. In 1492, Ferdinand and Isabel defeated the last remaining Muslim ruler.

Reconversion   The economic and social transition from the war effort to peacetime. Americans feared that reconversion might bring a return to the depression conditions of the 1930s.

Re-export trade   Marine trade between two foreign ports, with an intermediate stop in a port of the ship's home nation. United States shippers commonly engaged in the re-export trade during the European wars of the late eighteenth and early nineteenth centuries, when England and France tried to prevent each other from shipping or receiving goods. United States shippers claimed that the intermediate stop in the United States made their cargoes neutral.

Republicanism   A set of doctrines rooted in classical antiquity that held that power is always grasping and dangerous and presents a threat to liberty. Republicanism supplied constitutionalism with a motive by explaining how a balanced constitution could be transformed into a tyranny as grasping men used their power to encroach on the liberty of citizens. In addition, republicanism held that people achieved fulfillment only through participation in public life, as citizens in a republic. Republicanism required the individual to display virtue by sacrificing his (or her) private interest for the good of the republic.

Requerimiento **(the Requirement)**   A document issued by the Spanish Crown in 1513 in order to clarify the legal bases for the enslavement of hostile Indians. Each conquistador was required to read a copy of the *Requerimiento* to each group of Indians he encountered. The *Requerimiento* promised friendship to all Indians who accepted Christianity, but threatened war and enslavement for all those who resisted.

Safety-valve theory   An argument commonly made in the nineteenth century that the abundance of western land spared the United States from the social upheavals common to capitalist societies in Europe. In theory, as long as eastern workers had the option of migrating west and becoming independent farmers, they could not be subject to European levels of exploitation. Thus the West was said to provide a "safety-valve" against the pressures caused by capitalist development.

Scab   Slang term for a worker employed during a strike; a strikebreaker.

Scalawag   A derogatory term referring to southern whites who sympathized with the Republicans during Reconstruction.

Second-wave feminism   The reborn women's movement of the 1960s and 1970s that reinterpreted the first wave of nineteenth- and early twentieth-century feminists' insistence on civil rights and called for full economic, reproductive, and political equality.

Separation of powers   One of the chief innovations of the Constitution and a distinguishing mark of the American form of democracy, in which the executive, legislative, and judicial branches of government are separated so that they can check and balance each other.

Sharecropping   The practice of a tenant farming the landlord's ground for a share of the crop, sold when the harvest came in. This became a common form of employment for former slaves in the post–Civil War South.

Slave power   In the 1850s northern Republicans explained the continued economic and political strength of slavery by claiming that a "slave power" had taken control of the federal government and used its authority to keep slavery alive artificially.

Slave society   A society in which slavery is central to the economy and political structure, in contrast to a society with slaves, in which the presence of slaves does not alter the fundamental structures of the society.

Slavery   A system of extreme social inequality distinguished by the definition of a human being as property, or chattel, and thus, in principle, totally subordinated to the slave owner.

Social Darwinism   Darwin's theory of natural selection transferred from biological evolution to human history. Social Darwinists argued that some individuals and groups, particularly racial groups, were better able to survive in the "race of life."

Spoils system   The practice of politicians rewarding their friends with offices and contracts.

Stagflation   The unusual combination of stagnant growth and high inflation that plagued the American economy in the 1970s.

Strict constructionism   The view that the Constitution has a fixed, explicit meaning which can be altered only through formal amendment. Loose constructionism is the view that the Constitution is a broad framework within which various interpretations and applications are possible without formal amendment.

Subtreasury   A government-run bank in which farmers could get low-interest loans using their crops as collateral. The creation of subtreasuries formed a key plank in the Populist platform.

Suburbanization   The spread of suburban housing developments and, more broadly, of the suburban ideal.

Supply-side economics   The controversial theory, associated with economist Arthur Laffer, that drove "Reaganomics," the conservative economic policy of the Reagan administration. In contrast to liberal economic theory, supply-side economics emphasized that producers—the "supply side" of the economic equation—drove economic growth, rather than consumers—the "demand side." To encourage producers to invest more in new production, Laffer and other supply-siders called for massive tax cuts.

Tammany Hall   A fraternal organization in New York City that developed into a Democratic political machine, electing officials, mobilizing voters, and allotting contracts. Its enemies saw it as a symbol of corrupt, selfish, and incompetent government.

Tariff   A tax on goods moving across an international boundary. Because the Constitution allows tariffs only on imports, as a political issue the tariff question has chiefly concerned the protection of domestic manufacturing from foreign competition. Industries producing mainly for American consumers have preferred a higher tariff, while farmers and industries aimed at global markets have typically favored reduced tariffs. Prior to the Civil War, the tariff was a symbol of diverging political economies in North and South. The North advocated high tariffs to protect growing domestic manufacturing ("protective tariffs"), and the South opposed high tariffs on the grounds that they increased the cost of imported manufactured goods.

Taylorism   A method for maximizing industrial efficiency by systematically reducing the time and motion involved in each step of the production process. The "scientific" system was designed by Frederick Taylor and explained in his book *The Principles of Scientific Management* (1911).

Temperance   Moderation, or the use of something with restraint. In the Gilded Age, the temperance movement opposed the use of alcohol.

Trusts   Corporate arrangements to unify action in production and distribution among different firms. Shareholders handed over control of their stock to a board that held the shares in trust and operated the combined concerns.

Universalism   Enlightenment belief that all people are by their nature essentially the same.

Vaudeville   A type of variety show popular in the late 1800s and early 1900s. Vaudeville was family friendly and included songs, band performances, skits, comedy routines, and circus acts.

Vertical integration   The practice of taking control of every aspect of the production, distribution, and sale of a commodity. For example, Andrew Carnegie vertically integrated his steel operations by purchasing the mines that produced the ore, the railroads that carried the ore to the steel mills, the mills themselves, and the distribution system that carried the finished steel to consumers.

Virtual representation   British doctrine that said that all Britons, even those who did not vote, were represented by Parliament, if not "actually," by representatives they had chosen, then "virtually," because each member of parliament was supposed to act on behalf of the entire realm, not only his constituents or even those who had voted for him.

Voluntarism   A style of political activism that took place largely outside of electoral politics. Voluntarism emerged in the nineteenth century, particularly among those Americans who were not allowed to vote. Thus women formed voluntary associations that pressed for social and political reforms, even though women were excluded from electoral politics.

Waltham system   Named after the system used in early textile mills in Waltham, Massachusetts, the term refers to the practice of bringing all elements of production together in a single factory setting with the application of non-human-powered machinery.

Wampum   Shell beads used by Indians of the Eastern Woodlands to make jewelry and to memorialize political agreements; later used as currency in the trade networks established between Europeans and Indians.

Watergate   The name of the Washington, D.C., office and condominium complex where five men with ties to the presidential campaign of Richard Nixon were caught breaking into the headquarters of the Democratic National Committee in June 1972. "Watergate" became the catchall term for the wide range of illegal practices of Nixon and his followers that were uncovered in the aftermath of the break-in.

Whig Party   The political party founded by Henry Clay in the mid-1830s. The name derived from the seventeenth- and eighteenth-century British antimonarchical position and was intended to suggest that the Jacksonian Democrats (and Jackson in particular) sought despotic powers. In many ways the heirs of National Republicans, the Whigs supported economic expansion, but they also believed in a strong federal government to control the dynamism of the market. The Whig Party attracted many moral reformers.

Whitewater   With its echo of Richard Nixon's "Watergate" scandals in the 1970s, "Whitewater" became the catchall term for the scandals that plagued Bill Clinton's presidency in the 1990s. The term came from the name of a real estate development company in Arkansas. Clinton and his wife Hillary supposedly had corrupt dealings with the Whitewater Development Corporation in the 1970s and 1980s that they purportedly attempted to cover up in the 1990s.

Women's rights movement   The antebellum organizing efforts of women on their own behalf, in the attempt to secure a broad range of social, civic, and political rights. This movement is generally dated from the convention of Seneca Falls in 1848. Only after the Civil War would women's rights activism begin to confine its efforts to suffrage.

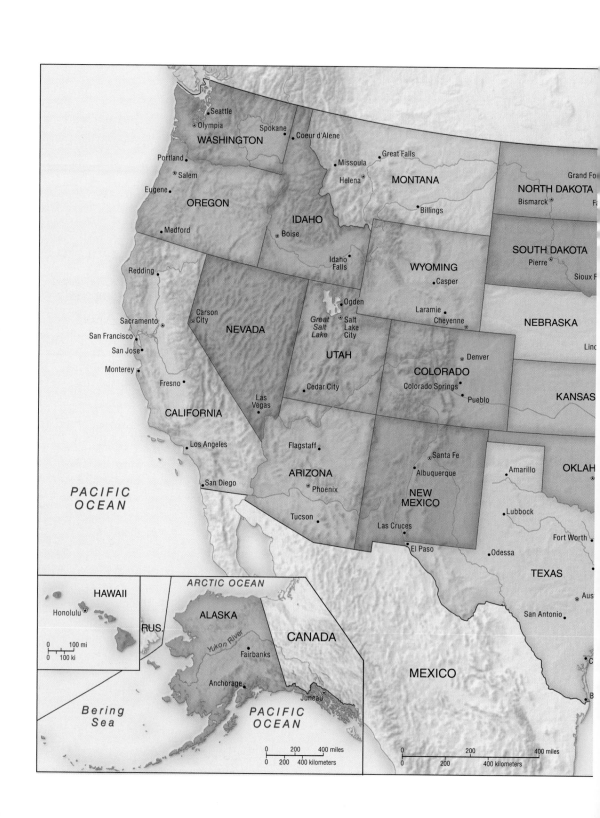

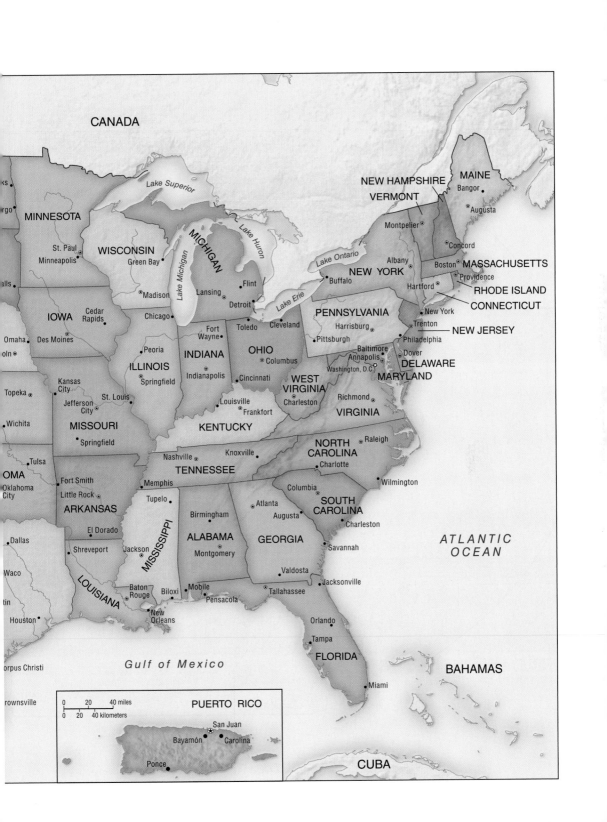

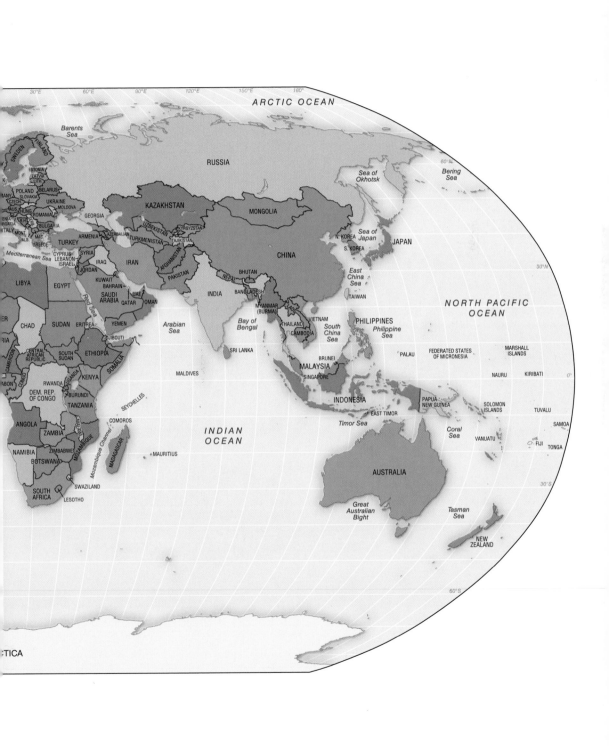